THE SOCIAL WORK EXPERIENCE

An Introduction to Social Work and Social Welfare

FIFTH EDITION

Curriculum Lab
College of Education Health & Human Services
University of Michigan-Dearborn

MARY ANN SUPPES
Mount Mary College
Milwaukee, Wisconsin

CAROLYN CRESSY WELLS
University of Wisconsin, Oshkosh

PEARSON

Boston   New York   San Francisco
Mexico City   Montreal   Toronto   London   Madrid   Munich   Paris
Hong Kong   Singapore   Tokyo   Cape Town   Sydney

Senior Series Editor: Patricia Quinlin
Editorial Assistant: Carly Czech
Senior Marketing Manager: Wendy Albert
Production Editor: Pat Torelli
Editorial Production Service: Elm Street Publishing Services
Composition Buyer: Linda Cox
Manufacturing Buyer: Debbie Rossi
Electronic Composition: Elm Street Publishing Services
Interior Design: Elm Street Publishing Services
Photo Researcher: Katharine S. Cebik
Cover Administrator: Linda Knowles
Cover Designer: Studio Nine

For related titles and support materials, visit our online catalog at www.ablongman.com.

Between the time website information is gathered and then published, it is not unusual for some sites to have closed. Also, the transcription of URLs can result in typographical errors. The publisher would appreciate notification where these errors occur so that they may be corrected in subsequent editions.

ISBN-13: 978-0-205-56939-7
ISBN-10:   0-205-56939-0

Library of Congress Cataloging-in-Publication Data

Suppes, Mary Ann.
    The social work experience : an introduction to social work and social welfare/
Mary Ann S. Suppes, Carolyn C. Wells.—5th ed.
        p. cm.
    Includes index.
    ISBN 978-0-205-56939-7
    1. Social service—United States.   2. Social service—Vocational guidance—
United States.   I. Wells, Carolyn Cressy.   II. Title.

HV10.5.S97 2009
361.3'202373—dc22

                                                                                                2008000392

Printed in the United States of America

10 9 8 7 6 5 4 3 2 1   12 11 10 09 08

With deepest gratitude to my husband, Fred,
for his unwavering love, his endurance, clear thinking,
and his numerous contributions to this book;
and to my mother, Lucille, whose spirit, spunk, and values
are transformed in the pages of this book.

To my beloved husband, Dennis Loeffler,
who inspires with his caring and critical thinking;
to my wandering brother, Ted Wells, who inspires
with his culturally sensitive regional planning all over the world;
and to my amazing sister, Merritt Stites, who inspires with her energy
and expertise as a clinical social worker.

NEW TO THIS EDITION

CHAPTER 1
THE SOCIAL WORK PROFESSION

- A new unit explores the profession's growing concern with global environmental issues, and the history section now offers a social justice perspective.

CHAPTER 2
THEORETICAL PERSPECTIVES FOR SOCIAL WORKERS

- New discussions include the global and environmental issues relating to social work practice and social welfare policy and spirituality in social work practice.

CHAPTER 3
SOCIAL JUSTICE AND SOCIAL WELFARE POLICY

- Health insurance accessibility is examined as a growing concern.
- An international perspective is provided with illustrations of social welfare policy in both Japan and Sweden.

CHAPTER 4
FAMILY AND CHILDREN'S SERVICES

- New discussions of immigrant families, family issues around the world, and ecological factors affecting families.

CHAPTER 5
SOCIAL WORK IN MENTAL HEALTH

- A new content unit examines the relationship between the degraded environment and mental health risk factors, such as suicide.

CHAPTER 6
SOCIAL WORK IN HEALTH CARE

- New unit discusses the impact of the environment on health care and social justice issues related to global health care.

CHAPTER 7
SOCIAL WORK IN THE SCHOOLS

- No Child Left Behind legislation, including recent research on the law's effects, is discussed in depth.
- An international example illustrates school social work in Ghana.

CHAPTER 8
SUBSTANCE ABUSE SERVICES

- New content areas include environmental issues; cross-national program development; and a critical review of the "war on drugs" social welfare policy, rife with human rights and social justice issues.

CHAPTER 9
SOCIAL WORK WITH OLDER ADULTS

- A new case study introduces Chapter 9.
- A new discussion of end-of-life issues examines death and dying, spirituality and religion, hospice services and complementary therapies, among others.

CHAPTER 10
CRIMINAL JUSTICE

- A new section describes human rights violations of international child labor laws and trafficking of women and children across borders for sexual exploitation.

CHAPTER 11
DEVELOPMENTAL DISABILITIES AND SOCIAL WORK

- A discussion of recent global efforts on behalf of people with disabilities is included.

CHAPTER 12
FUTURE CHALLENGES AND CLOSING NOTES

- A new case study drawn from international social work sets the stage for a global interconnectedness theme.

BRIEF CONTENTS

CONTENTS

PREFACE

One beautiful, crisp fall day two friends, both experienced social work educators, set off by car for a conference 200 miles to the north. We were those friends, and our conversation during that drive sparked the ideas that resulted in *The Social Work Experience*. We were both teaching introductory courses in social work that semester and, because our roots were in social work practice, we were frustrated by the lack of well-developed, contemporary case study materials in social work texts. Authentic, current case material, we were convinced, would help students identify with the real people who are served by social workers across the United States, and with the social workers themselves.

It occurred to us that we could create those materials from our own professional practice experiences and from the field learning experiences of our students. Our case studies could portray diverse populations in both client and social worker roles. Some could illustrate baccalaureate social work students in field work settings. We could synthesize real-life situations of people we had known and thus avoid exact duplication of any actual cases. With these ideas and commitments, the book emerged.

THE FIFTH EDITION

In the preceding four editions of this text, we designed case studies to illustrate generalist social work practice at different systems levels, carefully connecting case materials with theoretical content. Common themes were integrated into every chapter: generalist practice, social research, ethics and values, and human diversity. Beginning with the second edition, we augmented the human diversity theme to include an examination of poverty, populations at risk, and social justice issues. Our concern for special issues relevant to women helped frame several of the case studies as well as the didactic content of the text. The development of major social welfare programs in the United States was traced. The history of the social work profession was presented within each field of practice to acquaint students with the social and political context of the times and with the persons who provided strong leadership in the development of the profession. The primary focus of the book was entry-level generalist social work practice, but the linkage between generalist and specialist practice was also presented.

The common themes integrated into every chapter of the first four editions remain the same in the fifth edition. All information has been updated and augmented, however. The presentation of these materials has been enriched to include:

- New case studies, debate boxes, Internet sites, classroom exercises, research activities, and Internet research exercises.
- A new chapter, Social Justice and Social Welfare Policy, that explores the relationship between social justice issues and social welfare policy and programs.
- Ongoing examination of the effects of legislation on social welfare policy, social work practice, and the people served by social work practitioners that helps clarify the relationship of policy to practice.
- Human rights and social justice content incorporated systematically.
- Content on environmental concerns, globalization, and spirituality incorporated throughout the text.
- The problem-solving process as portrayed by case studies and further described in chapter content, illustrating social work practice with individuals, families, groups, organizations, and communities.
- Effects of welfare reform, the Earned Income Tax Credit, and other social programs designed to regulate the poor.
- Documentation of the increasing diversity of the American population, with discussion of potential ramifications.

Some of the specific changes in the fifth edition are described on a chapter-by-chapter basis in the following section.

FIFTH EDITION ORGANIZATION AND REVISIONS

All of the chapters in this text begin with case studies involving clients and social workers who are members of diverse groups. Case studies are provided to capture student interest and to provide appropriate context for the didactic material that follows. Each chapter includes content identified as important in the *Educational Policy and Accreditation Standards* of the Council on Social Work Education: generalist practice, social welfare policy, and professional values and ethics, among others.

Part I, Social Work and Its Context, consists of three chapters. **Chapter 1, The Social Work Profession,** introduces the generalist social worker, a professional who has earned the baccalaureate degree in social work from a program accredited by the Council on Social Work Education. Related professions are compared and contrasted; career opportunities are explored. A new section describes the breadth of practice environments that characterize the social work profession, contrasting these with the more limited variety of practice settings of nursing, teaching, physical therapy, and other professions. Another newly created unit explores the profession's growing concern with global environmental issues. The history section of Chapter 1 is reframed within a social justice perspective. Future employment projections are provided along with research that points to potential labor shortages for the social work profession.

Chapter 2, Theoretical Perspectives for Social Workers, examines theoretical perspectives important to generalist practice, focusing on the problem-solving/planned change process and the ecosystems approach. It also explores political perspectives that shape social welfare policy. The chapter includes a new discussion of global and environmental issues relating to social work practice and social welfare policy. It also includes a discussion of spirituality in social work practice.

Chapter 3, Social Justice and Social Welfare Policy, explores the relationship between social justice and social welfare policy. This chapter has two parts, the first focusing on major social justice issues and the second on social welfare policies and programs that have developed over time in response to some of these issues. How well contemporary welfare policy meets actual need is examined and explored as a social justice issue in itself. Updated statistics regarding populations at risk in the United States are provided, with a focus on population percentages and poverty. Health insurance accessibility as a growing concern is examined. An international perspective is provided, with illustrations of social welfare policy in both Japan and Sweden.

Part II, Professional Practice Settings, examines eight fields of professional social work practice. These include family and children's services, social work in mental health settings, social work in health care, in the schools, in chemical dependency settings, in criminal justice settings, with older adults, and with people who have developmental disabilities.

Chapter 4, Family and Children's Services, introduces readers to this field of practice. New content in this chapter includes a brief history of African Americans in the United States. A discussion of ecological issues affecting family welfare is introduced. The chapter includes a new discussion of immigrant families along with a discussion of family issues around the world. Spiritual concerns affecting social work with families are considered.

Chapter 5, Social Work in Mental Health, begins by outlining the knowledge, values, and skills needed for practice in mental health settings. The nature of practice with individual persons who have mental health problems, with families, the use of group intervention, and practice efforts aimed at changes in organizations and communities are described. New to this chapter is content on the social justice issues related to use of diagnostic labels, the inadequacy of treatment resources for people with no insurance coverage, and the disparity in access for racial and ethnic minorities. Another new content unit examines the relationship between our degraded environment and mental health risk factors such as suicide. In the fifth edition, increased attention is given to the impact of social policy on mental health services. A new Up for Debate box is provided as well as a thoroughly revised listing of current psychotropic medications.

Chapter 6, Social Work in Health Care, helps students understand how their liberal arts college education plus their social work generalist curriculum prepare them for practice in acute, long-term, and home health care as well as the evolving practice settings in hospice and insurance corporations. New to this edition are units on the impact of environment on health care and on social justice issues related to global health care. New exhibits include the National Association of Social Workers (NASW) policy statements on the environment and on linkages between health and human rights. New cross-national data on health care expenditures afford interesting insights when compared with data on health system performance across selected nations.

Chapter 7, Social Work in the Schools, now includes a brief history of Latino peoples in the United States. No Child Left Behind legislation, including recent research on the law's effects, is examined. The chapter now examines environmental factors that relate to sexuality and teen pregnancy. A new discussion of spiritual development and empowerment programs in selected schools is included. An international example is provided: school social work in Ghana.

Chapter 8, Substance Abuse Services, examines roles and responsibilities that generalist social workers assume in prevention and treatment programs, in addition to the evolution of social work services in this field. A new, internationally used assessment tool (the AUDIT) acquaints readers with the tests used to determine severity of abuse. Populations at heightened risk of substance abuse (women and children, youths, some minority groups, lesbian women and gay men, and persons with disabilities) are considered. Updated information on the substances of abuse is provided. Also new to the fifth edition are content areas on environmental issues, cross-national program development, and a critical review of the "war on drugs" social welfare policy that is rife with human rights and social justice issues.

A new case study introduces **Chapter 9, Social Work with Older Adults.** Statistics, including marital status, ethnicity, housing, and economic circumstances have been updated. The discussion of social programs assisting the elderly has been updated, including the critical examination of Medicare Part D. A new discussion of end-of-life issues has been included: death and dying, spirituality and religion, hospice services and complementary therapies, among others. An international perspective has been provided: social services for older adults in The Netherlands.

Chapter 10, Criminal Justice, introduces readers to the history of social work in the criminal justice field and the most common areas for generalist practice (law enforcement, the courts, and the adult and juvenile correctional systems). In a section that is new to the fifth edition, environmental perspectives are considered, with special emphasis on at-risk persons and communities. Spirituality, resilience, and restorative justice are shown to be strengths of communities that deal with crime on a daily basis. Careful attention is given to juvenile justice and social policies related to the death sentence. A final new section describes human rights violations of international child labor laws and trafficking of women and children across borders for sexual exploitation.

Chapter 11, Developmental Disabilities and Social Work, includes a discussion of recent global efforts on behalf of people with disabilities. The description of types of disabilities now includes emotional disturbance, and content on Asperger's disorder augments the discussion of autism. The role of spirituality in social work practice with people with disabilities is included.

Part III, A Look at the Future, concludes the text with a focus on events and forces that will define the future transformation of the world. A new case study drawn from international social work sets the stage for **Chapter 12, Future Challenges and Closing Notes,** with its view of social work as a profession at the edge of change. Much of the content for Chapter 12 is drawn from the work of futurists who think about the interconnectedness of people well beyond the narrow lens of international commerce. National and international strategic planning initiatives are identified. With global interconnectedness as a consistent theme, Chapter 12 addresses demographic, political, and economic trends as well as technological and biomedical advances that, along with an emerging crisis in environmental sustainability, will drive change. Woven throughout this discussion is the evolving role of the social work profession as a force for peace and a champion for human rights.

PEDAGOGICAL AIDS

- Up for Debate boxes are a unique pedagogical aid that contain a proposition regarding a current social welfare topic and then provide perspectives in favor of and against that proposition. The inclusion of these boxes should provoke much discussion among students regarding diverse issues of importance to the social work profession.

- Exhibits included in every chapter provide information from original sources to help students better understand issues discussed in the body of the text. Some of these materials are didactic; others include political cartoons, case studies, reflections on firsthand experience, and so on.

- Key terms are highlighted in every chapter and further defined in an extensive glossary.

- New Internet sites included in every chapter direct students to appropriate electronic data resources providing further information on various topics under consideration.

- Classroom exercises provide students with the opportunity to engage in small group discussion regarding various topics of interest to social work practitioners. A selection of these exercises is provided in every chapter.

- Every chapter includes discussion questions designed to provoke critical thinking.

- Research exercises are designed to encourage students to examine important contemporary issues in social work and social welfare outside the classroom setting.

- Internet research exercises are designed to engage students in the use of Web-based source materials that supplement chapter didactic content.

- An updated listing of additional readings accompanies each chapter.

SUPPLEMENTS

NEW for STUDENTS: MyHelpingKit is an electronic supplement that offers book-specific Learning Objectives, Chapter Summaries, Flashcards, and Practice Tests, as well as Video Clips and Interactive Activities to aid student learning and comprehension. Also included in MyHelpingKit is Research Navigator™, which gives students access to powerful and reliable research material. MyHelpingKit is available through an access code that can be shrinkwrapped with each new copy of this text at no additional cost to your students. Contact your local representative for special ISBN and ordering information: www.ablongman.com/replocator.

The fifth edition of the *The Social Work Experience* is accompanied by an ***Instructor's Manual/Test Bank,*** which includes chapter outlines, a complete test bank of objective and essay questions, and more. The *Instructor's Manual/Test Bank* is provided free of charge to instructors, and the Test Bank is available electronically. PPT slides to accompany this text are also available to instructors. Please contact your local Allyn & Bacon representative for more information on the above supplements at: www.pearsonhighered.com/replocator

IN APPRECIATION

Today, as we put the finishing touches on the fifth edition, we wish to acknowledge and thank those who assisted us in this project. While the book is basically our own creation, it has been substantially enriched by the critiques and contributions of its editors and reviewers. Pat Quinlin, Senior Series Editor of the fifth edition, has been absolutely essential in enabling the fifth edition to be published by Allyn & Bacon. Pat's constant encouragement and support have made the arduous work of developing the fifth edition much more enjoyable. We also wish to thank Karen Hanson, Editor-in-Chief, Social Sciences, for approving the acceptance of our manuscript by Allyn & Bacon.

For the fifth edition, we also wish to thank our Editorial Assistant, Carly Czech, and to express gratitude to our many anonymous reviewers. We are grateful to Pat Torelli, Production Editor; Kate Cebik, Freelance Photo Researcher; Karin Kipp, Project Manager; Laura Lee Manley, Marketing Manager; and Sue Nodine, Project Editor. Our gratitude is also expressed to those who provided materials for or helped to design our composite case studies: Isaac Christie, Jason Dietenberger, Joe Dooley, Georgia Giese, Pamela Awtrey Harrington, Linda Ketcher Goodrich, Karen Greenler, Sandra Hill, David Kucej, Julie Kudick, Maureen Martin, Sandra Miller, Melissa Monsoor, Malcolm Montgomery, Dolores Poole, Wanda Priddy, David Schneider, Sara Stites, Delores Sumner, Jody Searl Wnorowski, and Ellen Zonka. We appreciate the exceptional library research assistance of Laurel Privatt at Mount Mary College and the Internet research of Dr. William Bunge. We are grateful to Roberta Allickson, Margaret Schmidt, and Carolyn Sims for their technical assistance. We also wish to acknowledge and express special gratitude to Fritz Suppes for his "behind the scenes" contributions to library research, Internet exercises, photo selections, and countless technology consultations.

We are most indebted to the theorists and writers whose dreams of generalist social work practice have inspired us. Along with hundreds of other social work educators, we are committed to keeping alive and strong the concept of generalist practice articulated by Betty L. Baer and Ronald C. Federico, among others. It is our sincere hope that faculty and students alike will find this book helpful in understanding and appreciating the context and practice of Social Work.

MARY ANN SUPPES
CAROLYN CRESSY WELLS

ABOUT THE AUTHORS

MARY ANN SUPPES brings an unusual breadth of teaching, practice, and professional experience to the writing of *The Social Work Experience*. She is currently a professor of social work at Mount Mary College in Milwaukee, Wisconsin, where she has served as chair of the social work department for many years. She has provided curriculum consultation to numerous colleges and universities. A member of the Council on Social Work Education (CSWE), the Association of Baccalaureate Social Work Program Directors (BPD), the National Association of Social Workers, and the Wisconsin Council on Social Work Education, she has served for many years on the CSWE Commission on Accreditation, currently serves on the Council on the Social Work Education Continuum Committee, and has served several terms as a member of the board of directors of BPD. Her current responsibilities are that of chair of the BPD Social Work Education Continuum Committee. She has also been treasurer of the Wisconsin Council on Social Work Education and has chaired numerous CSWE site visits. Professor Suppes received both her undergraduate and graduate (MSW) degrees from the University of Wisconsin, Milwaukee, and did postgraduate work at the University of Chicago.

CAROLYN CRESSY WELLS is a professor of social work at the University of Wisconsin, Oshkosh, where she holds the Edward H. Rudoy Endowed Professorship. Previously she developed the social work program at Marquette University in Milwaukee, Wisconsin, where she served as program director for many years. She is a member of the National Association of Social Workers, the Association of Baccalaureate Social Work Program Directors, and the Academy of Certified Social Workers, and she has served on a number of accreditation site teams for the Council on Social Work Education. She is author of three other social work texts: *Social Work Day to Day: The Experience of Generalist Social Work Practice*; *Social Work Ethics Day to Day: Guidelines for Professional Practice*; and *Stepping to the Dance: The Training of a Family Therapist*. She maintained a small private practice for many years and currently serves as a hospice volunteer, playing Celtic harp at bedsides (certified as a Music Practitioner by the Music for Healing & Transition Program). She received her undergraduate degree in anthropology from the University of California at Berkeley and an MSSW and PhD in Child Development and Family Relationships from the University of Wisconsin, Madison.

SOCIAL WORK AND ITS CONTEXT

C hapter 1 introduces the generalist social worker, a professional who has earned the baccalaureate degree in social work from a program accredited by the Council on Social Work Education. Major competencies required by the generalist social work practitioner are identified, and social work's purpose and tasks are compared with those of related disciplines. Social work values and ethics are outlined, and their central role to the profession is discussed.

Chapter 2 examines theoretical perspectives for social workers that affect both professional practice and the social welfare policies that strongly affect practice activities and options. Systems theory, as well as its relationship to social work, is introduced. The highly related ecosystems perspective is discussed in detail. Generalist social work practice theory is presented and discussed, with an emphasis on the importance of a strengths perspective. Then, political perspectives shaping social welfare policies are examined, including classical conservative, neoconservative, liberal, neoliberal, and radical. How the political spectrum affects social welfare policy development is discussed.

Chapter 3 explores the relationship between social justice and social welfare policy. Part I of the chapter identifies major social justice issues and discusses why they comprise a growing concern in today's world. Populations at risk of poverty and discrimination are identified and discussed: children, women, older adults, racial and ethnic minorities, people with disabilities, and gay and lesbian persons, among others. Part II of the chapter examines social welfare as a system or institution and examines how its development relates to social justice concerns. How the social welfare institution in the United States derived primarily from that existing in England when the first settlers came to this continent is explained. Major contemporary governmental social welfare programs and how they may (or may not) adequately address social justice concerns today are then examined. ■

CHAPTER 1

THE SOCIAL WORK PROFESSION

OUTLINE
Susan Dunn

SUSAN DUNN

The telephone rang shrilly at the women's shelter at about 6:15 in the evening. The caller's voice was urgent, frightened, and intense, although little louder than a whisper. "I just called the crisis telephone line that was advertised on the radio," the woman began, "and the person who answered told me to try you. I need a safe place to stay, right now. Can you take me?"

"We may be able to," the social worker replied. "It depends on your situation. Our agency has been set up to help women who have been physically abused. Can you tell me something about yourself? What makes you need a place to stay just now?"

"I can't talk very long because I'm so afraid he'll come back soon," the caller responded, her voice slightly louder this time. "My husband just beat me up again, but he ran out when I threatened to call the police. The children saw the whole thing. I've decided I've had enough. But I don't know where to go. My friends are afraid to get involved. I've got two kids who have to go with me. I don't have any money of my own."

"Sounds like you're in a tough spot. My name is Pamela Wright. I'm a social worker here. Tell me if you need to stop talking. Call me back if you have to hang up. If you're in danger right at this moment, I can take your name and address and call the police for you."

"Oh no," the woman said. "The reason I didn't call the police in the first place is that I don't want to get my husband in trouble. I make him upset. Calling the police would embarrass the whole family. I couldn't possibly do that."

"You said your husband hurt you. Do you have injuries that may need immediate medical attention?"

"When he hit my face I tried to defend myself. I didn't want my face covered with bruises again. I put my hands up to my face. My right arm and shoulder hurt pretty badly now. I don't think I need to see a doctor or go to the hospital. I just need to get away from here."

"Do you feel it is safe for you to talk with me for a few minutes now?"

"Yes. The last time my husband got mad at me and left, he stayed away for a couple of hours. I'm pretty sure he'll do that again this time."

"Well," Pamela Wright said gently, "from what you say, this isn't the first time your husband has physically abused you. I take it that you want to be gone this time when he gets home?"

"Yes. He might come home drunk and hit me again. That's what happened last time. If it weren't for the children, I might take a chance and wait for him, because he might come home sorry and ready to make up. But the kids are awfully upset and scared. I want to get out of here this time."

"Have you any relatives who might be able to take you and the children tonight? You might feel a lot better if you had some family members around you to support you and help with the kids this evening. We'd be happy to help you here even if you were staying somewhere else. You could come in tomorrow, in fact, to talk with one of our counselors about things you could think about doing to deal with the physical abuse by your husband."

"I haven't got any family of my own around here. My parents live in another state, and so does my sister. My in-laws live near here, and they're good to me, but they would break down and tell my husband where I was. Then he'd come, and he might beat me up again. So I don't want anybody to know where I am."

Recognizing that this was an emergency situation, Pamela Wright said quickly, "We do have a room available in our shelter right now. I think that it is important for you to leave your home as quickly as possible. Will you be able to get yourself over here on your own if I give you the address?"

"Oh, I don't think I can. My husband took the car. My arm really hurts. I don't think I can carry anything. My 6-year-old can make it on her own, but the 2-year-old is too much trouble to take on the bus the way my arm hurts. And I'll need to bring some clothes and things."

"Have you any money at all right now?" Pamela asked. "We do have some special funds to send a cab in emergency situations, but those funds are very tight. Could you pay for a cab to get yourself and the kids over here?"

"Well, I have about $10 in my purse. My husband always keeps the checkbook with him, and he just gives me cash a little bit at a time. But if I spend what I have on a cab, I won't have any money at all to pay for my stay with you, or for anything else, for that matter."

"Our services are free. We can supply you with a small room for yourself and your children. We also provide meals. You can stay with us for up to a month. We will help you to decide what to do next. There will be rules about sharing household tasks and some other things, but I can explain more when you get here. You need to know, though, that we may want you to get checked out by a doctor. Sometimes people are more seriously injured than they initially think they are. Do you think you want to come?" After a moment's hesitation the caller whispered, "Yes, I do. Can I come with the kids right away?"

"Certainly," Pamela said. "But how bad is your arm? Will you be able to manage?"

"I think I can. I'll just have to pack with one hand. My 6-year-old can help. Is there anything in particular that we should bring?"

"Just bring the routine stuff—you know, toothbrushes, pajamas, toys, extra clothes, anything to keep you and the children as comfortable as possible."

"Okay. Thank you very much. I hope I'll be there soon."

"Fine. I'll give you our address. You are asked to tell it to no one but the cab driver, because for safety reasons we need to keep it secret." Pamela gave the woman the address of the shelter. "Now," she continued, "if your husband comes home before you get a chance to leave in the cab, do call the police right away, the minute you see him approaching. Or call us, and we'll call the police. Don't take the chance of another beating. Now, what is your name and address? I need to take your phone number, too, just in case." The address that the caller, Susan Dunn, gave turned out to be from a rather affluent suburban subdivision.

When Susan Dunn and her two children arrived at the shelter, their appearance betrayed some of their trouble. Susan's left eye was swollen and turning black. She held her sore right arm awkwardly and several fingers were bleeding and discolored. The eyes of both children were red from crying. Susan's clothes were rumpled and torn. She carried a small suitcase, and her 6-year-old daughter was wearing a backpack full of school supplies.

The newcomers entered the shelter, a crowded house in a busy city neighborhood, quite hesitantly and looked anxiously about the first-floor hallway with its worn brown rug and cheerful, hopeful posters. A dark-eyed child of 5 or 6 ran up to greet them. Pamela Wright introduced herself and the child, waiting for Susan to introduce herself in turn, along with her own children: Martha and Todd.

As Pamela Wright completed the introductions, Susan slumped into a chair and tears streamed down her face. She apologized, saying how grateful she was to be there. Pamela asked again about her injuries, and this time Susan replied, "Maybe I do need to see a doctor. My arm and my fingers hurt so much. Maybe something really is broken." Pamela immediately unloaded the children's and Susan's few belongings. "Would it be OK if Sara, our student social worker, helped the children get settled in with something to eat while I take you over to the emergency room to get checked out?" Susan reached for 2-year-old Todd and hugged him to her. She brushed away her tears and said, "I'd really like to get the children comfortable first, then I think it would be a good idea to get my arm checked out."

An hour later, with the children in Sara's gentle care, Pamela drove Susan to the hospital. In the car, Susan talked more about her husband, Jason, a recent college graduate who was building his future in the business world but with increasing stress and growing reliance on alcohol. X-rays demonstrated that Susan's left arm and two fingers were fractured. Pamela helped Susan when the police were contacted by the hospital staff and reports were filed. The ride back to the shelter was a quiet one. Pamela tried to help Susan to understand that she was doing the right thing for herself and her family by taking action to stop the abuse. Susan smiled weakly through her tears. ■

SOCIAL WORK: A UNIQUE PROFESSION

As the case study of Susan Dunn ends, you can probably imagine Pamela Wright's quick glance at Susan and Pamela's observation of the painful way she was moving her body and the grim, anxious expression on Susan's face. In her professional practice, this social worker had come to know well the terror and panic that threatened to overwhelm the women that arrived at the door of the shelter. Pamela's heart went out to Susan. She looked so frightened, so unsure of her decision. But, as a social worker, Pamela also had a good intellectual understanding of the dynamics of domestic abuse and the vulnerability faced by adults and children in at-risk situations. Pamela would review quickly in her mind the information she would need to obtain from Susan and the decisions that might need to be made quickly. She would prepare to use her social work expertise to listen to Susan's story and to offer Susan emotional support. Pamela, a baccalaureate-level social worker (BSW), was proud of her profession and confident in her ability to work with the people served by the shelter.

The Susan Dunn case was designed to introduce readers to this text and also to the profession of social work. Following Chapter 1, each of the chapters in the text will begin with a case study that will further illustrate the many dimensions of the profession, the diversity of the people social workers serve, and the social welfare system that forms the context for social work practice. We begin our exploration of this profession with a definition of social work:

> The major profession that delivers social services in governmental and private organizations throughout the world, social work helps people prevent or resolve problems in psychosocial functioning, achieve life-enhancing goals, and create a just society.

This definition underscores several important aspects of the profession. First, social work emerges out of the governmental and private organizations of nations; therefore, it is grounded in the human social welfare systems of countries. In conjunction with its focus on preventing and resolving problems in psychosocial functioning, the profession seeks to empower people and to identify and build on the strengths that exist in people and their communities. The ultimate goal of the social work profession is social justice.

While there are areas of overlap between social work and other human service professions, there are several ways in which social work is unique. Its dual focus on both the social environment and the psychological functioning of people differentiates social work from professions such as psychology and psychiatry. The social work approach of building on strengths within people and their communities further differentiates social work from these and other professions. The social work profession defines key values that, taken together, are unique among professions. The values guide and define the ethical practice of social workers. These values include belief in the dignity and worth of all persons, commitment to service, and the ultimate goal of social justice, among others. The values appear in the *National Association of Social Workers Code of Ethics* (National Association of Social Workers [NASW], 1996). The code, located in the Appendix, is referred to frequently throughout this book because it is so essential to social work practice.

Social work, then, is a profession that provides an opportunity for people who want to make a difference in their world. Social workers make this difference by helping individual persons, families, and communities, large and small. Social workers are employed by private nonprofit organizations, faith-based agencies, governmental organizations, for-profit organizations, and sometimes have their own private practices. While some social workers function primarily out of their offices, others work primarily in the field. This profession provides challenge, excitement, and splendid opportunities to work with very diverse populations. It also requires courage, ability to see strengths in difficult situations, and willingness to advocate for vulnerable people. As a profession, social work is uniquely committed to the fight for social justice.

PROFESSIONAL SOCIAL WORKERS

Using this basic understanding of the uniqueness of the social work profession as a frame of reference, we will next explore the different levels of professional practice in social work. We will begin with the baccalaureate level, the BSW. This book will emphasize social work at the baccalaureate level; therefore, more substantial information will be provided about BSW practice than the two more advanced areas, the master's (MSW) and doctorate degree levels of the profession.

Generalist BSW Social Workers

The BSW is the first or entry level into the profession. The degree is generally referred to in conversation as a BSW, but the actual degree awarded by colleges and universities ranges from a BA, BS, BSSW, to the BSW degree. All of these baccalaureate degrees are of equal value, assuming that the social work educational program in which the degree is earned is accredited by the Council on Social Work Education. The BSW can be completed in 4 years of college or university work, longer if the student is enrolled on a part-time basis. The BSW social worker, like Pamela Wright in the chapter case study, is professionally prepared as a generalist. What is a generalist? The authors of this text define the generalist social worker as:

> A professional social worker who engages in a planned change process—discovering, utilizing, and making connections to arrive at unique, responsive solutions involving individual persons, families, groups, organizational systems, and communities. Generalist social workers view clients and client systems from a strengths perspective to build upon the innate capabilities existing in all human beings. They respect and value human diversity. Generalists seek to prevent as well as to resolve problems. Generalist social work practice is guided by the NASW Code of Ethics. It is committed to improving the well-being of individuals, families, groups, communities, and organizations and furthering the goals of social justice.

Another way of understanding generalist practice is to look at what it is *not*. A generalist social worker is not a specialist in psychotherapy (treatment of mental disorder) with individuals or families. Nor is she or he an expert in working with groups, nor primarily a community worker. Yet a generalist social worker must often counsel with individuals and families; will often facilitate groups; and must often track down and mobilize, or even create, appropriate community resources.

The Council on Social Work Education, the organization that accredits social work education programs in the United States, requires that baccalaureate programs prepare students to become entry-level professionals in generalist practice. As a generalist with a 4-year baccalaureate degree, there are certain competencies that Pamela Wright must have achieved.

The Expertise of the BSW Social Worker

BSW social workers are well prepared to begin practice when they graduate from college. The courses and fieldwork they complete provide them with knowledge and skills—expertise—in specific areas. These areas of competence are defined by the Council on Social Work Education (CSWE). Although the CSWE educational policy changes somewhat over time, some areas of competence are critical to professional BSW social work practice. BSWs, for example, must be able to:

■ Implement a planned change process of engagement, assessment, planning, intervention, evaluation, and termination with individuals and families as well as groups, organizations, and communities.

■ Engage in practice that respects human difference and diversity.

■ Apply ethical principles in professional practice.

■ Apply bio-psycho-social-cultural-spiritual understandings of human behavior and the social environment to social work practice.

■ Use research to evaluate and improve practice, and use practice experiences to improve the quality of research.

■ Use critical thinking skills.

■ Engage in advocacy and policy practice to promote delivery of effective social work services.

■ Respond to and seek to shape organizations, communities, and larger social systems to promote sustainable, positive change in resources and in the delivery of social services.

■ Advocate for human rights and social justice.

■ Identify with the social work profession, and sustain conduct reflective of the ethics and values of the profession. (CSWE, 2001 and 2007)

Let's look at how Pamela Wright, in the chapter case study, demonstrated her professional competence. As the case study began, Pamela's expertise in telephone interviewing enabled her to quickly determine if Susan could be helped by the shelter. Using her critical, careful thinking skills, Pamela assessed Susan's crisis situation and determined that Susan could be admitted to the shelter. Notice how Pamela used engagement skills as she began to work with Susan. She communicated concern, caring, and respect, yet she obtained necessary information. On the telephone and in welcoming Susan to the shelter, Pamela showed no discrimination based on Susan's age, socioeconomic class, culture, or any other factor.

Pamela's professional competence enabled her to understand the abuse and oppression that Susan had experienced as a woman. Her social work knowledge and skills also enabled her to understand and respect other women at the shelter who were single parents, very poor, disabled, lesbian, or of diverse religions or cultures. Will Pamela Wright tell Susan to divorce her husband and never return to him again? Undoubtedly Pamela wants Susan and her children to be safe and to have a good quality of life, but

Social work field placement student leading a support group session in a domestic violence shelter.

Pamela would be violating one of the ethics of the social work profession if she took away Susan's right as a legally responsible adult to make her own decisions.

Pamela enjoyed working with families. Often she helped children and their mothers find ways to talk to each other about what was happening in their lives. Each evening Pamela conducted group sessions where the women talked about their day-to-day struggles and triumphs. Susan, for example, was astounded to learn in a group session about the exciting ways other residents were building new lives around jobs, further education, and reconnecting to family members. Individuals, families, and groups are three of the social systems that generalists work with.

Sometimes in group sessions at the shelter, issues emerged about the rules or procedures of the shelter. Pamela would advocate with the shelter's staff, executive director, or even the board of directors on behalf of the residents to get needed changes made. It was on the basis of her awareness of a growing number of Hispanic residents that special efforts were made to increase the Hispanic volunteers and staff members at the shelter and to develop educational materials on domestic violence in the Spanish language.

Susan Dunn and the other residents were grateful that the shelter existed, but Pamela and the other staff were deeply concerned that their shelter often had to turn people away. Pamela and the agency director, an MSW social worker who was her supervisor, formed a committee, which included several residents, to conduct research to identify factors related to the increase in domestic violence and possible solutions. Questions about the effectiveness of the current shelter program and the community domestic violence prevention programs were also researched. Pamela was one of the committee members who volunteered to study the changing social welfare policies that limited access to education for women receiving temporary financial assistance. This committee work excited Pamela. She felt especially good to be working toward goals that would further the quality of life of many people in her community. This ability to help individual people and also to make a difference in the larger community was exactly why Pamela chose social work as a career.

The Baccalaureate Social Work Curriculum: How Expertise Evolves

When Pamela was a sophomore student in college, she declared social work as her major. At that time she did not realize that the course of study for the major had been designed to be consistent with the standards of the Council on Social Work Education. In fact, CSWE has provided curriculum requirements for BSW programs since 1974 that begin with a liberal arts base and build on that base to offer a strong and well-integrated professional foundation curriculum. If a college or university's program is to be accredited, it must adhere to the educational policy set by CSWE.

Generally, students begin the social work major with just a few social work courses in the freshman and sophomore years. These courses usually introduce the social work profession and focus on social welfare, its history, current policies, and the impact of political decisions on the people whom social workers seek to help. The first and second years of the social work major are primarily taken up with liberal arts courses, which may include introductory courses in psychology, sociology, biology, college writing, philosophy, literature, and the arts—all courses that provide content that will be used later as professional courses unfold.

Important concepts for professional development appear in the introductory social work and social welfare courses taken in the first year or two of college. Professional ethics and values are among these concepts. A professional person's values significantly affect her or his practice. So, what are values? In general, *values* can be thought of as the philosophical concepts that we cherish as individuals, within our families, and as a nation. The values of the profession can be found in the National Association of Social Workers Code of Ethics, shown in Exhibit 1-1 along with the ethical principles that flow from them. Why are values important pieces of the social work curriculum? Well, society in the United States and in many other countries holds contradictory values concerning the needy. Some values found in society guide people toward helping the poor; others guide people away from helping the poor, either because poor people are viewed as unworthy or because they are viewed as potential competitors. Because we are all products of our society, an honest assessment of our own personal values may reveal that we have absorbed some quite negative values about certain people—the poor, for example. Yet that clearly conflicts with the profession's valuing of social justice.

Probably persons who do not relate to these values will drop out of social work courses as students or will leave the profession early in their careers. By contrast, persons who value human diversity and respect the dignity of others are more likely to be good candidates for a career in social work. Future chapters in this text will

---

EXHIBIT 1-1

NASW Values and Ethical Principles

Value: Service

Ethical Principle: Social worker's primary goal is to help people in need and to address social problems.

Value: Social justice

Ethical Principle: Social workers challenge social injustice.

Value: Dignity and worth of the person

Ethical Principle: Social workers respect the inherent dignity and worth of the person.

Value: Importance of human relationships

Ethical Principal: Social workers recognize the central importance of human relationships.

Value: Integrity

Ethical Principal: Social workers behave in a trustworthy manner.

Value: Competence

Ethical Principal: Social workers practice within their areas of competence and develop and enhance their professional expertise.

SOURCE: National Association of Social Workers. (1996). *NASW Code of Ethics* (rev. 1999). Washington, DC: National Association of Social Workers, pp. 5–6.

---

frequently refer to the National Association of Social Workers (NASW) Code of Ethics. The entire code is reprinted in the Appendix at the back of this book. The six major sections of the Code of Ethics are shown in Exhibit 1-2.

Social work ethics and values will thread their way through all of the junior and senior year courses, too, but the discussion becomes deeper and much more complex, especially in practice theory and field education courses. The introductory courses in social work and social welfare, and also the liberal arts courses in biology, sociology, and psychology, form a basis for one or more courses in Human Behavior and the Social Environment. That content area builds on the prerequisite courses to help students understand why people behave as they do. Studying the phases of human development promotes understanding of human behavior. Learning about social systems and how they interact to promote or deter human well-being adds other important dimensions to the social worker's knowledge base.

EXHIBIT 1-2

National Association of Social Workers Code of Ethics

Six Major Sections of the Code of Ethics

1. Social Workers' Ethical Responsibilities to Clients
2. Social Workers' Ethical Responsibilities to Colleagues
3. Social Workers' Ethical Responsibilities in Practice Settings
4. Social Workers' Ethical Responsibilities as Professionals

5. Social Workers' Ethical Responsibilities to the Social Work Profession
6. Social Workers' Ethical Responsibilities to the Broader Society

SOURCE: National Association of Social Workers. (1996). *NASW Code of Ethics* (rev. 1999). Washington, DC: National Association of Social Workers, pp. 7–27.

To work effectively on behalf of the people they serve, social workers need to understand the basic structures of local, state, national, and even international social welfare systems. Social workers are social change agents, and they want to be a part of the evolution that is constantly under way in the social welfare system. **Policy practice** is the term used for the conscious effort to effect change in the laws, regulations, and provisions of services of governmental and nongovernmental policies and programs.

Social work majors usually take several junior- and senior-year courses in social work practice theory. In these courses they learn how to interview effectively; how to develop respectful, effective relationships with the people they serve; and how to use the planned change process that is at the heart of generalist social work practice. Students learn how to uncover strengths in people and their environments, assess the problem situations faced by their clients, and work collaboratively with clients, not imposing their own solutions but engaging people in discovering new and more effective means for dealing with the difficult situations. Research is interwoven in practice courses and studied in one or more specific courses that help social work majors learn how to use systematic approaches for gathering data from interviews **(qualitative research)** and/or to use statistical, numerical data gathering and analysis to arrive at valid, reliable conclusions **(quantitative research)**. Research skills will help students evaluate the effectiveness of their own practice and also the effectiveness of social programs.

Respect for human diversity and growing understanding of the amazing diversity of the people they serve is another thread that weaves its way through all social work courses. Students learn about cultures, lifestyles, physical and mental health factors, socioeconomic differences, gender orientation, age-related issues, and spiritual values and practices that differ from their own. Understanding and valuing differences is not enough, however. Social workers must learn how to actively explore diversity in practice because it affects every phase of the intervention or problem-solving process. Because social justice is the ultimate goal of the profession, social work education provides special attention to populations that are most at risk of poverty, discrimination, and oppression. These are the unloved people of our society. Social work students need to learn strategies that will be effective in assisting individuals, families, and often whole communities of people. Advocacy strategies can be learned to attain social and economic justice on an individual **(case advocacy)** basis or for whole groups of people **(cause advocacy)**.

Field education generally occurs in the junior and or senior year, when most, if not all, of the other required social work courses have been completed. This is the part of the curriculum that students look forward to most eagerly. BSW students spend a minimum of 400 hours working with clients in one or more supervised field placements. The settings for field placements range widely but may include courts; child or adult protection settings; health care organizations such as hospitals, home health care, or nursing homes; adoption or foster care agencies; community centers; youth-serving organizations; domestic violence shelters; or mental health facilities. Field education is closely monitored and evaluated by social work faculty. By the time students complete field education, they have demonstrated all of the competencies of the generalist social worker. In other words, they are ready to begin professional practice!

BSW social worker interviews child at her school.

Advanced Practice: Social Workers with MSW and PhD Degrees

Advanced and specialized social work practice usually requires additional education. The master's degree in social work (MSW) is a 2-year degree following completion of a baccalaureate degree. Actually, however, an MSW can be completed in as little as 1 year for students who are awarded advanced standing because they have already completed a BSW. The MSW prepares social workers for advanced professional practice in an area of concentration. Although they differ among MSW programs, concentrations include various methods of practice (such as group work, administration), fields of practice (clinical social work or health care), social problem areas (poverty, substance abuse), or special populations (older adults, a cultural group such as Hispanic Americans). Advanced generalist practice is also an area of concentration for some MSW programs.

The domestic violence shelter in the case study employed an MSW social worker as well as Pamela Wright, BSW. Amy Sacks, MSW, received specialized training in working with individuals, families, and groups. Such a concentration is fairly common at the graduate level and may be called direct practice, micro-level intervention, or clinical social work. Amy's role at the shelter is focused and scheduled; she does individual, family, and group therapy by appointment.

Amy is responsible for overseeing the shelter's program in crisis couples' counseling and for the batterers' intervention program, where she works with groups designed specifically for people like Susan Dunn's husband who abuse their partners. In batterers' groups, which are sometimes court-ordered, members must confront their patterns of response to stress and explore new, nonviolent ways of expressing their needs and emotions. These group experiences may be difficult and extremely emotional and are sometimes confrontational; the group process is aimed primarily at personality change rather than at emotional support, which is the main goal for the evening women's groups at the shelter. In therapy groups and in couples' counseling, where personality change is a primary goal, specialized training for the leader or therapist is very important.

Pamela Wright's role at the shelter is broader and more flexible than Amy's. She too counsels individuals, families, and groups, but usually in a less formal manner, often as needed and not necessarily by appointment. In addition, she responds to crisis calls, intervenes in problems among the residents, trains volunteers, and supervises the myriad tasks involved in running a residential facility. She does not live at the shelter but coordinates the schedules of evening staff and occasionally receives calls at night from staff for help during emergencies.

The fact that the BSW is educated to be a generalist does not mean that on occasion she or he does not develop or learn specialized skills in a particular field of practice (or, for that matter, that the MSW cannot be a generalist). In the real world, where funding may not provide the means to hire enough professionals to do a given job, both BSWs and MSWs may end up doing approximately the same thing, but the MSW curriculum provides its students with specialized knowledge in an area of concentration that allows them to work at an advanced practice level. MSWs are also more likely to be promoted to administrative positions, especially in larger organizations. The work of the BSW is usually more diverse and more flexible, and it usually involves mobilizing a wide variety of skills and resources.

Doctorate degrees are also offered in social work. Doctorates are the highest degrees awarded in education. In social work, a doctorate could take 3 to 5 years to complete beyond the master's degree. The doctoral degree in social work, usually a PhD or a DSW, prepares people for teaching in colleges and universities, for specialized advanced practice, or for research and organizational administrative positions.

THE SOCIAL WORK PRACTICE ENVIRONMENT

Regardless of the degree they receive—BSW, MSW, or PhD—social workers tend to be employed in a remarkably wide array of settings. By contrast, teachers tend to be employed in schools, physical therapists and nurses in health care organizations, and psychologists in mental health settings. A misconception about social work, held by some people, is that all social workers are employed by governmental organizations and work with the poor or in child welfare, where they take children away from their parents. Social workers do have special concerns about poverty and social injustice, but social workers work with people of all income levels. They do not work only in governmental offices. And social workers make every possible effort to keep families together.

There are so many misunderstandings about the profession of social work! Many people would be surprised to learn about the range of settings in which social workers are found. To begin with, most social workers are employed by organizations, although some social workers are in private practice similar to the private practice of some doctors. Like many other professionals (e.g., teachers, lawyers, rehabilitation therapists), social workers are also government employees. Actually, a declining number of social workers (currently less than half) are employed in federal, state, or local tax-supported organizations. Increasingly, social workers are likely to be employed by nonprofit private agencies (such as the American Red Cross), denominational (church-sponsored) organizations, or for-profit businesses (most nursing homes fall into this category).

Child welfare or human service departments do employ many BSWs and MSWs, but this is just one area of practice. There is an amazing variety of additional social work employment environments as well. A sampling of these includes:

- Hospitals, emergency rooms, nursing homes, home health care, clinics.
- Police departments, probation and parole offices, juvenile detention facilities.
- Group homes or residential facilities that care for runaway children, persons with disabilities, or frail elderly persons.
- Legislative offices at all levels of government.
- Senior centers, older adult day care, planning councils for older adult programs.
- Immigrant and refugee centers.
- Schools.
- Disaster relief services.

New environments for social work practice constantly evolve. Genetic counseling, for example, has grown in recent years. Social workers who once specialized in child adoption placement now find themselves helping people locate their birth parents. War, terrorism, and natural disasters have resulted in a need for social workers who can help people get their basic needs met and deal with physical as well as psychological trauma.

While most social workers spend the majority of their working hours in their offices or their organizational settings, where their clients come to meet with them, this isn't true for others. Many social workers go wherever people are experiencing problems—to the places where people live, work, study, and play. Social workers who make home visits know that entering into the natural environment of people, entering into their world, often makes people more comfortable and is much less threatening than an office visit. Social workers may also meet their clients in a coffee shop, in a library, in a school or hospital, or even on the streets if they are doing outreach work to persons who are homeless, for example. When working with children in foster care or detention or in contested custody cases, social workers may spend hours in court. Daily practice brings social workers into contact with other professional people, including other social workers. Meetings in the community occur frequently as groups of professional people, including social workers, come together to advocate for new legislation, for example.

Regardless of their settings, social workers have offices where, generally, some clients, family members, or other professionals meet with them. Here, too, the social worker has access to telephone, fax, and files as well as computers. Even those social workers who primarily do outreach work or home visits need to spend many hours in their offices. Here, too, consultation with colleagues or a more experienced social worker, a supervisor, is attainable. Students doing an internship or field placement would also use the office as a home base.

A BROADER ENVIRONMENTAL PERSPECTIVE

The practice environment is actually much larger than just office settings and homes that are sometimes visited by social workers. While these may capture our attention, our social work focus should also be widened so that it brings into view the physical environment in which we work, play, and share our lives with the rest of the world. Early pioneers of the social work profession paid keen attention to the condition of the environment. Somewhere along the way, though, perhaps around the time that Freudian psychodynamic theory began to influence us, the profession gradually narrowed its sphere of concern. The profession became fascinated with the clinical context of human existence, and social workers began to focus their attention on the social and emotional relationships that influenced people's lives.

Today, however, the profession is beginning to awaken to the significance of our global physical environment. Natural disasters such as tsunamis and hurricanes have wreaked destruction in the recent past and seem to be occurring with increased frequency throughout the world. War and industrial pollution are claiming victims in many parts of the world. Our asthma-infected children and health threats from toxic contamination of produce being sold in our supermarkets have given many Americans a renewed concern about the physical environment.

Social workers are responding with increased interest in the relationship between human social welfare and ecology. Mizrahi and Clark, in *Social Work Speaks*, describe conditions of special concern to American social workers:

> The inextricable links among poverty, environmental degradation, and risk to human well-being cannot be denied. The relationships are clear in polluted inner-city neighborhoods where children of color suffer from high rates of asthma; in crop lands where poor migrant workers carry agricultural pesticides home to their families on their work clothes; in low-income Louisiana parishes along the industrial "Cancer Alley" stretch of the Mississippi River; and in the unsanitary, crowded, and hastily and poorly constructed maquiladoras that house Mexican plant workers along the United States–Mexico border. (2003, pp. 118–119)

What this means for social workers is that as students and practitioners, we need to be invested in building a healthy environment for all people. We need to develop our understanding of the relationship between poverty and the risks emanating from degraded environments. In our daily social work practice, we need to take special care not to further endanger people by placing them in unsafe housing, and we need to work with landlords, volunteer groups, neighborhoods, and communities to clean up degraded areas and create environments that can nurture children, families, and older adults. Of great importance is the advocacy that we engage in together with other environmental activists. Whether we are working with individual clients, families, or groups, or within organizations or communities, our professional behaviors must reflect a sense of responsibility for environmental concerns.

SOCIAL WORK PROFESSIONAL ROLES

The professional behaviors that comprise social work practice are referred to as professional roles. Whether we are assisting an individual client like Susan Dunn in the chapter case study or engaging in environmental advocacy at the state level, our generalist social work professional roles are at the heart of our practice. What are roles? If we were looking at *role* from a sociological perspective, we would think of behaviors that are prescribed or defined by culture, society, and perhaps families. Professional roles, then, are the behaviors that are expected from persons who are sanctioned by society through education and legal certification to provide service in a specific profession. Most of us, for example, have a pretty good idea of what to expect from a doctor or a teacher. For social work, role expectations are not quite as clearly understood by the general public. Perhaps this is because there are so many professional roles in social work. The number and diversity of social work roles, however, provide opportunity for a great deal of creativity in practice. Let us look at a few of these professional roles.

Probably the most frequently used role is that of communicator. Verbal, nonverbal, and written communication skills are critical for social workers. Skill must be developed in interviewing, which incorporates verbal and nonverbal communication across the full range of diversity represented by social work clients and communities. Interviewing also incorporates relationship building. Creating an emotional environment that will enable clients to feel sufficiently comfortable and trustful to tell their stories requires an ability to communicate acceptance of the client and sincere interest in the client's concerns. Communication can be quite a challenge, and it is a skill that should be nurtured and that should grow throughout one's career. The relevance of good writing skills is apparent when a social worker's letter of recommendation to a juvenile court judge will help the judge decide whether to sentence a child to a prison or to permit the child to be placed on probation. Letters are just one form of written communication. Social workers are also responsible for report writing, assessments of new clients, summaries of progress or at termination, and efforts to advocate on behalf of people. Environmental advocacy, as described in the previous section of this chapter, would surely require both verbal and written communication skills.

The role of counselor is one of the most frequently used roles in social work. Empowering people and helping them deal with feelings are characteristic of this role. Affirming personal strengths in clients helps them find energy and motivation to tackle problems and to relinquish apathy and resistance. The counselor role focuses on improving "social functioning by modifying behaviors, relationship patterns, and social and physical environments" (Miley, O'Melia, & DuBois, 2007, p. 17). It is also used to help people cope with stress, crises, or changing life circumstances. Psychotherapy could be considered an advanced level of counseling, in which specially trained and certified professionals, including social workers, "help resolve symptoms of mental disorder, psychosocial stress, relationship problems, and difficulties in coping" (Barker, 2003, p. 349). While counseling is an inherent part of nearly all social workers' practice, the psychotherapy role is reserved for the MSW social workers with clinical training.

Another frequently used role is that of advocate. An **advocate** is someone who fights for the rights of others or fights to obtain needed resources. When a social worker, after lengthy phone calls and a rather difficult meeting, is finally able to convince the director of a shelter to keep a family for a week beyond the allotted time, the social worker was a successful advocate. Social workers advocate with doctors, teachers, judges, landlords, and even employers in their effort to obtain health care, special education, reduced sentencing, improved housing, or employment accommodations for a disabled worker, for example. Advocacy efforts can be used on behalf of large populations of people, too, such as using the political process to create state or federal low-income housing or health care programs.

The **broker** role is somewhat similar to the advocate role. Brokering, however, usually doesn't require strongly assertive action. Instead, the social worker uses the process of referral to link a family or person to needed resources. A new mother, for example, might be given information about doctors or clinics that will provide immunizations and health care for her baby. Effective brokers do not simply provide information; they also follow up to be sure that needed resources were actually obtained. For the broker role, social workers need knowledge of the location and quality of services that are available, eligibility requirements, and fees, but they also need the ability to help people make effective use of services (Kirst-Ashman & Hull, 2002).

Professional roles are often intertwined. The case manager role blends elements of all the roles previously mentioned and adds some new dimensions. **Case management** typically involves planning, locating, securing, and monitoring quality of services for people who are unable to do this because of ill health or frailties. Persons with chronic mental illness, infirm elderly persons, children with disabilities, or homeless families may all benefit from case management. Case management services may be brief, but often they are needed over a very long time, sometimes for a lifetime. Counseling is nearly always a component of case management, especially counseling that enables clients to achieve maximum benefit from the services they receive. Case management in social work should not be confused with the case management sometimes used in health care where the goal is to increase economic profits of a facility by denying access to care. Social work case management, instead, has a goal of increasing access and ensuring that good quality care is provided.

Do you think of social workers as teachers? Perhaps not, but in their role of **educator,** social workers do teach people about available resources, how to use services, how to communicate effectively, even how to budget or to discipline children safely and lovingly. A hospital social worker may help a physician make a medical diagnosis understandable to a patient. When working with child neglect or abuse situations, social workers teach effective parenting skills. Coaching is an educational tool that may be used by a group worker to improve the socialization skills of lonely, insecure, socially immature adolescents. Speaking of groups, the **facilitator** role is prominent in social work with groups. As facilitators, social workers convene groups, introduce members, promote communication, and engage members in planning, decision making, and goal attainment.

In creating community change, the role of **organizer** is a powerful one. A social worker may, for example, bring representatives of several Native American social agencies together with members of environmental groups in an effort to build concerted, united opposition to legislation that proposes to open up forested reservation land to industrial exploitation. The organizer role could also be used to effect policy changes within a social agency, especially if the agency administrator or board of directors is resistant to the expressed needs of staff or clients.

Social workers create change. Professional roles shape and guide the action that generates change. Just a few of the many potential social work roles have been described here, but they offer some insight into how social workers practice their profession. Next we turn to an exploration of educational preparation for professional social work practice. Because this book's focus is on BSW social work, baccalaureate social work education will command our attention.

SELECTING A CAREER IN SOCIAL WORK

College students typically experience a great deal of pressure to select a major and begin a career path. Selecting a career is surely one of life's most exciting and most difficult challenges. Fortunately, many resources are available to help with decisions about choice of career. Career counseling centers in colleges and universities offer a variety of aptitude and interest tests. The Internet and libraries offer resources such as the *Occupational Outlook Handbook* of the U.S. Bureau of Labor Statistics. Professors and advisers are yet another source of career advice and information. In the end, however, the choice is a very personal one.

Many college students know very little about the profession of social work, yet some might think that social work could potentially be a career that would enable them to accomplish their desire of helping others. This text seeks to help you determine if a social work career is right for you.

You will find that every chapter in this text begins with a case study describing social workers in action. In the next several paragraphs, you will learn about the paths taken by several of the case study social workers as they launched their careers. This text is primarily focused on professional social work at the baccalaureate level, so the three social work career tracks introduced are of BSW social workers. (Please note that the people in the case studies are actually fictitious.) We will begin with Pamela Wright from this chapter's case study.

Pamela Wright

Pamela Wright entered college directly from high school. She had years of volunteer experience in the grade school where her mother was a teacher, and she knew the inner workings of hospitals through her father's employment as an accountant in a local hospital. Pamela knew that she wanted to be a social worker, and, while in college, she selected elective courses in some of the liberal arts areas that would enhance her social work competence: courses in psychology, Spanish, and political science. Her senior-year social work field placement was with an inner-city shelter for homeless families. As Pamela told her dorm roommate, she just loved her work at the shelter, especially her work with abused women and their children. Following graduation, Pamela was immediately employed by the shelter that provided emergency care for Susan Dunn and her children.

Alan Martin

In Chapter 10 you will meet Jamie Sullivan's parole agent, Alan Martin. The 2 years Alan spent working on the family farm after high school convinced him that farming was not his calling in life. Accounting, bank financing, and crop planning necessitated a lot of paperwork, allowing for minimal interaction with people. After his father's death, Alan and his mother sold the farm to pay off Alan's father's medical expenses. When Alan enrolled at the state university branch campus, he was not sure what major to declare, but he was certain that he wanted to work with people. At the start of his sophomore year, Alan enrolled in an Introduction to Social Work course. A guest speaker for his class, a social worker who was a probation/parole agent for the state, especially intrigued him. Neither Alan's student field placement nor his first job following graduation was in the criminal justice field. In his substance abuse position, however, several of Alan's clients were on probation, and his contacts with their probation agents reawakened Alan's interest in the criminal justice system. Alan decided to take the exam for a probation/parole agent position. Six months and several interviews later, Alan received notice that he had been approved for a position, and, luckily, it was with the office that served youths in the rural western part of the state. The best of both worlds! Alan really preferred living in a rural area. He also especially enjoyed working with youths. His new position was with the juvenile probation and parole unit. By the time Jamie Sullivan, an adolescent convicted of armed robbery, met with Alan for the first time, Alan had 4 years' experience in juvenile justice work.

Madeleine Johnson

Unlike Alan Martin, Madeleine Johnson grew up in a middle-class, primarily African American suburb of a large metropolitan city. Along with her two older sisters, Madeleine was involved in volunteer work with her church's youth groups. Madeleine's mother's volunteer service at a church was the inspiration for her first career. Madeleine completed an associate degree in nursing and worked in various hospitals and outpatient clinics for 5 years. Following her divorce and a period of personal unhappiness, Madeleine decided to pursue a second career. When she returned to college, she found that it would take a total of 3 more years to earn a social work degree, but Madeleine was determined to do this. Her life experience proved to be a real asset, making courses in history, philosophy, and research much more interesting than she had expected. Madeleine really enjoyed the role-play exercises in the social work courses; she could understand how clients might feel, and yet she could also sense compatibility with the role of the social worker. Because of her nursing background, Madeleine was initially interested in a hospital field placement but was challenged by the social work faculty to explore new areas. After careful thought, a public social service agency was selected. Here, Madeleine was given experience with nurturing groups for teen parents and with intensive, in-home services to families where child abuse had occurred. The panel that interviewed Madeleine when she applied for a position with the Salvation Army after graduation was impressed with her years of volunteer work, her experience as a nurse in health care, and her field placement with the public family and children's agency. You will learn about Madeleine Johnson's work with Dan Graves at the Salvation Army in Chapter 8.

The case studies introduce some social workers who struggled with career decisions, just as readers of this text may be struggling. "I want to help people. Which profession should I pursue? Am I in the right major?" These questions are asked over and over again by college students. Social work is an exciting career. There are few "dull moments" in a day for social workers. It is a career that enables people to make a difference in the lives of others. It offers opportunities to transform the world. But it isn't the right profession for all people. Students are encouraged to talk with social workers, to do volunteer work, or perhaps to test their ability to work with others through a part-time job in the broad area of human services. Taking an introductory course in social work or social welfare is a very useful way for students to further explore their suitability for a career in social work. We hope this book will increase our readers' understanding of social work as a profession. We hope, too, that it will provide a sense of the remarkable opportunities this profession offers to people who sincerely want to make a difference in this world that we share.

EDUCATION AND THE SOCIAL WORK CAREER LADDER

In selecting a career, it is important for college students to understand the concept of the career ladder, which includes a progression of career advancement opportunities within a single, recognized profession. A **career ladder** is constructed of the steps one must take to progress upward and therefore to advance in a profession or occupation. The notion of a career ladder is based on the assumption that it is possible to begin at a low level and then to move from one position to another, continuously progressing toward the top of the ladder.

In some occupations or professions, obtaining an entry degree enables a person to progress up the ladder without returning to school for graduate or postgraduate degrees, advancing based primarily on performance. In other professions, the career-ladder concept is viable only if additional academic credentials are obtained. Social work reflects an interesting mix. As Exhibit 1-3 shows, there are multiple educational levels within the profession. Each is explained next, along with typical responsibilities.

At the lowest rung of the ladder is the *preprofessional* (also referred to as paraprofessional) *social work or human service aide*. Although they do not have access to membership in NASW or to professional status, persons with bachelor's degrees in areas related to social work (e.g., psychology, sociology, and behavioral science majors) and persons with associate degrees are employed in human services. They assist clients by helping with complicated paperwork or performing tasks such as assisting chronically mentally ill

EXHIBIT 1-3

The Social Work Career Ladder and Professional Education

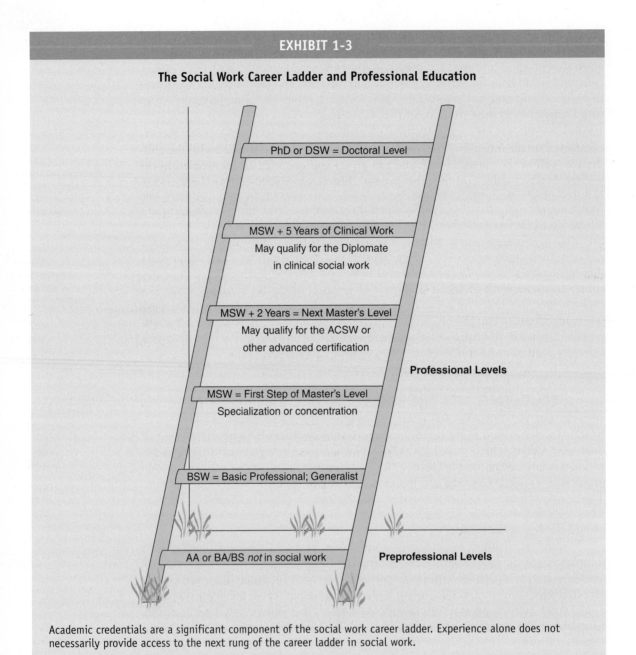

PhD or DSW = Doctoral Level

MSW + 5 Years of Clinical Work
May qualify for the Diplomate
in clinical social work

MSW + 2 Years = Next Master's Level
May qualify for the ACSW or
other advanced certification

Professional Levels

MSW = First Step of Master's Level
Specialization or concentration

BSW = Basic Professional; Generalist

AA or BA/BS *not* in social work

Preprofessional Levels

Academic credentials are a significant component of the social work career ladder. Experience alone does not necessarily provide access to the next rung of the career ladder in social work.

persons, frail elderly people, or persons with disabilities to obtain needed resources. Some preprofessional staff members are hired without regard for their academic credentials but, instead, for their extensive firsthand knowledge of the community served by the agency.

The *BSW* is the basic entry level. The academic credential for this category is precisely defined: a bachelor's degree from a college or university social work program that is accredited by the Council on Social Work Education. The basic professional level social worker has been prepared as a generalist and is able to engage in practice with individuals, families, groups, organizations, and communities. In this chapter's case illustration, a distinction is made between the responsibilities of Pamela Wright, the BSW, and those of Amy Sacks, who has an MSW degree. Pamela conducted intake interviews for the domestic violence shelter, worked with the children as well as the client herself, and ran group sessions with all the women in the shelter. As a recognized professional person, Pamela was able to engage clients, do an assessment of the problem, design and carry out an intervention plan, and then terminate and evaluate the intervention. Amy Sacks, in contrast, functioned at the MSW professional level.

The master's degree in social work, the *MSW,* must also be from a program accredited by the Council on Social Work Education. The curriculum of master's degree programs builds on generalist content to develop a concentration in a practice method or social problem area; some master's degrees focus on advanced generalist practice. The MSW social worker should be able to engage in generalist social work practice and also function as a specialist in more complex tasks. Amy Sacks, the MSW social worker at the shelter in the case study, received specialized graduate training in clinical social work. At the shelter Amy's role is more focused and the service she provides is in greater depth than Pamela Wright's. Amy does individual, family, and group therapy, usually by appointment. In addition, Amy is the executive director of the shelter.

At the top of the professional education classification system is the *social work doctorate.* Some doctoral programs have a research or teaching focus, whereas others prepare for advanced clinical practice. Although the number of doctoral programs has been growing, in a recent NASW study only 2 percent of licensed social workers had social work doctorates (Whitaker, Weismiller, & Clark, 2006).

EMPLOYMENT OPPORTUNITIES

Unfortunately, it is rather difficult to find research that accurately describes the full scope of employment of social workers. One very plausible reason for this is that social workers are so often employed under other titles. In some states, too, it is still possible for persons without degrees from accredited social work programs to obtain licensure or certification as social workers; research that included these persons would not provide a true picture of social work employment in that state. Researching the NASW membership base also fails to provide a clear picture of social work employment because not all social workers, whether BSWs, MSWs, or PhDs, hold membership in the social work national organization. While not providing a truly comprehensive survey of the profession, selected studies can provide useful data about employment in social work.

A Research Question: Where Do Social Work College Graduates Find Jobs?

Fortunately a valuable set of research data on employment of social work college graduates is available. It is collected annually from BSW social work programs by the Association of Baccalaureate Social Work Program Directors Inc. (BPD). This research is part of a nationwide effort to assess the outcomes of baccalaureate social work education and to determine if BSW programs meet the needs of their graduates as well as the needs of employing agencies.

Persons who graduated two years previously responded to the survey reflected in Exhibit 1-4. The graduates' responses about employment provide an answer to one of the most frequently asked questions about social work: Where do social work majors get jobs after graduation? As Exhibit 1-4 shows, child welfare settings accounted for the largest percentage (20.5 percent) of these social workers' primary employment practice settings, followed closely by mental health. An interesting pattern that emerged from this study was that no single type of employment setting accounted for much more than 20 percent of the social workers' practice settings. (This finding may reflect one of the purposes of baccalaureate social work education: to prepare generalist social workers who can competently work in a wide variety of settings.) If clusters of similar settings are combined, it can be seen that close to one-third of BSW social workers were employed in child and family services (child welfare and family services), and a similar portion were employed in health care (mental health, health/medical,

EXHIBIT 1-4	
Primary Fields of Practice of BSWs 2006	
Child welfare/child protection	20.5%
Mental/behavioral/CMH	15.7
Aging/gerontological social work	10.9
Family services	8.3
Health/medical	7.4
Mental retardation/developmental disabilities	5.7
Alcohol, drug, or substance Abuse	4.5
Crisis intervention/information and referral	4.3
School social work	4.0
Corrections/criminal justice	2.6
Other	16.1

SOURCE: V. Buchan, G. Hull, C. Pike, B. Rodenhiser, J. Rogers, & M. Smith. (2006). BEAP total reports: Primary field of practice of your current social work position. *BPD Baccalaureate Education Assessment Project*. Retrieved January 8, 2007, from http://beap.socwk.utah.edu

and alcohol, drug, or other substance abuse) (Buchan et al., 2006). The BPD survey findings related to fields of practice are not new. The surveys conducted by this organization have produced remarkably similar findings for more than 15 years.

Another way of looking at jobs for BSWs is to consider the auspices, public or private, of their employing organizations. The data from the BPD survey of graduates shown in Exhibit 1-5 are especially interesting because they demonstrate that an overwhelming portion of baccalaureate social workers are not employed by governmental agencies, as is often assumed. In fact, in the survey population, two-thirds of the graduates were employed in the private sector. This is a considerable shift! In 1999 just over half of BSW program graduates were employed by governmental agencies, and for at least the preceding 10 years survey data showed that 50 percent of BSW grads were employed by governmental agencies. Exhibit 1-5 also reflects private, for-profit sector employment of BSWs; this is another very new trend (Buchan et al., 2006).

The largest employer of BSWs, as shown in Exhibit 1-5, is the private, nonsectarian sector (the American Red Cross would be one example). The largest governmental employer in the BPD study proved to be state government. This could include state child welfare programs such as foster care, adoptions, or child safety services. It could also reflect employment in state aging programs, mental health, or probation and parole.

Employment Patterns for MSWs

Research on licensed social workers reported by NASW in 2006 provides a picture of social work practice of persons who hold primarily the MSW degree; 79 percent of the survey respondents had completed an MSW and 12 percent held BSW degrees as

EXHIBIT 1-5	
Employment Auspices of BSWs, 2006	
Private nonprofit nonreligious	37.4%
Private nonprofit religious	15.1
Private for profit	13.9
	66.4%
Public state	18.2
Public county, municipal, or town	11.9
Public federal nonmilitary	3.0
Public federal military	0.5
	33.6%
	100%

SOURCE: V. Buchan, G. Hull, C. Pike, B. Rodenhiser, J. Rogers, & M. Smith. (2006). BEAP total reports: Type of organization where you are currently employed. *BPD Baccalaureate Education Assessment Project*. Retrieved January 8, 2007, from http://beap.socwk.utah.edu

their highest degree earned in social work (Whitaker et al., 2006). The NASW study has somewhat different categories, but it is interesting to compare Exhibit 1-6, the primary practice areas of the MSW social workers, with Exhibit 1-4, which illustrates the primary practice areas of BSWs. The largest portion of BSWs was employed in child welfare, whereas the largest percentage of the NASW, primarily MSW group, worked in mental health (the second strongest area for BSW employment). Work with older adults attracted 10.9 percent of BSWs and 9 percent of MSWs. This is such an expanding field that one might expect this to be a strong growth area in the future. Both BSWs and MSWs were widely scattered across the many other areas of practice.

Private sector employment is growing significantly for BSW practitioners, although not as psychotherapists (a role that is appropriate only to MSWs or doctoral professionals). Private sector employment includes quite a variety of employment settings, but all are administered by privately funded organizations. Many of these organizations do seek out and use considerable amounts of governmental funds to conduct their programs. A nonprofit child welfare organization may actually contract with a state or county public welfare office to provide the child protection services that, in the past, the county had provided. Religious denominational organizations,

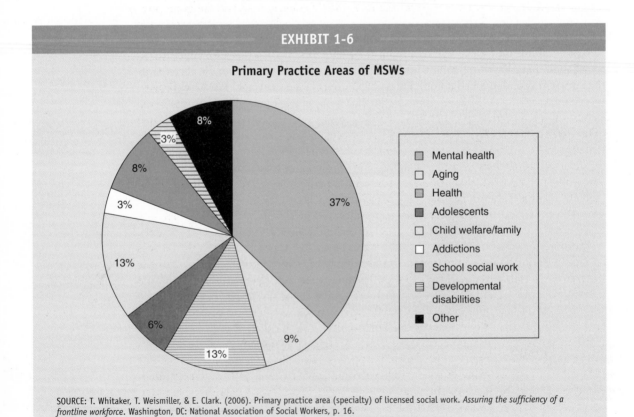

EXHIBIT 1-6

Primary Practice Areas of MSWs

Legend:
- Mental health
- Aging
- Health
- Adolescents
- Child welfare/family
- Addictions
- School social work
- Developmental disabilities
- Other

Pie chart values: 37%, 9%, 13%, 6%, 13%, 3%, 8%, 3%, 8%

SOURCE: T. Whitaker, T. Weismiller, & E. Clark. (2006). Primary practice area (specialty) of licensed social work. *Assuring the sufficiency of a frontline workforce*. Washington, DC: National Association of Social Workers, p. 16.

too, often seek grants or contracts with public agencies to support their programs. The newest area, at least for BSWs, is the for-profit sector. These organizations, as the name implies, must provide services in a way that ensures that the corporation will earn a profit for its owners. Counseling positions in mental health, house manager and group facilitation positions in group homes, telephone crisis and referral jobs in employee assistance programs—these are all examples of the kinds of for-profit employment opportunities that are increasingly available to baccalaureate social workers. The 2006 NASW study of licensed social workers, interestingly, found 66 percent of their study population employed in the private sector—the exact percentage of BSWs shown by the BPD study to be in the private sector.

Salaries and Demand for Social Workers

In recent years there has been a very uneven job market for social workers. In some urban areas of the United States it has been difficult for social workers to find employment. At the same time, however, states such as Texas, Iowa, and Arkansas were seeking social workers. Rural areas were so desperate for social work staff that they employed uncredentialed people because they were unable to attract professionally trained social workers.

The job search experiences reported in the BPD studies, however, are quite positive. Although some BSW respondents elected to go to graduate school after receiving their degrees and a small number sought employment in another field or were not successful in finding social work jobs, more than 75 percent consistently obtained social work employment. These recent graduates routinely provided information about their first social work job search for the annual BPD survey. Recent survey data showed that a considerable number, 34.8 percent, already had a social work job when they graduated from college, one that they had held before starting school or one they had obtained while they were in school. An additional 31.5 percent found social work positions within three months after graduation. By six months after graduation, 88.3 percent had taken a position in social work at the baccalaureate level (Buchan et al., 2006). These data are encouraging when we recognize that sometimes people need time for themselves or their families and therefore delay a job search for weeks or even months.

When looking at salary data, it is important to consider several factors. First, it is very important to keep in mind that social work salaries tend to increase every year. The salary information that we provide in this book is outdated as soon as the book is published, so the salary information we provide here is very likely to be *less* than the salary that social workers in the field are earning when you read this report, and the data reported here are likely to be considerably lower than the salaries students are likely to earn when they graduate. Social work salaries vary immensely by region of the country, years of experience, field of practice and auspice, and highest degree earned. Another important factor to remember is that commitment to vulnerable populations is a stronger motivation for some social workers than salary, and many accept employment with seriously underfunded organizations that pay extremely small salaries. This, then, tends to skew the earnings data on social work employment and to give an impression of lower salaries than the salaries that may, in fact, be available from other organizations. The Bureau of Labor Statistics' *Occupational Outlook*

Handbook (2006b) is a good source for current general salary information. The 2006–2007 edition (pp. 5–6) reported the following data on 2004 median annual salaries for social workers according to their field of practice:

Child, family, and school social workers	$34,820 annual; $57,860 for top 10%
Medical and public health social workers	$40,080 annual; $58,740 for top 10%
Mental health and substance abuse social workers	$33,920 annual; $54,180 for top 10%
All other social work fields of practice	$39,440 annual; $62,720 + for top 10%

An NASW study conducted by Whitaker, Weismiller, and Clark (2006) provides additional interesting data about social work salaries. In their survey, the median income for the study group (comprised primarily of MSWs but including some BSWs) was $47,640. Considering that some social workers choose to work in underfunded organizations because of the vulnerable populations they wish to serve, it is not surprising that there were some fairly low salaries even among MSWs. What might be surprising for some people is the fact that some salaries exceeded $100,000. The annual salaries of all social workers in the NASW study are depicted in Exhibit 1-7. Exhibit 1-8 demonstrates that the size of community in which the person is employed is also a factor in salary; perhaps the lower cost of living of the smaller or rural areas needs to be considered when thinking about the lower incomes that are shown to exist in those areas.

EXHIBIT 1-7

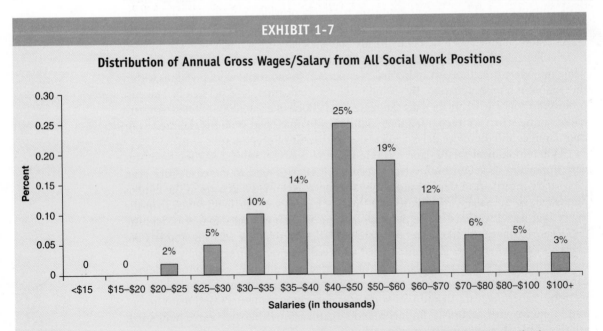

Distribution of Annual Gross Wages/Salary from All Social Work Positions

SOURCE: T. Whitaker, T. Weismiller, & E. Clark. (2006). Distribution of annual gross wages/salary from all social work positions. *Assuring the sufficiency of a frontline workforce.* Washington, DC: National Association of Social Workers, p. 28.

EXHIBIT 1-8

Median Salaries of Full-Time Social Workers, by Rural Urban Location and Sector of Primary Employment

Sector of Primary Employment	Metropolitan Area	Micropolitan Area	Small Town	Rural Area	Total
Private practice	$58,747	$47,820	$46,415	$34,266	$57,357
Private, not-for-profit	46,482	40,658	36,344	38,542	44,998
Private, for-profit	47,286	45,713	39,332	33,628	46,433
Government	51,833	39,681	41,123	37,906	48,351
Total	49,175	42,160	39,014	37,641	47,640

SOURCE: T. Whitaker, T. Weismiller, & E. Clark. (2006). Table 3, Median salaries of full-time social workers, by rural urban location and sector of primary employment. *Assuring the sufficiency of a frontline workforce.* Washington, DC: National Association of Social Workers, p. 29.

Again, a reminder: both MSW and BSW salaries tend to increase each year, so the salary information in these exhibits probably won't be a true representation of social work salaries when you read them, and they will be even less representative of social work salaries by the time you graduate from college. Salaries also vary considerably across the different geographic regions of the United States.

Future Employment Opportunities for Social Workers

Economic conditions, the political climate, social welfare policy decisions made by our government, even changing demographics and technological advances—all of these factors affect employment prospects in social work and other fields. Replacement needs as some social workers retire or leave for other reasons also influence the number of positions available.

"Landmark Study Warns of Impending Labor Force Shortages for Social Work Profession" was the headline for an NASW press release announcing findings from the 2006 Whitaker et al., study. Although MSWs were overrepresented in this study of licensed social workers, BSWs and even a very small number of persons without social work degrees were included. NASW, with a sense of urgency, reported these findings in the press release:

■ The number of new social workers providing services to older adults is decreasing, despite projected increases in the number of older adults who will need social work services.

■ The supply of licensed social workers is insufficient to meet the needs of organizations serving children and families.

■   Workload expansion plus fewer resources impedes social worker retention.

■   Agencies struggle to fill social work vacancies (Nadelhaft & Rene, 2006, pp. 1–2).

NASW's Center for Workforce Studies expects to continue to collect and disseminate data as emerging demographic trends challenge the profession's ability to produce sufficient social workers for the near future (Whitaker et al., 2006).

Already there are reports of shortages in social workers, not just in the United States but also in other parts of the world. As early as 2001 a *Social Worker Today* article, reporting on a California state assembly hearing, cited "a severe shortage of trained social workers and the lack of a candidate pool to fill employment positions" as well as an insufficient number of social work students graduating from state schools (Harvey, 2001, p. 20). In 2006, Hawaii's Department of Human Services reported a shortage of social workers for their child welfare department, and Kaui Castillo of the Queen Liliuokalani Center told a reporter: "We are seeing this in child welfare, gerontology, mental health, the criminal justice system, schools and health in general" (Lee, 2006, p. 1). In Capetown, South Africa, the Minister of Social Development stated that "a critical shortage of social workers [is] inhibiting the provision of welfare services . . . The extent to which we are able to provide social welfare services is fundamentally influenced by critical shortages in the supply of social workers and other social service professionals" (News 24, 2006, p. 1). Reports from Scotland and the United Kingdom also showed serious shortages of social workers. Efforts to recruit social workers in other countries, especially in Canada, have not been effective to meet the needs that exist in London and other metropolitan parts of the United Kingdom, according to a 2005 report (Community Action, p. 1). In Scotland, the Minister of Education expressed grave concern that children's welfare was potentially being jeopardized as a result of the social work shortage. She asked that the social work profession seek out new methods to recruit social workers in order to stop even a greater crisis to occur within social work departments across the country (SNP: It's Time, 2005).

Returning to the U.S. Department of Labor for data, we find that 562,000 social work jobs existed in 2004, a considerable increase from 468,000 in 2000. The Department of Labor's *Occupational Outlook Handbook 2006–2007* listed the following categories of social workers (2006a, p. 5):

Child, family, and school social workers	272,000
Medical and public health social workers	110,000
Mental health and substance abuse social workers	116,000
Social workers, all other	64,000

The *Occupational Outlook Handbook*, perhaps in answer to the question about social work shortages, reported that there tends to be more competition in cities for social work jobs. This is especially likely in cities where professional educational programs are present. In rural areas, however, the need for social workers is often very great and shortages of social workers are very apparent. In fact, rural areas appear to have great difficulty attracting and retaining social workers. In view of these data, what employment projections does the U.S. Department of Labor make for social workers?

"Employment for social workers is expected to increase faster than the average for all occupations through 2014" (Bureau of Labor Statistics, 2006b, p. 4). This prediction is a remarkably strong statement!

The U.S. Department of Labor categorizes social work, along with psychology and other human service professions, within the professional and related occupations area. The Labor Department's *Occupational Outlook Handbook* predicts that from 2004 to 2014, total employment in the United States will increase by 18.9 million, a growth rate of about 13 percent. The professional and related occupations group, however, "will grow the fastest and add more new jobs (6.0 million) than any other major occupational group" (Bureau of Labor Stastics, 2006c, p. 2).

The employment outlook for some professions within the general category of professional and related occupations is not as positive as for others. Employment positions in psychology, for example, are expected to increase by 18.7 percent (from 179,000 in 2004 to 212,000 in 2014) compared with a 22 percent increase (from 562,000 in 2004 to 686,000 in 2014) for social workers (Hecker, 2005, p. 85). The Labor Department also notes that in psychology, a doctorate degree is required for most clinical work, although the master's degree is acceptable for some positions in schools and industry. Few opportunities are projected for persons holding only a bachelor's degree in psychology (Bureau of Labor Statistics, 2006a).

Why will social work positions increase in the future? The increasing population of older persons is one reason. The U.S. Department of Labor projects rapid increases in social work positions in the field of gerontology. A rapidly growing aging population plus the aging baby-boomer generation will require services—services to assist with the stresses that accompany midlife crises related to career as well as personal issues. Increased demand for social workers is also expected in home health care, assisted living, and hospice programs. There is also anticipated strong demand for social workers in substance abuse areas as increasingly persons who abuse substances are being placed in treatment programs rather than given prison sentences. Additional growth areas include school social work and employee assistance programs (Bureau of Labor Statistics, 2006b).

The Internet Sites section in this chapter contains several sites that offer considerable additional information about employment in social work. Social work faculty members and college and university libraries are also good sources of information about career opportunities. Professional organizations such as the National Association of Social Workers and the Council on Social Work Education can also be contacted for additional information.

LEGAL REGULATION OF THE PROFESSION

State Licensure and Certification

Can doctors practice their profession without being licensed? Can pharmacists? Dentists? How about social workers? While there are some situations in which doctors, pharmacists, and dentists may practice without a license, these are relatively few. Medicine, pharmacy, and dentistry were among the first professions to be legally regulated in the United States (Biggerstaff, 1995). **Legal regulation,** according to *The Social Work Dictionary*, is "the control of certain activities, such as professional conduct, by government rule and enforcement" (Barker, 2003, p. 246). Today doctors, pharmacists, and dentists are licensed by the states in which they practice.

Social workers, too, are legally regulated in all states in the United States. The first statute providing for legal regulation of social workers was passed in Puerto Rico in 1934 (Thyer & Biggerstaff, 1989). There are several different forms of legal regulation governing social work. In most states social workers are licensed, generally at both the BSW and the MSW level. In a few states social workers are certified, not licensed. Canadian provinces generally use the term *registration* instead of licensure or certification for their legal regulation.

Licensure and certification in the United States are very similar. Both are created through passage of state law, so they are born out of the political process. State boards of regulation and licensing are responsible for administering licensing and certification of all professions. Only persons with appropriate credentials (usually degrees from CSWE accredited schools) are permitted to take the social work competency examinations that are required. A national organization, the Association of Social Work Boards (ASWB), provides examinations to the states; each state determines its own passing score. There is one important difference between certification and licensure. While certification protects the title "social worker," it doesn't prohibit uncertified people from practicing social work. They simply may not call themselves social workers. Certification is not considered to be as strong a form of legal regulation as licensure.

Although states determine the categories of social workers they will license or certify, the four categories most commonly seen and the academic degree and practice experience required are as follows:

Bachelor's: a baccalaureate degree in social work.

Master's: an MSW degree; no experience required.

Advanced Generalist: MSW degree plus 2 years of supervised experience.

Clinical: MSW degree plus 2 years of clinical practice. (Association of Social Work Boards, 2006)

Renewal of a state license or certification, which may occur every 2 years, usually requires documentation of completed continuing education. Earning a degree in social work is truly not the end of a social worker's education!

NASW Certification of Professional Achievement

There is a growing demand by consumers and insurance companies for affirmation of experienced professionals beyond the entry level and even beyond state licensure. NASW has met this challenge by creating specified credentials for social workers. NASW sustains authority over their affirmation process; it is not a form of governmental regulation such as licensing, although it often incorporates requirements for state licensing.

The ACSW was the first advanced practice credential offered by NASW. Developed in 1960, it is still the most respected and recognized social work credential. The ACSW designates membership in the Academy of Certified Social Workers. It is available to members of NASW who have an MSW degree, 2 years of additional MSW-supervised social work practice, professional evaluations that confirm their practice skills and values, and 20 hours of related continuing education (NASW, 2007).

Following the development and broad acceptance of the ACSW, NASW created the Diplomate in Clinical Social Work (DCSW) and the Qualified Clinical Social Worker (QCSW). They, too, have been very successful. Both are advanced practice credentials. The Diplomate, which requires 5 years of post-MSW or postdoctorate clinical practice, is the highest professional level authorized by NASW. The QCSW requires 2 years of clinical practice following receipt of an MSW or doctorate in social work, plus attainment of state licensure. Note that the ACSW, the Diplomate, and the QCSW are all designated by NASW as professional credentials.

In more recent years, NASW has responded to the need for additional acknowledgment of specialized expertise. It created specialty certifications to recognize specific practice expertise, as compared with the broader areas of the advanced practice credentials described earlier. NASW developed seven specialization certifications for MSWs and three for BSWs. Three new certifications recognize special expertise in practice with older adults: the Clinical Social Worker in Gerontology (CSW-G) and the Advanced

Social workers and students attend NASW social policy forum in Washington, DC.

Social Worker in Gerontology (ASW-G) at the master's level, and the Social Worker in Gerontology (SW-G) at the baccalaureate level. The ASW-G denotes practice expertise in macro and administrative practice with people who are elderly in contrast to the clinical focus of the CSW-G. The SW-G certificate affirms professionalism in care and case management in BSW practice. In general, all three of these certificates require membership in NASW, a minimum of 2 years (3,000 hours) of experience, 20 hours of continuing education related to practice with older adults, appropriate references, and attainment of state license or certification within the appropriate category (clinical practice or either MSW- or BSW-level state licensure; NASW, 2007). Clearly, the aging demographics surfacing in the United States and internationally are creating a market for social workers, especially social workers with recognized practice expertise with older adults. These are just the three newest NASW certificates.

Additional certificates offered by NASW for MSW social workers include those designated for practice in children, youth, and family social work (C-ACYFSW), in health care (C-SWHC), in the field of substance abuse (C-CATODSWO), in case management (C-ASWCM), and in school social work (C-SSWS). For BSWs, two additional certificates exist: the C-CYFSW for practice with children, youth, and families, and the C-SWCM to recognize practice in case management. The specific requirements for all of these certificates are similar to those described in the preceding paragraph (NASW, 2007). They can be accessed online in the "Credentials" area on the NASW website: http://www.socialworkers.org.

Credentials that testify to expertise in specialized areas of practice can provide a competitive advantage in the job market. They are also a way of alerting potential clients or referral sources to the knowledge and practice expertise of the social worker.

PROFESSIONAL SOCIAL WORK ORGANIZATIONS

This chapter has already referred to NASW and CSWE numerous times. Hopefully this signifies the remarkable importance of the two national social work organizations for the profession and for social workers. NASW and CSWE are, indeed, the most prominent, but many other professional social work organizations also exist.

The National Association of Social Workers

NASW has become the major professional membership organization in the United States. It was founded in 1955 when seven existing but quite separate social work organizations (such as the American Association of Medical Social Workers) joined together. The NASW has four major functions:

1. Professional development.
2. Professional action.
3. Professional standards.
4. Membership services.

Graduates of schools of social work that are accredited by the Council on Social Work Education are eligible for full membership in the National Association of Social Workers. Students in CSWE-accredited programs are eligible for student membership at reduced rates. NASW's journal, *Social Work*, is a respected source for research findings in various fields of practice (useful for writing term papers). The monthly publication of the national office, *NASW News*, provides information regarding new developments, social policy discussions, and updates on legislation of interest to social workers and their clients; it also advertises social work professional positions. All 56 chapters publish newsletters, keeping chapter members abreast of statewide developments. At the national level, NASW employs a lobbyist to represent members' views on policy issues known to Congress. Through PACE, the Political Action for Candidate Election wing of NASW, candidates for national as well as state offices are endorsed, and information about their positions is disseminated. There are approximately 150,000 members of NASW (NASW, n.d.). NASW is located in Washington, DC.

NASW's strong commitment to service is dramatically evident in its online resource, *Social Workers: Help starts here* (www.helpstartshere.org). This beautifully designed website provides stories of people who have experienced very difficult times but discovered organizations, experts (sometimes social workers), or even their own inner strength that enabled them to get through a problem or crisis. Helpful, readable, current information on subjects as varied as health and wellness, family problems, and issues facing older adults is offered. Readers are invited to share their own story about how a social worker helped them or a loved one. Under the heading of "Find a Social Worker," a link is provided to the NASW Register of Clinical Social Workers. This anonymous electronic resource is offered as a public service.

NASW also responds to national disasters by organizing its national office, state chapters, and social workers across the United States to meet the urgent needs of victims. In the immediate aftermath and in the months following Hurricane Katrina in 2005, social workers provided assistance with housing, health services, access to information about lost or missing family members, and grief counseling to residents of Gulf Coast states. Immediately following the terrorist attacks on September 11, 2001, the NASW national office provided information on its website on how to help and where social workers' services could best be used. The NASW website also put up "numerous links to disaster-response organizations, victim's services and information on coping with trauma" (O'Neill, 2001, p. 14). The New York City and New York State NASW chapters took leadership roles in disaster assistance work in New York City. The Metro Washington NASW chapter targeted the Pentagon crash site. Pennsylvania chapter members "participated in counseling and debriefings in Pittsburgh and the New York area and with members of the Secret Service" (O'Neill, 2001); they also operated a hotline, making referrals and providing information. NASW is an organization that social workers can be proud to support.

The Council on Social Work Education

Like NASW, the Council on Social Work Education (CSWE) is a private, nongovernmental organization. It is located in Alexandria, Virginia, but it has a membership of more than 3,000 individuals plus 700 or more institutional memberships of colleges and universities. CSWE is the only organization in the United States that is authorized to accredit social work educational programs. "CSWE works to ensure the preparation of competent social work professionals by providing national leadership and a forum for collective action. The main responsibility of CSWE is therefore to provide and maintain the high quality of social work education. In addition, CSWE strives to stimulate knowledge and curriculum development, to advance social justice, and to strengthen community and individual well-being" (CSWE, 2006).

CSWE has accredited MSW programs since its creation in 1952. In 1974 accreditation was expanded to include baccalaureate programs. Currently, nearly 200 MSW programs and approximately 460 BSW programs are accredited (CSWE, 2006). To date, doctoral programs in social work are not accredited by CSWE.

CSWE conducts a number of other activities in addition to accreditation. An annual conference, for example, showcases presentations of scholarly papers and current research. CSWE publishes books, a newsletter *(The Social Work Education Reporter)*, and a scholarly journal (the *Journal of Social Work Education*). A recent and ongoing project aims at strengthening the competence of social workers for work with the growing population of older adults. Through its members, the CSWE also seeks to influence social policy and funding, both governmental and private, to support social work education.

The National Association of Black Social Workers

The National Association of Black Social Workers (NABSW), like NASW, is a membership organization located in Washington, DC, but unlike NASW its membership is open to any Black person who is working in social work or human services; it does not specify academic credentials. NABSW was created in 1968 to address issues pertaining to the recruitment and education of Black social workers and the delivery of social welfare services to Black people (NABSW, n.d., History section).

The Code of Ethics speaks eloquently to the mission and purpose of this organization. It states, in part:

> I hold myself responsible for the quality and extent of service I perform and the quality and extent of service performed by the agency or organization in which I am employed, as it relates to the Black community.
>
> I accept the responsibility to protect the Black community against unethical and hypocritical practice by any individuals or organizations engaged in social welfare activities.
>
> I stand ready to supplement my paid or professional advocacy with voluntary service in the Black public interest.
>
> I will consciously use my skills, and my whole being, as an instrument for social change, with particular attention directed to the establishment of Black social institutions. (NABSW, n.d., Code of Ethics section, p. 1)

The NABSW has several publications, including *The Black Caucus Journal*. More than 100 chapters of NABSW exist throughout the United States with affiliate chapters in other countries such as South Africa, Canada, Ghana, and the Caribbean. Student units exist as well on college and university campuses. National conferences are held annually in key cities in the United States and are open to both members and potential members. Summer international conferences offer exciting opportunities to "experience African culture, heritage, and social institutions" in Ghana, South Africa, and globally where people of African descent live and have communities (NABSW, n.d., History section).

The National Association of Puerto Rican & Hispanic Social Workers

Founded in 1983, the National Association of Puerto Rican & Hispanic Social Workers (NAPRHSW) offers membership to social workers, students, and other professionals in the field of human services. Like the NABSW, it does not restrict membership to credentialed social workers. It seeks to organize social workers and others to enhance the general welfare of Puerto Rican/Hispanic families and communities. The organization's objectives, found at their website (http://www.naprhsw.org), are:

> To advocate in the interest of Latinos at the local, state and nationwide levels in private and public sectors.
>
> To establish connections with other community resources that further and solidify the position of the Latino population in addressing policy issues that impact the community.
>
> To disseminate knowledge for professional growth to its membership and increase the academic foundation for providing assistance towards that end.
>
> To be a resource to the Latino Community for information and advocacy.
>
> To continue efforts to recruit and encourage Social Workers and Human Service students in their professional aspirations. (NAPRHSW, 2007, Mission section, p. 1)

Members of the NAPRHSW have opportunities to attend conferences dealing with such issues as strengths and diversity of the Latino family, immigration reform, ethnic sensitive practice, substance abuse, and domestic violence. The organization also shares information on employment opportunities and engages members in political, educational, and social activities (NAPRHSW, 2007, Membership section).

Other Professional Organizations

There is a wealth of other professional organizations serving social workers. In addition to the NAPRHSW, there is a Latino Social Workers Organization that sponsors annual conferences and offers committee membership to students as well as professional social workers. Some of the emphases of this organization are training in cultural competency and recruitment and retention strategies. Founded in 1970, the National Indian Social Workers Association seeks to support Native American people, including Alaska Natives. It also provides consultation to tribal and other organizations. Other groups exist for gay and lesbian social workers, Asian American social workers, and American social workers who live and work in other countries. In addition there are practice-related organizations such as the National Association of Oncology Social Workers, the National Federation of Societies of Clinical Social Workers, and the North American Association of Christians in Social Work.

International Social Work Organizations

Social workers in countries outside the United States have professional organizations as well. Some examples are the Australian Association of Social Workers; the Canadian Association of Social Workers; the Nederlands Instituut voor Zorg en Weizijn (The Netherlands); the Chinese Association of Social Workers; and national associations of social workers in Ghana, Nigeria, and Israel, among others.

Civil unrest, war, famine, and more recently terrorist attacks have led to an increased sense of global interdependence among social workers. Even before the terrorist attacks on the World Trade Center and the Pentagon, U.S. social workers had become involved in the refugee camps of Bosnia and with health organizations fighting the AIDS epidemic in Africa.

One social work organization, the International Federation of Social Workers (IFSW), was initiated in 1956 to help social workers learn about the experience of their counterparts in other countries. Currently, the IFSW represents 84 countries and half a million social workers around the world. Although membership in the IFSW is limited to national social work organizations, individuals may join the Friends of IFSW. The organization publishes a newsletter and it is a sponsor of the journal, *International Social Work* (IFSW, 2005, General Infos section). The aims of the IFSW are listed in Exhibit 1-9.

EXHIBIT 1-9

Aims of the International Federation of Social Workers (IFSW)

The Constitution of the IFSW provides that the aims shall be:

■ To promote social work as a profession through international cooperation, especially regarding professional values, standards, ethics, human rights, recognition, training, and working conditions.

■ To promote the establishment of national organisations of social workers or professional unions for social workers and when needed national co-ordinating bodies (collectively "Social Work Organisations") where they do not exist.

■ To support Social Work Organisations in promoting the participation of social workers in social planning and the formulation of social policies, nationally and internationally, the recognition of social work, the enhancement of social work training and the values and professional standards of social work.

In order to achieve these Aims the Federation shall:

■ Encourage cooperation between social workers of all countries.

■ Provide means for discussion and the exchange of ideas and experience through meetings, study visits, research projects, exchanges, publications and other methods of communication.

■ Establish and maintain relationships with, and present and promote the views of Social Work Organisations and their members to international organisations relevant to social development and welfare.

SOURCE: International Federation of Social Workers. (2005, November 11). *Aims.* Retrieved January 3, 2007, from http://www.ifsw.org, p. 1.

Just as international trade has developed globally in the past decade so, too, have international efforts to improve the health and welfare of all people. Hopefully, the future will bring increasing cross-national and international social welfare development and advocacy efforts especially to war-torn and economically devastated areas. What a challenge for the next generation of social workers!

COMPARING RELATED OCCUPATIONS

To meet the challenges of the present as well as the future, social workers need to understand and develop cooperative working relationships with the professions and occupational groups that work alongside us in the social welfare arena. Currently, a great deal of overlap exists in the responsibilities and tasks of professions. In hospitals, for example, nurses as well as social workers assist patients with discharge planning. In mental health the overlap appears even greater. Psychiatrists, psychologists, social workers, and professional counselors all engage in psychotherapy with individuals, groups, and families. Each profession, however, has its own area of expertise. This can be confusing. In the paragraphs that follow, we will try to identify and compare roles and responsibilities across several professions or occupations.

Sociology

We will begin by looking at sociology, an academic area that is closely related to social work. In fact, social work students are likely to be required to take some sociology courses early in their social work major. Sociology is an academic discipline that examines society and the behavior and beliefs of specific groups in society. Sociologists study characteristics of all types of groups: ethnic minorities, families, children, men, women, gays, the elderly, juvenile delinquents, and many others. Sociologists also examine the class structure of society. Through careful research, they attempt to sort fact from fiction regarding the mythology surrounding various social groups. Sociologists develop theory regarding how and why people become what they are, and in particular they study the influence of the social environment on thought, behavior, and personality.

What students of sociology learn to do is to observe carefully, think systematically, develop theory, and perform research to test theory. Sociological knowledge is useful to the social worker, and many social workers developed their initial interest in social work by taking sociology courses. Hence there is often confusion regarding the two disciplines. Also confusing is the fact that there are branches of sociology developing today called "applied" and "clinical" sociology. Applied sociology involves the use of sociological research methods for community needs assessment and program evaluation. Clinical sociology involves the application of sociological theory to social intervention. Their domains and methods are not yet clearly defined. Because sociologists specialize in the study of various types of groups, however, it is likely that applied and clinical sociologists will focus on the applications of sociological theory to behavior in groups, organizations, and communities.

Although they need to study sociology, social workers are expected to apply their knowledge to working with people to solve problems. Sociology normally teaches students to observe and to research social problems, but it is social work that teaches interpersonal skills and techniques and that provides an analytical approach to problem solving. Sociologists with advanced degrees often apply their education by researching and teaching.

Psychology

Psychology is another field closely related to social work. Psychologists study individuals and try to understand how they develop as they do and the important internal factors that influence a person's mind and behavior. Many psychologists study perception and learning in the laboratory setting and try to understand the inner workings of the mind through experimental means. Like sociologists, many psychologists spend their careers researching, testing theory, and teaching. One branch of psychology is applied, so that some psychologists also counsel individuals and families and conduct IQ tests, personality tests, and the like. Psychologists who wish to specialize in psychotherapy usually earn a doctorate degree.

Social workers must study both sociology and psychology. They must utilize information from both of these fields to assess the problems of their clients appropriately and to develop workable intervention plans. Social workers cannot focus solely on the individual, as psychologists tend to do, or on the social environment, as sociologists do. Instead, they must examine aspects of both, and how they interact, to engage in constructive problem solving.

The U.S. Department of Labor lists multiple specializations for psychology. The primary ones are licensed clinical psychologist and counseling psychologist. Both require a doctorate degree. Other specialization areas are school psychology; industrial–organizational psychology; and developmental, social, and experimental or research psychology (Farr & Ludden, 2000). School psychologists may need only a master's degree. Yet another area of psychology, community psychology, overlaps social work in its interest in social issues and social institutions. Community psychologists are educated at both the master's and doctoral levels. Community psychology is said to have more of a research orientation than social work. It is also much less treatment focused than clinical psychology (Cook, 2001).

Counseling

Counseling is another profession that overlaps social work in many ways: counselors, too, serve the social and emotional needs of people in schools, mental health, and other settings where social workers are employed. Most counselors hold master's degrees from university programs in education or psychology, although some doctorates are also available in counseling. There is a confusing array of areas in this field, including mental health counseling; educational, vocational, or school counseling; rehabilitation counseling; substance abuse and behavioral disorder counseling; and gerontological counseling. The vast majority of counselors, more than 200,000, are employed as educational, vocational, or school counselors (Hecker, 2005). Recent legislation allowing some counselors to be reimbursed by insurance companies has increased the growth of private practice among counselors. Like social workers, counselors work with people who have personal, family, or mental health problems; however, counselors often have special expertise in helping people with educational or career planning.

Marriage and Family Therapy

This is another professional area that is somewhat confusing because persons from a number of different professions can be certified as marriage and family therapists (MFTs). To qualify for certification in most states, evidence must be presented of completion of a master's or doctoral degree in marriage and family therapy or in a program with equivalent content. In addition, at least 2 years of clinical experience (or 3,000 hours) are required. MSW social workers, psychologists, psychiatrists, and some nurses may qualify. According to the American Association for Marriage and Family Therapy, MFTs treat a wide variety of personal and mental health problems. The focus, even for an interview with a single person, is on the relationships in which the person is most significantly involved (American Association for Marriage and Family Therapy, 2002). Marriage and family therapy emphasizes short-term treatment.

Psychiatry

Psychiatry is related to social work, but psychiatry is a specialization of medicine. An MD (medical degree) must first be earned, and then the aspiring psychiatrist must complete a postdoctoral internship. Psychiatrists' primary focus on the inner person is grounded in their knowledge of physiology and medical practice. They may practice psychotherapy, but most do so very infrequently. Instead, their focus is on prescribing medications such as antidepressants and antipsychotics, the drugs used to treat psychoses (severe forms of mental illness). Psychiatrists frequently see people for 15-minute medication monitoring sessions.

Human Services

In its broadest definition, human services includes all occupations and professions seeking to promote the health and well-being of society: lawyers, firefighters, social workers, teachers, and so on. The narrower definition includes only those people who have completed an educational program with a major in human services or people who have been hired to work in the broad human services area without academic credentials. Human service academic programs generally offer a two-year associate degree, although sometimes they involve four-year degrees. While knowledge development is not ignored, the human service field emphasizes task completion and skill development. Graduates seek employment across multiple paraprofessional and professional job areas; these positions frequently offer only minimal opportunities for advancement.

In the 1980s, a National Commission for Human Service workers was initiated to credential and certify human service workers, but it has since disbanded. Currently, there is no national organization comparable to the NASW that establishes certification standards for human service workers (Woodside & McClam, 2005).

HOW PROFESSIONS RELATE

How might some of these professions become involved in a case such as that of the Dunn family in the case study at the beginning of this chapter? A sociologist might study the social problem of battered women or battering families; he or she might interview the Dunn family to learn what they have to say about the phenomenon from personal experience. The sociologist, as a result of this study, might publish research that might result in decreased domestic violence. The sociologist, however, probably would not be involved in direct assistance to members of the Dunn family. The professional person that the Dunn family is most likely to encounter in a domestic violence shelter is a social worker.

Through the counseling they receive from social workers while in crisis, Susan Dunn and her husband could decide there is enough hope for change for themselves that they will begin living together again. With encouragement, they may follow up on the social worker's recommendation that they attend longer-term marriage and family counseling with a family service agency. The Dunn's counselor at the family service agency might be either an MSW social worker, a PhD psychologist, or possibly a counselor. A consulting psychiatrist would be retained on the staff of the agency, to whom the Dunns could be referred if the primary counselor felt medication was required.

There could be several outcomes to this case. Let us say, for purposes of speculation, that as counseling progresses, Susan's husband voluntarily enters a group for batterers conducted by a professional counselor; a social worker or psychologist could also facilitate this group. Although he often feels like dropping out of the group, he continues with it as well as the family counseling. Over the months, several episodes of angry outbursts occur, but there are no further episodes of physical abuse. Gradually, both parents learn healthier ways of communicating with each other. Meantime, Susan Dunn has established a better relationship with her own family and begun to make routine visits back home. With the help of a vocational counselor, she has enrolled in a computer class at the local community college and has acquired several women friends from class. Susan now has a safety plan involving family and friends, in the event that she should need it. If Susan's husband continues to work very hard with the batterers group and no longer uses violence as a way of dealing with his frustrations, the future looks reasonably promising for this couple.

What would happen if, instead, Susan Dunn remains in clear physical danger? Let us say, for example, that her husband refuses to attend any kind of counseling with her and openly threatens future abuse. Susan might still choose to go home, believing that, if she behaves more carefully, she will be able to avoid "causing" her husband to physically abuse her. She is likely to have at some point another crisis requiring her to flee again to the shelter. At least this time she will know where she is going. If her husband is drinking or becomes violent at work and loses his job, Susan may find herself becoming involved with her country's financial assistance program called Temporary Assistance for Needy Families (TANF). The staff she encounters there will probably not have professional training in social work. Their role is a more clerical one that may also involve some employment counseling and referral to other resources.

Although Susan Dunn comes from a middle-class background and has remained a member of the middle class because of her husband's occupation, once she leaves her husband she is at risk of poverty. Almost overnight she could become a poor, single mother. The social worker at the shelter might be able to help her locate an inexpensive apartment. She might also file a legal restraining order through the district attorney's office, prohibiting her husband from threatening or even contacting her. She might file for divorce and child support; however, legal action against her husband could be very difficult without money. If fortunate, she might be able to secure inexpensive legal assistance from a legal aid society. Waiting lists for such programs are often long, however. Susan's social worker will help her assess her evolving situation and take whatever steps are necessary to ensure that Susan and her children are safe from harm. Susan's decisions, however, will be respected by the social worker.

The story of Susan Dunn and her family introduced readers of this chapter to the profession of social worker. The remainder of this text will delve into the work of social workers in much greater detail. Other social work clients will also be introduced as the chapters unfold. First, however, we can get a better grounding in the evolution of the profession by taking a brief look at the history of the social work profession.

HISTORY OF SOCIAL WORK: LINKAGE TO SOCIAL JUSTICE

Social work is an evolving, relatively young profession. As Morales and Sheafor point out, the profession of social work grew out of and has sustained commitment to a threefold mission: caring, curing, and changing society (2002). All three components are intrinsically related to social justice. From its earliest beginnings, the predecessors of social work have cared for the most vulnerable groups of people in society. Sometimes the caring was (and still is) prompted by humanitarian concerns; at other times it was mixed with less noble objectives. Persons who were not valued by society because they were too ill, too old or too young, too disabled, or otherwise not productive tended to be the very persons that social workers recognized as needing services and assistance. But social workers also have a history of helping people change, grow, and develop new skills. Persons with mental health or behavioral disorders have been helped through counseling and psychotherapy, immigrants have been helped to acquire citizenship, and prisoners have been empowered to rebuild their lives following incarceration. Some of the earliest social workers were reformers who sought change through labor laws, political action, and community development.

The Civil War in the United States is probably responsible for the first paid social work–type positions. These jobs were created in 1863 by the Special Relief Department of the U.S. Sanitary Commission to assist Union Army soldiers or their families with health and social problems related to the war. The impact of these workers and other humanitarians, such as Clara Barton who later founded the American Red Cross, helped pave the way of the future social work profession. Three subsequent social movements arising in the late 1800s, however, significantly contributed to the development of the profession. One major movement was the Charity Organization Society (COS); it began in England and took hold in Buffalo, New York, in 1877. Its most famous leader was Mary Richmond. Volunteers for the COS initially viewed the abject poverty of many urban dwellers, especially immigrants, to be the result of personal character defects. "Friendly visitors," usually wealthy women who were not permitted by social norms of the time to be employed, visited people in their homes to provide "moral uplift." Only as a last resort was material aid offered.

A second major movement contributed a strong social justice thrust to the developing young social work profession. This was the settlement house movement, which, like the COS, began in England. In the United States, Jane Addams was its most famous leader. Addams established Hull House in Chicago in 1889. Settlement workers brought a more compassionate view of poor people than the COS volunteers. They believed that poverty resulted from unjust and unfortunate social conditions. Settlement workers lived among the poor. They assisted in developing needed services such as day care for children of factory workers through mutual aid. They also advocated for better working conditions and protective legislation through various governmental bodies.

A third movement, more diffuse, and often not recognized for its historical impact on the development of the profession was the child welfare movement. This began with the Children's Aid Society founded in New York in 1853 and was strengthened by the Society for the Prevention of Cruelty to Children that was founded in 1875, also in New York City (Popple, 1995). The child welfare movement, over time, evolved into the entire area of foster care, adoptions, child protective services, and juvenile court services.

A growing desire for professionalization emerged by the late 1890s. Charity organization work and settlement house work were increasingly salaried, but as yet there was no name for this profession. By the early 1900s the broad field of applied philanthropy began to be called social work or social casework. The New York School of Philanthropy, established in 1904, was the first professional education program. Mary Richmond, leader of the Charity Organization Society, was among the original faculty. The school is now known as the Columbia University School of Social Work (Popple, 1995).

With increasing confidence in their new profession, social workers invited Abraham Flexner to address the 1915 National Conference of Charities and Correction. Flexner's critique of the medical profession was renowned for dramatically improving that profession's status and quality of care. Flexner's pronouncement that social work was not yet a real profession startled the social work world but unleashed new energy directed at rectifying the deficiencies he identified (Popple, 1995).

As Flexner's criticisms were attended to, large numbers of persons flocked to the profession expanding social work practice into new areas such as schools and hospitals. The theory base of the profession was developed and research began to be published. Freudian theory was widely adopted in the 1920s. The Great Depression turned public attention to the economic and social forces causing poverty. The result was the passage of the Social Security Act in 1935, legislation in which social workers played a prominent role. From its earliest days, then, the profession of social work embodied emphases both in social reform and in the psychosocial problems of individuals, families, and communities.

World War I and II further increased social workers' involvement in mental health as psychiatric casualties of the wars brought large numbers of social workers into military social work. Social workers with master's degrees dominated the profession by the early 1950s, but they tended to work in specialization areas such as child welfare, medical social work, or psychiatric social work. In a remarkable move toward unity, seven specialty areas merged to found the National Association of Social Workers in 1955. Until 1970, when baccalaureate social workers were added, NASW membership was exclusively limited to MSWs. The founding of NASW and enactment of the NASW Code of Ethics to ground the practice of all social workers firmly established social work as a profession.

In the years since the birth of the profession, social work has grown dramatically in numbers, in areas of practice, in the people it serves, and in status. In recent years it has achieved legal regulation (licensure or certification) in every state. The profession has struggled to retain its social reform legacy by lobbying against discriminatory legislation and by supporting social policies that promote human welfare and well-being. Social work and social welfare, therefore, remain intertwined today, as the next chapter in this text will explain. Because of its commitment to social and economic justice and its mission to work on behalf of people who are discriminated against, the profession of social work is sometimes not well understood nor even well accepted. Its values make social work a truly unique profession.

As we conclude our review of history and shift into contemporary times, we find that today social work practice makes increasing use of computer technology. Throughout this text we will invite you, the reader, to learn more about how to use the Internet as a valuable resource for information about the profession and the people served by social workers. So, before turning to the summary of Chapter 1, we encourage you to take a look at the following listing of Internet sites. They might be interesting to explore; all relate to the topics covered in this chapter, including a few sites related to domestic violence. You will find similar lists of Internet sites near the end of each chapter in this text. Following the summary, you will also find a list of key terms. They are the terms that have appeared in bold print within the chapter. If you aren't sure you understand them, you will find them in the Glossary at the end of this text. The discussion questions may be used in class. We truly hope that you will enjoy using this text.

INTERNET SITES

http://www.socialworkers.org	National Association of Social Workers
http://workforce.socialworkers.org	MediaWatch; NASW's Center for Workforce Studies
http://www.cswe.org	Council on Social Work Education

http://www.ifsw.org	International Federation of Social Workers
http://www.bpdonline.org	Association of Baccalaureate Social Work Program Directors
http://wall.aa.uic.edu/62730/artifact/HullHouse.asp	Hull House Museum
http://www.idbsu.edu/socwork/dhuff/XX.htm	The Social Work History Station
http://www.socialworker.com	The New Social Worker
http://www.ncadv.org	National Coalition Against Domestic Violence
http://www.vaw.umn.edu	Violence Against Women Online Resources
http://www.abanet.org/domviol/home.html	Commission on Domestic Violence, American Bar Association
http://www.bls.gov	U.S. Department of Labor, Bureau of Labor Statistics

SUMMARY

The case of Susan Dunn and her family, who are in need of social services from a shelter following an episode of domestic violence, introduces the chapter and also the profession of social work. A definition of social work is offered. The ways in which social work is unique among human service professions, its strengths perspective and social justice commitment, for example, are identified. Because the generalist perspective is a basic ingredient of all social work practice and lies at the heart of baccalaureate practice, the concept of generalist practice is explored. The generalist social worker is presented as one who engages in a systematic planned change process with a variety of social systems, including individual people, families, groups, organizations, and communities. Master's degree social workers are prepared for advanced practice within an area of concentration such as clinical social work or advanced generalist practice.

Social work educational programs prepare social workers at the baccalaureate (BSW), master's (MSW), and doctoral (PhD or DSW) levels. The chapter provided information about the curriculum at the baccalaureate level. Less information was presented about the MSW or doctoral curricula because they vary depending on the area of concentration offered by the program.

Pamela Wright was the social worker who assisted Susan Dunn and her family in Chapter 1's case study. Each chapter in this text will begin with a case study showing how social workers engage people and work with them to solve problems across many different social agency and community practice settings. Most people who consider a career in social work do so because they want to help people. Like Pamela Wright, they want their lives to make a difference. The chapter offers information about career options and employment opportunities in a profession that is devoted to making a difference—social work.

Social work, like most other professions, is legally regulated by state licensing boards to protect consumers from unethical and uncredentialed practice. Unfortunately, because states' social work license laws are not consistent, there remains much work to be done to ensure that persons who deliver social services and claim to be social workers really are social workers. Some states still have no licensure or certification for BSW social workers. It remains possible for persons without academic degrees in social work to obtain social work positions in a few states. NASW, the National Association of Social Workers, has led the effort to achieve social work licensure at all levels and in all states. Chapter 1 explains some of the other ways in which NASW serves its members and also tries to protect clients. Other social work professional organizations, such as the Council on Social Work Education and the International Federation of Social Workers, are also introduced in this chapter.

Social work is sometimes confused with other professions. Students often wonder, for example, whether they should major in psychology or social work, not knowing that social workers carry some of the same responsibilities for counseling and therapy as persons with degrees in psychology. Yet, while professions such as psychology and social work do overlap, all professions are unique and have their own areas of expertise. The chapter compares several related professions and highlights the uniqueness of the social work profession.

In the Chapter 2 case study you will meet another social worker, Stephanie Hermann, who applies her social work practice skills and knowledge to the problems faced by so many people that successful intervention required response from an entire community. The Stephanie Hermann case study leads to an exploration of the theories on which generalist social work practice is grounded. Inextricably connected to the theory of practice is an understanding of political perspectives and how they influence the well-being of people.

KEY TERMS

ACSW, *p. 33*

advocate, *p. 18*

BSW, *p. 6*

broker, *p. 18*

career ladder, *p. 21*

case advocacy, *p. 12*

case management, *p. 18*

cause advocacy, *p. 12*

communicator, *p. 17*

counselor, *p. 17*

educator, *p. 18*

facilitator, *p. 18*

generalist social
  worker, *p. 7*

legal regulation, *p. 32*

MSW, *p. 7*

organizer, *p. 18*

policy practice, *p. 12*

professional roles, *p. 17*

psychotherapy, *p. 17*

qualitative research, *p. 12*

quantitative research, *p. 12*

social work, *p. 6*

DISCUSSION QUESTIONS

1. What is the definition of social work given in this book? How would you explain social work to a friend?

2. What is a generalist social worker?

3. From what three social movements did the social work profession arise historically?

4. Name at least one person who contributed to the historical development of the social work profession. Explain that person's contribution.

5. How does the usual role of the baccalaureate-level social worker compare with that of the master's-level social worker?

6. There seems to be a common belief that the vast majority of social workers, especially BSWs, work for "the government." Is this true? What data are available to support your answer?

7. If your friend said to you, "There are no jobs in social work. Why are you going into this field?" what would you say? How would you substantiate your response to your friend?

8. Explain legal regulation of social work. How does licensure or certification protect the public? What are the benefits for social workers?

9. How does NASW provide recognition of special practice expertise? Identify at least one area for which NASW offers certification, and explain how someone would qualify.

10. Describe the roles or purposes of professional social work organizations, including the National Association of Social Workers and the Council on Social Work Education. Can you name any additional professional social work organizations?

11. What is the purpose of the NASW Code of Ethics? How do the values of the social work profession relate to the Code of Ethics?

12. Identify several professions related to social work. What characteristics distinguish social work from these other professions?

13. Can you think of examples that explain how you think about "social justice" or "social injustice"? Why would social workers want to fight for social justice in the world?

CLASSROOM EXERCISES

While not required, it is suggested that students break into small groups of three or four to discuss these exercises. It may be helpful to choose a scribe to record and report major points to the class after the group discussion.

1. Undergraduate students who want to work with people often have difficulty choosing among related majors. Discuss the relative merits of majoring in sociology, psychology, human service, or social work if one's goal is to obtain a position working with people soon after graduation with a baccalaureate degree. Be sure to review information provided in the text while conducting this exercise.

2. When students consider potential future careers, often they realize that they want their career to be one that will enable them to help others or to make a change in the world. Using content from Chapter 1, think of examples of ways in which social workers can help individuals and families. Can you also imagine circumstances in which social workers might advocate for or create change in communities or in society?

3. A major shift that is taking place in the world and certainly in the United States is that of increasing human diversity. Have you seen changes in the community that you come from or the community surrounding your college or university? Describe changes you are seeing in the ethnicity of people, or their religion, socioeconomic status, sexual orientation, physical or mental abilities, political thinking, age, or other areas.

4. Why are some people, children as well as adults, at risk of being poor and living in unsatisfactory, potentially unhealthy housing or experiencing discrimination? Can anything be done about it? How?

5. Sometimes people are discriminated against, treated disrespectfully, or even abused by professional people they had come to trust. How does the NASW Values and Ethical Principles statement (see Exhibit 1-1 in this chapter) address such situations? Can you think of examples of ways in which social workers or other professionals could be unethical in their practice?

RESEARCH ACTIVITIES

1. Conduct a series of interviews with a social worker, a sociologist, a psychologist, and another person from one of the human service professions. Compare and contrast their tasks and responsibilities.

2. Interview two baccalaureate-level social workers and two master's-level social workers. Compare and contrast their tasks and responsibilities.

3. Learn about your state NASW chapter. Where is it located? When, where, and how frequently does the chapter conduct meetings? Are students welcome to attend? What issues is your state chapter currently working on? Can students become involved?

4. Obtain information regarding legal regulation of social workers in your state. Does the law in

your state provide for licensure, certification, or some other form of regulation? What levels of practice are regulated? What is the procedure that is required for licensure (or certification)? Is there an examination? How have graduates of your program fared with the state licensure exam?

5. Research your local area or state to determine the range of salaries paid to social workers. Compare differences in salaries by checking specific factors (variables) such as the practice setting—child welfare, school social work, mental health, aging, and probation and parole are just a few. Compare differences between BSW and MSW salaries. Entry-level salaries could also be compared with upper-range salaries paid for experienced, advanced practice, and for organizational administrative or college/university teaching positions.

INTERNET RESEARCH EXERCISES

1. One of the most interesting and informative social work sites on the Web is the Social Work History Station, http://www.idbsu.edu/socwork/dhuff/XX.htm.

    a. Go to the section on this site entitled "The Professionals." What can you learn from this site about the effect of World War I on social casework? (*Social casework* was the term commonly used at that time to refer to social work with individuals.)

    b. What was the second major event identified in "The Professionals" section that affected social casework?

    c. What does the author identify as the leading edge of social casework in the 1920s?

    d. Who were two prominent social workers active in the Roosevelt administration during the depression?

2. Many other countries, like the United States, have national professional organizations for the profession of social work. Go to the website http://www.nlasw.ca, the site for the Newfoundland and Labrador Association of Social Workers. Find the page for "Mission and Goals."

    a. How does the NLASW mission differ from that of the National Association of Social Workers (NASW)?

    b. How similar are the goals of these two organizations?

    c. Go to the "Code of Ethics" page and read the philosophy. What is your impression? Could you live with this statement of philosophy?

3. When an individual wishes to advocate for specific issues, the World Wide Web offers numerous resources. An example would be the Action Network for Social Work Education and Research (ANSWER). This is part of the National Association of Social Workers (http://www.socialworkers.org/advocacy/answer/default.asp).

    a. What is the mission of this organization?

    b. What is the primary cause that is espoused by this site?

    c. One of the areas listed on the home page is "Loan Forgiveness." What kind of issues are addressed here?

FOR FURTHER READING

Guttmann, D. (2006). *Ethics in social work: A context of caring*. New York: The Haworth Press.

    This book was written to assist social workers in their complex task of caring for clients in a way that is effective and ethically honorable. The author is committed to the concept of caring, compassion, and doing good not just as a characteristic, but as an obligation of the profession. In the first half of his book, Guttmann explores the historical and philosophical context of social work ethics. The second half of the book takes on contemporary social work practice issues, approaches to ethical dilemmas, confidentiality dilemmas, and promises to keep clients' secrets. The final text chapter focuses on malpractice and professional misconduct. Because they do care about the people they serve, social workers are vulnerable to ethical errors that can be harmful to their clients, to families, or even to the social workers themselves.

Ginsberg, L. H. (2001). *Careers in social work* (2nd ed.). Boston: Allyn & Bacon.

Ginsberg's paperback may prove to be one of the best investments made by the baccalaureate or master's degree student ready to initiate an employment search. A wealth of nitty-gritty, practical information is offered from tips on effective employment interviews and résumé preparation to handling of salary and compensation issues. Of special interest is the content on social work in smaller communities, in employee assistance programs, and in international settings; this information tends not to be well covered in most social work texts. Examples of state and federal employment application forms are welcome additions to the appendix.

Martin, N. (2007). Classroom comes to life in HIV/AIDS field placement. *The New Social Worker*. Retrieved January 9, 2007, from http:www.socialworker.com

Students will find Nancy Martin's reflection on the meaning of her HIV/AIDS field placement especially interesting. In her brief article, Nancy Martin describes some of the responsibilities she assumed as a fieldwork student. She shares her thoughts about the centrality of the profession's values and ethics for her own fieldwork practice. This article is one of many that are now available to social work students and faculty free of charge on the website shown here. Until 2007, *The New Social Worker* was only available by subscription.

CHAPTER 2

THEORETICAL PERSPECTIVES FOR SOCIAL WORKERS

OUTLINE

The case study for this chapter introduces a community-level problem requiring social work intervention and then describes how a particular person, Sandra McLean, is affected. It illustrates how persons and environments interact and how social welfare policy influences social work practice. While the events described in this case took place a number of years ago, the generalist practice skills demonstrated by social worker Stephanie Hermann remain contemporary and impressive.

THE SEVERAL ROLES OF STEPHANIE HERMANN, BSW

S tephanie Hermann, BSW, waited impatiently for the mail that morning, for her boss had told her to expect an important memo. Stephanie worked as an assistant administrator in a regional office of the Division of Community Services, a part of her state's Department of Health and Social Services (DHSS). The office interpreted new DHSS policies pertaining to health and social service agencies in the region, both public and private. Stephanie consulted with agency administrators to clarify state policies and to document agency compliance.

Recently, the state DHSS office had received notice from the Federal Health Care Administration that people with developmental disabilities (DD) would soon lose eligibility for Medicaid funding in nursing homes. The intent of this policy was to encourage the development of community-based living settings for people with disabilities. A survey had been conducted around the state, and 2,025 adults with disabilities were found to be living in nursing homes. Among them was Sandra McLean, whose story will be a focus of this chapter.

This large number worried DHSS officials. They did not believe there were existing alternative community placement options that could care for anywhere near this number of people. Stephanie's boss had described the memo that was on its way as "at least trying to head us off from a bigger problem later."

The expected memo arrived: "The Department of Health and Social Services finds that an emergency exists . . . . This order amends the department's rules for nursing homes . . . to prohibit the admission of any person with a developmental disability, including mental retardation, to a nursing home for intermediate nursing care unless the nursing home is certified . . . as an intermediate care facility for the mentally retarded (ICF/MR)."

The memo explained that to obtain certification as an ICF/MR, a nursing home must identify staff skilled in working with persons with developmental disabilities and describe specific internal programs, supplementary services from other agencies, admissions policies, and individual care plans for each resident. The DHSS memo defined developmental disability as follows: "mental retardation or a related condition such as cerebral palsy, epilepsy, or autism, but excluding mental illness and the infirmities of aging."

Stephanie was excited by the new policy. She had long believed that most persons with disabilities should be placed in family-like settings. But few such places of residence currently existed. Adult family care homes (foster homes for adults) required families willing to take in persons with disabilities; small group homes required paid staff. Apartment living required monitoring and support. All required funding and neighbors willing to accept persons with disabilities.

BROCKTON MANOR

When Stephanie received the emergency order from the state DHSS, she decided to consult with every county in her region. At this point only new DD clients were prohibited from receiving Medicaid funding for nursing home care, so Stephanie believed that new placement options could be developed gradually. She also consulted with nursing homes that were currently caring for persons with disabilities, to assist them in developing state-certified ICF/MR programs.

However, only 2 weeks after the state's emergency ruling, Brockton Manor, a large nursing home in Stephanie's region, decided to phase out its services for people with disabilities. Administrators believed they could easily fill their beds with elderly people, who are less costly to serve. Brockton Manor offered to cooperate with county and state officials in developing alternative living arrangements so that each of its 49 residents with developmental disabilities would have a place to go.

Now Stephanie had an immediate situation to deal with. A worst-case scenario would be 49 new street people. But fortunately, Medicaid regulations required individual assessments and specific discharge plans, including places to live and active treatment. Active treatment involved individualized plans for training, therapy, and services to help achieve the highest possible level of functioning. But how did one find or develop such resources?

Stephanie determined that she would need to play several roles. The first would involve coordinating the efforts of various community agencies. Brockton Manor's major responsibility would be to provide individual plans of care for each DD resident; each county's primary responsibility would be to develop alternative living arrangements, and the state's responsibility would be to provide funding, with federal assistance through Medicaid.

A second community-organizing role would be to involve private voluntary organizations, such as the Association for Retarded Citizens (ARC), in planning efforts on behalf of Brockton Manor's DD clients. For example, the ARC might organize informational meetings and help locate alternative living settings.

Third, Stephanie knew she would have to mediate disputes among various county and state offices. Thirty-five of the 49 residents with developmental disabilities at Brockton Manor originally came from different counties. Their counties of origin were likely to refuse to resume responsibility because of the cost. Fourth, Stephanie planned to help assess the needs of DD residents of Brockton Manor and to help develop appropriate discharge plans.

Stephanie began to carry out her organizing role immediately. She arranged a meeting of representatives from all the key agencies that would be involved in relocating the DD residents, including Brockton Manor staff, county officials responsible for finding new living arrangements, administrators from the state DHSS offices, and members of Stephanie's own regional office. A Subcommittee on Relocation was established that met biweekly for more than a year. The subcommittee set up teams to assess all residents with disabilities at Brockton Manor. It also conducted a study to determine the probable cost of community placement for each resident.

Funding complications soon became apparent. Besides encouraging development of more family-like settings, community placement was intended to cut costs. Medicaid thus funded community care at only 60 percent of the institutional-care reimbursement rate for the same DD person. Yet the money was supposed to cover active treatment as well as room, board, and assistance in daily living tasks. Many of the people at Brockton Manor required 24-hour care and supervision.

Still, the subcommittee pressed on. It organized a large "stakeholders" meeting for all agencies and individuals who might be willing to get involved. Videotapes of several residents were prepared to educate the community and to enhance the "human-interest" side of the story.

The meeting spearheaded a flurry of community activity. Several voluntary organizations collected supplies for new apartments, the Kiwanis Club developed a proposal for public housing for people with disabilities, county departments of social service advertised for adult family care homes, and Brockton Manor solicited foster parents from its own staff. Two private social service agencies developed small group homes. Funding for these homes required creative planning; half the residents had to be taken from costly state institutions, because the Medicaid funding available for community placement for these persons was higher.

Through the development of small group homes and new family care homes, 15 of Brockton Manor's residents were soon placed into the community. One of these persons was Sandra McLean.

SANDRA McLEAN: THE EFFECTS OF INSTITUTIONALIZATION

Sandra McLean's mother had a long and difficult labor, and finally forceps were used in delivery. The forceps injured Sandra's skull. The result was mental retardation and grand mal epileptic seizures, commonly known as convulsions.

Mr. and Mrs. McLean raised Sandra at home until she was about 8 years old, by which time she was toilet trained, could walk, and could say "Mama" and "Papa." Then they sent her to public school. This was before the days of special education, however, and they soon decided they could educate her better at home. They were able to teach the child to bathe, dress, and feed herself.

When Sandra was about 10, her parents had a second daughter, a normal, healthy infant named Susan. After Susan's arrival, the McLeans did not have quite so much time for Sandra, but by then she was more independent. When Sandra was in her late teens, an activity center for people with disabilities was established in a nearby community. Her middle-class parents could afford the moderate fee, and so she was enrolled. To the McLeans' delight, Sandra blossomed. She began to talk and smile more. She was a favorite among the staff.

The blow struck when Sandra was 27 years old. First, her father died of a heart attack. Shortly thereafter, her mother had a stroke. Partially paralyzed, the mother was no longer able to care for Sandra. Susan was ready to go to college, and Mrs. McLean did not want to hold her back. The family doctor suggested that Sandra be placed in a state institution. Mrs. McLean, seeing no other option, reluctantly agreed. At the institution, Sandra was medicated heavily to control her seizures. There wasn't enough staff to provide her with the compassionate care she had received at home or to respond immediately if she were to have a seizure. She spent her days strapped into a wheelchair, eyes glazed, drooling.

Several years later, Sandra was transferred to Brockton Manor, and several years after that, she was referred for community placement by Stephanie Hermann's team. Stephanie arranged for the mother, then very frail, to visit. The team listened with amazement as Mrs. McLean described Sandra as a young girl, able to walk and talk. Stephanie contacted Sandra's sister, Susan, and heard the same story. Mrs. McLean talked about the activity center Sandra had participated in years before, so staff members there were contacted as well. A therapist who had known Sandra visited and was shocked to see her current condition. The therapist described the smiling person she used to know, who enjoyed socializing and who could walk, talk, feed, and toilet herself.

Stephanie and the assessment team called in a physician skilled in working with people with disabilities. The physician was willing to prescribe different medications. The assessment team then held a joint meeting with all the professional staff at Brockton Manor involved with Sandra's care. They explained that Sandra might begin to have seizures again, and they discussed how to deal with them. They suggested that occasional grand mal seizures might not be too high a price to pay if the young woman were able to learn to walk again and to communicate with people, at least in a limited way. The nursing home staff agreed.

The plan worked. Sandra did begin to have seizures again, but they were not too difficult to handle. With physical therapy she learned to walk again, and with occupational therapy she learned to dress and feed herself. The nurses taught her how to toilet herself again. Sandra became a social person once more and began to use limited words. She clearly recognized her mother and sister. Everyone felt deeply rewarded. Now the time had come to develop community-based living arrangements.

Although Mrs. McLean would have loved to have her daughter return home, she was not physically able to care for her. Sandra's sister, Susan, explained to Stephanie Hermann, with obvious distress, that she worked full-time and had two children to care for. She frequently helped her mother with routine household chores. She did not feel able to take on her sister's care as well. But both mother and daughter welcomed the idea of a family care home for Sandra.

A potential home was located and licensed by social workers from the county Department of Social Services. The foster parents, a childless couple in their mid-30s, had learned of the need through newspaper advertisements. They visited Sandra several times at Brockton Manor and took her home for a trial overnight visit before making a final decision. The Brockton Manor staff taught them about Sandra's special needs, especially about what to do during seizures.

Arrangements were made for Sandra to attend the local activity center for people with disabilities during the day, once she was living in her foster home. She enjoyed the social and recreational opportunities, such as exercise classes, educational games, and other small group activities very much. The placement worked out so well that her foster family took in a second adult with a disability.

ONGOING CHALLENGES OF COMMUNITY PLACEMENT

An adult family care home was provided for Sandra McLean by the Department of Social Services because federal funding through Medicaid and Supplemental Security Income (to be discussed in Chapter 3) was sufficient to pay all her bills, including foster care and active treatment at the local activity center. However, funding was not sufficient to permit community placement of residents who needed more care, and eventually many of them had to be transferred to different nursing homes that met the new federal requirements. ■

Young person with disability in
family care home.

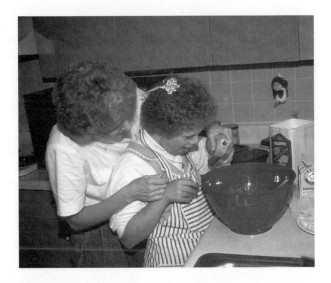

SOCIAL WORK AND SYSTEMS THEORY

As illustrated by this chapter's case study, social work is a profession that requires working
with systems of many sizes. For example, Stephanie Hermann was employed by a large
state organization, the Department of Health and Social Services. The DHSS was, in
turn, strongly affected by the policies of an even larger organization, the federal government. Stephanie, by publicizing and interpreting new federal and state policies, affected
the operations of the social service organizations and agencies in her entire region, both
public and private. She provided professional assistance to help these organizations and
agencies meet changing requirements. She also educated citizens' groups about new regulations and solicited their aid in developing new resources to meet community needs.

Besides working with larger systems, Stephanie worked with smaller ones. For
example, she helped establish a formal task group, the Subcommittee on Relocation,
which managed the job of finding and developing alternative living arrangements for
disabled residents of Brockton Manor. She met with this group for more than a year.
She also worked with a team of staff at Brockton Manor to assess the needs of each
resident with a disability.

As part of her work in assessing the needs of individual residents at Brockton Manor,
Stephanie worked with a yet smaller system, the individual named Sandra McLean
(among others). To help gain a better understanding of Sandra's potential capabilities and
needs, Stephanie met with Sandra's family members as well, Mrs. McLean and Susan.
These family meetings led Stephanie to contact another system or organization, the
activity center that Sandra had attended many years before.

As is obvious from Sandra McLean's story, improving the life of just one person
can involve skills in working with systems of many sizes. For this reason, social work is
a complex practice. It requires the guidance of a broad theoretical framework to help
organize and analyze large amounts of information. For many social workers, systems

theory provides that theoretical framework. Systems theory helps the social worker attend to and understand the dynamic interactions among the many biological and social systems that affect ongoing practice (Shaefor, Horejsi, & Horejsi, 2000).

Applying systems theory requires familiarity with certain basic concepts. A few will be introduced here. The term **system** has been defined in many ways, but perhaps the simplest is that a system is a whole consisting of interacting parts. These parts are so interrelated that a change in any one part affects all the others.

Let us consider an example of a biological system, the human body. The body is composed of many interrelated, interacting parts, including the skeleton, muscles, blood, and so on. What happens when one part is disturbed in some way? Let's say a piece of the skeleton is broken. Every other part of the system is affected. Muscles tighten, and blood circulation increases in the area of the broken bone. Nerves carry impulses to the brain that are translated as pain, which affects every other part of the body.

Each of the major parts of the system called the human body can itself be considered a system: skeletal system, muscle system, blood system, nervous system, for example. These smaller systems are themselves made up of parts even smaller: organs, molecules, atoms, particles of atoms. Sometimes smaller systems within larger systems are called *subsystems*. Whether something is considered a system or a subsystem depends only on where the observer decides to focus attention. The important point to keep in mind with respect to systems theory is the concept of interrelationships: a change in one part of a system affects all the other parts in some way. Smaller systems that are parts of larger systems affect each other and the larger system as a whole. Any change in the larger system (or *suprasystem*) affects all the systems and subsystems within.

The human body is an example of a biological system, and humans, as biological organisms, are part of a larger physical environment. But people are also social systems and parts of larger social environments. Both physical and social environments are made up of systems of various sizes to which people must adapt.

Consider the human family. The family constitutes a certain type of social system, a whole consisting of interacting parts, so that while its form may vary, family members know who belongs and who does not. A change in one part affects all others: people cannot join or withdraw without other family members responding in some way. In the McLean case, having to send Sandra to an institution undoubtedly affected her mother's well-being in a negative way. Research has even shown that if one family member is physically injured in the presence of another, the physical body of the observer will be affected (stress hormones will be released, muscles will tighten, and so on). For this reason, systems theory has been adapted for use in medicine, social science, social work, and other professions (Wells, 1998).

Compton and Galaway (1999) have identified five systems of special importance to social workers:

- Change agent system.
- Client system.
- Target system.
- Action system.
- Professional system.

EXHIBIT 2-1

Important Systems for Social Workers

Change agent system	Social workers and their agencies of employment
Client system	People who have requested social work services or who have entered into a formal or informal contract with a social worker
Target system	People who need to change in order for social work clients to meet their goals
Action system	All those who work cooperatively with the social worker to accomplish desired changes
Professional system	Social work education programs, professional organizations, and the social work professional culture, including values and ethics

---

The change agent system includes social workers and their agencies of employment. The client system includes people who have requested social work services or who have entered into a formal or informal contract. The target system includes people who need to change in order for clients to meet their goals, and the action system includes all those who work cooperatively with the social worker to accomplish desired changes. The last system, the professional system, is made up of social work education programs, professional organizations, and the professional culture, including values and ethics (see Exhibit 2-1).

THE ECOSYSTEMS PERSPECTIVE

Social workers have long promoted a person-in-environment perspective. General systems theory, proposed by biologist Ludwig Von Bertalanffy in the late 1960s, was adopted by many social workers as an overall framework for practice very much because it was congruent with their ongoing experience. The theory helped social workers remember and pay attention to the interactions between larger and smaller systems and thus provided a useful framework for analysis. However, according to Germain and Gitterman (1995), some theorists felt that systems theory was too abstract for practical use. They adopted instead a closely related outlook from biological science, which was itself derived from the basic assumptions of systems theory, the ecological or ecosystems perspective (Sommer, 1995). Many social workers now use an ecosystems or ecological perspective to guide their practice.

The ecosystems perspective encourages social workers to maintain simultaneous focus on person and environment, much as workers have done since the birth of the profession. Now, however, the practice is supported and strengthened by a theoretical model. The ecosystems focus on interactions between person and environment is perhaps a simpler way of expressing major concepts in general systems theory (such as the importance of interactional effects). The concept of "environment" as presented from the ecosystems perspective is virtually synonymous with the concept of a large or "suprasystem" from systems theory; "person" is simply an example of a smaller or subsystem (see Exhibit 2-2).

Useful concepts for social workers who use an ecosystems perspective include person/environment fit, life stressors, and adaptation, among others. The *person/environment fit* is the actual fit between human wants and needs and the environmental resources available to meet them. *Life stressors* include issues and needs that exceed environmental resources. *Adaptations* are the processes people use to try to improve the fit between themselves and their environments (Johnson & Rhodes, 2005).

To apply ecosystems concepts to the situation of Sandra McLean, consider how Sandra's environment affected her personally. Her life became completely different in the institutional setting from what it had been at home or at the activity center. Sandra's experience and behavior became so changed that she might as well have been a different person. The heavy dose of drugs that was administered to control her seizures acted as a physiological stressor that suppressed her capacity to adapt, and she essentially became a human vegetable. Only when federal policy changed, and Sandra was viewed as a whole person with human rights despite her disability, did she have

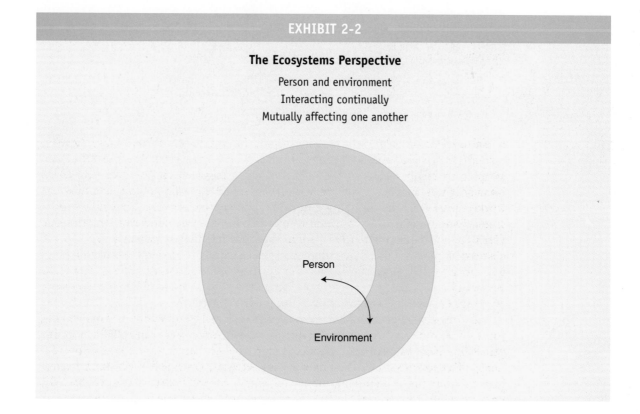

EXHIBIT 2-2

The Ecosystems Perspective

Person and environment
Interacting continually
Mutually affecting one another

Person

Environment

a chance to live a more normal life. In her case, that required changes in state and local social policy, which led in turn to changes in the medical and social services available to her. Sandra couldn't live a fulfilling life of her own until new opportunities were created in the wider environment by changed social policies and by professional practices committed to carrying out those policies.

EXHIBIT 2-3

An Ecosystems Perspective: Sandra McLean Case

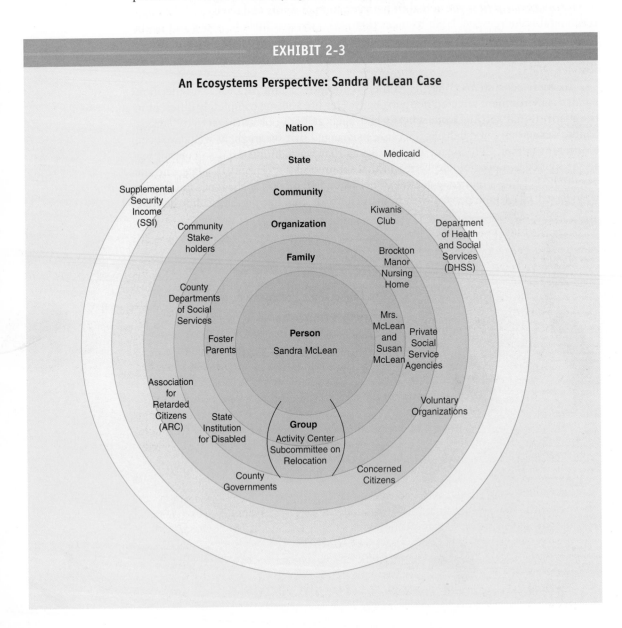

Changes in Sandra herself also affected her environment. For example, her new abilities affected various medical professionals, who were astounded at what she could accomplish and who then were willing to consider modifying medications for other people with disabilities as well. Sandra's new opportunities also affected the people who became her foster parents and those whom they later took in with her. Sandra's good fortune affected staff at the activity center, who rejoiced for her and were inspired to develop new activities to assist in her recovery. Her mother and sister rejoiced also: a family tragedy had been transformed by what seemed like a miracle. (See Exhibit 2-3.)

THE GENERALIST APPROACH

The **generalist approach** to social work practice is strongly rooted in systems theory and its descendant, the ecosystems perspective. As described earlier, systems theory and its attention to systems interactions served as a useful guide for social work practice soon after biologist Von Bertalanffy published his ideas in the 1960s. The ecosystems perspective that developed out of systems theory provided the conceptual framework for the development of the generalist approach to social work practice. Thus, the generalist approach involves attention to multiple **levels of intervention** (discussed in the next section); the term *level*, as used in this context, is virtually synonymous with the term *system*.

The ecosystems perspective helps the social worker recognize that intervening on one systems level will prompt all other systems levels to adapt in some way. The worker must assess these adaptations because she or he may then have to intervene on multiple levels (individual, family, group, organization, community, etc.) to achieve the desired result. A generalist practitioner such as Stephanie Hermann, as she begins to intervene at a large system level (the community), is guided by the ecosystems perspective to attend to changes occurring on smaller systems levels due to adaptation processes (Brockton Manor, the McLean family, Sandra McLean as an individual, etc.).

The generalist approach, in addition to an ecological perspective and attention to multiple levels of intervention, requires a careful problem-solving or planned change process (to be discussed later). While each CSWE-accredited baccalaureate social work program develops its own definition of generalist practice according to accreditation guidelines, the following is typical:

> The generalist approach to social work practice, supported by concepts drawn from social systems theory and using an ecological perspective, is attentive to person and environment and their interactions. Generalist practice is based on research-guided knowledge and uses a planned change or problem-solving process to determine the level or levels of intervention—individual, family, group, organization, and/or community—appropriate to addressing the issues presented. It recognizes the profession's dual purpose and responsibility to influence social as well as individual change.

Levels of Intervention

Note that the preceding definition explains that the generalist approach involves not only an ecological perspective but the use of multiple "levels of intervention" and a planned change process. The planned change process will be discussed further on. At this point, let us describe the various levels (systems) of intervention identified in the definition of generalist.

Individual   Intervening at the individual level involves working one-on-one, either to help a person better adapt to his or her environment or to modify the environment so it better meets the needs of the person. In this chapter's case study, Stephanie Hermann worked with Sandra McLean individually to help assess her abilities and needs.

Family   Intervening at the family level may involve working with whole families or parts of a family, such as a mother and child or a pair of parents. Stephanie Hermann worked with members of Sandra's family in planning for her care. Some types of family work can be much more intensive. Family therapy, for example, assists families in overcoming interpersonal conflicts and power imbalances among members.

Group   Intervening at the small group level may involve working with many different types of groups. Stephanie Hermann developed and worked with a task group, the Subcommittee on Relocation, at Brockton Manor. The activity center where Sandra received services ran activity groups and support groups for its clients.

Organization   Intervening at the organizational level involves assessing needs within an organization and planning and coordinating efforts to meet those needs. For example, Stephanie alerted Brockton Manor about new federal regulations regarding care for residents with disabilities. When the nursing home administration decided not to serve these clients any longer, Stephanie helped coordinate the organization's efforts to develop responsible discharge plans.

Community   Intervening at the community level involves evaluating community needs and planning and coordinating efforts to meet those needs. Stephanie Hermann helped her region of the state to evaluate its capacity to provide family-like care for citizens with disabilities and coordinated the efforts to expand resources and options (please review Exhibit 2-3).

Some social workers prefer to talk of micro-, mezzo-, and macropractice rather than practice with individuals, families, groups, organizations, and communities (Zastrow, 2007). Professionals differ, however, in their understanding of which levels of intervention these terms include. This text, to simplify, will refer to specific levels of intervention: individual, family, group, organization, and community. However, we must remember that as our world shrinks and we all become more interdependent, our concept of community must extend to include the whole planet (see Exhibit 2-4).

EXHIBIT 2-4

Social Work Levels of Intervention

Community
Organization
Group
Family
Individual

Global, Environmental, and Spiritual Considerations

While the generalist approach to social work practice traditionally encompasses individual, family, group, organization, and community levels of intervention, the profession is awakening to the increasing impact of wider environmental issues. These issues extend beyond any particular community—they are global, affecting everyone on earth today and future generations as well. Social workers need to be aware of global and environmental issues because they affect absolutely everyone, not only ourselves and our clients. Spiritual awakening can help empower people as they struggle to save planet earth, currently under siege.

As an illustration of the magnitude of the environmental problem, Bauerlein (2006) writes:

> According to the vast majority of government and other scientists, . . . the past few years have brought overwhelming evidence that pollution at currently permitted levels is sickening and killing thousands of people. . . . For example, 30,000 people die each year from power-plant pollution alone, according to a study by a firm that trains EPA (Environmental Protection Agency) staffers—almost twice as many as are killed by drunk drivers and 50% more than are murdered. As in Chicago, the study found that simply enforcing air-quality laws would save two-thirds of those lives. (p. 58)

Michael Lerner (2006) issues another powerful warning:

> We live in an Age of Extinctions. This is the sixth great spasm of extinctions in the history of our planet. We are driving biodiversity back 65 million years, to its lowest level of vitality since the end of the Age of Dinosaurs. Climate change, ozone depletion, toxic chemicals, habitat destruction, and invasive or infectious species are five of the principal drivers of this Age of Extinction. (p. 543)

For students who are already socially and politically aware, looking toward the future can be frightening at this time in human history. Preceding generations have been exceedingly short-sighted, and many economic institutions today have built-in

EXHIBIT 2-5

Air Quality Index

pressures to remain short-sighted. (For example, the stock market responds to short-term profits, regardless of how those profits are made. Most corporations, therefore, do whatever they can to increase short-term profits, regardless of the affect on planet earth. Few investors are willing to invest in a company that does not show a profit, so that clearly, we are all culpable at some level.)

Lerner notes that health issues continue to increase worldwide due to the factors he identifies in the preceding extract (ozone depletion, toxic chemicals etc.). He also finds that "the impact of poverty on health is an overwhelming reality, especially in developing countries" (2006, p. 545). Poor people simply do not have access to the health care that might help protect them or the political clout that might enable them to prevent waste dumps from being established in their neighborhoods, as one example.

However, Lerner is not a pessimist. He believes that there is a path to saving the planet and its people and that this path is already being blazed by a growing environmental health movement. He believes that mothers who want to breast-feed their babies with milk that is toxin-free, health professionals who care about their clients, environmental justice groups who want to save endangered species, religious groups who literally want to save human souls, and many other potential allies will recognize the power of joining forces. Out of this alliance, Lerner believes a movement can arise strong enough to stop the race toward destruction of our good Earth. The task is incredibly challenging, and one in which the social work profession can and hopefully will play an important role.

That Lerner's optimism is warranted can be found in the insights of contemporary theologians such as Diarmuid O'Murchu, who writes powerfully of the importance of ecological sustainability: "Sustainability is not merely a form of ecological sensitivity and economic prudence; it is above all else an aspect of God's own wisdom and grace" (2000, p. 141). This respected theologian asserts that all animal and plant life on earth co-exists for mutual benefit and enrichment of the greater whole, and that no part (including humans) can flourish if others are injured or destroyed.

Another hopeful development is that even some members of the conservative evangelical Christian movement are calling for awareness of the dangers of today's environmental degradation, particularly global warming. For example, Reverend Richard Cizik, Washington spokesperson for the National Association of Evangelicals, recently urged national action toward reducing global warming based on the biblical demand for "creation care," or stewardship of the land provided by the creator (Lampman, 2006). Cizik developed his concern after talking with an Evangelical scientist based at Oxford University who laid out the scientific consensus on the issue.

In addition, there is evidence that even some of the most serious polluters on the planet, American corporations, now understand that global warming is increasing at such a rapid rate, and is so hazardous to human life, that government regulation is necessary. General Motors, for example, in 2007 joined a list of companies urging federal policies to tighten standards on vehicle emissions. This is finally taking place because some chief executive officers (CEOs) have truly "gotten religion" on what they see as major threats to the ecosystem and the economy; others, more pragmatic, want to "have a seat at the table" when policies are written and to have advance knowledge of what regulations are likely to involve (Trumbull, 2007).

The Intervention Process

To continue our more mundane discussion of the generalist approach to social work practice, the third major component (besides the ecosystems perspective and the use of multiple levels of intervention, as previously described) is the planned change, intervention, or problem-solving process. This third component has traditionally been known as the **problem-solving process,** and that terminology is still used today by many social workers. The terms *planned change process* and *intervention process*, however, are sometimes preferred because some think they better encompass the idea of preventive work. For example, parents who wish to maintain a safe neighborhood may request assistance in developing a community center for teens who might otherwise become involved in gangs. However, many social workers point out that "problem solving" can also encompass preventive work.

Regardless of the terminology used, a careful, step-by-step process must be employed in professional social work practice. It is all too easy for a caring person to hear about a situation that needs to change and immediately jump in to try to "do something," unintentionally causing serious complications.

An explicit intervention process alerts responsible social workers to think carefully before acting and provides guidelines regarding how to think critically. This text will usually use the terms planned change or intervention process to describe the painstaking methodology employed in professional social work practice. Acting after hearing just one person's side of a story neglects other people's experience and points of view. The intervention process involves several steps, as described in the CSWE Educational Policy and Accreditation Standards (CSWE, 2001):

> Social work practice content is anchored in the purposes of the social work profession and focuses on strengths, capacities, and resources of client systems in relation to their broader environments. Students learn practice content that encompasses knowledge and skills to work with individuals, families, groups, organizations, and communities. This content includes engaging clients in an appropriate working relationship; identifying issues, problems, needs, resources, and assets; collecting and assessing information; and planning for service delivery. It includes using communication skills, supervision, and consultation. Practice content also includes identifying, analyzing, and implementing empirically based interventions designed to achieve client goals; applying empirical knowledge and technological advances; evaluating program outcomes and practice effectiveness; developing, analyzing, advocating, and providing leadership for policies and services; and promoting social and economic justice.

Obviously, this process is involved and requires expertise! To translate for beginning students (see Exhibit 2-6), the generalist social worker usually *begins with a situation in which change is desired.* Let us use this chapter's case study as an example. Government officials in the state where Stephanie Hermann worked desired to change the situation in which people with developmental disabilities were routinely placed in nursing homes. Stephanie's job as a social worker in her regional government office was to assist the desired change to come about. She engaged her client system, in this case the social service providers in her region, by alerting them to the coming policy changes that would affect them. She helped them identify and define important issues involved, and assisted them in gathering and assessing as much relevant information as possible (e.g., How many nursing home residents would be affected? What alternative placements were available for them?).

EXHIBIT 2-6

The Intervention Process

Engaging the client system	Contracting
Identifying and defining important issues	Implementing plans of action
Gathering and assessing data	Evaluating outcomes
Identifying plans of action	Terminating

Once Brockton Manor decided to seek alternative placements for all its residents with developmental disabilities, Stephanie, in collaboration with the nursing home and various other community agencies and organizations, identified possible plans of action. She helped develop agreements (contracts) regarding differing responsibilities and roles of the various stakeholders. She then helped implement mutually determined plans of action using the best knowledge and technological advances available (involving, e.g., medical evaluations and video services). She displayed leadership in developing new resources (the new group homes and family care homes for people with disabilities). Stephanie then monitored and evaluated outcomes. When the situation was improved to the clients' satisfaction, she formally terminated her involvement. It goes without saying that excellent analytical and communication skills were required throughout this process.

The planned change process helps the generalist social worker determine which level or levels of intervention to involve in resolving the issue or concern at hand. In Stephanie's case, resolving the issue involved working at every level of intervention: the community (Stephanie's region of the state); the social service agencies and voluntary organizations within that region; and several families, small groups, and individuals like Sandra McLean. On the other hand, generalist intervention may involve working only with a single individual or a particular family, group, or organization. The important point is that the plan of action determined by the generalist worker depends on the nature of the circumstances and careful implementation of the planned change process. The plan of action is not determined according to a method that simply happens to be preferred by the worker—for example, one-on-one counseling or group work.

VALUES, ETHICS, AND HUMAN DIVERSITY

The trend toward community placement of people with developmental disabilities was a welcome one for the social work profession. Social work values, as identified in Chapter 1, include the dignity and worth of each person. It is easy to recognize the dignity and worth of fortunate individuals with no apparent disabilities, who can live independently as expected in our society. But what about persons like Sandra McLean, who, no matter how hard they may try, will require ongoing assistance throughout their lives? A basic ethical principal in social work requires that social workers respect the inherent worth and dignity of all. Sandra, despite her disabilities, was a whole person who deserved respectful treatment designed to meet her special needs, treatment that would help maximize her potential.

Sandra was a member of a population known as people with disabilities. The many challenges of diverse populations will be explored in a later chapter, but it can be stated here that the dignity and worth of people with disabilities is frequently overlooked, as is their right to self-determination (another basic social work value). In fact, **ableism** is identified by Berg-Weber (2005, p. 104) as a practice in which people without disabilities exclude and/or oppress those who do. Sadly, the worth and dignity of the disabled person may be overlooked by the wider community because that community simply wants to spend the least amount of money for care possible. Self-determination may never even be considered, so many people with disabilities are drugged to unconsciousness to make them easier to manage, as was Sandra McLean. Yet in many instances, people with disabilities are able to make many decisions for themselves, and in all cases, worth and dignity should be honored. Fortunately, respectful care often leads to treatment, which turns out to be less expensive than warehousing in institutions, as in Sandra McLean's case.

SOCIAL JUSTICE AND POPULATIONS AT RISK

As will be discussed in more detail in Chapter 3, certain populations in this society are especially at risk of poverty, discrimination, and oppression. People with disabilities are among the populations at risk. Social workers can serve as advocates to assist them to live happy, productive lives. Social work values and ethics challenge us to work with people with disabilities: a major professional value promoted by the National Association of Social Workers is **social justice,** with the related ethical principle of challenging social injustice. People with disabilities are often treated unjustly and require active intervention and advocacy. They do not choose their disabilities, of course, and they do not deserve to be ignored, isolated, and oppressed because of them. Instead, social workers should provide assistance in achieving their goals, which are as varied as the goals of people without disabilities. They may range from simply enjoying the love and companionship of others to engaging in a professional career, depending on the individual situation.

The Strengths Perspective: Resilience and Empowerment

Dennis Saleebey pioneered what has become known as the strengths-based approach to social work practice. He reminds us that it is of great importance to seek and identify strengths in all client systems. Focusing only on problems and deficits tends to discourage workers and clients alike. Saleebey (2006) notes that despite the difficulties our clients may have experienced, they have also developed many skills and attributes that have helped them to meet and overcome difficult challenges. People often exhibit remarkable resiliency in the face of adversity.

Glicken (2004) points out that the strengths perspective always views clients in a hopeful and optimistic way, regardless of the complexity of their issues. Like Saleebey, Glicken believes that all clients have innate strengths and abilities. Social workers can enhance these strengths when they focus on positive and successful client behaviors, which can be found in even the most difficult situations. Glicken counsels social workers to do a conscious "asset review" of a client's many positive behaviors and qualities.

The strengths-based approach is especially appropriate in working with clients with disabilities. The focus can and should be on strengths and abilities, not deficits. Consider the example of Sandra McLean. Despite being warehoused in institutions for many years, this remarkable woman rebounded courageously when given a chance. She turned out to be an amazingly resilient human being. She relearned how to walk, talk, feed, and toilet herself, and she was especially talented in the area of social relations.

Assisting clients to discover and honor their own strengths and powers of resilience may be our very best service to them as individuals. In addition, many external environments, even seemingly the poorest and most harsh, offer important resources that can make a difference in our clients' lives. The practitioner's challenge is to help find these resources and assist clients to utilize them.

A strengths perspective leads naturally to the idea of empowering clients; recognizing and honoring strengths is a firm foundation for empowerment. According to Miley, O'Melia, and Dubois (2004), empowerment involves both personal and political aspects. *Personal empowerment* involves one's own sense of competence, control, mastery, and the like. *Political empowerment* involves resource accessibility and the power to make choices. Genuine options must be available in the wider environment, and people need the power to choose them (or not) to have political empowerment.

POLITICAL PERSPECTIVES

The concept of empowerment leads to a discussion of political perspectives and their importance to social workers and their clients. Remember that the impetus for Stephanie's region to provide community placements for people with disabilities came from changing *government* policies at the *federal* level. These policy changes were a result of political action by various groups of people with disabilities and their advocates, including social workers. It was a positive result of long years of work by those who wanted people with disabilities to have the option to live in family-like settings in order to lead more fulfilling lives. It was an achievement that helped empower many people with disabilities. However, even if enough family care and small group homes were available to care for all, many disabled people would be unable to pay for them. That is because people with disabilities are especially at risk of poverty and discrimination. Without government help, many people with disabilities are simply unable to secure the financial resources to pay for community care.

Preschool children from economically deprived families learn new skills at a Head Start Center.

UP FOR DEBATE

Proposition: Should the federal government develop programs designed to assist poor people?

YES	NO
People are naturally industrious and will use such assistance responsibly to better their lives.	People are naturally lazy, and government assistance will only make them more lazy and irresponsible.
Environmental conditions such as discrimination may hold a person back unless government assists to "level the playing field."	Individuals are autonomous and achieve according to their inborn talents; they have complete free will.
Government programs are necessary to help meet basic human needs for all.	The free market economy is the best way to fulfill individual needs.
A free market economy needs intervention and regulation by government to ensure that competition is fair.	Government's role should be to support, not regulate, the free market.

Helping poor people achieve their needs and goals is considered a legitimate government function by some in America today, but not by others. The political parties differ markedly in their views on this matter. Thus, it makes sense for students considering the social work profession to become informed voters. Social work clients frequently belong to populations at risk who experience poverty and other ongoing challenges. Government assistance can be crucial in allowing them to obtain the resources necessary to improve their lives. One way social workers can help their clients is by voting for the candidates whose policies will genuinely assist the poor and disadvantaged. Even better, professional social workers can develop active political careers themselves.

To help students make thoughtful choices in the voting booth, this chapter will discuss political perspectives known as conservative, liberal or progressive, and radical. It will also briefly describe neoconservative and neoliberal views. The discussion here will be very basic; students are encouraged to read as much as possible from additional sources and to examine the Up for Debate box. Suggestions for further reading can be found at the end of the chapter.

The Political Spectrum

It is probably fairly common for people to vote as their families, friends, or neighbors do early in their voting careers. That is certainly the easiest way to decide for whom to vote. But it makes better sense for citizens to inform themselves about the positions that candidates take on major issues and to vote for those candidates whose views are most nearly in accord with their own. Of course it is important to think through one's own views carefully, so that one's vote is cast intelligently. All too often we let our friends or family do our thinking for us, so that we vote against our own best interests. For example, in the 2004 election an acquaintance of this author, a minimum-wage worker who constantly worried about making ends meet, voted for the political party that opposed raising the minimum wage. The reason? "Oh, I've always voted Republican—our family's just that way. I don't like thinking about politics myself." Another salient illustration involves Abbie Heinrich (not her real name, of course), who serves as Chapter 9's case example. Abbie, a physically disabled older woman totally dependent on Medicaid to pay for her nursing home care, voted for the party that she knew was most likely to cut her lifeline, Medicaid. The reason? Fundamentalist TV evangelists had persuaded her that the Republicans would protect the moral purity of the country against "filthy homosexuals" and gay marriage. (Issues used to persuade vulnerable citizens such as this to vote against their own best interests are known as "wedge issues.")

Learning about political parties can help students and other voters select candidates in an informed manner because the parties themselves take different positions on important issues. That is what party "platforms" are about. The platform tells the position of the party on many public issues such as health care, education, affirmative action, women's reproductive rights, Social Security, and the like.

Political parties in the United States today fall along a political spectrum, described as "right" to "left." Those on the "right" are considered relatively "conservative"; those on the "left" are considered relatively "liberal" or "progressive." The major conservative political party in the United States today is the Republican party, and the major liberal party is the Democratic party. There are parties even further "right" (or more conservative) than the Republican, however, and parties further "left" than the Democratic.

Webster's Dictionary defines "liberal" as "favoring reform or progress, as in religion, education, etc.; specifically, favoring political reforms tending toward democracy and personal freedom for the individual; progressive" (Guralnik, 1984, p. 814). It defines "progressive" as "favoring, working for, or characterized by progress or improvement, as through political or social reform" (Guralnik, 1984, p. 1135). *Webster's* defines "conservative" as "tending to preserve established traditions or institutions and to resist or oppose any changes in these (conservative politics, conservative art)" (Guralnik, 1984, p. 302). These definitions are useful in understanding basic differences in perspective between liberals or progressives and conservatives in the United States.

People who find themselves on different ends of the political spectrum tend to have different attitudes toward change; different views of individual behavior, human nature, and the family; different views toward the social system; and different perspectives on the proper role of government with respect to the economic market (Popple & Leighninger, 2005). We will discuss some of these differences next.

Conservative Perspectives

The word *conservative* is derived from the verb "to conserve" or "to save." So it should come as no surprise that people who are conservative tend to want to keep things as they are and to resist change. People want to keep things as they are for many good reasons, but perhaps the simplest is that these individuals tend to be "haves" who want to keep what they have, or who believe that the current system will provide them with the best opportunity to become "haves."

In particular, conservatives believe that government should not interfere with the free market forces of supply and demand. They want to preserve the traditional free market economic system because this is the system that got them where they are, or else it is the system they believe can best take them where they want to go.

Conservatives tend to believe that people are fully autonomous and have total free will, so that whatever a person achieves in life he or she deserves, be it wealth or poverty. They also tend to believe that economic insecurity is *necessary* because, in their view, most people are naturally lazy and would not work without fear of poverty (Karger & Stoesz, 2005; Popple and Leighninger, 2005.)

Given these perspectives, it follows that conservatives do not believe that government should use its powers to help poor people. In the conservative view, that would only increase laziness. Government should, instead, provide tax breaks for the rich, because wealthy people invest money in the economic market. New investment theoretically could lead to new jobs for poor people, who would be better off with more work. This perspective is popularly known as the "trickle down theory" or, more formally, as "supply-side economics."

The conservative orientation goes beyond economics. Preservation of social traditions such as the nuclear family is also strongly promoted. Thus, political conservatives generally oppose such potential public services as government day care programs because, from this perspective, child care should be provided only by a wife within the family household. Single parenthood, sex outside of marriage, abortion, homosexuality, and so on, are also generally opposed by conservatives because these practices are not considered traditional (Ginsberg, 1998). This type of conservatism, sometimes called cultural conservatism, results in major contradictions, however. While conservatives insist that government take a hands-off (laissez-faire) position with respect to intervention in the economic market, many conservatives push hard for government intervention restricting reproductive choice, access to sex education in the schools, and the like.

The major conservative political party in the United States today is the Republican Party, as mentioned earlier: that of Presidents Nixon, Ford, Reagan, and George H. W. and George W. Bush. Other conservative parties include the Traditionalists, who believe that Christian doctrine should become the law of the state, and the Libertarians, who oppose virtually all government regulation (including taxation), except when one individual threatens the physical safety of another (Karger & Stoesz, 2005).

Liberal or Progressive Perspectives

The liberal or progressive worldview is quite different from the conservative. First of all, the conception of human nature is more optimistic. Liberals believe that people are naturally good and do not need to be controlled or forced to work. Rather, they need to be protected from corrupting influences in the wider environment (Popple & Leighninger, 2005). Liberals believe that people are industrious by nature and will take pleasure in hard work and personal accomplishment if conditions are humane.

While liberals do not deny human autonomy and free will totally, they believe that conditions in the social environment strongly affect people's chances to develop their talents and achieve a fulfilling life. From this viewpoint, if people are poor, it is in large part due to lack of opportunity, societal discrimination, oppression, and the like—problems that lie in the external environment.

Unemployed worker interviews at a job placement service.

It only makes sense that worldview affects political perspectives. Liberals or progressives, believing in the inherent goodness of people and the fact that unfavorable conditions in the wider environment may cause harm, support government intervention in the workings of the economic market to try to level the playing field for groups they believe are disadvantaged. For example, they tend to support government social welfare programs that provide monetary assistance to poor children and their families. They tend to support affirmative action programs to provide better access to jobs for women and ethnic minorities. They support national programs such as Head Start, which provides early environmental and educational enrichment for poor children to give them a better chance to fully develop their talents (see Exhibit 2-7).

EXHIBIT 2-7

The Political Spectrum

Liberal or Progressive Perspectives	Conservative Perspectives
Change can make the world a better place	Change should be resisted; tradition should be maintained
People are naturally good and industrious	People are naturally lazy, corrupt, and irresponsible
People are strongly influenced and shaped by their environment	People are autonomous and guided entirely by free will
Family is an evolving institution; family forms may change	The traditional family should be upheld; programs designed to help nontraditional families should be opposed
The social system needs regulating; government should intervene in the economic market to assist disadvantaged populations	The social system functions correctly as is; government regulation threatens individual liberty and smooth functioning of the economic market

SOURCE: Adapted from P. Popple & L. Leighninger. (2005). *Social work, social welfare and American society* (6th ed.). Boston: Allyn & Bacon.

The major political party in the United States today that supports a liberal or progressive perspective is the Democratic Party, that of Presidents Kennedy, Johnson, Carter, and Clinton. There are other parties more liberal than the Democratic in the United States; they are much smaller, however. The Green Party is an example. It promotes environmental sustainability, community-based economics, grassroots democracy, nonviolence, respect for diversity, feminism, and social justice, among other progressive policies. The party began in Germany and is now a worldwide movement (Karger & Stoesz, 2005).

International news media may confuse Americans when the terms *liberal* or *conservative* are used to describe governments abroad. For example, while in the United States the term *liberal* is typically associated with increased government support for social programs, the term has different meanings in other parts of the world. In the United Kingdom, for example, it is usually applied to a philosophy of limited government influence. In Australia, the "liberal" party is "conservative" according to U.S. definition while the "labour" party is "liberal" (Abbott, 1999). In this text, we will use the terms *liberal* and *conservative* as they are generally understood in the United States.

Neoliberalism and Neoconservatism

Confusing to many students today is the fact that there are *neoconservative* and *neoliberal* perspectives, which are also important forces on the political scene. While a great deal could be said about them, it will be stated here only that both are to the "right" of their parent movements, the conservative and the liberal. American politics in general shifted greatly to the right toward the end of the 20th century, and the momentum has been so strong since the turn of the century that many liberals try to distance themselves from the term *liberal*, using the word *progressive* instead. For neoconservatives, the shift to the right has involved adopting stands that are strongly culturally conservative, such as opposing choice for women, banning gay people from the military, and banning gay marriage. Their stance could be described as "reactionary," opposing any policy empowering minorities. For neoliberals, the shift to the right has involved adopting favorable policies toward big business.

Bill Clinton was among the founders of the neoliberal movement, believing that a more favorable attitude toward big business would help him get elected. This attitude may have been what persuaded him, as president, to sign the bill (to be discussed in a later chapter) known as the Personal Responsibility and Work Opportunity Act, which, in 1996, ended the entitlement of all poor children to public welfare in this country. To be sure, the bill was passed by a Congress largely composed of neoconservatives. "Neos," especially neoconservatives, strongly oppose public welfare programs for the poor, or any increase in minimum wages, because they fear such assistance to the poor might limit corporate profits.

Radical Perspectives

The radical perspective, which may be described as "left" of the liberal, is held by a much smaller number of people in this country than either the conservative or liberal, but it is still influential. The radical view of human nature parallels that of the liberal or progressive—that people are inherently good and naturally industrious. They will work hard and take pride in their achievements given reasonable working conditions.

Like liberals, people who take a radical perspective believe that environmental influences may prevent people from achieving their full potential. But while liberals believe that the environment can potentially be made fair *within* the capitalist system by enlightened government intervention, radicals believe that capitalism itself is the problem. They believe that a wealthy and powerful elite make decisions that further their own interests at the expense of others, so that fairness is not possible under this system. Instead, society must be entirely restructured to redistribute wealth and power among all the people (Popple and Leighninger, 2005).

Probably the major party in the United States today that most nearly reflects the radical perspective is the Socialist party, although it is very small (see Exhibit 2-8).

The Political Spectrum and Social Welfare Policy

Liberal and conservative positions fall toward opposite ends of the political spectrum, as described earlier. Conservatives oppose government intervention in the workings of the free market, except to bolster big business, and liberals support intervention to correct imbalances and empower citizens who fall outside the mainstream. By the late 20th century, these positions had polarized, and at the beginning of the 21st century, as this text is being written, polarization is increasing. A Democratic majority elected to both houses of Congress in 2006 helped limit the power of the neoconservative executive branch, but discourse continued to be strident. Our greatest challenge in the future may be finding a way for people of differing political perspectives to enter constructive dialogue.

The fear that swamped the nation after the September 11, 2001, terrorist attacks seemed to pull our nation together for a time, but then President George W. Bush used that fear to lead the nation to war, not only against Afghanistan, where terrorists were sheltered, but against Iraq. As is now believed, Iraq had nothing to do with the

---

EXHIBIT 2-8

The Political Spectrum

Left				Right
Radical	Liberal	Neoliberal	Conservative	Neoconservative

←- →

Socialist	Green	Democratic		Republican Libertarian

This exhibit portrays where the author believes certain political parties lie today along the "left–right" political spectrum. This illustration is made according to the author's best understanding, but other views may differ. In some ways, it is incorrect to place

Libertarian to the "right" of Republican, as Libertarians strongly promote individual liberties, including those of the less powerful, so they do not promote legislation limiting women's right to choice, gay marriage, etc.

2001 attacks on the World Trade Center and Pentagon, nor did it maintain stockpiles of weapons of mass destruction as claimed by the Bush administration. However, war is profitable for large American corporations, especially those involved in the defense industry. The lure of potential profits may have clouded the nation's decision-making processes.

Increasing distrust between the major political parties at the time of the 2004 presidential election led to serious concern that the Bush victory could be illegitimate due to voting fraud. While a thorough investigation will probably never be conducted, Senator Barbara Boxer, a Democrat, formally challenged the election on the floor of the U.S. Senate on January 6, 2005. Her protest went unheeded. However, by 2006 at least six states had initiated lawsuits to block the purchase or use of computerized voting machines, due to their vulnerability to software tampering and lack of printed records that can be hand-counted in case of dispute (O'Driscoll, 2006).

As this text is being written in 2007, the cost of ongoing war in human, economic, and moral terms continues to mount and divide the nation. With billions of dollars committed to the war effort, fewer and fewer resources are available to assist people in need in this country and abroad. The great tsunami of 2004 and the hurricanes flooding New Orleans and the southeastern coast of America in 2005 highlight the problem. Resources needed at home and abroad to assist people in natural disasters are often already committed to military engagements abroad, which may cause even greater internal disasters.

EXHIBIT 2-9

'You needn't worry, sir. I don't think these rules apply to selling a war.'

To return to our chapter's case study: regarding a politically powerless but personally plucky individual like Sandra McLean, would there be any way that people from both ends of the political spectrum might be willing to assist her? Remember that it was a policy change at the *national* level that prompted reassessment of her care in the *local* nursing home and her subsequent rehabilitation and foster home placement. What could a conservative approach do for Sandra? Under what conditions might the free market have an interest in helping her? Should Sandra be helped even if the free market has no interest in her, given that she is unable to work? If so, why? If not, why not? Students are requested to keep such questions in mind as they read further in this text and others.

INTERNET SITES

http://www.democrats.org	The Democratic National Committee
http://www.rnc.org	The Republican National Committee
http://www.greens.org	The Green Parties of North America
http://www.lp.org	The Libertarian Party
http://www.policyalternatives.ca/	Canadian Centre for Policy Alternatives
http://www.congress.org	Current issues, votes, debates
http://www.hudson.org/wpc/	Welfare Policy Institute
http://www.acosa.org	Association for Community Organization and Social Administration
http://www.euro.centre.org	The European Centre for Social Welfare Policy and Research

SUMMARY

This chapter begins with the case study of Sandra McLean, a young woman who suffered a head injury at birth and cannot live independently. Sandra's situation is used to help illustrate the importance of two major types of theoretical perspectives necessary for competent social work practice: those that guide daily practice and those that guide social welfare policy decisions and strongly affect practice.

With respect to social work practice theory, the chapter discusses the influence of systems theory and an ecosystems perspective on today's generalist approach to practice. Levels of intervention included in the generalist approach are discussed as well as the systematic planned change or intervention process. The importance of a strengths-based orientation and recognition of client resilience is discussed. The chapter notes that appropriate levels of social work intervention today may extend beyond former notions of community to include global, ecological, and environmental considerations.

The chapter then discusses basic political theory to help social work students understand different views on government action that will strongly impact practice with clients, who often fall outside the mainstream. Conservative perspectives are contrasted with liberal or progressive and radical viewpoints.

Neoconservative and neoliberal points of view are introduced.

The chapter concludes with a discussion of the political spectrum and how it affects social welfare policy decisions. Social work students are challenged to think about which political perspective might best assist their clients and to attempt to find ways to encourage people who fall on opposite ends of the political spectrum to work together to improve the lives of all.

KEY TERMS

ableism, *p. 67*

active treatment, *p. 53*

community placement, *p. 53*

conservative, *p. 70*

cultural conservatism, *p. 72*

ecosystems perspective, *p. 58*

empowerment, *p. 69*

family care homes, *p. 54*

generalist approach, *p. 61*

levels of intervention, *p. 61*

liberal or progressive, *p. 70*

neoconservative, *p. 70*

neoliberal, *p. 70*

planned change or intervention
   process, *p. 66*

problem-solving process, *p. 65*

radical, *p. 70*

resilience, *p. 69*

social justice, *p. 68*

strengths perspective, *p. 69*

system, *p. 57*

worldview, *p. 72*

DISCUSSION QUESTIONS

1. Considering the story of Sandra McLean provided in this chapter, can you think of ways in which social welfare policy may affect social work practice? Can you think of ways in which social welfare policy directly affects the lives of people whom you may know?

2. How is the generalist approach to social work practice defined in this text? Is this the only way the concept can be defined? What are the three main components of the generalist approach as identified in our definition?

3. Define the concept of *system*. How is this concept reflected in the ecosystems perspective? How can a systems approach or an ecosystems perspective be helpful to social workers?

4. What are the levels (or systems) of intervention that are involved in the generalist approach to social work practice?

5. Identify and discuss the steps of the intervention or planned change process as identified by the Council on Social Work Education. Why is it important that social workers use a systematic process in their work?

6. Describe and discuss the worldview of political conservatives. How does the worldview of conservatives lead people of this persuasion to promote a free market but not government intervention to try to make a better world? Which major American political party can be described as conservative?

7. Describe and discuss the worldview of political liberals or progressives. How does the worldview of liberals lead people of this persuasion to promote government intervention to try to make a better world? Which major American political party can be described as liberal?

8. Are the "neo" movements within the Democratic and Republican parties to the "left" or "right" of the parent parties? Do these movements tend to make the parties more liberal or more conservative?

9. What major piece of legislation relating to children in America was signed by President Bill Clinton, who helped found the neoliberal movement? How does this legislation reflect conservative philosophy? How did this legislation affect children in America who are poor?

10. Describe and discuss the worldview of political radicals. Why do they believe that using the regular political process to improve conditions in the United States will not work?

11. From reading about the political spectrum of the United States as briefly described in this text,

where do you believe that you personally fit on this spectrum? Would you say that you occupy the same place on the spectrum as your parents? Your siblings? Your friends? Why or why not?

12. Which political perspective do you believe can best assist people like Sandra McLean in this chapter's case study? Please give your reasons.

CLASSROOM EXERCISES

While not required, it is suggested that students break into small groups of three or four to discuss these exercises. It may be helpful to choose a scribe to record and report important points to the class after the group discussion.

1. Think about an issue that has been troubling you in your own life, an issue that you are willing to share with your classmates. How much of the issue seems located in the wider environment (beyond your person)? How much seems personal only? How do person and environment interact to produce or maintain this issue? How do you think they will need to interact to best resolve it?

2. If a social worker were to become involved in assisting you to resolve your issue, what levels of intervention do you believe the worker should employ? Why?

3. Many ordinary people are assisted by government social welfare programs, even while they mistakenly believe that these programs only help "other" people. Tax deductions for home mortgages, Social Security benefits, and student loans are common examples of government welfare programs that help many of us. Identify those that may have helped you or your family now or in the past.

4. Sometimes people are categorized as "haves" or "have-nots," meaning that some people have sufficient resources at their disposal and some do not. Suppose that you are "have-not." Which political philosophy, conservatism or liberalism, do you believe would work best on your behalf? Why?

RESEARCH ACTIVITIES

1. Read your local newspaper to find out what social welfare–related issues are active in your area. For example, perhaps a controversy exists over the location of a low-income housing project in your city or town, or over a zoning variance required to establish a group home for people with disabilities in your neighborhood.

2. Visit the local offices of the Democratic and Republican parties, and examine their literature (and other political party offices, if available). Find

out the types of policies these parties support on issues of concern to you.

3. Attend a session of your state legislature, and observe the political debate process. If you live too far from your state capital, find out where a local governing body meets and attend a meeting.

4. Talk with your family and friends about their political affiliations, and ask them to tell you the reasons they have made their choices.

INTERNET RESEARCH EXERCISES

1. The National Alliance for the Mentally Ill has a very informative website. Their Policy Research Institute has a web page entitled "Spending Money in All the Wrong Places" (http://www.nami.org/ Template .cfm?Section=policy_research_institute&Template= ContentManagement/ContentDisplay.cfm&Content ID14596).

a. What are the issues for which they have prepared fact sheets?

b. To whom is this information aimed?

c. How effective do you feel this approach can be?

2. The Canadian Research Institute for Social Policy represents an example of an organization dedicated to conducting policy research (http://www.unb.ca/crisp/index.php).

   a. What is their mission? (Hint: click "Overview," then click "Mission.")

   b. What is their approach?

   c. Describe three of their current projects.

3. An interesting website, Global Alliance for a Deep Ecological Social Work (http://www .ecosocialwork.org/), presents a platform for the ecological perspective for social workers.

   a. Click on "Mission." What is the stated mission of GADESW?

   b. What are its objectives?

   c. Click on "Perspectives." On this page Dr. Fred Besthorn says, "I see the contours of a Deep-Ecological Social Work as coalescing along three dimensions." What are these dimensions?

FOR FURTHER READING

Abramovitz, M. (2000). *Under attack: Fighting back: Women and welfare in the United States.* New York: Monthly Review Press.

This excellent little book describes American women's long history of struggle for economic rights. Abramovitz shows clearly that the 1996 Personal Responsibility and Work Opportunity Act, which ended entitlement for government aid for poor mothers and their children, was simply another setback in a long struggle for equality and respect for women's rights in this country.

Compton, B., & Galaway, B. (1999). *Social work processes* (6th ed.). Pacific Grove, CA: Brooks/Cole.

A classic text on social work practice that has survived through several editions, this is an excellent source of information on systems theory and how it can be used in social work practice.

Germain, C. B., & Gitterman, A. (1995). Ecological perspective. In *Encyclopedia of social work* (19th ed., pp. 816–822). Washington, DC: NASW Press.

Germain and Gitterman describe their concept of the ecological perspective in detail in this article. They outline and define multiple concepts that are important in this perspective, including ones that have been newly added by contemporary theorists.

Ginsberg, L. (1998). *Conservative social welfare policy: A description and analysis.* Chicago: Nelson-Hall.

Ginsberg provides a detailed historical perspective on the development of American social welfare policies and identifies persistent themes. He then examines how political orientation shapes perception of those themes. He examines conservative political policies and their impact on social welfare legislation, and the impact of conservative economic perspectives on social policy.

Karger, J. K., & Stoesz, D. (2005). *American social welfare policy: A pluralist approach* (4th ed.). Boston: Allyn & Bacon.

A very readable text on social welfare policy, this book examines the American political economy and describes the impact of the American political continuum on social welfare policy in the first chapter. Further discussion of the impact of multiple political perspectives on American social welfare policy is found throughout the book.

Popple, P., & Leighninger, L. (2005). *Social work, social welfare and American society* (6th ed.). Boston: Allyn & Bacon.

This text provides an in-depth discussion of competing perspectives of social welfare in the first chapter. The worldview of conservatives, liberals, and radicals is explained in-depth, including attitudes toward change, views of human nature, views of the family, and views of government and the economic system. Further discussion of these topics is found throughout the book.

CHAPTER 3

SOCIAL JUSTICE AND SOCIAL WELFARE POLICY

OUTLINE

Juanita Chavez

JUANITA CHAVEZ

J uanita cheered when she was offered the job as a social worker at Urban Neighborhood Center. A recent BSW graduate, Juanita knew she was competing for the position with more experienced workers. But she had an important skill: she spoke both Spanish and English fluently. Moreover, as part of the requirements of her social work major, she had served her senior-year field placement in an alternative school where Spanish was the first language of many of the students. Urban Neighborhood Center was located in an area where many residents were of Hispanic origin. Juanita hoped her bilingual abilities would help her get the job. They did.

Juanita had now been working for several months. She felt she was developing a broad understanding of the needs of the neighborhood as a whole that surrounded the agency. As part of her job, she was expected to help identify major needs of community residents, to inform residents about the services available at the center, and to provide them with information concerning community resources that might help meet their needs. The Center provided after-school recreational programs for school-age children, limited tutoring services, and a food pantry staffed by volunteers. Lately, however, the food pantry had been short on supplies and hungry people had been sent home empty-handed. That bothered Juanita very much. While she liked the fact that her position gave her a broad perspective of the neighborhood in which she worked—indeed of the midsized city of which the neighborhood was a part—that knowledge could be disturbing. She now knew that resources needed by many of the poorer residents were frequently not available.

Juanita's first crisis call on the job related to TANF (Temporary Assistance for Needy Families, to be discussed in more detail later in the chapter). She remembered the phone call well. A volunteer helping supervise a recreational program had called Juanita just as the new social worker was trying to organize her tiny office. Two children much too young for the agency's after-school programs, and much too young to be out on the streets alone, had been brought in by a school-age child who regularly came to the agency. The child said she had found the toddlers on the sidewalk, crying and apparently lost. Juanita soon encountered the young children, ages approximately 2 and 3, who said their names were Tomas and Tomacita. They could not provide an address or last name. They said they had been put to bed for a nap by their mother, but when they awakened, she was gone. Frightened, they began to search for her.

Juanita decided that she would have to call Protective Services to report abandoned children. Because the situation was not perceived as an emergency by the city's overburdened department, however, no worker arrived at Urban Neighborhood Center for several hours. Toward the end of the day, one of the longtime agency social workers returned after having made some home visits. By good fortune, this worker recognized Tomas and Tomacita and knew that they were siblings of a teenage girl who sometimes attended tutoring programs at the agency. There was a family telephone number on file. A call was made immediately, and a distraught mother answered. She had had to report to job training that day under the rules of the TANF program, she explained. Her older daughter, who usually babysat, was involved in a field trip with her school class, and the mother had not wanted her to miss it. The neighbor who had promised to substitute had been unavailable at the last minute. The children's mother didn't dare miss her job training as she could then be eliminated from the TANF program. That would take away her only source of money for food and rent. She knew people who had missed a single day of training due to lack of child care who had already been dismissed. So Tomas and Tomacita's mother had opted to take a serious risk, leaving her children alone after putting them to bed for a nap, hoping against hope that they would remain asleep.

The children's mother and the Protective Services worker arrived at Urban Neighborhood Center at almost the same moment. Only the advocacy of the agency social worker who knew the mother prevented the children from being taken into the foster care system then and there. Had that happened, months might have passed before Tomas and Tomacita were returned home. Their mother promised, of course, never to leave the children again without a babysitter. The Protective Services worker scolded her for not taking advantage of child care that was supposed to be provided by the TANF program. The mother explained that she had applied for child care months before but that it hadn't come through yet.

Juanita learned later that child care, while theoretically available to poor mothers enrolled in TANF in her city, in reality involved a long waiting list. While her state permitted child care assistance for poor mothers under an option allowed by federal TANF legislation, funding was inadequate to meet the need. Tomas and Tomacita's older sister missed school regularly so that the mother could attend job training. The ability to secure a pay check to purchase food and shelter was naturally perceived by this family as more important than education. Juanita soon became aware that many other families who lived near Urban Neighborhood Center were in the same situation. Many parents, languishing somewhere on TANF waiting lists for child care, depended on older children to babysit so they could go to work. Others with regular jobs earned wages too low to afford child care and also depended on their older children, especially teenage girls, to babysit. These helpful teens risked truancy proceedings, adding to family difficulties. Juanita was beginning to collect data on a number of high school girls in her area who were routinely missing school to babysit for younger siblings. She hoped eventually to influence legislators to appropriate more funds for child care. Juanita also hoped to see a Spanish-speaking day care center established by her agency because none yet existed in the city. She even made an appointment to speak with her agency's board of directors about establishing such a service. She was excited when the board appointed a special committee to study the situation *and* appointed Juanita a member. The committee then authorized Juanita to conduct a door-to-door survey to find out how many families would take part in a Spanish-speaking day care center if one were available. In this way, the social worker became engaged in community organization work, along with her other responsibilities at the neighborhood center.

As Juanita walked up the steps of a tiny, single-family cottage one day collecting data for her survey, she noticed that one of the special school vans that transport students with disabilities was pulling up to the door. The driver honked, and then asked Juanita to knock, since he needed to deliver a child. No one answered the door, however, and the driver explained that he would have to take the child back to school. Juanita could see the sad face of a little girl peering out of the side window of the bus. Her head was misshapen and too large for her features. The driver muttered something about irresponsible mothers, shook his head, and drove away.

Juanita returned to the cottage later that day. This time her knock was answered by a young woman who appeared to be in her early 20s. Juanita explained who she was and why she had dropped by earlier. The woman looked blank, and then said haltingly, with a heavy accent, "I no speak English." Juanita then greeted the young woman in Spanish. Her reward was an enormous, engaging smile. When Juanita mentioned the incident with the bus, however, the young woman's face took on an alarmed expression. She invited Juanita inside. She introduced herself as Carla Romero. "You say you are a social worker from Neighborhood Center?" she asked in Spanish. Juanita nodded. "Maybe you can help me, then," Carla continued.

"Tell me how I can assist," Juanita replied in Spanish, and the young woman began her story.

Carla told Juanita that her young daughter, Maria, was physically and cognitively disabled due to complications of birth that had resulted in permanent swelling of the brain. Now 6 years old, Maria functioned at a 12-month level. She had to be constantly supervised. But Carla had to work to support herself and the child. Her ex-husband, father of the child, kept in touch but had returned to Puerto Rico from where the couple had come. Child support checks were few and far between. Carla went to work when Maria began public school at the age of 3. The little girl received skilled service at school: occupational, physical, and speech therapy. Lately, however, there had been an embarrassing problem. The school nurse had sent Maria home with head lice. Carla had bought a number of products from the neighborhood pharmacy and used them carefully, but a few nits, or eggs, seemed to persist no matter what Carla did. The child continued to be sent home.

Carla, since she could not speak English, had already had a neighbor call the school to explain that she was doing all she could. The neighbor asked politely if the child could remain in school in spite of a few nits because her mother, Carla, had to work to provide food and shelter for the family. But the school nurse insisted that Maria could not attend school unless she was nit-free. The next day Juanita called the nurse. She got the same story: no exceptions. Juanita called the health department for assistance. There she learned that certain strains of lice were currently resisting all remedies available in the store. The health department had effective treatments, a nurse there told her, but due to funding cuts, the staff could no longer provide services to help with this problem. Lice were no longer considered a "communicable disease" under current funding definitions! The nurse suggested taking the child to a doctor and fumigating the house.

Carla was fortunate in that, while her job was very low wage and did not provide any benefits such as health insurance, she was nevertheless able to take her daughter to the doctor and to save enough money to pay for fumigating the house. That was because Maria qualified for both Medicaid and Supplemental Security Income (programs authorized under the Social Security Act) as a severely disabled child. The doctor told the young mother, however, that he did not know of any better treatment for lice or nits than the over-the-counter remedies she was already purchasing in the local stores. Carla then bought another standard treatment at the neighborhood pharmacy. She also had the house fumigated. But the problem continued.

Carla called Juanita at Urban Neighborhood Center in desperation after her daughter was sent home from school for the third month in a row. Her neighbor was babysitting regularly now, but she was not happy about it, and the cost was taking up most of Carla's food budget. The young mother frequently had to turn to Neighborhood Center's food pantry, but sometimes even the pantry was out of supplies. Juanita called the health department again, explaining that Carla had done everything she could but still her child was being sent home from school. The department continued to insist that they had no staff to deal with the problem. In desperation, Carla shaved Maria's head. Even that did not work! Tiny nits persisted, and Maria continued to be sent home. Juanita had angry words with the school nurse, explaining that the little girl, through no fault of her own, was missing out on valuable therapies at school and that her physical condition was deteriorating as a result. But the nurse, perhaps understandably, was unmovable.

Then Juanita had an inspiration. She called the social worker at the school Maria attended. That worker was aware of the problem and had already tried to intervene with the school nurse, but to no avail. But this worker and Juanita agreed that they would both make impassioned pleas to the health department. The health department refused once more, pleading budget cuts. Finally, the school social worker had her supervisor call the health department. That worked. At last, a public health nurse visited the Romero home. Juanita was present at the appointment, serving as translator and family advocate. The nurse promptly diagnosed Maria's strain of lice precisely and provided an effective remedy. Little Maria went back to school. But she had lost out on four months of education and therapy at an important developmental stage.

The Romero family's problem was not unique, of course. In Juanita's rounds of the neighborhood to collect information for her survey, she found that little Maria was not the only child missing school because of resistant strains of head lice. She also found several teenage girls at home taking care of babies, sometimes their younger siblings but sometimes their own children. Unable to afford the child care that would have enabled them to stay in school, and lacking any hope of reaching the top of the TANF waiting list for child care, they dropped out. The teen mothers were lucky if their parents let them continue to live at home, because most jobs available to people without high school degrees paid too low a wage to cover rent, food, clothing, and child care.

In addition, Juanita found several children in the neighborhood who stayed out on the streets after school because their parents had to work long hours and could not be home to supervise. Local schools offered a few sports programs for boys, but similar programs for girls were lacking. She also learned to her surprise that many of the families who used the agency's food pantry included full-time workers; some of the larger families included two full-time working adults yet they still could not make ends meet. Wages were simply too low to cover expenses for a family, so cupboards stood empty at times.

Juanita decided to take the results of her survey back to the committee who had appointed her and to the full Urban Neighborhood Center board of directors as well. Now, besides a Spanish speaking day care center for young children, she was interested in developing an after-school sports program for girls, as none currently existed in the area. Perhaps she could work with neighborhood schools to this end. Juanita also wondered if there might be a way to increase the supplies in her agency's food pantry. She hoped that, with a number of caring minds working on the problems she documented, effective solutions might be generated, including ways to raise funds to finance new programs. The agency's budget was limited, she knew. But as a social work professional, Juanita believed she could make a difference, especially if she could combine her problem-solving efforts and energies with those of other dedicated people committed to the agency and the surrounding community. ■

PART I
SOCIAL JUSTICE: A GROWING CONCERN

SOCIAL JUSTICE, POVERTY, AND POPULATIONS AT RISK

Little Tomas and Tomacita and Carla and Maria Romero belonged to a population at risk, or a population likely to suffer poverty in the United States. In fact, they belonged to several. Tomas, Tomacita, and Maria were children; Tomacita, Carla, and Maria were female; all were members of the ethnic minority group known as Hispanic or Latino. Children, women, and ethnic minorities are all populations at risk in this country. Prejudice against populations at risk, particularly against ethnic minorities and women, is common. Poverty, a basic issue of social and economic justice, is a common experience for members of these groups. *Poverty* may be defined broadly as the lack of resources to achieve a reasonably comfortable standard of living.

As mentioned in Chapter 1, social and economic justice and populations at risk constitute a curriculum area required of all baccalaureate degree programs by the Council on Social Work Education. They are intertwined in the real world. Social welfare policies and programs have been developed in many times and many places to help promote social and economic justice, to help improve the lives of people at risk. Sometimes these efforts have been successful, sometimes not. Some programs, unfortunately, seem to have been designed more to control people who are poor than to alleviate poverty or promote other forms of social or economic justice.

Social and Economic Justice

Let us begin with a discussion of social and economic justice. The *Social Work Dictionary* (Barker, 2003, p. 404) defines *social justice* as "an ideal condition in which all members of a society have the same basic rights, protection, opportunities, obligations, and social benefits. Implicit in this concept is the notion that historical inequalities should be acknowledged and remedied through specific measures. A key social work value, social justice entails advocacy to confront discrimination, oppression, and institutional inequities." Economic justice can be understood to be part of the larger concept of social justice, relating specifically to people's right to an adequate income and standard of living.

The United Nations' *Universal Declaration of Human Rights*, adopted in 1948, is an inspirational document comprising 30 articles that outline important elements of social justice. Hodge (2007) notes that this is still the most widely accepted human rights declaration in the world today. Article 1 affirms that "all human beings are born free and equal in dignity and rights. They are endowed with reason and conscience and should act towards one another in a spirit of brotherhood." Many other articles specify conditions necessary for the attainment of social justice as an overall ideal. Article 25 relates most specifically to economic justice (UN, 1948):

> Everyone has a right to a standard of living adequate for the health and well-being of himself and of his family, including food, clothing, housing and medical care and necessary social services, and the right to security in the event of unemployment, sickness, disability, widowhood, old age or other lack of livelihood in circumstances beyond his control.

> Motherhood and childhood are entitled to special care and assistance. All children, whether born in or out of wedlock, shall enjoy the same social protection.

Cynthia Rocha and Andrea McCarter (2003/2004) note that economic justice is not yet a well-developed concept in social work education. They state that much work needs to be done to help students understand how the concept relates to trends in the economy and to social welfare policies and programs. This text will try to further that understanding. This chapter's case study, for example, illustrates how poverty can result in young children left without parental supervision, lost educational opportunities, entire families experiencing hunger, and mothers forced to work outside the home although badly needed within. It introduces some of our national poverty programs purporting to ease the plight of the poor. But do our current policies and programs advance social and economic justice? Do they provide adequate "special care and assistance" to poor mothers and children as advocated by the UN Declaration of Human Rights?

Although the United States is the wealthiest nation in the world today, poverty is widespread. More than one child in six lives in poverty, and the number is growing. Thirty-seven million Americans overall live in poverty and that number is growing also. Approximately 35 million Americans suffer food insecurity (not enough food for healthful living; hunger), and more than 13 million of them are children. The United States, to its shame, has the highest child poverty rate of any industrialized nation in the Western world, (USA news in brief, 2006; *The state of America's children*, 2005; *Over 13 million children face food insecurity*, 2005; Despeignes, 2004). What does it say about a nation's commitment to social and economic justice when so many people, especially children, suffer poverty, malnutrition, and lack of health care?

The Impact of Poverty

What is the matter with being poor? After all, some believe that poverty is beneficial, motivating family members to work hard, pull together, and practice frugality. Indeed, self-help efforts have assisted many poor people to survive. However, poverty is almost always harmful, because it substantially limits people's choices. Where it is severe, the means for securing necessities such as food and shelter are lacking, so that poverty can literally steal people's lives.

As noted by May-Chahal, Katz, and Cooper (2003):

> Parents living in deprived circumstances find it difficult to meet the needs of their children, and poverty and social exclusion prevent their being able to discharge their parenting role effectively . . . (p. 49)

Childhood poverty is of particular importance in terms of social policy, not only because children suffer disproportionately to other groups, but also because their experiences in childhood will have implications for their adult lives: childhood lays the foundations for adult abilities, interests, and motivations and, hence, is the keystone for assuring equal opportunities for adults.

EXHIBIT 3-1

Cartoon: "Very Low Food Security"

CARLSON©2006 Milwaukee Sentinel. Reprinted with permission of UNIVERSAL PRESS SYNDICATE. All rights reserved.

A nation's social policies, if that nation so wills, can prevent child poverty and lay the foundations for a fulfilling, competent adulthood. This has been proven by the experiences of other countries, particularly the Scandinavian and some of the other European nations. But policies that create social and economic justice and eliminate poverty require an aware populace with the value base, political savvy, and determination to bring them about.

POPULATIONS AT RISK

Everyone in the world is, to some degree, "at risk" of poverty and other hazards. But not everyone is at risk to the same degree. Those people who fall into the categories that research has found most likely to experience poverty, for reasons beyond their own control but not due to chance or laziness, are known as **populations at risk.**

Members of populations at risk make up the clientele with whom social workers do most of their work. Tomas, Tomacita, Carla, and Maria of this chapter's case study are members of various populations at risk; Sandra McLean of Chapter 2 is at risk because she is female, and further at risk because she has a disability. Susan and Martha Dunn of Chapter 1 are at risk because they are female, and Martha and Todd Dunn are at risk because they are children. Members of two or more categories of risk, such as children who are female or members of ethnic minorities, suffer increased risk.

Children

Sadly, children comprise America's largest population at risk. During the 1980s, growth in child poverty rates led to the coining of the term **juvenilization of poverty.** Today, more children are poor than 38 years ago, and children are more likely to be poor in America than in 18 other wealthy industrialized nations. Child poverty has been rising for the past few years even among working families (more than 7 out of 10 poor children live in families with an employed relative). Three-fifths of all the children who have fallen into poverty since 2000 have fallen into "extreme poverty"—their families live at less than half the poverty level, scraping by on less than $20 per day (*The state of American's children*, 2005). These figures, serious as they are, belittle the problem, because America's formula for determining the poverty line (to be discussed later in the chapter) severely underestimates the number of people who actually experience poverty.

While the poverty rate among all children is high, the proportion of poor children who are members of ethnic minorities is even higher They suffer myriad undeserved privations. An interview with a Hispanic teen in Harlem illustrates how children raised in deprived urban environments feel about how they are valued in this society (Kozol, 1996, p. 38):

> "Think of it this way," says a 16-year-old named Maria————. "If people in New York woke up one day and learned that we were gone, that we had simply died or left for somewhere else, how would they feel?"

"How do you think they'd feel?" I ask.

"I think they'd feel relieved. I think it would lift a burden from their minds. I think the owners of the downtown stores would be ecstatic. They'd know they'd never need to see us coming in their doors, and taxi drivers would be happy because they would never need to come here anymore. People in Manhattan could go on and lead their lives and not feel worried about being robbed and not feel guilty and not need to pay for welfare babies."

"It's not like, 'Well, these babies just aren't dying fast enough,'" Maria says. "'Let's figure out a way to kill some more.' It's not like that at all. It's like—I don't know how to say this—." She holds a Styrofoam cup in her hands and turns it slowly for a moment. "If you weave enough bad things into the fibers of a person's life—sickness and filth, old mattresses and other junk thrown in the streets and other ugly ruined things, and ruined people, a prison here, sewage there, drug dealers here, the homeless people over there, then give us the very worst schools anyone could think of, hospitals that keep you waiting for 10 hours, police that don't show up when someone's dying, take the train that's underneath the street in good neighborhoods and put it above where it shuts out the sun, you can guess that life will not be very nice and children will not have much sense of being glad of who they are. Sometimes it feels like we've been buried six feet under their perceptions. This is what I feel they've accomplished."

Clearly, in America we do not enjoy the situation often piously described as "women and children first." Children especially often come last, and if the interview just quoted is evidence, they apparently know it. Children often feel unappreciated and unloved as well as poor and deprived. However, the situation is not necessary or inevitable, but the result of choices our elected representatives have made in major social policy decisions (see Exhibit 3-2).

EXHIBIT 3-2

Poverty Kills

Poverty kills. It also maims and stunts the growth and eclipses the dreams of hundreds of millions of children around the world. Yet the fact that more than 20,000 people worldwide will die in extreme poverty will not make tomorrow's headlines. Similarly disregarded is the irony that America's poorest residents continue to be worse off than those of almost any other country in the developed world.

Poverty in America is a political problem, caused less by a lack of resources than by a failure to come to terms with reality. It is universally understood that food, shelter, health care, and other basics are crucial to the well-being of children and families. What is largely ignored by our leaders, the news media, and the public, however, is the fact that millions of families do not have adequate income to provide these necessities.

SOURCE: Quoted from *The state of America's children*® *2005*. Retrieved June 17, 2006, from Children's Defense Fund website, http:www.childrensdefense.org/publications/greenbook/default.aspx

Women

Women compose another population at risk. Although progress has been made over the past two decades, that progress, unfortunately, may be less than most people believe. Part of the problem is lack of access to high-paying professions. Women's limited ability to earn is shown by the disparity in average earnings between female and male full-time workers in the United States. In 2007, the average woman worker earned less than 77 cents for every dollar earned by a man with similar work efforts, slightly lower than 10 years earlier. The disparity was even greater for women of color. Moreover, a year after graduation, college women, who outperformed men in every field of education including math and science, earned only 80 percent of what their male peers earned. Ten years after graduation, college women made only 69 percent of what their male counterparts did (Oliver, 2007).

That gender discrimination is perceived to be a serious issue by many women today is illustrated by a number of recent class action sex discrimination lawsuits against several large employers such as Wal-Mart and Morgan Stanley (Navetta, 2005). Achieving equality through legal action is not easy, however. For example, in May 2007, the U.S. Supreme Court ruled against a female employee of Goodyear Tire and Rubber Company, Lilly Ledbetter. After being employed by Goodyear for many years, Ledbetter learned via anonymous letter that she was earning several thousand dollars per year less than her male counterparts. She filed a legal challenge within a month of receiving the letter, but the Supreme Court ruled against her on the grounds that she had not filed within 180 days of original employment (a 180-day limit is currently stipulated by Civil Rights law). Ruth Bader Ginsburg, the only woman on the court, wrote a powerful dissent to this ruling, calling on Congress to enact legislation to correct the "high court's parsimonious reading of pay inequity claims" (Terzieff, 2007).

While many women have branched out into nontraditional professions (women have increased their representation since 1989 in 106 of 497 occupations tracked by the U.S. Labor Department), most remain clustered in lower paying jobs such as sales workers, secretaries, cashiers, nurses, elementary school teachers, hairdressers, receptionists, and so on (Francis, 2001). Moreover, women do the bulk of the caregiving in this society. They provide most of the care for children, elders, and other dependent persons—both within their own homes and out in the paid workforce. However, our economic system undervalues caregiving work. It completely overlooks the fact that caregiving is work when provided in the home. Because wages are not involved, caregiving work at home does not qualify a woman for her own Social Security benefits or for unemployment insurance if she is "fired" by her husband. It no longer entitles her to public assistance under the Social Security Act when she has dependent children, even though women shoulder most of the burden of the child rearing in cases of divorce or birth out of wedlock. Outside the home, caregiving is poorly paid, exposing many female wage earners to poverty. It is not surprising that in 2004, nearly 42 percent of female-headed families lived in poverty, and the number continues to grow (*The state of America's children*, 2005). The substantial poverty of women has led to the coining of the term feminization of poverty.

Older Adults

Older adults compose another population at risk. There is some good news, however, for this group. Social Security amendments passed in the 1960s and 1970s [primarily Medicare and Supplemental Security Income (SSI), to be discussed later in the chapter] helped reduce poverty for people over age 65 from more than a third to about 10.2 percent in 2005, slightly below the overall poverty rate for the nation (*General information on Social Security*, 2005).

If older adults now enjoy a poverty rate lower than that for the population as a whole, how can they be considered at risk? The fact is that the overall figures hide wide discrepancies among older people. Older women and ethnic minorities have a much higher poverty rate. And without Social Security, nearly half of all older adults would live in poverty (*General information on Social Security*, 2005). A danger faced as this chapter is being written is the fact that the G. W. Bush administration continues to push to "privatize" Social Security, which would leave many of our future elderly in serious jeopardy. It seems, though, that he is unlikely to succeed. This issue will be discussed in more detail in a later chapter.

Elderly people in financial need frequently face discrimination in the workplace, and elderly women and members of ethnic minority groups are even more likely to face it. For those fortunate enough to receive a pension upon retirement, the pensions are almost always less than wages earned previously. Many people do not receive pensions at all. Companies are not legally required to offer pension plans, and those that do may go bankrupt and be unable to honor their commitments. Some older adults lose their pensions because they are intentionally laid off just before reaching retirement age. Today, many pension plans have been replaced by tax-sheltered annuity options, which involve substantial employee contributions and financial risk.

The percentage of older adults who are considered to live in poverty would rise significantly if the standard for measuring poverty were updated, critics believe. The poverty line used as today's standard was established in the early 1960s. It resulted from surveys taken from 1955 through 1961 that indicated that the ratio of food consumption to all other household expenditures was 1:3. A basic food budget was then generated by the Department of Agriculture and was multiplied by 3 to determine the **poverty line.**

The food budget developed for the elderly was lower than that for younger people, so the official poverty line for the elderly was lower as well. In 2006 it was $9,669 for a single older adult as compared with $10,488 for a younger person (*Poverty threshold 2006*). The percentage of older adults who are recognized to be poor today would go up considerably if the poverty line used were the same as that for younger people. Moreover, the formula for determining the poverty line has not changed since the 1960s except to account for inflation. Later surveys have indicated that the current ratio of food costs to other necessary household expenditures is more nearly 1:5 (Kart, 1994, p. 275).

Racial and Ethnic Minority Groups

Racial and **ethnic minority groups,** those with distinct biological or cultural characteristics different from the majority, are other major populations at risk. Groups that are considered minorities differ from country to country and from region to region. For example, although Hispanics are a minority group in the United States, that is not the case in Mexico or Latin America. The term *race* usually refers to physical or biological characteristics. In the United States, four racial **minority groups** are usually distinguished: Native Americans, African Americans, Hispanics, and Asian Americans. This can be confusing, because not all members of these groups are people of color. Persons who consider themselves Hispanic, for example, include both whites and nonwhites. Thus "Hispanics" can more accurately be considered an ethnic group rather than a race.

Ethnic groups share certain cultural characteristics that distinguish them from others, such as customs, values, language, and a common history. An ethnic group may contain members of different races, as in the example of Hispanics, or it may differ culturally from the race it most resembles physically.

Racial and ethnic minority groups, earlier in this country's history, were expected to become part of a national "melting pot." Minority groups were thus pressured toward giving up cherished aspects of their cultural identities. Today, however, a new paradigm, or model for understanding, is emerging: **cultural pluralism** and ethnic diversity, in which difference is expected, acknowledged, tolerated, even celebrated. This paradigm is increasingly embraced by social workers, and **cultural competency,** or the skill of communicating competently with people of contrasting cultures, is becoming an increasingly important expertise in social work practice (Lum, 2007). One simple reason: almost one in three Americans today, more than 100 million persons, are members of racial and ethnic minority groups (Bernstein, 2007).

Many older adults, especially racial minorities, suffer from poverty and neglect.

What minority groups have in common in the United States is that they have less power than the majority group. Lack of power renders minority group members vulnerable to discrimination and devaluation. (In this sense, females are considered a minority group, even though they constitute a numerical majority.) Discrimination in the United States influences the amount minorities are likely to earn so that they suffer a greater risk of poverty. For example, in 2005, while the poverty rate for whites was 8.3 percent, the rate for Asian Americans was 11.1 percent. The rate for Hispanics was 21.8 percent, and for African Americans 24.9 percent (*Poverty among individuals*, 2005). The poverty rate for Native Americans was highest of all, 26 percent in 2004 (*Senators urge native leaders to cry out louder*, 2004, p. 6).

Sometimes a person's racial or ethnic heritage affects where he or she can live more directly than income alone. Those who succeed financially despite discrimination may find themselves unwelcome and may be actively harassed in areas predominantly inhabited by persons of European background. (Fortunately, due to civil rights activism and legislation in the 1960s, such harassment is no longer legal. See Exhibit 3-3.)

In some cases, the cultural heritage of a minority group has been actively suppressed, not only in historical times but also in the present. In the worst-case scenario, sometimes members of majority ethnic groups try to exterminate others entirely. The example of the Holocaust against Jewish and Gypsy people, among others, under Germany's Nazi regime during World War II is a case in point. In the United States, hundreds of thousands of Native Americans were exterminated during the migration of white people across the continent. Millions of people in Tibet were massacred by the Chinese in the 1960s and 1970s. The recent ethnic cleansings in Bosnia, Rwanda, Kosovo, Darfur, and other areas of the world, including Iraq, provide chilling evidence that people still have not learned that the example we set today plants seeds for the future.

Since the terrorist attacks in New York City and Washington, DC, in the fall of 2001, the United States has experienced a powerful new challenge relating to minority ethnic groups. Because the men who hijacked the planes crashing into the World Trade Center and the Pentagon were of Middle Eastern origin, people of that ethnic

EXHIBIT 3-3

Segregation for African Americans

The segregation of African Americans survives at extraordinary levels throughout the nation, although it is generally a little worse in the North and in larger, more modern cities. It is much higher now than in 1860 or 1910. In 1930, in northern cities, except for Chicago and Cleveland, the average African American lived in a neighborhood dominated by whites; by 1970, this was totally reversed, and blacks in all northern cities lived far more often with other African

Americans than whites. The average African American in major northern cities lived in a neighborhood that rocketed from 31.7% black in 1930 to 73.5% in 1970.

Although it is often equated with poverty, racial segregation afflicts affluent as well as poor African Americans. Indexes of segregation remain about as high for them as for poor blacks.

SOURCE: Quoted from Michael B. Katz. (2001). *The price of citizenship*. New York, Metropolitan Books, p. 48.

group immediately became suspect. Thousands, including students, were arrested without delay. Congress soon passed the USA Patriot Act, legislation that diminishes many cherished American civil liberties. For example, student records can now be subpoenaed if a judge agrees they might obtain information pertinent to terrorist investigations, and any person's residence can now be searched without that person's knowledge or consent.

The fear that understandably arose from the 2001 attacks was used by President G. W. Bush to declare war on Afghanistan and then Iraq, despite strongly expressed disagreement by the United Nations and most other nations of the world. Bush then declared, as America's commander-in-chief, that people captured in these wars were enemy combatants without any legal rights, as opposed to prisoners of war protected under the Geneva Convention.

Torture was used against the prisoners at Guantanamo Bay, and other terrorist suspects were kidnapped all over the world and taken to nations where torture was widespread, a practice called *extraordinary rendition* (Anti-torture efforts on Capitol Hill, 2006). The purpose was to extract information from prisoners in ways that would not normally be legal in this country under our Constitution. The U.S. Supreme Court has overturned certain aspects of the Bush administration's policies (Civil liberties and human rights, 2004), and the United Nations Committee Against Torture

EXHIBIT 3-4

" I THINK ASHCROFT'S GETTING CARRIED AWAY WITH THIS ETHNIC PROFILING OF MIDDLE EASTERNERS..."

Bill Shorr/United Feature Syndicate, *The Christian Science Monitor*, December 3, 2001, p. 10. ©United Feature Syndicate, Inc.

has called upon the United States to close the detention camp at Guantanamo Bay (Richey & Feldman, 2006).

Early in 2006, information was "leaked" to the press that the federal government has been routinely tapping, without judicial warrants, the telephone conversations of all persons suspected of communicating with suspected "terrorists" (e.g., telephone conversations with persons overseas); it has been collecting telephone records of every citizen in the United States.

Many Americans agree with the Bush policy, placing national security concerns above human rights, but legal and humanitarian protections lost to one are lost to all. If the President can remove legal protections and thus dehumanize anyone by declaring that person an "enemy combatant," who among us, besides the President, is free?

As noted by Grier (2001):

> Once bullets begin to fly, government officials must judge how much danger the nation is in, where those dangers lie, and whether the defense against them requires some abridgement of much-cherished individual rights—all under the pressure of onrushing time. History shows that they don't always get it right. The World War II internment of those of Japanese ancestry is today widely seen as a blot on the nation's honor. (p. 8)

People with Disabilities

People with disabilities are another population at risk, because people who do not have disabilities may hold negative attitudes toward those who do. An extreme example of the inhumane treatment that may result took place in Nazi Germany, where many were sent to concentration camps and exterminated. In the United States, historically, many people with disabilities were sent to public institutions and sterilized so they could not reproduce. Today, persons with disabilities may find themselves subject to social ostracism, ridicule, job discrimination, and the like. The civil rights movement in the United States in the 1950s and 1960s helped develop an awareness of social justice issues for the disabled, and they and their families began to advocate for legal rights and protections. Legislation important to persons with disabilities in the United States will be discussed in Chapter 11.

Societal definitions of disability differ with time and are hotly debated; the consequences are serious because certain protected populations can benefit from legislation from which others are excluded. For example, tens of thousands of poor children lost their federal disability benefits as part of 1996 welfare "reform" legislation simply because of changes in the legal definition of disability.

Persons with disabilities experience many barriers, both social and economic, to full participation in today's world. Many suffer unemployment or underemployment. For this reason, many qualify for Supplemental Security Income (SSI), as did little Maria in this chapter's case example, but SSI rarely lifts a person with a disability above the poverty line. The Americans with Disabilities Act of 1990 was designed to help people with disabilities improve their chances of escaping poverty. It has had mixed results, and will be discussed in more detail in Chapter 11.

Gay and Lesbian Persons

Discrimination is a fact of life for most gay and lesbian persons, and, unlike other groups who suffer this problem, federal civil rights protections have not yet been extended to include them. The reason seems to be that many people, because of their personal or religious values, do not accept those whose sexual orientation is toward persons of the same gender. While people have the right to choose their own values, discrimination against gays and lesbians is nevertheless discrimination against our fellow human beings.

Without civil rights protections, people who are gay and lesbian can be fired from their jobs, denied home mortgages, refused apartment rentals, and so on, without legal recourse. To protest these and other discriminatory practices, hundreds of thousands of gays, lesbians, and other civil rights activists marched on Washington in 1993 seeking to obtain civil rights protection under the law. The efforts failed to obtain their immediate objective, but gay rights did gain recognition as a national issue.

In 1994, a Republican Congress was elected, slowing progress toward equality considerably. Concerned that the state of Hawaii was about to legalize gay marriages, Congress responded by passing the Defense of Marriage Act of 1996. This act permitted states not to accept as legal gay marriages performed in any other state.

In 2000, gays and lesbians won a joyful victory in Vermont, when the state legislature approved civil unions for same-sex couples, legally equivalent to marriage (Marks, 2000). Another step forward was taken when the Massachusetts Supreme Court ruled in 2003 that barring persons to marry solely because those persons wanted to marry persons of the same sex violated the Massachusetts constitution (Paulson & Stern, 2003).

However, gay people in America have been experiencing a backlash over the past several years. By 2003, 37 states had passed acts barring recognition of gay marriage; others continue to put such issues on the ballot. Missouri, for example, passed a constitutional amendment in 2004 banning gay marriage (Kramer, 2004); New York and Georgia ruled in 2006 that gay marriage was not permitted (Scherer, 2006); Wisconsin passed a constitutional amendment banning gay marriage in 2006.

Gays and lesbians have responded with courage to discrimination against them. When the state of Colorado passed a ban against antidiscrimination protection laws for gays and lesbians, activists scored a victory when they appealed the ban to the Supreme Court. In the 1996 case of *Romer v. Evans*, the Supreme Court ruled that Colorado's prohibition was unconstitutional (Segal & Brzuzy, 1998). Today, however, when states put gay marriage bans on the ballot, gays and lesbians usually lose. President George W. Bush proposed constitutional amendments to ban gay marriage throughout the nation virtually every year of his administration (Feldmann, 2006). Still, glimmers of hope remain. Oregon passed a bill recognizing same-sex couples as "domestic partnerships" in 2007, granting them the same rights as married couples and banning discrimination in employment, housing, and public accommodations (Huang, 2007).

POTENT FORMS OF DISCRIMINATION IN THE UNITED STATES

Although Americans proclaim an overall belief in equal justice for all, and although various social movements have produced important legislation to protect the rights of minority groups, a marked discrepancy still exists between principle and practice today. Certain potent societal "isms" are clearly still in evidence.

Isms are prejudices common to large segments of society that relegate people who are perceived as different to a lower social status. Isms in the United States stem from cultural teachings such as white is better, male is better, young is better, and heterosexual is better. Isms have many consequences, including the fact that minority populations are "at risk." Risk can vary from milder forms of social discrimination such as lack of access to certain jobs and lower pay to attempted extermination of the devalued population. Sadly, people who suffer discrimination often take their poor treatment to heart so that they suffer loss of self-esteem as well.

Racism

Racism is the belief that one race is superior to others, a belief that tends to justify exploiting members of other races. In the United States, the majority race includes a variety of white-skinned ethnic groups of European origin, who tend to consider themselves superior to people with darker skin. Racism leads to discrimination against people of color perpetrated by both individuals and social institutions such as governmental bodies and private organizations. Institutional racism, or patterns of racial discrimination entrenched in law and custom, lives on in many subtle forms today. It was far more blatant, of course, before the civil rights movement of the 1960s and early 1970s. The civil rights movement was sparked in 1955 by Mrs. Rosa Parks's courageous refusal to obey a white man's demand that she give up her seat on a Montgomery, Alabama, bus, as required by racist laws.

Today, overtly racist laws have been ruled unconstitutional, but subtler institutional racism and personal affronts continue. Ongoing racism is clearly illustrated in the United States today by the residential segregation visible throughout most of the nation.

Sexism

Sexism is the belief that one sex is superior to the other, usually that males are superior to females. This belief tends to justify exploiting females economically and sexually. Sexism is undergirded, unfortunately, by various organized religions that cite ancient texts alleging the superiority of the male. However, modern scholars have found substantial evidence indicating that these texts were selectively edited over time to conceal the value of female roles and to stifle women's leadership potential. Whole books have been written about this fascinating subject, including *The Gnostic Gospels* by Elaine Pagels (1979), *Beyond Belief*, by the same author (2003), and *The Chalice and the Blade* by Riane Eisler (1987).

Although numerous laws have been adopted in recent times to help create equal opportunity for females, a constitutional amendment, stating simply, "Equal rights under law shall not be denied or abridged by the United States or by any State on account of sex," was never ratified. Many women helped fight to maintain gender inequality, fearing loss of certain legal protections such as exemption from military draft. However, it is unlikely that the draft, if reinstated in the future, would exclude women anyway. Women's contributions to the paid labor force are simply too important to ignore today.

Discrimination against females has important effects. Girls and young women tend to limit their aspirations to the types of positions they perceive they can get. Unskilled women, for example, tend to fill service positions, while educated women disproportionately select service professions like nursing, teaching, and social work. Women are characteristically paid less than men, even with the same education, the same job position, and the same number of years of paid work experience. This injustice forces many women to remain economically dependent on men (Navetta, 2005).

Ageism

Ageism is the belief that youth is superior to age, that old people have outlived their usefulness and therefore are of little value. Ageism involves such stereotypes as that the majority of old people are senile, old-fashioned, and "different." These stereotypes tend to justify discrimination against the elderly.

Recently, a "new ageism" has taken shape, emanating from a perception that the elderly have made significant economic gains as a result of Social Security benefits. Robert Butler (1994), the social scientist who originally coined the term *ageism*, describes this phenomenon as "a dangerous viewpoint that envies the elderly for their economic progress and, at the same time, resents the poor elderly for being tax burdens and the nonpoor elderly for making Social Security so costly." He notes that many older adults are, in fact, still very poor.

Butler also pointed out a peculiar irony many years ago that is still true today. Most people dream of a long life, and in general this hope is being realized. However, instead of celebrating, younger people view the elderly as potential economic burdens. They fear that the Social Security system will be bankrupt by the time they become old. Butler points out that this fear is greatly exaggerated because, due to the falling birthrate, the total dependency-support ratio (ratio including dependents both below 18 and over 64 to working adults in a given family) has been steadily declining since 1900. It will continue to do so until 2050.

Myths that most older adults are senile and physically debilitated are simply that: myths. Most elderly describe their health as reasonably good. Memory loss is associated more with stress than with age, and it is usually reversible. The exception is memory loss caused by medical factors, such as Alzheimer's disease (see Chapter 9). Younger people, however, can be victims of this disease as well. Various studies have shown that what appear to be characteristics of aging, such as decreased mobility and memory loss, can also afflict younger people. These difficulties can often be reversed even among the very old with proper health and mental health care.

Heterosexism and Homophobia

Heterosexism is the belief that heterosexuals are superior to homosexuals. **Homophobia** is the fear, dread, or hatred of people who are homosexual. Both lead to social and economic discrimination against people who are gay or lesbian. There was a time when homosexuality was viewed as a mental disorder. However, research has led to the knowledge that sexual orientation has nothing to do with one's mental health (except, of course, that discrimination can result in fear and depression). For this reason, homosexuality is no longer listed as a pathology in the Diagnostic and Statistical Manual of Mental Disorders used by mental health professionals. Gays and lesbians are similar to other people in every way except their sexual orientation. No one understands the causes of homosexuality, but it generally is not considered a personal choice; hence, most gays and lesbians prefer to speak of **sexual orientation** rather than "sexual preference."

PART II
SOCIAL WELFARE POLICY: A SOCIETAL RESPONSE TO SOCIAL JUSTICE ISSUES

SOCIAL WELFARE POLICY AND SOCIAL JUSTICE

Discriminatory treatment, such as that described in the preceding "Isms" section, tends to result in ongoing poverty by many members of populations at risk. Social justice remains a major, even a growing, issue today. However, many organized attempts have been made to alleviate the suffering of poor people over the past centuries. Assistance is sometimes informal: for example, private acts of charity have been carried out by individuals, families, and religious groups from time immemorial. But in recent centuries, social justice issues have also led to government legislation creating formal public social welfare policies and programs designed to assist at least some of the poor.

Social welfare policy establishes the goals and procedures that enable social welfare programs to commence and to operate. Such policy is often established by government legislation. For a glimpse of public social welfare programs sanctioned by government social welfare policy in the United States today, let us consider this chapter's case example.

While many families living near the Urban Neighborhood Center were very poor, a few public programs were available that assisted them to some degree. Tomas and Tomacita's mother was enrolled in the **Temporary Assistance for Needy Families (TANF)** program. Maria Romero was assisted by Supplemental Security Income (SSI) and Medicaid because she was a severely disabled child. TANF is a cash benefit program (requiring work or work training) run by the county but established under state law according to federal guidelines. SSI is a cash benefit program for certain categories of poor people administered by the federal government, and Medicaid is a federal program administered by the state that provides medical care for certain categories of poor people. These programs are part of our nation's system or institution of social welfare.

What is **social welfare**? The *Social Work Dictionary* (Barker, 2003, p. 408) defines it as "a nation's system of programs, benefits, and services that help people meet those social, economic, educational and health needs that are fundamental to the maintenance of society." Is social welfare the same as social work? Not exactly, although the two are certainly related.

Social work, as described in Chapter 1, is a profession with the purpose of assisting people to improve their lives. Social welfare, in contrast to social work, is a system or institution (set of established practices) within a given nation. The purpose of the social welfare institution is not only to help individual people meet their basic needs but also to help the nation as a whole maintain stability. Social work is really only one profession among many that can be considered part of our nation's institution of social welfare. Other professions that also contribute to helping people meet social, economic, educational, and health needs are medicine, education, library science, and law, to name only a few. Because many of the decisions and referrals a social worker makes rely on familiarity with the various programs available within the social welfare system, we will focus on them before turning to the fields of practice explored in Part II of this book.

SOCIAL WELFARE POLICY IN THE OLD WORLD

Social Welfare Concepts: Residual versus Institutional

Wilensky and Lebeaux (1965) pointed out more than 50 years ago that our country holds two dominant conceptions of social welfare: residual and institutional. These distinctions are valid today.

Those who endorse the residual approach to social welfare believe that people should normally be able to meet all their needs through their own family or through the job market. Only after the family and the job market have "failed" should the formal social welfare system get involved. Under these circumstances the assistance is considered "residual"; it is activated only as a temporary, emergency measure. Services are accompanied by the stigma of "charity," as they imply personal failure. The intent is that they be short term, lasting only for the duration of the emergency.

Under the institutional conception, social welfare services are viewed as "normal, first line functions of modern industrial society" (Wilensky and Lebeaux, 1965, p. 138). According to the institutional view, social welfare services should be offered routinely as part of normal, nonemergency, problem-solving processes; they should be available without stigma to help prevent further problems. This approach assumes that in a complex society, everyone needs assistance at times. For example, even the best workers may lose their jobs when a company downsizes.

The social welfare system in the United States today reflects both the residual and the institutional approaches. Historically, the residual approach is older. Developments during and after the Great Depression of the 1930s pulled the social welfare system strongly toward the institutional concept, however. Then, during the 1970s, conservative politicians and presidential administrations began to pull it back toward the residual approach. This pull is extremely powerful today. The two concepts of social welfare are outlined in Exhibit 3-5.

Now, let us examine the historical roots of the social welfare system in the United States, because what happened in the past has shaped what the system looks like today.

Old World Historical Roots

Social welfare policy is controversial today, and perhaps it always has been. Questions inevitably arise about who to help and how much. We may think we want to help our neighbor, but how much? And are we interested in helping a stranger at all?

The earliest form of assistance for the needy was probably mother caring for child. Mutual aid among adults familiar with each other would be another example of help for the needy in early times, when reciprocal helping roles were provided by extended family members or members of one's tribe.

Only when more formal institutions had developed could a concept like "aid to the stranger" arise. One of the earliest known forms of aid to the stranger was provided by religious groups. The idea that services to the poor should be provided by "faith-based organizations," as espoused by President George W. Bush today, clearly goes back a long way! In Judeo-Christian tradition, almsgiving was commonly practiced. The commandment "Love thy neighbor," accentuated in the New Testament but based on early Scripture, motivated people to give of what they had. Many believed that aiding the needy would provide a means of salvation in the next world. Some religious groups established formal tithes, with a portion of the money raised being used for assistance to the poor. Such assistance was residual in nature, because it was offered as temporary charity in times of emergency.

EXHIBIT 3-5

Residual and Institutional Concepts of Social Welfare

RESIDUAL APPROACH	INSTITUTIONAL APPROACH
■ Needs are to be met through family and job market.	■ Social welfare system is viewed as part of first line of defense.
■ Aid from welfare system is considered "abnormal."	■ Aid from government welfare system is considered "normal."
■ Aid is offered after family and job market have already failed.	■ Aid is offered before family breakdown, for preventive purposes.
■ Aid is temporary, emergency, and as little as possible.	■ Aid is preventive, ongoing, and adequate to meet needs.
■ Stigma is attached.	■ No stigma is attached.

England provided the model for social welfare provisions in its colonies in America, and so we will focus on the social welfare history of that country. Responsibility for the poor in England remained primarily a function of the church until the arrival of the Black Death (bubonic plague) from continental Europe in 1348. So many people died that a labor shortage resulted. In 1349, a law was passed called the Statute of Laborers, which forbade able-bodied people to leave their parishes and required them to accept any work available. Alms were forbidden to the able-bodied (Karger & Stoesz, 2006). Such a law clearly reflected the interests of the ruling class. Since the time of the plague, many secular laws relating to the poor have been designed to control the labor supply at least as much as to relieve the suffering of the destitute.

Throughout the 1500s the Commercial Revolution grew, and feudalism declined. Tenants were evicted from the land, sometimes to make room for sheep, whose wool was increasingly valuable in the manufacture of cloth. Large numbers of destitute people went looking for work in the cities, where they found themselves crowding into urban slums. The resulting poverty and social need led to government assumption of more responsibility for social welfare. In England, legislation culminated in the famous Elizabethan Poor Law of 1601 (Whitaker & Federico, 1997). The Elizabethan Poor Law was brought by the first colonists to America. Its concepts still influence current thinking about provisions for the poor in this country and, hence, affect current law.

The Elizabethan Poor Law and the Act of Settlement

The Elizabethan Poor Law of 1601 was the first public legislation establishing a governmental system to meet the needs of the poor. The law established which unit was responsible to assist whom. By establishing which categories of people were eligible for what kind of assistance, the law also was geared toward social control (Segal & Brzuzy, 1998).

The local governmental unit, usually the parish (a geographic area similar to a county), was to maintain its own poor, and taxes could be levied for this purpose. An overseer of the poor—a public official, not a member of the clergy—was to be appointed. Families were to take care of their own members (reflecting the residual concept of social welfare). Whenever possible, grandparents were responsible for the care of children and grandchildren, and similarly, children and grandchildren were responsible for parents and grandparents.

Poor people were divided into categories, and relief was provided according to the category. Two of the categories, the impotent poor and dependent children, were considered "deserving" and so were offered aid. Children were to be indentured, or placed in the service of whoever would charge the parish the least amount of money for their care (the "lowest bidder"). The impotent poor (the old, the blind, and people otherwise disabled) were to be either put into an **almshouse (indoor relief)** or offered aid in their own homes **(outdoor relief),** depending on which plan would be least expensive to the parish.

The category of able-bodied poor was not considered deserving. These people were treated punitively. Alms were prohibited. People who came from outside the parish **(vagrants)** were to be sent away. Able-bodied poor who were residents were to be forced to go to a **workhouse,** where living conditions were hard and work was long and tedious. If they refused, they were to be whipped or jailed or put in stocks (Trattner, 1999; Federico, 1984).

The intent of the Elizabethan Poor Law of 1601 was that almshouses and workhouses should be separate institutions, with the almshouses meeting the special needs of the "deserving" sick and infirm. In practice, most communities that built such facilities combined them into one building for the sake of expense. Records indicate that people dreaded going into such places (see Exhibit 3-6).

Quadagno (1982, p. 95) writes that "overseers, conscious of the desire of ratepayers to keep rates down, did all they could to prevent paupers from becoming chargeable to the parish." The Settlement Act of 1662 required every person to be enrolled as a resident in some parish somewhere. Procedures establishing residency were complex. Persons who could not prove legal residence in the parish where they were living could be declared vagrants and sent away, in order that they not become financial burdens on the parish in the future.

Minor adjustments to the law were made over the years, but the Settlement Act of 1662 increased parish control over poor people.

New Concepts in Poor Law

Two acts were passed in England in 1795 that temporarily improved the condition of the poor. One act forbade parishes to drive nonresidents away unless they actually

---

EXHIBIT 3-6

A Workhouse Experience

Q: And, in your opinion, many of the old people in your union would rather die than go to the workhouse?

A: Very many of them; they would rather, sir . . .

Q: Did you find that work severe?

A: No, not severe; monotonous. You did not know what to do. You could not go out to write a letter, or to read, or to do anything: you had no time of your own; in fact, it was a place of punishment, and not relief. . . .

Q: Would you state any other objections you have to the treatment of the aged poor?

A: I think the taskmaster is very much more severe than he should be.

Q: In what way?

A: Well, when you go to dine, or to breakfast, or anything like that, he says, "come quicker," and pushes you partly into the seat; that is a very trifling thing. I had a sore throat, and he objected to my wearing a scarf around my throat and he said, "I will pull those rags off you when you come back

here again." That is, if I went back again. "You must not wear such things as this." I said, "I have a sore throat," and he says, "I don't care whether you and your father and your grandfather had sore throats." My father died of starvation through his throat growing together, and he suffered with sore throat. I suffered with sore throat, but not much; still, sufficient.

Q: Did you complain to the master of the workhouse of the language and treatment by the man you call the taskmaster?

A: No, my lord, not the slightest good in doing that.

Q: Why?

A: Whatever the taskmaster wished the master to say, the master would say. They were all under one control, even the doctor, and everybody was the same.

SOURCE: Quoted from Jill Quadagno. (1982). *Aging in early industrial society: Work, family, and social policy in nineteenth century England.* New York: Academic Press, pp. 107–110.

applied for relief. The other, the Speenhamland Act, introduced new concepts into poor law. This act was a humane response to the rising price of wheat. Rather than force poor able-bodied people into workhouses after they were destitute, the law established a wage supplement to help prevent destitution. The size of the supplement was determined according to both the number of children in a family and the price of bread.

Improvement of the condition of the poor was temporary under this act because the law did not include a requirement for a minimum wage. The gentry tended to lower the wages they paid, and the difference was picked up through the wage supplement that was financed by taxes paid by small farmers (Quadagno, 1982). Hence, before long, taxpayers strongly opposed the law.

In 1834 the New Poor Law reinstated most of the provisions of the Elizabethan Poor Law and introduced a new principle known as **less eligibility.** This was based on the idea that "pauperism was willful and the condition of the pauper who was relieved should be worse than the condition of the poorest, independent, self-supporting laborer" (Quadagno, 1982, pp. 97–98).

Today, as a similar example, our nation has a minimum wage law, but the minimum wage, even with the increase approved to begin in summer 2007 ($5.85 per hour), leaves a family of two (e.g., parent and child) with an income below the poverty level. A full-time worker with a family thus may qualify for public relief such as food stamps and/or the Earned Income Tax Credit (discussed later). Taxpayers' anger tends to focus on people who receive such assistance rather than on employers who profit from low wages.

POOR RELIEF IN THE UNITED STATES

Each colony in America enacted its own version of the Elizabethan Poor Law of 1601; Plymouth Colony was the first, in 1642. Ideas such as settlement and less eligibility, although codified under English law after the original colonization of America, continued to influence colonial attitudes.

After the American Revolution, the U.S. Constitution separated functions of state and federal governments, and assistance to the poor became a state prerogative. The federal government did not become involved until the end of the Civil War, in 1865, when the first national agency for social welfare was established: the Freedmen's Bureau. Through the Freedmen's Bureau, federal taxes supported free educational programs and financial assistance for former slaves for a few short years (Lieby, 1987). The bureau was disbanded in 1872 as a result of political infighting.

Values

Values strongly affected American poor law, and like the law itself, the major religious and cultural values of the United States originated in the Old World. Religious doctrines of various traditions taught that rich and poor alike should give what they could for others, motivated by love and compassion, not fear.

During the Protestant Reformation of the 16th century, many of these teachings were questioned. A Protestant ethic of salvation by hard work challenged the older notion of salvation by helping people in need. Puritan Calvinists, for example, "decreed one either saved or damned, a member of the elect or not. Charitable works could not alter this decision, for it was made eternally by God. One could, however, find out or at least seek indications of one's future celestial status" (Tropman, 1989). While no one could know for sure, many people came to believe that prosperity indicated one was among the elect and that poverty meant one was not among the elect. From this point of view, why help the poor?

Also in conflict with older religious and humanitarian ideals to help the unfortunate were new ideas from philosophy and economics. In *The Wealth of Nations* (1776), Adam Smith argued in favor of the principle that became known as *laissez-faire:* that government should not interfere in the "natural functioning" of the market by imposing interference such as taxes. The market should be allowed to perform solely according to the influences of supply and demand. Taxation to support poor people interfered with the rights of the wealthy and only created dependency among the poor, according to Smith's argument.

Thomas Malthus, an economic philosopher and clergyman, published *An Essay on the Principle of Population* in 1798. In it, he argued that relief for the poor contributed to overpopulation and that surplus population would result in disaster. Also contributing to reluctance to help the poor was Herbert Spencer's philosophy known as *social Darwinism.* Influenced by biological theories of evolution discussed in Charles Darwin's book *On the Origin of Species* (1859), Spencer preached that only the fittest people should survive. Poor people should be allowed to perish as they are demonstrably unable to compete (Karger & Stoesz, 2006). Such an argument overlooked the fact that no individual member of the human species could survive without the cooperation, as opposed to the competition, of others. For example, not a single person could survive infancy without the assistance and cooperation of others.

Do any of these arguments for or against aid to poor people sound familiar? Although some are centuries old, these ideas and values still affect societal responses to poor people today. Obviously, the value base underlying the social welfare system is complicated and conflicting. Conflicting values in social and political arenas affect what happens in social welfare legislation; in turn, social welfare legislation affects the resources available to social work practitioners and their clients.

The Charity Organization Society and the Settlement House Movement

The effects of values on approaches to social welfare in the United States are seen particularly clearly in two movements in private charity that strongly affected relief measures beginning in the 1880s. These movements, the Charity Organization Society and the Settlement House Movement, were introduced in Chapter 1 and are discussed more fully here because they, along with a more scattered child welfare movement, led to the birth of the social work profession. The two movements differed markedly in philosophy and methods.

The Charity Organization Society (COS) began in England in 1869; its first office in the United States opened in Buffalo, New York, in 1877 (Popple, 1995). Leaders of the COS believed that many poor people were unworthy, so applicants for aid should be carefully investigated. Records were to be kept about each case, and a central registry was developed to ensure that no person received aid from more than one source. The principal form of help to be offered should be "moral uplift," which was to be provided by "friendly visitors." Most of the visitors were women recruited from the upper class. Not only were these the persons who had the most time to volunteer, but, due to the patriarchal nature of the era, church-related, unpaid work was among the few outlets for these women's talents.

The methods developed by the COS were used as models for local public agencies; organization, investigation, and written records proved very useful in welfare work. Mary Richmond, a well-known leader of the COS movement in the United States, taught in the first social work training school, the New York School of Philanthropy (now the Columbia University School of Social Work), begun in 1898. The COS replaced most friendly visitors with paid staff by the early 1900s, partly because there were not enough volunteers and partly because volunteers were found to lack appropriate expertise (Popple, 1995).

The settlement movement, in contrast, involved concepts of self-help and mutual aid rather than moral uplift. Jane Addams, one of the movement's most famous leaders, established Hull House in Chicago in 1889. Settlement work arose in response to continuing pressures of the Industrial Revolution, which brought large numbers of immigrants to American cities, where they were forced to work long hours in factories under dangerous, unhealthful conditions.

Settlement houses brought idealistic young people, including many women of upper-class backgrounds, into the slums to live and work with less fortunate people.

EXHIBIT 3-7

Charity Organization Society and Settlement House Movement Compared

Charity Organization Society	Settlement House Movement
LEADER	
Mary Richmond	Jane Addams
TYPE OF WORKER	
"Friendly visitors"	Volunteers who lived among poor
TYPE OF AID OFFERED	
Central registry of poor	Mutual aid
Short-term charity	Self-help
Moral uplift	Social and political action
PRIMARY LEVEL OF INTERVENTION	
Casework with individuals and families	Group work; work with families, organizations, and communities

Settlement staff assisted immigrants in organizing into self-help groups and established mutual aid services ranging from day nurseries to garbage collection to organization of cultural events. In addition, settlement house staff and neighborhood participants became involved in political processes, advocating for better working conditions in the factories, better sanitation in the cities, and protective legislation for women and children (see Exhibit 3-7).

SOCIAL WELFARE IN THE UNITED STATES IN THE 20TH CENTURY

The history of social welfare in the United States in the 20th century revealed, according to James Lieby, an increasing role over time for both public and private nonsectarian agencies (agencies not affiliated with particular religious groups). Lieby (1987) believes:

> It is helpful to analyze this general trend in three periods: 1900–1930, when the action was at the level of local and state governments and local private agencies organized under the Community Chest; 1930–1968, when the federal government took important initiatives; and since 1968, when the progress of the "welfare state" has seemed to stop if not turn back. (p. 765)

Lieby made this observation many years ago; it is clear today that he was right—progress toward the welfare state has indeed turned back. That trend was highlighted by the passage of the Personal Responsibility and Work Opportunity Act (PRWOA) in 1996, which will be discussed later. In the early 21st century, the Republican administration of President George W. Bush engaged in an attack on the poor that was not limited to mothers and their children, but targeted the elderly and disabled as well, via a push to "privatize" Social Security. See the time line in Exhibit 3-8.

The Progressive Years, 1900–1930

The early 1900s were a time of reform in the United States. World War I slowed down reform efforts but did not entirely eliminate them. Women, for example, first gained the vote after the war, in 1920. A few women began to go to college, and some started to use ways to plan their pregnancies. Magazines designed to appeal to women appeared, such as *Good Housekeeping*, helping women begin to relate to other women. Activists such as those involved in the Settlement House Movement advocated, and in many cases secured, laws for the protection of women and dependent children, for better sanitation, and for better safety conditions in the factories. Forty states enacted mother's pensions, although only for those considered "fit": the widowed mothers (Bartkowski & Regis, 2003). By 1920, 43 states had passed workers' compensation laws. Federal guidelines were soon established; today all states have workers' compensation laws that meet federal guidelines. National leadership in protective legislation

EXHIBIT 3-8

Time Line: Major Historical Events in Social Welfare and Social Work

1348	Black death. Feudal system begins to break down
1349	Statute of Laborers (England)
1500s	Accelerated breakdown of feudal system (Commercial Revolution)
1601	Elizabethan Poor Law (England)
1642	Plymouth Colony enacts first colonial poor law, based on English Poor Law
1662	Settlement Act (England; idea migrates to colonies)
1795	Speenhamland Act (England)
1834	New Poor Law (England)
1865	Freedmen's Bureau (United States—ends in 1872)
1869	First Charity Organization Society (COS), London, England
1877	First COS in United States, Buffalo, New York
1884	First settlement house (Toynbee Hall, London)
1886	First settlement house in United States (Neighborhood Guild, New York City)
1889	Hull House, Chicago
1898	First formal social work education program (summer training by COS in New York City; evolves into New York School of Philanthropy, later Columbia School of Social Work)
1915	Flexner's report concluding social work is not a full profession
1917	First organization for social workers, National Workers Exchange
1919	American Association of Schools of Social Work formed (AASSW)
1921	American Association of Social Workers formed (from National Social Workers Exchange)
1928	Milford Conference; determines social work is a single profession
1929	Stock market crash leads to Great Depression International Council on Social Welfare (ICSW) founded in Paris
1933	President Franklin D. Roosevelt launches "New Deal" program
1935	Social Security Act signed into law
1936	National Association of Schools of Social Administration (NASSA) established
1952	Council on Social Work Education (CSWE) forms, merging AASSW and NASSA; accredits MSW programs
1955	National Association of Social Workers (NASW) forms, merging seven separate social work organizations; accepts MSW only
1956	International Federation of Social Workers (IFSW) established; membership consists of national social work organizations
1957	Greenwood article declares social work a full profession
1964	President Lyndon Johnson launches the War on Poverty
1967	The Work Incentive Program (WIN) established under the Social Security Act
1970	NASW admits baccalaureate social workers as members

(Continued)

EXHIBIT 3-8 *(Concluded)*	
1974	CSWE begins accreditation of baccalaureate social work education programs; Supplementary Security Income program established under the Social Security Act for aged, blind, and disabled; category of poor children omitted
1981	WIN program eliminated under the Reagan administration
1988	Family Support Act; parents receiving aid for dependent children under the Social Security Act must work when child is 3 years old
1996	Personal Responsibility and Work Opportunity Act signed into law by President Bill Clinton; eliminates right of poor children and parents to aid under Social Security Act; establishes Temporary Assistance to Needy Families (TANF) program
2000	Push by President George W. Bush to privatize formerly public assistance programs and provide federal funding to "faith-based" programs
2004	Medicare Part D signed into law by President George W. Bush, providing limited assistance to older adults in purchasing prescription drugs; law prohibits government from negotiating drug prices.

for children was provided by the Children's Bureau, established in 1909 as part of the U.S. Department of Labor.

Voluntary organizations also expanded during this period. Examples include the establishment or significant growth of the Boy Scouts and the Girl Scouts, the American Cancer Society, the National Association for the Advancement of Colored People, the National Urban League, and the Red Cross.

Federal Initiatives, 1930–1968

A great economic depression followed the stock market crash of 1929. Voluntary organizations and state and local governments did what they could to meet what seemed like unending financial need. But soon local treasuries were empty, including both private charities and relief-giving units of local government. People turned to the federal government for help. President Herbert Hoover was a proponent of laissez-faire economic theory and a political conservative. He believed that the federal government should not interfere with the economic market. Desperate Americans, however, began to perceive the widespread and rapidly increasing poverty as a **public issue** (an issue affecting so many people that it is considered beyond the "fault" of each affected individual) rather than a **private trouble.** Franklin D. Roosevelt was elected president in 1932 because he promised to involve the federal government in solving the crisis.

Roosevelt ushered in a series of emergency programs on the federal level to meet immediate needs for **income maintenance** and employment. His overall program was known as the New Deal. The New Deal offered temporary cash assistance and work-relief programs to needy people regardless of race. Roosevelt's major long-term proposal was the Social Security Act, passed by Congress in 1935. Since 1935, almost all additional federal social welfare policy has been adopted as part of this act (Segal & Brzuzy, 1998).

The Social Security Act is a complex piece of legislation that has been amended many times. The 1935 law established three types of federal provisions: (1) **social insurance,** (2) **public assistance,** and (3) health and welfare services.

Social insurance and public assistance are quite different. Insurance programs require the payment of taxes (in this case, the Social Security, or FICA, tax) earmarked for a special fund available only to the insured. Following rules relating to the amount of money contributed, benefits cover the "expected" problems of a modern industrial society, such as the death of a breadwinner.

Public assistance programs, on the other hand, are funded out of general tax revenues, usually income tax revenues, and people may receive benefits even if they have never paid taxes themselves. One qualifies according to whether one fits a specified category (e.g., elderly person) and in addition meets a **means test,** or has an income below a certain level specified by law. A stigma is often attached to public assistance benefits, because they are considered unearned.

The social insurance provisions of the original Social Security Act were Old Age and Survivors Insurance (OASI) and unemployment insurance. OASI was intended to provide income for retired workers, widows, and minor children of deceased workers. Later, in 1957, coverage was extended to include disabled persons. In 1965, Title XVIII, Medicare, was added to the act. (Medicare and Medicaid, Title XIX, will be examined in detail in Chapter 7.)

Three categories of people were originally eligible for aid under public assistance: the blind, the aged, and dependent children. Later, Aid to Dependent Children was expanded to include the mother and in some cases the father; the program became known as **Aid to Families with Dependent Children (AFDC).** A fourth category of people eligible for aid, the permanently and totally disabled, was added in 1950 (McSteen, 1989). In 1965, Title XIX, Medicaid, was added to the act.

Initially, most Black Americans were barred from Social Security benefits because of the power of southern Democrats, who insisted that domestic and agricultural workers be excluded from the law. They argued that such benefits would undermine the work ethic of their servants and laborers of whom, respectively, African Americans comprised 50 and 60 percent (Tyuse, 2003). It was not until 1950 that agricultural and domestic workers were finally included.

In 1974, to equalize benefits nationwide and to help remove stigma, public assistance income-maintenance programs for the blind, the aged, and the disabled were combined into one program known as Supplemental Security Income (SSI). SSI is funded and administered by the federal government, and people apply for benefits through federal Social Security offices, not local welfare offices.

AFDC was not included in the SSI program. Why? The answer seems to be that some categories of poor people are still considered undeserving of aid. Political passion can be inflamed by criticizing poor mothers without husbands or men who for whatever reason fail to provide. Their children suffer accordingly. AFDC remained a poor relation of SSI, with benefits that varied from state to state but, on the average, maintained recipients well below the poverty line, until 1996. In August of that year, the Personal Responsibility and Work Opportunity Act (PRWOA) ended the AFDC program and all entitlement of poor children and their mothers to government assistance. The PRWOA will be discussed more fully later in this chapter.

Reflecting the rescinding of all legal right to assistance in the United States for poor children and their mothers, Bartkowski and Regis (2003, p, 58) note: "The compassion of the maternalistic state manifested in the early decades of the 1900s had, by century's end, given way to the discipline and austerity of paternalistic governance."

General Assistance   One category of people has never been eligible for assistance under the Social Security Act, able-bodied adults between the ages of 18 and 65 (age 60 for widows) who have no minor children. Sometimes able-bodied adults in need can receive help from local programs known as general assistance, or poor relief. These programs varied widely across localities in the past, but in most places today they have simply been discontinued. Conservative ideologies focus on decreasing taxes rather than helping the poor. General assistance, where it exists, is strongly residual: aid is temporary and carries a stigma. Repayment is usually required.

Food Stamps and Other Federal Voucher Programs   The food stamp program was established by Congress in 1964. The program is administered by the U.S. Department of Agriculture, but state and local welfare departments process the applicants and provide the stamps. The program is means-tested, and allotments are based on family size and income. Food stamps are **vouchers,** or coupons, that may be used to buy most food items available at the supermarket.

Originally, many poor adults who qualified for no other aid could receive assistance in the form of food stamps. But in 1996, the Personal Responsibility and Work Opportunity Act (PRWOA) enacted large cuts in food stamp availability, cutting the program's funding by nearly $28 million over the 6-year period to follow. Most legal immigrants were cut off by the new law, and benefits were authorized for only 3 months in any 3-year period to unemployed adults without children. In 1998, food stamp benefits were restored to about 250,000 of the 935,000 immigrants who had previously been eligible, those who were disabled or elderly, or immigrants seeking political asylum (*Bills tackle welfare, patients' rights,* 1998).

From a high of 27.5 million people in 1994, only 17.3 million received food stamps in 2001. By 2006, however, 26.7 million people were receiving them, nearly the level of a dozen years before and indicating the high level of need. This despite complicated application processes and an average per person benefit of only $94.27 per month (*Food stamp program annual summary,* 2007).

In addition to food stamps, the federal government offers other voucher programs, such as fuel assistance, rent subsidies, and infant nutritional supplements. The Women, Infants, and Children program, known as WIC, is one of the best known of the latter. It provides supplemental foods to pregnant and breast-feeding women and their children up to age 5. The program is means-tested; applicants with pretax incomes up to 185 percent of the poverty line are eligible. Coupons or vouchers for specific food items are provided for purchases at grocery stores. The program is not an entitlement; funds may not be available to serve every woman who meets eligibility criteria. Yet WIC is very important as it serves approximately 45 percent of all U.S. infants today (Karger & Stoesz, 2006).

Post-Depression Trends   The Great Depression came to an end in the 1940s, when World War II provided full employment. The nation began to look at poor people as unworthy again. The 1950s set the stage for the social activism of the 1960s, however. Women who had worked full-time in paying jobs during World War II were sent back home to make room in the job market for returning veterans. Although returning to the home was more a philosophical idea than a reality for many women (especially for the poor and those from ethnic minorities, who often had no choice but to work outside the home), the 1950s gave rise to feminist activism based on women's loss of status and access to employment equality. The decade also harbored the beginning of the civil rights movement, sparked by Rosa Parks's refusal to give up her seat to a white man on a bus in Montgomery, Alabama, in 1955.

Then in the 1960s came the War on Poverty, under the leadership of presidents Kennedy and Johnson. This movement was stimulated by Michael Harrington's book, *The Other America*, originally published in 1962, which exploded the myth that people in poverty deserve their own misery. Much liberal legislation was initiated in the 1960s, furthered by the civil rights movement as well as by renewed understanding of societal causes of poverty. The AFDC-UP (Unemployed Parent) program, the food stamp program, WIC, the Head Start program, educational opportunity programs, college work-study programs, job training programs, Peace Corps, Vista (Volunteers in Service to America), Medicare, and Medicaid all were instigated during this period (Champagne & Harpham, 1984; Karger & Stoesz, 2006).

Increasing welfare rolls led to new public outcry, which led to the passage of the Work Incentive Program (WIN) in 1967. WIN was designed to encourage welfare recipients to take paid employment. Those who could find jobs were allowed to keep part of their welfare grant up to a certain earnings level. The program was unable to reduce welfare costs, however, as not enough jobs were available, and funds were lacking to provide adequate job training. In addition, day care facilities and inexpensive transportation were lacking (Champagne & Harpham, 1984).

Cutting Back the Welfare State, 1968 to the Present: Earned Income Tax Credit and Welfare Reform

Earned Income Tax Credit   Major efforts to reform the welfare system were made by Nixon's Republican administration from 1969 to his resignation in 1974 and by the Democratic Carter administration from 1977 to 1981, but their plans were not accepted by Congress. However, President Gerald Ford (Republican, 1974 to 1977) signed into law an important provision of the tax code, the Earned Income Tax Credit (EITC), which has become the largest means-tested income transfer in the United States today. Low-income families with children can receive an earnings supplement of up to 40%, to a maximum of about $4000 for families earning under $12,000. Depending on the number of children in a family, the EITC phases out so that families earning slightly over $30,000 no longer qualify. The EITC is popular today because benefits go only to the working poor, perceived as worthy (Bane, 2003; Segal & Brzuzy, 1998). Yet, in effect, through this legislation taxpayers pay wages for employers who can increase their profits in this way. There is a danger that, as in the

---

EXHIBIT 3-9

Issues with EITC

The EITC can be considered a guaranteed income support for poor working families with children. In contrast, there is no longer a federal guarantee for those outside the labor market, since Congress eliminated the entitlement of impoverished children to AFDC in 1996. One critical issue concerning the U.S. family policy is the absence of a major public safety net for the most impoverished group of children whose parents are not attached to the labor force. In addition, this group excluded from the public safety net is more likely the children of unmarried/never married parents. Through welfare reform and the EITC expansion, the nation has created two subclasses of children within the low-income class—one with and the other without a public safety net, based solely on the parents' employment and marital status. The assumption underlying this discriminatory treatment is that children of the nonworking and/or unmarried are unworthy and undeserving of public support. That is, the public value of children is determined by their parents' employment status and lifestyles. The nation appears to believe that the children of this "underclass" have no vested value for America's future.

SOURCE: Quoted from R. Kim. (2001). The effects of the earned income tax credit on children's income and poverty: Who fares better? *Journal of Poverty, 5*(1), 21.

---

time of the Speenhamland Act, the public will eventually instigate a tax revolt and repeal the wage supplement, rather than insist that employers pay a wage sufficient to support an average family (see Exhibit 3-9).

Welfare Reform   The president who was able to get major welfare reform proposals accepted was Ronald Reagan (Republican, 1981 to 1989). President Reagan was elected in 1980 with an apparent public mandate to lower taxes and inflation and to repair the budget deficit. Elected with massive financial support from right-wing conservatives, he and his administration were politically committed to investing in the military. Cutting taxes while building up the military obliged President Reagan to drastically reduce federal expenditures for income maintenance programs. The savings thus incurred were very small compared with the massive amounts of new money being poured into the military. The budget deficit became astronomical during Reagan's two terms of office. (President Reagan did not accomplish these deeds alone, but with the sanction of a Democratic Congress.)

The political agenda of the 1980s involved forcing able-bodied people, including the working poor, off welfare. The concept of aid returned to the old residual idea to assist helpless children on a temporary, emergency basis, and only as a last resort (an approach popularly called the *safety net*). The result was the 1981 Omnibus Budget Reconciliation Act. The financial incentive built into the WIN program (described earlier) was eliminated. Most of the working poor opted to keep their jobs despite loss of welfare benefits, but their financial circumstances were severely hurt, especially as many lost eligibility for Medicaid as well.

President Reagan signed another major welfare bill in 1988, the Family Support Act, just before he left office. This one was designed to force mothers who had remained on AFDC into the job market. All parents with children over 3 years old (1 year at states' option) were required to work or enter job training programs (if available) under this bill.

However, it wasn't until 1996 that poor children lost all entitlement to aid under the provisions of the Social Security Act. The Personal Responsibility and Work Opportunity Act was signed into law by President Clinton, a Democrat, in August of that year, ending six decades of guaranteed government aid for economically deprived children and their families. Clinton's acceptance of this law, proposed and passed by a Republican Congress, was seen by many liberals as a betrayal of the poor. The former AFDC program was eliminated by this bill. In its place, a new program called Temporary Assistance for Needy Families was established. TANF was to be funded by federal block grants to the states. Block grant funding is very different from the former open-ended funding for AFDC; each state receives a fixed sum of money for TANF and no more, regardless of need (Tyuse, 2003).

Under TANF, no family or child is entitled to assistance. Each state is free to determine who can receive assistance and under what circumstances. If a state runs out of money in a given year, it can simply stop providing aid, and poor families will have to wait until the following year for assistance. Besides the fact that assisting needy families is optional for states, regulations are complex and confusing under TANF. Some of the most significant requirements are that states are not allowed to assist anyone for longer than 5 years. They must require parents to work after 24 months of assistance. When parents work, the state may, but is not required to, provide child care assistance. Minor parents may not be assisted unless living at home and attending school. Assistance must be eliminated or reduced if the family is uncooperative with respect to child support–related requirements (e.g., if the mother does not name the father). Assistance may be denied to children born into families already receiving public assistance. Karger & Stoesz (2006) describe TANF legislation as a type of "welfare behaviorism," or social engineering. The law is designed to force poor parents to work outside the home regardless of suitability of jobs available or adequacy of wages. If they do not comply, punishment is severe (hunger, homelessness, loss of children to foster care, etc.).

While this law was touted as a way of ending welfare dependency, no national programs were created to help address the many external factors keeping poor people on the welfare rolls (e.g., lack of affordable day care, lack of a family-supporting minimum wage, lack of educational opportunities, lack of adequate job training programs, lack of jobs in the skill range of many recipients or in the geographic areas where they live, and lack of affordable transportation to places where jobs are available).

Fortunately, Medicaid was not included in the TANF block grant, and poor families who meet the previous income guidelines continue to be eligible for this program. However, many poor families who are eligible today do not receive either Medicaid or food stamps. The reasons are not fully understood, but it is believed that many people lack the information they need to apply (Thompson & Raikes, 2003).

SOCIAL WELFARE POLICY IN THE 21ST CENTURY

As noted by Goldberg (2002a), if any nation has the means to lift its poor out of poverty, it is the United States. Instead, however, welfare provisions for poor Americans have steadily eroded over recent decades. The trend toward diminishing social welfare policies and programs apparent in the beginning of the 21st century began, of course, in the 20th. Aid for poor families today is work based and thoroughly residual, forcing mothers to take jobs outside the home at paltry wages, with no attempt on the part of the nation to develop decent employment opportunities. "In the post-welfare era," Bane (2003, p. 57) writes, "the old poor law system has made a comeback . . . Welfare reform legislation of 1996 . . . has thrust us back into the Elizabethan past of poor laws and local oversight—if not local overseers."

A few of the major 21st century welfare programs are summarized in the following sections.

Temporary Assistance for Needy Families

TANF, as discussed earlier, is not an entitlement program. No needy child or poor parent in this nation has a legal right to aid today. Bane (2003) notes that only about one-fifth of poor families actually receive aid through TANF. Amendments hard-fought by organizations advocating for the poor, such as the National Association of Social Workers and the Children's Defense fund, have resulted in some ameliorating provisions, thankfully. For example, states may now opt to allow battered women to postpone employment for a time. States may also opt to provide child care assistance for longer than 5 years, as child care is not classified as a cash benefit. However, conservatives in Congress and the White House have recently increased work requirements under this program.

The Working Poor and the Earned Income Tax Credit

The federal government and several of the states provide earned income tax credit programs. The EITC lifts more children out of poverty today than any other federal program—far more than TANF. Yet millions of children remain poor today, and the number is growing due to unemployment and the low minimum wage. While the EITC does help many poor families, it also helps businesses by allowing them to keep wages low and thus reap higher profits at the expense of the average taxpayer.

Privatization

Privatization involves shifting the provision of social services and financial benefits from publicly operated government programs to private organizations, either non-profit or for-profit. For example, many states now contract with private agencies and organizations to operate TANF programs.

The political philosophy behind privatization is conservative, that government should have a minimal role in promoting the public welfare especially when it involves provision of economic assistance to the poor, as this might interfere with the economic market. (Workers might be unwilling to labor long hours for low wages if given an alternative.) This philosophy asserts that competition among private businesses as the most economical way to provide services and benefits.

Boy Scout troop helps conduct food drive for poor.

The Faith-Based Trend

Since the election of President George W. Bush, the term *faith-based initiative* has become part of the common parlance. This administration strongly promotes transferring the provision of formerly public social services and programs to private, religious organizations.

"Charitable choice" language first appeared in the 1996 Personal Responsibility and Work Opportunity Act (PRWOA). This legislation permits public funds to be used for religiously oriented social service programs. While denominationally sponsored social service programs have been eligible for public funds for many years, these earlier faith-based programs have separated their social services from religious proselytizing. By contrast, charitable choice language in the PRWOA broadened eligibility to allow public funding for church-sponsored programs that incorporate pervasive religious content.

Promoting the provision of social services by faith-based groups comes at a risk. Religious organizations, for example, are exempt from employment nondiscrimination laws. Stoesen (2004, p. 4) notes in the *NASW News* that the Salvation Army has "come under scrutiny due to some of its policies about hiring and providing services to lesbian, gay and bisexual people." In other organizations, beneficiaries in great need may find themselves required to espouse certain religious beliefs before they can receive food or shelter.

Faith-based programs supported by public tax dollars may be coming under closer scrutiny. By 2006, federal funding to religious groups received 11 percent of all moneys allocated to community groups, a percentage increasingly enhanced by executive order of President G. W. Bush. But in a court case that could serve as an important precedent, a federal district judge in Iowa ruled in 2006 that a faith-based prison ministry program in an Iowa prison, requiring participating inmates to attend weekly revivals, religion classes, and prayer services where Jesus Christ was presented as the sole means of salvation, overstepped the hazy line governing church-state relations (Paulson, 2006).

There is another important concern, however. The provision of social services by faith-based groups can allow the federal government to bow out of any responsibility to care for its poorest and most vulnerable citizens and divert its tax revenue instead to huge increases in military spending. That is exactly what has been happening under the administration of President George W. Bush. Most faith-based organizations are not capable of providing widespread services to large numbers of people. It was the inability of faith-based and other voluntary organizations to meet the public need during the great depression that led to the passage of the Social Security Act in 1935.

SOCIAL JUSTICE ISSUES IN THE 21ST CENTURY

Social justice issues in the 21st century are myriad. Their importance, of course, varies with the perspective of the observer. The following are issues of great concern to the profession of social work.

Poverty Programs That Maintain Poverty

Most of our nation's financial assistance programs leave beneficiaries far below the poverty level. The less eligibility factor is probably involved, although it no longer is stated explicitly in the law. For example, in our chapter's case example, Tomas and Tomacita's mother was attempting to support her family on income she earned through participating in her state's TANF job training program. Her stipend was just under $700 per month, or about $8,400 per year. Her budget looked roughly like this:

Income:	$700	Income from TANF
	275	Food stamps
Total	$975	
Expenses:	$440	Rent (heat included)
	300	Food for three
	50	Electricity
	35	Laundry
	50	Transportation to TANF program
	65	Clothes (including diapers)
	35	Telephone
Total	$975	

By comparison, the poverty line for a family of three (including two children) in 2006 was $16,242 (*Poverty threshold 2006*), more than $4,000 more per year than what this family was trying to survive on. No wonder the mother couldn't afford a babysitter. No wonder she and many other TANF participants in her neighborhood frequently relied on Urban Neighborhood Center's food pantry to help keep body and soul together. Note that there was no room in this budget for child care, miscellaneous items, emergencies, or recreation. It seems as if we like to punish the poor just for being poor, as if they have no right to enjoyment or security of any kind.

Poverty Line Determination Method

The method of determining the nation's poverty line has not been revised or updated for many years, except for inflation. When developed in the 1960s, it was based on the price of food. The Department of Agriculture's least expensive food plan was multiplied by 3, because an earlier study showed that the average family at that time spent about one-third of its income on food (Fisher, 1998). Today, however, housing, utilities, child care, and medical care make up a much higher proportion of the average family's budget. Many experts believe that a true analysis of modern costs of living would require a much higher poverty line.

In 2002, however, conservative elements in the government challenged official poverty statistics, believing not that they underestimated the number of poor people in poverty but that they overestimated them because poverty rates were determined by assessing earned income only. Noncash assistance such as food stamps, housing subsidies, medical care, and geographical differences were not factored in. But using alternative definitions of poverty suggested by a special panel, the percentage of people in poverty actually came out higher than under the official measure (*FAQ: who was poor in 2004?*).

Mother seeking provisions at food bank to provide for her children.

Poverty and the Minimum Wage

U.S. social policy seems based on the idea that anyone can find a job and that, by working, people can pull themselves and their families out of poverty. The problem is that this idea does not represent reality for large numbers of Americans today. Many people simply do not possess the educational qualifications or the technical skills required to get the jobs that are available. And in many places today, jobs that pay wages that can lift a family out of poverty simply do not exist.

Many people who work full-time remain in poverty. This problem is rooted in government policy. The federal minimum wage in 1968 was set so that a worker employed full-time at that wage could maintain a family of three (husband, wife, and child) at 120 percent of the poverty line. The minimum wage, however, has never been indexed to inflation. It remained at $5.15 per hour for a full 10 years, from 1997 until early 2007, when a new Democratic Congress was able to pressure President Bush into signing an increased minimum wage law. The new minimum wage was set to rise to $5.85 in the summer of 2007, to $6.55 in the summer of 2008, and to $7.25 in the summer of 2009 (Labor Law Center, 2007).

Even with the full increase taking place in summer, 2009, a full-time employee earning minimum wage would still take home less than a poverty level income for a family of three. And sadly, approximately one-fourth of the American workforce earns just poverty-level wages. One-third of all women do; fully 40 percent of Black women and more than half of Hispanic women suffer this indignity (Goldberg, 2002a). Thus the low minimum wage is an important factor in the growing feminization/juvenilization of poverty.

The Children's Defense Fund points out that if the minimum wage had increased at the same rate as the pay of CEOs between 1990 and 2005, the minimum wage would have been $23.03 per hour, not $5.15 per hour, in 2005! The low minimum wage has devastating effects on children. For example, approximately 42 percent of children in female-headed families, where the mother is likely to rely on the minimum wage, are poor (*The state of America's children*, 2005).

Affirmative Action Policies: Under Attack

Affirmative action policies are designed to try to "level the playing field" for populations at risk. Due to historical exploitation, prejudice, discrimination, and the "isms" discussed earlier in this chapter, members of populations at risk suffer economic hardships through no fault of their own. There are two main approaches in the United States to address this injustice: **nondiscrimination** and **affirmative action.** Nondiscrimination laws simply ban discrimination. The Civil Rights Act of 1964 was the first powerful national legislation to bar discrimination, carrying with it the power of the courts. Title VII of this act, as amended in 1972, prohibits employment discrimination on the basis of race, color, religion, sex, or national origin. Today, age and disability are protected categories as well.

Despite the Civil Rights Act, discrimination remained widespread, so courts began to require companies who lost discrimination cases to engage in "affirmative

EXHIBIT 3-10

Clay Bennett/North America Syndicate. Reprinted with permission.

action" efforts to improve compliance with the law. Affirmative action required targeted outreach toward minorities.

This approach has always been controversial, because a member of a protected minority might be recruited ahead of an equally qualified member of a nonprotected category. Such instances have led to accusations of *reverse discrimination*. Court decisions since 1978 have been inconsistent, sometimes upholding affirmative action efforts and sometimes not. In general, with conservative political trends, affirmative action is under attack and policies have become weaker. The most recent assault on affirmative action came with the Supreme Court decision in 2007 not to allow race as a deciding factor in assigning students to certain schools. Many public school systems had used race as a factor in school assignment to maintain racially integrated school populations. The decision was 5–4; had Sandra Day O'Connor not left the Court, to be replaced by President Bush's choice of an ideologically conservative justice, Samuel Alito, the decision would likely have gone 5–4 the other way (Richey, 2007). (See the Up for Debate box.)

UP FOR DEBATE

Proposition: Affirmative action programs should be maintained to assist in provision of equal opportunity for all.

YES	NO
Affirmative action programs help correct past discriminatory hiring practices by seeking qualified applicants of color and women.	Affirmative action programs may discriminate against people who are white, especially white males.
Affirmative action programs help ensure that jobs are genuinely and equally accessible to qualified persons without regard to sex, racial, or ethnic characteristics.	Affirmative action programs may hire women and people of color rather than others who are equally qualified.
Affirmative action programs help ensure that qualified persons of merit gain employment, even if minority or female, rather than applicants who simply happen to be white and male.	Affirmative action programs may help qualified minorities and females gain employment rather than white males who may be equally qualified.
In a democratic, multiracial society, integrated institutions can provide higher levels of service than agencies run entirely by one sex and race.	The most qualified applicants should always be hired, even if they all happen to be white and male.

Social Policy and the Growing Gap between Rich and Poor

The old saying, "the rich get richer and the poor get poorer" has been the reality for our nation over the past several decades. Today, the Children's Defense Fund reports that the richest fifth of American households has 15 times the median income of the lowest fifth. This is the largest gap on record at the U.S. Census Bureau (*The state of America's children*, 2005). The wealth gap between rich and poor Americans is even greater than the income gap. Shockingly, the top 1 percent of Americans owns one-third of all the wealth in the nation, as contrasted with the bottom 40 percent that owns only 0.3 percent (that's point 3 percent; Skenazy, 2004). In addition, the top 1 percent has almost doubled its share of the total income of the nation in recent years (*Democracy and the death tax*, 2006).

The gap between rich and poor is growing in large part due to deliberate social policies at the national level justified by conservative ideology. The shamefully low minimum wage (shamefully low even after the small recent increase) is one such policy. The personal income tax reduction tremendously favoring the rich is another. But perhaps even more devastating is a tax policy that has led to the decrease of manufacturing jobs in the United States, a policy that allows U.S.-owned multinational corporations to avoid paying taxes on profits earned in other countries (Rocha & McCarter, 2003/2004). As a result, large numbers of these companies have moved their operations abroad, and thousands upon thousands of Americans have lost jobs that paid union wages. New jobs have primarily been available in the service and retail sectors of the economy, in which wages are much lower (and benefits much poorer, if available at all).

Rocha and McCarter (2003/2004) make the discouraging observation that 4 to 6 years of postsecondary education are required to gain a high-skilled, better paid service job. They note that a 2-year, postsecondary occupational training program doesn't add significantly to the income predicted by a high school degree only. Many workers with 2-year post-secondary degrees continue to earn poverty-level wages.

Health Insurance Accessibility

A huge number of Americans under the age of 65—nearly 47 million in 2005—lack health insurance, and the number continues to grow. The number increased by nearly 7 million between 2000 and 2005. More than 8 in 10 of the uninsured came from working families (National Coalition on Health Care, 2007). Nine million are children, and millions more children are underinsured (*Nine million uninsured children*, 2007).

Because the cost of insurance is rising, many industries that formerly provided health insurance to working families are dropping coverage or increasing employee contributions drastically, and many firms are canceling coverage for retirees. Insurance rates have been rising so rapidly in recent years that it is uncertain how long the average American will be able to pay. Many Americans who are self-employed or without jobs today forego health insurance altogether because policies are financially out of reach for them.

Administrative Barriers to Aid

A different type of concern is that our welfare system often discourages even eligible categories of people from applying for aid. Forms are lengthy and complicated; they are especially confusing to people with limited education or whose first language is other than English. Work requirements under new TANF programs can be confusing and discouraging to people who lack child care provisions, adequate clothing for work, or transportation. Even if needy people decide to apply anyway, they may end up languishing on waiting lists, like Tomas and Tomacita's mother, who was still waiting for child care assistance in this chapter's case example. Such complications are known as administrative barriers to aid.

AN INTERNATIONAL PERSPECTIVE

How does the United States compare with other advanced nations of the world with respect to promoting the common welfare of its citizens? A rather sobering assessment has been compiled by the Children's Defense Fund. In its data sheet "Where America Stands" (2004), this important advocacy organization notes that among industrialized countries today, the United States ranks:

1st in military technology.

1st in military expense.

1st in gross domestic product.

1st in number of millionaires and billionaires.

1st in health technology.

1st in defense expenditures.

12th in living standards among our poorest one-fifth.

13th in the gap between rich and poor.

14th in efforts to lift children out of poverty.

16th in low birth weight rates.

18th in the percent of children in poverty.

23rd in infant mortality.

Last in protecting our children against gun violence.

The same data sheet also notes that Black infant mortality rates in Washington, DC, exceed those in 50 nations, including Barbados, Cuba, Dominica, and Oman, and that the United States and Somalia are the only two nations in the world that have refused to ratify the UN Convention on the Rights of the Child.

Americans have always liked to think of themselves as a people who care about human life, especially children. What do the preceding numbers suggest about this idea? With fewer tax dollars coming into the federal Treasury today because of huge tax cuts (mainly benefiting our richest citizens), and with billions more dollars going out in military spending, what does that mean for the ordinary citizen? Certainly there will be fewer resources to help people who are in need. President Bush's 2006 budget called for reductions in many programs, including child survival and disease programs, Head Start, American Indian education and health services, refugee assistance, the office of violence against women, the Peace Corps, lead hazard reduction programs, housing assistance, and many other programs that help vulnerable citizens (Frances, 2004).

"Guns or butter" is an old saying in our nation's common folk wisdom. Can the United States really be secure when millions of its citizens, especially children, lack access to basic necessities? Are guns a better collective investment than food, shelter, education, and health care for all American citizens? That is perhaps the most crucial question for the future (see Exhibit 3-11).

The United States is not the only nation where welfare has been diminishing—in fact, this unfortunate situation has been occurring even in nations with generous, long-established policies of social provision, such as Sweden. An excellent book examining this phenomenon, *Diminishing Welfare* (2002) by Gertrude Goldberg and Marguerite Rosenthal, finds that wherever governments have failed to defend full employment policies, social welfare programs have been cut back. This is because without full employment, a nation's tax base isn't broad enough to provide adequate resources for a strong social welfare system. At the same time, sadly, without full employment more people need assistance. So, many must go without.

The trend toward diminishing welfare among industrial nations seems to relate to the increasing power of international corporations. Corporations do not usually favor full employment policies or comprehensive social welfare programs because they prefer cheap labor. Corporations use their considerable assets to lobby against social welfare provisions nation by nation and to convince the general public through

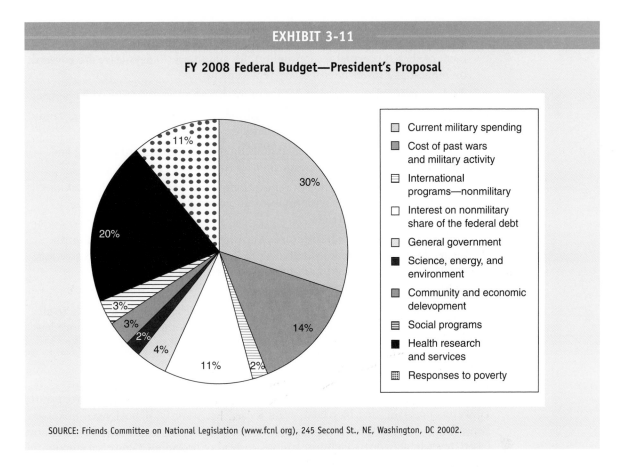

EXHIBIT 3-11

FY 2008 Federal Budget—President's Proposal

30%

14%

2%

11%

4%

2%

3%

3%

20%

11%

- Current military spending
- Cost of past wars and military activity
- International programs—nonmilitary
- Interest on nonmilitary share of the federal debt
- General government
- Science, energy, and environment
- Community and economic delevopment
- Social programs
- Health research and services
- Responses to poverty

SOURCE: Friends Committee on National Legislation (www.fcnl org), 245 Second St., NE, Washington, DC 20002.

advertising that social welfare programs cause budget deficits (obscuring the real culprits: tax cuts favoring rich individuals and rich corporations along with increased military spending). Ordinary citizens without political savvy and without ready access to jobs and/or adequate social welfare provisions do not have the information or clout to fight for better jobs or better wages. And unemployed and underemployed citizens cannot provide the tax base necessary to support a generous social welfare system.

Sweden

While Sweden has cut back its social provisions in recent years, its system is still extremely generous by American standards. This nation invests nearly twice the percentage of gross domestic product in social expenditures as the United States (Goldberg, 2002b). The following are social programs benefiting Swedish citizens, which are only a dream to Americans:

■ A universal children's allowance, with child support advances to single parents in situations where an absent parent fails to pay.

■ Parental leave for birth and adoption with salary replacement of 80 percent for 360 days as long as each parent takes at least 30 days' leave (note encouragement of shared parental responsibility). An additional 90 days leave are covered on request at a lower rate of salary replacement.

■ 60 days' annual leave for sick child care, with a wage replacement of 80 percent.

■ Highly subsidized child care centers utilized by 80 percent of two-parent families and 90 percent of single parent families.

■ Highly subsidized, publicly owned housing so that substandard housing and homelessness are virtually unknown.

■ Generous funding of apartment renovations for older adults to help maintain independence; assistance with transportation and shopping available; many subsidized adult day care centers.

■ Universal, virtually free health care. A small co-pay has recently been introduced, but total payment is limited to $125 per year. All health care is free for children under 20. Most prescription drugs are free.

■ Free dental care for children under 20.

■ Social assistance (means-tested general assistance programs) are available to all unemployed adults, without any time limit, when unemployment insurance has been exhausted. Retraining programs are provided (often required) by the government.

Truly, life for a Swede is not nearly as insecure as for an American. Poverty is rare. However, program cuts in recent years mean that poverty is no longer unknown. Pensions for the elderly have been especially weakened in the past decade. They are now based on each individual's lifetime earnings, instead of providing a universal amount for everyone (some credit is given for years of study and child care). A 2.5 percent payroll tax is earmarked for investment in private accounts, providing no guarantee of future yield (the same policy recently proposed in the United States).

Japan

Japan is the most advanced industrialized country outside of Europe and North America, and has the seventh largest population in the world. Yet it spends an even smaller proportion of its gross domestic product on social welfare programs than the United States (Goldberg, 2002b).

While Japan does have a few public welfare programs, Nomura and Kimoto (2002) estimate that less than a tenth of the eligible population actually receives benefits. They list three reasons:

1. Nearly one third of Japan's labor force works in large firms or government units that provide welfare services such as housing, medical care, and pensions. This circumstance has its roots in World War II, when conditions were so

terrible that strong labor unions arose. Organized labor demanded and won many benefits.

2. Nearly one-fifth of Japan's labor force is self-employed or family employed. While this percentage of the population is lower than in the past, it is still politically strong. The national government, to maintain loyalty, provides protection via implementing policies such as restricting competition from large-scale retail chains.

3. The agricultural sector is organized and has political clout, and farmers have won protection by the government from outside competition. Thus, small family businesses and farms usually earn an income adequate to maintain a decent standard of living. In return, families are expected to support their own members.

In Japanese families today, the wife of the eldest son is expected to care for his parents for life, and nearly half of Japan's elderly do live with family members. Full-time work among women outside the home is discouraged by a tax policy in which the husband loses a tax deduction if his wife earns over a certain limited amount, and the wife then has to contribute to the public pension system. Full-time homemaking for women is encouraged by a tax policy in which she may receive a basic public pension (described later) without contributing any money to the fund.

Government assistance to single mothers involves a severe means test and carries a strong stigma, so most women in this situation must get a job. Japan has had a children's allowance since the early 1970s, but it is not intended to fully support a child. There is so strong a social stigma against single-parent families that they are virtually nonexistent (only 1.3 percent of households). Nearly all pregnant teens get abortions. The divorce rate is very low and the remarriage rate high.

With respect to health care, all Japanese workers must purchase medical insurance, and there are different programs for different categories of workers. Those who work in large businesses receive most of their care from company programs. Japan's pension system for the elderly has three tiers. The first tier is a basic program for all insured, partially funded by the state. Full-time housewives are eligible. Beyond the basic program, additional tiers are funded by large employers in both private and governmental sectors. Benefits relate to a worker's before-retirement income. Despite these programs, fully one-quarter of elderly Japanese over 65 today work out of necessity. Beginning in 2000, all Japanese over 40 must contribute to a system of nursing care insurance for the elderly. The program is designed to supplement family care, not replace it.

Japan's unemployment program targets full-time workers and provides short-term benefits. Only about one-third of part-time workers are assisted. As in the United States, when unemployment benefits run out, there is no further assistance offered. Families are expected to provide. In some situations, subsidies for tuition for retraining programs are available.

Japan thus has very limited national social welfare programs. Its tax and protectionist policies for small family firms and farms, however, assist families to provide for the basic needs of their members to a much greater extent than their counterparts in the United States.

Progress of Social Justice Today

The United Nations' *Declaration of Human Rights*, parts of which have been quoted earlier, states that everyone has the right to a decent standard of living, including food, housing, medical care, and security in the event of unemployment, illness, and the like. The *Declaration* asserts that motherhood and childhood should receive special care and assistance.

This *Declaration* was made more than a half-century ago. Has progress been made toward achieving its goals? The answer varies according to the nation under consideration. Sweden, for example, has made a good deal more progress (despite recent cutbacks) than the United States or Japan.

Unfortunately, overall commitment to social justice seems to have decreased worldwide in recent years. Assistance to poor people has diminished at the very time that economic insecurity has grown. Goldberg and Rosenthal's research (2002) indicates that even the long-established programs of social provision in nations such as Sweden have diminished. This trend is continuing well into the 21st century. By the summer of 2007, resources of international aid associations were stretched very thin, partly due to a substantial rise in basic food costs (21 percent since 2005), a 30 percent rise in the cost of key commodities such as corn, and a 30 percent rise in the price of oil required to transport food relief. According to UN estimates, chronic hunger and malnutrition affects approximately 850 *million* people around the globe. Approximately a billion people live on $1 a day (Trumbull, 2007).

The National Association of Social Workers finds it increasingly important to advocate for poor people in these times. To that end, it has developed guiding principles and programs to advance human rights, some of which are discussed here. It has also begun to ally itself with other organizations committed to achieving social justice throughout the world.

NASW Welfare Reform Principles and Ongoing Human Rights Efforts

As part of its efforts to help achieve humane social policy, the NASW has developed several principles for welfare reform in the United States. These principles, released in 1994, are outlined in Exhibit 3-12. While few, if any, of these principles appear on the national agenda at the beginning of the 21st century, they remain important to consider and understand.

The NASW Social Work Congress of March 2005 adopted twelve "Social Work Imperatives for the Next Decade." Several are listed here:

- Take the lead in advocating for universal health care.
- Address the impact of racism, other forms of oppression, social injustice, and other human rights violations through social work education and practice.

EXHIBIT 3-12

NASW Welfare Reform Principles

1. The goal of reform should be to prevent and reduce poverty, not just reduce the use of public assistance.

2. Investing in human capital through universal opportunities, supports, and services is the best strategy for preventing poverty.

3. Under no circumstances should reform efforts jeopardize the well-being of children whom our welfare system is designed to serve.

4. No one should be penalized for the inability to secure employment due to depressed labor market conditions. A range of contributions, be they social or economic, should be recognized and rewarded.

5. Qualified, properly trained staff and manageable workloads are a necessary part of improving the welfare system.

6. All families are entitled to an adequate standard of living, regardless of workforce attachment.

7. The heterogeneity of the welfare population requires that services provided and expectations for self-support reflect each family's unique strengths, needs, and circumstances.

8. The obligations imposed upon welfare recipients should be no greater and no less than those applied to the rest of the population.

9. As consumers of services, welfare recipients should be involved in all decision-making related to reform efforts, and their rights should be scrupulously protected.

10. Recipients of public assistance should not be stigmatized.

SOURCE: Quoted from National Association of Social Workers, Office of Governmental Relations. (1994, March). *Welfare reform principles.* Washington, DC: NASW.

■ Mobilize the social work profession to actively engage in politics, policy, and social action, emphasizing strategic use of power.

■ Continuously acknowledge, recognize, confront, and address pervasive racism within social work practice at the individual, agency, and institutional levels.

■ Strengthen social work's ability to influence the corporate and political landscape at the federal, state, and local levels.

To help promote social justice, the NASW has also established a Human Rights and International Affairs Department. This department houses the organization's efforts on behalf of women, gays and lesbians, and racial and ethnic groups. It addresses such issues as diversity, discrimination, affirmative action, and cultural competence. The NASW has also recently joined an alliance of U.S.-based international and humanitarian nongovernmental organizations called InterAction, the American Council for Voluntary International Action. This alliance comprises more than 160 organizations working to advance social justice around the world, and it includes many well-known advocacy organizations such as CARE, Oxfam America, and Save the Children (Association Joins Global Coalition, 2005).

Clearly, social justice throughout the world can be achieved only by committed, intensive, long-term, cooperative efforts.

INTERNET SITES

http://www.nchc.org	National Coalition on Health Care
http://www.appam.org/home.asp	Association for Public Policy Analysis and Management
http://www.publicwelfare.org/	Public Welfare Foundation
http://www.aphsa.org/Home/home_news.asp	American Public Human Services Association
http://www.cbpp.org	Center on Budget and Policy Priorities
http://www.bath.ac.uk/gwlibrary/	The E-Library for Global Welfare
http://www.fcnl.org	Friends Committee on National Legislation
http://www2/rgu.ac.uk/publicpolicy/introduction/introf.htm	An Introduction to Social Policy
http://www.womenenews.org	Women's eNews
http://www.urban.org/	The Urban Institute
http://www.un.org/millenniumgoals/	UN Millennium Goal Project

SUMMARY

The cases of Tomas and Tomacita and of Carla and Maria Romero dramatize the predicament of people who are dependent on a variety of income maintenance and social service programs in this country. The recent introduction of programs such as Temporary Assistance for Needy Families, replacing AFDC, along with cuts in funding for other public programs such as public health, powerfully affects the lives of poor children and families.

Populations at high risk of poverty in this nation are identified and discussed, along with various "isms" that increase this risk through stigma and an undermining of political strength. These populations include children, women, older adults, racial and ethnic minorities, people with disabilities, and gays and lesbians. They are the ones usually in most need of assistance from the social work profession.

To understand why our income maintenance programs operate as they do, generally keeping recipients well below the poverty level, we must begin with the Old World background of the contemporary social welfare system in the United States. The Elizabethan Poor Law of 1601 was the law that English settlers brought to the colonies in America. The U.S. system has gradually evolved under the influence of values, politics, issues,

and concerns stemming out of the American experience. A history of social welfare movements and income maintenance programs in the United States reveals a shifting political impact of two ways of thinking about our nation's social welfare system: the residual and the institutional. Residual services dominated the colonies and the nation as a whole up until the Great Depression (1929). Experiences during the Great Depression brought about the temporary dominance of the institutional approach to social welfare, and national programs such as Social Security were developed that lifted many people out of poverty. The trend of the 1980s and 1990s toward the residual view, which continues at an ever-increasing pace in the beginning years of the 21st century, has meant less aid for poor people and fewer resources to sustain the social worker's referral system of financial and material aid.

Issues for the future involve a rethinking of the nation's institution of social welfare. A contemporary, contrasting model from Sweden is introduced for consideration, as is a model from Japan not unlike that of the United States's in many ways, except that tax policies in Japan are clearly designed to help small family businesses and farms to flourish, so as to be able to support family members adequately.

Welfare reform principles developed by the NASW are presented. The United States needs to determine how much interference with the free market is appropriate to alleviate poverty, which is deepening today among poorer women and children.

KEY TERMS

Aid to Families with Dependent Children (AFDC), *p. 111*
affirmative action, *p. 120*
ageism, *p. 99*
almshouse, *p. 103*
cultural competency, *p. 93*
cultural pluralism, *p. 93*
ethnic group, *p. 92*
feminization of poverty, *p. 91*
heterosexism, *p. 100*
homophobia, *p. 100*
income maintenance, *p. 110*
indoor relief, *p. 103*
isms, *p. 98*

juvenilization of poverty, *p. 89*
less eligibility, *p. 105*
means test, *p. 111*
minority groups, *p. 93*
mutual aid, *p. 107*
nondiscrimination, *p. 120*
outdoor relief, *p. 103*
populations at risk, *p. 89*
poverty, *p. 86*
poverty line, *p. 92*
prejudice, *p. 86*
private trouble, *p. 110*
privatization, *p. 116*
public assistance, *p. 111*

public issue, *p. 110*
racial group, *p. 92*
racism, *p. 98*
sexism, *p. 98*
sexual orientation, *p. 100*
social insurance, *p. 111*
social and economic justice, *p. 86*
social welfare, *p. 101*
Temporary Assistance for Needy Families (TANF), *p. 100*
vagrants, *p. 103*
voucher, *p. 112*
workhouse, *p. 103*

DISCUSSION QUESTIONS

1. What are the major populations at risk in the United States today? Why are they considered "at risk"?

2. Define *prejudice*. How do prejudice and "isms" increase risk?

3. What is affirmative action? How does it differ from nondiscrimination?

4. Why were affirmative action policies first adopted in this country? Why do you think they are under attack today? What evidence provided in this chapter indicates that these policies are still needed?

5. What is the relationship between social work and social welfare?

6. Compare and contrast the residual and institutional approaches to social welfare. Which approach do you think better meets the needs of modern industrial society? Why?

7. What major societal values affect the American social welfare system? Do these values complement one another or create conflict? How do they affect social welfare legislation today?

8. Define *social justice*. How are social justice and social welfare legislation related? Does social welfare legislation always promote greater social justice?

9. What country in the Old World provided the model for early American social welfare programs? What law was particularly influential? Why?

10. What were the four major provisions of the Elizabethan Poor Law of 1601? What categories of poor were established? What assistance was offered to each category?

11. How did the concept of *deserving* or *worthy* poor affect poor relief in the Old World? Does this

concept affect the American social welfare system today? How do you know?

12. What were the major innovations of the Speenhamland Act of 1795? What happened to this law, and why? Are there parallel occurrences in this country today?

13. Describe the concept of less eligibility. What do you think of this approach to aiding poor people? Why?

14. Compare and contrast the Charity Organization Society and the Settlement House Movement in the United States. Comment on their purposes, goals, types of aid offered, and levels of intervention or methods used.

15. What were some major social accomplishments of the progressive years?

16. How did the federal government respond to the Great Depression with respect to relief of the poor? Which President ushered in the New Deal?

17. What were the major provisions of the Social Security Act of 1935? Which categories of persons obtained assistance? Which category did not? Which racial and ethnic groups tended to be left out? Why?

18. Was the Personal Responsibility and Work Opportunity Act signed into law by President Clinton in 1996 a shift of the American welfare system toward the institutional or the residual? Do you think this legislation was based on findings from careful research? Why or why not?

19. Has the George W. Bush administration pushed the American social welfare system more toward the residual or the institutional?

20. Which political philosophy, liberal or conservative, tends to support a residual approach to social welfare? Which a more institutional?

CLASSROOM EXERCISES

While not required, it is suggested that students break into small groups of three or four to discuss these exercises. It may be helpful to choose a scribe to record and report major points to the class after the group discussion.

1. Imagine that you are a single parent with custody of a 2-year-old toddler. Would you prefer to care for your child at home or work at a paid job outside the home and purchase child care? Why? Which arrangement do you think would be better for your child? Why?

2. Work out a budget sufficient to meet the needs of a single parent and a 2-year-old child to the best of your ability. Then determine the wage that this parent would need to earn to make ends meet.

3. Given that American children have already suffered more poverty than those of most major Western industrialized nations, why do you believe a Republican Congress enacted and a Democratic president (Clinton) signed the Personal Responsibility and Work Opportunity Act of 1996?

4. What do you think about the fact that poor children whose parents earn wages receive an income supplement through the Earned Income Tax Credit, but poor children whose parents do not earn wages are not entitled to financial assistance from the federal government?

5. The Speenhamland Act was passed in England in 1795 to help poor working families. In what ways was this wage supplement legislation similar to today's EITC? In what ways was it different? Do you think the same issues that led to the downfall of the Speenhamland Act may endanger the EITC? Why or why not?

6. Many people today do not understand the reasons for affirmative action, especially members of the majority group. Identify those cited in this text supporting affirmative action, and think of three more from your own experience.

RESEARCH ACTIVITIES

1. Select one of the major populations at risk discussed in this chapter, and research it to gather the most recent information regarding the percentage of the current population that its members represent, the percentage of its members experiencing poverty, the percentage suffering unemployment, and so on.

2. Examine the buildings on your campus to find out whether they are accessible to people with disabilities. If not, what major barriers did you find? Conduct interviews with campus administrators to find out if they are aware of accessibility problems and whether plans are being developed to improve accessibility.

3. Since the passage of the Personal Responsibility and Work Opportunity Act of 1996, every state has developed its own program or set of programs to aid poor families. Many of these programs are called Temporary Assistance for Needy Families (TANF). Use your college library and the Internet to find out about the program your state has developed.

4. Interview social workers and other staff who work at one of your state's TANF offices. Find out what these workers see as the strengths of the current program. What problems have they observed? Alternately, simply go and observe how applicants are treated.

5. Use your library and the Internet to find out about what a nearby state is doing to aid needy families under the TANF program. Compare and contrast your own state's efforts with those of the nearby state.

INTERNET RESEARCH EXERCISES

1. Settlement houses are certainly not a thing of the past. Examples of two settlement houses that are very much alive are Toberman Settlement House Inc. (http://www.toberman.org) and East Side House Settlement (http://www.eastsidehouse.org).

   a. Has the purpose (or mission) of these settlement houses changed over the years since their founding? If so, how?

   b. What are the sources of funding for these agencies?

   c. If a student social worker served his/her field practicum in one of these houses, what activities would you expect him/her to perform?

2. A group of social workers/educators have formed a very useful and productive group called "Influencing State Policy" (http://statepolicy.org).

   a. Click "About us." What is this group's mission? What is their goal?

   b. Click "Liaison at Each Social Work Program." Does your school have a named liaison with this organization? What is that person's name?

   c. Click "Resources." This organization has compiled an extensive list of web links to serve its mission. To what purpose do you think you could put this material to better serve your clients?

3. Annually the United States Department of Health and Human Services publishes poverty guidelines (http://www.atdn.org/access/poverty.html). (Note: you may have to search for subsequent years.)

   a. What are some of the uses for these guidelines?

   b. The website cited states "The poverty guidelines apply to both aged and non-aged units." As a social worker, how does the word "units" strike you?

   c. How does your personal income compare with the poverty guideline listed for a single person? Do you think you could live on a poverty-level income?

FOR FURTHER READING

Bane, M. J., & Mead, L. M. (2003). *Lifting up the poor,*
a dialog on religion, poverty, and welfare provision.
Washington, DC: Brookings Institution Press.

At a time of heightened interest in the role of religion in
the provision of welfare services to the general public, this
dialog (in book form) was jointly commissioned by the Pew
Forum on Religion and Public Life and the Brookings
Institution. It involves a spirited debate between two social
scientists of different religious backgrounds and views, illustrating their different visions of welfare provisions in America
and their reasons, both faith and research based.

Bryner, G. (1998). *The great American welfare reform*
debate, politics and public morality. New York:
W. W. Norton.

This text thoroughly examines the politics of social welfare reform and identifies several major areas that were not
addressed, such as income provision for poor children without
working parents, domestic abuse issues, provision of realistic
employment opportunities, and the like. It discusses the
importance of addressing the American position in the global
economy, which will involve investment in a workforce that
has skills sufficient to meet the needs of the 21st century.

Goldberg, G. S., & Rosenthal, M. G. (Eds.) (2002).
Diminishing welfare, a cross-national study of social provi-
sion. Westport, CT: Auburn House.

Social provisions (social welfare programs) of nine major
industrialized nations are examined in this well-researched
text: the United States, Canada, Sweden, the United
Kingdom, France, Germany, Italy, Hungary, and Japan. The
authors note a consistent theme: that as full employment is
abandoned as a national priority, usually replaced by the goal
of low inflation, social welfare provisions tend to diminish. As
international corporations extend their influence over national
policy, full employment loses its priority, and welfare programs begin to unravel.

Karger, H. K., & Stoesz, D. (2006). *American social wel-*
fare policy: A pluralist approach (5th ed.). Boston: Allyn
& Bacon.

A very readable text on social welfare policy, this book
examines the American political economy and describes the

impact of the American political continuum on social welfare
policy. Discussion of the influence of multiple political perspectives on American social welfare policy is found throughout the book. Cutting-edge issues include technology and
social welfare policy, the fringe economy, religion and social
policy, and the transformation of public assistance policy into
labor policy.

Lum, D. (2007). *Culturally competent practice* (3rd ed).
Pacific Grove, CA: Wadsworth.

The third edition of Lum's classic text on culturally competent practice covers topics such as cultural differences and
the importance of cultural competence to social work practitioners today. The book illustrates major skills necessary to
understand, measure, and evaluate cultural competence. Case
studies help illustrate important points throughout the text.
Issues confronted by two families portrayed in the case studies, one Hispanic and the other Arab, help the student master
the knowledge and skills necessary to work effectively with
diverse client groups.

Stretch, J. J., Burkemper, E. M., Hutchison, W. J., &
Wilson, J. (Eds.) (2003). *Practicing social justice.* New
York: Hayworth Press.

This timely book includes a diverse collection of articles
highlighting innovative programs targeted toward vulnerable
populations. It raises critical questions regarding how society
should justly provide for the economic well-being of its children, with a critique of the Temporary Aid for Needy Families
legislation and its probable long-term impact on disadvantaged youth. It discusses various theories of social justice and
exposes the forms, extent, and sources of social injustice in our
daily lives.

Wilensky, H., & Lebeaux, C. (1965). *Industrial society*
and social welfare. New York: Free Press.

A classic, this book provides a thorough examination of
the ways in which industrialization has affected social welfare.
Part 1 of the book examines the development of urban-
industrial society and the emergence of related social
problems; Part 2 discusses social problems and the supply
of welfare services; Part 3 describes the organization of
welfare services in the United States.

PART II

PROFESSIONAL PRACTICE SETTINGS

P art II is the heart of this text. Part I provided background information defining social work, explaining the role of the generalist social worker, and discussing the choice of social work as a career. It introduced theoretical perspectives important to social workers, including those that affect practice activities and those that influence the political processes affecting social policy development. In addition, Part I explored issues of social and economic justice, poverty, populations at risk, and major social welfare programs designed to assist people in need. In this section the focus on generalist social work practice is sustained as the details of what social workers do are examined.

Regardless of where they practice, regardless of the socioeconomic population or problem situation they work with, all social workers need an understanding of current social welfare programs to serve clients effectively. It is not possible to understand social work in health care, for example, without some understanding of the Medicare and Medicaid programs, HMOs, and the politics of health care, all of which are described in detail in Chapter 6.

Eight different settings were selected from the numerous areas in which social workers practice: family and children's services, mental health, health care, schools, chemical dependency programs, services for older adults, criminal justice settings, and programs for people with disabilities. Each chapter focuses on one specific field of practice and reviews the history of the profession of social work in that area. Each explores the knowledge and skills needed by professionals in that field, and each examines the ethical and value issues that the social workers encounter. The populations that are served, especially those at greatest risk, are introduced. Legislation and public social policy are explored, and research that both evaluates and guides social work practice is described. Finally, each chapter features an extensive case study that examines clients representing diverse ethnic, racial, age, and socioeconomic groups.

Through our discussions we explore the richness and variety of social workers' day-to-day work, the social problems encountered in contemporary society, and the challenges facing professional social workers. ■

CHAPTER 4

FAMILY AND CHILDREN'S SERVICES

OUTLINE

LaTanya Tracy

LATANYA TRACY

L aTanya Tracy's great-grandmother, Ruby Bell Lowe, called Protective Services in a panic early one morning. Ruby had become exhausted from trying to care for LaTanya, an infant of only nine months. The baby had been crying all night, and Ruby had gotten little sleep. In her mid-80s, the elderly woman had been caring for LaTanya single-handedly for the past 3 weeks, ever since Natasha Tracy (Ruby's granddaughter and LaTanya's mother) had asked her to babysit late one evening. Ruby had felt uneasy accepting at that hour, suspecting that Natasha planned to go out drinking, but she had agreed for the baby's sake.

Natasha had not returned the following morning as promised, and LaTanya was keeping Ruby awake night after night. Exhausted and angry, Ruby remembered that a social worker from the County Department of Protective Services had been helpful a few years before when Natasha neglected her parental responsibilities to her son, Martin, because of a drinking habit.

The intake worker with whom Ruby spoke at Protective Services checked the computer files, and found that Natasha Tracy, 24 years old, had indeed been referred to the department previously. At that time, Natasha's young son, Martin, had been placed temporarily in foster care due to neglect, or failure to provide appropriate care, brought on by Natasha's drinking. (For reasons of confidentiality, the worker did not relay this information to Ruby, although Ruby probably already knew.) Martin had been returned to his mother after 8 months, and the case had been closed. That was because Natasha had entered an alcohol treatment program and had followed all court orders carefully. There had been no further referrals for child neglect until Ruby's anxious telephone call. The intake worker at Protective Services, on consultation with her supervisor, accepted the case for investigation and referred it to the social worker who had worked with Natasha previously, an experienced professional named Lauren White.

Lauren White, BSW, like Natasha, was a woman of African American descent. She knew from personal as well as professional experience that black families have many strengths. In times of difficulty, for example, extended family members such as Ruby frequently pitch in to help care for young children. Grandparents, great-grandparents, aunts, uncles, older siblings, even neighbors frequently help out when needed. Lauren checked her files to assist in recalling the facts of the former case. Four years before, the paternal grandmother had called to report neglect of Natasha's then-infant son, Martin. At that time Natasha was abusing alcohol, marijuana, and cocaine. A single parent, she was trying to cope with a baby with no assistance from that baby's father.

The case with Martin had a satisfactory ending, at least at the time. Once the little boy had been placed in foster care, Natasha had been willing to work hard to meet the conditions required by the court to get him back: regular participation in an alcohol and drug abuse treatment program and in a parenting class. Once court conditions had been met, Martin had been returned home, and the case had been closed shortly thereafter.

Lauren White's first step was to call Ruby Bell Lowe. She remembered the great-grandmother from her previous work with Natasha. Besides, no current telephone number had been given for Natasha, and the number on file was no longer working. From Ruby, Lauren learned that Natasha's telephone had been disconnected. Ruby could not take the bus to visit Natasha to talk with her as she was too frail to climb the vehicle's steep steps with an infant in her arms. She could not afford a cab. Ruby told Lauren that she didn't think she could keep LaTanya much longer. The baby had severe asthma attacks that frightened the old woman and sometimes kept her up many hours of the night. Ruby gave Lauren Natasha's address. She explained that she believed her granddaughter was abusing alcohol and possibly other drugs again. When Lauren asked where Natasha's son, Martin, was currently staying, Ruby didn't know.

Natasha Tracy opened the door of her apartment hesitantly at Lauren's knock, wearing an old bathrobe and smelling of alcohol although it was early in the afternoon. She recognized her former worker and invited her in with an embarrassed smile. She offered Lauren a seat on an ancient sofa and sank into a nearby chair with a sigh. "I know," she said, "I'll bet my grandmother called you."

Lauren replied that the elderly woman had done just that. "Ruby is very worried about you, Natasha," the worker continued sternly, "and LaTanya is hard for her to care for, as you can imagine. What has happened that you felt you had to leave LaTanya with your grandmother?"

Thus began a long, hesitant conversation in which Natasha seemed almost grateful to have someone to talk with, even if that someone was a social worker from Protective Services with the power to take away her children. Natasha explained that things had gone well enough for a couple of years after her son, Martin, had come home. But then she had become involved with an abusive boyfriend, LaTanya's father. This man frequently struck her when he was angry and ridiculed her when she cried. Then, just before LaTanya was born, the boyfriend had been arrested for armed robbery. He was now serving a long prison sentence. That solved the abuse problem, at least temporarily, but left Natasha alone with a young son and an infant with severe asthma.

After LaTanya's father went to prison, Natasha applied for Temporary Assistance for Needy Families (TANF; see Chapter 3). Under her state's program, TANF required Natasha to find a job right away since LaTanya was more than 12 weeks old by then. The young mother complied but soon felt exhausted by her dual responsibilities—sole parent to a baby and full-time employee at a fast-food restaurant. Even worse, the child care promised by TANF did not come through. There was a substantial waiting list for this service. Most of LaTanya's relatives and friends were working outside their homes as well, many of them required to do so by the same TANF program. They could only occasionally help Natasha. Soon, Natasha lost her new job because she was absent caring for LaTanya too often. Discouraged, the young mother began to drink again. Eventually, realizing she was unable to care for her children properly, she took LaTanya to her grandmother's house and Martin to the home of his paternal grandmother. That was 3 weeks earlier. Now, Natasha's drinking was completely out of control, and she was in debt to her landlord for her rent, facing eviction.

Lauren White realized that here was a young woman with multiple problems, but that she and her extended family had many strengths. First, there were two elderly grandmothers willing to help as long as possible. Probably other relatives could be found to help from time to time as well. Second, Lauren knew from past experience that Natasha was a good mother when she was not drinking. She had even been responsible enough to find other caretakers for her children when she realized her drinking was getting out of control again.

Gently, Lauren asked the young mother what she wanted for herself and her children. Did Natasha want to continue in the direction she was now heading, addicted to alcohol and in danger of losing her children, or was she willing to accept assistance toward recovery? Lauren *asked* Natasha because self-determination is a core social work value, to be implemented to the greatest extent possible even with involuntary clients. Clients who feel heard and respected will usually work harder to meet their goals.

Natasha's eyes filled with tears as Lauren asked her what she wanted to do with her life. She admitted that she had a substance abuse problem and said she was ashamed that she wasn't caring for her children. She knew she needed help.

Lauren had her work cut out for her to find resources to assist Natasha, but she was success-ful. An aunt was able to help Ruby Bell Lowe care for LaTanya until Natasha felt ready to take the baby home again. The paternal grandmother was willing to care for Martin a little longer. Family members loaned the young woman enough money to pay her back-rent. Lauren was able to arrange counseling for Natasha at the Islamic Family Center. While Natasha was not a Black Muslim, the Islamic Family Center was willing to accept her as a client even though Natasha's only way to pay was through Medicaid, a health insurance program for certain categories of poor people, which has a very low payment schedule (see Chapter 3). Natasha's counselor at the Islamic Family Center connected her with an Alcoholics Anonymous (AA) group that met in her neighborhood. Partly moti-vated by the provisions of a court order that Lauren White secured, and partly motivated (and increasingly empowered by) the encouragement and support she now received in counseling, Natasha attended her AA group faithfully. She regained control of her drinking.

Within a few weeks, Natasha stopped drinking entirely. After that, she was able to bring her children home under Lauren White's supervision. She found another job and was able to work regu-larly enough to keep it. She was able to work regularly this time because, as a Protective Services client, she was eligible for immediate child care services through a Protective Services program. Natasha continued counseling at the Islamic Family Center and attending her AA group.

After a few months passed, Lauren knew that Natasha was ready for release from supervision from Protective Services. She was worried, however, because once Natasha ceased to be a Protective Services client, funding for child care through that agency would stop. Lauren realized that she would need to become involved in advocacy for Natasha with the TANF program to assist her in being readmitted and to help ensure continuity in child care. Without that, Natasha would be right back in the situation that precipitated her previous substance abuse. Lauren knew that her task would not be easy, but she was willing to go beyond the call of duty to do what she could to ensure a decent future for LaTanya, Martin, and Natasha Tracy. ■

CHALLENGES OF AFRICAN AMERICAN FAMILIES: A BRIEF HISTORY

As noted in the chapter-opening case study, both Natasha Tracy and Lauren White were of African American descent—members of a minority group that has suffered immense challenges in the United States both historically and in contemporary times.

Many, like Natasha, still struggle to meet basic needs. Others, like Lauren, have secured the education that allows them to enter the professional world. Lauren's path was easier, of course: she did not have two young children to provide and care for.

As is well known, African Americans have endured a history of slavery in this nation, enriching others at terrible cost to themselves. But the first African Americans came to the colonies in 1619 not as slaves but as indentured servants. The institution of slavery did not take firm hold in this country until the late 1600s, when the South developed an agricultural economy dependent on slave labor (Lum, 1992).

The legacy of slavery is profound and reaches to the present day. Africans were different from other immigrant groups because the vast majority, including most of the indentured servants, were brought to this country as captives against their will. Unlike other immigrant groups, they had no stable community of free kinsmen or countrymen to turn to for assistance upon arrival. Instead, slave traders systematically separated families and tribal members and sold them apart from one another to reduce chances of coalition and revolt. Native languages and religious traditions were forbidden. Every attempt was made to suppress the spirit of the slaves. Laws denied them the right to marry, to maintain families, to assemble in groups, to learn to read and write, or to sue for redress of grievances. Slaves were legally not persons but property.

Slavery existed at first in both northern and southern states and territories. Rhode Island was the first state to free its slaves, in 1784, a few years after the American Revolution (Quarles, 1987). By the time of the Civil War there were approximately half a million free blacks in the nation (Logan, Freeman, & McRoy, 1990). They were strictly regulated, however. All had to carry special papers certifying their free status, and they could be sold back into slavery if their papers were lost or stolen. In most states they were denied the right to vote, hold public office, or testify in court.

The Civil War from 1860 to 1865 freed the slaves, but at great cost. One in four died from disease and deprivation related to the terrible conflict (Logan et al., 1990). The first federal social welfare agency, the Bureau of Refugees, Freedmen, and Abandoned Lands, known as the Freedmen's Bureau, was established 2 months before the end of the war, in anticipation of the enormous human need that would follow. The Freedman's Bureau distributed food, clothing, and medical supplies to starving blacks and whites alike. It also established 46 hospitals, several orphan asylums, and more than 4,000 schools for African American children. It established institutions of higher learning for African Americans, including Howard, Atlanta, and Fisk universities (Axinn & Levin, 1992). Unfortunately, the Freedman's Bureau was terminated in 1872. Had it been allowed to continue, the conditions for African Americans as a whole today would be much improved.

After slavery, all former states of the Confederacy except Tennessee passed "Black Codes" that limited the property rights of African Americans and forbade them to hold skilled jobs such as craftsman or mechanic. In Georgia, unemployed African Americans could be rounded up and put on chain gangs as criminals. State and local welfare programs for blacks were inferior to those for white people. Orphaned black children in Mississippi, for example, were apprenticed, and their former "masters" were given preference. No guarantees for adequate food, clothing, or education were written into the terms of indenture, as were included for white children (Axinn & Levin, 1992).

Under such difficult conditions, mutual aid and self-help were crucial for the survival of African Americans. The extended family rescued thousands of orphaned children, and churches organized orphanages, day care centers, and kindergartens. Churches also helped care for sick and elderly members and arranged for the adoption of children. African American lodges like the Masons and the Odd Fellows raised funds and provided needed services, as did various women's organizations (Logan et al., 1990).

African Americans today make up about 13.3 percent of the U.S. population, totaling more than 40 million people (Bernstein, 2007). Today they constitute the second largest minority group, after Hispanics. Among the many strengths of African American people is the fact that mutual aid extends beyond nuclear family boundaries. Aid is routinely offered to extended family members, friends, and neighbors, permitting the survival of many in need. Aid from the extended family network was crucial to the survival of LaTanya Tracy and her family in this chapter's case study.

It is important for social workers to remember that there is no single African American family structure. African American families may be nuclear (including two biological parents or blended in a variety of ways) or single parent; they may be wealthy, middle income, or poor. However, because of the realities of discrimination and limited opportunity, a disproportionate number are poor, increasing the chances of involvement with the social service system.

HISTORICAL PERSPECTIVES ON FAMILY AND CHILDREN'S SERVICES

Children and families in need have been helped by family members and other members of their villages or tribes since well before written history. Otherwise, we could not have survived as a species. Given that human infants are born almost totally helpless, it is cooperation among various members of humankind, not competition, that has enabled humanity to survive. Early human beings foraged for food and shelter at the mercy of an unpredictable environment. Survival was precarious, as it still is today in impoverished areas of the United States and other parts of the world.

Formal services to help those in need are a relatively recent invention. In earlier times, infanticide and abandonment were the primary means available for families to deal with infants they couldn't care for. In the ancient Greek city of Athens, a child's birth was recognized socially only 5 days after the biological event. Before that, he or she could be disposed of. In situations of great poverty today, families still occasionally resort to infanticide or abandonment.

As recently as the middle of the 18th century, nearly half the children born in London died of disease or hunger before they were 2 years old. In 18th-century France, two-thirds of all children died before they reached age 20 (Kadushin & Martin, 1988). A high death rate is probably a major reason rates of childbirth were so high in the past and remain high in poorer countries even today: adults have multiple offspring in the hope that one or two will survive.

Both Jewish law from the Old Testament and early Christian teachings stressed the importance of caring for needy children and families. The Catholic Church, in particular, exhorted the sanctity of all human life and taught (as it still does) that not only infanticide but also birth control and abortion were unacceptable. By preaching against all methods of regulating family size, the church obligated itself to help needy parents care for mouths they otherwise could not feed. A portion of church revenues was set aside for this purpose as early as the 2nd or 3rd century. Infants were often abandoned at church gates (Kadushin & Martin, 1988).

Under secular law, in early Europe there was no recognition of the rights of the child; the father had absolute control and no obligation to protect or maintain a child. Many babies were abandoned. The first known asylum for abandoned infants was founded in Milan in the year 787. After that, many other orphanages were established, among them the London Foundling Hospital, opened in 1741, "to prevent the murders of poor miserable children at birth and to suppress the inhuman custom of exposing newborn infants to perils in the streets, and to take in children dropped in churchyards or in the streets or left at night at the doors of church wardens or overseers of the poor" (Kadushin & Martin, 1988, p. 43).

Other mutual aid groups that helped children and families were the guilds (small groups of merchants and craftsmen that generated basic income to meet family economic needs of their members). However, with changes in technology, guilds ceded their function to factories, which were large, impersonal places of work with no sense of obligation to those who labored. Secular law began to provide some assistance to replace or supplement informal charity by church or guild. Life was still very hard, and assistance was extremely limited in kind and form. By the mid-1500s the average human life span was only about 30 years, and children were earning their own living by age 7 or 8. An English statute of 1535 reads, "Children under 14 years of age and above 5 that live in idleness and be taken by begging may be put to service by the government of cities, towns, etc., to husbandry or other crafts of labor" (Kadushin & Martin, 1988, p. 47).

The English Poor Law of 1601 codified many previous laws dealing with the needy. As described in Chapter 3, aid was usually offered only in almshouses or workhouses. The death rate in these institutions was extremely high because the sick and insane were usually housed with everyone else. Destitute families were separated, as children were apprenticed out to whoever offered to take them for the least cost to the parish.

English poor laws were brought to the New World in the 1600s, and help for needy children and families in America through the mid-1800s remained roughly the same: the almshouse for most destitute people, with children being apprenticed out as soon as possible. Death rates and sheer human misery were high. Some towns did offer temporary "outdoor relief" (assistance in one's own home), but this practice was rare.

In 1853 Reverend Charles Loring Brace took an innovative approach to helping poor children with the founding of the New York Children's Aid Society. Brace developed training schools, workshops, and living quarters for the city's destitute children, but the magnitude of their needs and the growing problem of juvenile delinquency alarmed him. He responded by devising a plan to ship the children out of the city to farmers in the West who could use their labor. He viewed this as a way of finding foster homes for the children and also to "drain the city" of a serious problem. Beginning in 1854, more than 50,000 children were sent west on Brace's "orphan trains." They were generally turned over to anyone who would take them. Many people opposed the plan, of course, including parents who hated to see their children go but were too poor to support them. Charity workers sometimes called the program "the wolf of indentured labor in the sheep's clothing of Christian charity." The westward transport continued, however, for more than 25 years (Trattner, 1999, p. 118). A positive legacy was a growing public interest in foster care for needy children.

The federal program that assisted African American and destitute white families in the south for a brief period after the Civil War (between 1865 and 1872), the Freedmen's Bureau, was almost revolutionary in concept. It was the first federal program to aid the poor. As discussed earlier, it provided education, work, land, and relief directly to families in the home setting. Unfortunately, this remarkable program fell victim to partisan politics after only 7 years of operation.

In the late 1800s, the settlement house movement, originating in England, came to the United States. Inner-city settlement houses began to offer services to poor families with children by helping to organize cooperative child care and other self-help programs. Jane Addams, as noted in a previous chapter, founded the famous Hull House of Chicago in 1889.

Partly due to activists in the settlement movement, laws began to be passed in the United States in the late 1800s against the use of "mixed almshouses," institutions in which destitute young children were housed with the sick and the elderly. One result was that more orphanages began to be established. Unfortunately, most excluded African American children, so Black people were forced to continue to rely on a strong network of extended family, friends, African American churches, and other African American voluntary organizations for basic survival.

Also in the late 1800s a major organization committed to helping families stay together in times of need, the Charity Organization Society, took shape, first in England and then in the United States. Mary Richmond was the major leader of the movement in this country. "Friendly visitors" were sent into poor people's homes to counsel parents toward better ways of living. The distribution of material aid to people's homes was centrally coordinated. Early friendly visitors believed poverty could be relieved by "moral uplift" of the poor. Later on, as workers became more knowledgeable about causes of poverty (such as low wages and poor health), they began to advocate for social reform in collaboration with settlement house workers. (The Charity Organization Society, the forerunner of today's family service agencies, and the settlement house movement were discussed in Chapter 3.)

The Child Welfare Movement and Protective Services Programs

The child welfare movement was a major contributor to the birth of the social work profession. Its roots can probably be traced to Charles Loring Brace's founding of the New York Children's Aid Society in 1853. While the practice of shipping children west became controversial, as it divided families and subjected children to serious trauma, Brace's efforts publicized the plight of poor children and orphans. Many Children's Aid Societies were founded in other cities. By the 1870s, some of these societies began to board impoverished children in family homes instead of sending them west, the beginning of foster care and adoption programs in this country (Karger & Stoesz, 1998).

Public debate arose around the use of orphanages versus foster homes for needy children. This question was resolved, at least in theory, with the 1909 White House Conference on Children. The conference was attended by Jane Addams, famous leader of the settlement house movement. It recognized the importance of families and unequivocally recommended foster rather than institutional care. Although many children continued to be placed in large institutions due to funding considerations and lack of available homes, the 1909 conference focused national attention on the plight of poor children. It was so successful that the conference has reconvened every 10 years except during the Reagan administration.

The need for protective services, the type of social services mobilized in the LaTanya Tracy case described in this chapter, formally came into recognition around 1875. The catalyst for protective services for children was a 10-year-old girl named Mary Ellen Wilson (see Exhibit 4-1).

Because of increased public awareness of abuse to children as a result of the Mary Ellen case, many societies for the prevention of cruelty to children were created throughout the country in the late 1800s. These were private, voluntary agencies. In some parts of the nation they still exist; in other parts they have merged with various other social agencies serving children.

Formalized public services to protect children were not mandated by law in the United States until passage of the Child Abuse Prevention and Treatment Act of 1974. Federal funds were provided to the states for this purpose, and a national

---

EXHIBIT 4-1

The Case of Mary Ellen

Mary Ellen Wilson was badly abused by a woman to whom she had been indentured at 18 months of age. The woman later admitted in court that Mary Ellen was the illegitimate daughter of her deceased first husband. Neighbors tried to help the girl because she was beaten regularly and kept as a virtual prisoner in her home. In 1874, they enlisted the help of a visitor to the poor, who appealed for assistance to the police and various charitable societies. As no assistance was forthcoming, the visitor then appealed to the president of the New York Society for the Prevention of Cruelty to Animals (SPCA), who sent an investigator. Due to conditions documented by the SPCA, a court order was obtained to temporarily remove the child from the home. The president of the SPCA then took Mary Ellen's case to court as a private citizen. He called it to the attention of the *New York Times* as a means of publicizing the problem of cruelty to children. The newspaper story succeeded in arousing widespread public concern. Mary Ellen was removed from the abusive home permanently, and her foster mother was sentenced to a year in prison.

SOURCE: Based on Sallie A. Watkins. (1990, November). The Mary Ellen myth: Correcting child welfare history, *Social Work 35*(6), 501–503.

Center on Child Abuse was established. Title XX of the Social Security Act was also passed in 1974 and provided block grants to the states, which helped finance child abuse programs (Segal & Brzuzy, 1998; Samantrai, 2004). Some states had provided these services on their own initiative for a number of years, but all states created protective services programs by 1978.

Establishment of protective services programs was accompanied by new laws requiring certain categories of professionals, such as doctors and social workers, to report suspected child abuse to designated authorities, a requirement known as "mandated reporting." Mandated reporting, not surprisingly, resulted in a great increase in reports of suspected child abuse and neglect. Unfortunately, however, most protective services programs are seriously underfunded and understaffed, so workers generally can provide service only in situations of crisis proportions (Karger & Stoesz, 1998; Samantrai, 2004).

Families who are reported to protective services units are often referred for more intensive counseling to private family service agencies, those connected historically with the Charity Organization Society. These agencies provide remedial services such as counseling to help improve conditions for neglected or abused children. They also usually provide preventive and educational programs. For example, member agencies of Family Service of America all provide family counseling, family life education programs, and family advocacy services.

The Family Preservation and Support Services Act was passed as part of the Omnibus Budget Reconciliation Act of 1993. This law aims to strengthen families by providing funds to states to develop new family support and preservation services. Responsibility for developing plans for specific programs rests with the states, which must target services in areas of greatest need and utilize community-based strategies that involve community groups, residents, and parents in the planning process (Allen, Kakavas, & Zalenski, 1994; Samantrai, 2004).

Children's Rights as International Law

The idea that children have rights is rather new. The United Nations, in November 1954, proclaimed through the General Assembly's Declaration of the Rights of the Child that children all over the world have certain rights (see Exhibit 4-2). These rights became international law in 1990 as the Convention on the Rights of the Child. Ninety-six percent of the world's children now live in countries that have ratified the convention, but unfortunately the children of the United States are not among them. The United States signed the Convention in 1995, but, except for Somalia, is the only nation in the world that has refused to ratify it. The Bush administration believes that the Convention infringes on U.S. sovereignty (Steinberg, 2006).

Underscoring the importance of children's rights, the International Federation of Social Workers developed a specific policy supporting the Convention on the Rights of the Child. Hopefully, the United States will ratify the Convention in the foreseeable future.

United Nations Declaration on the Rights of the Child

Every child in the world has rights.

Every child has the right to have a name and a country.

Every child has the right to have enough food to eat, a place to live, and a doctor's care.

Every child who is handicapped has the right to special treatment and care.

Every child has the right to grow up in a family feeling safe, loved, and understood.

Every child has the right to go to school and to play.

Every child has the right to be watched over and taken care of in times of danger.

Every child has the right to be protected from cruelty or unfair treatment.

Every child has the right to grow up without fear and hatred and with love, peace, and friendship all around.

SOURCE: From the Convention on the Rights of the Child, 1990. Reprinted by permission of the Secretary of the Publications Board, United Nations. Quoted in C.S. Ramanathan and N. J. Link. (1999). *All our futures, principles, and resources for social work practice in a global era.* Belmont, CA: Brooks/Cole, p. 10.

SERVICES AND THEIR PROVIDERS: A CONTINUUM OF CARE

A significant percentage of child and family services are offered by professional social workers. The 1980 Adoption Assistance and Child Welfare Act recommends a minimum of a baccalaureate-level degree in social work (but unfortunately does not require it). While this important work is often performed by people without appropriate training or experience, the social work degree remains the best professional preparation for the field. Workers with this background can be instrumental in improving the quality of service.

Least Restrictive Environment

Services to children and families, like services to other populations at risk, should be offered in the least restrictive environment, the setting that provides the least interference with normal life patterns yet provides the most important and needed services. The least restrictive environment for children is normally the biological family home.

Services offered to children in need can be classified in several ways, but one of the simplest is to divide them into two major categories: in-home (the least restrictive environment) and out-of-home. (Be careful not to confuse these contemporary service categories with *indoor* and *outdoor relief* as offered under historic English poor laws.) A continuum of care from least restrictive environment to most restrictive is illustrated in Exhibit 4-3.

In-Home Servics

In-home services (see Exhibit 4-3) are provided to a family to help members live together more safely and harmoniously in their own homes. They are preventive in orientation. Paradoxically, some (like day care) may be offered outside the home,

---

EXHIBIT 4-3

A Continuum of Care

Least Restrictive: In Home

↑

Financial aid

Family life education

Homemaker services

Day care

Family therapy

Protective services

Family-based services

Foster care

Group home

Adoption

Institutional care

The judicial system

↓

Most Restrictive: Out of Home

---

but the goal is to assist families to stay together. In-home services are described in this section. A discussion of out-of-home services appears further on. There is some overlap between in-home and out-of-home services, of course. For example, adoption, while classified here as an out-of-home service because it removes children from their biological homes permanently, also *provides* needy children with homes.

Financial Aid   Many families require financial aid to survive. The major programs available were described in Chapter 3 and will be reviewed briefly here. The federally administered Social Security program provides income to families in which a breadwinner who has paid sufficient Social Security taxes has died, become disabled, or retired.

States *may* provide limited financial aid to poor families for no more than 5 years in a given parent's lifetime under the Temporary Assistance for Needy Families (TANF) program. This option is authorized under the federal Personal Responsibility and Work Opportunity Act of 1996. TANF replaced AFDC, Aid to Families with Dependent Children, a program previously *entitling* poor children to aid under the Social Security Act.

Medicare and Medicaid programs provide funding for medical care for many families in need. They are authorized by amendments to the Social Security Act. Medicare primarily provides funds for elderly and disabled people. Medicaid is available to certain categories of poor people who pass a means test. Most people who qualify for TANF also qualify for Medicaid.

Food stamps provide financial assistance to families in voucher form. The amount of aid given depends on the number of people in a household and on the combined household income. Eligibility for food stamps has become more restrictive in recent years, as described in Chapter 3.

Other forms of financial aid include subsidized school lunch programs, surplus food distributions, and rent assistance provided by the U.S. Department of Housing and Urban Development. Availability of these and other aid programs varies according to year, state, and locality. In general, funding for these programs tends to be cut under conservative administrations.

Family Life Education   Family life education is an in-home social service intended to prevent as well as to help solve family problems. This type of educational program is often offered at traditional family service agencies and also at family support centers that are being developed in some areas of the country. Usually family life education classes are held at the sponsoring agencies, but sometimes workers go out into the home setting. Topics covered vary with the setting, but typically they include information about the developmental stages of childhood, weaning and toilet-training issues, building self-esteem, parenting skills, communication skills, and constructive methods of discipline.

Homemaker Services   Homemaker services may be provided to families in which one member is too ill, too old, or too emotionally unstable to carry out normal household tasks. Such services may also be provided on a short-term basis to care for children when a parent is temporarily absent because of physical illness or mental breakdown. Sometimes a homemaker is assigned to a family that has been reported to protective services for neglect, as a temporary corrective measure. In these cases, homemakers assume a teaching or modeling role.

The provision of homemaker services can allow families to stay together in their own homes under circumstances that might otherwise break them up. Services may include cleaning, shopping, cooking, laundry, and child care. They are offered at low cost to eligible families that meet a means test, through both public and private social service agencies. In most cases, services are provided by aides rather than social workers.

Day Care   Day care is considered an in-home social service, even though it is often provided outside the home. This service permits a working parent who has no partner, or two working parents, to maintain their young children as part of the household.

Too common are "latchkey children," who spend part of their day in school and part at home alone, having let themselves in. Even this arrangement, however, is not feasible for families with infants and toddlers; without day care, these very young children would require foster care. For this reason, many states and counties have established programs in which day care is publicly subsidized, and a sliding fee is charged according to the income of the parent(s). The replacement of AFDC by TANF makes subsidized day care programs particularly imperative today since most poor mothers have to work outside the home. Yet there is still no national requirement for such a service.

Day care centers that serve special populations of children are probably most likely to have social workers on staff. For example, some centers offer care for children with developmental disabilities or for those adjudicated by the courts as **children at risk.** At-risk children usually come through the recommendation of protective services social workers, who have determined that these children would be reasonably safe at home if their parents were relieved of child care responsibilities during all or part of the day.

Family Therapy   Family therapy is a service available to families experiencing many different kinds of distress. Although it usually is conducted in professional offices, it is considered an in-home service because it assists family members to live together more safely and harmoniously.

Family therapy is a practice concentration within the social work profession, and it requires a master's degree. Family therapy may be provided by members of related professions as well, such as psychologists or psychiatrists. Sometimes family therapists work in teams in which a psychologist administers psychological tests, a psychiatrist administers medication, and both serve as consultants to the social worker, who usually provides the ongoing counseling.

Protective Services   **Protective services** are designed to shield children from maltreatment, including both abuse and neglect. Lauren White of the LaTanya Tracy case was a protective services worker. The Child Abuse Prevention, Adoption and Family Services Act of 1988 provides a general federal definition of maltreatment (quoted in Gustavsson & Segal, 1994, p. 75):

> The physical or mental injury, sexual abuse, or exploitation, negligent treatment or maltreatment of a child by a person who is responsible for the child's welfare, under circumstances which indicate that the child's health or welfare is harmed or threatened thereby, as determined in accordance with regulations prescribed by the Secretary of the Department of Health and Human Services.

While each state has its own definition of child maltreatment, the preceding federal definition specifies that it may be physical, mental (including emotional), or sexual, and it may involve active abuse or negligence.

Protective services workers usually begin by investigating and monitoring a referred child's own home. They counsel both children and parents; inform parents of legal requirements; and use as motivation for positive change both skillful professional relationships and sanctions, or penalties for noncompliance, provided by the court. In situations of extreme risk (and when such resources exist), protective services workers may mobilize family preservation teams for intensive in-home intervention as described later. Where safety issues remain serious, children may be placed in foster care (Reich, 2005). Children removed from parental homes are ideally placed in homes of relatives, as in the LaTanya Tracy case.

The primary goal of protective services programs under the Adoption Assistance and Child Welfare Act of 1980 was to preserve families while providing safe environments for children at risk. This law emphasized rehabilitation of parents so that children could leave the limbo of foster care and return to their own homes (McKenzie & Lewis, 1998; Reich, 2005). However, despite the good intention of this law, many children then remained in the limbo of foster care awaiting parental rehabilitation, in situations where the parents indicated little or no interest in change. The Adoption and Safe Families Act, signed into law by President Clinton in November 1997, acknowledges the importance of family preservation and support services but also encourages more timely **permanency placement,** recognizing children's developmental

Family struggling in the wake of TANF sanctions.

need to have a permanent home. The bill authorizes bonuses to states to increase adoptions of children and also speeds up timelines for holding hearings initiating proceedings to terminate parental rights (Adoption and Safe Families Act, 1997). States receive "report cards" on performance factors such as the number of adoptions completed and the shortness of stay in foster care (Samantrai, 2004).

Family-Based Services   Family-based services were prompted by the federal Adoption Assistance and Child Welfare Act of 1980, which required states to maintain children in the least restrictive environment possible (Smith, 1998). They include both family support and family preservation services for the purpose of keeping families together, healthy, and safe. Toward this end, all the other services described in this section may be employed.

Family support services are generally designed to promote the stability and well-being of families, and to prevent family problems from escalating to a crisis point where out-of-home placement might be required. These services are usually targeted toward at-risk families—those where there is increased risk of abuse or neglect—and may include a variety of health, mental health, social, and educational benefits. Usually no time limit is imposed.

Family preservation services are designed specifically to help families that have been reported to public authorities for problems of neglect and abuse, when the children are at immediate risk of placement outside the home. Crisis workers may spend many hours per week in the family home on a short-term basis, focusing on parenting skills. Family preservation services are usually employed only after all other assistance has failed (Samantrai, 2004).

Out-of-Home Services

Sometimes, regardless of the amount of effort invested by protective and other supportive services, family circumstances still remain unsuitable for the upbringing of a child. In these cases, out-of-home services must be substituted, short or long term depending on the circumstances (see Exhibit 4-3).

Foster Care   The type of foster care provided to LaTanya and Martin Tracy was perhaps the very earliest form available: care in a relative's home. Placement may be informal, purely a family matter. However, placement by a government agency such as a department of child welfare involves a foster home licensing process. Requirements for licensing include such factors as the amount of space in a house compared with the number of people living there, the number of bedrooms, and compliance with building codes and fire safety regulations. In addition, prospective foster parents must be investigated with respect to character, reliability, and parenting skills. Usually, social workers are the professionals who conduct foster home studies and recommend acceptance or rejection.

Once a foster home is accepted, social workers supervise the home. They visit on a regular schedule and talk with both foster parents and children to make sure that a constructive relationship is developing. When there is a problem, social workers become involved in solving it. Some foster homes are specialized; they are licensed to care for children who have unusual needs, such as physical or mental disabilities, behavioral disturbances, or emotional illness.

Normally, while a child is in foster care, the social worker works with the biological as well as the foster parents. The purpose of this work is to enable the natural parents to prepare for the successful return of their child, wherever possible.

Group Homes   Group homes are usually licensed to house eight people, a number large enough so that residents can have a variety of others to meet and talk with but small enough so that they can receive individual attention. Homes for children usually have a stable staff of youth care workers, often BSWs, supplemented by a housekeeping staff and child care aides. The aim is to make the setting as family-like as possible.

This type of out-of-home service meets several needs. First of all, given the shortage of licensed foster homes, group homes can provide shelter when regular foster homes are not available. In some cases, group home care may meet a particular child's needs better than a foster home can. For example, some teenagers cannot make the emotional investment necessary to develop close relationships with foster parents. They may be much more willing to relate to peers in a group home.

Shelters for runaways have emerged in many cities over the past two decades. Originally founded by volunteers, many shelters have become licensed as foster group homes. Runaway shelters usually provide bed, board, and crisis counseling, and their ultimate goal is to reunite families under conditions that are safe for the children.

Shelters for battered women and their children, which were introduced in Chapter 1, can be thought of as another type of group home for family members who are "running away from home." These shelters provide short-term bed and board. In addition, most provide information and referral services and crisis counseling. Usually, shelters are more widely available for battered women than for battered men. This is because women are most often the victims of battery and because women activists (including social workers) have usually been the driving force behind the creation of the shelters.

Adoption   Sometimes out-of-home substitute care goes beyond the temporary and becomes permanent by adoption. Adoption benefits needy children by providing a permanent plan of care. It provides children and their adoptive parents the same legal rights and responsibilities with respect to one another as are available to biological parents and their children. Children become available for adoption only when the rights of both natural parents have been terminated. Occasionally parental rights are terminated involuntarily by court order—for example, in circumstances of extreme, documented battery to the child. More often, biological parents themselves decide that they are not in a position to provide the kind of parenting they wish for their child.

The Adoption and Safe Families Act of 1997, as discussed earlier, encourages increased recognition of children's need for permanent homes. To this end, incentives are offered to speed up adoption procedures in situations where evidence is persuasive that the biological parents cannot provide suitable homes.

Social workers often provide counseling for people trying to reach the difficult decision of whether or not to place a child for adoption or even, in recent times, whether or not to continue a problem pregnancy. Termination of pregnancy is potentially an option in many circumstances, although the U.S. Supreme Court's 1989 Webster decision provided states with more regulating power. In recent years, more and more states have used this power to enact restrictive laws, and in early 2006 the U.S. Supreme Court overturned a nationwide injunction aimed at preventing violence at abortion clinics (Roth, 2006). Thus, women may again be intimidated by extremist groups from trying to obtain abortions.

Children who have special characteristics or needs (such as those who are older, part of a sibling group, of mixed race, or disabled in some way) are hard to place and may spend their lives in foster homes. These are the children that single people or older couples are encouraged to adopt. An important task for social service agencies is the recruitment of adoptive placements for children who might otherwise never find permanent homes.

States are authorized under the Adoption Assistance and Child Welfare Act of 1980 to provide adoption subsidies for hard-to-place children. The medical costs of raising physically fragile children, for example, can be exorbitant. Subsidies make adoption a more realistic choice for many families (Gustavsson & Segal, 1994).

Adopted children may want to try to find their biological parents at some point in their lives. In recent years laws have been changed in many states, allowing adopted persons (after becoming adults) to obtain some of their social service agency records, or, as in New Hampshire, to obtain copies of their original birth certificates (Collins, 2005). Parents who terminate their rights and place a child for adoption today may opt, in some states, to note in the records that they would be willing for the adult child to contact them.

Institutional Care   Institutional placement is another out-of-home option for the care of minor children. In the recent past, children who lost their parents were often placed in large institutions known as orphanages. Most such facilities have now been closed, replaced by foster homes and small group homes. Where large child care institutions still exist, they usually provide specialized treatment or short-term emergency shelter for children awaiting placement in less restrictive environments.

Some children are placed for a year or more at a type of institution known as a residential treatment center. These children usually have been determined by professional evaluation to be seriously emotionally disturbed; they often are referred by courts in an effort to control delinquent behavior. Residential treatment centers often provide a comprehensive range of services that include behavior modification programs (an approach sometimes called milieu therapy), individual counseling, family therapy, and instruction by teachers skilled in working with the emotionally and behaviorally disturbed.

The children who are placed in residential treatment facilities usually have been referred first to special education services in their respective community schools. Federally mandated special education policy requires treating children in the least restrictive environment possible, so a given child will initially be placed part-time and then full-time, if necessary, in a special education classroom. Only if these interventions fail will a child be referred to a residential treatment center.

The Judicial System   If a child has committed frequent and/or severe-enough crimes, he or she may be sentenced by the court to what amounts to a jail for minors. Pending a court hearing for an alleged offense, a child may be held temporarily in a detention center. This step is truly a last resort, and it usually represents the failure of other services. This is what is likely to happen when a child needed residential or other treatment earlier in life but the care was not provided because of monetary cost. Attention to short-term budgetary concerns without consideration of long-term costs, both human and monetary, has been tragically characteristic of social planning in the United States (see Exhibit 4-4).

EXHIBIT 4-4

Child Welfare in the United States Milestones

1642	Plymouth Colony enacts poor law similar to Elizabethan Poor Law of 1601.
	Destitute children and orphans are apprenticed.
1790	First publicly funded orphanage in United States: Charleston, South Carolina.
1853	Reverend Charles Loring Brace founds Children's Aid Society, New York City.
1865	Freedmen's Bureau founded, first federal welfare agency; in action until 1872.
1877	Society for Prevention of Cruelty to Children founded in New York City.
	First Charity Organization Society in United States founded in Buffalo, New York.
1886	First Settlement House in United States founded in New York City.
1889	Hull House founded in Chicago by Jane Addams.
1909	White House Conference on Children.
1912	U.S. Children's Bureau founded.
1935	Social Security Act: dependent children who are poor receive entitlement to aid.
1974	Child Abuse Prevention and Treatment Act.
1993	Family Preservation and Support Services Act.
	Family and Medical Leave Act.
1996	Personal Responsibility and Work Opportunity Act ends entitlement of poor children to aid under Social Security Act. Establishes Temporary Assistance for Needy Families (TANF) program at *states' option*.
1997	Adoption and Safe Families Act.

CLIENT SELF-DETERMINATION AND PROFESSIONAL DECISION MAKING

The social work profession holds as an important principle the right of clients to make their own decisions. A major principle of the social work Code of Ethics, 1.01, deals specifically with **self-determination** (see the Appendix). It states:

> Social workers respect and promote the right of clients to self-determination and assist clients in their efforts to identify and clarify their goals. Social workers may limit clients' right to self-determination when, in the social worker's professional judgment, clients' actions or potential actions pose a serious, foreseeable, and imminent risk to themselves or others.

The LaTanya Tracy case is a good example of a situation in which a social worker, Lauren White, in her professional role as a protective services worker, determined that Natasha Tracy's actions were posing a serious risk to herself and her children. Thus, while the principle of self-determination would normally guide a social worker to honor a client's own decisions, Natasha's substance abuse presented a substantial enough risk to justify Lauren's intervention ethically as well as legally. However, Lauren maximized her profession's ethical principle of self-determination to the greatest extent possible under the circumstances. She listened respectfully to Natasha; helped the young mother identify the many problems in her life that needed addressing; helped her sort out her own goals, which included caring for her children; and assisted in developing a plan of action that would solve many of the problems and permit the children to return home.

WOMEN, CHILDREN, AND ETHNIC MINORITY GROUPS: POPULATIONS AT RISK

Is raising children a task that is of value to our nation as a whole, not a particular family only? If all parents vanished, leaving the children behind, would it be worthwhile for the adults who were left to raise those children—not due to compassion but to self-interest?

In this country, we are so accustomed to thinking of child rearing as a family responsibility that we forget that the nation as a whole benefits. In addition to what children add to the tapestry of human experience, their survival is essential to carrying on the fundamental tasks of the economic market. Today's productive adults will grow old and die; they will need replacement. Thus, despite appearances, it is in the national interest, not just the interest of the individual family, to provide for children so that they can grow up to be emotionally stable, well educated, and capable of contributing to the common good (see Exhibit 4-5).

EXHIBIT 4-5

Should Single Mothers Be Forced to Work outside the Home?

Poor single mothers already shoulder a double burden in parenting; should social policy require them to perform yet another job? The issue is not whether women with care-giving responsibilities should enjoy full opportunity and equality in the labor market. Of course they should. The issue is coercion. Why should poor single mothers—and *only* poor single mothers—be forced by law to work outside the home?

Care-giving, especially for young children—and 63 percent of mothers on welfare have children under age 5—involves more than baby-sitting. It includes managing a household, doing housework, and most important, nurturing, loving, and comforting. Meeting the basic challenges of family work—nutritious meals with very little money, schlepping to the laundromat without a car, attending to a child's schedule of needs, cleaning, mending, caring—takes time, effort, energy, and responsibility (the very skills and sacrifices assigned economic value in the outside labor market). For a solo care-giver who is poor, it can be a labor-intensive, full-time job.

SOURCE: Quoted from Gwendolyn Mink. (1998). *Welfare's end.* Ithaca, NY: Cornell University Press.

Because we don't seem able to recognize the value of raising children in America, however—to recognize child rearing as valid work—we do not consider the task worth paying for (if provided by the mother). The Personal Responsibility and Work Opportunity Act (PRWOA) rescinded any national responsibility to assist poor parents in their child rearing job. Thus, as described in our chapter's case example, when the men in Natasha Tracy's life abandoned her to raise her two children alone, so did the nation. She then faced an impossible dilemma. Natasha needed to hold a paying job to feed herself and her two children, but her paycheck wasn't large enough to purchase child care. She needed to purchase child care to keep her paying job. This dilemma is experienced by millions of poor women today. The TANF program (see Chapter 3) can help for a time, if it is offered, but it requires a mother to work outside the home. In many states, even where a TANF program is provided, assistance with child care is not available.

Has the PRWOA and its TANF program helped poor people in this country, as trumpeted enthusiastically by supporters? It was supposed to reduce welfare "dependency," thus producing proud, self-supporting mothers previously too lazy and dependent to work outside the home. In the years since the PRWOA was passed, welfare caseloads have indeed dropped by about half. This has been touted as a great national success.

However, the reduction in case loads has meant that millions of poor people, mostly women and children, have simply lost access to assistance. Only about 60 percent of the adults forced off welfare found jobs, and only about half of those earned enough to pull their families above the poverty line. Rarely did the jobs they found provide decent pay or benefits such as health insurance. Only a third of the newly employed were able to work continuously for a full year. Many who enrolled in TANF were forced off the program due to **sanctions** (Hays, 2007). Many were sanctioned as they were unable to meet TANF work or training requirements due to child care needs.

It is clear that TANF can help some young parents—perhaps 10 to 15 percent are in a better position now than they would have been if the PRWOA law had not been passed. Some have been provided with valuable training, work clothes, bus vouchers, child care subsidies, and income supplements, at least for a time. However, many others have been unable to meet TANF requirements and have experienced what happened to Natasha Tracy and her children—they were simply dropped from the program (Hays, 2007).

States have various options under the PRWOA: they may require a mother to work outside the home before her child is 24 months old, the federal mandate, as was the case in Natasha Tracy's state; they may institute a lifetime policy benefit shorter than the federal limit of 5 years; they may deny additional benefits to children conceived by women receiving assistance; and they may choose weak, moderate, or strong sanctions for recipient infractions such as missing work due to child care needs.

A team headed by Soss (2004) wondered if state policy choices would follow a "color line." Specifically, the team hypothesized that tougher policies would be adopted in states where Blacks and/or Hispanics made up a higher proportion of the welfare caseload when the PRWOA was passed. Sadly, their study confirmed the hypothesis. States with higher percentages of Black and Hispanic clients in 1996 were significantly more likely to adopt harsher policies, especially stricter family caps and stricter time limits for assistance.

How are poor people faring since the passage of the PRWOA? As mentioned in a previous chapter, at least 35 million are hungry (USA News in Brief, 2006). The number fluctuates but is higher today than before the law was passed. Preliminary data from a U.S. mandated national count in 2006–2007 reveals that homelessness is growing alarmingly across the nation, approaching 800,000 in 2007 (Jonsson, 2007). There is also an increase in the number of homes housing multiple generations (Miller, 2005), as younger people (including young parents) find it difficult to make it on their own and have to move back in with their own parents. A growing number of people—nearly 47 million, or more than 16 percent of the population—lack health insurance (National Coalition on Health Care, 2007).

How have social workers been affected by the PRWOA? Mimi Abramovitz (2005) writes that they have found themselves facing serious ethical dilemmas. The code of ethics requires maximizing client self-determination, protecting confidentiality and promoting social justice, whereas TANF policy requires imposition of sanctions on vulnerable clients for relatively minor and entirely reasonable infractions (absence due to lack of transportation, lack of child care, illness in the family, etc). Abramovitz finds that conflicts between professional ethics and welfare reform policy are creating increased stress and burnout for social workers. On the positive side, many workers are deeply involved in advocacy for their clients and actively lobbying for change.

From the perspective of many in the social work profession, welfare reform has abandoned America's most vulnerable people, especially children but also women and ethnic minorities. The primary effort has been to force poor parents, most of them single women, into low-wage employment outside the home (see the Up for Debate box) regardless of how much they are needed within the home.

UP FOR DEBATE

Proposition: Poor children should be entitled to public assistance.

YES	NO
Children, especially young children, need a parent to care for them at home for consistent parental bonding, supervision, and a sense of security.	Even in many intact, middle-class families today, both parents have to work to make ends meet.
Day care services affordable to poor parents who have to work outside the home are likely to be unregulated and of poor quality, putting poor children at increased disadvantage.	Day care services may be available in centers offering a sliding fee. Besides, babysitting for other people's children can provide welfare mothers a means of earning an income.
Poor parents usually have been disadvantaged with respect to education; they often must accept jobs at or near minimum wage, which is too low to raise their families out of poverty.	If public assistance is offered to poor children, their parents may opt not to work outside the home, thus depriving potential employers of low-wage workers.
Many studies, both national and international, have shown that good welfare programs do not increase birth rates in single-parent families. Besides, regardless of the circumstances of their birth, all children deserve a minimum standard of living even if their biological parents cannot provide.	Assisting poor children may encourage poor, single mothers to have more children whom society does not want.

Reproductive Rights and Single Parenting

Ironically, at a time when the nation is abandoning its poor children, it continues to deny poor mothers the means to terminate unwanted pregnancies. In 1973, the Supreme Court ruled that women have a constitutional right to safe and legal abortions *(Roe v. Wade)*, but the "Hyde amendment" of 1976 denied Medicaid funding for abortions to poor women. That amendment remains in force today. Since the 1973 ruling, all women have found it increasingly difficult to get an abortion, poor or not. Many states have passed restrictions such as parental notification for minors and mandatory waiting periods. More than a hundred clinics have been shut down by disruptive demonstrations and threats on people's lives. The National Organization for Women secured a court injunction preventing demonstrators from blocking clinic entrances, but the Supreme Court overturned the injunction in early 2006 (Roth, 2006).

The Supreme Court also made abortions more difficult to obtain by allowing a late-term abortion ban in 2007. It was a 5–4 decision extremely dangerous to women as it allowed no exception to safeguard a woman's health. Justice Ruth Bader Ginsberg, the only woman on the court, blasted the majority for using "flimsy and transparent justifications" for upholding the ban (Richey, 2007).

EXHIBIT 4-6

©Mike Keefe, The Denver Post and PoliticalCartoons.com. Reprinted with permission.

A hopeful development is the recent approval granted by the U.S. Food and Drug Administration (FDA) allowing nonprescription sale of an emergency contraception pill to women over 18. This pill can prevent fertilization of the woman's egg "the morning after" unplanned intercourse; minors who need the pill must procure a physician's prescription (Erickson, 2006a).

No one knows for certain what the future will bring with respect to reproductive rights in the United States, but neo-conservative President George W. Bush appointed two judges to the Supreme Court whose records did not look promising for women at the time and have proved not to be so (e.g., the subsequent late-term abortion ban). Reproductive rights are clearly in jeopardy. Hostility of lawmakers toward women who become pregnant out of wedlock may help explain the government's paradoxical refusal both to fund abortions for poor women and to help them finance raising the children that Medicaid policies force them to bear. After all, lawmakers in this country are overwhelmingly male (see Exhibit 4-7).

One goal of welfare reform was to encourage single women to marry, in part by making marriage more economically imperative. However, research shows that fewer new marriages have taken place per year since the 1996 PRWOA was passed. Researchers point out that we have much to learn about factors that lead to marriage (Campbell, 2004). Economic desperation by legislation does not seem to be sufficient incentive.

EXHIBIT 4-7

Welfare Reform to Punish Nontraditional Families?

The drive to reform welfare that began in the early 1980s and culminated with the PRWOA in 1996 was never about welfare alone. In fact, the attack on welfare helped to fulfill other political agendas. Liberal politicians bashed welfare and the poor to establish their conservative credentials. Business and industry turned against welfare arguing that it undercut their profits. The social conservatives used welfare reform to promote their own version of family values that ruled out all but the two-parent, heterosexual household.

SOURCE: Quoted from M. Abramovitz. (2000). *Under attack, fighting back, women and welfare in the United States.* New York: Monthly Review Press, p. 17.

Ecological Issues

Ecological research alerts us that not only are poor people at risk on this good earth, but all people are—in large part because the population is exploding (Nadakavukaren, 2006). The population of the United States reached 300,000,000 in October 2006; the population of the world is currently more than 6.5 billion and projected to reach 9 billion by 2050. In addition to the danger of people outgrowing the food supply as farm lands succumb to housing and industry, the natural environment is in grave danger (Francis, 2006). Global warming is on the rise, due in part to high carbon emissions into the atmosphere from human use of fossil fuels. The ice caps are melting, glaciers are receding, and large chunks of ice are dropping into the oceans, threatening to redirect the course of the Gulf stream. Temperatures in the Northern Hemisphere have been significantly warmer in the last 30 years than at any time since the U.S. government began collecting data in 1895 (Kaufman, 2007). In addition, a vast hole in the ozone layer is growing because of chlorine atoms emitted by consumer goods such as hairspray, refrigerants, pesticides, plastics, and fire retardants (Ornes, 2007).

What must be done to save the environment, so that the human species can survive along with it? Scientists are working hard on this issue, although many politicians are avoiding their counsel. Certainly the United States needs to cooperate with international treaties designed to reduce emissions, as discussed in Chapter 3. But more than that, population stabilization measures are desperately needed, not only in this nation but around the world (Nadakavukaren, 2006). Family planning services that include voluntary termination of pregnancy need to be available to all. A sound education for all children is imperative, along with programs alerting all to the need for conservation. American children are in special need of conservation education: the average American consumes 20 times as much energy as the average African (Francis, 2006).

Education and family planning services hopefully can allow world population to stabilize through voluntary means. Many studies have shown that women with access to family planning services, educational opportunities, and rewarding careers decrease their family size voluntarily. The alternative has been demonstrated in China, where a burgeoning population led the government to restrict families to a single child. Involuntary abortion, increased voluntary abortion and infanticide (abortion and infanticide especially of female babies), and an alarming imbalance in the ratio of

EXHIBIT 4-8

males to females are among the results. Chinese families restricted to a single child tend to keep the male, as the male child is expected to marry a wife who is expected to care for her husband's parents. But where will the wives come from now?

Gay and Lesbian Families

According to Benkov (1994, p. 323), "It is no accident that the rise of lesbian parenting has coincided with the burgeoning of single heterosexual women choosing to have children. The idea that women could shape their intimate lives according to their own standards and values rather than conform to constricting social norms was powerful in its own right."

Still, heterosexism and homophobia are very much alive in the United States. It is important that social workers maintain not only a broad cultural perspective but an understanding of the conditions in their own communities. While self-disclosure may help many gays and lesbians create a more integrated life, it can expose others to real danger (Pardess, 2005). Social workers who counsel gay and lesbian persons need to understand the challenges this minority faces and consider both empowerment and safety issues.

Gay couple cares for adopted children.

How to become parents presents practical problems for both lesbian women and gay men. Adoption is a possibility for some, although many programs discriminate against people of same-sex orientation. Those who want to become biological parents face a different challenge. Some women may ask male friends to consider becoming sperm donors, while others may turn to sperm banks. Use of medically administered sperm banks eliminates the potential danger of later court battles for parental rights (donors in medically controlled donor insemination programs waive parental rights and responsibilities), so many women prefer this option. Gay men, on the other hand, unless they or their partners have custody of children from prior heterosexual relationships, must find surrogate mothers. For them, the risk that a surrogate may later sue to gain custody is a real concern.

Sperm banks have been available for decades, but people have become more aware of them in recent years, and some interesting questions have arisen. For example, are multiple women inseminated by the same man? Is it likely their children might meet in the future? Do children conceived in this way want to locate their fathers?

According to Engbur and Klungness (2000), most sperm banks have developed policies to limit the likelihood of encounter with half-siblings. Sperm from a given donor may be used for only a limited number of pregnancies, and sperm is shipped all over the nation, not just to a local area. Thus, the likelihood of a child later entering a relationship with a half-sibling is extremely small.

When the practice of artificial insemination was first begun, secrecy was practiced. Donor records were destroyed to protect the privacy of the adults involved. However, similar to adoptive children, some children conceived through artificial insemination wish to meet their biological fathers. Many sperm banks today provide an option for donors to be contacted by children once they have turned 18. Some require potential donors to grant grown children that right.

Many gays and lesbians share parental responsibilities with committed partners who may try legally to adopt the biological children of their mate. Such adoptions have been difficult to obtain in court, although spouses in heterosexual marriages where children have been conceived through alternative means are automatically considered the legal parents of these offspring. Legal marriage for gays and lesbians would provide a child conceived by alternative means two legal parents, but so far only Massachusetts has provided this opportunity. Sadly, there is a backlash movement in that state to ban it again via constitutional amendment. Misinformed, frightened, and prejudiced citizens of many states have passed constitutional amendments forbidding gay marriage in recent years.

According to Savin-Williams and Esterberg (2000), research indicates that children who are raised by lesbian or gay parents exhibit no differences from those raised by heterosexuals with respect to gender identity, sex-role behavior, self-concept, intelligence, personality characteristics, or behavioral problems. They are also no more likely to suffer any kind of sexual abuse.

Given this research knowledge, the NASW defends gay families. For example, the NASW filed a legal brief defending a lesbian foster family in the *In re: A. W.* case. A. W., a minor child, was removed from his grandparents' home by the Department of Children and Family Services (DCFS) because the grandparents had fractured his skull and tibia and inflicted a number of other serious injuries. The child had previously been removed from his mother's home due to similar serious abuse. The DCFS placed A. W. in the home of Rosemary Fontaine; Ms. Fontaine's home included another foster child and her long-term partner, Tammy Johnson. A. W. received excellent care there and bonded well with Ms. Fontaine and her partner. But the court-appointed guardian ad litem (attorney to protect the rights of a minor) worked for Central Baptist Family Services, an agency with a religious orientation proclaiming lesbian relationships unacceptable. The guardian ad litem secured a court order to have Central Baptist Family Services take over guardianship of A. W. from the DCFS with intent to return the child to his abusive grandparents.

Fortunately, the NASW brief helped prevent the child from being sent back to such a dangerous environment; the Illinois State Supreme Court restored custodial guardianship to the DCFS, including authority to consent to the child's adoption (Stoesen, 2005). A. W. could remain in his foster home with Ms. Fontaine, possibly to become her adopted child.

The fact that Central Baptist Family Services considered a severely abusive home with grandparents preferable to a safe and loving home with lesbian foster parents indicates the extent of prejudice in some places against gays and lesbians, a minority group often lacking protection under the law.

Multiracial Families

Multiracial families are now a part of the American scene, although as yet a fairly small part. For the first time in 2000, the U.S. census permitted people to classify themselves in more than one racial category. Approximately 2 percent took advantage of the opportunity (Belsie, 2001). Interracial marriage is one way to form a multiracial family; another is to adopt a child of a different race. Each process presents its own opportunities and challenges.

The modern family may be multiracial.

According to Diller (1999), children raised in multiracial families are quite capable of developing healthy ethnic identities. They can integrate different cultural backgrounds into a single sense of self, and they tend to welcome the opportunity to discuss who they are ethnically with other people. Children may meet special challenges in school, where the question "what are you" requires a skillful response. Teens especially may be pushed by peers to adopt part of their racial identity and reject another; their single-race parents may have difficulty understanding the pressures involved. Still, supportive parents can make an important difference in helping interracial children cope with a complex, sometimes hostile world.

Interracial couples face special challenges; it is common for at least one set of in-laws to reject the chosen partner, for example. Interracial couples may find themselves socially isolated not only from families of origin but from former friends. In response, many associate mostly with other interracial couples. Moreover, each partner brings different cultural expectations to the marriage, so role expectations may require skillful negotiation. Many couples meet these challenges successfully, however.

Intercultural adoptions involve a different set of challenges. They are usually opposed by people of color, especially African Americans and Native Americans, who believe that white parents cannot provide minority children appropriate exposure to their cultural heritage or teach them how to cope with discrimination in the wider society. Many children of color adopted by white parents in the United States today come from overseas. Special efforts must be made to help these children learn about their cultural heritage.

Immigrant Families

Like multiracial families, immigrant families face myriad challenges although they differ in nature. Fathers often find that the vocational and educational skills they worked so hard to achieve in their nation of origin are not transferable to the

United States; former professionals may find themselves performing unskilled labor, earning incomes too meager to adequately support a family. Financial need may require the wife, who probably did not work in the nation of origin, to find a job to supplement the family income. In the new work setting she may learn that gender roles in the United States allow more freedom to women and that she has new legal rights. She may begin to challenge the gender roles of her nation of origin, leading to marital strife. Men may begin to feel a loss of power and self-esteem while the wife gains more power and authority (Delgado, Jones, & Rohani, 2005).

Children in immigrant families can feel the strain as well. They are likely to learn English much faster than their parents, for example. Serving as translators for parents can burden children by exposing them to adult issues before they are ready, leading to premature independence and a power shift in the family. Children taking on adult roles prematurely can virtually skip their own childhood. They can lose confidence in their parents as they see them changing from competent caretakers to overwhelmed individuals dependent on translation services of their children. They are likely to challenge their parents' authority at an early age.

Language may become a serious communication barrier within immigrant families as well. Children may adopt English as their first language and forget what they ever knew of their language of origin, whereas members of the grandparent generation, who may have immigrated with the family, never learn English at all. Children may become ashamed of members of their extended family who cannot speak English and who maintain customs from their nation of origin (Delgado et al., 2005). Family therapy could help family members appreciate each other's strengths, but immigrant families rarely seek out such services. This may be due to lack of information as well as cultural norms that teach that family issues should remain within the family.

DIVERSE FAMILY STRUCTURES AND SOCIAL WORK'S ETHIC OF CULTURAL COMPETENCE

Social workers today frequently work with families to help strengthen the relationships among members, foster nonviolent parenting skills, assist in finding financial and material resources, help protect abused and neglected children, help arrange foster care, provide home studies for adoption, and the like. For this reason, it is very important that workers recognize, understand, and respect family diversity, whether ethnic, cultural, lifestyle, socioeconomic, or whatever.

The social work Code of Ethics, 1.05(c), states:

> Social workers should obtain education about and seek to understand the nature of social diversity and oppression with respect to race, ethnicity, national origin, color, sex, sexual orientation, age, marital status, political belief, religion, or mental or physical disability.

Social workers who work with families today need to recognize and respect the increasingly diverse forms. They may need to seek new information and gain new skills to provide the most effective service. Hence, the importance of the quoted provision of the professional social work Code of Ethics.

Carter and McGoldrick (2005) point out that diverse groups have very different cultural expectations relating to the family, including the importance attributed to different life-cycle transitions, intergenerational relationships, gender roles, and the like. For example, the Irish place great emphasis on the wake, viewing death as the most important life-cycle transition. African Americans also emphasize funerals. But Italian and Polish families place greatest emphasis on the wedding; Jewish families emphasize the bar mitzvah and bas mitzvah, the transition to adulthood for boys and girls, respectively. With respect to intergenerational relationships, families of British heritage may feel they have failed if their children do not move away from the home as adults. Italian families may feel they have failed if their children *do* move away! Italian and Greek children are taught at an early age that it is their responsibility to care for their parents in old age. But older adults of British heritage tend to consider dependence on adult children a tragic situation.

Because expectations relating to the family differ so much among diverse cultural groups, it is important for social workers to educate themselves about the characteristics of the populations they serve. There are variations *within* populations as well, so that the worker's knowledge must constantly be refined and updated.

SPIRITUALITY, RELIGION, AND SCIENCE

Social work literature has reflected an increasing interest in spiritual issues in recent years, and many social workers on the front lines have felt a growing need for a vision of society and the human person that transcends the material. In the United States, a person's worth is often measured in dollars only, and those who serve the less fortunate may experience a hunger to find a measure of human worth providing more dignity and hope.

Some find solace in traditional religions, but others look toward what can perhaps be a more all-embracing source of strength, spirituality. Spirituality can be defined most simply as the universal search for meaning and purpose. It is an aspect of humanity common to all: atheist, Christian, Jew, Buddhist, Muslim, traditional Native American, whomever. It involves a loving appreciation for all that exists, allowing almost mystical new perspectives, increasing one's understanding and ability to cope with human suffering (Lindsay, 2002).

Most Western educational institutions (with the possible exception of theological schools and departments) avoid any discussion of spiritual issues in the classroom. After all, Western science has "proven" that people are material only, that one's life ends at death, that the soul is a fictional concept, etc. Meantime, sadly, traditional religions often battle one another trying to impose their particular interpretations of reality on others.

Spirituality shares much in common with religion, but does not claim any particular "truth" nor does it try to impose anything on others. Instead, spiritual seekers remain open to new understandings involving ongoing growth and change and may or may not affiliate with a particular religious group.

Oddly enough, new understandings involving ongoing growth and change of perspectives seem to be emerging from an unexpected source: Western science! Dr. Larry Dossey, for example, a physician of internal medicine, has written a series of intriguing books examining a number of modern, controlled, double-blind research studies that provide highly statistically significant evidence that prayer and human intention promote healing—not only in humans (where a "placebo affect," or the power of expectation, might confound these experiments) but in a variety of animals, bacteria, fungi, cancerous tissues, and enzyme preparations. Prayer has even been demonstrated to make plants grow faster (Dossey, 1989 & 2003).

A highly publicized study at Duke University, initially indicating no effect of distant prayer on the primary clinical outcome for heart patients, was widely touted across the nation as evidence that prayer has no effect. A follow-up study 6 months later was not so widely publicized, yet found that 6-month mortality was lower for patients who had been provided with music, guided imagery, and touch (MIT) at bedside, with *the lowest absolute death rates observed in patients treated with both prayer and bedside MIT.* Patients treated with "two-tier" prayer (patients whose prayer groups were prayed for by a second prayer group; prayer groups included Christians, Jews, Buddhists, and Muslims) had absolute 6-month death and rehospitalization rates approximately 30 percent lower than control patients (DukeMedNews, 2005).

Dr. Dean Radin, laboratory director at the Institute of Noetic Sciences in Petaluma, California, has conducted several studies demonstrating, with overwhelming statistical significance, that the human mind can affect matter. For example, human intention can increase growth in brain cells cultured in the laboratory—and can even slightly skew the output of numbers produced by random number generating machines (Radin, 2006).

On an entirely different tack, Dr. Gary Schwartz, who received his PhD in psychology from Harvard University and is now a professor at the University of Arizona and director of its Laboratory for Advances in Consciousness and Health, has been investigating a phenomenon considered impossible by most Western scientists—survival of consciousness after death. He has tested several well-known psychic mediums under controlled conditions to find out if they can give accurate information about loved ones who have died (information consistent among independent mediums and confirmed by knowledgeable family and friends). He has found evidence strong enough to convince himself, his team, and many others (Schwartz, Simon, & Chopra, 2002).

Most of the preceding research has been ignored by mainstream scientists as it lies outside the Western paradigm of thought. But Dr. Marilyn Schlitz, vice president for research and education at the Institute for Noetic Sciences, known for her double-blind experiments on the power of human intention to promote physiological changes in other humans (and having produced statistically significant evidence that it can), finds herself pondering the meaning of Schwartz's work (see Exhibit 4-9).

EXHIBIT 4-9

Hope for the Bereaved?

Does this mean that we can communicate with the dead? No. But we also don't know that we can't. As studies of mediums are combined with other efforts, such as investigations of reincarnation, out-of-body experiences, and near-death experiences, scientists are formulating a new image of death. We are moving from an image of the grim reaper, cutting us off from our loved ones, to what psychiatrist Raymond Moody described as "the being of light." From this perspective, death is seen as a continuum rather than an either/or condition. By reframing death, we may engage in levels of transpersonal growth that can provide us with connections to the subtle, causal, and ultimate realms of reality.

This exploration of the possible survival of consciousness, even in the absence of definitive answers, can offer comfort to the bereaved. The burden of grief, the lingering fears and doubts, may be tempered by hope and possibility. Through this process, we may move outside a limited paradigm of separateness and finality and toward a larger sense of self and our connections to the whole.

SOURCE: M. Schlitz. (2005). Consciousness beyond death. In M. Schltz, T. Amorok, & M. Micozzi (Eds.). *Consciousness and healing, integral approaches to mind body medicine*. St. Louis, MO: Elsevier, pp. 222–223.

FAMILY POLICY, DOMESTIC AND INTERNATIONAL: RESEARCH RAISES QUESTIONS

Is the United States meeting the needs of its children and families? While lip service is given to family values in the United States today, few governmental supports exist to provide assistance to those in need. The result is unfortunate: for example, research data reveal that United States falls far down on the list of comparative world infant mortality rates: it is 23rd. The Black infant mortality rate in Washington, DC, exceeds that of 50 nations, including Barbados and the Bahamas. Twice as many Black children die in their first year as White children in this nation (Where America stands, 2004; United States fails to meet key health goals for infants and mothers, 2006). Yet despite the fact that many American families are very poor and in obvious need of attention, a Republican Congress and Democratic (neo-liberal) President Clinton repealed all entitlement to aid in 1996 (see Chapter 3 and Exhibit 4-10).

How do other nations help keep their children out of poverty? Many different approaches are taken, but virtually all Western industrialized nations except the United States provide universal health care. Many nations also provide universal, non-means-tested children's allowances to help keep families out of poverty in the first place, recognizing that children bring additional expenses to every family. Some countries provide an additional stipend if a noncustodial parent fails to keep up with child support payments. Many nations provide universal day care, either free or on a sliding scale. Others provide paid maternity and/or paternity leaves for as long as a full year, with the guarantee that one has a job when one is ready to return to work. Unfortunately, however, all these benefits are in jeopardy today because of intense international competition from global corporations and trends in privatization of social services (Ford, 2005).

EXHIBIT 4-10

Children at Higher Risk in Red States

Michael R. Petit, the president and founder of Every Child Matters Education Fund and an NASW member, has released a book with statistics showing that the well-being of children living in "red states" (those that voted Republican for President, e.g., for Bush) is worse than that of children living in "blue states" (those that voted Democratic for President, e.g., for Gore or Kerry). . . .

Petit's book, *Homeland Insecurity*, offers data showing that anti-tax and anti-government policies place children at greater risk for low birth weight, infant mortality, premature death, child abuse, lack of health insurance, and poverty. . . .

Petit used U.S. Census data and other governmental sources to compare and rank states on outcomes for children. He developed a "child vulnerability index," based on 11 statistical measures, such as the percentage of uninsured children, child mortality rates, child abuse fatailties, juvenile incarceration rates, child welfare spending, and other factors.

For overall child vulnerability rankings, based on the 11 measures, 9 of the 10 best-ranked states were blue states. All of the 10 worst-ranked states were red states.

Petit also compared the U.S. with other developed countries. The U.S. has higher rates of incarceration, homicides and firearm deaths than the United Kingdom, Canada, Germany, Italy, France, or Japan. The U.S. also has the lowest life expectancy and the hightest infant mortality rate among these countries.

SOURCE: Quoted from L. Stoessen. (2007, March). Children said at higher risk in red states. *NASW News*, p. 11.

The good news is that government programs can make a difference to children and can help strengthen families. A distinct low point in U.S. child poverty rates was achieved in 1969, and it was not due to any accident, but rather was the result of the combined effects of important programs in the War on Poverty at that time. The War on Poverty was not lost because it could not be won, but rather because the money was diverted to the military budget and the conflict in Vietnam (Van Wormer, 1997).

The bad news is that now our nation is at war again, in what is proving to be extended combat on many fronts. Our preemptive war against Iraq unleashed a massive civil war there. As this chapter is being written, President Bush has intensified the war in Iraq and threatened to invade Iran and Syria. A terrible humanitarian disaster may be in the making, not only for the people that our President considers enemies but for poor Americans.

"Guns vs. butter" has been the subject of persistent debate: which is more important, military action or humanitarian aid at home and abroad? In recent years, guns have clearly trumped butter; as a result, hunger and homelessness have been growing in the United States. The good news is that a network of emergency food providers has arisen to try to meet the need. One of the largest is America's Second Harvest (A2H). This organization conducted a study in 2005 that found that it had served approximately 25 million unduplicated people that year, averaging about 4.5 million unduplicated people each week. More than one-third were children. Two-thirds of households had incomes below the federal poverty level. Twelve percent of the people served were homeless (Hunger in America 2006). The work of A2H is admirable—but that so many people are so poor today is quite an indictment of the values of the leaders of the United States, the wealthiest nation in the world.

There is also the problem of rising homelessness in the United States. The National Alliance to End Homelessness conducted a study in January 2005, which identified 744,313 people who were homeless in that month alone. Preliminary data from a 2006–2007 study found 800,000 homeless (Jonsson, 2007). Among the people counted as homeless in the 2005 study were 98,452 families with children. Fifty-six percent of the homeless were living in shelters, but sadly, 44 percent had no shelter at all (First nationwide estimate of homelessness population in a decade announced, 2007).

Research thus indicates a growing need for basics such as food and shelter for poor citizens in the United States, at a time when tax revenues are increasingly being directed toward the military. A new Democratic Congress may be able to slow this trend, but Democrats hold very small majorities in both the House and Senate as this text is being written; a Republican President still holds the power of the veto. Government, therefore, is not likely to offer much if any aid to needy families in the near future. Americans may well be increasingly on their own trying to provide for their families. Will they be able to meet their needs in the workplace?

HOW FAMILY-FRIENDLY IS THE AMERICAN WORKPLACE?

Given that the shrinking of government programs is forcing more and more parents to work outside the home, the question of whether the workplace is family-friendly becomes increasingly important. Studies show, unfortunately, that the workplace in the United States has a long way to go in this area.

A recent study by the Center for WorkLife Law at the University of California–Hastings found that pregnancy discrimination lawsuits in the United States rose from a mere 97 in 1996 to 481 in 2005. A woman is all too likely to be transferred or terminated if she becomes pregnant, especially if she requests family leave. Men have been terminated as well for requesting family leave. Employers frequently refuse to consider women for promotion if they are pregnant or have young children. Few firms allow flexible schedules, crucial for parents with young children, or allow a new parent to phase-in the return to work. Nevertheless, such provisions are increasingly necessary given that two-thirds of women in the workforce have children under 18, and a high percentage of older workers are nearing retirement (Gardner, 2006).

Recognizing this problem, the state of California recently passed an innovative public policy designed to help families. While the California law does not guarantee time off for new parents, it does provide parents whose employers grant family leave with 55 percent of their regular salaries for up to 6 weeks. The program is operated through the state disability system and is financed entirely by employees. Young parents find this provision tremendously helpful in meeting their parental responsibilities (Gardner, 2006).

As discussed in a previous chapter, the president of the National Association of Social Workers, Elvira Craig de Silva, reminded social workers in 2006 that the United Nations adopted two covenants in 1966 involving human rights, the International Covenant on Civil and Political Rights and the Covenant on Economic, Social and Cultural Rights. These include rights to liberty, health, and education and the right to work, protect one's family, and earn a decent standard of living. Because the United States has not lived up to these covenants, the NASW has become a partner of the ONE campaign, a worldwide movement to end poverty (de Silva, 2006).

The National Organization of Women (NOW) is also trying to move the United States toward meeting the terms of these U.N. covenants, thus working toward achieving a more just nation and a more family-friendly workplace. When the United States filed a report with the U.N. claiming compliance with the International Covenant on Civil and Political Rights in October 2005 (10 years late), circumventing many issues such as prisoner abuse, domestic wiretapping, and infringement of civil liberties in the guise of fighting terrorism, this report asserted that American women have full protection under the law from sex discrimination. Disputing this assertion, NOW Foundation filed a "Gender Shadow Report" with the U.N. in July 2006, asserting that:

- The U.S. government has failed to adopt effective laws that address persistent pay inequity for women.
- Laws against sexual harassment and discrimination in employment and education in the United States are inadequate and poorly enforced.
- Family support policies are seriously lacking in the United States and their absence makes it nearly impossible for women to achieve equality in the workforce. Family and medical leave provisions are among the most unfriendly of all developed nations, providing only unpaid leave and requiring only about half of all employers to provide even this.

The effort to highlight U.S. problems such as these to the U.N. was successful: the U.N. Human Rights Commission's concluding observations on U.S. compliance, after considerable subsequent investigation, was that the Commission was "especially concerned about the reported persistence of employment discrimination against women" (Erickson, 2006b, p. 17).

Discrimination against women affects families directly. Someone has to care for infants, transport young children to day care, attend parent–teacher conferences, take children to medical appointments, care for the sick, and the like—the father can do this as well as the mother, of course, but both parents require workplace flexibility if they are to meet the needs of their offspring.

FAMILY ISSUES AROUND THE WORLD

The United States is not the only Western nation with problems relating to families. The European social model of providing strong welfare programs for its citizens is in jeopardy given the requirements of the European Union, which requires "free and unfettered competition" among members. While Finland, Sweden, Denmark, and Norway have remained highly competitive even with generous social welfare provisions, other nations such as Germany and France have made substantial cuts. At the same time, unemployment rates in Europe have been growing, reaching 10.2 percent in France in 2005 (Ford, 2005). A problem of homelessness in France brought popular demonstrations in 2006. No one knows how democratic socialism will evolve in relationship to raw capitalism in Europe, but it seems clear that economic security for the average citizen is in jeopardy.

Another European issue is that the number of children born to unmarried couples has risen sixfold since the 1970s. More than one child in three is now born out of wedlock, from 4 percent of children in Greece to 56 percent in Sweden. Whether this is a problem depends on a person's point of view. In France, unmarried couples and their children enjoy the same legal rights as married couples; virtually no social distinction is made. In Sweden, numerous social programs provide single-parent families with economic and social security. On the other hand, legal protections for children born out of wedlock in many other countries are not as strong, and the average nonmarital union does not last as long as the average marital union. The income of a single-parent family is usually lower than that of a married couple. Thus, while most European countries are cutting back on welfare benefits, the actual need may be growing (Ford, 2006).

In Latin America, Chile recently adopted an innovative policy relating to families. Public health clinics across the nation will distribute the "morning-after" pill to women age 14 and older. That is because almost 14 percent of Chilean girls become mothers by age 14; 40,000 babies are born annually to women younger than 19. Both Chile's health minister, Maria Soledad Barria, and the nation's president, Michelle Bachelet, are women; this is probably not an insignificant factor in the decision to adopt the new policy. The decision to distribute morning-after pills defied strong pressure and legal action from the Catholic Church, necessitating a ruling by Chile's Supreme Court. The Court's ruling that permitted distribution centered on the fact that the pill is not abortive, but works to inhibit ovulation, thus preventing fertilization (Ross, 2006).

The nation of Japan is facing a problem of rising income inequality reminiscent of the United States. A poll conducted in 2006 found that 81 percent of Japanese respondents were worried about their financial situation, startling in a nation where 90 percent have traditionally considered themselves part of the middle class. Another survey found that two-thirds of respondents believed that income inequality was too high in Japan. Factors involved were recent labor law changes permitting employers to take on more part-time and temporary workers and reducing subsidies for public works. Many Japanese fear they are heading toward a society of economic "winners and losers" (Miks, 2006).

CURRENT TRENDS IN THE UNITED STATES

William Clinton came into office as president in 1993 with an apparent agenda to improve family well-being in the United States. His administration provided support for families when it first took office by initiating passage of both the Family and Medical Leave Act of 1993 and the Family Preservation and Support Services Act of 1993. The Family and

Medical Leave Act permits 12 weeks of unpaid leave for people working for businesses with 50 or more employees. Leave can be taken when a child is born, adopted, or taken into foster care or for medical reasons to provide health care for a relative or for oneself. The leave is unpaid, however, so many people who are eligible cannot afford to take it. The Family Preservation and Support Services Act was intended to provide services to all families, not only families at risk. Its implementation is a collaborative effort between the states and the federal government.

As is well known, however, the Clinton administration was unable to pass legislation to provide universal health care, so poor Americans still find access to such care extremely limited. And as discussed previously, the program that President Clinton actually signed into law that affected poor families in this country the most eliminated their entitlement to government aid under the Social Security Act. The PRWOA of 1996 permitted, but did not require, states to develop their own programs of assistance to poor families within certain federal guidelines, and limited any such aid offered to 5 years in a given parent's lifetime.

George W. Bush took office as president in 2001 without a popular mandate. He was not elected by a majority of Americans and there is much speculation that he would have lost the electoral vote as well if the Supreme Court had allowed a fair and detailed recount of the votes cast in Florida. In 2004, Bush did win a majority, in part because the country was at war and Americans hesitate to change leaders during times of crisis.

Bush took office with major political obligations—to wealthy businessmen, the religious right, and the National Rifle Association, among other conservative constituencies that financed his campaign. Hence, it is not surprising that in his early days in office he proposed and was able to pass a substantial tax cut favoring the wealthiest of Americans. He included an increase in the tax credit for minor children, from $500 per child to $1,000, but that credit only benefits wealthier families who have enough tax liability to claim it.

At the same time, Bush proposed a $200 million cut in child care subsidies for low-income families (Gardner, 2001). He reinstated the "gag rule" so that federally funded family service agencies could not inform pregnant women of their option for abortion. He pledged to privatize social service programs and proposed public funding for faith-based organizations (see the discussion in Chapter 3). Even more telling, he proposed a substantial build-up in military spending, a major benefit for big business, well before the events of September 11, 2001. His spending on war-related efforts has exploded over the years.

The Republican preference regarding "guns over butter" is clear. And for many years that policy enjoyed strong public support given a citizenry afraid and upset by the terrorist attacks in New York and Washington, DC, and constantly reminded of danger, real or otherwise, via ongoing terrorist alerts.

By now, however, public support for the war has decreased. In fall 2006, national elections, both the U.S. House of Representatives and the U.S. Senate, gained slight, but significant, Democratic majorities. The election was widely interpreted as a repudiation of President Bush's military policies. It remains to be seen, however, if the new majorities in Congress can be effective in shifting national policy from guns toward butter. There will be an enormous challenge in doing so: the Middle East is in chaos (which the United States helped create), and financing the war there has increased our national debt enormously. In situations regarding balancing budgets, it is usually social welfare programs that are cut, regardless of need. Poor people have little political clout.

In the meantime, income inequality in the United States is growing at an alarming rate. Since the election of President Reagan in 1980, the share of American income taken by the top 10 percent has more than doubled, while the share of income going to the remaining 90 percent has declined. George W. Bush's tax cuts for the rich have exacerbated this trend. The top 1 percent of households now owns one-third of the wealth and 40 percent of all financial assets in America (Yule, 2006). Taking into consideration a different measure, the ratio of CEO to worker compensation in the United States in 1980 was 42:1; in 2005 it was 411:1. The average American worker literally has to work for more than a year to earn what the average CEO makes in a day. The average worker's salary in 2005 was $28,300, contrasted with a CEO's $11.6 million (Trumbull, 2007, February 2). By comparison, Mexico, the country with the next highest inequality record, sports a CEO to worker compensation ratio of "only" 60:1. The ratio in Japan is 11:1, a situation considerably more equitable (Trumbull, 2007, January 4).

Middle and working classes in America have been struggling to make ends meet in recent years. For the first time since the Great Depression, the savings rate of Americans dropped into the negative in 2005, with households borrowing 14.6 percent of their disposable income by late summer of that year. The situation improved slightly by late summer of 2006, but families were still borrowing to make ends meet (Trumbull, 2007, January 2). An increasing number of families have fallen into serious debt and have found it necessary to declare bankruptcy. In response, the Republican Congress made it more difficult to file for bankruptcy beginning in 2005. The new law, which required a means test for bankruptcy, affected more than a million people with major debt burdens from circumstances such as medical expense, job loss, and divorce. Families whose income was above the state median 6 months prior to filing can be required to repay their creditors whatever they can (as determined by a judge) over a 5-year period rather than having their debts forgiven.

At the same time, credit card companies are allowed to raise interest rates on people's credit cards if a cardholder misses a single payment—and not just on the card in question, but on any card the cardholder possesses (Kirchheimer, 2005). The past few years have clearly been very difficult for the average citizen and consumer.

The outlook for American families is beginning to look more hopeful, however. The new Democratic Congress, upon taking control of the U.S. House and Senate in 2007, immediately voted to raise the minimum wage. President Bush did not veto the change. Congressional committees in both the House and Senate began to investigate the war in Iraq and to challenge President Bush's call for an increase in troops. (Congress was not successful in preventing this move, however.) Huge compensation packages for CEOs came under investigation.

Given the enormous national debt, it is unlikely that American families will see changes that can benefit them very soon, but there is a possibility that tax breaks for the rich will be repealed in the foreseeable future, providing more resources to help the poor, the working, and the middle classes. Subservience to the producers of "guns" may give way to consideration of the need for more "butter," or meeting the human needs of ordinary American citizens.

Although 28 states have approved the addition of marriage discrimination amendments to their state constitutions since 1998, glimmers of hope are appearing in this area too. While bans against gay marriage were approved by more than 70 percent of voters in 2004, in 2006 these votes were not as overwhelming. The anti-marriage measure in South Dakota passed by only a 52–48 margin, and a ban was defeated in Arizona, the first defeat (Vives, 2007). Oregon voted to permit civil unions for gay and lesbian couples in 2007. Entrenched attitudes take time to change, but a shift may be under way.

Volunteer organizations, often assisted by grants from both governmental and nongovernmental sources, continue to work toward social justice. Important examples have been discussed previously in this chapter such as America's Second Harvest, which has been feeding hungry families, and the National Alliance for the Homeless, which has been advocating for homeless families. Pathways to Housing is another innovative nonprofit organization that provides permanent housing for homeless people regardless of mental health or substance abuse challenges; the program is spreading to hundreds of cities across the nation. Pathways' research demonstrates that providing housing to homeless people actually cuts costs to the community, largely by preventing expensive emergency hospitalization (Home at last, 2007).

The good news is that small programs can be tailored to meet specific needs of specific communities. The bad news is that such efforts are fragmented, without dependable funding, and not available to all who need them. What is needed today is a nationwide, coordinated effort to meet the basic needs of all citizens.

INTERNET SITES

http://www.aamft.org	American Academy for Marriage and Family Therapy
http://www.acf.dhhs.gov	The Administration for Children and Families
http://www.fosterparentnet.org/	The Foster Parent Net
http://www.nfpn.org	National Family Preservation Network
http://www.childrensdefense.org	The Children's Defense Fund
http://www.msa.md.gov/msa/refserv/html/afro.html	Maryland State Archives African American Resources
http://endhomelessness.org	National Alliance to End Homelessness
http://www.hungerinamerica.org	Hunger in America
http://www.cbpp.org	The Center on Budget and Policy Priorities

http://www.unicef.org/crc

http://www.foundlingmuseum.org.uk

UNICEF—Convention on the Rights of the Child

The Foundling (Hospital) Museum—London

SUMMARY

This chapter's case study describes the circumstances of LaTanya Tracy, an infant who has been left in the care of her great-grandmother. Unable to cope, the great-grandmother calls for help from her local protective services program. The case study illustrates how the problem was successfully resolved through the skilled intervention of a baccalaureate social worker, Lauren White.

The social work value of self-determination guides and challenges Lauren White in working with the Tracy family. Ms. White's primary client is an infant whose mother has become neglectful due to substance abuse. How can the value of self-determination be applied in a situation like this? The social worker skillfully finds ways to work with the mother, maximizing her self-determination and thus her cooperation, in this way best protecting the interests of the child.

A historical context is provided for family and children's services. Mutual aid among family members came first, supplemented later on an emergency basis by churches. Secular law eventually provided certain kinds of assistance, such as the categorical aids under the Elizabethan Poor Law of 1601. Formal assistance to families beyond the financial and material came even later. For example, the first protective services case was not taken to court until 1875, and then it was brought by the president of the SPCA, a private organization to help animals. Not until the 1970s did the federal government, through Title XX of the Social Security Act, require all states to provide protective services for children. Legislation requiring protective services did not mandate adequate funding, however, so many neglect and abuse cases reported today are never investigated.

It is believed that services to assist families should be offered in the least restrictive environment; the least restrictive environment for families is usually the home. In-home services available to meet special needs of children and families in the United States today include (limited) financial aid, family life education, homemaker services, day care, family therapy, protective services, and family-based services. Among out-of-home substitute services are foster care, group homes, adoption, institutional care, and the judicial system.

Research reveals that public assistance to families is decreasing in the United States and many other nations, although aid is especially limited in the United States. The possible relationship of family diversity to the curtailment of public assistance in this country is considered. Data revealing mixed results of welfare reform are discussed. Social policies and services that assist families in other industrialized countries are compared with those in the United States. Findings indicate that families in the United States receive many fewer supports than families in other industrialized nations.

Ecological issues such as pollution and global warming and their relationship to population growth are explored. Family planning policy and its impact on population growth is examined. Research finds that women limit family size voluntarily when family planning services are available along with educational and vocational opportunities. Mandatory limits in childbearing as practiced in China today have resulted in a skewed gender ratio toward males, portending future problems.

Spirituality is explored as a resource for both social workers and clients in our increasingly challenging world. A spiritual orientation is introduced as a means of developing strength in these complex and difficult times. Research demonstrating efficacy of prayer and human intention in double-blind scientific studies is introduced, along with a discussion as to why this research is largely overlooked.

Finally, trends in family policy are discussed. While family supports have been decreasing in America in recent decades, there is an indication that family issues may gain renewed attention. Among the first actions of the Democratic Congress that took office in 2007 was an increase in the minimum wage, assisting many poor Americans.

KEY TERMS

abuse, *p. 138*

children at risk, *p. 149*

gay, *p. 161*

guardian ad litem, *p. 163*

in-home services, *p. 146*

least restrictive environment,
p. 146

lesbian, *p. 161*

neglect, *p. 137*

out-of-home services, *p. 151*

permanency placement, *p. 150*

protective services, *p. 149*

sanctions, *p. 156*

self-determination, *p. 155*

spirituality, *p. 166*

DISCUSSION QUESTIONS

1. In child protective services, why are major attempts made to keep children in their own homes whenever possible and, if that is not possible, to place children in the homes of relatives?

2. Which do you think is more important, if a choice must be made: guaranteeing a child's safety by providing permanence in an adoptive home or making every effort to reunite a child with his or her biological parents? Why?

3. What types of in-home services are provided to children and families under the social welfare system? Describe each briefly. Why are in-home services generally considered preferable to out-of-home services? (Explain the concept of least restrictive environment.)

4. What types of out-of-home services are available under the American social welfare system? Describe each briefly.

5. What is the social work principle of self-determination? Where specifically is it identified as an ethical principle for social workers? How did Lauren White exercise this principle, given that her primary client was a minor under law?

6. In what year were formal public services to protect children established by federal law in the United States? By what year did all states actually provide these services? Are the services provided adequate today?

7. For how long have social workers been working with families in this country? Compare and contrast the approaches taken by the Children's Aid Society of Charles Loring Brace, Societies for the Prevention of Cruelty to Children, Charity Organization Societies, and settlement houses.

8. What factors seem to be involved in the substantial amounts of poverty found in American families today?

9. What do you think about the idea that government aid to families may have been cut to punish female heads of households and nontraditional families? Do you think this is a realistic theory? Do you think curtailing such aid to encourage traditional families is a good idea? Why or why not?

10. What family policies in other countries help prevent child and family poverty? What do you think of these policies? Why?

11. What major pieces of legislation were passed early in the Clinton administration that can help strengthen American families? What major legislation failed to pass Congress?

12. What are the major provisions of the Personal Responsibility and Work Opportunity Act? What have been some early results? Do you think this legislation will strengthen American families? Why or why not?

13. How can family-planning policies affect the wider environment, both locally and globally? What can happen if voluntary access to full family-planning services including abortion is not provided? What lessons can we learn from the situation in China today?

14. Can a spiritual orientation be of assistance to a social worker? Why or why not? To a client? Why or why not? Has science provided any evidence that there may be more to humankind than material substance?

CLASSROOM EXERCISES

While not required, it is suggested that students break into small groups of three or four to discuss these exercises. It may be helpful to choose a scribe to record and report interesting points to the class after the group discussion.

1. Think about all the families you know. About what percentage are "traditional," meaning that they include both biological parents and their children? Then think about the nontraditional families you know. How many alternative family types can you identify (single parent, separated, widowed, or divorced; single parent, never married; heterosexual unmarried couple with children; gay or lesbian couple with children; blended families with stepparents; etc.)? Identify as many as you can from the families that you know.

2. We have long had a dialogue in our nation concerning whether mothers should remain at home to care for their children. The 1996 PRWOA no longer allows poor mothers to do so. What do you think about the wisdom of this policy? What factors make it more difficult for a single mother to work outside the home as compared with a mother who has a partner? What types of supports do other Western industrialized nations provide to working single-parent families to help avoid destitution?

3. If you could improve the 1993 Family and Medical Leave Act to make it more available to all American families, what would you do?

4. What is the cost to American families of the high military budget? Which do you believe leads to a more secure nation, "guns or butter"? Why?

RESEARCH ACTIVITIES

1. Pay a personal visit to a family service agency in your city or county. Is the agency public or private (run by the government or by a voluntary organization)? If private, is it a for-profit or nonprofit agency? Find out what kind of services are offered. What do the various services cost? Are sliding fees available?

2. Interview a social worker employed by the protective services program in your area. Find out about the worker's educational background and how helpful the worker believes it was. Find out what the worker finds most challenging about his or her job. What does the worker find rewarding about the work?

3. Interview four friends to learn about their family structures, both current and in the past. How much diversity do you encounter?

4. Visit a local Head Start program, where many of the children come from disadvantaged backgrounds. If you can, interview teachers, social workers, and parents. In what ways do these different sets of people believe the program enriches the children's lives? Do you find any similarities in perspective? Any differences? What social justice issues can you identify as a result of your interviews?

INTERNET RESEARCH EXERCISES

1. A growing concern among health professionals is the influence of the worsening environment on the health and welfare of families and children. A group formed to address this concern is "The Collaborative on Health and the Environment" (http://www.healthandenvironment.org).

a. What is the mission of this organization?

b. What are some of the goals as envisioned in the area of the site entitled "CHE Vision"?

c. How does this organization break up the work on various goals and subject areas?

2. An interesting organization formed in 1985 whose mission is to promote and ensure fair, accurate, and inclusive representation of individuals and events in all media as a means of eliminating homophobia and discrimination based on gender identity and sexual orientation. The Gay and Lesbian Alliance Against Defamation (GLAAD) has a website to help achieve these goals (http://glaad.org).

   a. After reading the section "About GLAAD," what methods do you understand that this group uses to achieve its goals?

   b. What is a media resource center? Has GLAAD's media resource center been used by the media?

   c. Do you feel that this group has made progress toward achieving its stated goals?

3. An organization called "Children's Rights" appears to be quite effective in working for the improvement of child protection (http://childrensrights.org/site/PageServer?pagename-home_page).

   a. What methods does this foundation use in its advocacy work?

   b. One of this group's main issues is child fatalities. What are the two causes of death due to maltreatment?

   c. To what does the term "aging out" refer?

FOR FURTHER READING

Carter, B., & McGoldrick, M. (2005). *The expanded life cycle, individual, family and social perspectives* (3rd ed.). Boston: Allyn & Bacon.

This classic text examines life cycle issues from the perspective of the family system. It provides an in-depth analysis of the impact of culture, class, gender, and ethnicity on human development. The text also provides a scholarly assessment of the ongoing evolution of the American family, especially changes in family structure, and then provides an in-depth discussion of clinical applications for social workers.

Delgado, M., Jones, K., & Rohani, M. (2005). *Social work practice with refugee and immigrant youth.* Boston: Allyn & Bacon.

This book provides a guide for social workers who are trying to develop effective interventions with refugee and immigrant youth. It explores the unique experiences faced by these youth and provides a conceptual framework that can be utilized in social work intervention efforts. The book identifies potential forces that may facilitate or hinder the use of this framework and presents several case studies illustrating its effectiveness.

Demo, D. H., Allen, D. R., & Fine, M. (Eds.) (2000). *Handbook of family diversity.* New York: Oxford University Press.

This edited volume provides a wealth of information about diversity in American families today. The first section provides historical perspectives on family diversity. Subsequent sections discuss gender dynamics, family structure issues, racial and cultural diversity, class diversity, and applications to family social work.

Lindsay, R. (2002). *Recognizing spirituality, the interface between faith and social work.* Crawley, Western Australia: University of Western Australian Press.

This impressive little book explores the relationship between spirituality, social work education, and social work practice. It explores the concept of spirituality and traces the development of the concept; it also examines research carried out by Australian social work educators regarding spirituality and religion and its relationship to education and professional practice. The book examines models of spiritual development and develops the argument that modern spirituality presupposes certain underlying values that are compatible with social work practice.

Petit, M. R. (2007). *Homeland insecurity.* Washington, DC: Every Child Matters Education Fund. (This book can be downloaded free at www.everychildmatters.org/homelandinsecurity/)

All too important today, this book offers detailed data illustrating how anti-tax and anti-government policies place children at greater risk for low birth weight, infant mortality, premature death, child abuse, lack of health insurance, poverty, juvenile incarceration, and other distressing conditions. It also compares infant mortality and life expectancy rates in the United States with those of other nations that have more generous social welfare policies to assist the poor.

Reich, J. A. (2005) *Fixing families, parents, power, and the child welfare system*. New York: Routledge.

In a serious effort to improve child welfare services, this book examines the interactions between child welfare workers and the families they serve, exploring numerous factors that confound and disrupt communication. To provide greater understanding of these interactions, the book examines, in depth, the inner workings of several cases in the child welfare system of a particular county in northern California, involving social workers and other service providers, clients, attorneys, courts, and judges.

Samantrai, K. (2004). *Culturally competent public child welfare practice*. Pacific Grove, CA: Brooks/Cole-Thompson Learning.

This book emphasizes that professional practice does not take place in a vacuum, but requires knowledge of the culture of the client. It provides a conceptual model to assist child welfare workers to carry out their practice in the most effective manner possible. It is comprehensive in that it includes information on both child welfare policy and practice and how they interact, and presents a culturally sensitive paradigm for practice.

CHAPTER 5

SOCIAL WORK IN MENTAL HEALTH

OUTLINE

David Deerinwater

Knowledge, Values, and Skills for Mental
Health Work

Areas of Responsibility: Knowledge and Skill

Values and Integrity

Specific Knowledge Base for Mental Health

Generalist Practice with Groups and
Communities

Working with Groups in Mental Health

Community Practice

Generalist Practice in Case Management

Social Workers Respond to Disaster:
Dealing with Psychological Trauma

Acute Traumatic Stress

Posttraumatic Stress Disorder

Social Justice Issues in the Mental Health
Field

Environmental Perspectives on Mental
Health

Practice with Diverse Populations

Native American History and the
Cherokee Experience

DAVID DEERINWATER

Roberta Sholes, a BSW with several years of experience at the Oklahoma State Mental Health Center, had just returned from vacation in the eastern part of the state, where she had visited Oklahoma Indian country. Now she would be working with a newly admitted Cherokee man who was from that area. Psychiatric staffings (multidisciplinary patient care meetings) always excited Roberta's interest, but today she was especially eager to meet David Deerinwater, her new client.

Sadly, the first of the five persons discussed by the team was a young woman who was critically ill following an aspirin overdose. Next was a 55-year-old attorney who had been readmitted following an episode of frenetic behavior; he had discontinued taking the medication prescribed for his bipolar disorder. Following him were two elderly women who had been admitted with severe depression. Then the psychiatric resident who had admitted David Deerinwater began by sharing what he knew about his case.

David Deerinwater had come to Tulsa from a ranch in the Goingsnake District of Oklahoma about 10 years ago, in search of employment. Living in a series of one-room, inner-city apartments, he sustained himself with odd jobs and some janitorial service work; he had few social contacts, although he seemed to identify strongly with his tribal people. David had been living on the streets for at least 6 months and seemed to have no possessions and no family or friends in the city. Increasingly isolated, his energy seemed to decline, and he lost weight. On admission, speech was of a muttering, incoherent quality, and his gestures suggested that he might be hearing voices. David voluntarily admitted himself to the hospital through the assistance of a social worker from the hot meal site where he had obtained food for the past 6 months. The admitting diagnosis was schizophrenia, undifferentiated type, a severe form of mental illness.

As David Deerinwater was being wheeled into the staff meeting, Roberta was startled to see the cold, distant expression in his dark eyes. He stared straight ahead, completely unresponsive to the questions that were asked, yet Roberta sensed that he had some awareness of what was happening around him. After he left, it was confirmed that Roberta would be the social worker for David.

When Roberta went to see David later in the day, she found him in his wheelchair on a sun porch, staring at the trees and park area beyond the window. She was pleased when he motioned her to sit down. Remembering the quiet pride of the Cherokee men she had seen, Roberta sat beside him for a time, not speaking. After a while and without turning to her, he asked, "Well, what do you want?" It was a good sign that he acknowledged her presence, and Roberta was pleased. She explained simply that she wanted to help. He replied, "That is not possible." Roberta then introduced herself slowly and said again that she wanted to help. Several minutes passed before he replied, "Then you will help me to get out of here." Roberta told David that she would need his help for that and that she would work with him to accomplish it. She wasn't sure he heard her. He no longer seemed aware of her as he stared into the distance.

The next morning David Deerinwater greeted Roberta with an almost imperceptible wave of his hand. She again sat quietly beside him. Then, because it was a beautiful, warm day, Roberta asked David if he would like to go outdoors with her for a few minutes. For a moment his expression appeared to be one of startled disbelief. Then a somber, closed expression again came over his face, but he nodded assent. Roberta wheeled his chair outdoors and across the carefully tended lawn to the shade of the ancient catalpa trees. David inhaled deeply. He was silent, perhaps more peaceful than she had seen him previously. Roberta began telling him about the hospital, its location, its purpose (to help people get well and return to their homes), and the staff and how they worked together. Again, Roberta stressed that she would need his help, adding that she needed to understand about his life, his growing up years, his family. Again David nodded his head, acknowledging that he understood, but he added, "I am very tired now."

The following morning Roberta was surprised to find David Deerinwater waiting for her at the nurse's station. He was no longer using a wheelchair, she noted. She took him to the sun porch. Once there, he spoke: "You said that you could help me to get out of here." She replied that was just what she aimed to do, but that she wanted to be sure that he was feeling better and that he would have a place to go. He replied, haltingly, that he was eating and sleeping much better now, but he was feeling cooped up and didn't think he could stay much longer. Although he was not an easy person to interview, Roberta appreciated the quiet dignity beneath David's cool, distant gaze. She tried not to hurry him as she gently asked about his family and his experiences as a child.

Slowly and somewhat hesitatingly, over the next half hour, David gave Roberta a picture of his youth in the Goingsnake District, including memories of stomp dances (social events centering on spiritual dances), green corn feasts in the fall, and much hard work on the ranch. He spoke, too, of having been sent to boarding school with other Indian children, and of the pain he felt when teachers spoke degradingly of Cherokee Indian life and reprimanded the children for speaking in their Cherokee language. He recounted serene times with family as well as hardship and poverty. David's father had been chronically ill with diabetes and had died when David was 16. Joe, 3 years older than David, had taken on major responsibilities for his mother, David, and three younger girls. The family had relied on help from friends and neighbors and had worked their small ranch and summer garden; that was how they had survived. Roberta realized that David was beginning to develop some trust in her when he willingly signed a form giving Roberta permission to share information about him with his family and with the Health and Social Services Department of the Cherokee Nation.

Roberta had not worked with a Cherokee Indian before, and she realized that she would need to acquire a better understanding of this ethnic group before she could adequately assess David Deerinwater's situation and begin to develop a plan with him for life beyond the hospital. She placed a long-distance telephone call to the Health and Social Services Department of the Cherokee Nation and found that Dorothy White, one of the social workers in the office, knew the Deerinwater family.

Dorothy White offered to drive to their small ranch and ask David Deerinwater's mother to telephone Roberta the next day from the Cherokee Nation office because the family had no phone. She also volunteered to send Roberta information about the Cherokee Nation's services. She suggested it might be important to David's potential recovery, both physically and mentally, that he return to his home. She said she suspected that he really needed to be back with his people and in his natural environment where he would be understood and cared for by his family. Through the Cherokee Nation clinic, he could receive medical, rehabilitative, and mental health services that incorporated the beliefs and values of the Cherokees. She explained that the clinic offered group services, for example, that helped people come together to achieve harmony with each other, the community, and the natural world.

Dorothy White proved to be extremely helpful. When she called Roberta the next day, she had both David's mother and Joe (David's brother) in her office. David's mother was very eager for news about her son. She was especially concerned about David's weakness and nutritional state, and she concluded by saying, "We will bring him home. He needs to be with his people." Roberta explained that David was not yet well enough to leave the hospital and that he would have to determine for himself whether he wished to return home or remain in Tulsa. For now, however, he needed to gain strength and to continue taking his medication. David's mother replied that she knew what he would eat; she would cook for him. Then Joe Deerinwater came to the phone and said that he and his wife would drive to the city the next day. They would stay with friends and could visit David daily. They would bring food prepared by his mother. Roberta replied that she would be eager to see them.

In the days that followed, David Deerinwater benefited greatly from the visits of family members, and his nutritional status improved considerably. He also seemed to be responding well to his psychotropic medication (drugs prescribed by doctors to influence mental functioning, mood, or behavior). Although increasingly coherent, he remained isolated, interacting minimally with other patients. Roberta explained to the staff that David, like most Native Americans, did not engage readily in frivolous social conversation and would be unlikely to socialize unless he had a reason to do so. He also was probably quite frightened of the institution. Roberta had learned to adjust her own sense of time when speaking with David, and she had learned to respect periods of silence. She helped other staff communicate more effectively with him, too.

In the final staffing before discharge, the psychiatric resident described David Deerinwater's response to medication as being very good. The psychologist's summary of the psychological testing he had completed supported the early diagnosis of schizophrenia. The staff was very interested in Roberta's assessment, which included a history of David Deerinwater within the context of his family and his ethnic community and his sense of unity with nature. Roberta was not as convinced as the other team members that David Deerinwater's mental illness was as serious as the diagnostic label, schizophrenia, suggested. He was much more oriented to reality than was usual for schizophrenic patients. She explained the perspective of the Cherokee Nation health center that often behaviors that are appropriate in one culture (such as an Indian's seeing signs in birds or the sky) are considered to be very inappropriate, sometimes even to be indicators of mental illness, in another culture.

Fourteen days after admission, David Deerinwater was released. His discharge diagnosis remained schizophrenia, undifferentiated. David had decided to return home to live with his mother, but he would be receiving follow-up care from the Cherokee Nation health center, which provided a full range of mental health services, including access to tribal medicine men and spiritual healers. He could also see the vocational rehabilitation counselor at the Cherokee Nation about future employment and career options. Roberta was satisfied that David would receive social work services and health care that respected his cultural heritage.

As she said farewell to David, Roberta thought about the Cherokee people and the Deerinwater family. She realized how much she had learned from this person, his family, and community and how much they had enriched her life.[1] ■

KNOWLEDGE, VALUES, AND SKILLS FOR MENTAL HEALTH WORK

Areas of Responsibility: Knowledge and Skill

Roberta Sholes is a good example of a competent generalist BSW social worker. Take, for instance, the interviewing skills she demonstrated. She spoke quietly, gently, and slowly to David Deerinwater, helping him focus on her words. She reassured him yet confronted him with reality. Roberta's respect for the culture of the Cherokee people and the value of Cherokee family life was clearly present in her interviews with the Deerinwater family and the action she took to involve the Cherokee community in David Deerinwater's mental health care. Would this have been the approach used by David Deerinwater's psychiatrist, nurse, or other mental health professionals? Probably not, but it is uniquely consistent with social work intervention in mental health.

To prepare for a career in mental health, Roberta Sholes might have had a field placement in a mental health setting, although even if she did not, there is a good likelihood that any field placement would present opportunities to work with people who are experiencing mental or emotional problems. The courses Roberta completed for her social work major probably didn't have titles such as "therapy" or "counseling," but, as can be seen from Roberta's competence, the social work courses prepare students well for work in the mental health field. Roberta might also have taken elective courses such as abnormal psychology if she planned to seek employment in the mental health field.

BSW social workers are not expected to take responsibility for complex psychotherapy. That is the role of MSWs, and if Roberta decided that she would like to become a therapist, she would need to pursue a master's degree. The MSW curriculum, or course, has a generalist practice base, but most MSW programs provide

---

[1] Contributions to this case study were made by Dr. Wanda Priddy, former practicum program coordinator, and Dr. Dolores Poole, Northeastern State University Social Work Department, Tahlequah, Oklahoma; Delores Titchywy Sumner, Comanche tribe, assistant professor of library services, special collections librarian, John Vaughn Library/Learning Resources Center, Northeastern State University, Tahlequah, Oklahoma; Linda Ketcher Goodrich, ACSW, deputy director of the Cherokee Nation Health Service, and Beverly Patchell, RN, MS, program director, Jack Brown Center of the Cherokee Nation, Tahlequah, Oklahoma; and Isaac Christie, Malcolm Montgomery, and Jan Mowdy, Behavioral Health Unit, W.W. Hastings Hospital, Tahlequah, Oklahoma.

an opportunity to complete a concentration in mental health or clinical social work. With additional experience, MSWs can be licensed to practice psychotherapy. MSWs routinely provide individual, family, and group therapy as well as marriage counseling. They may also be found in administrative positions in mental health hospitals and clinics. In some parts of the United States where MSWs are in short supply, BSWs assist and sometimes even assume major responsibilities for therapeutic work, especially in state hospitals and with persons who have persistent and major mental disorders. BSWs, however, do not claim to be psychotherapists, and they are alert to situations that require assistance from or referral to someone with advanced expertise.

Mental health crises or emergencies are not uncommon in generalist social work practice across all possible settings; therefore, BSWs do need to have confidence in their ability to work with people with a wide range of problems. BSWs in mental health settings such as hospitals often provide crisis intervention, work with the families of patients, and counsel persons individually and in groups. They serve as the hospital's link to the community, teaching its staff about the population while at the same time offering preventive mental health education within the community.

In many community-based programs, BSWs carry important responsibilities for people who are chronically mentally ill. Dorothy White, the social worker in the Cherokee Nation's Health and Social Services Department, was also a BSW who provided advocacy, counseling, and case management services to Cherokee families. After David Deerinwater's discharge from the hospital, Dorothy or another social worker in the department would serve as his case manager. A **case manager** coordinates and ensures that all the services needed by a client (medical, financial, legal, and so on) are, in fact, provided. The case management function requires that the social worker be skilled both in working within the community and in working individually with lonely, isolated, and sometimes resistant persons. The generalist preparation of BSWs—especially their courses in practice methods and field experience—prepares them with the knowledge and skills they need for the diverse and challenging practice responsibilities they can expect to have in the mental health field.

Psychotherapy is the realm of the MSW. In the past, a social worker who was qualified to engage in psychotherapy was called a psychiatric social worker. Today the term used most often is **clinical social worker.** The NASW expects social workers who engage in private practice of psychotherapy to be recognized by the ACSW (Academy of Certified Social Workers) at a minimum. As Chapter 1 noted, the NASW also recognizes with QCSW (qualified clinical social worker) certification persons who have achieved certain standards, including 3,000 hours of clinical experience. The DCSW (diplomate in clinical social work) is reserved for advanced clinical social workers with 5 years of post-MSW clinical experience (NASW, 2007). Many states also license clinical social workers.

All social workers in mental health settings, whether BSWs or MSWs, are responsible for collecting and assessing data that contribute to the mental health team's diagnosis and understanding of individual people in relation to mental health. These social workers are responsible, too, for creating intervention plans in collaboration with people, for implementing the intervention, for monitoring and evaluating the outcomes, and for terminating relationships with clients. Knowledge of the community and its resources is one of social work's unique contributions to the mental health team. The social worker also brings to the team an understanding of social policy and its impact on programs that exist and programs still needed to prevent and treat mental illness. An understanding and sensitivity to the culture or lifestyle of diverse groups is another contribution made by social workers in mental health settings. When Roberta Sholes provided information about the Cherokee Indian culture and cautioned members of the mental health team not to assume psychosis in David Deerinwater, she was making this kind of contribution. In sharing knowledge about cultural practices, social policy issues, or even community resources, social workers continually educate others.

Values and Integrity

Knowledge and skills alone, however, do not make a good social worker. A third dimension is essential: values. Social workers demonstrate integrity when their personal values and actions are compatible with those of the profession. Professional social work values compel attention to and respect for the uniqueness and intrinsic worth of each person. Social workers empower clients and encourage them to be as self-directing as possible. They are very careful to respect privacy and confidentiality. Their professional values compel social workers to go even further. They urge social workers to work to make social institutions more humane and more responsive to people's needs. In mental health settings, these values take on special meaning. Our society tends not to respect the mentally ill, especially those who are chronically ill. Thus, social workers often have to advocate on behalf of the mentally ill. Within their communities and especially within the health care institutions that employ them, social workers attempt to create an environment that deals humanely with persons who are mentally or emotionally ill.

In this chapter's case study, Roberta Sholes demonstrated much sensitivity for David Deerinwater as a client. Her respect for his uniqueness and worth led her to learn more about Native American ethnicity. Even if she believed that returning to his home community was in David Deerinfield's best interests, she did not force this plan on him. Instead, she engaged him in making decisions about his own posthospital care. Because of Roberta's respect for confidentiality, she obtained written permission before sharing information with his family or other agencies.

Few professions stress values in the way that social work does. This is especially apparent when a social worker practices in a **secondary setting** (one in which social work is not the primary function), such as mental health. Schools and courts are other examples of secondary settings. Not only do social workers in secondary settings need conviction about their values, but they also need to acquire an understanding of the primary function of the setting that they are in. In field practicum courses and on the job, social workers learn about the organizational context in which they work.

Specific Knowledge Base for Mental Health

The settings in which social workers are employed almost always require an additional layer of knowledge and skills. Because social workers are flexible and tend to move from one area to another during their professional careers, this gives them a splendid opportunity to acquire a rich array of specialized knowledge. When they become field placement students or are employed with organizations that serve people with HIV/AIDS, or in domestic abuse settings, social workers quickly begin to learn about those specific problem areas. In secondary settings, such as school social work and health care, skills must be developed in interdisciplinary teamwork relationships.

Teamwork Relationships   The ability to work as a part of an interdisciplinary team is an important skill in the mental health field. Teamwork skills are key among the credentials sought by employers. The traditional mental health team consists of a psychiatrist, a psychologist, a psychiatric nurse, and one or more social workers. Roles overlap considerably in mental health. All team members provide psychotherapy, often as co-therapists in family and group therapy. Each team member also performs a unique function (see Exhibit 5-1). This traditional team may be supplemented by speech, recreational, art, and occupational therapists. Teachers are an added component in children's mental health programs.

In addition to direct work with the consumers of mental health services, the roles for social workers in mental health have expanded considerably to include administration of mental health programs; teaching of psychiatric residents as well as nursing and social work students; community mental health education; proposal writing and lobbying for funding; advocacy; crisis intervention; discharge planning; case management;

EXHIBIT 5-1

Social Work in Mental Health: The Traditional Mental Health Professional Team

- *Psychiatrists* prescribe medication. They hold the MD (doctor of medicine) degree and have additional training in psychiatry. Some also engage in psychotherapy.

- *Psychologists* administer and interpret psychological tests. They generally hold the PhD degree in clinical psychology, although in some areas persons with a master's degree in psychology may serve on the professional team. Clinical psychologists may provide psychotherapy as well as testing.

- *Psychiatric nurses* have training in nursing, which enables them to administer prescription medications, give injections, and assist in various other medical procedures. They generally hold a master's degree in nursing; again, however, in some regions of the country, nurses with a baccalaureate degree in nursing (BSN) serve on mental health teams.

- *Social workers* have specialized knowledge about community resources. They generally obtain the social history of a patient (a chronology of the individual's life events related to a potential mental health problem), which assists the team in arriving at a diagnosis and a treatment plan. Both BSWs and MSWs function as members of the mental health team; MSWs carry primary responsibility for psychotherapy, but both BSWs and MSWs provide counseling, facilitate groups, and provide case management.

and, of course, therapy for individuals, families, and groups. It is not surprising, then, that mental health teams often comprise several social workers but just one psychiatrist, one psychologist, and one or two nurses.

In our case study, the psychiatric facility's mental health team consisted of:

1. The chief psychiatrist, who served as team leader, conducted staffings, supervised residents, wrote prescriptions, and did some individual therapy.

2. Three psychiatric residents, who were assigned for a 6-month period. (Because they were students, they carried a limited number of cases and were under the supervision of the chief psychiatrist.)

3. Two psychiatric nurses, who administered all nursing and bedside care of patients, participated as co-therapists in group therapy, and supervised student nurses.

4. Three MSWs and one BSW, who provided individual, family, and group therapy; obtained social histories; and linked the hospital with the community.

5. One clinical psychologist, who administered and analyzed psychological tests and engaged in individual, family, and group therapy.

The mental health team in the case study was fairly typical of the teams in teaching hospitals. In hospitals that are not connected with a university medical school, the mental health team generally has no medical or nursing students and hence is much smaller. Considerable effort is required to keep a team in any setting functioning smoothly, for friction is inevitable when professional roles overlap. Team members learn quickly that they need to understand the perspectives of other professionals who make up the mental health team.

Classification and Treatment of Mental Disorders   Social workers in mental health settings clearly need an understanding of mental illness. They need to be able to use the terminology of the current psychiatric mental illness classification system. Social work students at the baccalaureate level and in master's programs are generally introduced to the classification system as part of their coursework. Becoming truly adept at its use usually occurs with employment in a mental health setting (or in substance abuse or any other settings that use the same system of classifying mental disorders). The system widely used in the United States was created by the American Psychiatric Association and is known among mental health professionals as the *Diagnostic and Statistical Manual of Mental Disorders* (DSM). The 2000 version of the manual, which is currently in use, is known as the DSM-IV-TR. It comprises five major sections called *axes*. The axes incorporate a numerical coding system that is used on hospital and insurance forms in place of lengthy descriptive terms. More than 200 specific diagnostic categories are listed under the five DSM-IV-TR axes. Exhibit 5-2 provides an abbreviated overview of the diagnostic system (American Psychiatric Association [APA], 2000). The next revision of the DSM is expected in approximately 2010. The International Classification of Diseases, referred to as ICD-10 because it is in its 10th edition, is another categorization of mental disorders. It is used by most countries outside the United States. It is almost identical to the DSM, except it gives much less attention to eating and sexual disorders.

EXHIBIT 5-2

Overview of DSM-IV-TR Classification System Using a Fictitious Case

Axis I   **Clinical Disorders**

Example: 296.23, Major Depressive Disorder, Single Episode, Severe, Without Psychotic Features

Axis II   **Personality Disorders** and **Mental Retardation**

Example: 301.6, Dependent Personality Disorder

Axis III   **General Medical Conditions**

Example: Overdose of Aspirin

[*Note:* The numerical code for general medical conditions comes from a source other than *DSM-IV-TR.*]

Axis IV   **Psychosocial and Environmental Problems**

Example: V61.1, Divorce

Axis V   **Global Assessment of Functioning**

Example: GAF52, Some danger of hurting self or others

[*Note:* The GAF number comes from the patient's score on the Global Assessment of Functioning scale.]

SOURCE: American Psychiatric Association. (2000). Examples of how to record results of a *DSM-IV-TR* multiaxial evaluation. In *Diagnostic and statistical manual of mental disorders: DSM-IV-TR* (4th ed., rev.). Washington, DC: American Psychiatric Association, p.35.

The current DSM explains that definitions of **mental disorder** are not precise. Instead, the definitions reflect behavioral patterns that occur in individuals and that cause suffering, pain, or some level of disability to the person. "Mental disorders are defined by clusters of persistent, maladaptive behaviors that are associated with personal distress, such as anxiety or depression, or with impairment of social functioning, such as job performance or personal relationships" (Oltmanns & Emery, 2007, p. 9). An understandable and culturally sanctioned behavioral response to an event (e.g., a grief response to death) is not considered a mental disorder. Behaviors considered deviant by society (religious, political, or sexual behaviors), or conflicts between individuals, are also not mental disorders unless there are symptoms of dysfunction. The DSM states clearly that it isn't people who are diagnosed; their disorders are. So it is not correct to speak of a "schizophrenic," but it is appropriate to refer to a "person with schizophrenia" (APA, 2000).

In the past decade a great deal was learned about how the human brain functions physiologically. Building on this knowledge, researchers of multiple disciplines are now exploring the impact of our biological and genetic makeup, our physical and social environments, and also our emotions and our thinking as these evolve into the human behavior that is seen by others as mental health or mental illness.

In this chapter's case study, David Deerinwater was diagnosed as having a psychosis, schizophrenia. Because cultural factors related to David's behaviors complicated the diagnosis, neither the social worker nor the Cherokee community mental health center staff were convinced that this was the correct diagnosis for David; however, they recognized that he did need treatment, especially treatment that was culturally sensitive in the way it was delivered. Culture, age, socioeconomic status, and intellectual ability are just a few of the factors that may complicate the assessment and diagnostic process. The frequent revisions of DSM, too, suggest that even the experts' understanding of psychosis is still evolving; however, **psychosis** is generally considered to be a serious form of mental illness, with schizophrenia the most serious of the eight psychoses. DSM-IV-TR suggests several slightly different ways of looking at psychosis. Its narrowest definition requires the presence of **hallucinations** or **delusions.** Delusions are disorders of thinking in which a person holds a strong but inaccurate belief about reality, often believing herself or himself to be persecuted. Hallucinations are also misperceptions of reality, often accompanied by responses to voices the person believes that she or he hears. In both cases the person's behavior may be very inappropriate. The broadest definition requires neither hallucinations nor delusions but the presence of symptoms such as disorganized speech or catatonic behaviors (e.g., immobility or peculiar movements of the limbs).

Schizophrenia is a form of psychosis that is serious but that can be successfully treated. Sadly, schizophrenia often makes its appearance in young adulthood, and it may require treatment for the remainder of the person's life. This, however, is not always the case. There are many misconceptions about this mental disorder—most commonly, that it entails one personality that has split into two or that multiple personalities have emerged out of a single personality. Although such symptoms can occur, they are not usual or necessary in order for a diagnosis of schizophrenia to be made. In fact, the characteristic symptoms of schizophrenia include:

■ Delusions.

■ Hallucinations.

■ Incoherent and very disorganized speech.

■ Grossly disorganized or catatonic behavior. (APA, 2000, pp. 297–298)

Schizophrenia is a likely diagnosis if hallucinations or delusions have been clearly present for the greater part of 1 month and present at some level in the previous 6 months.

Anxiety disorders, mood disorders, and personality disorders are also among the more prevalent mental health problems that social workers may encounter. The DSM-IV-TR classifies a large number of anxiety-related states under the heading **anxiety disorder.** Panic attack and posttraumatic stress conditions, for example, are considered anxiety disorders.

Mood disorder, as the name implies, is a category that focuses on disturbances of mood. This is a relatively new diagnostic category, one that contains both very serious as well as more minimal dysfunctions of mood. Depressive (low mood) and manic (abnormally high mood) states are represented, as well as bipolar states in which periods of both depression and mania occur. Among the **personality disorders** there are multiple subcategories as well. Examples would include the paranoid personality (characterized by pervasive suspicion and distrust of others) and the schizoid personality (where inability to form close social relationships occurs, usually coupled with emotional coldness).

In total, DSM-IV-TR presents 17 major mental disorder classifications with approximately 20 subcategories. It is anticipated that the next revision of the DSM will introduce still more mental disorders. While assessment and diagnosis are far more scientific now than in the past, they remain an imprecise procedure. The mental health professionals, MSW social workers included, who are responsible for diagnosing mental disorders must exercise great care in their assessments. BSW social workers who are employed in mental health settings, like Roberta Sholes in the case study, learn a great deal about the specific mental disorders in the course of their professional work. BSWs do not diagnose, but they are responsible for gathering data that will be combined with the information obtained by other members of the interdisciplinary mental health teams in their diagnostic work.

Diagnosis, of course, is just the beginning. Treatment of mental disorders is complex. In mental health care today, medication is widely utilized in the treatment of many of the mental disorders. Learning about some of the psychotropic medications used in treating mental illness also became a reality of Roberta's job. She found that although psychiatrists are no longer the only members of the mental health team who have the sole authority to prescribe medication, at her institution they did retain primary responsibility for writing prescriptions. All of the other team members, including social workers, needed to develop some familiarity with these medications, their uses, and their side effects so that they could be alert to possible complications. Almost all medications, Roberta found, do have some potential side effects, and some side effects are more extreme than others.

Some of the drugs that typically produce remarkably positive results in the treatment of psychosis can have negative side effects for the persons who must take them: loss of sense of balance, trouble walking, even severe emotional reactions. Sometimes the side effects are so serious that people have to be hospitalized so their medications can be changed or so additional drugs can be prescribed to suppress negative side effects. When unpleasant side effects occur, people sometimes discontinue taking their prescribed medication, and this may result in reoccurrence of the mental illness. The newer medications that have come on the market in recent years have fewer side effects than drugs previously used to treat mental disorders. They have been of significant benefit to large numbers of people. With the newer drugs, though, some people feel so well that they discontinue taking their medications. They are then at high risk of relapse. Other people are unable to afford the extraordinarily high cost of some of the newer psychotropic drugs—costs may be as much as $6,000 per month!

Among the medications used to treat some forms of mental illness are tranquilizers. Tranquilizers can be dangerous, even life threatening, if taken with alcohol. They can also create lethargy and such overwhelming sleepiness that the person has considerable difficulty holding a job or studying. The opposite effect, hyperactivity, can occur with drugs prescribed for depression. Weight gain is a less-threatening side effect. These are examples of the complexities of psychotropic medication treatment.

Social workers, however, are taking increasing responsibility for monitoring medication use by their clients. Monitoring includes education regarding use of medications for both the client and family members, who may not be well informed. Ongoing communication with the physician who has written the client's prescriptions is also a part of the social worker's monitoring function.

Some of the psychotropic drugs currently used in the medical management of mental disorder are listed in Exhibit 5-3. A list such as this cannot remain up to date for long, because breakthroughs in pharmaceutical research may result in new medications being added and older drugs dropped in just a short time. Some people

EXHIBIT 5-3

A Sample of Major Psychotropic Medications

Drug Type	Examples of Disorder Treated	Generic Name	Brand Name	Usual Daily Dosage
Antipsychotic	Schizophrenia, bipolar disorders, major depressions, organic mental disorders	chlorpromazine chlozapine fluphenazine haloperidol olanzapine risperidone aripiprazole	Thorazine Clozaril Prolixin Haldol Zyprexa Risperdal Abilify	75–900 mg 300–900 mg 2–20 mg 2–100 mg 5–20 mg 1–8 mg 15–30 mg
Antidepressant	Major depressions, dysthymia (persistent minor depression), adjustment disorders	fluoxetine sertraline paroxetine phenylzine tranylcypromine amitriptyline escitalopram imipramine	Prozac Zoloft Paxil Nardil Parnate Elavil Lexapro Tofranil	10–80 mg 50–200 mg 10–60 mg 45–90 mg 20–60 mg 75–300 mg 10–20 mg 75–300 mg
Mood Stabilizer	Bipolar disorder	lithium carbamazepine divalproex lamotrigine	Eskalith Tegretol Depakote Lamictal	400–1200 mg 300–1600 mg 750–3000 mg 100–500 mg
Antianxiety	Anxiety disorders (including panic disorders, phobias, obsessive-compulsive disorder, posttraumatic stress disorder)	alprazolam clonazepam diazepan lorazepam oxazepam chlordiazepoxide buspirone	Xanax Klonopin Valium Ativan Serax Librium Buspar	0.5–10 mg 1–6 mg 4–40 mg 1–6 mg 30–120 mg 15–100 mg 5–30 mg
Psychostimulant	Attention deficit hyperactivity disorder	dextroamphetamine methylphenidate	Dexedrine Ritalin	20–40 mg 20–40 mg

SOURCE: Based on J. N. Butcher, S. Mineka, & J. M. Hooley. (2008). *Abnormal psychology: Core concepts.* Boston: Allyn & Bacon, p. 89–90, 94–95; and F. F. Oltmanns & R. E. Emery. (2007). *Abnormal psychology* (5th ed.). Upper Saddle River, NJ: Pearson, Prentice Hall, p. 70.

today, however, are very reluctant to take prescribed medication; recently, there has been renewed interest in use of vitamins and herbs as a substitute for drug treatment of mental disorders.

Social workers, too, have ethical questions related to use of psychotropic medications, especially when they are prescribed for children. Concerns relate to the appropriateness of drugs (e.g., use of amphetamines for children), possibility for negative side effects, and the potential development of psychological dependence on drugs. There is concern that children could learn to cope with normal stresses by taking medication rather than learning healthy adaptive behaviors. When children are in foster and institutional care and in the custody of the state, there are times when social workers must make decisions on the child's behalf about medical care. These are not easy decisions, as the Up for Debate box suggests. Social workers are often in the unique position of being able to make clear to the physician the preferences and circumstances of the child's parents or the client, if the client is an adult, and to help these people understand the medical situation and available options. The social worker is the professional who "spends more time with the client and family than others on the treatment team; he or she may be best informed about their perspectives regarding medication and other interventions" (Bentley & Walsh, 2001, p. 131).

Today treatment of mental disorders often consists of a combination of medication, monitoring, various forms of psychotherapy, and patient education. The treatment programs that deliver these services have come to be known as behavioral health care. According to the Joint Commission on Accreditation of Healthcare Organizations, behavioral health care services cover a very broad area, including mental health, mental retardation, developmental disabilities, and cognitive rehabilitation

---

UP FOR DEBATE

Proposed: Medications should be used routinely to help children with Attention-Deficit/Hyperactivity Disorder (ADHD).

YES	NO
Research has shown that medications such as Ritalin have a quieting effect on hyperactive children.	There are numerous known side-effects of medication, especially Ritalin, including decreased blood flow to the brain, insomnia, and disruption of normal growth in the body, including the brain.
Medication can increase the alertness of hyperactive children at the same time it is decreasing overactivity.	The long-term effects of medicating hyperactive children are not well researched or well known.
With medication, many children with ADHD can function at an acceptable level in the classroom and progress in learning.	Medication does not cure hyperactivity.
The aggressiveness of hyperactive children is lowered through the use of medication, making them less of a threat to their siblings and classmates.	The chemical composition of Ritalin is similar to that of cocaine, and there are instances of recreational use and abuse of Ritalin by college students.

services. These may be provided during hospitalization or on an outpatient basis (Joint Commission, 1998). Hospitalization, when needed, tends to be much briefer than in the past, in part due to psychotropic medications but also due to curtailed length of stay dictated by insurance or managed care corporations. Many patients (like David Deerinwater) now remain hospitalized for only a matter of days, followed by outpatient treatment to continue psychotherapy and to monitor the medication. Monitoring is necessary because sometimes people are still too heavily medicated when they leave the hospital, and then find either they cannot function properly or they become discouraged and discontinue medication.

Hospitalization and, for that matter, even medication are not necessary for all persons who are experiencing mental health problems. Social workers are among the professionals who provide counseling and psychotherapy for individuals, families, and groups with the objective of preventing and treating mental and emotional disorders. The many ways in which social workers, including BSWs, contribute to the prevention and treatment of mental disorders are described in the next section.

GENERALIST PRACTICE WITH GROUPS AND COMMUNITIES

The David Deerinwater case study is an example of generalist social work intervention occurring simultaneously at several different systems levels: the individual client, the family, the mental health team, and the community. The primary focus of Roberta

Social work field placement student develops a contract with a new group member.

Sholes's social work service, however, was the individual client, David Deerinwater. We now examine social work in other types of mental health settings and in practice situations in which the target for intervention is not an individual but a group or a community.

Working with Groups in Mental Health

In social work, groups are used with people of all ages for providing therapy, counseling, teaching skill development, raising self esteem, and for problem solving of many kinds. The following is an example from a chapter in Gitterman and Shulman's classic social work text, *Mutual Aid Groups* (Vastola, Nierenberg, & Graham, 1994). In this example, children were referred to a mental health clinic for emotional problems that they experienced after the death of a parent or someone of considerable significance to them. Each of five children was first seen in an individual session where the group was described; all the children expressed a desire to participate.

In the first group session, the social worker asked the children to introduce themselves. She asked if anyone knew why the group was meeting; the children readily responded that it was a group for children whose parents had died. She explained in more detail how the group was planned to help kids help each other through this difficult time. She asked the group, "What do you think about being here?" Several children said that the group was a good idea. Then, spontaneously, they began to tell their own stories, identifying who had died and how it had happened. In the next weeks the children continued to work out their grief. There were several episodes of angry outbursts. In one a child cried out, "I don't want anyone talking about my grandfather. . . . I just don't want anybody saying that he died!" Other group members agreed: "Nobody really wants to talk about a person's dying, it's too hard" (Vastola et al., 1994, p. 87).

But they did talk. They also shared personal experiences, such as nightmares, that they could not discuss with anyone else. The social worker encouraged group members to bring in pictures or personal mementos. In one touching episode, a boy removed from his jeans pocket a tattered, frayed picture of a beautiful young woman—his mother when she was a teenager. The social worker was able to help this child have the picture laminated so that he could retain this treasured object. The children also had curiosity and many unanswered questions about funeral homes, autopsies, and the decomposition of human bodies. Their questions were respected, and factual information was provided. They needed to be reassured that, if their present caretaker died (one child had lost both parents and was living with an aunt), there would be someone who would care for them.

Although the children found it difficult to terminate the group at the end of 12 weeks, the social worker encouraged the children to verbalize their painful feelings about ending the group. She also helped them review what they had gained from the group and think about how they might be able to apply their newly acquired skills in the future. These children had named their group "The Lost and Found Group."

Community Practice

In addition to practice with individuals and groups, social workers seek to assist communities, at-risk populations, or organizations to promote mental health or to design programs for people with mental health problems. Examples of community practice often appear in *NASW News*, the monthly publication of the National Association of Social Workers.

Sarah Hamil, a social worker who works with child, adolescent, and family therapy, provided community education about the dynamics of bullying in an article in the *Jackson Sun*, a Tennessee newspaper. The newspaper story enabled her to explain that bullying is hazardous both to the bully and to the child who is victimized. She pointed out that bullying is not normal behavior but that this aggressive behavior may occur when children do not have other means of getting their needs met. She explained how parents can better understand and learn to deal with bullying in their child. The parents of children who are victimized by bullies also need to protect their children including providing a safety plan for them (Social work in the public eye, 2006, p. 11). Bullying has recently become a major concern for parents and for school systems. It is increasingly an issue confronting social workers in mental health, family and childrens' services, and also school social workers.

When Timothy's Law was passed by the state of New York, it ensured that many people, including children, would receive insurance coverage for mental health care at the same level as that for other forms of health care. This so-called parity law was named after Timothy O'Clair, a 12-year-old child with an emotional disorder who committed suicide. It took an enormous amount of political action before Timothy's Law was successfully passed. Social workers across New York participated in rallies, made multiple telephone calls seeking support for the legislation, and met with their state legislators. Elizabeth Clark, the executive director of NASW and former director of the New York State Chapter of NASW, wrote to Governor George Pataki urging him to sign the legislation (Pace, 2007). Social workers will continue to seek enactment of a national mental health parity law but, at least in New York State and a growing number of other states, parity with ~ insurance now exists.

As the Timothy's Law example shows, social wo
they work for change in mental health care in communi
ing consumer movement in mental health, composed p
experienced poor treatment by the mental health systei
workers. In some communities, social workers join attori
whose legal rights have been violated by illegal detainm
improper use of restraints and medication, or by inapprop

The National Association of Social Workers, represe
the United States, seeks to influence our government's
benefit vulnerable people, including people at risk of r
NASW's concern about inadequate availability of mental he
the NASW Policy Statement on Mental Health. The NAS
Exhibit 5-4.

EXHIBIT 5-4

NASW Policy Statement on Mental Health

To further improvements that have been made in the prevention, diagnosis, assessment, and treatment of mental illness, it is the position of NASW that:

■ All people in the United States, including immigrants and refugees, be entitled to a comprehensive system of person-centered mental health care, both for severe and persistent mental illness and for acute and episodic mental health problems that impair the individual's functioning.

■ Mental health treatment be provided in parity with treatment for other types of illness in all health care plans.

■ Social workers should advocate for the elimination of stigma associated with mental illness.

■ Social workers should recognize outreach services as an important part of mental health services.

■ Managed health care and other health care plans should rely on the best judgment of mental health clinicians in conjunction with consumers' judgment about the type and duration of services needed. Mechanisms for appeal of treatment decisions are needed to ensure protection of both the consumer and the provider.

■ The preventive functions of social work practice, including education, consultation, and early intervention, should be recognized and fully funded, with the goal of maximizing individual and family wellness and fostering resilience.

■ Social workers should be knowledgeable about and involved in emergency preparedness planning and policy development as well as direct intervention with the affected individuals, families, and communities.

■ [So]cial workers, in collaboration with the consumer, [shoul]d involve family members and significant [others i]n assessment and treatment planning. [Consumers] should be given choices among service [options to] meet their needs and individual

[preferences.] [Social workers sh]ould seek to maximize family [involvement, with an e]mphasis on all levels of

■ Family members should have access to supportive services to help them cope with the problems posed by the mental illness of a loved one.

■ The correctional system should not be used as a de facto mental health system. In addition, incarcerated individuals should have access to mental health services, including assessment, screening, medication, counseling, discharge planning, and referral.

■ A more integrated system of care should be developed, with an emphasis on empowerment and recovery.

■ Social workers should support a broader range of housing and vocational services to improve the quality of life, enhance independent community living, and build effective and stable interpersonal relationships.

■ Services should be fully integrated for consumers with severe mental illness and co-occurring disorders such as substance abuse and mental retardation.

■ People with substance abuse disorders and mental illness should be treated fairly in assessing functional capacity and in rendering social insurance, public assistance, and social services.

■ Social insurance and public assistance payments should be increased to a level equal to or above the federal poverty standard.

■ The efforts of people with mental illness to work should be encouraged and should not result in negative sanctions from social insurance, public assistance, or other programs.

■ The Omnibus Budget Reconciliation Act, the Americans with Disabilities Act of 1990, and related legislation should be fully enforced so that people with mental disorders can achieve full inclusion in all aspects of life in the least restrictive environment.

■ Social workers have a vital role to play in mental health research and should be encouraged to seek research funding to test their treatment methodologies and outcomes. In addition, social workers should engage in research or advocate for further research on mental health issues, with particular emphasis on traditionally underrepresented populations, including,

(Continued)

EXHIBIT 5-4 *(Concluded)*

but not limited to, children and adolescents, women, members of racial and ethnic groups, elderly people, and people with disabilities.

■ In light of the trend toward involuntary outpatient commitment, careful evaluation must be done to ensure protection of consumers' right to self-determination and safety of family members in the community.

■ Culturally responsive treatment in the most therapeutic and least restrictive environment, including use of the consumer's native language, should guide the practice of social work.

■ Social workers should take the lead in advocating for viable, comprehensive, community-based mental health services.

■ Social workers specializing in mental health should be accorded the same status as other core mental health professionals.

■ Social workers play a key role in educating the public about mental illness as a means of fostering prevention, encouraging early identification and intervention, promoting treatment, and reducing the stigma associated with mental illness. This responsibility includes efforts to influence public policy in ways that will foster improved prevention and diagnosis and promote comprehensive, continuous treatment of mental illness for all individuals who need these services and not only those who might be considered a threat to society.

SOURCE: E. C. de Silva & E. J. Clark. (2006). Mental health policy statement approved by the NASW Delegate Assembly, August 2002. *Social work speaks: National Association of Social Workers policy statements 2006–2009* (pp. 266–274). Washington, DC: NASW Press.

Another way in which social workers practice their profession within the community is through case management. Case management focuses more on work with individual people, however, and less on community change. In many mental health community support case management jobs, social workers meet with their clients out in the community: where they live, shop, visit a doctor or dentist, work, or go to school.

GENERALIST PRACTICE IN CASE MANAGEMENT

So, what would social work case management in mental health look like? To begin with, the same generalist practice, multiple-phased change process is used that was described in Chapter 2 of this book. The process begins when the social worker reaches out and seeks to engage the client, establishing a sound working relationship. At the same time, information is gathered about the nature of the mental health problem, other issues in the client's life, and the strengths that the client brings to the situation. Then, with the collaboration of the client, a plan is developed and the case management intervention implemented. Monitoring is done regularly by the social worker and client to ensure that the client's needs are being met. The case management relationship may be terminated because the client no longer needs this service, because the social worker leaves the agency and a new case manager is assigned, or because the client chooses to end the service.

Case management often, although not always, involves long-term work with people who have multiple and complex problems. In mental health work, these may be persons with severe and persistent mental illness. Some clients may be resistant. Some may have been or currently are homeless and living on the streets. Case managers seek to connect clients with needed services. At times, strong advocacy is needed to convince an organization or professional person to provide needed care. Finding a dentist who will see a 45-year-old man who has not had dental care in 25 years may not be easy. Helping the client agree to accept the needed service and keep follow-up appointments may be no easier, but accomplishing these challenges can be very rewarding.

Exhibit 5-5 provides an example of case management involving a 36-year-old Asian woman. The social worker writers of this case study point out that case management is a more comfortable fit with many Asian people than the traditional clinical service model of American outpatient mental health care. Asian people tend to view health and well-being holistically, with mental, physical, emotional, and spiritual elements inseparable. Family relationships are highly valued, and a person's self-concept is intrinsically related to her or his involvement with family. When refugees have endured war, separation from family, and political persecution before coming to the United States, they may transfer their sense of family obligation to others, especially people of their same culture, but they may be very guarded and reluctant to trust professional people or service providers. They may appreciate home visits, however, and may gradually accept help from a social worker who sustains contacts and demonstrates concretely his or her willingness to help (Eng & Balancio, 1997).

EXHIBIT 5-5

A Case Management Case Study: Sue Xiong

Sue Xiong (not the client's real last name), a 36-year-old single Cambodian woman, was referred to an outpatient mental health clinic following her third hospitalization within a year. She was unemployed, had no family, and had come to the United States 3 years previously. She was diagnosed with a bipolar disorder and had never kept the previous outpatient appointments given her on discharge from the hospital. She had also not taken any of the medications previously prescribed. She was said to be in denial about her psychiatric diagnosis but to have complaints about physical disorders.

The social work case manager who was assigned visited Sue Xiong at the hospital before discharge in order to begin the engagement, relationship-building process and to obtain information about her diagnosis and medical recommendations. It quickly became apparent to the social worker that the client believed her three hospitalizations resulted from problems associated with her menstrual cycle. She refused to accept appointments at the outpatient mental health clinic but did agree to regular home visits after the social worker volunteered to take her to a medical clinic to have her concerns about her menstrual irregularities assessed. She was also very relieved when the social worker agreed to help her apply for temporary financial assistance.

In the next 2 months, the social worker met with Sue Xiong regularly and also accompanied her to the women's health clinic and the financial aid office. She often spoke to Sue about mental health and helped her understand more about how mental health services are provided in this country. The client gradually became more comfortable and open to considering use of medication to treat the stressful mood-related symptoms she now acknowledged.

After 2 months Sue Xiong decided to come to the mental health clinic to meet with a psychiatrist. She accepted the medication that was prescribed and, with the social worker's encouragement and support, took the medication regularly. Two years after their first visit, Sue Xiong was employed, having also accepted assistance from the vocational rehabilitation service that the social worker connected her with.

SOURCE: A. Eng, & E. F. Balancio. (1997). Ch. 25, Clinical case management with Asian Americans. In E. Lee (Ed.), *Working with Asian Americans: A guide for clinicians* (pp. 400–407). New York: The Guilford Press.

Social workers at many different educational levels are involved in case management. Doctoral-level social workers may provide consultation and expert backup for case managers. MSW social workers may supervise case management programs or may provide clinical case management themselves. BSW social workers provide extensive case management services. You may recall that Chapter 1 described the NASW certifications available to BSW and MSW social work case managers, the C-ASWCM (for MSWs) and the C-SWCM (for BSWs). Other professionals—such as nurses, psychologists, and professional counselors—also provide case management services. Some organizations use persons with no academic credentials beyond a high school degree to assist professional staff or to provide case management with special populations.

Case management is just one form of intervention in mental health practice. It incorporates a great deal of counseling, advocacy, and monitoring. These and other well-honed generalist practice skills are truly put to the test when large-scale community disasters strike.

SOCIAL WORKERS RESPOND TO DISASTER: DEALING WITH PSYCHOLOGICAL TRAUMA

When disaster strikes, generalist practice skills enable social workers "to intervene immediately, actively, and directively from a client-centered, problem-focused perspective" (Gelman & Mirabito, 2005, p. 481). According to Ken Lee, social workers may be the best equipped of all mental health professionals to respond to disasters. Lee, a social worker from Hawaii and member of the American Red Cross Air Incident Response Team, is also a mental health trainer for the Red Cross. He was one of countless mental health professionals who assisted at the Ground Zero site following the terrorist attack on the World Trade Center in New York in 2001.

In an *NASW News* story (Social work in the public eye, 2002), Lee identified intervention strategies used by social workers at the time of that disaster. The immediate strategy is to provide basic needs such as food and water to victims, family members, or rescue workers. This creates a bridge that enables the social worker to touch and care for raw emotional needs. Helping people tell their story—offering affirmation, support, and encouragement—is the core of crisis intervention. Defusing, a related strategy enabling people to ventilate—to talk, cry, scream, express rage—takes "the fuse out of a potentially explosive situation" (p. 15), according to Lee. Defusing often frees people to engage with the social worker or family members in the immediate problem solving that must be done in the wake of the disaster.

Group treatment for survivors of disasters and for volunteers as well is recommended by both the American Red Cross and the Substance Abuse and Mental Health Services Administration (SAMHSA). The focus is present-centered, avoiding vivid details of the actual trauma but listening to the pain of the emotions and helping group members to support and bond with each other. Effort is made to prevent people from retraumatization through exposure to the grim details of their own or others' detailed accounts of the event, but the emotions, pain, and consequences of the experience are thoroughly validated. Energy is directed to "helping locate missing family members, providing food and water, filling out forms" (Johnstone, 2007, p. 40) for federal assistance and helping each other reconnect with family, friends, and spiritual forms of support. Whether disasters are caused by terrorist attack, shootings at a school, or natural events such as hurricanes, earthquakes, tornadoes, floods, or forest fires, social workers respond.

Acute Traumatic Stress

During and immediately following disasters, people may be subjected to overwhelming physical and psychological distress, often known as **acute traumatic stress.** Normal reactions cover a wide spectrum of behaviors. Emotionally, people may experience shock, feeling as though they are in a fog, an unreal world. They may feel numbness and have no physical pain even in the presence of profound injuries. Or they may react with terror, panic, anger and hostility, grief, or a marked sense of isolation. They may be confused and disoriented, have difficulty making decisions, experience "racing" thoughts, or replay the experience over and over again in their minds. Lee, in the *NASW News* article, described the faces of rescue workers as they reflected "pain, fatigue, and black stares" (Social work in the public eye, 2002, p. 15). Withdrawal and difficulty communicating is a common behavioral response to traumatic exposure. So is pacing, aimless walking, or an exaggerated startle response. Physical symptoms, including rapid heartbeat, stomach upset, and difficulty breathing, need prompt medical evaluation, of course (Lerner & Shelton, 2001). The stages of acute traumatic stress management are shown in Exhibit 5-6.

Posttraumatic Stress Disorder

Social workers and other mental health professionals know that immediate mental health intervention at the time of the disaster or traumatic experience may prevent or minimize the development of an enduring stress disorder. That is why the kind of crisis intervention provided by persons trained in disaster work, like Hawaiian social worker Ken Lee, is so critical in the first hours following a disaster. When the symptoms listed earlier last beyond a month, however, or depression or intense anxiety persist, the person should be evaluated for possible **posttraumatic stress disorder (PTSD).** According to the National Institute of Mental Health, "most people with PTSD try to avoid any reminders or thoughts of the ordeal" that they experienced (NIMH, 2001, p. 1). Unless it is treated, PTSD may impair children as well as adults, making it nearly impossible for them to study, work, sustain parenting responsibilities, or even maintain self-care.

People recover from trauma in their own time, using their own strengths and with the support of their family, friends, and community. Life may never be the same again, especially if there has been a death or permanent disability. Many people, however, do survive disasters, and there are even people who actually grow and thrive as a result of their experience. In the weeks that follow the traumatic experience, there is first a period of disorganization with depression and anger and then a period of reorganization when new patterns for functioning evolve and new relationships are built (Lerner & Shelton, 2001).

EXHIBIT 5-6

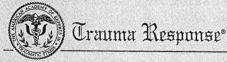 Trauma Response®

PRODUCED AS A PUBLIC SERVICE OF
THE AMERICAN ACADEMY OF EXPERTS IN TRAUMATIC STRESS, INC.
368 VETERANS MEMORIAL HIGHWAY, COMMACK, NEW YORK 11725
TEL. (631) 543-2217 • FAX (631) 543-8977
WWW.ATSM.ORG • WWW.TRAUMATIC-STRESS.ORG • WWW.AAETS.ORG

 *Infosheet*™

How Do People Respond *During* Traumatic Exposure?

Reprinted from *Acute Traumatic Stress Management*™
by Mark D. Lerner, Ph.D. and Raymond D. Shelton, Ph.D.
© 2001 by The American Academy of Experts in Traumatic Stress, Inc.

The following emotional, cognitive, behavioral and physiological reactions are often experienced by people *during* a traumatic event. It is important to recognize that these reactions do not necessarily represent an unhealthy or maladaptive response. Rather, they may be viewed as *normal* responses to an *abnormal* event. When these reactions are experienced in the future (i.e., weeks, months or even years after the event), are joined by other symptoms (e.g., recurrent distressing dreams, "flashbacks," avoidance behaviors, etc.), and interfere with social, occupational or other important areas of functioning, a psychiatric disorder may be in evidence. These individuals should pursue help with a mental health professional.

Emotional Responses during a traumatic event may include *shock*, in which the individual may present a highly anxious, active response or perhaps a seemingly stunned, emotionally-numb response. He may describe feeling as though he is "in a fog." He may exhibit *denial*, in which there is an inability to acknowledge the impact of the situation or perhaps, that the situation has occurred. He may evidence *dissociation*, in which he may seem dazed and apathetic, and he may express feelings of unreality. Other frequently observed acute emotional responses may include panic, fear, intense feelings of aloneness, hopelessness, helplessness, emptiness, uncertainty, horror, terror, anger, hostility, irritability, depression, grief and feelings of guilt.

Cognitive Responses to traumatic exposure are often reflected in impaired concentration, confusion, disorientation, difficulty in making a decision, a short attention span, suggestibility, vulnerability, forgetfulness, self-blame, blaming others, lowered self-efficacy, thoughts of losing control, hypervigilance, and perseverative thoughts of the traumatic event. For example, upon extrication of a survivor from an automobile accident, he may cognitively still "be in" the automobile "playing the tape" of the accident over and over in his mind.

Behavioral Responses in the face of a traumatic event may include withdrawal, "spacing-out," non-communication, changes in speech patterns, regressive behaviors, erratic movements, impulsivity, a reluctance to abandon property, seemingly aimless walking, pacing, an inability to sit still, an exaggerated startle response and antisocial behaviors.

Physiological Responses may include rapid heart beat, elevated blood pressure, difficulty breathing*, shock symptoms*, chest pains*, cardiac palpitations*, muscle tension and pains, fatigue, fainting, flushed face, pale appearance, chills, cold clammy skin, increased sweating, thirst, dizziness, vertigo, hyperventilation, headaches, grinding of teeth, twitches and gastrointestinal upset.

*Require immediate medical evaluation

SOURCE: M. D. Lerner & R. D. Shelton (2001). *Acute traumatic stress management*. The American Academy of Experts in Traumatic Stress, Inc. Reprinted at http://www.aaets.org and retrieved September 29, 2001.

Posttraumatic stress disorder, if it occurs, can be treated through individual or family counseling, or with group therapy. Some therapeutic models focus on helping the person cognitively, by increasing their intellectual comprehension of the experience and their reaction to it. Behavioral methods seek to change ineffective responses to behaviors that strengthen the person's ability to cope. Medication is sometimes used in conjunction with counseling. Social workers tend to use a holistic approach that identifies strengths in the person and connects people with others who can help: family members, friends, and co-workers. Spiritual beliefs are another source of support that is valued. Referrals are made to community resources if appropriate.

Mental health treatment for posttraumatic stress disorder or for any other mental health problem is much like treatment for a physical ailment. It can be taken care of very quickly in some cases, or it may require ongoing care and monitoring. Injustice at several levels, however, can sabotage mental health care.

SOCIAL JUSTICE ISSUES IN THE MENTAL HEALTH FIELD

Social justice concerns abound in the field of mental health. The very diagnostic labels described earlier may cause damage. To label someone as schizophrenic, for example, can be very damaging; a person so labeled is expected to perform (or not to perform) in a specific, predetermined manner. When this label is known to hospital or clinic staff, schools, correctional facilities, employers, or other organizations, other people are likely to assume or to anticipate the expected behaviors. Political careers or administrative promotions can be jeopardized if it is discovered that a person was ever labeled, correctly or incorrectly, with a psychiatric diagnosis. Diagnostic labels can follow a person for life. Although medical information is supposedly confidential, private, and protected by law, in reality it is remarkably available to a large number of persons the client has never even seen. A child's school record, for example, is passed from one teacher to another, complete with psychological evaluations. Medical records are handled not only by doctors, nurses, and therapists of many kinds, but also by clerks, aides, medical records personnel, and insurance staff.

Persons with psychiatric labels may be stereotyped or subjected to bias by others, but something even more devastating may occur when people begin to define themselves by a label. Sometimes, even when people do not know their specific diagnosis, they do understand that they have been labeled with some kind of mental problem. Because of the stereotyping and discriminatory attitudes of society, this knowledge may be devastating! It certainly does not create positive self-regard, nor does it promote motivation to engage in treatment.

Social workers Herb Kutchins and Stuart Kirk have been studying the *Diagnostic and Statistical Manual* over many years and through several of its revisions (Anello, Kirk, & Kutchins, 1992; Kirk & Kutchins, 1992; Kutchins & Kirk, 1989). Their book, *Making Us Crazy: DSM—The Psychiatric Bible and the Creation of Mental Disorders* (1997), attracted national attention with its critique of the DSM-IV. In this book, Kutchins and Kirk severely criticize the ever-lengthening list of mental disorders that may be used to label human behavior. They report that this growing list serves the insurance industry but stigmatizes people whose problems are those of daily living, of coping with the stresses of life, not true medical situations. With DSM-V on the horizon, the expectation is that this next version of the manual for diagnosing mental disorders will only further expand the number of recognized forms of mental illness.

Another perspective on social justice and mental health relates to the inadequacy of treatment resources for persons who lack financial resources—possibly as a result of their mental health problem. Reflecting on the presence of high levels of mental illness among people who live on the streets, Ezra Susser, noted psychiatrist and epidemiologist, remarked: "I don't think we would allow people with multiple sclerosis to live in the streets. It wouldn't be morally acceptable. So why is it acceptable for people with disabling mental illnesses to live in such conditions?" (as cited in Wortsman, 2006, para. 11). For most social workers, the inhumane living conditions of homeless persons, especially people with chronic mental illness, is unjust.

Equally unjust is the disparity in access to mental health care experienced by racial and ethnic minorities that was so carefully documented in the 2001 report of the Surgeon General of the United States, David Satcher in the report, *Mental Health Culture, Race, and Ethnicity* (U.S. Department of Health and Human Services, 2001). The research of Satcher and others (Cunningham & Freiman, 1997; Wells, Klap, Koike, & Sherbourne, 2001) consistently points to inability to obtain needed care as well as poor or inadequate care when it was available. Some examples of poor quality care include decreased likelihood of appropriate prescription medication provided to African Americans with depression, when compared with Whites, and failure to recommend continued outpatient care. These research findings persisted even when factors such as income and age were taken into account.

Social workers, among others, seek to change social policy and provide programs that will ensure a reasonable standard of living and access to mental health services to homeless persons and all persons in need of care. The NASW Policy Statement on Mental Health, shown earlier in Exhibit 5-4, clearly states the profession's commitment to the development of resources that provide not only treatment in the least restrictive environment but also housing, vocational services, educational opportunities, and other services that maximize wellness and encourage resilience (de Silva & Clark, 2006).

ENVIRONMENTAL PERSPECTIVES ON MENTAL HEALTH

It is not difficult to imagine how their unsafe and hazardous environments put mentally ill persons living on the streets at great risk of physical health problems, rape, and criminal victimization. While untreated mental health problems may create behaviors that alienate people from their families and leave them homeless, the sometimes toxic environmental context of homelessness can exacerbate existing mental health problems. Not surprisingly, homelessness may precipitate emotional crises as well.

As social workers trained in an environmental perspective, we cannot ignore the physical surroundings of the people we serve. The environmental context is increasingly a focus for mental health practitioners as well as social planners. Environmental degradation affects the physical well-being and also the mental health of people around the globe. Mental health practitioners have learned to respond to the long-term emotional needs of victims of nuclear accidents, such as in Chernobyl, and to the trauma created by industrial accidents, war, and natural disasters as well as toxic physical and social environments.

The World Health Organization report, *Quantifying Environmental Health Impacts* (2007), described mental health and behavioral risks that are linked globally to environment. Suicide, for example, was shown to be linked to work-related stress and stress stemming from degraded environments. Environmental factors varying from country to country were shown to affect access to the means used by people to commit suicide. These ranged from ingestion of pesticides in Trinidad, Sri Lanka, and Malaysia to use of charcoal fumes in China and gunshot in the United States. "Globally, an average of 30% (22–37%) of all suicides were attributable to the environment" (p. 54). The report noted that lives could be saved by improving chemical safety and limiting access to guns. Similarly, interpersonal violence could be reduced globally by reducing access to firearms and improving street lighting. The report also found depression to be linked to occupational stress, some Parkinson disease was linked to exposure to chemicals, and some forms of mental retardation were associated with lead poisoning.

Epidemiologists, persons who study occurrence and distribution of a disease within a population, increasingly look at risk factors occurring at multiple levels—for example, looking at early brain development, at the life course of the disease within an individual, and looking at the macro level of the community or society. Schizophrenia has been linked to genetic impact on brain development prior to birth. In many persons, schizophrenia is also known to lie dormant during childhood, only to appear in late adolescence or early adulthood. Recently, scientists have discovered clues to societal level influences on the development of this disease. The relatively high incidence of schizophrenia among Afro-Caribbeans who immigrated to the United Kingdom and Moroccan immigrants to the Netherlands intrigued epidemiologists, especially when it

Without needed medication or consistent medical health care, persons with serious and persistent mental health problems may be forced to live on the streets in precarious circumstances.

was found that second-generation persons of these groups born in Europe had an even higher rate of the disease. "Currently, the pattern of results across numerous studies suggests that the social experience of discrimination contributes to this high incidence" (Susser, Schwartz, Morabia, & Bromet, 2006, p. 419).

Can social workers avoid the messages inherent in this research? If social workers are committed to advocating for change, fairness, and an end to discrimination and inequality, then environmental issues must become significant in our work in the mental health field. While we can provide counseling and psychotherapy for individuals, families, and groups, we must also focus our skills on changing the societal factors that affect access to care, quality of care, and nature of the environment in which we live. In other words, we will become much more knowledgeable about and actively involved in the social policies and legislation that affect mental health.

PRACTICE WITH DIVERSE POPULATIONS

Commitment to social justice and increasing appreciation of both the physical and social environment has enriched social workers' valuing of human diversity. Unfortunately, in the past social workers and other mental health professionals have not always been very sensitive to ethnic differences in the people they serve. Today, however, social work education is seeking to prepare students to work with an increasingly wide range of populations in ways that will empower individuals and their communities and will safeguard the integrity of family life, as it is defined by diverse populations. This concept, referred to as cultural competence, was introduced in Chapter 3 of this text, but it is a theme that is repeated throughout the book.

Cultural competence involves knowledge of the history and patterns of oppression experienced by cultural and ethnic groups, the traditions, and the values of those groups. It requires appreciation for differences in cultures. Cultural competence includes, first, the "development of academic and professional expertise and skills in the area of working with culturally diverse populations" (Lum, 1999, p. 3), then putting that knowledge into actions that will generate social change and lead to realization of social justice (Lum, 2007). In this process, social workers need to look carefully at their own ethnic and cultural backgrounds. Because many of us as social workers come from backgrounds with mixes of culture, race, socioeconomic status, spirituality, and other forms of diversity, looking at our own ethnic identity is definitely not easily done. Yet our appearance, the way we talk, and the way we present ourselves immediately convey messages more powerful than we know to clients of contrasting cultures and backgrounds. If we are to begin to develop skill in utilizing culturally appropriate interventions, we do need to build self-awareness and appreciate our own uniqueness as well as that of each individual client. Social work researchers such as John Red Horse provide guidelines that aid our understanding of the intensity and the differences in our own and our clients' identification with cultural roots.

Many years ago, John Red Horse (1988) classified Native American families along a spectrum from traditional to panrenaissance. Family members in a *traditional* family, he explained, use their native language in the home and community, practice the native religion, and sustain tribal beliefs regarding disease. These families rely on traditional rituals and ceremonies to rid them of mental and physical illness and to bring their minds and bodies back into harmony with the spiritual world and the universe. One step from traditional families is *neotraditional* families, in which some members use the English language and have adopted new rituals and spiritual healers; most family members, however, retain traditional beliefs. The *transitional* family uses English in the community but speaks the native language at home. Traditional beliefs are retained, but family members often travel a considerable distance back to the homeland to participate in religious and ceremonial rituals; these family members gradually begin to use contemporary American health care. *Bicultural* families speak English and retain traditional beliefs in the Great Spirit but begin to adopt some non-Indian spiritual beliefs. American health care systems are used, but family members prefer Native American health care services that are parallel to those in the larger community. *Acculturated* families have lost their native language, religion, and often even their extended kinship system; they rely on American contemporary health care systems. Finally, *panrenaissance* families seek to renew their native language fluency and to revitalize some aspects of the traditional religion. Some members of these families are very critical of American health care systems and actively pursue the expansion of all-Indian parallel health care services that respect traditional beliefs and practices.

Incorporating these understandings into interviews—along with warmth, empathy, and respect—takes time to learn but will become a part of every student's professional preparation for a career in social work. Classroom role-plays of interviews plus actual experience in fieldwork are just the beginning of cultural competence, which is acquired over a professional lifetime.

In the David Deerinwater case at the beginning of this chapter, Roberta Sholes demonstrated sensitivity throughout her work with the client, his family, and the Cherokee community. The result was that Mr. Deerinwater was reunited with his family, and he gained access to a whole set of support networks that would perhaps otherwise not have been available to him. Roberta's newly gained knowledge of Cherokee history, beliefs, traditions, even food preferences helped other members of the hospital's mental health team to understand this client and others like him. Perhaps it also helped to humanize the institution, resulting in increased respect and social justice for future Native American clients.

NATIVE AMERICAN HISTORY AND THE CHEROKEE EXPERIENCE

Roberta Sholes's respect for the Cherokee people grew as she researched the history of Native American people in the United States and, more specifically, the Cherokee Nation. Aware that Native Americans, also known as **First Nations People,** were the first Americans, Roberta found that scientists now believe that the ancestors of today's Native Americans probably migrated across the Bering Strait from Asia. By the time the first Europeans arrived, there were approximately 1.5 million native peoples thriving in North America, representing a wide variety of tribal groups, customs, and languages (Lum, 1992).

For Native Americans the coming of the Europeans was a catastrophe. Europeans immigrated in massive numbers, dangerously armed with the power of the gun and bringing new diseases that decimated many Indian populations. They drove the Indians from their lands and frequently massacred those who resisted. This genocide is depicted in the story of the Cherokee's Trail of Tears, written by Wilma Mankiller (Mankiller & Wallis, 1993), a social worker and also the first woman to hold the position of principal chief of the Cherokee Nation. According to Mankiller, Cherokee people had long been living in the Great Smoky Mountain region when European settlers arrived on the coast of the United States. The Cherokees developed remarkably advanced communities, attaining wealth through their farms and plantations as well as commercial trading contracts with merchants in European countries. The discovery of gold on Cherokee land in Georgia ultimately led to broken treaties with the U.S. government and to President Andrew Jackson's order for removal of the Cherokee people to western lands. In 1835, 7,000 federal soldiers arrived; they rounded up Cherokee families, held them in stockades, and then forced them westward at gunpoint for the historic Trail of Tears. It is believed that of the 18,000 persons forcibly removed, approximately 4,000 died. According to Wilma Mankiller:

> Old ones and small children were placed in wagons, but many of the Cherokees made that trek by foot or were herded onto boats. Some were in shackles. Thousands perished or were forever scarred in body, mind, and soul. It was not a friendly removal. It was ugly and unwarranted. For too many Cherokees, it was deadly. The worse part of our holocaust was that it also meant the continued loss of tribal knowledge and traditions. (Mankiller & Wallis, 1993, p. 47)

The first winter in Oklahoma resulted in additional deaths from starvation and freezing. By 1839, however, homes were built and communities established. A new constitution was written, and Tahlequah was established as the Cherokee capital. Always respectful of education, the Cherokee Nation created a public school system by 1841, and in 1851 male and female seminaries were established for higher education. The strong work ethic and tribal pride of the Cherokees resulted in the rapid development of commerce, farms, government, and a judicial system. In 1862, during the Civil War, Cherokee land was invaded and taken by the Union Army. War destroyed ranches, homes, and the Cherokee economy. Following the Civil War, which ended in 1865, Congress decreed that all Indians were wards of the government; no tribal sovereignty would be honored, regardless of previous treaties. Native Americans were then confined to reservations. In the 1870s railroad expansion brought homesteaders from the East. Despite the protest of Indians, the federal government sold previously protected Indian Territory to white settlers.

The General Allotment Act (the Dawes Act) of 1887 dealt a severe blow to Indian territories across the United States. The act provided private ownership of parcels of former reservation land—allotments—to individual Indians, with the remaining lands reverting to the U.S. government for homesteading or other purposes. Many Cherokees unknowingly sold their parcels of land for little or nothing and were left destitute. The Dawes Act dispossessed Indians in Oklahoma and across the country of nearly all their holdings. The next blow to Indian independence and self-rule came in 1898 with passage of the Curtis Act, which ended tribal courts as of that year and tribal government by 1906.

Beginning in the early 1900s additional efforts were made to destroy Native American culture. Children were forced to attend white boarding schools far from their reservations. They were forbidden to speak their own languages or to honor their own religious traditions. This practice continued into very recent times. It was only in 1924 that Native Americans were finally granted full U.S. citizenship.

In 1934, the Indian Reorganization Act signaled a change in U.S. policy. Providing for the reestablishment of tribal governments, it was strongly supported by John Collier, a former social worker and President Franklin D. Roosevelt's appointee as head of the Bureau of Indian Affairs. Collier was a crusader for the welfare of Native Americans. The Cherokee and many other Indian tribes were able to regroup and rebuild their governmental structures and communities under the provisions of the Indian Reorganization Act.

The history of the Cherokee Nation reflects the history of Native American people generally. All shared common experiences of broken treaties and harsh treatment from the U.S. government. All tribes today continue to struggle with poverty; discrimination by the majority society persists. Despite this, there are vast differences among Native American people today. The U.S. 2000 Census identified 4.1 million Native Americans, representing approximately 500 different nations or tribes. Some Indian nations are quite small, with fewer than 100 members, while others may have in excess of 100,000 members. Some have very large land holdings, with families often living in isolated rural areas, while others, such as the Cayuga of New York, have no actual land holdings at all. "These nations differ in terms of language, religion, social structure, political structure, and many other aspects of their cultures" (Lum, 2007, p. 256).

The former Cherokee Female Seminary now houses faculty offices and classrooms, including those of the Northeastern State University (Oklahoma) Social Work Program.

While Indian leaders such as Wilma Mankiller have engendered increasing self-respect and pride among native people, the historical tearing of family structures that resulted from the Trail of Tears and all other Indian removal programs is only now beginning to be addressed. Treatment programs—especially in Indian mental health and substance abuse programs—promote Native American intergenerational healing by focusing on both the strong survival skills and the unhealthy coping behaviors that people used when faced with a hostile environment. Although the history of broken treaties and oppression of Native American people goes back many years, it has links to our time. Maria Yellow Horse Brave Heart, a social work practitioner and educator, is another respected authority on Native American history of trauma. Writing as a Native person herself, she reports that almost all Indian families today include someone who was humiliated and traumatized by Indian boarding schools or who lost family members—generally children—taken by Indian agents or social workers, sometimes even given over by parents for adoption into non-Indian homes to avoid overwhelming poverty (2004). In her work she frequently deals with the unresolved grief and historical trauma of Native people. Clearly, much healing remains to be done because the scars remain deep and painful.

MENTAL HEALTH POLICY AND SOCIAL WORK PRACTICE: HISTORICAL PERSPECTIVES

As social workers today attempt to help people heal from many kinds of traumatic experiences and provide services to diverse populations with complex mental health needs, they do so within the context of governmental policy that creates or limits access to mental health programs. Sometimes it is really difficult to understand government policy and a societal climate that fails to provide care. Unfortunately, attitudes toward mental illness today still reflect the mixture of repulsion, fear, and even amusement with which the mentally ill were regarded for centuries. But progress has been made both in our understanding of and attitudes toward mental illness and in our professional technologies for treating it.

Gradual Enlightenment

To understand the mental health system in the United States today, we must look back to its roots. The colonists who first came to the United States from European countries brought with them attitudes that were harsh and notions about caring for the mentally ill that stressed containment and coercion, whips, and chains. The first state hospital for the mentally ill in the United States was opened in Williamsburg, Virginia, in 1773. Before this, the mentally ill were cared for by their families or in poorhouses (almshouses) that also provided for poor people, people with tuberculosis and other contagious diseases, and persons with physical or cognitive disabilities.

Almost simultaneously in the United States and Europe during the late 1700s and early 1800s, leaders emerged whose reform activities produced a shift in societal attitudes toward mentally ill persons. In Paris, Phillipe Pinel, a physician, attracted

Dorothea Lynde Dix: pioneer social reformer in the field of mental health.

public attention in 1779 when he struck off the chains of the mentally ill men at Bicêtre, a "lunatic asylum." A Quaker religious community in York, England, provided funds to William Tuke to develop an institution for the humane treatment of mentally ill persons (no chains were permitted). In the United States, Dr. Benjamin Rush, a physician and one of the signers of the Declaration of Independence, instituted many reforms at Pennsylvania Hospital; he also wrote the first American text on psychiatry.

A Courageous Researcher and Reformer: Dorothea Dix

The most famous reformer, however, was Dorothea Lynde Dix, an activist and reformer whose work in the mid-1800s brought attention to the inhumane treatment of the mentally ill in the United States. A schoolteacher, Dix volunteered to teach a Sunday school class at the East Cambridge women's jail near Boston in 1841. Here she discovered that it had become common practice to place mentally ill poor people in prisons. She was horrified by the inhumane conditions in which they were kept, and she felt compelled to do something about it. Dix's well-trained mind told her that only carefully conducted research to document the conditions of the mentally ill would elicit the attention of public officials. Accordingly, she set about visiting every jail, prison, and almshouse in Massachusetts. The following description of her visit to a Saugus, Massachusetts, poorhouse one Christmas Eve is characteristic of what she uncovered:

> They ascended a low flight of stairs into an entry, entered a room completely unfurnished, no chair, table, bed. It was cold, very cold. Her conductor threw open a window, a measure imperative for the digestive stability of a visitor. On the floor sat a woman, her limbs immovably contracted, knees brought upward to the

chin, face concealed, head resting on folded arms, body clothed with what looked like fragments of many discarded garments. They gave little protection, for she was constantly shuddering.

"Can she not change positions?" inquired Dorothea. No, the contraction of her limbs was caused by "neglect and exposure in former years," before, it was inferred, she came under the charge of her present guardians.

"Her bed." As they left the room the man pointed to an object about three feet long and from a half to three-quarters of a yard wide, made of old ticking and containing perhaps a full handful of hay. "We throw some blankets over her at night." (Wilson, 1975, pp. 109–110)

Dix systematically recorded her findings: a woman kept in a cage; another fastened to a stone wall with chains; a man whose feet had been damaged by frostbite who was kept in a box; many mentally ill persons kept in woodsheds without light, heat, or sanitation. The dates, places, and details of her investigations were all documented in a 30-page report that was presented to the Massachusetts legislature in January 1843. According to one biographer, on reading the report, the legislature "exploded like a bombshell. Years later a commentator would refer to it as 'the greatest sensation produced in the Massachusetts legislature since 1775.' Another would call her investigation 'the first piece of social research ever conducted in America'" (Wilson, 1975, p. 124). Legislation authorizing the building of hospitals to treat persons with mental illness was passed in Massachusetts as a result of Dix's investigations, but her work was not done.

Despite ill health, Dix traveled throughout the United States and Canada, continuing her research and reporting on inhumane treatment of people with mental illness. Through her efforts, the Canadian government authorized construction of a new mental hospital for western Canada, and the Kentucky legislature approved construction of a new wing for an existing hospital in Lexington. Illinois, Tennessee, and many other states appropriated funds for hospitals. Because many states were either unwilling or unable to finance hospitals for the mentally ill, Dorothea Dix decided to go to the federal government for help. Through her tireless efforts, a bill was passed by Congress that would have permitted funds from the federal government's sale of western lands to be used to care for the mentally ill, but President Franklin Pierce vetoed the bill in 1854.

Unfortunately, the new state hospitals—founded on the principle of humane treatment—soon deteriorated, causing alarm for Dix and her followers. Mental hospitals became dumping grounds for society's problems. For example, hospital wards were filled with immigrants, and anti-foreign sentiment defined institutional policy. The foreign-born were housed separately from nonimmigrants and often in inferior quarters. African American people—in those states that even admitted them to state hospitals—were also segregated. By 1900 conditions in state hospitals were investigated and were vividly described in news articles. Across the country, reformers, inspired by the earlier work of Dorothea Dix, demanded strict guidelines for the proper care of the mentally ill.

In 1908 Clifford Beers's book, *A Mind That Found Itself*, captured a more receptive public than might have been the case had it not been for the work of Dorothea Dix, Benjamin Rush, and others. The book told the author's personal story. Beers, a

Yale University graduate, suffered a mental breakdown and endured years of inhumane treatment in both private and state facilities. He eloquently described what he saw and heard from attendants and others, even when he was severely ill and in a catatonic state. The book aroused the interest of the public as well as professional people. Beers subsequently founded the Connecticut Society for Mental Hygiene and assisted in the development of the national and international mental hygiene movement, which advocated for federal government intervention in the problem of mental illness.

The Past 100 Years

The Social Work Profession Emerges   Even in the earliest days of the profession, the early 1900s, social work pioneers were involved in mental health work. In 1907, Mary Antoinette Cannon was hired by Massachusetts General Hospital to work with mentally ill patients. She was the first social worker to enter this field of practice. Mary Jarrett was employed in 1913 as the first director of social services at the Boston Psychopathic Hospital, where she is said to have coined the term *psychiatric social worker.* Soon social workers began to be routinely hired by hospitals and clinics to provide therapy.

Social casework, emerging from the work of the Charity Organization Society, was the primary social work method in the mental health field. The pivotal work done by Mary Richmond, the founder of social casework, in her seminal texts, *Social Diagnosis* (1917) and *What Is Social Casework?* (1922), demonstrated the strong relationship between poverty and the mental health, personality development, and well-being of social work clients.

World War I, from 1914 to 1918, resulted in battle casualties that were psychological as well as physical. *Shell shock* was the term used to describe psychiatric problems created by war experiences. Mental health staff, including social workers, was needed. Recognizing the need for social workers trained to work with psychiatric disorders, Mary Jarrett initiated a specialized psychiatric social work training program in 1918 at what is now the Smith College School for Social Work.

Sigmund Freud's writings were introduced into the United States in the early 1900s, and by the 1920s, Freudian theory was well accepted as the most useful approach to the treatment of mental illness. Freud taught that mental illness derived from unresolved conflicts and that patients could best be helped by remembering and discussing early events, even dreams, with a trained person. As Freudian theory was popularized in the 1920s and 1930s, public and private mental clinics began hiring many social workers to provide psychotherapy. These were still the early years of the profession, and the mental health movement gave the profession of social work a real boost. Social workers became valued parts of mental health treatment teams.

The demand for social workers to staff the clinics and hospitals spurred growth of the profession. The American Association of Psychiatric Social Workers, founded in 1926, became a strong force within the profession. In 1955 it merged with other specialized social work organizations to form the National Association of Social Workers.

Bertha Capen Reynolds was one of many social workers who provided leadership in the field of mental health practice. This feisty intellectual, clinical social worker, and educator is also remembered for her social activism, strong support for labor unions, and critique of capitalism. In her work and in her writing, Reynolds was committed to fighting against wars, oppression, and human degradation. Her thinking was influenced by Christianity, Marxism, and Freudian theory. Her books, *Between Client and Community* (1934), *Learning and Teaching in the Practice of Social Work* (1942), and *Social Work and Social Living* (1935) reflect her understanding of the need for social workers to meet psychological and emotional needs of clients and families while at the same time devoting energy to social change efforts in communities and society. Bertha Capen Reynolds is remembered as a leader in progressive social work.

The first book on child psychotherapy, *The Dynamics of Therapy in a Controlled Relationship* (1933), written by Jessie Taft, was based on her experiences with a social work agency, the Children's Aid Society in Pennsylvania. Taft, a psychologist, was strongly influenced by the psychoanalytic work of Otto Rank, and she brought his theoretical base to her teaching at the Pennsylvania School of Social Work. Taft and Virginia Robinson, a social worker on the school's faculty, developed what came to be known as the functional school of social work. Use of time and time-limited casework was a major focus of functional theory, thus making the functional school a precursor of modern-day brief, or time-limited, therapy.

When World War II began in 1939, officer-level positions for psychiatric social workers were created by the army, and social workers functioned on military neuropsychiatric teams. During the war, approximately 1 million patients with neuropsychiatric disorders were admitted to U.S. Army hospitals (Callicutt, 1987). This resulted in an expansion of psychiatric social services, especially group work, for the military and their families. By the end of the war, in 1945, the military services and the Veterans Administration hospitals had become the largest employers of professional social workers (Leiby, 1987).

Evolving Social Policy Affects Service in Mental Health The first major piece of mental health legislation passed by the U.S. government was the National Mental Health Act of 1946. The act provided federal funding for research, training, and demonstration projects to help the states develop programs for the prevention and treatment of mental illness. The act set the stage for the creation of the National Institute of Mental Health (NIMH) in 1949. The leadership and authority of this federal organization came to be well recognized, and it had a major impact on the development of state mental health programs.

During the 1950s, social work continued its growth in the mental health field. Within the profession itself, social casework dominated practice from the 1940s through the 1960s. Prominent among the theorists and writers were Helen Harris Perlman, whose book, *Casework: A Problem-Solving Process* (1957), integrated the theories of the functional school (Taft and Robinson) and the diagnostic approach (Hamilton), and those of Florence Hollis, author of *Social Casework: A Psychosocial Therapy* (1964). Hollis's work has been described as the springboard for the clinical social work movement (Meyer, 1987).

The Community Mental Health Centers Construction Act of 1963 was the next major piece of federal legislation related to mental health policy. With the strong support of President John F. Kennedy, this act gave credibility to the leadership and commitment of the federal government in mental health. It provided grants for the construction of the community mental health facilities that were to provide care for the persons released from hospitals for the chronically mentally ill. It defined the continuum of care to be given and required that care be provided even to patients who could not afford to pay for it. Many historians believe that this legislation revolutionized the mental health system in the United States, because it resulted in large-scale development of community mental health programs as well as the deinstitutionalization of patients.

Over the next decade, as the effectiveness of psychotropic medication grew, the length of inpatient stay declined and the shift to outpatient services dramatically expanded. The plan to provide deinstitutionalized persons with well-integrated, publicly funded community mental health services did not materialize. While some persons received needed care, many others did not. The numbers of homeless, chronically mentally ill persons increased dramatically, calling public attention to the inadequacies of the community mental health centers in meeting the needs of this population. In the 1970s, the National Institute of Mental Health sponsored programs to test new forms of service delivery, many of which incorporated case management.

Decisions in the 1970s by the U.S. Supreme Court *(O'Connor v. Donaldson)* and the U.S. Court of Appeals for the Fifth Circuit *(Wyatt v. Stickney,* an Alabama case) set precedents in the areas of mental health and developmental disability. The rulings directed that mental patients who had been committed to a hospital had a right to release (assuming they were not dangerous to themselves or others) if they were not receiving treatment. Care for mentally ill or retarded persons was to be provided in the least restrictive (i.e., the least confined and most homelike) setting possible.

By the 1980s case management was being used for cost-containment purposes and at the same time, private insurance corporations began to cover mental health services, although not at the same level as other health care. With insurance money available, private general hospitals expanded their inpatient and outpatient facilities. States began to gradually turn over their mental health programs to private enterprise to administer. A system that had once been largely a governmental operation was slowly transformed to a nonprofit and then, increasingly, to a for-profit economy.

A consumer movement emerged at this time and grew remarkably quickly. The National Alliance on Mental Illness (NAMI) was founded in 1979 of consumers (this term is preferred to patients), family members, and concerned professionals. Today NAMI continues to support research, education, and social policy and political activity that will enhance access to community-based services. The organization is supported by members and now has affiliate offices in all 50 states and affiliates in 1,100 local communities (NAMI, 2007).

The Mental Health Systems Act of 1980 continued funding for community mental health centers and attempted to address the ramifications of deinstitutionalization. Across the country, many thousands of persons who had lived many years in state hospitals, receiving only custodial care, had been released. Some had been living on the streets for many years. To meet the basic needs of homeless mentally ill persons and others needing follow-up care, the act authorized the use of case management. Almost immediately, many new programs for homeless persons and others with persistent and serious mental illness were put into place.

Then came the 1980s. The Omnibus Budget Reconciliation Act of 1981, supported by President Ronald Reagan but opposed by social workers and many people in the mental health field, discontinued the federal government's leadership in the development of mental health services. (Previously, as governor of the state of California, Reagan had proposed closing all state mental health institutions.) This act effectively repealed the Mental Health Systems Act and shifted responsibility for funding and future development of mental health programs to the individual states in the form of block grants. Most states had already closed or substantially reduced their mental health facilities. With minimal infrastructure to provide care and with new responsibility for mental health, many states developed contractual arrangements with counties and with private organizations to provide community-based services to persons with more serious and chronic forms of mental illness. This led to fragmentation of services; however, it also expanded private practice opportunities for clinical social workers and other mental health professionals, and it increased the number of case management positions.

The election of President Bill Clinton in 1992 signaled a readiness for new approaches to health care financing, and, indeed, many Americans supported some form of national health care. But the Clinton administration's plan met with a great deal of opposition, and eventually it was withdrawn. When it was apparent that health and mental health reform would not be accomplished in the way that he had hoped, President Bill Clinton spearheaded a **Mental Health Bill of Rights.** This set of principles tried to ensure that basic consumer rights would be met. The bill of rights was implemented in Federal Employee Health Benefit Plans in 1997 but was intended to provide guidance for state and private mental health service providers as well. The bill addressed consumers' rights to information about their health plans, their rights to information about the professionals who deliver services, the right to a reasonable choice of providers, access to emergency services, the right to participate in treatment decisions, the right to receive respectful care, confidentiality, and the right to appeal decisions of the health care plan (KEN Publications/Catalog, n.d.). In an unprecedented move, nine professional organizations, representing more than 500,000 mental health practitioners, collaborated and jointly published a Mental Health Bill of Rights (shown in Exhibit 5.7). This policy statement was stronger and more inclusive than the set of principles set forth by the Clinton administration. NASW was one of the nine sponsors. This initiative reflected the level of professional practitioner support for patients' rights reform and an end to stigmatization and discrimination for persons who suffer from major or minor mental disorders.

Mental Health Parity Legislation Years of reduced access to mental health care—from deinstitutionalization of the 1970s, to Reagan's Omnibus Budget Reconciliation Act of 1981, to managed care—led to public outcry in the 1990s. Consumers of mental health services and their watchdog organizations, NAMI and

EXHIBIT 5-7

National Association of Social Workers Mental Health Bill of Rights Project Joint Initiative of Mental Health Professional Organizations: Principles for the Provision of Mental Health and Substance Abuse Treatment Services
A Bill of Rights

Our commitment is to provide quality mental health and substance abuse services to all individuals without regard to race, color, religion, national origin, gender, age, sexual orientation, or disabilities.

RIGHT TO KNOW

Benefits: Individuals have the right to be provided information from the purchasing entity (such as employer or union or public purchaser) and the insurance/third-party payer describing the nature and extent of their mental health and substance abuse treatment benefits. This information should include details on procedures to obtain access to services, on utilization management procedures, and on appeal rights. The information should be presented clearly in writing with language that the individual can understand.

Professional Expertise: Individuals have the right to receive full information from the potential treating professional about that professional's knowledge, skills, preparation, experience, and credentials. Individuals have the right to be informed about the options available for treatment interventions and the effectiveness of the recommended treatment.

Contractual Limitations: Individuals have the right to be informed by the treating professional of any arrangements, restrictions, and/or covenants established between third-party payer and the treating professional that could interfere with or influence treatment recommendations. Individuals have the right to be informed of the nature of information that may be disclosed for the purposes of paying benefits.

Appeals and Grievances: Individuals have the right to receive information about the methods they can use to submit complaints or grievances regarding provision of care by the treating professional to that profession's regulatory board and to the professional association. Individuals have the right to be provided information about the procedures they can use to appeal benefit utilization decisions to the third-party payer systems, to the employer or purchasing entity, and to external regulatory entities.

CONFIDENTIALITY

Individuals have the right to be guaranteed the protection of the confidentiality of their relationship with their mental health and substance abuse professional, except when laws or ethics dictate otherwise. Any disclosure to another party will be time limited and made with the full written, informed consent of the individuals. Individuals shall not be required to disclose confidential, privileged or other information other than: diagnosis, prognosis, type of treatment, time and length of treatment, and cost.

Entities receiving information for the purposes of benefits determination, public agencies receiving information for health care planning, or any other organization with legitimate right to information will maintain clinical information in confidence with the same rigor and be subject to the same penalties for violation as is the direct provider of care.

Information technology will be used for transmission, storage, or data management only with methodologies that remove individual identifying information and assure the protection of the individual's privacy. Information should not be transferred, sold or otherwise utilized.

CHOICE

Individuals have the right to choose any duly licensed/certified professional for mental health and substance abuse services. Individuals have the right to receive full information regarding the education and training of

(Continued)

EXHIBIT 5-7 *(Continued)*

professionals, treatment options (including risks and benefits), and cost implications to make an informed choice regarding the selection of care deemed appropriate by individual and professional.

DETERMINATION OF TREATMENT

Recommendations regarding mental health and substance abuse treatment shall be made only by a duly licensed/certified professional in conjunction with the individual and his or her family as appropriate. Treatment decisions should not be made by third-party payers. The individual has the right to make final decisions regarding treatment.

PARITY

Individuals have the right to receive benefits for mental health and substance abuse treatment on the same basis as they do for any other illnesses, with the same provisions, co-payments, lifetime benefits, and catastrophic coverage in both insurance and self-funded/self-insured health plans.

DISCRIMINATION

Individuals who use mental health and substance abuse benefits shall not be penalized when seeking other health insurance or disability, life or any other insurance benefit.

BENEFIT USAGE

The individual is entitled to the entire scope of the benefits within the benefit plan that will address his or her clinical needs.

BENEFIT DESIGN

Whenever both federal and state law and/or regulations are applicable, the professional and all players shall use whichever affords the individual the greatest level of protection and access.

TREATMENT REVIEW

To assure that treatment review processes are fair and valid, individuals have the right to be guaranteed that any review of their mental health and substance abuse treatment shall involve a professional having the training, credentials and licensure required to provide the treatment in the jurisdiction in which it will be provided. The reviewer should have no financial interest in the decision and is subject to the section on confidentiality.

ACCOUNTABILITY

Treating professionals may be held accountable and liable to individuals for any injury caused by gross incompetence on the part of the professional. The treating professional has the obligation to advocate for and document necessity of care and to advise the individual of options if payment authorization is denied.

Payers, and other third parties may be held accountable and liable to individuals for any injury caused by gross incompetence or negligence or by their clinically unjustified decisions.

(Continued)

EXHIBIT 5-7 *(Concluded)*

PARTICIPATING GROUPS

- American Association for Marriage and Family Therapy (membership: 25,000)
- American Counseling Association (membership: 56,000)
- American Family Therapy Academy (membership: 1,000)
- American Nurses Association (membership: 180,000)
- American Psychological Association (membership: 142,000)
- American Psychiatric Association (membership: 42,000)
- American Psychiatric Nurses Association (membership: 3,000)
- National Association of Social Workers (membership: 155,000)
- National Federation of Societies for Clinical Social Work (membership: 11,000)

SOURCE: NASW On-Line. (1999, November 21). Mental Health Bill of Rights Project; Joint initiative of mental health professional organizations: Principles for the provision of mental health and substance abuse treatment services. Retrieved August 25, 2001, from http:www.naswdc.org/practice/mental.htm.

Mental Health America (formerly the National Mental Health Association), along with social work and other mental health professional organizations actively sought public support for meaningful mental health parity legislation. This forced an increasingly conservative U.S. Congress to pass the Mental Health Parity Act of 1996 and many states to pass their own parity acts. *Parity*, here, refers to efforts to equalize benefits for physical and mental health care. (Note the areas of parity specified in the Exhibit 5-7 Bill of Rights.) The 1996 act was breakthrough legislation and widely acclaimed, but it failed to meet expectations. Its limitations became apparent quite quickly: only employers of 50 or more were mandated to comply and only if they offered provisions for mental health care. Not surprisingly, some employers immediately discontinued any mental health care in their health insurance. The law also allowed insurance plans to limit the number of outpatient visits it would pay for and limit hospital stays; it also permitted charging higher co-payments than people were asked to pay for their physical health care.

Social workers, including NASW lobbyists, sought passage of legislation that would rectify the limitations of the 1996 legislation. A number of bills were introduced between 1999 and 2001. None passed, including the Mental Health Equitable Treatment Act of 2001, a bill that had broad political sponsorship plus the enthusiastic support of NAMI and other organizations. This bill covered the full range of mental disorders, unlike the 1996 Act, and it prohibited unequal limits on mental health benefits. Just a handful of conservative members of the House of Representatives were responsible for defeat of mental health parity legislation in the final days of 2001 (Wyffels, 2001).

Momentum continued to build, however. States as diverse as Connecticut, North Carolina, and Texas passed mental health parity laws. At the federal level, several bills were introduced into the Senate and House of Representatives in 2007. The extent of support for meaningful mental health parity legislation can be seen in the fact that the Paul Wellstone Mental Health and Addiction Equity Act of 2007 had 268 sponsors, almost two-thirds of the House. The Senate bill, the Mental Health Parity Act of 2007, also had strong support from both Democrats and Republicans. Both bills represented an improvement over the Mental Health Parity Act of 1996 (which was scheduled to terminate in 2007). The bills were somewhat different, with the House bill giving less decision-making power to insurance companies than the Senate bill. The bills, however, seek to address existing inequities. Both attempt to prohibit group health insurance corporations from limiting treatment or from imposing financial require-ments that are more restrictive of mental health care than of physical health care in their insurance plans. Both bills incorporate substance abuse care along with mental health services in their definition of parity. As this book goes to press, it seems likely that some version of federal mental health parity legislation will soon be passed.

POLICY AND PRACTICE: FUTURE ISSUES

Regardless of which version of the 2007 mental health parity legislation becomes law, some serious issues remain unresolved. The masses of people who are not currently covered by health insurance of any kind may have little to gain by a mental health parity law. The primary continuing problem compelling political action by social workers and other health care advocates is the basic issue of access to health care, including substance abuse and mental health care, for all citizens. Until some form of universal health care law is passed, millions of people will have no health insurance; therefore, the mental health parity law will not help them.

It seems probable, too, that organizations that employ fewer than 50 persons will not be required to comply with the provisions of the 2007 mental health parity law. The millions of persons employed by smaller companies, then, will also receive no benefits from the law. Another concern is that health insurance companies may retain responsi-bility for determining which forms of mental illness—which DSM diagnoses—will be covered. According to Connecticut State Representative Christopher Murphy, "Insurance mandates never work perfectly. There are always loopholes and caveats for insurers to find" (Lightman & Waldman, 2007). Murphy added that changing the stigma that mental health problems are somehow different from physical health problems may be one of the biggest benefits of mental health parity law.

In addition to access, the quality of mental health care will also continue to be an issue for the future. The system of managed care, used to control cost of health care, has had a major impact on the persons receiving care and on the practice of social workers. The traditional, open-ended therapies used in the past by social work psychotherapists and the long-term involvement so characteristic of many BSW caseloads have given way to brief, highly focused approaches to practice. In many settings, intermittent services have replaced long-term case contact. Managed care has encouraged the use of groups, often with a psychoeducational focus instead of indi-vidualized psychosocial therapy, for inpatient as well as community-based practice. The use of standardized protocols, sometimes referred to by insurance companies as preferred practices, is another response to the demand for short-term, highly focused intervention. These protocols, or preferred practices, are directives that determine the practices to be followed for specific client problems (Mitchell, 1998). All these practices may have benefits for some people and for cost containment, but persons with persistent, serious mental health problems often fall between the cracks of this system.

Mental health social and economic policies will continue to influence social work practice in the future, and new forms of practice are likely to evolve. Short-term approaches may be increasingly demanded. Some that have emerged recently derive from more traditional practice. Cognitive behavioral therapy, for example, seeks to retrain clients whose difficulties result from the use of dysfunctional or negative thought patterns. Strategic or solution-oriented approaches help clients focus narrowly on ineffective behaviors and reframe or obtain new perspectives that enable the achievement of goals. Time-limited family and group interventions, even single-session treatment approaches and Internet therapeutic techniques, continue to evolve. Social workers are becoming skilled in the use of computerized Internet groups and computer-assisted therapy, enabling caregivers of persons with Alzheimer's disease, for example, or chronically ill children to benefit from groups in privacy and without leaving their homes (Schopler, Abell, & Galinsky, 1998).

The Internet has also provided social workers with rapid access to updated information about mental disorders and their treatment as well as pending mental health legislation. The Internet also provides opportunities for mental health professionals and concerned citizens to organize efforts to affect mental health policy. (See the Internet Sites for further information on mental health and also to find social and political action resources that support mental health legislation.)

Future trends in mental health social work practice will surely continue to be strongly influenced by the evolution of health care policy. Cost containment is likely to remain a pressing issue. With insurance companies imposing time limits, social workers and other mental health practitioners will work under considerable pressure to achieve results in meeting clients' needs more quickly. Social workers of the future will be challenged to design new practice approaches; to demonstrate with clear evidence that they are achieving their goals in meeting client needs, they will retain leadership in creating and administering mental health programs, and they will need to become more active in political process and policy development. Is this a big job? Yes! Clearly it calls for well-educated and prepared professionals who are strongly grounded in compassion for clients and commitment to professional values and who are equipped with advocacy skills to seek the kind of social change that will lead to increased health and well-being for all people.

INTERNET SITES

http://mentalhealth.samhsa.gov/cmhs	Center for Mental Health Services
http://www.nimh.nih.gov/	National Institute of Mental Health
http://www.nmha.org/	Mental Health America

http://www.nami.org/	The National Alliance on Mental Illness
http://www.cmha.ca/bins/index.asp	Canadian Mental Health Association
http://www.wfmh.com/	World Federation for Mental Health
http://narmh.org/	National Association for Rural Mental Health
http://www.suicidology.org/index.cfm	American Association of Suicidology
http://www.healthyplace.com/site/childhood_psychiatric_disorders.asp	Childhood Psychiatric Disorders
http://twhj.com	The Wounded Healer
http://www.ptsdinfo.org	Gateway to Post Traumatic Stress Disorder Information
http://www.who.int/mental_health/en	World Health Organization: Mental Health

SUMMARY

Roberta Sholes's work with David Deerinwater demonstrated the unique contribution that social work can make to the mental health team. Her sensitivity to the cultural dimensions of the case enriched her work with the client and enabled her to help other professional staff in their work. Most significantly, this BSW social worker helped David Deerinwater achieve his goal and reintegrate with his family and his people. As a generalist social worker, Roberta had the skills to work within a complex organizational structure, with families as well as individuals, and she was able to understand and use community systems.

Although they are not educated in a medical profession and they have serious concerns about the use of certain diagnostic labels, social workers whose careers are in mental health settings must learn the diagnostic terminology used by members of the mental health team. The chapter, therefore, introduced readers to the *Diagnostic and Statistical Manual of Mental Disorders* of the American Psychiatric Association. An introduction to the more commonly used psychotropic medications was also provided.

Social workers in mental health encounter significant social justice issues. The chapter identified concerns related to the use and abuse of diagnostic labels. Inadequate access to mental health care, especially for persons who are unemployed, homeless, and those with persistent, serious mental illness, was also identified as a concern. Environmental causes of mental illness or contributors to mental health problems were also discussed.

The chapter also traced the development of the U.S. response to mental illness from colonial times to the present. Key figures in reforms of the mental health system were Dorothea Lynde Dix, whose research and publications called the nation's attention to the inhumane treatment of the mentally ill, and Clifford Beers, whose book, *A Mind That Found Itself,* furthered public understanding of mental illness and helped promote an emerging mental hygiene movement. Mary Antoinette Cannon, Mary Jarrett, Jessie Taft, and Virginia Robinson were instrumental in the development of professional social services for the mentally ill and of training programs for social workers. Sigmund Freud's works resulted in improved approaches to treatment of mental illness, approaches that were quickly incorporated into the curricula of schools of social work as well as medicine, psychology, and nursing.

Social policy initiatives were described. These included federal legislation that created the National Institute of Mental Health and other laws such as the Community Mental Health Centers Construction Act of 1963 and the Mental Health Systems Act of 1980, all of which promoted programs for the mentally ill. This period of growth, however, ended in the early 1980s as federal budget deficits resulted in cutbacks of funding for programs. The Omnibus Budget Reconciliation Act of 1981 shifted primary responsibility for leadership in the development of mental health services to the individual states. Concern about increasing health care costs and growing public reluctance to support health and human services marked the 1990s, signaling shifts in the way that social workers and all mental health professionals would provide care. Policies designed to curtail rising costs nourished the growth of managed care in the field of mental health.

When access to mental health care declined, diverse national organizations, including NAMI, NASW, and other mental health professional groups, promoted media attention to the growing problems in the mental health field. Nine professional mental health organizations, including the NASW, disseminated a joint Mental Health Bill of Rights. Discriminatory and abusive treatment of persons with mental disorders increasingly became an issue of concern to the public. The Mental Health Parity Act of 1996 was a step in the right direction. As it was about to terminate in 2007, new mental health parity legislation was nearing passage. Some

states also developed limited mental health parity laws. One of the most pressing needs in the United States is for health insurance that will cover all U.S. citizens so that the massive number of uninsured persons will have access to health care, including mental health care. This concern will be discussed further in the next chapter.

This chapter concludes with trust that the spirit of openness to new knowledge that has pervaded the social work profession since its inception will keep social workers in the future alert to new learning for their work in the field of mental health. Firm grounding in professional values will also guide social workers of the future as they continue to provide leadership and strong advocacy for vulnerable populations such as persons with mental and emotional disorders.

KEY TERMS

acute traumatic stress, *p. 202*

anxiety disorder, *p. 191*

behavioral health care, *p. 194*

case manager, *p. 186*

clinical social worker, *p. 186*

delusions, *p. 191*

Diagnostic and Statistical Manual of Mental Disorders (DSM), *p. 189*

epidemiologists, *p. 206*

First Nations People, *p. 208*

hallucinations, *p. 191*

mental disorder, *p. 190*

Mental Health Bill of Rights, *p. 217*

Mental Health Parity Act of 2007, *p. 221*

mood disorder, *p. 191*

National Alliance on Mental Illness (NAMI), *p. 216*

personality disorders, *p. 191*

posttraumatic stress disorder (PTSD), *p. 202*

preferred practices, *p. 222*

psychosis, *p. 191*

psychotropic medication, *p. 184*

schizophrenia, *p. 182*

secondary setting, *p. 187*

staffing, *p. 182*

DISCUSSION QUESTIONS

1. Consider what might have happened to David Deerinwater if social workers at Oklahoma State Mental Hospital were not responsible for assisting with discharge planning. What might the outcome have been if a nurse or other staff member had been responsible for the discharge plan?

2. What social work values apply to practice in mental health? In what ways did Roberta Sholes demonstrate adherence to social work values?

3. Which professions make up the traditional mental health team? In what ways are these professions different? In what ways do they overlap?

4. Why are social workers skeptical about the use of classification systems such as the DSM-IV-TR? Are there any advantages to using such a system to classify mental disorders?

5. Why is Dorothea Dix important in the history of mental health care?

6. Identify some of the pioneering social workers in the field of mental health, and describe their contributions.

7. What is meant by the statement that social workers overidentified with Freudian psychology?

8. What were the positive and negative implications of deinstitutionalization for the mentally ill? For their families? For the community?

9. What is acute traumatic stress? What are the behavioral reactions of people when they are in acute traumatic stress? Give examples of situations that might result in acute traumatic stress. How can social workers be helpful?

10. What environmental or ecological situations might cause or contribute to mental illness?

11. What do you consider to be the most significant mental health policy issue of the immediate future? Why? What populations might be most negatively affected if this issue is not resolved?

CLASSROOM EXERCISES

While not required, it is suggested that students break into small groups of three or four to discuss these exercises. It may be helpful to choose a scribe to record and report important points to the class after the group discussion.

1. Why do many hospitals that treat people with mental illness have policies requiring that social workers be part of their mental health team? What special expertise do social workers bring to a mental health team, as illustrated in the Deerinwater case?

2. How has the National Association of Social Workers been involved in influencing national social policy affecting people at risk of mental health problems?

3. From information provided in this chapter, do you think the primary purpose of case management is client service or cost containment? Explain your reasons.

4. What are two major thrusts of recent national social policy reform efforts that are attempting to assist people with mental illness? What are the pros and cons of these policy efforts from the perspective of the general public? How might social workers look at the issues differently?

RESEARCH ACTIVITIES

1. What specific concerns do consumers of mental health services and their families have? Contact a local unit of NAMI or your local or state Mental Health America (formerly known as the Mental Health Association) to learn about the needs and issues of people with mental disorders who live in your area. Your state NASW chapter may also be a good source of information. Consider volunteering with one of these organizations to assist with political activity in support of programs that serve persons with mental illness. Find out, too, how volunteers can be helpful in other ways.

2. Select a specific mental disorder as a research topic. Use both the Internet and your school's library to obtain information about this form of mental illness and its treatment. Be sure to use professional social work periodicals for some of your research.

3. Study the many types of mental health resources in your community. Select one that provides prevention services and one that focuses on treatment. Interview a social worker in each setting to obtain information about the nature and goals of social work services provided. Consider if you would like to have a career in this field in the future.

4. Conduct a small, informal survey in your neighborhood to learn how people might react if a group home for the mentally ill was proposed. If their responses are negative, consider what you might say to educate them about the reality of mental health problems.

INTERNET RESEARCH EXERCISES

1. The National Institute of Mental Health offers information on bipolar disorder on its website (http://nimh.nih.gov/health/publications/bipolar-disorder/summary.shtml).

   a. What percentage of the U.S. adult population suffers from bipolar disorder?

   b. What are the symptoms of (1) depression and (2) mania?

   c. What evidence is given to support the thesis that bipolar disorder has some sort of genetic basis?

2. The National Alliance on Mental Illness (NAMI) has an informative page entitled "About Mental Illness" (http://nami.org/Content/Navigation Menu/Inform_Yourself/About_Mental_Illness/About_Mental_Illness.htm).

   a. How many people in America are affected by mental illness according to this site?

   b. What is this site's estimate of the economic cost of mental illness each year in the United States?

   c. What does NAMI cite as the main barriers to effective treatment and recovery from mental illness?

3. The National Center for Posttraumatic Stress Disorders has been established through the U.S. Department of Veterans Affairs (http://www.ncptsd.va.gov/ncmain/index.jsp).

   a. What is the purpose of this center?

   b. Is the center designed strictly for veterans? If not, who else might make use of its facilities?

   c. What is the name given to the largest interdisciplinary database of literature on traumatic stress? Check it out. What is your impression?

4. The World Health Organization has a website devoted to their WHO MIND project (http://www.who.int/mental_health/policy/en).

   a. What does WHO MIND stand for?

   b. What are the four elements in the Mental Health Improvements plan?

   c. What does this site see as the outcomes from treating and preventing mental disorders?

FOR FURTHER READING

Bentley, K. J. (Ed.). (2002). *Social work practice in mental health: Contemporary roles, tasks, and techniques.* Pacific Grove, CA: Brooks/Cole.

   Although this text is targeted for MSW as well as BSW readers, the focus on professional roles makes the book highly useful for generalist social workers employed in the mental health field. Chapters emphasizing the following roles may be of special interest to BSW students: crisis counselor, mediator, skills trainer, case manager, medication facilitator, consumer and family consultant, interagency and interdisciplinary teamwork, advocate, and community organizer. Chapters are readable and practical. They consistently address relevant empirical research and theory base, social work tasks and responsibilities across systems levels, skills and techniques, model programs, and special challenges for social workers. Most chapters include a "case dilemma" that depicts the real-life challenges for social workers.

Bentley, K. J., & Walsh, J. (2001). *The social worker and psychotropic medication: Toward effective collaboration with mental health clients, families, and providers* (2nd ed.). Belmont, CA: Brooks/Cole.

   Baccalaureate-level social workers in mental health settings are likely to become involved with clients' medication issues in ways that they probably never anticipated as college students. This text is a splendid aid in understanding psychotropic medications. The text explains how and why psychotropic medications are used and the many potential roles of social workers in medication management, educating clients and families, and the legal and ethical concerns related to client refusal to comply with prescribed medication regimens. The text demonstrates social workers' unique opportunities to assist clients with their medication-related concerns. The authors suggest ways for social workers to assist physicians and psychiatrists in understanding the cultural and socioeconomic factors that underpin clients' fears and concerns about psychotropic medications.

Corrigan, P. W. (2007). How clinical diagnosis might exacerbate the stigma of mental illness. *Social Work*, 52(1), 31–39.

This article is a refreshing look at the negative effects of diagnostic labeling with an eye toward solution to the stereotyping problem that occurs. Corrigan provides ample evidence of the manner in which persons with mental illness, the public, and even mental health practitioners become caught up in stereotypical thinking as a result of diagnostic classifications of mental illness. The unintended effects for people with mental illness may include failure to participate in mental health treatment in an effort to avoid being labeled, blocked opportunities in life, and self-stigma. Corrigan suggests that a dimensional approach to diagnosis would refocus the practitioner as well as the client toward change from one level of symptoms on a continuum, an action orientation, rather than the categorization approach currently in use. Corrigan also suggests that during their training, practitioners have contact with persons who have recovered from mental illness, thus grounding the practitioner in an understanding that pathology is not a necessary life course. Corrigan also urges mental health professionals to be open to the research evidence that supports recovery and to replace their expectations of poor prognosis with the assumption of recovery.

Derezotes, D. D. (2006). *Spiritually oriented social work practice*. Boston: Pearson, Allyn & Bacon.

Students or social workers who are looking for a method for integrating spirituality into practice will want to look at Derezotes's text. A strength of the text is that it is grounded in a biopsychosocial-spiritual-environmental perspective that continually seeks wholeness in individuals, couples, families, groups, organizations, and communities. The author believes that spirituality is most clearly expressed through the loving kindness shown by a person toward other people and toward the environment and all living things. The chapter on spiritually oriented practice in mental health settings proposes that spiritually oriented practice in mental health continues to use current treatment methods, but it adds the dimension of a wholistic understanding of symptoms, disorders, and suffering. The therapist helps the person to co-create well-being and move toward a new stage of personal consciousness through such work as teaching respect of others and the environment, teaching forgiveness and compassion, using religious rituals, and becoming involved in communities of spiritual diversity.

Kirk, S. (Ed.). (2005). *Mental disorders in the social environment: Critical perspectives*. New York: Columbia University Press.

The authors and researchers who contributed to this book include some of the most respected critical thinkers and contributors to social work literature. The intent of the editor, Stuart Kirk, was to offer a counterpoint or at least another, more critical perspective to the literature on mental disorders and mental health treatment that social workers are typically exposed to. He succeeds remarkably well. The 24 chapters of the text are organized under the following headings: Assessment and Diagnosis; the Social Context of Intervention; Evidence-Based Practice; Psychotherapy and Social Work; Questioning Psychiatric Medications; and Ethics, Laws, and Regulations.

Sullivan, W. P. (2005). Mental health services in the 21st century: The economics and practice challenges and the road to recovery. *Advances in Social Work*, 6(1), 193–201.

Sullivan presents a very clear history of the Community Mental Health Centers Program from its inception in 1963 to the present time, demonstrating the impact of politics and economics on this program. While he finds challenges related to current and future funding, he also finds much to be optimistic about, especially in terms of the services that are now being provided to persons with persistent, serious mental health disorders; the pharmacological advances that make treatment more effective and humane; and the growing acceptance by practitioners as well as consumers of the concept of recovery. The future will necessitate increased attention to short-term treatment approaches, evidence-based practice, and increased interdisciplinary work in community settings.

CHAPTER 6

SOCIAL WORK IN HEALTH CARE

OUTLINE

Katherine Lewandowski

KATHERINE LEWANDOWSKI

A s Linda Sanders walked down the corridor on the third floor of St. Anne's Hospital, she smiled at some of the nurses she passed. She was just beginning to know the staff, now that she was entering the second month of her senior-year social work field placement at this community general hospital. After all the years of classroom courses, it felt really good to finally be in a program that permitted her to do field work and apply what she had learned.

Linda was thinking now about the patient she was about to visit. Katherine Lewandowski was an 86-year-old widow who had been placed in a nursing home two months ago because she had suffered several minor fractures as a result of osteoporosis, a bone-thinning disease most commonly found in women over 50. Because of her condition she could no longer live at home. Linda liked the silver-haired, frail woman who spoke both Polish and English. Katherine had a hearty sense of humor, but it was revealed infrequently during her hospitalization, for she was frightened of the medical setting and of staff in white uniforms. Fortunately, she had related well to Linda from the start.

As she approached the patient's room, Linda recalled her two previous visits with Katherine. She had provided emotional support, which the elderly woman badly needed at the time of her arrival at St. Anne's. In the days that followed her admission to the hospital—necessitated by a fall at the nursing home, which had fractured her hip—Linda had tried to help Katherine understand and accept the recommended surgical procedure to repair the break. The surgery, performed three days ago, had gone well.

Linda tapped lightly on the door and entered the room. She glanced at Katherine and was startled by her appearance. Katherine's eyes were closed, but there were tears on her cheeks. Her color was poor. From her movements it was clear she was in pain. When Linda spoke a quiet, gentle greeting, Katherine opened her eyes. Linda delivered the message she had come with, that the doctors felt Katherine could return now to her nursing home; an ambulance would take her there in the morning. Linda had spoken with Katherine's daughter, Loretta, who had said that she would visit her mother at the nursing home the next evening. Katherine's response to this message was to turn her head toward the wall. Linda asked if Katherine had any questions, if there was anything she could do. Katherine closed her eyes; then, after a silence, she said, "No." Gently, Linda asked, "Katherine, are you okay? You seem to be upset. Can we talk about whatever is troubling you?" Katherine turned her face even more toward the wall. When she said, "I am all right," her tone was one of dismissal.

Linda was troubled as she left the room. She wondered whether Katherine was really ready to be discharged from the hospital. Katherine was in pain, and she was weak and obviously distressed. Linda discussed her concerns with Katherine's nurse, but the nurse said that she had already been in the hospital more than 5 days, and that most patients with hip fractures were able to leave in that period of time. Linda then spoke with her field instructor, who advised her to contact Katherine's doctor. The physician seemed somewhat annoyed with Linda's call and indicated that Katherine had used all the days of hospital care allowed by Medicare. She could recuperate just as readily in the nursing home.

Again Linda sought clarification from her field instructor, an experienced social worker whom Linda admired and respected. Marge O'Brien helped Linda review carefully what she had observed in Katherine's behavior. Then Marge explained that Medicare paid the hospital based on diagnosis, and this determined length of stay. The Business Office had notified the doctor that Katherine was reaching the end of her predetermined hospital stay. The doctor's discharge plan for Katherine was final unless it was clearly inappropriate or threatened the patient's well-being. Linda had already alerted the doctor to her concerns, which was a very important form of advocacy, because the doctor would continue to be responsible for Katherine in the nursing home. Marge was very sensitive to Linda's concerns about Katherine. Premature hospital discharges were increasing, she said, because of efforts to reduce the high cost of medical care. Hospital social workers were increasingly alarmed about the risk to patients. Marge directed Linda to report her concerns to Katherine's daughter immediately and also to the social worker at the nursing home.

When Linda telephoned Katherine's daughter, Loretta said she was concerned, too, but she felt the doctor must surely know what was best. Linda encouraged Loretta to remain in close contact with the doctor and to advise him of any change in her mother's condition. Then, as she made ambulance arrangements and gathered medical information for the nursing home, Linda was alert to any additional data that she could use to seek a delay in Katherine's discharge. There were none. Linda faxed the necessary forms and medical records to the nursing home; then she telephoned the social worker there to report her observations and her concerns about Katherine.

Two days later, when Linda returned to the hospital for her next field placement day, she asked about Katherine. The nursing staff reported that Katherine had been discharged and returned to the nursing home without incident. Linda continued to think about Katherine, however, knowing that the discharge to the nursing home—which was still not "home" for her—and the uncomfortable ambulance ride might have been quite difficult.

On Sunday evening Linda picked up the section of the Sunday paper that contained the classified ads and the obituary column. She thought she would check the advertised social work positions. Suddenly the obituary column caught her attention. There was Katherine! She had died 3 days after returning to the nursing home. Linda was stunned. She reviewed her telephone call with Katherine's daughter, her last conversation with Katherine, and her phone call to the doctor. Could Katherine's death have been prevented? Had she given up too quickly? What else could she have done? As she thought about it, Linda realized that it was possible that Katherine might have had additional health complications after returning to the nursing home. She turned back to the newspaper. Then she recognized the name of another patient who had been discharged recently, and then she saw another name she knew. Reading on, she counted five recently discharged elderly patients' obituaries. Feeling very troubled, Linda put the newspaper down. She knew that she would have many more questions to ask her field instructor.

Still troubled by Katherine's death, Linda noted some especially interesting research findings as she worked on a term paper for one of her classes. In an NASW publication article by Munch and Shapiro (2007), Linda learned that osteoporosis is frequently undetected in men as well as women (citing the National Osteoporosis Foundation, 2007), that there is an increase in the diagnosis in young women as early as their 20s and 30s (citing Petras, 1999), and that depression has been cor-related with bone density loss in some studies (citing Cizza, 2006). Linda carefully reviewed this article and its recommendations and then reported her findings at the next staff meeting of the hos-pital social work department.

The staff had not seen this research, but the social workers were very interested, especially when Linda proposed the development of an interdisciplinary study group to determine how best the hos-pital could assess and work with people, men as well as women, found to have loss of bone density which could lead to osteoporosis and related depression. Citing the article's recommendations, Linda suggested prevention efforts that could be initiated, too, through community outreach and educa-tion. Dietitians, nurses, physical therapists, and doctors could all participate. Social workers could take leadership roles in creating this change in the way that the hospital as an organization dealt with both inpatient and outpatient osteoporosis prevention and treatment. Older adults like Katherine Lewandowski would no longer be sent off to nursing homes following surgery for osteoporosis-related fractures without careful assessment of their psychological and emotional well-being. ■

APPLYING GENERALIST PRACTICE THEORY TO HEALTH CARE

Linda Sanders realized that she and the hospital social workers needed to work on several social systems levels simultaneously. As they assisted individual persons like Katherine Lewandowski and her family, they also needed to create change within the hospital as an organizational system. Ultimately they would need to collaborate with other health care professionals and public citizens to seek the kind of political change that would make health care truly responsive to the needs of people in the local community and elsewhere. In the meantime, however, Linda and the social work staff decided to focus on changing procedures and creating new programs within the hospital.

Starting with the Liberal Arts Base of Social Work Education

Using knowledge acquired in math, sociology, speech and writing courses, statistics, political science, and research courses, Linda could have input into an action research project that would engage and hopefully energize other health care professionals. Linda felt confident that her liberal arts courses had prepared her for this challenge. Initially, Linda's field instructor, Marge O'Brien, encouraged Linda to deliver her ideas verbally to the social work staff. When Linda's suggestions were well received, Marge asked Linda to write up a proposal for an action plan that would initially focus on data gathering from each of their perspectives by nurses, dietitians, and other health care staff. As a student in her first field placement, Linda was prepared to participate in but not direct the social work action that lay ahead. The director of the social work department would probably assume the primary leadership role. Marge, however, wanted to give Linda opportunities to experience the research, education, and advocacy that would be primary strategies in changing the hospital's procedures. Linda anticipated learning a lot about the political systems that operated within large organizational systems and was excited about the challenges and the learning she could gain in this field placement!

While Linda assisted the social workers with creating new programs and procedures for St. Anne's Hospital, she would also work beside and learn from them as they continued their regular professional responsibilities. This included seeing patients on a one-to-one basis to counsel, intervene in crises, and help families with discharge plans. Often, too, Linda and the social workers referred patients and their families to other community resources, such as nutrition or hot meal programs and substance abuse treatment. Generally, hospital social workers did not engage in long-term counseling with individual patients; therefore, patients who needed ongoing, intensive counseling were referred to local social service agencies or to private practitioners in social work, psychology, or psychiatry. Some hospital social work staff worked with groups of patients such as those newly diagnosed with cancer or who were dependent on alcohol or drugs. One social worker had developed a support group for people who had had strokes and for their friends and families. As a field placement student, Linda was able to acquire group work skills by assisting with the group. Linda's field placement gave her a strong sense of growing professional competence.

Births and deaths, accidents and injuries, acute illnesses and chronic diseases—these are the concerns in health care settings. Social workers must have a solid knowledge base if they are to further other health care team members' understanding of the emotional factors in illness. Coursework in the liberal arts provides a basic understanding of the biological sciences as well as the social, psychological, and cultural sciences. As we saw in Chapter 1, unlike the training of other health care providers, the social worker's professional education stresses the person within his or her environment. The generalist social worker is prepared to intervene with individual persons, like Katherine Lewandowski; with entire families or with selected family members (Katherine's daughter, for example); with small groups; with organizations (like St. Anne's Hospital); and with large groups, neighborhoods, and communities.

Social work students begin their education with liberal arts courses in such areas as literature, writing, philosophy, sociology, and psychology. By the sophomore and junior years, the curriculum includes professional courses in practice methods, research, human behavior in the social environment, cultural diversity, and social policy. The liberal arts courses teach students to think critically, to question, and to analyze. They also provide knowledge about human beings, society, and different cultures that professional courses later build upon. This is especially true of the courses in human behavior and social policy. Coursework in practice methods provides the skill base and the knowledge of social work practice theory that leads to competent social work practice in health care or other settings. Beginning in the second semester of the junior year or in the senior year, baccalaureate students spend a minimum of 400 hours in field work. It is in field

Poverty places families, especially children, at risk of malnutrition, disease, and accidents.

work that all the theory is applied and that students acquire the competence to practice social work when they graduate.

Hospitals like St. Anne's generally employ both BSW and MSW social workers. MSWs generally staff specialized services such as cardiac intensive care and neonatal nurseries because of their complex nature and immediacy of the services needed by patients and families. Especially fast-paced areas such as the ER (emergency room) also require very skilled, experienced social workers; except in small hospitals and sometimes in rural areas, MSWs are given these responsibilities. The MSW curriculum is also based on liberal arts preparation and a generalist perspective, but advanced, specialized courses are also taken.

Values and Ethics in Health Care Social Work

Hospitals and other health care settings work daily with frightened, hurting, vulnerable people. As organizational systems, hospitals often deliver services in ways that seem cruel and heartless to patients. Social workers in health care, guided by the values of the profession, can help humanize the health care environment for people and teach staff how to individualize patients. Among the values that the profession holds are regard for individual worth and dignity, the right of people to participate in the helping process, and the right of clients to make decisions that will affect them.

These values and the Code of Ethics of the National Association of Social Workers were introduced in Chapter 1. The Code of Ethics, which is reprinted in the Appendix of this text and incorporated in social work students' coursework, provides guidelines that further support ethical social work practice. Health care is a field of practice that challenges social workers to sustain their commitment to professional values and ethics. The health care environment itself sometimes contradicts social work values. This is especially true when the policies of our country, our states, and even our employers' insurance companies eliminate or reduce access to health care for poor persons, or where health care organizations make huge profits but deny some people access to health care, and when salaries range from hundreds of thousands of dollars for some and barely minimum wage for other health care employees.

Linda Sanders, the student social worker, was shocked by Katherine Lewandowski's death and by the depression that she saw in many other persons who were discharged to nursing homes or back to their families following treatment for fractures caused by osteoporosis. She began to think about the ethical questions related to the care of these people. Was it possible that people were being discharged from the hospital prematurely, without adequate assessment and treatment for depression? If so, was this happening because the professional staff was not aware of the high rate not only of depression but even of death following osteoporosis-related fractures? The National Osteoporosis Foundation reported that in the United States, 24 percent of people who experience a hip fracture will die within a year (2007). Was it instead possible that premature discharge was encouraged by the health insurance companies who sought to expedite discharge to contain costs?

Biomedical ethics is not a concern for physicians alone. Social workers too, especially those in the health care field, encounter ethical and value-laden issues in daily practice. Often social workers assist patients and families with decisions about continued use of life-support systems for terminally ill persons or for profoundly disabled infants. Social workers frequently serve as the "conscience" of institutions as they challenge policies and procedures that have negative impacts on people. Students preparing for careers in social work develop an understanding of moral and ethical problems through liberal arts courses, such as philosophy and theology, and through content regarding ethics and values in their social work courses.

Focusing on the Community and Populations at Risk

The health care social worker is the essential link between the patient, the health care facility (whether hospital, clinic, health department, or nursing home), and the community and its resources. Knowledge of the community means more than a mere listing of community resources, which would be available to any hospital employee. Truly understanding the community means understanding the diverse racial and ethnic groups that make up that community, their traditional beliefs about illness and health care, and any special "healers" that people might turn to. The faith and spiritual values of the community must be understood and respected by social workers. Often such values are the one vital, sustaining source of strength for a patient or a family. In health settings, social work has traditionally been the professional discipline that interprets the ethnic, class, or cultural roots of beliefs and behaviors that have influenced patients' responses to illness. Armed with knowledge of cultural diversity and the community, social workers sometimes help families design remarkably creative plans for posthospital care or as an alternative to nursing home placement.

Disparity of health care services and the near-absence of public health services in the United States places many persons at risk of accident or injury or of acquiring (and transmitting) communicable diseases.

There has been a long history of disparity of health services to lower-class and minority people in the United States. Of serious concern to social workers are the poor (especially members of racial and ethnic minority groups), people with disabilities, and suspected AIDS carriers. These are populations that are seriously at risk, because some health care professionals avoid or even refuse to treat them (Reamer, 1993). The number of underinsured poor and middle-class persons is increasing, too. It has become extremely difficult for social workers to locate health services for persons in poverty and those without adequate health insurance. Sometimes it is even difficult to sustain contact with culturally diverse patients whose needs are not met or whose health care has been delivered in an insensitive, disrespectful manner. As Devore and Schlesinger point out, "advocating for the poor, for those who do not speak English, and for those who have greater faith in the spirits than in modern medicine requires a high degree of self-awareness and comfort with the identity 'social worker'" (1987, p. 260).

For social work students, awareness and appreciation of human diversity and community norms is built gradually. This learning starts with the liberal arts courses taken in the freshman and sophomore years. Courses in literature, history, political science, and sociology help prepare social work students to understand the influences of class, gender, race, and ethnicity. Students begin to understand such concepts as social norms and roles and to appreciate the rich contributions of many cultures to contemporary society. Social work courses taken in the junior and senior years further prepare students for practice within the community and with a variety of populations.

The field practicum that concludes the baccalaureate-degree program enables students to demonstrate competent social work practice, not in a classroom but out in the community.

Preparing to Practice in Health Care

Accidents, injury, and illness all have impact. Pain, often both psychological and physical, occurs. There may be days lost from work or school. This can mean getting behind on schoolwork or projects on the job. It could even mean loss of a job and loss of income. Understanding the social systems and ecosystems perspectives (as described in Chapter 2), social workers in health care anticipate that there will almost always be consequences for persons beyond the patient. There may be impact on the job site, for example, if a person is hurt at work. If a parent is ill or injured, there are consequences for the family. Loss of income could have devastating results for the family, potentially even homelessness. Young children don't understand illness or disability well; they may be very upset emotionally by the events unfolding in their family. In a single-parent family, severe or prolonged illness of the parent may require placement of the children with a relative or even in foster care if relatives are not available. In any event, health care problems of the parents often change the quality of nurturing available to the children. In some cases, too, older children must take on greater family responsibility, which may include staying home from school to care for younger brothers and sisters.

The generalist practice theory that social work students acquire, based on social systems theory and the ecosystems perspective (described in Chapter 2), provides a basis for understanding the impact of illness and injury on individuals and families as well as larger social systems. In practice methods courses, students learn the interviewing techniques and communication skills that are needed in health care social work practice as well as many approaches to problem solving with individuals and families. They also apply their understandings of how organizations and communities function as systems and learn how to help organizations, like St. Anne's Hospital in this chapter's case study, change procedures and initiate programs or engage in efforts to prevent illness and injuries.

Whole communities suffer when there are epidemics of flu or much more serious contagious diseases, so social work efforts in prevention are important. Every day social workers help young parents understand the preventive care needed by new babies or young children. Illnesses threaten masses of people in society when the health care system of our nation does not ensure that everyone has access to health care. Social workers, through the NASW and other organizations, continue to be strong advocates for health care reform in the United States. Social work students learn the skills of political action, and they learn to analyze as well as to affect social policy in their practice and social policy courses. The research methods they acquire are among the skills they use when their generalist practice in health care leads to social action or social reform at the largest social systems levels. Like Linda Sanders in the case study, students have opportunities in their fieldwork experiences to apply the theory and skills they have learned in the classroom. Because health care is such a large and diverse part of our society, health care field placements may occur within a wide variety of community organizations.

HEALTH CARE SERVICES

Linda Sanders's social work field placement was in a community general hospital, but hospitals are not the only health care settings that employ social workers. The U.S. health care system, fueled by a desire to sustain profitability while controlling rapid increases in health care costs, has created a wide variety of new health care ventures. In metropolitan areas, many inner-city hospitals closed and public health services cut back. Meanwhile, mergers and acquisitions of hospitals, nursing homes, subacute centers, HMOs, pharmacies, and diagnostic testing centers created giant, profitable, in some cases multinational health care corporations (Weiss, 1997). Users of health care and all of the health care professions have been impacted by these changes. Dramatic change in health care is likely to continue.

The result of ongoing change throughout the system is that social workers may now be found in a very wide variety of health care settings (see Exhibit 6-1 for a sampling of settings). As the list of settings suggests, social work is a viable profession in a growing number of health-related community organizations. Studies reported in Chapter 1 done by NASW and the Association of Baccalaureate Social Work Program Directors showed that many BSW and MSW social workers are employed in the health field.

Acute Care

The majority of health care social workers today are employed in **acute care** (facilities that provide immediate, short-term care): hospitals, inpatient and outpatient clinics, rehabilitation centers, and **subacute centers.** Subacute centers provide intensive medical services for people who do not need to remain in the hospital but also may not

---

EXHIBIT 6-1

Settings for Health Care Social Work

General hospitals	Women's health centers
Children's hospitals and other specialized hospitals	Health planning boards
Physicians' offices	Specialized health organizations (American Cancer Society, National Kidney Foundation)
Public health clinics	Hospice programs
Health maintenance organizations (HMOs)	Insurance companies
Rehabilitation services	Private social work practice
Nursing homes and subacute centers	Homeless shelter health clinics
Home health care organizations	Outpatient clinics

need, or hopefully can avoid, long-term care. Subacute care—while lengthier and somewhat less expensive than hospitalization—is fast paced. Subacute care facilities are not yet available in all communities. This is one of the areas in which evolution in the nation's health care systems has produced a new area for social work practice.

> Services provided by the acute care social worker are usually short-term, episodic, and intensive, because average length of stay in acute care is now less than two days. Service functions traditionally include social risk screening, discharge planning, psychosocial interventions, case consultation, collaboration, health education, information and referral, quality assurance, agency planning, program consultation, and community planning. (Poole, 1995, p. 1162)

Hospital social work is changing dramatically, as hospitals themselves are changing. Once there were hospital social work departments headed up by MSW social workers. Now social workers are employed by hospitals, but they often work out of designated units such as cardiac intensive care, the spinal cord injury area, or the unit that cares for high-risk newborns (neonatal intensive care). Social work service to hospital emergency rooms is taking on increased importance. Twenty-four-hour social work staffing is now provided in many busy metropolitan hospitals. Nonetheless, as Keigher states, "hospitals no longer dominate the field [of health care]. Indeed, they have become remarkably limited, providing mainly specialty treatment and highly technological diagnostics" (2000, p. 7). The shift away from hospitals to outpatient, community-based, and in-home health services means that hospital social work is evolving into a broader concept: health care social work.

The National Association of Social Workers has developed a policy statement that addresses some of the political issues related to health care. The statement (see Exhibit 6-2) is based on social work values and principles. It clearly supports the right of all persons to a full range of health care services.

Long-Term Care

Although most people think of a nursing home when they think about long-term care, a growing number of services are, in fact, included within the purview of long-term care. In addition to nursing homes, some of the community-based services include home health care, assisted-living facilities, home-delivered meals, and adult day care. **Long-term care** consists of any combination of nursing, personal care, volunteer, and social services provided intermittently or on a sustained basis over a span of time to help persons with chronic illness or disability to maintain maximum quality of life.

Not all users of long-term care are the elderly, but with the population of older persons increasing, a growing segment of long-term care consumers are likely to be older persons. **Cost containment** concerns—concerns about the need to control rising health care costs—have limited the funding available for home-based care from both Medicare and private insurance. These programs and Medicaid are more likely to provide for nursing home care. Social work researchers among others have pointed to the need to lower the eligibility requirements to accommodate larger numbers of

---

EXHIBIT 6-2

NASW Policy Statement on Health Care

PROMOTING THE RIGHT TO HEALTH CARE

NASW supports a national health care policy that ensures the right to universal access to a continuum of health and mental health care to promote wellness, maintain optimal health, prevent illness and disability, treat health conditions, ameliorate the effects of unavoidable incapacities, and provide supportive long-term and end-of-life care. These policies are based on the principle of universality available to all people in the United States, regardless of financial status, race, ethnicity, disability, religion, age, gender, sexual orientation, or geographic location. NASW supports:

■ Efforts to enlarge health care coverage to uninsured and underinsured people until universal health and mental health coverage is achieved.

■ Economic, social, occupational, and environmental policies that contribute to maintaining health,

recognizing the relationship between these factors and quality and longevity of life.

■ The coordination of NASW chapter efforts to influence state and federal health care policy.

■ Giving all patients the opportunity to retain or regain their social roles and functional capacities within the limits of their mental, physical, sensory, and chronic condition.

■ Giving all patients and their families necessary and appropriate care and benefits.

SOURCE: Adapted from E. C. de Silva & E. J. Clark (2006). Health care: Policy statement approved by the NASW Delegate Assembly, August 1999. *Social work speaks: National Association of Social Workers policy statements 2006–2009*. Washington, DC: NASW Press, p. 190. Exhibit 6-2 represents only a partial listing of the policy statement.

---

persons in community-based care (Robert & Norgard, 1996; Slivinski, Fitch, & Wingerson, 1998).

The 1999 U.S. Supreme Court Olmstead decision encouraged states to develop programs to ensure that older adults and persons with disabilities can live in the least restrictive environment possible. With some pressure from the federal government, states are continuing to evolve programs that enable elderly persons to avoid nursing home placement or return to community living if they have been placed in a nursing home.

Nursing homes are one of the most common forms of long-term care. In the United States, a large portion of nursing homes are owned by proprietary (for-profit) corporations. There are also private, nonprofit homes (some operated by religious denominations) plus federal (Veterans Administration), state, and county public facilities. Nursing homes are licensed by the state. Nursing services are provided 24 hours per day, augmented by physical, occupational, and activity therapists, dieticians, and social workers, among others.

The newest development in long-term care is assisted-living facilities for older adults who are fairly independent. Assisted-living units are often attached to existing nursing homes, thus providing for a range of care, depending on need. Assisted living is an evolving area for social work practice and an interesting one. Residents of assisted living have intellectual, social, political, and spiritual interests and considerable capacity to enjoy them, thus making field trips, even travel, a possibility. Groups of many kinds can be used by creative social workers to meet the social, intellectual, and emotional needs of residents.

Federal law requires that nursing homes provide social services to help residents obtain the highest possible physical and psychological functioning. Homes with 120 or more residents are required to have at least one full-time social worker, but other homes must make social work services available (NASW, n.d.).

The NASW listing of clinical indicators for social work in nursing homes identifies the following as major functions and services that are provided by social workers:

1. Facilitating the admissions process.
2. Developing an individualized plan of care.
3. Facilitating the social and psychological well-being of residents and their families.
4. Involving the entire facility in meeting psychosocial needs of residents.
5. Planning discharges to ensure appropriateness and continuity of care for transfers within and discharges from the nursing home. (1993, pp. 4–5)

In thinking about the ways in which social workers implement the NASW clinical indicators policy statement, we can recall the case study from the beginning of this chapter. We might ask: what might the nursing home social worker have done at the time of Katherine Lewandowski's admission to the nursing home to help this elderly woman? If social history information had been obtained at the time of admission, the social worker would have learned that Katherine Lewandowski had a very strong sense of family, of identity with her Polish ethnicity, and of faith in the Catholic religion. The social worker would have understood the cultural origin of Katherine Lewandowski's sense of abandonment: the highly valued Polish custom of caring for elderly persons within the family, with nursing home placement used only as a final resort. The social worker would also have recognized that Katherine's despair was heightened by significant losses: the death of her husband 5 years ago, the death of a son from cancer 18 months ago, and the loss of control over her own body as she became increasingly frail and handicapped by osteoporosis.

Katherine Lewandowski could have benefited from encouragement and reassurance provided by the social worker during frequent visits to her room and also to the hospital when Katherine had surgery. The social worker could have helped other nursing home staff understand Katherine and be more sensitive to her needs. The activities staff, for example, could have been urged to engage Katherine in socialization activities with other Polish women in the nursing home, thereby helping her to reestablish her sense of identity and linkage to a familiar community. The Catholic chaplain or a priest from Katherine's parish might have been a significant resource, helping her find comfort in her faith and thereby engage another source of strength. Too often the spiritual life of clients is ignored in hospitals and nursing homes.

Nursing home social work offers unique opportunities for long-term involvement with people during a phase in their lives when many crises may occur. This area of social work practice also offers opportunities to work with families and with groups, to provide education for resident care staff, and to be one of the decision makers that influences the organization's policies and procedures. Nursing home social workers have remarkable opportunities to become very strong advocates for their clients.

Home Health Care

Home health care is the provision of health care services, including social services, to people in their own homes. The resurgence of home health care in recent years has been generated by economic concerns, by the growing number of terminally ill elderly and AIDS patients, and by humanitarian interests that seek to provide care to loved ones within the comfort and security of their own homes.

Home health services are provided by organizations such as the Visiting Nurse Association, by hospitals, by public health departments, and by proprietary (for-profit) corporations. Social workers are key members of the home care team today. Through counseling, they help family members, especially those in caregiver roles, work through their feelings of frustration, anger, grief, and pain. Supporting the family and preventing personal and group breakdown during the caregiving time is an objective of the social workers. They also help the family locate needed resources, such as financial aid and bedside nursing equipment. Others routinely on the team are physicians, who provide supervision, and nurses. Ancillary staff often include homemakers, physical therapists, and dieticians.

With their professional colleagues, home care social workers increasingly deal with ethical dilemmas related to questions about how much autonomy and self-determination to support with elderly persons who have physical or cognitive disabilities, or when family caregivers become overburdened (Healy, 1998). Home health hospice programs—which now serve children and adults of all ages with AIDS, cancer, and heart disease—raise similar ethical questions. Nonetheless, this is a growing field of service and one that offers considerable satisfaction as well as challenges.

Insurance Companies

Financing of the U.S. health care system today functions primarily through health insurance companies. Because of buyouts and mergers in the 1990s, these are increasingly large, often multinational corporations. Employers and private persons purchase insurance through these companies, which assume responsibility for contracts with and payment to health care providers. Even the federal government Medicare and Medicaid programs use private insurance companies as their carriers.

A new but fledgling development in health care social work is the establishment of social work services within insurance companies. In recent years, some insurance companies have hired social workers, often BSWs, to provide preventive care to the insurance company's Medicaid subscribers immediately following the birth of a baby. Social workers review educational information with the mothers about risks such as lead poisoning if the baby eats lead-based paint chips and about immunizations and other health care the new baby will need. Assessment is done and referrals made if other needs exist, such as special assistance for a single mother with cognitive disabilities or if domestic violence is threatened in the home. Mothers are assisted with the names and telephone numbers of primary care physicians for their babies, with the paperwork needed to obtain Medicaid care for the new baby, with information about lead screening, and with any other community service referrals needed. Some insurance companies have added prenatal care coordination and child care programs, too, that enable social workers to do home visits and case management. These services within insurance companies, however, are a recent development, and it is not yet clear if they will prove to be sufficiently feasible economically to be sustained into the future.

Hospice and Palliative Care

Hospice refers to a specialized approach in caring for terminally persons, not to any specific place. Hospice care is a program that can be provided at home, in a hospital, or in a facility designed specifically for the purpose of serving persons who are dying. Some nursing homes are now adding hospice care units. The central treatment approach used by hospices is **palliative care.** The World Health Organization defines palliative care as the

> active total care of patients whose disease is not responsive to curative treatment. Control of pain, of other symptoms, and of psychological, social, and spiritual problems, is paramount. The goal of palliative care is the achievement of the best quality of life for patients and their families....Palliative care affirms life and regards dying as a normal process, neither hastens nor postpones death...provides relief from pain and other distressing symptoms. (Doyle, Hanks, & MacDonald, 1998, p. 3, as cited in Csikai & Chaitin, 2006, p. 107)

The term *hospice* dates back to medieval times when hospices were way stations, generally run by religious orders or monks or sisters, that provided rescue and assistance to travelers. The St. Bernard Hospice in the Alps between Switzerland and Italy, for example, used St. Bernard dogs to rescue travelers lost in snowstorms and avalanches. Cicely Saunders, a nurse and social worker, worked at a hospice in Ireland that served dying people. Saunders's commitment to humane care of the dying led her to obtain a medical degree, and, in 1967, she established the famed St. Christopher's Hospice (Richman, 1995). The first hospice programs in the United States emerged around 1970 and were patterned after the model for humane care established by Cicely Saunders.

Hospice care is provided by an interdisciplinary team comprised of doctors, nurses, social workers, and clergy, often supplemented by a core of volunteers. Many insurance programs, including Medicare, cover hospice care because it is less costly than hospital or nursing home care. Medicare and many insurance policies require a physician's certification that the potential hospice patient is within 6 months of death. The patient must agree to forego curative treatment. On admission to the hospice program, patients are usually assigned to a team that will remain with them through death. Hospice programs provide care to infants and children as well as young and older adults, although older adults comprise the largest cohort of hospice patients.

The NASW policy statement on hospice care notes that "The hospice concept is the embodiment of social work values and principles" (de Silva & Clark, 2006, p. 215). The NASW policy statement affirms that "every dying person is of value and deserves individualized care while being served by hospice" and that "client self-determination is inherent in the provision of hospice care so that the dying can choose how they live until their death" (p. 214).

Social workers in hospice programs are an integral part of the health care team. Social workers counsel patients and their families prior to death and offer a great deal of emotional support. They assist dying people to deal with the physical and emotional pain that is so often part of the destruction and end of life. They provide crisis intervention and engage in advocacy to ensure that clients' needs are met. They help both the dying person and family members and friends with anticipatory grieving. In fact, on admission the assessment done by the social worker seeks to identify the strengths previously achieved as people have coped with other losses (Dziegielewski, 2004). Following death, hospice social workers continue to assist family members and friends with bereavement.

EMERGENCY ROOM: TRAUMA AND CRISIS AMID HUMAN DIVERSITY

Hospitals that operate large, active emergency care facilities employ social workers on all shifts, 7 days a week. In smaller facilities, social workers staff emergency rooms during periods of high demand and they function on an on-call basis during less busy periods. Every television viewer knows well the life-and-death drama of the hospital emergency room. For the social worker, emergency room practice means fast-paced crisis intervention work and brief contact with clients. For example, the 17-year-old who took an overdose of aspirin when her boyfriend threatened to end their relationship needs someone to help her sort out her embarrassment and shame, after the aspirin has been removed from her stomach. The social worker makes a rapid assessment of the young woman's psychosocial situation and determines that referral for counseling is needed both for the young woman and for her family.

Consider another example: a 5-year-old boy is treated for multiple fractures suffered in a car accident. He will be admitted to the hospital after receiving initial care in the emergency room. Every 15 minutes the social worker provides information to the parents—information obtained from the doctors and nurses who are with the boy. The parents, a young Puerto Rican couple, show their immense concern about their son very openly. The wife, who is pregnant, is extremely nervous and is breathing irregularly, and she appears to be about to have an *ataque* (an episode similar to a seizure; *ataques* are sometimes experienced during periods of severe emotional stress and are recognized in the Puerto Rican culture as a cry for help). The husband's anger with the hit-and-run driver who injured his son takes the form of angry threats, loudly voiced, and of demands that the hospital staff do something to save his son. The social worker provides emotional support to the parents and helps them to a room where they have more privacy and where additional family members can be with them as soon as the social worker is able to contact them.

Before the evening ends, the social worker will also have helped a 55-year-old, white, middle-class woman whose husband's life could not be saved following his third heart attack; an elderly Catholic nun who required admission to the hospital because of pneumonia; and a poor, inner-city African American mother and infant who were hungry and whose heat had been turned off by the landlord for nonpayment of rent. The emergency room social worker interpreted medical information to waiting families, offered psychological strength, demonstrated concern and caring, confronted inappropriate behavior, used crisis counseling techniques, and connected people with needed community resources. In addition, the social worker helped the doctors and caregivers understand and appreciate the cultural dimensions that influenced patients' responses to pain and their families' responses to crisis.

When disaster strikes a community, hospital emergency rooms receive injured and psychologically traumatized patients. All hospitals have disaster plans, so social workers and other staff know their roles in advance. Emergency care of medical needs must take priority, of course. Social workers are important members of the team. They assess and comfort children and adults whose injuries do not appear to require immediate care, if all medical staff are needed for more seriously injured persons. They provide emotional assistance to persons whose trauma is threatening their mental health status. In fact, they provide many of the psychosocial services for persons in acute traumatic or posttraumatic stress that were described in Chapter 5.

Hospital social workers' responsibilities during community disasters vary according to the nature of the disaster. In war situations or terrorist attacks, the profound sense of loss of personal security and safety may immobilize or impede both health care staff and the persons they are trying to serve. In the volatile and chaotic environment of terrorist attacks in Israel, for example, social workers' own personal responses need to be dealt with so they can continue to provide care to civilian casualties and their families (Somer, Buchbinder, Peled-Avram, & Ben-Yizhack, 2004). In general, however, hospital social workers must focus on rapid psychosocial assessment. Immediate counseling must be offered, providing considerable emotional support for injured persons who may be overwhelmed with pain, fear of death, or grief over the loss of family members or co-workers. Social workers assist with efforts to locate or provide information to friends or family members. Sometimes they deal with the emotional outbursts of injured persons or other people that may interfere with hospital staff's efforts to give medical attention. In this very demanding environment, social work skills facilitate communication and assist the health care organization to provide emergency medical care. All of this is done with appreciation for the diversity of the people involved and for the community environment.

Social workers' well-developed interdisciplinary teamwork relationships are extremely valuable when serious emergencies strike. The experience and expertise hospital social workers develop in their day-to-day work with persons who are ill, injured, dying, or recovering from surgery and facing a bright new future—all of this serves the social worker, the health care team, and traumatized persons who are helped during times of disaster.

HEALTH CARE IN RURAL AREAS

The nature of the community in which health care is provided is also significant in contemporary social work practice. Health care facilities in rural areas, for example, often require considerable community involvement from the social worker. In rural settings, social workers call on all their generalist practice skills as they work with families and communities to provide care following hospitalization or to help people obtain health care. Long distances between health centers, isolated dwellings, poverty, and lack of transportation make it difficult for many rural people to obtain high-quality health care. Pregnant rural women, for example, are at increased risk because they often have inadequate access to prenatal care. Their generalist practice skills were enormously helpful to several Pennsylvania social workers when they organized rural community leaders and developed health and social services for pregnant women. Included were a mobile unit for prenatal care, an information and referral service, health education, and clinical care and follow-up services (Pistella, Bonati, & Mihalic, 1999).

Hospitals in rural areas or small towns generally have no more than 50 to 100 beds. Complex and expensive medical services such as **hemodialysis** (a procedure to cleanse the blood of persons with chronic kidney disease) are often not provided. Severe financial pressure is often experienced by small hospitals.

Usually the hospital employs only one or two social workers. Generalist practice skills are vital. Social workers in small health care facilities have to be very knowledgeable about the local community and its resources. Often, when needed resources such as home health care are not available, the social worker helps to create them or calls on clergy, police, or neighbors for assistance. In small towns friends, neighbors, and co-workers sometimes provide exceptional help, as this single mother of a son with AIDS explains:

> And then when he was deteriorating so bad in December, I just decided that I needed to be at home with him. I was given an open-ended leave, and when my accumulated hours of pay were used up, they let people donate hours to me, and I never lost a paycheck. I work with a really super group of people . . . very caring, very giving. (McGinn, 1996, p. 276)

Rural communities sometimes lack information about medical conditions such as AIDS. This may exacerbate existing lack of tolerance for diversity. Sometimes negative responses to people who are HIV-positive stem from concerns about contagion and also from moral judgments that derive from very strong religious values. Social work support for the patient and family then is needed to deal with the emotional burden, with social isolation, and also with the lack of resources in the community.

The rural health care facility—a rehabilitation center, hospital, or nursing home—often serves people from a very large geographical area. The social worker must have a good understanding of several counties' welfare and human service resources. One county may have a Meals on Wheels program, for example, while

Family members from distant areas gather at the bedside of a seriously ill family member. Distance from health care settings is characteristic in many rural areas.

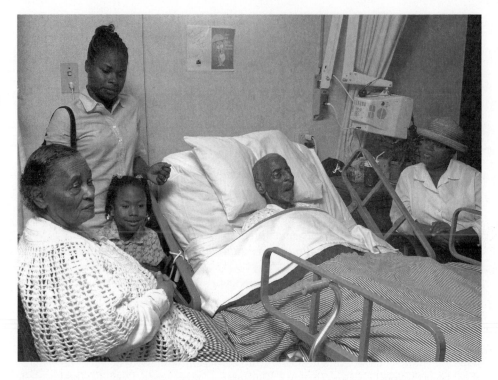

another does not or can provide only general nutrition but no special diets (such as a diabetic diet). A large geographical area may also mean long-distance travel for the social worker when a home visit is needed.

Social workers in rural health care settings often work independently without the support of social work colleagues in similar settings in the area. Professional isolation is a problem. Even within the health facility the social worker must make decisions without the assistance of a social work supervisor, consultant, or another social worker. Continuing education programs of the NASW and state universities provide important support. In many areas, regional organizations have sprung up and are often the rural social worker's professional lifeline.

ENVIRONMENTAL ISSUES

Rural communities were once assumed to be free of the environmental conditions in cities that create hazards to health and well-being. As increasing understanding is developed about the forces causing destruction of the biosphere, however, it is increasingly apparent that environmental degradation and disease are created in rural areas by agricultural practices such as the use of chemical fertilizers and pesticides, permitting polluted water to flow into crop irrigation systems, and as a result of deforestation practices. Of course, the industrial smokestacks and vehicle emissions of metropolitan areas are responsible for major environmental impacts that may have consequences for health and well-being.

Concern about threats to public health actually goes back to the mid- to late 1900s, when social reformers in England came to believe that overcrowding in urban areas was toxic to the physical and mental health of the population (Susser & Morabia, 2006, p. 16). The social reformers perceived that the rapid urbanization, poor sanitation, overcrowding, and stark inequalities of the Industrial Revolution were responsible for the concurrent spread of disease. Awareness that environmental toxins such as mercury and lead could contribute to specific physical and mental illnesses, however, has evolved steadily over the years until today, a great deal is known about the relationship between environmental issues and health.

In the United States, social work as a profession has been slow to embrace environmental concerns. Yet, according to De Silva and Clark, the president and executive director of NASW, respectively, "social work is unique among the helping professions in its emphasis on the person-in-environment prospective" (2006, p. 136). Carol Germain and Alex Gitterman were two of the early social work contributors to the ecological systems theory that underpins practice today. Their 1980 text, *The Life Model of Social Work Practice*, incorporated a great deal of content related to the natural environment. The profession, however, seemed more eager to apply the text's social systems theory than its environmental theory to practice.

In the mid 1990s Berger, in a series of articles in the journal *Social Work*, challenged social workers to stop ignoring the perilous reality that all of humanity faced as a result of ongoing environmental degradation. In 1995 Berger pointed to accumulating evidence that human immune systems were increasingly compromised, asthma and allergies were more prevalent, and diseases such as lupus, multiple sclerosis, Graves disease, and rheumatoid arthritis had also begun to increase. In 1994 Hoff and McNutt published *The Global Environmental Crisis: Implications for Social Welfare and Social Work*, clearly demonstrating how all areas of social work practice are affected by and respond to environmental issues.

In 1999 NASW adopted an Environmental Policy statement. Portions of that statement appear in Exhibit 6-3. Gradually, the profession began to respond. Besthorn, for example, wrote about a shift he believed was occurring in the way that Western society was beginning to evolve a new "sense of self" characterized by increased appreciation for the natural environment and for nonhuman beings that share that environment. He perceived that the true essence of human development would be achieved through nature. In social work practice, he saw potential in exposing clients to wilderness experiences and other activities involving therapeutic contact with natural environments (2002). One entire issue of the journal *Health and Social Work* was devoted to the social work research, practice, and community initiatives that were being implemented to secure healthier community environments (Galambos, 2003).

Meantime, Saleebey (pioneer developer of the "strengths perspective") began to urge social workers to pay more attention to the spaces in which social work clients live their daily lives. He pointed to many small but meaningful changes that could be made within clients' homes (e.g., repairing a broken window), in neighborhoods (community garden projects or creating a children's play area in a neglected lot), in local school buildings or to school playgrounds, even to brighten and improve agency

---

EXHIBIT 6-3

NASW Policy Statement on the Environment

All people share a common need for and right to a fair share of the Earth's resources, including a clean, safe, and healthy environment. Social workers are in a unique position to influence the distribution of resources and to participate in efforts to protect the environment. Environmental exploitation violates the principle of social justice and is a direct violation of the NASW Code of Ethics (Hoff & Rogge, 1996). Citizens of the world need to embrace a moral code that recognizes the realities of technological advancement and the vulnerabilities of the natural environment. Therefore, it is the position of NASW that:

■ Social workers have a vested interest in the viability of the natural environment, including the noxious effect environment degradation has on people, most especially on oppressed individuals, families, small groups, and communities.

■ Social workers have a professional obligation to become knowledgeable and educated about the precarious position of the natural environment, to speak out and take action on behalf of it, and to help their clients act in an environmentally responsible manner.

■ We support vigorous enforcement of environmental protection laws; funding to promote research into prevention and treatment of environmentally

related diseases such as multiple chemical sensitivity, asthma, allergies, and emphysema; and the enforcement of the rights of people afflicted with environmental diseases.

■ In the United States, the U.S. Environmental Protection Agency and state and local counterparts must have the necessary resources and authority to establish and enforce environmental protection in accordance with generally acceptable scientific standards and data. Similar policies should be adopted and enforced by the appropriate offices within the United Nations and other appropriate organizations and governing bodies throughout the world.

■ Individuals who work in hazardous jobs must be protected by strict national and international environmental standards, including effective enforcement mechanisms.

■ We advocate for a secure affordable food system free of toxic chemicals and pesticides for all individuals.

SOURCE: E. C. de Silva & E. J. Clark (2006). Environmental policy. Policy statement approved by the NASW Delegate Assembly, August 1999. *Social Work Speaks: National Association of Social Workers policy statements 2006–2009*. Washington, DC: NASW Press, pp. 140–141. Exhibit 6-3 represents only a partial listing of the policy statement.

---

waiting rooms (2004). Social workers and even social work student organizations could readily take on such initiatives. These small projects hold power to transform otherwise forbidding and nonnutritive environments.

Perhaps it will take today's students and a whole new generation of social workers, who are enlivened by an appreciation of the natural environment, to truly implement the action that the NASW policy statement envisioned. Clearly there is much work to be done if social workers are to take the kind of leadership on environment that the profession is capable of.

SOCIAL JUSTICE AND HEALTH: GLOBAL PERSPECTIVES

The NASW policy on the environment, in part, states: "Global justice cannot exist unless all people of the world share the Earth's resources. Global justice cannot exist when a minority of people in technologically developed countries consume a disproportionate share of the available resources" (de Silva & Clark, 2006, p. 140). Health and well-being, too, are amazingly dependent on the state of the environment and on equitable sharing of resources. According to Lee Jong-wook, director-general of the World Health Organization, "today's global health situation raises urgent questions about justice" (2003, p. 3). The World Health Organization's data demonstrate serious inequities in health care resources between developing countries and industrialized nations and inequities in access to care even within some of the wealthiest nations.

In many of the world's poorest regions, especially Africa, current levels of child mortality are actually higher today than they were in 1990, according to the World Health Organization (Jong-wook, 2003, p. 8). HIV/AIDS remains a factor, too, in child deaths in sub-Saharan Africa. In rich nations as well as poor nations, children are at much higher risk of dying if they live in poverty and are malnourished. In the world's poorest nations, social, political, and economic instability contribute to deteriorating rates of adult survival, too. In recent years this has been dramatically demonstrated in mortality rates exceeding those of 30 years ago for countries such as Zimbabwe, Botswana, Swaziland, and Lesotho in Africa (p. 8).

The essential interdependence between health and social justice is well illustrated in Exhibit 6-4. Violations of human rights that potently threaten the health and well-being of people include such current practices as trafficking in women and children. **Trafficking** refers to the use of physical or psychological coercion in transporting persons, often for financial gain; women may be trafficked for commercial sex or domestic labor purposes, while children may be transported for sexual purposes, to provide low cost labor, or for illicit adoption. The U.S. Department of State estimates that "600,000 to 800,000 people of all ages are trafficked across international borders each year, mostly for sexual exploitation and forced labor" (USAID, 2007, p. 1). An estimated 100,000 children are trafficked internationally each month (Dottridge, 2004, as cited in Lyons, Manion, & Carlsen, 2006). Homeless children worldwide and those in very poor families are more vulnerable to exploitation of many kinds. Ethiopia, for example, "has one of the highest rates of child labor in the world. With more than 50 percent of the population below the age of 14 and a fertility rate of seven children per woman, poorer households have seen children begin to work at an earlier age, sometimes before the age of five" (Admassic, 2003, as cited in Lyons et al., p. 143).

Human rights violations of the kind described put both children and adults at great risk of ill health, injury sometimes leading to death, and sexually transmitted disease (including HIV/AIDS), regardless of the country in which the exploitation occurs. When people are transported from one country to another, diseases of many kinds travel with them, thus placing other populations at risk. War, famine, and poverty—all facets of social injustice—carry negative implications for health and human rights.

Even within wealthy industrial countries like the United States, race and socioeconomic status adversely affect human well-being. The links among poverty, environmental degradation, race or ethnicity, and illness are apparent when minority residents of polluted inner-city areas suffer high rates of asthma, when the families of migrant workers suffer illness from the toxins and pesticides brought home on work clothes and human skin, and when young children suffer lead poisoning from eating lead-based paint chips from the walls of their slum homes. Inequality in income has

EXHIBIT 6-4

Linkage between Health and Human Rights

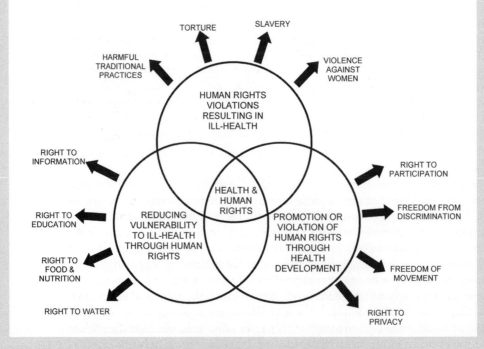

LINKAGES BETWEEN HEALTH AND HUMAN RIGHTS

 World Health Organization

Promoting and protecting health and respecting, protecting and fulfilling human rights are inextricably linked:

- Violations or lack of attention to human rights can have serious health consequences (e.g. harmful traditional practices, slavery, torture and inhuman and degrading treatment, violence against women and children).

- Health policies and programmes can promote or violate human rights in their design or implementation (e.g. freedom from discrimination, individual autonomy, rights to participation, privacy and information).

- Vulnerability to ill-health can be reduced by taking steps to respect, protect and fulfil human rights (e.g. freedom from discrimination on account of race, sex and gender roles, rights to health, food and nutrition, education, housing).

Examples of the linkages between health and human rights:

TORTURE   SLAVERY

HARMFUL TRADITIONAL PRACTICES   VIOLENCE AGAINST WOMEN

HUMAN RIGHTS VIOLATIONS RESULTING IN ILL-HEALTH

RIGHT TO INFORMATION   RIGHT TO PARTICIPATION

HEALTH & HUMAN RIGHTS   FREEDOM FROM DISCRIMINATION

RIGHT TO EDUCATION   REDUCING VULNERABILITY TO ILL-HEALTH THROUGH HUMAN RIGHTS   PROMOTION OR VIOLATION OF HUMAN RIGHTS THROUGH HEALTH DEVELOPMENT

RIGHT TO FOOD & NUTRITION   FREEDOM OF MOVEMENT

RIGHT TO WATER   RIGHT TO PRIVACY

SOURCE: World Health Organization (n.d.). *Linkages between health and human rights*. Retrieved June 14, 2007, from http://www.who.int/hhr/HHR%20linkages.pdf

been shown by numerous studies to be related to incidence of disease and mortality (Kawachi, 1999; Muenning, et al., 2005; Wennemo, 1993; & Wilkinson, 2005, as cited in Moniz & Gorin, 2007, p. 229). Similarly, numerous studies have pointed to disparity based on race. The 1985 U.S. Department of Health and Human Services study of differences in health status among people of color, the 1999 Kaiser Family Foundation's study of access to care, the 2002 Institute of Medicine's *Unequal Treatment* report, and the 2004 *National Healthcare Quality Report* of the Agency for Healthcare Research and Quality—these studies all showed disparity in access to care for racial and ethnic minority populations in the United States.

Perhaps it is not a big surprise, then, that researchers have found that the wealthiest of countries do not consistently demonstrate the strongest indicators of health. The United States, for example, spends far more on health per citizen than any other country, yet data collected over many years show that the United States lags behind approximately 20 other countries (including most all of the European countries) in health (Moniz & Gorin, 2007). Of course, the European Union countries and many others as well all have one thing in common that the United States does not yet have: a national health system that ensures access to health care for all citizens.

HISTORICAL PERSPECTIVES

The chapter content now shifts to history. We begin with a quick look at the origin of hospitals and then trace the history of social work within health care. Following the history section, the chapter introduces the social policy that has shaped health care in the United States. An undercurrent that is subtly present in both the history and the social policy areas is that of social justice. Social justice concerns brought social workers into the health arena, and social justice concerns perplex social policy planners and activists as health care policies and programs continue to evolve.

Early History: Caring for the Poor and Sick

It is not clear when health care institutions were developed, but archaeologists have uncovered ruins of what may have been such facilities dating from the sixth century B.C. The tithing of the early Christians produced funds that churches could use for the care of the poor and the sick. Around the third century A.D., monks of the Roman Catholic Church began to provide rescue service and health care to avalanche victims in shelters known as hospices. The victims were mostly southern Europeans who were fleeing from famine and economic hardship and were trying to reach northern regions in search of a better life. They were unfamiliar with and unprepared for the harsh weather of the mountains. Gradually the term *hospice* came to be used for institutions that cared for ill persons. In western Europe hospices housed not only the sick but, until almshouses were organized, the poor as well. Gradually hospices developed into larger institutions that were run primarily by religious orders of priests or sisters. (Even today, in most of Europe, a nurse is called "sister.") In England during the mid-1500s, monasteries were confiscated by the Crown in the historic dispute between Henry VIII and Rome. With the seizure of religious holdings, the settings that cared for the sick were gradually converted into publicly held institutions.

Origins of Health Care Social Work

The English forerunners of today's health care social workers were the **lady almoners,** persons who provided food and donations to the poor. In 1895 a lady almoner was stationed at the Royal Free Hospital with the understanding that she was to interview patients to determine who would receive free, or partly free, medical service, "and to exclude those unsuitable for free care. But in serving this restricted purpose the worker was soon aware that many patients accepted for medical treatment were in sore social difficulties as well" (Cannon, 1952, p. 8). This early social worker, like many today, preferred to define the nature of her professional practice herself, rather than permitting hospital authorities, physicians, or others to govern how she understood and carried out her professional responsibilities. In fact, she became an advocate for patients, fighting for the rights and needs of the poor and underserved, those whom the Royal Free Hospital saw as "unsuitable." The use of social workers spread throughout British Commonwealth hospitals, and their role soon broadened to include advocacy, referral to other community resources, patient education, and counseling.

The Emergence of Health Care Social Work in the United States

The person who is generally considered the originator of medical social work in the United States is Ida Cannon. As a young woman, Ida Cannon had worked as a visiting nurse in the slum areas along the Mississippi River in St. Paul, Minnesota. Inspired by Jane Addams, the great settlement house worker, Cannon became interested in social work and went to Boston to pursue her studies at the Boston School of Social Work. In 1905 Dr. Richard Cabot, whose concerns about poverty and its impact on illness paralleled her own, asked Ida Cannon to join the staff of Massachusetts General Hospital.

In her professional practice, Cannon was not only a competent social worker but also a dynamic leader, a teacher of medical and social work students, and an articulate author. Health care social workers were the first among the various social work specialty groups to organize professionally. Ida Cannon was among the founders of the American Association of Hospital Social Workers in 1918. This organization, later known as the American Association of Medical Social Workers (AAMSW), published its own journal, *Medical Social Work.* The AAMSW eventually merged with other independent social work organizations to become the National Association of Social Workers (NASW) in 1955. Cannon's 1952 text, *On the Social Frontier of Medicine: Pioneering in Medical Social Service,* describes the early years of hospital social work.

Soon after Ida Cannon developed the social service department at Massachusetts General Hospital, Bellevue Hospital in New York hired a social worker. Slowly hospitals across the country, including specialized facilities, copied these examples. Public health concerns about patients with tuberculosis and venereal disease resulted in employment of social workers by state health departments and tuberculosis sanatoriums. The passage of the Social Security Act in 1935 resulted in entitlements that further encouraged the expansion of social work in health care settings. Both the American Hospital Association (AHA) and the American Public Health Association developed standards and requirements for social workers in the facilities they regulated.

One of the most influential persons in shaping health care social work over ensuing years was Helen Rehr. For more than 30 years she provided leadership, creating many innovative programs within the Social Work Department at Mount Sinai Medical Center in New York. A prolific author, she published many works related to health care social work, among them: *Medicine and Social Work: An Exploration in Interprofessionalism* (1974) and *Advancing Social Work Practice in the Health Care Field* (1982). Although now retired, this health care social work pioneer continues to consult, to contribute to her community, and to publish; her most recent book is *The Social Work-Medicine Relationship: 100 Years at Mount Sinai* (2006).

SOCIAL POLICY: POLITICS AND ECONOMICS IN HEALTH CARE

By 1905 when Ida Cannon initiated the first hospital social work department, the U.S. health care system had evolved from one delivered by women within their own households, relying primarily on homemade medical preparations, to an industry dominated by specialized professionals, pharmaceutical corporations, and institutions. Massive hospitals, first built during the Civil War, utilized new techniques of hygiene and by the early 1900s vastly increased the number of surgical procedures performed, thanks to the development of diagnostic X-rays and anesthesia.

By 1912 many European countries (England, Germany, Austria, and others) and Russia had initiated compulsory health insurance programs, and increasing interest in such programs was emerging in the United States. Jane Addams and social workers in the settlement house movement, well aware of unmet health needs—especially of women and children—threw their support behind presidential candidate Theodore Roosevelt when he advocated compulsory health insurance for the United States. With the advent of World War I and the Bolshevik Revolution in Russia, however, the U.S. public began to perceive anything that appeared German (e.g., compulsory health insurance) as negative and threatening or anything Russian as Communistic. Jane Addams and other proponents of compulsory health insurance were branded as traitors. Even the Federation for Social Service of the Methodist Church faced extremely adverse publicity. The American Medical Association (AMA) changed course and began what was to become a lengthy history of opposition to any form of what they called "socialized medicine" (Moniz & Gorin, 2007).

Social workers and other health care policy reformers did not give up, however. Julia Lathrop and Grace Abbott, both former colleagues of Jane Addams and former residents of Chicago's Hull House, disseminated research findings showing that the United States's exceptionally high rate of infant mortality was related to inadequate prenatal care and poverty (Trattner, 1999, as cited in Moniz & Gorin, 2007). Another social worker, Jeanette Rankin, serving as the first woman elected to the U.S. Congress, introduced and achieved passage of the Sheppard-Towner Infancy and Maternity Act of 1921. This legislation provided funding to states for numerous public health programs aimed at improving the health or women and children. With the advent of the Great Depression and concerted opposition from the AMA, which saw public health services as interfering with their right to free enterprise, the Sheppard-Towner Act was terminated in 1929 when Congress discontinued funding for it. The establishment of Blue Cross and Blue Shield insurance programs in the 1930s "laid the foundation for a third-party payment system, completely changed health care financing, and led the way for employment-based insurance" (Moniz & Gorin, 2007, p. 26).

In the 1930s, social workers again provided courageous leadership in health care reform efforts. Harry L. Hopkins, a social worker who had worked with Franklin D. Roosevelt in New York when Roosevelt was governor, became a trusted adviser of Roosevelt when he was elected U.S. President. Hopkins and Frances Perkins, another social worker and Roosevelt's Secretary of Labor (the first woman to occupy a cabinet position), both supported compulsory health care and hoped to have it included in the Social Security Act of 1935. As a result of a flood of opposition orchestrated by the AMA, compulsory national health insurance was removed from the final version of the Social Security Act (Moniz & Gorin, 2007).

By the 1940s, "former charity hospitals transformed themselves into profit-making, or surplus-generating (among the nonprofit institutions) businesses, increasingly dependent on cash-paying customers and third-party payers (for example, insurers)" (Weiss, 1997, p. 13). Blue Cross and Blue Shield, instituted in the 1930s, were controlled by hospitals and physicians, thereby ensuring payment for medical services delivered by the private sector. Public health services, which had served the nation through several waves of infectious diseases and provided health care to low-income populations, were politically crushed by the strength of the entrepreneurial, for-profit, health care industry.

> By the 1960s, however, it was clear that private health insurance was not capable of providing benefits to large numbers of people and that it was not capable of containing costs. At the same time, nationwide pressure was building for national health insurance. (Weiss, 1997, p. 86)

Medicare

The federal government's involvement in health care financing became a reality in the 1960s with the enactment of the programs known as Medicare and Medicaid. **Medicare** was created in 1965 with an amendment, Title XVIII, to the Social Security Act. Labor unions strongly supported this legislation while the American Medical Association (AMA), the AHA, "and the insurance industry engaged in a bitter, vitriolic battle to keep government out of health care. These interests perceived government involvement as a threat to the realization of maximum profit and to professional autonomy" (Weiss, 1997, p. 153). It may be that the compromises made to secure passage of Medicare are partially responsible for some of the program's current problems with skyrocketing costs, fraudulent charges by health care providers, and mismanagement. Compromises won by the AMA and the AHA included limiting government control over reimbursements for services and, a major victory, allowing for Blue Cross and Blue Shield (and other insurance companies) to be the conduit for payments made to providers.

Medicare currently covers 43 million Americans who are:

- People who are 65 years old.
- People who are disabled.
- People with permanent kidney failure (Medicare).

Medicare has four parts. Part A provides insurance for hospital care and 100 days in a nursing home. Medicare comes from payroll taxes paid while people are working; however, it is definitely not free. It requires substantial co-payments. Hospice care is provided for terminally ill persons, but only if they are expected to die in 6 months. Many qualifications must be met before a person may receive home health care under Medicare.

Part B is different from Part A. It closely resembles a private health insurance program. It is entirely voluntary, but it is vital to most people because it pays for some of the health care expenses not covered by Part A. Like private insurance, there are monthly payments ($93 monthly in 2007). The payment amount is almost always increased when there is a raise in Social Security. Part B is often thought of as outpatient insurance since it provides payment for physicians, laboratory services, medical equipment such as wheelchairs or walkers, and outpatient surgeries.

To the surprise of some people, Medicare does not cover all medical expenses of the elderly. In fact, with growing concern about the cost of this program, recent legislation has decreased Medicare coverage substantially. Often social workers must explain the limitations of Medicare to disbelieving elderly persons who have trusted that the money they paid into Social Security would take care of all of their medical needs in old age. (Could concern about the cost of her medical care have caused some of Katherine Lewandowski's depression in the case study at the beginning of this chapter?) Services not provided by Parts A or B include:

- Long-term nursing or custodial care.
- Dentures and dental care.
- Eyeglasses.
- Most prescription drugs.

It should be noted, however, that Medicare provides an option in the form of managed care plans that sometimes do cover some of the services listed above. These are **capitated plans,** prepaid by Medicare, in which comprehensive health care is provided and services are coordinated by the plan. Clients may not receive any health care services outside the plan.

Under increasing political pressure, several options to Medicare were initiated in 1997 as Part C. Also known as the Medicare + Choice Program or Medicare Advantage Plan, it includes a variety of managed-care plans plus Medical Savings Accounts. The

Medical Savings Accounts require a very high deductible payment (approximately $6,000 a year) plus monthly premiums. If illness occurs, the $6,000 amount (which is likely to change over time) has to be paid before the plan takes over, but when it does, it pays all remaining medical expenses.

An advantage of the Medicare + Choice programs was that many included prescription drug coverage. A critical complaint of Medicare Parts A and B was their failure to provide coverage for prescriptions. The prescription drug issue became so volatile that in 2003, as part of the Medicare Modernization Act, a prescription drug benefit plan was created. It became Part D of Medicare. Effective in 2006, it is a prescription medication insurance program for Medicare-eligible persons. This plan is administered by private health insurance companies, sold to individuals on a competitive basis, and requires a monthly premium. While there are numerous plans for persons to chose from, each of the plans must adhere to some degree to basic elements of a "standard plan." In the standard plan, after a $250 deductible, most subscribers pay a monthly premium (possibly $35 per month) and a percentage of their prescription costs (possibly 25 percent) up to approximately $2,250 in total drug costs per year. If the person has very expensive medications and reaches the magical $2,250 amount, most plans offer absolutely no coverage for the next $2,850. This must be paid by the person. This period of time when the subscriber receives no prescription drug coverage at all is referred to as "the donut hole." After the subscriber has paid $2,850, coverage resumes at a rate of 95 percent; subscribers are then only responsible for the remaining 5 percent of their prescription costs.

There is amazing complexity in the Medicare Part D program, and few people understand it well. To complicate matters, people in most states must chose from 40 to 50 different plans, and the plans change (sometimes quite dramatically) from year to year. In a hearing before the U.S. Senate Committee on Finance, an attorney from the Center for Medicare Advocacy testified regarding some of the problems with Part D. Foremost was the complexity of the program, which makes it extraordinarily difficult for subscribers to understand, but which also makes it ripe for marketing scams and unscrupulous practices by sales agents. Also of significant concern was the large number of persons with minimal incomes who experience devastating financial circumstances when they reach the "donut hole," despite the supposed availability of emergency subsidies. Other issues involved the inefficient and inaccurate system for transferring information to beneficiaries. The primary concern, however, for the Center for Medicare Advocacy was that with each of the recent private Medicare reform efforts, the "private plans have shown that they are unable to provide the same services as the traditional Medicare program at reduced costs without drastic subsidies from the federal government" (Center for Medicare Advocacy, 2007). So it would seem that the private sector programs offered in recent years have not provided an answer to the prescription drug financing problem that faces America.

Medicare, despite its failings, is a remarkable program. It provides health care to millions of people, many of whom could otherwise not afford it. It is expensive and it has problems, one of which is the millions of dollars lost each year in fraud that is perpetrated by laboratories, managed care plans, physicians, hospitals, nursing homes, and others, sometimes including patients.

Medicaid

Social work as a profession has a special commitment to people who are poor or vulnerable. Of course, this includes people who are at risk of or who have existing physical and mental health problems. Because **Medicaid** is the largest U.S. financial aid program for poor people, it is obvious that social workers need to know something about Medicaid. Most social workers, however, will not need to know all of the intricate details; they do need to know where they can find information about Medicaid. One of the best sources is the Medicaid website, currently at http://www.cms.hhs.gov/home/medicaid.asp. Some very basic information about the Medicaid program follows.

Medicaid, also known as Medical Assistance, was enacted in 1965 as Title XIX of the Social Security Act. It is administered and partially funded by states, but the federal government also partly funds Medicaid and provides some oversight of the program. Initially designed to provide health care funding for poor older people, it was expanded over time. It now covers approximately 58 million people, including people who receive SSI (Supplemental Security Income) because they are blind, aged, or have disabilities. Pregnant women and children with a family income below 133 percent of the poverty line, in general, are also eligible. Medicaid is a lifeline for poor people because it pays for prescriptions, laboratory tests and X rays, inpatient and outpatient hospital care, skilled nursing home care, and home health care.

Medicaid is a means-tested program. Applicants must provide proof of poverty according to their state's definition. Many people find the application procedure humiliating. All persons become eligible for Medicare at age 65, so there is no means test for it. This dramatically differentiates Medicare from Medicaid.

In recent years, the states' power over Medicaid has increased considerably. Now each state:

- Establishes its own eligibility standards.
- Determines the type, amount, duration, and scope of services.
- Sets the rate of payment for services.
- Administers its own program.

As political pressure mounts to cut the costs of Medicaid, states have been given special authority to design their own programs. Some have trimmed Medicaid to its bare bones while others have provided more generous benefits. Cost-cutting methods have included eliminating some health care benefits, moving people out of nursing homes, putting all persons into managed care programs, and cutting mental health services.

Myths that minority, low-income women with many children accounted for most of the expenditures were unfounded; in fact, data indicate that approximately $1,500 is spent per year on children while $13,000 is spent per person for those who have disabilities and $11,000 per person per year is spent on elderly persons (The Henry J. Kaiser Family Foundation, 2007). One author's analysis of the politics of Medicaid is shown in Exhibit 6-5. The future of the Medicaid program depends, ultimately, upon

---

EXHIBIT 6-5

An Analysis of the Politics of Medicaid

Business interests—typically a well-organized lobby—generally want to discredit Medicaid and cut benefits in order to reduce their tax burden.... Hospitals and providers, also with well-organized lobbies, are interested in maximizing Medicaid income through high reimbursements on the one hand but want to weaken federal and state oversight as much as possible on the other. Medicaid beneficiaries—low-income persons, female-headed single parent families, disproportionately minority, elderly, or disabled—are among those with the least political power to influence Medicaid inequities. Legislators commonly want to pass laws that appear to benefit the poor, elderly and disabled but that objectively meet the needs of the business community and providers.

SOURCE: Quoted from L. D. Weiss. (1997). *Private medicine and public health: Profits, politics, and prejudice in the American health care enterprise.* Boulder, CO. Westview Press, pp. 180–181.

---

the political and economic decisions Americans will make concerning the financing of health care.

Financing Health Care

In 1983 the federal government instituted a hospital payment program that almost overnight changed the way hospitals provided service. The program came to be known as the **diagnostic-related group (DRG) plan.** It provided payment to hospitals based on a specific dollar amount per diagnosis. The implementation of DRGs resulted in reduction of hospital stays, increased use of outpatient care, and some level of cost containment. Although designed for Medicare, the DRG plan has evolved into today's **prospective payment system (PPS).** It is widely used by managed care organizations and private insurance plans as well. The PPS sounds more confusing than it really is. With this system, hospitals are paid a fixed amount, a lump sum of money, based on the patient's diagnosis. If the hospital can discharge the patient early, it makes a profit. If the patient outstays the fixed amount, the hospital could lose money. Obviously this system of health care financing offers powerful incentives to hospitals to discharge people very quickly.

Katherine Lewandowski, the client in this chapter's case study, is an example of an elderly person whose discharge from the hospital was dictated, at least in part, by the PPS hospital reimbursement plan. Social workers are among the health care professionals who have expressed concern about the impact of this hospital payment plan on vulnerable patients.

Health Care Reform

Health care reform has been pushing its way to the top of the political agenda since the 1990s. The first proposed large-scale health care reform proposal was the Clinton Health Security Act of 1993, which would have achieved universal coverage if it had become law. According to *The Social Work Dictionary,* "**Universal programs** are social welfare programs that are open to everyone in a nation who falls into a certain category. These programs do not subject people to individualized tests of income or need.

Social Security and Medicare are examples of universal programs in the United States . . ." (Barker, 2003, p. 450). **Universal coverage,** then, would typically refer to a health care program in which every citizen would receive health care benefits at the same rate and without regard to their economic status.

When Hillary Rodham Clinton campaigned across the country seeking support for the Clinton Health Security Act, her message was not well received. According to one magazine, she "invokes the rhetoric of rights and morality. Health care is the 'right' of all Americans, she says, and assuring that they get it is a matter of 'social justice.'" (Barnes, 1994, p. 15). Opponents argued that universal health care was so expensive that it would destroy the country's economy. Liberals failed to support the Clinton proposal because it retained private insurance corporations as program administrators (hence huge administrative costs and built-in profitability) and failed to require a single-payer system. A **single-payer system** exists when either the government or a selected corporation administers the insurance program. The Clinton Health Security Act would have given states control over the system, including the right to select and use a private enterprise single-payer system, but the federal government would have had oversight.

What happened to defeat this major piece of health care reform legislation? Gorin's analysis (2000) provides insight:

> Although the Health Security Act would have preserved the employer-based system of coverage and the private insurance industry, it also would have transformed our health care and political systems. Establishing a right to health care would have dealt conservatives a severe blow and strengthened efforts to expand the social safety net. Interestingly, conservatives had a clearer understanding of this relationship than many progressives did. William Kristol, a key Republican strategist, warned that the Health Security Act posed "a serious *political* threat to the Republican Party" (Skocpol, 1997, p. 145). He warned that the plan's enactment would revive faith in government and enable the Democrats to pose as the "protector of middle-class interests." Conversely, the act's defeat would be a "watershed in the resurgence of a newly bold and principled Republican politics" (Skocpol, p. 146). (Gorin, 2000, p. 141)

So the Health Security Act went down in defeat. Even before the act was voted down, managed care was expanding rapidly and moving with dizzying speed into all segments of the health industry. Once the Clinton national health care reform was clearly dead, "vast sums of federal money (Medicare and Medicaid) were already flowing through private, for-profit MCOs [managed-care organizations]" (Davidson, Davidson, & Keigher, 1999, p. 164). The failure of the Health Security Act proved to be a watershed indeed. A **national health insurance** plan would not be politically acceptable again in the very near future.

What made the failed piece of legislation a national insurance plan? National insurance plans are those systems of a given country that ensure participation in comprehensive health care insurance for all citizens. Sometimes there is confusion, especially in the political rhetoric, between **national health service** and national health insurance. A national health service is a country's ownership and administration of health care facilities and services where all citizens may receive care. England and Germany, for example, have such systems. In the United States the Veterans Administration operates health care facilities that serve veterans; the U.S. military also administers and provides health facilities for military families. A national insurance plan, by contrast, is merely the insurance that is provided to ensure that citizens can access health care. In national health insurance, the government may operate the insurance program or it may contract with one (a single-provider system) or multiple private insurance companies. National insurance plans and national health services both provide universal coverage. In fact, most industrialized countries except the United States do have some form of universal coverage.

Change   There is no doubt that our health care system is already changing but is it changing in the direction that we would want? Currently, workers who only a few years back received free or low-cost health insurance as a fringe benefit of employment are finding that employers are shifting more of the health insurance costs to them. They now make co-payments each time they see a doctor or get a prescription refilled. They also pay much larger monthly fees for employer-sponsored health care insurance. Yet these employees are lucky. Employees of small businesses may receive no employee health insurance at all. Small, private hospitals have merged into giant corporations that own not only the hospital but also the outpatient clinics, pharmacy, behavioral health system, and nursing homes. Doctors have lost control over hospital admissions and discharges, since they are increasingly determined by the corporation's business office. Freedom to choose one's health care provider—once a hallmark of the American system, a factor that separated it from the systems of other countries—has quietly vanished. More importantly, vast numbers of Americans (15.9 percent or 46.6 million people) have no health insurance at all (U.S. Census Bureau, 2004).

Today, change is in the wind. Indeed, it seems inevitable. Between 2006 and 2007 Massachusetts and Vermont passed health care reform laws, and approximately 20 additional states had legislative proposals for some form of health care reform. Lack of action on the part of the federal government resulted in state action to deal with growing numbers of uninsured persons, mostly young adults and children. Some of the bills required citizens to purchase health care insurance, possibly through their employers, and created disincentives for employers who failed to provide insurance coverage. This amounts to a major overhaul of state health systems. Other states moved more slowly and incrementally, with plans focusing on only portions of their uninsured citizens. Interestingly, some of the leadership in health care reform is coming from Republican state governors such as Arnold Schwarzenegger of California and Mitt Romney, the former governor Massachusetts. Citizen action groups range from a diverse group called Health Care for All to physicians' groups dedicated to health care policy reform and social workers through the national NASW office and state NASW chapters. U.S. Senator Barbara Mikulski (Democratic Senator from Maryland), who is also a social worker, is a strong supporter of universal health care for the United States.

Health care reform could be initiated with small, incremental steps, such as creation of programs targeted to specific vulnerable groups, or it could mean a major overhaul of the existing health care system. Options would include development of a governmental health care system similar to that of some European countries, where the government owns and operates hospitals and other health care facilities; such an option is probably not likely to garner support in the United States. Reform could also mean a federal funding to states to develop programs that would ensure quality health insurance for all citizens, with most existing systems remaining in place. Or it could require a single-payer program such as the Canadian system, whereby each state negotiates with a single insurance corporation to handle all claims, thereby dramatically reducing bureaucracy as well as billing, marketing, and other health care administrative costs. Some public citizen health advocacy groups are convinced that the single-payer approach is the only option that will make universal coverage affordable (Wolfe, 2006). Private enterprise would perhaps oppose government-administered health care with tax supports, preferring that individual citizens be required by law to purchase insurance from any insurance provider whose plan met prescribed requirements. Other options also exist. Do we now have the political will to change? With skyrocketing costs under the current system, can we afford not to create change?

Cost-Benefit Analysis   The United States is not the only country with increasing health care costs. Costs appear to be rising everywhere; however, it is instructive to see what benefits we currently achieve from our health care dollars. Today, as Exhibit 6-6 shows, the United States expends a considerable percentage of its gross national product on health care. But what has this investment purchased?

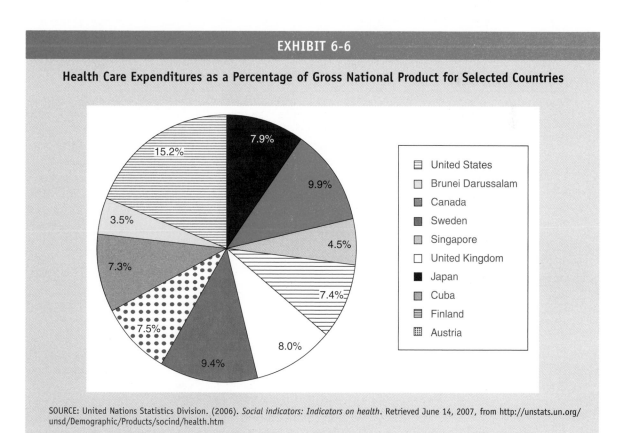

EXHIBIT 6-6

Health Care Expenditures as a Percentage of Gross National Product for Selected Countries

15.2%
7.9%
9.9%
4.5%
3.5%
7.3%
7.4%
7.5%
8.0%
9.4%

Legend:
- United States
- Brunei Darussalam
- Canada
- Sweden
- Singapore
- United Kingdom
- Japan
- Cuba
- Finland
- Austria

SOURCE: United Nations Statistics Division. (2006). *Social indicators: Indicators on health*. Retrieved June 14, 2007, from http://unstats.un.org/unsd/Demographic/Products/socind/health.htm

For many years health-index statistics have been tracked by country, so it is now possible to compare critical indicators of health across many nations. Two prominent measures traditionally used to evaluate health systems' performances are infant mortality rates and life expectancy. Compare the health-index data in Exhibit 6-7 with the

EXHIBIT 6-7

Measures of Health Systems' Performance

Country	Infant Mortality (Deaths per 1,000 Live Births)	Life Expectance at Birth (Years)	
		Male	Female
Isle of Man	2	74	80
Japan	3	78	85
Sweden	3	78	82
Singapore	3	77	81
Iceland	3	79	83
Hong Kong	4	79	85
Finland	4	75	82
(6 additional countries)	4		
Austria	5	76	82
United Kingdom	5	76	81
Israel	5	78	82
Canada	5	77	82
(10 additional countries)	5		
Cuba	6	75	79
Cypress	6	76	81
Brunei Darussalam	6	74	79
(3 additional countries)	6		
United States of America	7	75	80
Croatia	7	71	78
Malta	7	76	81
(3 additional countries)	7		
Chile	8	75	81
Macao	8	78	82
Slovakia	8	70	78
(2 additional countries)	8		

SOURCE: United Nations Statistics Division. (2006). *Social indicators: Indicators on health*. Retrieved June 14, 2007, from http://unstats.un.org/Demographic/products/socind/health.htm

per person health care expenditures in Exhibit 6-6. Even though other factors such as healthier lifestyle may account for some of the differences seen, it is apparent that in the United States the cost per citizen is not achieving the results on these important indicators that national health care systems attain in the other industrialized countries. Note that the lowest rates of infant mortality came from countries like Sweden and Japan (only three deaths). The United States, which ranked 22 among countries in 1998, had slipped to 26 by 2000 and 34 by 2005. Exhibit 6-7 also provides data for selected other countries.

As U.S. citizens seek answers to the health care dilemmas in this country, some look to the Canadian system. Enacted in 1971 and known as Medicare, it is of considerable interest, because Canadians share many of the values and beliefs of Americans. An overview of the basic principles of the Canadian system is provided in Exhibit 6-8. Because Canada has a single-payer system, there are minimal expenses for billing. It is estimated that approximately half of the differences in costs between Canadian and U.S. hospital costs relate to administrative expenses. Canada also expends only minimal time and costs in determining who is eligible for care and what the extent of their insurance coverage is; Canadians merely present their provincial health identification card. Hospitalization is covered so they are not billed (Armstrong, Armstrong, & Fegan, 1998).

Access   Although no Canadian is denied health care based on financial ability, what happens for the many uninsured or underinsured Americans is that they postpone preventive or diagnostic care. The result is more expensive care, debilitation, and even premature death. The underinsured are also discharged from care prematurely, which also brings long-range health (and cost) hazards.

It does seem likely that at present the United States has more technology for organ transplants, diagnostic imaging, and other complex procedures, but the Canadian system is not far behind and routinely performs open heart surgeries and other major operations. Access to high-tech medical procedures is more uniformly available to Canadian citizens than to U.S. citizens. In terms of pioneering new technology, Canadian doctors, too, have made important contributions: the discovery of

---

EXHIBIT 6-8

Basic Principles of the Canadian Health Care System

1. **Universality.**   Everyone is covered and has the same benefits.

2. **Portability.**   Benefits are not linked to employment or province of residence.

3. **Comprehensiveness.**   Benefits include full coverage of medical and hospital care, long-term care (covered separately and differently, depending on the province), mental health services, and prescription drugs for people over 65 and for people with catastrophic illnesses, and other services.

4. **Public, nonprofit administration.**   The system is publicly run and publicly accountable, with provincial governments as the single payers of physicians and hospitals.

5. **Freedom of choice of provider.**

SOURCE: T. Mizrahi, R. Fasano, & S. N. Dooha, (1993). National health line: Canadian and American health care: Myths and realities. *Health & Social Work, 18*(1), pp. 7–8.

insulin for the treatment of diabetes, the pioneering of lung transplants and bone marrow transplants, and the development of very lightweight batteries to supply power for artificial hearts.

Waiting lines are another issue related to access. The myth is that Canadians must wait in long lines to see doctors but that Americans don't. The reality is that while waiting definitely can be a problem in Canada, it should be recalled that those Americans who cannot afford private doctors must use emergency rooms and clinics, where waiting lines do exist. Similarly, in rural areas and underserved metropolitan neighborhoods, waiting lines are long. In the early 2000s, Canadians did encounter waiting lists, especially for surgeries such as hip and knee replacement and cataract repair. In 2005 a Supreme Court case brought the issue to a head, and the Canadian government recognized that it would either have to develop a two-tier system whereby portions of the population with sufficient income would obtain surgery or other specialized care on a private basis while others would endure lengthy waits, or action would need to be taken to restore the promise of the Canadian Health Act to provide truly universal care. The government responded by putting $4.5 billion into a 6-year plan to reduce waiting times for treatment, increasing funding to the provinces by an additional $3.5 billion over 2 years, and earmarking an additional 6 percent per year in anticipation of rising health care costs. By 2008 it was expected that waiting lists would have been substantially reduced and the promise of the Canadian Health Act would be respected (CBC News, 2006).

Bureaucracy Americans are highly suspicious of bureaucracy. This suspicion then generates fear about government regulation and centralized authority. It is a mistake, though, for Americans to think that our health care system is not bureaucratized and regulated: it is increasingly regulated by thousands of insurance and managed-care corporations so impersonal that patients have not even had the right to appeal decisions or sue for malpractice. Our system isn't centralized. Sometimes that is an advantage, but when it leads to fragmentation and lack of access to needed care, it can be a serious limitation. The Canadian system is also not managed by a single government bureaucracy; instead the 10 Canadian provinces (similar to U.S. states) administer their own services. The Canadian federal government partially funds the system and requires that each province meet the system's principles (see Exhibit 6-8).

The growing state of crisis in the U.S. health care system suggests that change is necessary, either incremental change or large-scale, fundamental change. There are probably many different directions that the United States could go. The inequity and huge administrative costs of the present system suggest the inevitability of change. The Up for Debate box offers arguments for and against a national health plan for the United States that would be based on the Canadian system. In this plan private as well as public hospitals would continue to exist and doctors could be employed in public health or could operate private practices.

A single-payer system (where one insurance plan selected by the state or federal government pays hospitals and providers directly) would eliminate the multiplicity of insurance carriers and administrative overhead that inflate health care costs. Other options exist and still others are yet to be created as the political discussion continues.

UP FOR DEBATE

Proposition: The United States should adopt a national health insurance plan based on a single-payer system that would provide universal coverage.

YES	NO
Access to health care should not depend on one's economic status.	Persons who work hard and carry substantial responsibility are entitled to receive whatever level of health care their income affords them.
Use of a single, public system to process claims based on standardized forms would save billions of dollars in health care costs.	The nation's economy would be adversely affected by the demise of the health insurance industry.
The kind of competition that improves service and reduces waiting can be built into a national plan.	The likelihood of waits for nonemergency yet needed services, including surgeries, is a big risk.
All citizens would be covered even if they were between jobs, were employed part-time, or had a preexisting condition.	The current mix of public and private health care plans fuels the economy and generates diverse health plans that meet most people's needs.
Equal access to health care is a moral right of all citizens.	There is no constitutionally defined right of citizens to health care.

Hopefully, the outcome will be a system that provides excellent quality, dignified health care to all Americans. If we have the political will to do so, we can accomplish this social justice goal.

FUTURE TRENDS FOR SOCIAL WORKERS

The enactment of Medicare and subsequent legislation related to Medicare profoundly influenced the profession. One result was an expansion of the number of social workers hired by hospitals. Hospitals became increasingly alert to the credentials of the persons who provided social services as gradually all of the states passed laws requiring certification or licensure for social workers (some, however, only at the MSW level of practice). Other health care providers, such as nursing homes and home health care agencies, also increased their hiring of social workers.

In the 1980s, when Medicare cost containment became a serious concern, prospective pricing was introduced through the DRG procedure described earlier in this chapter. Many MSWs found the discharge planning responsibilities of the DRG program less appealing than the more therapeutic services they had been providing. As a result, some hospitals increased the number of BSWs and made discharge planning their primary responsibility. But other hospitals began using nurses as discharge planners. Then, as the 1990s brought increased pressure to cut costs, hospitals ceased expansion of social work departments and, in some cases, reduced the number of social workers.

The Bureau of Labor Statistics' publication *Occupational Outlook Handbook* predicts that "employment of social workers is expected to *increase faster than the average* for all occupations through 2014. The rapidly growing elderly population and the aging baby boom generation will create greater demand for health and social services, resulting in particularly rapid job growth among gerontology social workers" (2006, p. 4, emphasis added). Their experts anticipate that the growth of hospital social work positions will be slower than other areas because hospital stays have become so brief. This trend has resulted in growth in home health care, assisted-living centers, hospices, and nursing homes.

The elderly, mentally ill persons, people with chronic health problems, and families in crisis are expected to need increased services in the future from health care providers. These are the very people that social workers will be seeing in long-term care facilities, subacute centers, home health care, hemodialysis units, rehabilitation and other specialized care centers, HMOs, and health clinics. Within hospitals, social work responsibilities will continue to shift toward emergency and trauma centers, cardiac and intensive care units, oncology and hospice programs, and perinatal centers. The growth of community-based centers, including outpatient surgeries and diagnostic centers, is predicted to provide more employment opportunities, too. With fewer services offered under some managed care plans and large numbers of families who are under- or uninsured, social work advocacy skills will be needed in both clinical and policy arenas (Poole, 1995). A new area for further development is social work within insurance companies: in community education, in prevention programs for new parents, in case management with frail older adults, and in management and policy-making positions.

Health care is one of the most rapidly changing fields of social work practice. It brings social workers into some of the most emotional and sensitive experiences of human lives—life-saving surgeries, births, minor as well as serious injuries, and deaths—some experiences welcomed and some filled with anger and despair. Social workers will need to sharpen their skills for work in these very challenging areas. The professional education that has equipped social workers to "treat the whole person," to understand and locate strengths in the environment, and to advocate for social justice—these will remain the hallmark of health care social work practice.

INTERNET SITES

http://www.napsw.org	The National Association of Perinatal Social Workers
http://www.nrharural.org	National Rural Health Association
http://www.nlm.nih.gov/pubs/factsheets/nichsr_fs.html	National Information Center on Health Services Research and Health Care Technology
http://www.aosw.org	Association of Oncology Social Work
http://www.who.int/	World Health Organization
http://www.kidney.org/professionals/CNSW	Council of Nephrology Social Workers of the National Kidney Foundation

http://www.medicareadvocacy.org/	Center for Medicare Advocacy, Inc.
http://www.medicare.gov/	The Official U.S. Government Site for Medicare Information
http://www.kff.org/about/kcmu.cfm	Kaiser Commission on Medicaid and the Uninsured
http://www.aascipsw.org	American Association of Spinal Cord Injury Psychologists and Social Workers
http://www.hospicenet.org	Hospice Net
http://www.who.int/hhr/en	World Health Organization – Health and Human Rights
http://medlineplus.gov	Medline Plus

SUMMARY

Linda Sanders, a senior social work student in field placement, introduces the reader to the field of health care. Because her courses are preparing her for generalist social work practice, Linda is able to assess the tragedy of Katherine Lewandowski's death within the context of a whole population of frail elderly persons who might be at risk because of premature discharge from the hospital. The case study is designed to illustrate why it is necessary for social work students to acquire knowledge and skill not only in counseling and one-on-one work but also in advocacy and larger systems change. These practice skills are needed in health care as much as—perhaps even more than—in any other field of social work practice.

Social workers frequently serve as members of health teams that grapple with ethical dilemmas. Often decisions are made by the team as a whole, leaving no one person to make a decision alone. Ethics and values content pervade the social work curriculum and are also derived from philosophy, theology, and literature courses, giving social work students in health care settings a basis from which to examine ethical issues. In addition, the Code of Ethics of the National Association of Social Workers provides guidelines for ethical practice.

The health care field encompasses much more than hospitals. Indeed, social workers are employed in rehabilitation centers, nursing homes, hospices, hemodialysis units, home health care services, insurance companies, and other specialized care centers—in large cities, in small towns, and in rural areas. The community itself, including its economic well-being, its potential environmental risks, and its racial and ethnic characteristics, must be understood by the health care social worker to provide a bridge between the community and the health care facility. Social justice issues related to health must also be understood from a global perspective.

The history of social work in health care is a proud one. Not only have social workers in this field helped patients and their families, but for 100 years they have worked to make health care organizations and social policy more responsive and more sensitive to the needs of people.

Today the impact of public policy is immense. The entire health field seems to be in crisis. At the center of the debate is health care financing. Increasing numbers of people are underinsured in the United States, and others have no health insurance coverage at all. As health care costs keep rising, business corporations and nonprofit organizations are less willing to pay for employees' health insurance. The cost containment procedures that have been implemented have the potential result of leading to inadequate medical care or premature discharge of hospital patients. Reform of the U.S. health care system is needed, but public support for a comprehensive national program is uncertain. Social workers, who witness the tragedy of inadequate health care, will undoubtedly continue to fight for comprehensive reform that ensures universal health care coverage for all.

To meet the challenges of this exciting and rapidly evolving field of practice, social workers will need to sustain commitment to their professional values just as social workers have since the days of the lady almoners at the Royal Free Hospital in London.

KEY TERMS

acute care, *p. 237*

capitated plans, *p. 255*

cost containment, *p. 238*

diagnostic-related group (DRG)
 plan, *p. 258*

hemodialysis, *p. 245*

hospice, *p. 242*

lady almoners, *p. 252*

long-term care, *p. 238*

Medicaid, *p. 257*

Medicare, *p. 254*

national health insurance,
 p. 259

national health service, *p. 259*

osteoporosis, *p. 229*

palliative care, *p. 242*

prospective payment system
 (PPS), *p. 258*

single-payer system, *p. 259*

subacute centers, *p. 237*

trafficking, *p. 249*

universal coverage, *p. 259*

universal programs, *p. 258*

DISCUSSION QUESTIONS

1. Why do you think Katherine Lewandowski, the patient in the case study, was discharged from the hospital when she apparently did not want to leave?

2. Could the nursing home social worker have done anything to prevent Katherine Lewandowski's death? What could she have done?

3. Discuss the hospital procedure and policy changes that could result from social workers' intervention following the Lewandowski case.

4. Chapter 1 described generalist social work practice. What knowledge, values, and skills does a generalist social worker need to work effectively in health care?

5. In what ways is health care social work different in rural areas than in urban areas?

6. Social work is one of many professions providing health care. What are some of the others? How might these various professional roles overlap?

7. In the discussion of the emergency room as a health care setting, a young Puerto Rican woman who is pregnant experiences an *ataque*. How could the social worker's understanding of their culture help the family in this situation? Should Katherine Lewandowski's Polish culture have been of significance to social workers at the hospital (or at the nursing home)? Why?

8. Medicare and Medicaid have been presented in detail in this chapter. Outline the differences between the two programs.

9. What environmental conditions create health hazards in the United States or elsewhere in the world? How can environmental problems in one country affect other parts of the world? Give examples.

10. Cite several health problems in the United States that reflect or involve social injustice. Give examples for other parts of the world.

11. Analyze the costs and benefits of the present U.S. health care system. In what ways does the United States spend more than other countries on health care? Do these additional expenditures benefit American citizens?

12. What kind of incremental change do you think might take place in health care policies in the United States in the future? What are the prospects for fundamental health care system reform? How might this come about?

13. What do you expect the impact of the current administration to be on Medicare? Medicaid? Other components of the American health care system?

14. What are the prospects for social work employment in health care? In what types of health care settings is employment likely to increase for social workers in the future?

CLASSROOM EXERCISES

1. This chapter notes that more than 46 million Americans are without health insurance today. Discuss possible reasons this is so. Do you think a large uninsured population is good for the nation overall, in that it makes people more economically insecure and thus more willing to work, a classic conservative argument?

2. The chapter's case example regarding Katherine Lewandowski illustrates a policy or system known today as PPS, or prospective payment system, used not only by Medicare but by managed-care organizations and private insurance plans. According to this sytem, a hospital is paid a fixed fee for a patient's care according to the diagnosis. Identify as many pros and cons of this policy as you can. Overall, do you think it is a good one for Americans in need of care? Why or why not?

3. The text compares and contrasts the Canadian health care system with the American system. What are the differences? The similarities? Overall, which nation's plan does the author believe better meets the health care needs of its citizens? Review the evidence provided in the text. Do you agree with the author? Why or why not?

4. Should health care be universal in the United States? Why or why not? If health care were to become universal, which approach do you believe would best serve the needs of Americans, a national health service or universal health insurance? If universal health insurance, which approach do you believe would be more cost effective, a single-payer system coordinated by the government or multiple systems run by private insurance companies? Cite evidence provided in the text to support your position.

RESEARCH ACTIVITIES

1. Using library resources, identify five countries that have a universal health care plan, and find out how each of these plans functions.

2. Explore the full range of health care settings in your community in which social workers are employed.

3. What professional social work periodicals does your school's library have that focus on social work in health care? Read the table of contents of a couple of the most recent issues. What topics appear to be of special concern to social workers in health care? Do any of these topics directly or indirectly relate to the profession's ultimate goal of social and economic justice, or to subjects that have ethical implications?

4. When toys made in China with lead-based paint are sold in U.S. Wal-Mart stores to low-income families, children may be exposed to lead poisoning. What can be done to prevent this? List other diseases that could potentially be spread from one country to another. Discuss the ways in which these transmissions might occur, and consider constructive ways to resolve the problem.

INTERNET RESEARCH EXERCISES

1. The Kaiser Family Foundation prepared a fact sheet on Medicaid's role in long-term care (http://www.kff.org/medicaid/upload/Medicaid-and-Long-Term-Care-Services-PDF.pdf).

   a. How many people in the United States need long-term care?

   b. How many people under age 65 require some form of long-term care?

   c. What does the term "300 percent rule" mean with reference to Medicaid availability?

2. A very complete explanation of hemodialysis as a treatment method for advanced and permanent

kidney failure is available on the website of the National Institutes of Health (http://kidney.niddk .nih.gov/kudiseases/pubs/hemodialysis/index.htm).

a. What is kidney dialysis, and when is it necessary?

b. What is a dialyzer?

c. What functions do the kidneys serve besides removing wastes and extra fluid?

3. The Century Foundation has a web page entitled "Universal Health Coverage: Coming Sooner Than You Think" (http://www.tcf.org/Events/ 07-27-05/coverage7-27-05 trans.pdf).

a. What two conditions have changed in recent years that account for changing societal attitudes on universal health care coverage?

b. Discuss the observation that "the United States is the only developed country that bases health coverage on employment status."

c. What is the crux of the proposed plan discussed in this paper?

4. The Urban Institute has posted an extensive paper on "Why Do People Lack Health Insurance?" (http://www.urban.org/UploadedPDF/411317_lack_ health_ins.pdf).

a. According to the findings in this report, who are the individuals most likely to be uninsured?

b. What two factors are cited as the most common reasons for being uninsured?

c. What does the paper report as to the current effectiveness of ESI (employer-sponsored insurance) in providing protection from the growing costs of health care?

FOR FURTHER READING

Almgren, G. (2007). *Health care politics, policy, and services: A social justice analysis.* New York: Springer.

Tremendous changes are taking place in health care in the United States. Medical advances offer increased life span, replacements for malfunctioning body organs, improvements in cancer detection and treatments that promise longer survival rates, and numerous other advances. At the same time, however, disparities in access to health care are more visible than ever before, especially for persons who are poor, for undocumented immigrants, and for those with disabilities. This book examines several philosophical perspectives on social justice within the health care environment. It uses social epidemiology as a lens for understanding the social determinants of health care policy. The concluding unit of the text provides useful social policy arguments that support the positive right of all persons to health care. It forces examination of the question: incremental change or fundamental reform?

Cannon, I. M. (1952). *On the social frontier of medicine: Pioneering in medical social service.* Cambridge, MA: Harvard University Press.

Anyone who is interested in the history of social work will find Ida Cannon's classic text very informative. The book provides a rare opportunity to read about the development of an area of social work practice from the perspective of the woman who led the movement. Her sensitive analysis of the social problems of her time—problems such as poverty and industrial hazards—will give readers a perspective on contemporary social problems. It is difficult to read this book without gaining inspiration from the intellect, energy, and compassion of Ida Cannon.

Dziegielewski, S. F. (2004). *The changing face of health care social work: Professional practice in managed behavioral health care* (2nd ed.). New York: Springer.

Sophia Diegielewski's clear understanding of today's managed care environment threads its way through this book's description of the practice of social work in acute care, long-term and restorative care settings, home health care, emergency room services, case management, and hospice programs. She urges social workers to become skilled in their ability to validate their practice and their cost effectiveness as a way of fighting for the future of the profession in the highly competitive health care industry.

Moniz, C., & Gorin, S. (2007). *Health and mental health care policy: A biopsychosocial perspective.* Boston: Pearson, Allyn & Bacon.

This excellently researched book makes health care policy come to life. The authors carefully trace history, present meaningful data, and examine previous evidence-based research to provide a lucid, clear, understandable presentation that never loses its grounding in social work values and ethics. Readers will learn to appreciate the depth of existing health care disparities in the United States and the clear need for health care financing reform. The concluding "highlights" section of each chapter effectively uses bullet points to ensure that significant content is noted and preserved.

Weiss, L. D. (1997). *Private medicine and public health: Profit, politics, and prejudice in the American health care enterprise.* Boulder, CO: Westview Press.

Weiss exposes the flaws, abuse, and deceit of the current for-profit health care system in the United States. Using research, trial documents, personal accounts, and statistical data, he uncovers the political power used by physicians' professional groups, hospitals, and the pharmaceutical and insurance industries to fend off a national health care program. This small book is highly readable yet sure to deliver new understandings about the forces that make systemic change so difficult—and so necessary.

White House Domestic Policy Council (1993). *The president's health security plan.* New York: Times Books, Random House.

This paperback book supplies both the original draft of President Clinton's Health Security Plan and a report prepared by the White House Domestic Policy Council. It is a fascinating source of information about a U.S. national health care plan that almost happened.

CHAPTER 7

SOCIAL WORK IN THE SCHOOLS

OUTLINE

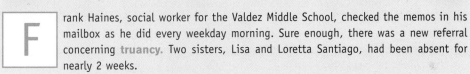

LISA AND LORETTA SANTIAGO, CHILDREN AT RISK

Frank Haines, social worker for the Valdez Middle School, checked the memos in his mailbox as he did every weekday morning. Sure enough, there was a new referral concerning truancy. Two sisters, Lisa and Loretta Santiago, had been absent for nearly 2 weeks.

Children whose primary language was Spanish, such as Lisa and Loretta, could learn basic subjects like math and reading in their native language at this school, enrolling at the same time in English as a Second Language (ESL). Other Spanish-speaking children who had a better grasp of English could take most classes in English, and a bilingual teacher would assist them in Spanish as needed. Frank Haines, the social worker, was not Latino, but he spoke a fair amount of Spanish. In his former training to be a Catholic priest, Frank had traveled to two Latin American countries and had also served as a street worker among Latino youth. He recognized that there were great differences as well as similarities among Latino families and that linguistic dialects and cultural norms differed significantly among Spanish speakers from Mexico, Puerto Rico, Cuba, South America, and the southwestern United States.

Frank had eventually changed his career goals to social work because he wanted to have a family of his own. He then earned the MSW, the degree most commonly required for this type of employment in the public schools. He also took courses in education to obtain certification in school social work, as required by his state's department of public instruction.

To begin his work with the Santiago sisters' case, Frank examined the girls' school files for records of attendance, conduct, and grades. He found that the two sisters had transferred from a school in Texas 3 years before. Their attendance had been regular until recently. The younger girl, Loretta, a seventh-grader, had good grades up to the most recent report. Lisa, an eighth-grader, had only fair grades the previous year, but her grades for the first quarter of this year were absolutely terrible. Frank wondered if something might have happened recently to upset the children, especially Lisa.

Frank then checked with the children's teachers. Loretta's teachers expressed concern for the girl and worried about her absence, but otherwise reported that she was a good student. Her homeroom teacher had sent the parents a note about attendance, but there had been no response.

Lisa's teachers reported that ever since summer vacation, the girl had seemed "different." The mathematics teacher and the ESL teacher said that Lisa stared at the classroom walls for long periods of time. Sometimes she would cry or chew on her knuckles. Teachers had sent notes home, asking for a conference with the parents, but so far, no one had responded.

Frank's next step in his investigation was to try to talk with the parents. No one answered his first several telephone calls. Finally, a young woman answered who said that she was the children's stepmother. She told Frank that the girls had run away 2 weeks before. Frank made an appointment for a home visit late the next day, when Mr. Santiago would be home from work. He mentally crossed his fingers, hoping he would get his work done in time to have supper with his family. All too frequently, Frank's work hours conflicted with his precious time at home.

Fortunately, both Mr. and Mrs. Santiago were present when Frank arrived for his appointment. In the Latino culture it is often considered improper for an unrelated man to visit alone with a woman, even on official school business. Frank greeted the couple in Spanish, which warmed the atmosphere immediately. Mrs. Santiago served the two men coffee and then withdrew to manage several small children. Frank began the interview with Mr. Santiago in his best halting Spanish, but the latter, with a broad smile, responded in imperfect but much better English. "Spanish is a beautiful language," he said, "but I think perhaps it will be easier for you to speak in English. I understand you are here because of my two older daughters, Lisa and Loretta. You see," he said, "they come from my first wife, who still lives in Texas, and sometimes they cause me a great deal of trouble."

Frank soon learned that Mr. Santiago had been battling with his former wife over custody of Lisa and Loretta for years. The court had awarded him custody because his second marriage was intact, whereas the biological mother was not legally married to her live-in boyfriend in Texas. Mr. Santiago loved Lisa and Loretta as well as his five younger children by his second marriage, but, like many urban men of Mexican descent, he translated his love for his daughters into powerful protectiveness and control.

The girls had run away, he said, because Lisa broke his rule against dating. Lisa had taken Loretta with her on the date as a family chaperone, but that was not enough to satisfy the father. When he learned what had happened, he became very angry, gave them both a severe lecture, and grounded them for 2 weeks. Then he locked them in their bedroom, but they broke out and ran away. Mr. Santiago knew where they were, he said: with his current wife's sister. They were afraid to come home, he said, because they knew he was so angry he "might be tempted to use the belt."

"How will the girls learn that you are ready to let them come home without that kind of punishment?" Frank said. "You know that's not a good way to discipline your children."

"Oh," Mr. Santiago replied breezily, "if I tell my wife it's OK, they'll be home soon enough."

Frank suspected that the father might be ready for an excuse to let his daughters come home, as he cared enough about them to let them stay in a safe place until he calmed down. The social worker seized the moment to tell Mr. Santiago that he was very worried; the father was breaking the law by allowing his daughters to remain truant. If they stayed out of school much longer, a parental conference would have to be set up with the principal. That would mean Mr. Santiago would miss work and could lose hours of pay.

After a few minutes, Mr. Santiago said he had decided it was time. He would speak to his wife and she would bring the children home. Two days later, Lisa and Loretta were back in school. Frank called them into his office for a conference. Both girls moaned to Frank that they would never be able to lead a normal life. All their friends were allowed to go out with boys when they were in junior high, they said.

"All of them?" asked Frank. "You know, I've heard that girls from Latino families are often not allowed to date, at least without a brother or sister along."

"But I took my little sister," Lisa wailed, "even though I know lots of girls who don't have to. None of the Anglo kids have to do that."

Frank empathized with the girls, but he pointed out that because they lived with their parents, they would have to obey their parents' rules.

"But we don't live with our parents," Lisa wailed again, "and these aren't our parents' rules. We live with our father, and they are our father's rules. And I hate him," Lisa said suddenly in a much different tone, intense and furious. "He was mean to my mother, very mean. Last summer I was visiting her in Texas, and he was staying with my grandparents there. I was walking with my mother when my father saw us on the street. He came up and stood in her way and wouldn't let her by. He called her horrible names and shoved her until she nearly fell. I thought he was going to hit her. My mother was shaking all over. He made her cry, and I heard every terrible word he said. I hate him."

Now Frank understood why Lisa was acting so troubled and defiant. She had been through an emotionally traumatic experience. He let both girls talk at length. He wondered out loud if they might want to see a counselor either by themselves or with their father and stepmother. But they insisted a counselor wouldn't help.

A few weeks later, Lisa and Loretta violated their father's curfew again. When they returned home, Mr. Santiago lost his temper and began shouting at his daughters, yelling that they were no good and would be grounded for a month. They would not be allowed to go on a school trip they had been counting on. The girls retaliated by calling their father every nasty name they could think of, in both English and Spanish. Mr. Santiago locked them in their room, but they left through the window.

Soon afterward, the girls showed up at Frank's office door at school, sobbing angrily. Fortunately, no one else was there, so he invited them in right away. Before Frank could find out what was wrong, however, Mr. Santiago himself arrived, clearly in a rage. Lisa immediately began to scream and curse. Mr. Santiago shouted for her to be quiet and then yelled at Frank that he had had all the disrespect and disobedience from his daughters that he could take. "Listen to that!" Mr. Santiago shouted, jabbing at Lisa and Loretta with a powerful forefinger. "Listen to how my daughters defy me! Listen to the kind of language they use with their own father! These girls are runaways, Mr. Haines! I want you to call the police! They are no longer welcome in my home!"

Lisa and Loretta continued to cry and yell. The more they carried on, the angrier Mr. Santiago became. Suddenly, he turned abruptly and began to stalk out of the office.

Frank stopped him. "Obviously, Mr. Santiago," he said quietly, "you have had a very difficult time. But I think we need to talk a little longer to decide what to do now."

"I will not talk any more!" Mr. Santiago shouted. "I have had all the disrespect I can take from these children! They must be punished! I want you to call the police. I will not allow these girls to darken my door again." He stormed out of the office and was gone.

After calming Lisa and Loretta as best he could and finding out what had happened at home, Frank determined that it would not be safe for the girls to return there. He called the protective services unit of the county social services department. No one was free to come to the school. Underfunding and understaffing are perennial problems of protective services programs. Frank thus took the girls to protective services in his own car, a personal risk for him, beyond his professional obligation. If he had had an accident, his automobile insurance company might not cover him because he was doing work-related driving.

The social worker on duty tried to place Lisa and Loretta temporarily with their step-aunt, the person they requested. But the woman declined a formal arrangement, saying it might ruin her relationship with her brother-in-law. So the girls were placed with strangers. And unfortunately, soon afterward, their foster father was charged with sexually molesting a former ward. The girls could not be left in that home. The protective services worker consulted with Frank. Should Lisa and Loretta be transferred to a different foster home, enduring another major adjustment, or should Mr. Santiago be approached about taking the girls back again? The worker said she had already looked into sending the girls to their mother in Texas, but lengthy court action would be required because of the prior custody battle and interstate regulations. Additional time in foster care would be required during that process.

Frank felt compassion for the children. They had been through a great deal. But he thought that Mr. Santiago and his second wife basically meant well. The problem was that Mr. Santiago set rigid rules that drove his daughters to disobey. The rules were within the bounds of his cultural norms but different from those of many of the girls' Anglo friends. The father verbally assaulted Lisa and Loretta when they disobeyed and gave them lengthy punishments, but the girls provoked him further with their own harsh words. If the cycle of provocation could be stopped, Frank believed that this family could learn to live together more peacefully and happily. As the discovery of sexual abuse in the foster home illustrated, life elsewhere was no bed of roses either.

Frank felt the best plan for the girls would be to go back home, with family counseling to help improve communication and understanding among the generations. He knew, however, that the girls should be consulted first and that the father would need some persuading. The protective services worker was more than willing to let Frank take on those tasks.

Frank talked with the girls the following day and learned they were ready to return to their father and stepmother. They were lonely and afraid in the foster home. He made an appointment with Mr. Santiago through the stepmother. When he arrived, he was not surprised to hear Mr. Santiago announce that the girls were no longer welcome in his home. Frank called on his former training for the priesthood to help accomplish his goal of having the children return. Given Mr. Santiago's cultural heritage, he expected that the man would be a devout Catholic. So he told the story of the Prodigal Son in somber, measured tones, inviting this father to forgive like the father in the Bible. Eventually, Mr. Santiago was persuaded to take his daughters back and to participate in family counseling if a Latino counselor could be found. Mr. Santiago's job provided very limited insurance benefits, so a very low cost provider would have to be found. Frank took on the challenge. He soon found a Latino social worker with expertise in family counseling, Ramon Garcia, who was willing to see the family free of charge providing that he could use the opportunity to train two graduate students in field placement. Mr. Santiago agreed, and Frank arranged the first session personally.

A week passed, and then another. Lisa and Loretta both attended school regularly. There were no more incidents of truancy. At a meeting with Frank, they explained that Ramon had helped family members talk to each other without fighting so much. At a follow-up home visit, Frank learned that the parents were pleased with the counseling experience as well. They believed they understood the girls better. They had become a little more flexible with their rules, and the children no longer tested them so severely. Life for the family was much happier. ■

PEOPLE OF LATINO OR HISPANIC HERITAGE: A BRIEF HISTORY

Lisa and Loretta Santiago and their parents were members of the largest minority group represented in the United States today, Latinos. Latinos are classified as Hispanics by the U.S. Bureau of the Census, but "Latino" is the term more commonly used. Including people from 26 countries, Latinos form a rapidly growing, diverse minority group that constitutes approximately 14.8 percent of the U.S. population, overtaking African Americans in 2003 to become the nation's largest minority group. They comprise more than 44.3 million people (Bernstein, 2007). Approximately 58.5 percent are of Mexican origin, 9.6 percent are Puerto Rican, 3.5 percent are Cuban, and 2.2 percent are from the Dominican Republic. Of the remaining Latino population, no other single country of origin accounts for more than 2 percent. Today, half of the Latino population resides in two states, California and Texas. Three-quarters of the population lives in just seven states, California, Texas, Arizona, New York, Florida, Illinois, and New Jersey. New Mexico, although not one of these seven states, has the highest percentage of Latinos in its population, 42 percent (Jolly, 2004).

Texas, California, Arizona, and New Mexico originally belonged to Mexico. There were border disputes in Texas and California between white settlers and Mexicans, however. Texas declared its independence from Mexico in 1836, and the United States admitted it as a state in 1845. President Polk accepted the boundary claimed by Texas rather than that claimed by Mexico and ordered General Zachary Taylor to enter the eastern bank of the Rio Grande to defend the disputed territories, thus precipitating the Mexican–American War. Mexico City was captured in 1848, resulting in the Treaty of Guadalupe Hidalgo. Under this treaty, the United States took ownership of the disputed territories.

Social worker discusses stresses at school with troubled youth.

Mexicans who lived in the formerly disputed territories (lands that became Texas, California, Arizona, and New Mexico) were allowed to stay, with American citizenship, or to leave for what remained of Mexico. Those who chose to stay in the United States were supposed to keep ownership of the lands they held before the war. However, the burden of proof of ownership was placed on the Mexicans, and many legal records were deliberately destroyed during and after the war. Gradually, people of Mexican heritage who stayed lost their land, becoming second-class citizens (Lum, 1992).

After losing their land, Mexican Americans resorted to work as laborers, primarily in agriculture. And because economic conditions in Mexico were poor, other Mexicans crossed the border to seek work in the United States. These immigrants, legal and illegal, formed the backbone of the migrant laborers who traveled the nation to harvest crops according to the season. Low wages, poor housing, and lack of sanitation and health care greeted them in many places. As a result, strong efforts were made to win the right for farm workers to form unions and engage in collective bargaining. In the late 1980s, the work of self-advocacy organizations such as La Raza resulted in amnesty being offered to many illegal aliens who had lived in the United States for a significant period of time.

Today, the challenge continues as desperately poor people from Mexico continue to pour into the United States illegally, looking for work. These persons are viewed by many industries as a good source of cheap labor, so they are often hired—angering many American workers who view them as competitors. The status of illegal laborers continues to be debated across the nation today.

Puerto Ricans form another major group of Hispanic or Latino people in the United States. Puerto Rico became part of a commonwealth of the United States in 1917. Many Puerto Ricans later migrated to the mainland to pursue economic opportunity, usually settling in New York City. Today most still live in the northeastern region of the country. Unfortunately, many subsist in inner-city neighborhoods and suffer high rates of unemployment.

Cubans migrated to this country in large numbers in the early 1960s to escape Fidel Castro's government. They settled primarily in Florida. Early immigrants from Cuba were usually professionals and businesspeople who were economically advantaged. Later, however, many of the immigrants arrived destitute and required numerous services for basic survival. Latino immigrants from Central America have also come primarily as refugees. In particular, wars in Nicaragua and El Salvador forced many to seek asylum in the 1970s and 1980s. Numerous people were denied entry and returned forcibly to dangerous situations. The needs of those who were allowed to stay strained the resources of agencies and programs designed to assist them (Lum, 1992). In recent years, there has been widespread pressure in the United States to modify immigration policy.

Given such multiple origins, it is easy to understand that Hispanic peoples are racially as well as ethnically diverse. When asked to describe their cultural heritage, most Latinos refer to their national identity (e.g., Mexican or Puerto Rican). Not all speak Spanish, and not all have surnames that appear Spanish in origin.

Like other minority groups, Latino Americans face discrimination and limited economic opportunity in the United States. Fully 82 percent of Latinos in a 2002 national survey reported that discrimination was a problem that kept them from succeeding in general and that it was a particular problem in the workplace (78 percent) and at school (75 percent). Two-thirds reported being unable to save any money for future needs; nearly one-third reported having been laid off from their job in the previous year (Politics & Opinion, 2002).

HISTORY OF SOCIAL WORK IN THE SCHOOLS

School social workers do what they can to assist all students, including Latinos, to succeed in school. Frank Haines, the social worker who assisted Lisa and Loretta Santiago, came from the proud but relatively short tradition of school social work. The history of this field is described in this section. It is important to realize, however, that even today many schools lack social workers. In many other schools, these hardworking professionals may have to educate administrators and teachers as to their potential roles.

Early Years

As with many of the fields of professional social work today, social work in American public schools began with the far-sighted efforts of voluntary organizations (see Exhibit 7-1). In 1906 two New York City settlement houses, Hartley House and Greenwich House, assigned "visitors" to do liaison work with three school districts. One of these visitors, Mary Marot, was a teacher and a resident of Hartley House. A natural leader, she formed a visiting teacher committee at the settlement house. The Public Education Association of New York became interested in her work and asked her if she would make her committee part of their organization. She agreed, and the association publicized the concept of "visiting teacher." At about the same time, the Women's Education Association in Boston established a "home and school visitor" to improve communication between the home and school settings. In Connecticut, the director of the Psychological Clinic of Hartford hired a "special teacher" to assist him in making home visits and to act as a liaison between the clinic and the school (Hancock, 1982).

The fact that the concept of visiting teacher took hold at about the same time in three separate cities indicates that this was an idea whose time had come. Initially, visiting teachers were financed by settlement houses or other private associations or agencies. But from about 1913 to 1921, various school boards began hiring them, beginning with Rochester, New York, in 1913 (Dupper, 2003). The movement gradually expanded from the eastern to the midwestern states. The early focus of these workers was community based; settlement houses in particular lent an orientation toward finding ways to alter the environment to improve individual lives. Visiting teachers tried to find ways to intervene in the school and community settings to help prevent delinquency, improve attendance, and develop scholarship.

The passage of compulsory attendance laws during this time reflected growing societal awareness of the importance of education and that every child had not only a right but an obligation to go to school. Compulsory education laws increased the

EXHIBIT 7-1

Timeline: History of School Social Work

1906–1907	School social work services begin independently in New York City, Boston, and Hartford.
1913	Rochester, New York, becomes the first school system to finance school social work services.
1921	National Association of Visiting Teachers is established.
1923	Commonwealth fund of New York increases the visibility of school social workers by providing financial support for a program to prevent juvenile delinquency that includes the hiring of 30 school social workers in 20 rural and urban communities across the United States.
1943	The U.S. Office of Education recommends that a professional school social work certificate be a master's degree in social work (MSW).
1955	NASW by-laws provide for the establishment of a school social work specialty.
1959	Specialist position in school social work is established by the U.S. Office of Education.
1969	"Social Change and School Social Work" is the national workshop held at the University of Pennsylvania, and its proceedings resulted in the publication of the book entitled *The School in the Community* (1972).
1973	NASW Council on Social Work in the Schools meets for the first time.
1975	Costin's school–community–pupil relations model of a school social work practice is published.
1976	The first set of standards for school social work services are developed by NASW. These standards emphasize prevention as an important theme.
1985	NASW National School Social Work Conference "Educational Excellence in Transitional Times" is held in New Orleans, Louisiana, and results in the publication of *Achieving Educational Excellence for Children at Risk*, which contains papers from this conference.
1992	The school social work credentialing exam, developed by NASW, the Educational Testing Service, and Allen-Meares is administered for the first time.
1994	NASW launches school social work as its first practice section.
1994	The School Social Work Association of America (SSWAA) is formed, independent of NASW.

SOURCE: D. Dupper. (2003). *School social work, skills and interventions for effective practice.* Hoboken, NJ: John Wiley & Sons, p. 12.

employment of visiting teachers (Costin, 1987). Increasing numbers of visiting teachers led to the establishment of the National Committee of Visiting Teachers in 1921 (Freeman, 1995).

During the 1920s, the initial emphasis on community liaison and change gradually shifted toward concentration on adjustment of the individual child. Attention was focused on reducing delinquency and improving mental health, not so much through improving school and community conditions as through helping the child personally to adjust. This shift in emphasis paralleled the growth in popularity of Freudian psychology, which strongly focused on individual treatment rather than social change.

The Great Depression of the 1930s drastically reduced employment for social workers in the schools. Early in this period, those who retained their jobs tended to become heavily involved in locating and distributing food, shelter, and clothing. When the federal government began to provide these necessities, social workers gradually resumed their trend toward becoming caseworkers with individual students and their families. This orientation was well in place by the 1940s.

Middle Period

Throughout the 1940s and 1950s, with the federal government providing many basic financial and material needs to American families, social workers tended to maintain a clinical orientation, which increased their prestige in the school setting. Refinement of practice techniques to help individual students adjust to their environments then became the primary goal. Florence Poole, however, helped shift the focus from the "problem pupil" alone to a perspective that pupils and schools need to mutually adapt to each other, using the rationale that children had a right to an education. As early as 1949, Poole wrote that it was the responsibility of the school to offer its students something that would help them benefit from an education (Constable, 2006).

The 1960s brought a number of social protest movements, and with them came a shift in emphasis to changing the school environment to help better meet the needs of diverse students. Social workers were to pursue this goal in collaboration with other school personnel. In the 1970s, development of systems theory and the ecological perspective helped focus social workers' attention on the complex problems of schools and communities, including racism and students' rights. Not all workers made the transition, however (Freeman, 1995). During this time, the term *visiting teacher* gradually changed to *school social worker.*

Employment of school social workers expanded in the 1960s and continued to expand in the 1970s. One reason was that legislation provided a variety of new employment settings. For example, the Economic Opportunity Act of 1964 created Head Start programs, which often employed social workers full- or part-time. Moneys appropriated under the Elementary and Secondary Education Act of 1965, an act that sought to improve educational opportunities for disadvantaged children, sometimes were used to employ social workers. In 1975 the Education for All Handicapped Children Act created new roles for social workers as part of a special education team. This act later evolved to become the Individuals with Disabilities Education Act, or IDEA (Dupper, 2003).

In the mid 1970s the National Association of Social Workers developed standards for school social work. This project was initiated by the NASW Task Force on Social Work Services in the Schools and completed by its successor, the Committee on Social Work Services in the Schools. The basic purpose of these standards was "to provide a model or measurement that school social workers can use to assess their scope of practice and their practice skills" (Hancock, 1982). The standards identify three major targets of service: pupils and parents, school personnel, and the community. Clearly, the intent of the standards is that school social work services maintain a strong preventive, ecological perspective.

Recent Times

In the 1980s, school social workers began to pay more attention to students' rights, cultural diversity, parental involvement in the schools, and school-community-family partnerships. The impact of IDEA legislation in particular encouraged active parental involvement in educational planning for their children. The 1997 Individuals with Disabilities Education Act Amendments established the Individualized Education Program (IEP) as the major tool in assisting every student to progress; every IEP requires parental input. Social workers have assumed much of the responsibility to make the goals of the act a reality. They frequently provide information to parents about programs and services, serve as mediators in conflicts regarding educational decisions, and provide mental health services in the classroom (Freeman, 1995; Dupper, 2003).

The growth of child poverty and homelessness over the past several decades has presented school social workers with increasing challenges, given the associated negative impact on attendance, achievement, and graduation rates. The impact of poverty on school performance will be discussed in more detail in a later section.

SOCIAL WORK ROLES IN THE SCHOOLS

As noted by Boyle-Del Rio, Carlson, and Haibeck (2000), the role of the school social worker is constantly changing to meet shifting school, community, and societal needs. Social workers must be creative, innovative, and proactive in developing, implementing, and interpreting new roles in this challenging setting. Nevertheless, like all social workers, they utilize a variety of levels of intervention, as discussed in the rest of this section.

Working with Individuals

Social workers perform a variety of roles in the schools. First of all, as illustrated in the Santiago case, social workers frequently counsel with individual students. Students may be referred for a variety of reasons, among them truancy, undesirable behavior, and pregnancy. In schools where there is a guidance counselor, such cases may be assigned either to the counselor or to the social worker, depending on who has more time available.

School social workers today work with individual school personnel in a variety of ways as well: consulting with teachers about the needs of particular children, sharing with teachers and each other knowledge about cultural factors in the educational process, informing staff about important community resources, consulting with teachers about classroom relationships, and so on.

Some school social workers become involved in screening individual students for material aid, such as free or reduced-fee lunch programs. Some schools also distribute donated books, clothing, writing materials, and the like to needy children. Often it is the social worker who identifies the children who need this material help.

Family Work

Another type of social work service in the school setting involves working with parents and families. The social worker is the main link between the family and the school; the worker is often the *only* person from the school who can make home visits. Parents are contacted to gain information that may help teachers work more effectively with particular children. The worker may also make suggestions about parenting techniques in the home.

When a student is referred to special education for evaluation, especially for suspected emotional or behavioral disturbance, the school social worker usually interviews the parents to learn more about that child's early development and about how he or she currently behaves in the home and community settings. This responsibility will be discussed in more detail in a later section of this chapter. When appropriate, school social workers refer families to community agencies for material assistance, counseling, or other services.

Group Work

School social workers also often develop and lead groups of students. Group work utilizes peer processes and other motivational techniques to help resolve attendance, academic, and social difficulties (Rose, 1998; Pawlak, Wozniak, & McGowen, 2006). Topics are sometimes controversial, such as pregnancy prevention, sexual orientation, preventing sexually transmitted diseases, and coping with parents who are drug abusers. Groups can become the focus of heated community debate because some parents want these topics to be discussed only at home.

School social workers may also become involved in leading groups of parents and/or teachers, with topics depending on circumstance and need. Some school social workers become involved in leading groups to promote change in the school system or the wider community.

Working with Organizations and Communities

In accord with the generalist approach, educating and organizing school personnel and the wider community is an important part of school social work. The social worker is often the major link between the school and the wider community. This role is increasingly important today as children's problems grow and school resources shrink. For example, more and more children today find themselves with nothing to do and no place to go after school, because most parents work outside the home. Social workers increasingly find themselves doing community assessments to find resources for after-school programs, only to end up organizing these programs themselves within the school setting using laboriously recruited volunteer staff, including both parents and teachers (Wells, 1999).

Involvement with school-linked, integrated services (discussed later) is another undertaking that requires skill in working with organizations and communities.

Teamwork

Perhaps the most important thing to note about teamwork in the schools is that the school presents the social worker with a secondary social work setting, or host setting,

---

EXHIBIT 7-2

The Secondary Social Work Setting

The social work job function is affected in major ways when it is performed in a secondary, or host, setting. For example, most of the employees in a school are teachers; if there is a social worker, usually there is only one employed in that setting. This can be a lonely position because nobody else is likely to have the same knowledge, values, and skills. In addition, many social workers are assigned to several schools. They may not have private offices but instead must share space with other staff, holding interviews in temporarily empty classrooms or even utility closets. Private telephones may be unavailable, so scheduling home visits or discussing family problems by phone is difficult if not impossible. Organizing the political support required to secure needed changes is not easy in a secondary setting where the social worker may be the sole representative of his or her profession.

---

for employment (see Exhibit 7-2). The primary purpose of the school system is educational. The position of the social worker within the school setting is to support the educational function of the institution. In contrast, a family service agency is an example of a primary social work setting for a social worker. The primary purpose of the family service agency is to enhance social functioning, which is also the primary purpose of the social work profession; thus, the majority of the staff are social workers.

Social workers almost always function as part of a team in school social work. That team might consist only of the social worker and a referring teacher, working together to meet the educational needs of a particular child. It might be a multidisciplinary team assessing a student referred for special education evaluation. In the latter situation, the team might include the regular classroom teacher; a special education teacher; the school principal, guidance counselor, and school nurse; a county social worker; and one or more parents. Teams are constructed by their members according to the need at hand; decision making is collaborative, implying shared ownership of problems and solutions. Teamwork is an important element in planning and carrying out change in the wider school environment as well. Because social workers value cooperation and are trained to communicate well across disciplinary boundaries, they are often assigned to work as team coordinators and leaders (Constable & Thomas, 2006).

School-Linked, Integrated Services

A movement toward school-linked, integrated services is under way in many communities across the United States. The intent is to make schools "hubs" for the delivery of a full range of services, involving various health, mental health, and social service agencies from the wider community (Franklin, 2000). Sometimes these services are provided at the schools themselves, and sometimes they are simply coordinated by school personnel.

Schools where coordinated community services are actually delivered on site are sometimes called "full-service" schools. They have been developed in several states to help children at risk: those who arrive unprepared for the educational process and unable to concentrate on school work due to abuse, neglect, homelessness, poverty, and poor health. Services such as counseling, family intervention, and group work may be targeted toward children displaying specific at-risk behaviors. Some full-service schools also offer comprehensive health and mental health services. Other, more broadly based services may be available as well, such as case management, advocacy, child care, and transportation.

Only a few schools have achieved full-service status today. One interesting example is a middle school in the Washington Heights section of New York City, which has teamed with the Children's Aid Society to create a settlement house right in the school facility. Other New York City schools are less comprehensive but are working toward the full-service model. Located in low-income areas, they describe themselves as "community schools," and seek to serve as "nerve centers" for comprehensive neighborhood revitalization (Constable & Kordesh, 2006).

THE IMPACT OF CULTURAL DIVERSITY IN THE SCHOOLS

Cultural diversity has been increasing rapidly in the United States over the past few decades. The impact of cultural diversity on the city school system where Lisa and Loretta Santiago attended was considerable. When Latino children first began attending the public schools, they were a small minority and were placed in classrooms where English only was spoken; some of these children swam, but many of them sank. No help was offered to those who could not handle the experience. This is still the situation in many schools in the United States today. Rural school systems are particularly devoid of resources for children whose native language is other than English. Yet in recent decades, the Latino population has been growing more than seven times as fast as the rest of the nation, and by 2030 Hispanics are expected to constitute 25 percent of the total school population (Ginorio & Huston, 2001).

The American cultural myth of the melting pot has lulled many people into assuming that children who are not native speakers of English can assimilate the language effortlessly. Yet many children struggle and cannot keep up in basic subjects like math and history. Crucial early learning time, the foundation for more advanced study, is lost (see Exhibit 7-3).

Many schools have devised innovative programs to meet the needs of children from diverse backgrounds. The primary thrust came from educators, but social workers provided strong support. Two models for teaching children whose native language is not English have emerged. The **bilingual** model allows students to take courses like math and history in their native languages, while studying English in specialized **English as a Second Language (ESL)** courses. The other model plunges students immediately into intensive **Sheltered English Immersion (SEI)** to get them up to grade level in English and into regular classrooms as quickly as possible (Llana & Paulson, 2006).

The model used at the Valdez Middle School that Lisa and Loretta Santiago attended was bilingual. Hispanic children could take all their classes in Spanish, if desired, enrolling concurrently in ESL courses. Students with more understanding of

---

EXHIBIT 7-3

Children from Non-English-Speaking Homes: One in Five

[Approximately] 9.9 million children, or 22 percent of the school-age population, live in a house where a non-English language is spoken. . . . Children of racial minorities and non-English speaking children tend to come from families occupying a lower socioeconomic position. Their parents are often poorly educated and somewhat mystified by the educational process and all of the special programs. Moreover, their parents also may not have a command of the English language.

These children generally find entry into the public school difficult because they lack the family resources and experiential background that usually lead to successful achievement in what has been called a middle-class institution.

SOURCE: Quoted from S. Kopels. (2000). Securing equal educational opportunity: Language, race, and sex. In P. Allen-Meares, R. O. Washington, & B. L. Welsh, *Social work services in schools* (3rd ed., p. 216). Boston: Allyn & Bacon.

---

the English language were mainstreamed, or educated in English in as normal a fashion for an American child as possible, while still having bilingual teachers available who could assist them in Spanish when needed (see the Up for Debate box).

California passed a law in 1998 eliminating bilingual education from its public schools, followed by Arizona and Massachusetts. The rationale was that students would learn English faster in an "immersion" type program and that they would be able to join their English-speaking peers in less than a year. However, a recent study in Massachusetts found that 83 percent of its SEI students were unable to join regular classrooms after a year, and more than half had not achieved fluency in English after 3 years in an SEI classroom. No study has actually shown that students learn

UP FOR DEBATE

Proposition: Bilingual education should be provided in the public schools.

YES	NO
Children learn more easily in their native language, especially complex concepts.	Children need to learn the language of the majority culture as quickly as possible.
Children feel more comfortable in an environment where their native language is spoken.	Children need to learn to feel comfortable in an English-speaking environment in the United States.
Teaching in one's own language affirms children's cultural identity and thus enhances self-esteem.	Pride in one's cultural heritage and in oneself can be taught in English.
Some children simply fail when they must learn in a language that is not their own.	Some children will fail regardless of the language in which they are taught.
America needs bilingual citizens to maintain an enlightened place in the world.	All Americans should speak English as their primary language.

faster in an English immersion classroom; many educators today believe that the most effective programs are "dual language," or programs where children learn in their native language for part of the day and study in English for part of the day. These educators also argue that in today's shrinking world, it is important for at least some Americans to be fluent in more than one language and knowledgeable about more than one culture, so maintaining bilingual education is good for the nation as a whole (Llana & Paulson, 2006).

Bilingual teachers, social workers, and other staff are needed in schools where a large proportion of children speak languages other than English; however, these professionals need to know about the cultural backgrounds of their students as well. Frank Haines, for example, secured his job at the Valdez Middle School partly because he spoke basic Spanish but also because he had direct experience working with various Hispanic peoples in his prior training for the priesthood. To work effectively at the Valdez school, for example, Frank needed to know about dating customs constraining young Hispanic girls, and to understand normal disciplinary practices among Hispanic families living near the school. He needed to understand sex-role behaviors and authority patterns (see Exhibit 7-4).

Social workers can learn what behavior is appropriate in a given culture or subculture by talking with other workers who are knowledgeable, by observing behavior directly, by talking with members of the subculture in question, by taking classes, and by reading. Many sources of information are available, but they must be conscientiously pursued.

Another important impact of cultural diversity in the schools involves the fact that the children learn from each other. Norms that might go unquestioned within a single culture may be questioned as the children learn that there are other ways of doing things. On the positive side, this can lead to flexible, informed, tolerant citizens later on in life. On the negative side (as in the case of the Santiago sisters), it

---

EXHIBIT 7-4

Exploring Cultural Diversity in Today's Schools

Cultural assessment of the child and family requires that the school social worker be open and willing to learn from the client, and to use that knowledge on the client's behalf. In every culture, there exist some expectations and codes of behavior around areas of discipline, time, health, and religious beliefs. A worker's understanding of what these values are, where they fall on a value continuum of traditional to modern, and how they interface with behavioral expectations of the education system regarding children's learning is a key element of cross-cultural practice in school settings.

People from diverse racial and ethnic groups have experienced different forms of oppression and racism in their interactions with the majority culture. Placing these concerns into a cross-cultural perspective involves exploring the client's historical experiences with the majority culture and, if applicable, with migration and immigration. This history may include movement both within the United States and across foreign borders. In this connection, there may be historical conflicts among or between certain cultural groups that will need to be explored.

SOURCE: F. S. Caple & R. M. Salcido. (2006). A framework for cross-cultural practice in school settings. In R. Constable, C. Massat, S. McDonald, & J. Flynn (Eds.), *School Social Work, practice, policy, and research* (6th ed., pp. 299–320). Chicago: Lyceum Books.

may lead to rebellion against family norms and expectations because other alternatives are readily in evidence.

Particularly during the teenage years, most children enter a period of rebellion as they attempt to define who they are. A major developmental task of adolescence is to differentiate the emerging self from parents and other family members. Cross-cultural issues complicate this normal process. Social workers may need to reach out to contact children who are experiencing difficulty because some cultural norms do not promote a tendency to seek professional help. On the whole, the value of exposure to differences and the learning that children must undertake to deal with conflicting information probably far outweigh the discomfort of temporary confusion or rebellious behavior.

Alternative Schools and Charter Schools

Another impact of cultural diversity in the schools is a proliferation of what are known as **alternative schools,** schools that operate outside the regular public system. Although these schools are usually privately run, at least two cities, Milwaukee and Cleveland, provide taxpayer money to poor parents to help finance tuition. In some places, alternative schools develop formal agreements with public schools and even share staff. Alternative schools are not limited to children of ethnic minority background, but minority parents have become strong advocates (Baldauf, 1998).

Probably a reason many minority parents have become advocates for alternative schools involves the fact that cultural or religious teachings may be incorporated into the regular curriculum. Also, these schools often have much smaller classes than regular public schools, providing students with more personal attention. A problem, however, is that most lack the resources to provide special education services.

Baccalaureate social workers usually have a better chance to be hired in alternative schools than in regular public schools. Moreover, many alternative schools hire full-time social workers on staff, sometimes more than one. By contrast, a single social worker is often shared among several schools in the regular school system.

Charter schools are a type of alternative school growing rapidly in states that permit them. They are public schools (financed through tax revenues like regular public schools) that are operated independently. They are regulated at the state level and deal with complex financial and management challenges. Most emphasize the particular academic philosophy that motivated their creation. Minnesota was the first state to enact charter school legislation in 1991; today there are well over a thousand charter schools, with Arizona having the largest number, followed by California and Michigan (Hare, Rome, & Massat, 2006).

INVOLVEMENT IN SPECIAL EDUCATION

Since 1975 many social workers have been hired by schools to work with special education programs. Before that time, many students with special needs were simply refused admission to public school. In 1975, however, landmark federal legislation—Public

Law 94–142, the Education for All Handicapped Children Act—changed public education forever. This law is now known as the Individuals with Disabilities Education Act, or IDEA, promising free and appropriate public education to all children with disabilities (Dupper, 2003). Amended in 1997, it was reauthorized as the Individuals with Disabilities Education Improvement Act of 2004, aligning many of the principals of IDEA with the No Child Left Behind Law to be discussed later in this chapter (Constable & Kordesh, 2006).

While a great boon for the students and families it helps, the law has placed a strain on state and local community financing. That is because while the federal government under the law is committed to providing 40 percent of the funding per student, it actually pays less than 20 percent. Because the cost of providing special education per student per year is more than twice that of regular education (approximately $16,921 per year vs. $7,552), the federal underfunding leads to local school budget shortfalls, undermining educational opportunity for all students (*Special education*, 2007).

IDEA requires that social workers be part of a multidisciplinary team (sometimes called an M-team, pupil planning team, etc.) that evaluates referrals. Students are referred to special education services for a variety of reasons: speech or language impairment, physical disability (including visual or hearing impairment), learning disability, cognitive or other developmental disability, emotional or behavioral disturbance, pregnancy or health impairment, autism, and traumatic brain injury. Many children who never would have received an education, or completed one, now have a much better chance.

Part C of IDEA 2004 reinforces federal legislation originally passed in 1986 extending the right of special education services to infants and toddlers with disabilities. Part C has a strong focus on family; it signals a change in philosophy for early childhood intervention from child-centered to family-centered services. The family-centered model guides social workers toward family–professional collaboration whether they are working directly with families or developing policy, programs, or evaluation strategies (Bishop, 2006).

Social workers in special education programs assume many roles, but a prominent one involves evaluating children who are referred because of suspected "emotional disturbance" (sometimes labeled "behavioral disturbance"). Essentially, these are the children who are identified by teachers as behaving in harmful or inappropriate ways. School social workers often need to become involved before evaluation of a referral can take place, because under special education law all parents must consent in writing. Usually a child's referring teacher contacts the parents about a referral and the reasons it was made. Then a permission slip is sent for the parents to sign. If the parents do not return the form, the social worker usually makes a home visit to explain the situation further and try to obtain permission.

Once permission to do an evaluation has been obtained, the social worker's next responsibility is to interview the parents to determine whether a referred child exhibits disturbance in the home or community environment. If a referred child misbehaves at school but gets along well in the home and community settings, then perhaps the problem lies with the school and not with the child.

A multidisciplinary team (M-team) will meet to determine whether a referred child qualifies for special education services. Social workers serve on many of these teams, particularly if a child is referred for emotional disturbance. The M-team will comprise a variety of professionals depending on the nature of the referral (e.g. regular education teacher, special education teacher, psychologist, nurse, guidance counselor, social worker, school principal, etc.). The referred child's parents are also invited to be part of the team.

Once a child has been accepted into special education, the law requires that the educational program be in the least restrictive environment and in an environment tailored to each child's special needs; an Individualized Education Program (IEP) must be developed for each child. An important role for social workers is to mobilize a variety of services to help attain IEP goals. Social workers may provide direct services themselves to assist these children, such as individual or group counseling, and they may assist teachers and parents in developing behavior management programs (Dupper, 2003).

Educational Evaluations as Applied Research

What the evaluation team does when activated by a school special education referral is an example of applied research. Each member of the multidisciplinary team seeks information about the referred child in his or her area of expertise. Results of these research efforts are used in joint decision making. Within 90 days, the M-team must meet together to determine whether the child is indeed qualified to receive special services and, if so, what kind. This type of applied research has serious, immediate consequences for a given child.

School social worker interviews parents at home regarding truancy of their child.

The social worker researches the child's developmental history and also investigates his or her current behavior at home and in the community. When researching the child's developmental history, the social worker gathers information that will help determine if the child has developed "normally" or not. How did the parents feel about the child's birth? Did the child walk and talk at about the same age as most children? What kind of concerns about the child, if any, did the parents have in the past? How has the child related to the parents? How does he or she behave at home? What types of discipline seem to work best with this child? Are there any brothers or sisters? If so, what was the birth order? How has the child related to the siblings? Has the child been in any sort of trouble in the community? If so, what kind? What concerns do the parents have about the child today? About the school? These are only a few of the questions a social worker might ask.

Sometimes parents are anxious about having their child evaluated by the school. They become distressed about giving certain information that would be helpful in assessing the child because talking raises sensitive issues or painful memories. In these circumstances, the social worker must use his or her best relationship skills and assure the parents that any information they provide will be shared only with the special education evaluation team. The assurance of confidentiality helps parents overcome their fear of providing sensitive information. Sometimes a social worker must make many visits to the parents of a referred child because time is needed to obtain the parents' trust and cooperation. The social worker may also assist the school in obtaining signed releases from parents to gather medical and other pertinent diagnostic information.

While the social worker is conducting his or her part of the investigation, other members of the evaluation team will also be at work. The psychologist may be conducting a battery of psychological tests designed to indicate evidence of emotional disturbance and may also administer an IQ test. The teacher for the emotionally disturbed will observe the child in the regular classroom, taking detailed notes to document the percentage of the time the child is doing assigned work ("on task"), as opposed to how much time the child spends misbehaving, wandering around, daydreaming, and the like.

After the various members of the multidisciplinary team have gathered their data, an M-team meeting will be held to which the parents are invited. At this meeting, the team will determine whether the child demonstrates needs that qualify him or her for special education services. Parents must then agree in writing for their child to receive these services. They may also refuse services, or they may appeal an M-team decision that has determined that the child does not need special services.

The social worker's role on the school's special education team then often involves securing cooperation and information from the family. Both BSWs and MSWs perform this type of work, although BSWs will usually find greater opportunities in rural areas, where the professional labor supply is limited. Additional training in child development and education is desirable for both BSWs and MSWs. Appropriate expertise is especially important in school social work because the lives of children with special needs are affected so directly.

Unfortunately, the beliefs and actions of people in the wider society sometimes *create* clients for social workers in special education. In an ideal society, special education evaluation would be a waste of time for these children because, given acceptance by others, they would have no problems to evaluate. The following is an example of such a circumstance, sadly still common today.

School Social Work with Other Special-Needs Children: The Ordeal of Two Gay Brothers

Todd Larkin was about 11 years old when he began to sense he was different. As early as the sixth grade he sometimes felt very alone. His buddies made cracks and catcalls at the girls, and the girls flirted in return. Everyone seemed to share some sort of secret. Todd, who had many friends who were girls, couldn't grasp what it was all about. He liked girls as people, but the flirting and catcalls left him bewildered. However, he didn't talk to anyone about his confusion because he was afraid there might be something wrong with him. Since he was handsome, athletic, and gregarious, nobody noticed his pain.

When Todd was in his early teens, he noticed a strong attraction to his male friends. No other boy mentioned such an attraction, so he felt confused and scared. Other boys were starting to date, but they dated only girls. Todd felt a desire to date boys. Increasingly, he wondered if something was wrong with him. He was afraid to talk with anyone about his fears, however. He didn't even have the words in his vocabulary to help him name his difference from other children.

Then, by chance, Todd saw a movie on television one evening at home. The movie was called *The Truth about Alex*. The movie's hero, Alex, was handsome, athletic, and outgoing, just like Todd. And also like Todd, he was physically attracted to boys, not girls. Alex kept his difference a secret for a long time, but eventually he told a close friend in high school. As a result, Alex was labeled homosexual and ostracized by all his former friends.

Todd began to believe that he was homosexual too; but, given Alex's experience in the movie, he determined to remain absolutely silent. He even began to date girls to make sure no one would ever suspect. He "passed" very successfully. He was popular among the young ladies. But he graduated from high school with the whole burden of worry about his sexuality on his own shoulders. He didn't even talk with his parents about it.

Because Todd felt so lonely and misunderstood in high school in his small, rural town, he decided to go away to college in a large city. He hoped he might be able to talk with someone there about his concerns. Being extremely bright and an academic achiever, he was admitted to a prestigious private urban university. But his first days at college were disappointing. Right across the hall from his dorm room, for example, a large poster was displayed making fun of gay and lesbian people. And in theology class, Old Testament scriptures were quoted that rebuked gay people. Again, the boy felt lonely and afraid.

One day a hall director found Todd staring at the poster on the door across from his room. The director, a sensitive young woman who also served on the Campus

Ministry staff, asked Todd if the poster offended him. Todd admitted that it did. The director agreed and suggested that Todd talk with a certain priest at the college, who felt the same way.

For several weeks, Todd tried to find the courage to call the priest. He was afraid, however, of being overheard in the dorm. Finally, he decided to call from a pay phone. Slumping down in the booth, Todd dialed the priest's number six times in a row. Each time his call was answered, he hung up in embarrassment and confusion. At last, on the seventh call, a warm, gentle voice spoke before the boy could hang up. "Come to my office today at 3 p.m.," Father Healy said.

Todd arrived at the priest's office door feeling sick to his stomach and not sure what to say. However, Father Healy's gentle sense of humor broke the ice. "Hello, son," the man began with a smile as he saw the boy's tense face. "I hate hang-ups. Come on in, and let's talk." Todd did just that. By the time he left Father Healy's office, he had been invited to attend a group of **gay** students run by Campus Ministry, co-led by the priest and Todd's own hall director.

When the boy didn't appear after a couple of weeks, Father Healy called to tell Todd he was sending a student to fetch him. In this way the priest gave Todd a chance to refuse and yet actively expedited his appearance. The hall director met Todd at the door of the meeting and eased his way into the group by finding a place for him to sit. It took several weeks for the boy to tell his story. But in the nurturing environment provided by the Campus Ministry gathering, Todd began to understand that his worth and dignity as a spiritual being were not diminished by his sexual orientation. He began to open up. Six months into the school year, Todd decided that he was, indeed, gay and that it was time to come out of the closet.

Encouraged by his support group, Todd began by telling his mother about his sexuality. To his shock, Todd's mother told him that she had suspected he was gay for some time and that she was glad he was finally able to tell her. Todd's mother eased the boy's way toward acceptance in the family by telling his father and stepfather for him. Todd's stepfather accepted the news fairly well; his biological father was more ambivalent. Neither man, however, totally rejected Todd, as he had feared they would.

The one person Todd pledged his mother not to tell, however, was his younger brother Tim. Todd felt that Tim, having weathered his mother's divorce and remarriage, needed a stable male role model in his life. Todd believed he was that role model, and feared Tim would be upset at a critical time in his life if he learned that Todd was gay. The mother consented.

Ironically, Tim was struggling with questions about his own sexuality. Like his brother before him, he was afraid to talk to anyone. At age 11 the boy began to abuse drugs, perhaps to mask his worries and confusion about his sexuality. At age 13 Tim took a major overdose and had to be hospitalized to save his life. It was there, by Tim's bedside at the hospital, that Todd learned what his brother had been going through. As Todd sat in the visitor's chair and asked Tim what was wrong and why he had tried to kill himself, he heard the younger boy say things like "I'm all alone" and "No one understands me."

For a while, Todd could not understand what his younger brother was trying to tell him. But suddenly, he recognized his own feelings and experiences in high school.

Was it possible that Tim had doubts about his sexuality too? Finally, Todd asked. Tim began to cry, and then Todd cried, and the two brothers shared as they never had before.

It would be nice if the story ended happily here, but life had more trials in store. Two weeks after the suicide attempt, Tim decided to confide in a close friend in junior high. He chose the friend carefully, hoping to be accepted.

But Tim was not accepted. A terrible replay of *The Truth about Alex* began to take place in his small, rural town. Within a week, everyone seemed to be pointing at him. The boy felt betrayed, angry, confused, ashamed, and scared. His family's house was pelted with eggs, and his mother's car tires were slashed. When the family appealed for help from the police, the police did nothing.

A couple of weeks after that, a boy in Tim's eighth-grade class pointed at him rudely and jeered loudly, "You're a fag, Tim Larkin! You're a fag!"

Tim's teacher should have protected him. But, instead, the man pointed a long finger at the boy. "Well, Tim," the man said, looking down his considerable nose, "is it true?"

Tim couldn't speak at first. Then he took a deep, slow breath. "I don't know, Mr. Humphrey," he replied bravely. "I'm not sure yet."

The class roared with laughter. The teacher glared and said, "I thought so; I thought so."

Mr. Humphrey's tone was so harsh, and the laughter in the classroom so derisive, that Tim couldn't bear to stay in his seat. He leaped up and ran home, shut the window shades, and locked the door. He refused to go back to school. When his mother and stepfather were able to persuade him to go back a few days later, Tim found himself thrown against lockers, spat upon, and beaten up. The school principal refused to help. "We aren't in the business of protecting people from discrimination here," he said, when Tim's parents went to the school to complain.

When Tim continued to refuse to go to school, the school administration threatened to prosecute for truancy. At this point Tim's mother appealed for help at the state level, wanting to know her and her son's rights. She also took Tim to a social worker in private practice, an MSW who specialized in family counseling.

The social worker helped Tim and his mother understand that confusion about sexual orientation was a normal part of adolescence. She helped the mother provide Tim with much-needed understanding and support so that despite the harsh daily reality of rejection from the outside world, Tim did not attempt suicide again. Instead, he brought his troubles and frustrations to the safe haven of home or a counseling session. On the suggestion of the state office of public instruction, Tim's mother also referred the boy for special education services at the school. The social worker who was counseling privately with the family wrote a powerful letter to the evaluation team describing the school as an environment hazardous to Tim's physical and mental health. The team then determined that Tim was a student at risk and authorized homebound instruction.

Tim continued to face difficulties, however. He was harassed when he went to school to pick up his assignments for homebound instruction. So the family enrolled him in a home-schooling organization. However, trapped in the house, afraid to go out even to the grocery store, Tim couldn't concentrate on his studies by correspondence. He then decided to work for his GED (general equivalency diploma) at a technical school in a neighboring town. Again, however, the boy suffered ridicule by students who had heard of his situation.

Discouraged, Tim dropped out of the GED program. About this time, hoping to help create positive social change, Tim's mother courageously agreed to take part in a public radio program discussing challenges for parents with homosexual children. When she returned to her job (she had been a caretaker for an elderly woman for more than 15 years), she found her belongings piled on the front porch, the door of the house locked, and a note telling her she was fired. She was never allowed to speak with her former client, a shut-in, again.

With such truly depressing experiences, one could hardly blame this family for becoming bitter and giving up. But instead, they maintained hope and overcame the odds with help from people who cared. For example, a dedicated teacher tutored Tim outside the regular GED program; he passed the exam! Tim's family, excited and relieved, gave him a formal graduation ceremony along with Todd's partner, who completed his GED at approximately the same time. Many celebrating friends and family members attended. Tim was accepted into college. Todd now has his MSW and counsels gay and **lesbian** youth.

Tim's mother explains that she maintains a safe haven for her two sons at home. It is still dangerous for them to walk alone in the neighborhood. She declares that antigay people, even long-term family friends, are not allowed in the house when her sons are present. This impressive woman has also paid attention to her own needs. Not only has she survived being fired from her job, but she has updated her nursing credentials and developed entrepreneurial skills as well. Today she runs her own bridal shop.

SOCIAL WORK VALUES IN THE SCHOOL SETTING: POLICY IMPLICATIONS

Social work professional values strongly affect the policies social workers promote in the school setting. The Santiago and Larkin cases will be used as illustrations followed by a discussion of other serious school issues that tend to be addressed in very different ways depending on value orientation.

The Santiago Sisters

Let us begin with the Santiago sisters. Years ago, truancy would have been viewed simply as bad behavior, and the response of the school system would have been punitive. However, over the years more enlightened values in the fields of education and social work together have led to the development of a more individualized approach to truancy. Today, many schools have a policy of assigning a social worker to approach the investigation not as an effort at social control but as a fact-finding task. The uniqueness of each child's personal circumstance is recognized, and the worth and dignity of each child is respected. Usually the truant child needs assistance with some underlying problem.

The very existence of bilingual education illustrates how values have affected policy in the schools. The primary thrust for the development of bilingual education came from the profession of education, of course, but social work values such as self-determination strongly support it if that is what minority people request. Recognition of minority languages and cultures in public schools not only helps children learn but also shows respect for the worth and dignity of all persons. Such attention helps children gain self-esteem and pride in their own heritage.

Values also were the fuel for development of special education programs in the public schools. Certainly it is easier for a school system simply to refuse admission or to expel children who bring with them special problems and needs. But over time, the values of fairness and individual worth and dignity have led to the recognition that children don't have much of a chance to make it in this society without an education. Even children with special problems should thus have a right to public education. Committed organizing and political strength were required to translate these values into public law, however.

The Larkin Case

The Larkin case is an example of what happens when conformity rather than diversity is valued by a school administration. Social work values, by contrast, honor the worth and dignity of all persons, and they teach respect for diversity. If social work values had been activated in Tim's school during his ordeal, new school policy would have been proposed, at the very least, to protect the rights of minorities. However, no one on the staff stepped forward to organize for change. Ideally, such a task would have been taken on by a school social worker (see Exhibit 7-5). Unfortunately, evidence suggests that

---

EXHIBIT 7-5

Challenge of Gay Youth for Social Work

Educational systems need to develop programs that increase faculty and student awareness of homosexuality as a normal variation on sexual orientation. Accurate information about homosexuality should become a part of school sex education curriculums, and faculty in-service training must be provided in this area. School social workers, with their ethical commitment to the uniqueness and individuality of all people, can be instrumental in providing or arranging for such training. Administrative discrimination in the hiring of gay and lesbian teachers must cease; these teachers should be sought as positive role models for lesbian and gay youths in the same way that culturally diverse teachers are hired to serve as role models for their respective cultures. . . .

Sanctions need to be implemented to end lesbian and gay discrimination, harassment, and violence in the schools. These sanctions must be enforced for students, teachers, and administrative personnel alike. . . .

Finally, social workers must work to dispel negative stereotypes, myths, and discrimination aimed at lesbian and gay individuals. Social workers must become role models of respect and acceptance of diversity among people, including gay and lesbian people.

SOURCE: Quoted from D. F. Morrow. (1993, November). Social work with gay and lesbian adolescents. *Social Work, 38*(6), pp. 655–660.

many social workers themselves are **homophobic,** or at least **heterosexist** (Berkman & Zinberg, 1997).

Who knows how many children with questions about their sexual orientation are currently hiding their pain, dealing with their confusion and fear all alone? Who knows how many parents are struggling with their own confusion and fear as well?

Punitive attitudes toward diversity, rather than respect, do not just hover in the abstract. They have concrete and horrific results. One study of gay and lesbian students, for example, found that 22 percent of males and 29 percent of females experienced physical injury by other students because of sexual orientation. Other studies have found that gay and lesbian students attempt suicide at a rate two to seven times higher than their heterosexual counterparts. Almost 40 percent have problems with truancy, and 30 percent drop out of school. These are tragedies relating to harassment, yet school personnel rarely view stopping harassment as part of their job (Dupper, 2003).

How different life for gay and lesbian students would be if school personnel, including social workers, took a serious interest in this issue and worked hard to solve it! Schools can be ideal settings to provide education about sexual orientation because almost all children and families become involved in them. School programs can help teach understanding and acceptance of diversity to students and parents alike, given the commitment to do so.

To assist school social workers to better serve lesbian, gay, bisexual, and questioning (LGBQ) students, the NASW sponsored a professional development workshop in June 2006. It addressed several issues of concern for school social workers, in particular the role of the social worker in addressing health and mental health issues of LGBQ students. The workshop also offered information on prevention of HIV and other sexually transmitted diseases and unintended pregnancy. NASW today considers working effectively with LGBQ youth a "core competency" required of all school social workers (Stoesen, 2006).

Beyond the school setting, social work values support protective laws for people with same-sex orientation and their families. Without such laws, people like the Larkins may find it difficult to obtain police protection when harassed, and they may be without recourse when fired from their jobs.

Violence in the Schools

Almost everyone today is aware of violence in the schools. The mass shooting at Columbine High School in Littleton, Colorado, in April 1999 awakened everyone to its frightening reality. The massacre at Virginia Tech in April 2007 reawakened such fear in a manner horribly reminiscent of the Columbine killings. The student who murdered 30 of his peers at Virginia Tech and then killed himself imitated the clothing and stance of the Columbine killers and called them martyrs in videotapes that he left behind (O'Driscoll, 2007).

How can such horrors be prevented? As far back as 1994, the federal government mandated **zero-tolerance** policies in the public schools under President Bill Clinton's Gun-Free Schools Act. Zero tolerance means that a student *must* be expelled from

School social worker talks with troubled student in school setting.

school for a calendar year if caught carrying a weapon (although administrators are given slight latitude according to the circumstance). After the mass shootings at Columbine, many schools began bringing in police, posting hall monitors, installing metal detectors and surveillance cameras, requiring student ID badges, and the like. Students began being disciplined for very minor infractions. The major response to safety concerns in many schools has thus been one of increased security and punitive measures.

Is zero tolerance and strict disciplinary action the best way to prevent violence? Many social workers disagree. Our professional values stress the worth and dignity of every person and the provision of options and choices, not repression. Perhaps surprisingly, many other professionals also advise that preventing attacks involves far more than punitive measures. Many children who threaten or disobey in school have been bullied themselves by peers or teachers. Surveillance measures may only make them feel more afraid (see Exhibit 7-6).

Personnel surveyed in school-based clinics after the Columbine murders reported that there was a tremendous need for more mental health professionals in the schools (Button & Rienzo, 2002). Professionals, including police, continue to stress the importance of good relationships between staff and students in the school setting, listening, spotting warning signs, and persuading students to report threats (Paulson, 2005). Preventive efforts such as conflict resolution and peer mediation programs, after-school programs, and family intervention programs have significant, positive effects. Research indicates that even preschool programs have significant long-term effects, reducing the frequency and severity of juvenile delinquency by the age of 18 (Mann & Reynolds, 2006).

Disciplinary action may be necessary to help create pro-social behavior. However, social skills training and counseling are far more lasting, transformative experiences and help create a much more positive, trusting wider environment. School social workers can provide the expertise needed to create and carry out such programs.

EXHIBIT 7-6

Surveillance: The Best Answer to Violence?

A collaborative study between the DOE (U.S. Department of Education) and the U.S. Secret Service of 37 acts of violence in American schools found that the incidents were rarely impulsive. It showed that someone almost always knew of the plot. The perpetrators had often been bullied, experienced a significant personal loss, and exhibited striking changes in behavior. . . .

Mr. Modzeleski (a security specialist at the DOE) and others are convinced that the answer lies not in more metal detectors or school guards, but in a shift in culture. "It's easy to focus in on shootings, but we also need to look at what we're doing about harassment, teasing, bullying," he says. The real key is "putting adults in there that kids can talk to when they have a problem, making sure they can listen, that they have the willingness to listen, and can provide them with guidance."

SOURCE: Quoted from A. Paulson. (2005, March 25). Schools using many lessons of Columbine. *The Christian Science Monitor*, p. 10.

Sexuality and Teen Pregnancy: Environmental Factors

Sexuality and teen pregnancy are issues for schools because sexual behavior often begins while children are still students in school. Early sexual activity is particularly risky among children today because girls are physically maturing earlier and thus at greater risk of pregnancy. As Dr. Jocelyn Elders (2001), former U.S. Surgeon General, puts it, "In the good old days the mean age of menstruation was 17—time to get married. In the 1800's it was 15 or 16—time to date. Now it's 11 years and 4 months—time to educate!"

No one is certain why girls are maturing physically so much earlier than in previous times, but many scientists believe that environmental pollution is a major culprit. Dr. Joseph Mercola (2001) warns that certain synthetic chemicals in the environment mimic estrogens (female hormones). These are derived in many cases from plastics, ingested through food (commonly wrapped in plastic), water, and mother's milk. Mercola cites evidence from the *Journal of Epidemiology* that contamination of foods by the chemical polybrominated biphenyl (PBB) is associated with early puberty; and plasticizer chemicals called phthalates are also associated with early puberty in a major study published by the *Journal of Pediatrics*. Dr. William Hobbins (2007) cautions that in addition, hormones ingested for purposes of birth control or to cope with hot flashes in menopausal women often end up in the sewage system. These are not removed by normal sewage plant treatments and can end up in the water supply.

Regardless of the reasons young girls are maturing sexually so early, whether schools should get involved in sex education has been a controversial issue for decades. Many people insist that sex education should take place in the home only. Yet Dr. Elders reports that only 36 percent of teens surveyed said they had had a helpful conversation about sex with their parents (Dr. Jocelyn Elders, 2001). Many people oppose sex education in the schools because they fear it may increase sexual activity. However, a review of 250 programs teaching teens how to avoid pregnancy found that these efforts did *not* lead to increased sexual activity. Instead, many resulted in the opposite. The most successful programs employed an "abstinence plus" approach, promoting abstinence but also encouraging teens who were sexually active to protect themselves from sexually transmitted diseases and pregnancy (Study: Safe-sex programs don't increase sexual activity, 2001; see Exhibit 7-7).

Many school social workers today are involved in sex education programs, frequently working in teams with school nurses, guidance counselors, physical education teachers, and others. Social workers are likely to take on the important task of developing parental support for these programs. The good news is that teen pregnancy and birth rates have declined overall in the United States by about one-third since the 1990s. But this nation, to its shame, still has the highest teen birth rate in the industrialized world. Foster children are at especially high risk; by age 19, almost half of young women in foster care have been pregnant, as compared with approximately one-fifth of those never in foster care. Moreover, Latina teen pregnancy is almost twice as high as the national average (National Campaign to Prevent Teen Pregnancy, 2007).

One approach to the problem is simply to blame the teens and walk away or else to inflict punishment such as expulsion (usually of the pregnant girl). This was the norm not so many years ago, justified as a deterrent to other students. Another approach, however, is to honor the worth and dignity of all youth and to provide them with more genuine choices and opportunities to maximize their potential. The latter is the approach in accord with social work values, and it is probably more effective in terms of school retention. For example, while statistics often correlate early pregnancy with dropping out of school, and many social scientists assume that pregnancy *causes* the dropping out, evidence sometimes indicates that the relationship may be the other way around. Discouragement at school can lead to pregnancy as a means of escape.

What can social workers do to help make schools more hospitable places for their students so that they want to stay and learn? When the question is posed in this way, many creative ideas can be generated. For example, cultural events that help members of ethnic minority groups feel more comfortable can be organized. Family outreach and family-life education programs can be developed, along with after-school tutorial and recreational programs, sex education and self-defense programs, support groups

---

EXHIBIT 7-7

Sex Education in the Schools?

One of the most difficult subjects schools teach is sex education. Pressure from parents and community members often results in sexual education ending up on the "evaded" curriculum—never discussed, and its side effects ignored and relegated to the area of "personal problems." Even if sex education is taught as part of the formal curriculum in health class, *meaningful* school-based support systems for teen mothers are still relatively rare. Teen mothers rarely have good options for child care and alternative scheduling that will allow them to work toward, and complete, their high school degree. "Sex education school initiatives tend to place primary responsibility for adolescent pregnancy on girls."

SOURCE: Quoted from A. Ginorio & M. Huston. (2001). *Si, se puede! Yes we can, Latinas in school.* Washington, DC: AAUW Educational Foundation, p. 26.

for pregnant teens and young mothers, day care for their children, and the like. Myriad possible programs may help prevent early pregnancy or at least help young parents complete high school.

No Child Left Behind?

In another effort designed to help children succeed in school, the No Child Left Behind Act (NCLB) was signed into law by President George W. Bush in January of 2002. The NCLB involved a sweeping reform of Title I of the Elementary and Secondary Education Act that was originally passed in 1965. Title I was intended to assist states to provide additional resources for educationally disadvantaged children (Hare, et al., 2006).

The NCLB has impressive goals: to set high standards for achievement and to establish strong accountability measures via ongoing standardized testing. Students are to be tested in grades three through eight to assess their progress in reading and mathematics; results are to be tabulated for multiple subgroups including minority, low-income, special education, and limited-English students. By 2014, every American child is supposed to meet specified achievement standards in reading and math (Paulson, 2007).

Many problems became evident as the law was implemented, however. For example, while states can set their own achievement standards, the NCLB requires that every school in a given state, including every subgroup in every school, achieve the same standards. The underlying NCLB assumption is that schools by themselves can achieve major leaps in educational achievement for all students in a very short time, and that if this does not happen, the fault lies entirely with the school and its teachers (Sunderman, Kim, & Orfield, 2005). Not taken into account is what some people have described as "America's dirty little secret": a substantial proportion of American children live in dire poverty. A shamefully large number are homeless. Children whose lives are scarred by poverty and homelessness can rarely concentrate long enough to complete a standardized test, much less achieve a desirable score. Schools and teachers alone simply cannot solve the issue of educational achievement in American schools (see Exhibit 7-8).

A further problem with the NCLB is that the promised increase in federal funding enacted into the law to assist with the cost of testing did not materialize after the first year. Schools find implementation a heavy burden both in terms of financial cost and the time required to administer the tests. Additionally, schools whose students do not achieve at the required rate for 2 years in a row are sanctioned—they may lose funding, and their students are allowed to transfer. This means in practice that schools with the greatest majority of poor and minority students, the very schools that need assistance the most, are the ones most likely to lose funding under the NCLB (Sunderman et al., 2005; Paulson, 2007).

The NCLB was to be reauthorized by Congress in 2007, but due to its controversial nature, debate was postponed. A coalition of 100 groups, including the NAACP (National Association for the Advancement of Colored People) and the National Education Association, have signed a list of 14 requested changes to the law,

EXHIBIT 7-8

Challenges of Children in Poverty

Children from economically disadvantaged families are more likely than their middle-class or wealthy peers to suffer preventable illnesses caused by inadequate health care, lack of health insurance and contaminated living spaces. They're more likely to experience hunger and homelessness, to go without meals, without shelter and warmth. They're more likely to live in neighborhoods with unsafe levels of environmental pollutants, to lack safe places to stay, safe water to drink, safe air to breathe.

Regardless of whether a child living in poverty wants to learn, regardless of whether she's determined to make the best life for herself, she must first overcome enormous barriers to life's basic needs—the kind of needs that middle-class people, including most professional educators, usually take for granted: access to health care, sufficient food and lodging; reasonably safe living conditions. . . .

Whenever somebody refers to education as the great equalizer, we must remember the injustices listed above. We must remember that in almost every conceivable way, the very structure of the U.S. education system denies students in poverty the opportunities and access it affords most other students.

SOURCE: Quoted from *Teaching tolerance, a question of class*. Retrieved April 7, 2007, from the Teaching Tolerance website, http://www.tolerance.org/teach/magazine/features.jsp?is=40&ar=777

including a lowering of proficiency targets; giving schools credit for making strides toward meeting standards, even if they fall short of proficiency; encouraging testing designed to measure higher thinking skills and performance throughout the year; providing more assistance to failing schools; and getting rid of sanctions altogether (Paulson, 2007).

Teen Drop-out Rates

The problem of teens dropping out of school is a serious one; while the drop-out rate can be difficult to determine, a recent study found that approximately one-third of students who started high school 4 years earlier did not graduate on time. The rate for minorities was even higher, with more than half dropping out in some cities. The official drop-out rate nationally is currently about 10 percent, but studies indicate that teens who have left school have been severely under-counted for the past several decades. Because teen drop-outs are far more likely than other teens to land in prison, on public assistance, or unemployed, this is a major social problem (Paulson, 2006). Unfortunately, the No Child Left Behind Act does not provide incentives to keep students in school. NCLB may even be a factor promoting dropping out, as schools needing to raise overall achievement scores to avoid sanctions may quietly ignore the exit of underachieving students.

Latino students, sadly, have the highest school drop-out rates of all; Latinos also have the highest rates of illiteracy and enrollment at below grade-level in American schools. Only about 45 percent of Latino teens complete high school, and of those who do, a large proportion cannot go on to college because they have enrolled in vocational tracks. The dismal statistics regarding Latino school success contributes to the reasons this group as a whole remains at the lower rungs of the economic ladder today (Hinkelman, 2005).

Social work values promote the goal of assisting all students to succeed at school, to help them achieve better opportunities in life, and to maximize their potential. Such goals clearly involve access to good schools so that students are motivated to stay, but they involve much more: a decent standard of living for all students, a safe environment, and parents (or parent-figures) who have the means to participate in their children's education (e.g., parents who are not forced by low wages to work multiple jobs so that it is impossible for them to attend parent-teacher conferences; fluency in the English language, etc.). That is why school social workers must advocate for students and their families not only in the school setting but in the wider political arena.

Spiritual Development and Empowerment

Helping empower students to develop the inner strength to remain in school, a challenging environment under the best of circumstances, can involve some unusual and creative strategies. For example, biofeedback techniques can dramatically reveal to students the connection between the inner workings of the mind and the mind's effect on the physical body. Students can actually *see* on biofeedback monitors how their angry thoughts lead to increased muscle tension and decreased hand temperature. Students can teach themselves how to calm their own minds and reduce their own physiological stress. A calm mind and reduced physiological stress permit much greater impulse control. Biofeedback can be an excellent tool not only in learning anger management, for example, but also in developing self-understanding and thus personal empowerment.

While merely a technique for physiological monitoring if viewed narrowly, biofeedback also provides a view into the workings of the inner self. It provides new self-awareness and the ability to modify, intentionally, one's own emotional and physiological stress responses. Many professionals believe that increasing understanding of the mind-body connection, along with the ability to bring about desired emotional and physiological changes, can lead to enhanced personal and spiritual growth (Matuszek & Rycraft, 2003).

Helping assist in the development of students' spiritual growth in the school setting must be done with care, as spirituality and religion are often confused. Because of the required separation of church and state, religion must not be taught in the public schools. But there are effective ways to assist in the development of spiritual growth and personal empowerment that are compatible with any religion. One contemporary approach is known as **social-emotional learning (SEL)**. SEL involves recognizing emotions and using a variety of methods to regulate responses to stress such as contemplative practice or meditation and breathing exercises (see Exhibit 7-9). Social workers can be effective SEL promoters and practitioners in the school setting. They can also be instrumental in organizing such programs.

EXHIBIT 7-9

Social-Emotional Learning

Arthur Zajonc, physicist and director of the Center for Contemplative Mind in Society, says that he sees education "as the sole means for interior harmony, which in the end is the capacity for *freedom and love.*" Yet in modern secular educational systems, directly providing the tools that lead to this harmony have been problematic because many practices stem directly from spiritual and religious traditions, potentially breaching the separation of church and state. Patricia Jennings, director of the Garrison Institute's Initiative on Contemplation and Education (ICE), cautions, "We need to be sure that the language we use is scientific and secular, and that the techniques do not require any kind of belief system to work." Despite this challenge, a dedicated corps of educators has been bringing "social-emotional learning" (known by its acronym, SEL) and contemplative practices into public schools.

Though solid definitions are sometimes hard to come by in this emerging educational field, SEL usually includes recognizing emotions in oneself and others; regulating responses to conflict and stress through breathing exercises, meditation, or yoga; and intentional moments of silence and reflection, among other practices.

SOURCE: Quoted from *The 2007 shift report, evidence of a world transforming*. (2007). Petaluma, CA: The Institute of Noetic Sciences, pp. 57–58.

AN INTERNATIONAL COMPARISON: SCHOOL SOCIAL WORK IN GHANA

A brief discussion of social work in Ghana, a nation on the west coast of Africa just north of the equator, demonstrates both the similarity and differences in social work services offered in the United States and in this former British Colony.

Ghana was the first African nation colonized by the British to win its independence. It did so in 1957, only to fall into a dictatorship. This dictatorship was eventually overthrown, and various governments, mostly military, ruled until 1992. At that time a fourth republic headed by an elected president was established, and the nation remains a republic today.

Ghana is ethnically diverse, home to more than 100 distinct ethnic groups. More than 50 languages and dialects are spoken. Thus it should be no surprise that English, the language introduced by the British, is used as a *lingua franca* (a language used for communication between different peoples). The government and the public schools use English as their official language.

More than half of Ghana's population is under the age of 18. Since 1996, education has been free, compulsory, and universal. With so many children to educate, many Ghanaian schools have instituted "shift" systems: one group of children attends school in the morning and another in the afternoon. No special school programs are available for physically disabled children. These children are integrated into regular classrooms; some may receive treatment at state rehabilitation centers. There are no special provisions for children with learning disabilities. Each teacher does the best she or he can to assist as needed.

The British government initiated social work services in Ghana in the 1950s under its Department of Social Welfare, but in 1967 the Ghana Education Service established its own social work service, the School Welfare Service. Truancy and delinquency had increased by that time to alarming proportions. Due to a need for more trained professionals, the Ghana Education Service contracted with the University of Ghana in 1975 to provide professional training for social workers. A 2-year graduate program was developed, leading to a diploma in social administration, recognized by the International Council for Social Work Education. In 1990, the University of Ghana initiated a 3-year undergraduate program in social work.

School social workers in Ghana serve multiple roles. Families in this nation are matrilineal, which means that children are supported by their mothers' extended families, primarily their mothers' brothers—not their fathers. While Ghana's extended family system was strong prior to colonialism, today the family structure is in disarray due to colonialism's after-effects. Men are frequently missing, searching for work far away. Poverty is widespread, so many children are mired in child labor or abandoned on the streets. School social workers (known as welfare officers) do their best to assist children who are hungry, homeless, neglected, abandoned, abused, exhausted, and frequently truant. They assist children who are engaged in prostitution; addicted to alcohol, drugs, and gambling; bullied; and/or challenged with various physical and other disabilities.

Recognizing the widespread problem of hunger, school social workers were the professionals who organized Ghana's school meal program, helping provide at least one balanced meal to each student every day. School social workers currently serve as nutrition officers, making sure that school meals are nutritional and properly prepared. In addition, they serve not only as consultants to teachers regarding the learning needs of particular students, but they directly assist new teachers in finding accommodations for themselves and their children. They arrange school placements for teachers' children, and make sure that teachers' salaries are paid on time. They ensure that each teacher understands his or her duties, obligations, and rights. They organize seminars for teachers on the latest teaching techniques and methods designed to meet the psychological needs of their students.

Ghanaian school social workers serve as the primary link between the school and the family. They make home visits to assist families to become more active in their children's education and to help resolve any problems between the school and the home. They assist parents to develop positive parenting techniques and provide family-life education programs. They assist parents with special needs children to keep their children in school and to find additional resources such as state rehabilitation centers. They refer parents to appropriate community resources to help resolve other issues such as marital problems and child support disputes.

School social workers in Ghana also help develop and run parent–teacher associations. The main purpose is to bring parents together to identify common interests and to provide forums for joint parent–teacher discussion and collaboration.

Overall, school social work services offered in Ghana are designed to be preventive—the parent–teacher associations, home and school collaborative activities, nutritional programs, and family-life education programs are all designed to help parents, teachers and schoolchildren prevent school-related problems or to alleviate them before they become serious (Sossou & Daniels, 2002).

CURRENT TRENDS

Social workers are challenged today, and will continue to be challenged, by the many issues and trends discussed in this chapter. In the United States these include meeting the needs of an increasingly diverse student population, especially greater numbers of children of ethnic minority heritage, children whose first language is other than English, and gay and lesbian students. It involves dealing constructively with violence, teen sexuality and pregnancy issues, and new school accountability measures (including holding those measures *themselves* accountable so as to find ways to make them fairer for children who are poor, underprivileged, and overstressed).

Schools serve almost all children in this country today and can thus be primary sites for preventive efforts and early intervention. What better locus for social work leadership? Not surprisingly, whenever possible social workers today are increasingly involved in macro-level intervention to stretch scarce resources and prevent problems from arising. Efforts are myriad in scope, including organizing after-school programs, child care programs, weekend recreational programs, parenting classes, substance abuse prevention programs, and the like. Increasingly, efforts include securing the funds to support these programs and require sophisticated grant-writing skills (Wells, 1999).

Ironically, as discussed earlier, schools in poverty-stricken areas that need help the most are the ones most likely to find themselves losing funding under the No Child Left Behind Act. That is because disadvantaged students are among those most likely to score poorly on standardized tests, resulting in sanctions being taken against their schools. The NCLB does not take into account factors external to the schools, including other government policies (e.g., the very low minimum wage and TANF program requirements) that tend to increase poverty, hunger, and homelessness among children, directly obstructing their school performance.

The trend toward increased numbers of alternative and charter schools has also been discussed earlier. In addition, increased summer school enrollment will affect social work practice. Particularly in large cities, summer school enrollment has been burgeoning in recent years. Summer school enrollment in Chicago, for example, increased 10-fold over a 5-year period so that more than half of its student body was enrolled in summer school by 2001. This trend is partially fueled by standardized testing and the curbing of social promotion. Other factors involve increasing numbers of single-parent and two-working-parent households that welcome summer programming for their children (Sappenfield, 2001). So far teachers have been most affected, but school social workers may find their employment contracts running more on a year-round basis in the foreseeable future.

Issues relating to gender diversity remain serious. According to a report on gender gaps in the schools conducted by the American Institutes for Research (1998) and commissioned by the American Association of University Women Educational Foundation, the cumulative effect of poverty, abuse, and other family or community problems is even worse for girls than for boys. The report notes that about 20 percent of girls have been sexually or physically abused, 25 percent show signs of depression, and 25 percent do not receive needed health care. Sexual harassment interferes with the learning of both boys and girls in schools. Substance abuse is a widespread problem; in boys it is tied to a higher school dropout rate than for non-substance-abusing boys, in girls to a higher rate of criminality than for non-substance-abusing girls. Boys are much more likely to be diagnosed with learning disabilities than girls, although the reasons are not fully understood. How can the differing needs of both boys and girls be met? Some people are beginning to suggest an old idea: single-sex schools (Tyre, 2006).

Special-needs populations today include children with developmental disabilities, emotional and behavioral disorders, cognitive disabilities, physical disabilities, and the like. Early assessment and planning for services in the least restrictive environment remain important tasks for the school social worker today. Assessing how home and community environments affect student development is another important focus of today's school social worker (Dupper, 2003).

School social work is a strong and growing field today. The number of state associations for school social workers has continued to grow. In the early 1990s, school social workers developed the first specialty practice section within the NASW, the School Social Work Section. Such associations are important because they provide forums for development and discussion of important issues in the field and for dissemination of current research findings. They can also, ideally, lead to the development of political action groups to lobby for needed legislation and funding.

INTERNET SITES

http://www.sswaa.org/	The School Social Work Association of America
http://www.lehman.cuny.edu/faculty/jfleitas/bandaides/	Band-Aides and Blackboards
http://www.nationalsave.org	Students against Violence Everywhere
http://www.socialworkers.org/practice/standards/NASW_SSWS.pdf	NASW Standards for School Social Work Services
http://internationalnetwork-schoolsocialwork.htmlplanet.com	International Network for School Social Work
http://www.panic-anxiety.com/phobias/didaskaleinophobia	School Phobia
http://www.nabe.org/	National Association for Bilingual Education
http://www.rong-chang.com/main.htm	English as a Second Language
http://members.aol.com/Horsemom2/	Support for Parents & Gay Kids during the Never-ending Coming-Out process
http://www.doe.state.in.us/sservices/socwork.htm	School Social Work National and State References
http://www.special-ed-careers.org/career_choices/profiles/professions/social.html	National Clearinghouse for Professions in Special Education—School Social Worker
http://online.onetcenter.org/link/summary/21–1021.00	Occupational Information Network—School Social Worker

SUMMARY

This chapter begins with a case study of two Latino sisters who were referred to the school social worker because of attendance problems. The social worker approaches the referral from a generalist perspective, finding out what the girls' past history of attendance has been and consulting with the parents, teachers, and the girls themselves to determine the nature of the problem. He does not assume that the problem lies with the girls, but he explores the possibility that family, school, or other environmental factors might be contributing to their truancy. After gathering and assessing data concerning the problem and determining appropriate goals (reducing conflicts at home, increasing school attendance), the social worker develops a plan of action, referring the children and their family to appropriate resources. The social worker thus mobilizes the resources of family, school, and community.

The impact of cultural diversity on the schools is clearly illustrated in this case study by the organization and planning invested in making a bilingual, bicultural program available for Latino children. Social work values such as self-determination support the development of such programs. Not only can the children learn better and faster in their own language, but self-esteem is enhanced in circumstances where the children's heritage is recognized and honored. The nation itself benefits from bilingual, bicultural citizens.

The public school is a gathering place for most of the children of America. For that reason, representatives of almost every minority will be found there. This chapter's second case study concerns two brothers with a homosexual orientation. It is offered to illustrate the serious challenge the social work profession faces in helping to expand tolerance for diversity in the school setting. Social work values affirming the worth and dignity of every person serve as a beacon to help guide the

worker through circumstances involving ignorance and intolerance.

The school is a secondary, or host, setting for the social worker, so the social work role is often as a member of a team. The social worker serves as the major link between the school and the home. On the special education team, the social worker is the designated liaison between school and family; she or he gathers information about children's developmental histories and behavior patterns in the home and community settings. Special education evaluations can be viewed as applied research with important consequences pertaining to multidisciplinary team decision making.

Social work values help orient social workers in influencing and implementing policies in the schools that deal with issues such as violence, sexuality and teen pregnancy, and accountability. How policies may differ according to value orientation (e.g., the orientation toward educating, developing new social skills, and maximizing potential, rather than controlling or punishing) is discussed. Student spiritual development and empowerment are discussed as means of assisting these young people to deal with challenging school environments.

School social work services in Ghana are described as a means of comparison and contrast with services offered in the United States. Many services are the same, including those involving assisting poor, hungry, homeless, neglected, and abused children and their families. In both nations, social workers are the primary link between the school and the home.

Social work roles in the schools are generalist in nature, ranging from working with individuals and families to working with small groups, organizations, and communities. Problems such as violence in the schools have their roots in the community as a whole, so that intervention on a single level will not suffice.

KEY TERMS

alternative schools, *p. 288*

bilingual, *p. 285*

emotional or behavioral
   disturbance, *p. 283*

English as a Second Language
   (ESL), *p. 285*

gay, *p. 293*

heterosexist, *p. 297*

homophobic, *p. 297*

homosexual, *p. 292*

lesbian, *p. 295*

mainstreamed, *p. 286*

multidisciplinary team
   (M-team, pupil planning
   team), *p. 289*

norms, *p. 287*

primary social work
   setting, *p. 284*

DISCUSSION QUESTIONS

1. What two major educational models to assist minority children at school have developed over the past several years? How are these models of education in accord with social work values? Why are they considered important?

2. Imagine you were a child entering public school with no knowledge of English. Which educational model do you think would have worked better for you? Why?

3. What were Frank Haines's initial hypotheses with respect to the truancy of the Santiago sisters? How accurate did his hypotheses turn out to be? How useful were they in shaping his initial investigation?

4. What is a culture? A subculture? Which cultures or subcultures are represented in the Santiago case example described in this chapter? Why is the concept of culture important in social work practice?

5. How did social workers originally become involved in work in the schools? How has the school social work role changed over time? In what ways has it remained the same?

6. What are school-linked, integrated services? What kinds of services do full-service schools provide in addition to an education? What are some strengths of this kind of collaborative effort? Can you think of any problems that might arise?

7. What is the social worker's role on a special education evaluation team? How is this role an example of applied research? How does this role affect children and families referred to special education?

8. How can biofeedback and social-emotional learning (SEL) programs be used by social workers to assist students in meeting the challenges inherent in the school environment? Do you think issues of spirituality should be addressed? Why or why not? How do social-emotional learning (SEL) programs address this issue?

9. If you could develop a policy pertaining to students with a homosexual orientation for your school, what key provisions would you include? Why?

10. Violence in the schools may relate to the fact that American communities themselves are violent. Do you agree? Disagree? Why? What has been your own experience?

11. Many social workers believe that sex education should be offered in the schools. What do you think about this? Why? If a student becomes pregnant, do you believe that services should be offered to help keep that student in school? If so, what kind of services do you think would be most helpful?

12. What are your views on standardized testing in the schools? What evidence is provided in this chapter that accountability measures such as these can have unexpected side effects? How do you think the social work profession should respond to accountability measures in the schools? Why?

13. Compare and contrast social work services in the United States and Ghana.

CLASSROOM EXERCISES

While not required, it is suggested that students break into small groups of three or four to discuss these exercises. It may be helpful to choose a scribe to record and report interesting points to the class after the group discussion.

1. Think about something school related that you did or considered doing that teachers or other staff would describe as at-risk behavior, something you are willing to share with the group. Examples might include truancy, substance abuse, withdrawn or disruptive behavior, and the like. Given the perspective of time, why do you think you did what you did, or why *didn't* you? On reflection, what school policies or programs do you think could have helped you? If some of them were already present in your school, what held you back from using them?

2. In your high school, how prevalent were troubles such as violent behavior, sexual harassment, or teen pregnancy? What policies, if any, did the school implement to address these issues? What policies do you believe could have been helpful?

3. Were accountability measures such as standardized testing practiced at your school? Describe measures you were aware of. What effects, if any, did they have on you? On your classmates?

4. If you were to develop policies to promote the best possible atmosphere in your school to help enhance student learning and cooperation, what policies would you develop? What would be the role of the school social worker? Would you include biofeedback and/or social-emotional learning techniques? Why or why not?

RESEARCH ACTIVITIES

1. Where these schools are available, arrange to interview a social worker who works in a regular public school, a second social worker who works in a charter school, and a third who works in an alternative school. Compare and contrast their educational backgrounds, satisfaction with their positions, and descriptions of their work roles and responsibilities.

2. If your town or city has a full-service school, arrange to talk with social workers employed by community agencies stationed at the school. What is their perception of the major needs of students

at the school? How does their work help meet these needs? What needs of the students still are not met, from their point of view?

3. Find out about special education services in the school system in your town or city. Are there special classrooms for children with disabilities or is the full-inclusion model in operation? Interview both a teacher and a social worker who work with the special education program. What do they think about full inclusion as an educational model for students with disabilities? What are their reasons?

INTERNET RESEARCH EXERCISES

1. A position statement on school violence was issued in November 2006 by the National Consortium of School Violence Prevention Researchers and Pactitioners on the NASW website (http://www.socialworkers.org/practice/school/110206.asp).

a. What are the four key elements that this paper cites as necessary for safer schools?

b. What is the thrust to the statement on "snitching" and how do you think it could be accomplished?

c. How do you suggest that the problem of "marginalized" could be handled?

2. An organization called Gay, Lesbian, and Straight Education Network (GLSEN) has commended and promoted the signing of a comprehensive safe schools bill in Iowa (http://www.glsen.org/cgi-bin/iowa/all/library/record/2042.html).

   a. At the time of this posting, how many states had passed similar bills in the United States?

   b. How effective can bills such as these be in bringing about a safer and more productive climate in the schools? Explain.

   c. The specific citation of "sexual orientation or gender identity/expression" is considered especially important. Why?

3. At the University of Illinois at Chicago the Psychology Department has an organization called CASEL, the Collaboration for Academic, Social and Emotional Learning (http://casel-org/).

   a. Click on "About CASEL." What is the mission or purpose of this group?

   b. Click on "Basics" and the "Definition." How would you paraphrase the definition of SEL, in one or two sentences?

   c. On what is SEL based? What does research demonstrate as the benefits of SEL?

FOR FURTHER READING

Constable, R., Massat, C., McDonald, S., & Flynn, J. (Eds.). (2006). *School social work, practice, policy, and research* (6th ed.). Chicago: Lyceum Books.

   The sixth edition of *School Social Work* addresses many key issues facing school social workers today. Chapters developed by multiple authors with diverse expertise address the history of school social work; policies and programs for developing social services in the schools; assessment, consultation, and planning issues; and practice applications in the schools. This timely text employs multiple case examples that illustrate how contemporary legislative changes have placed major new demands on educational institutions and how school social workers have served as catalysts for development of creative responses both within and beyond the school setting.

Dupper, D. (2003). *School social work, skills and interventions for effective practice.* Hoboken, NJ: John Wiley & Sons.

   The author developed this text specifically to provide school social work students and practitioners with a compendium of promising and appropriate interventions that can address a wide variety of problems frequently encountered in the school setting. The book begins with a discussion of the history, roles, and functions of school social work, goes on to illustrate and discuss various student-focused interventions and systems-focused interventions, and concludes with a carefully developed discussion of outcome evaluation.

Huxtable, M., & Blyth, E. (Eds.) (2002). *School social work worldwide.* Washington, DC: NASW Press.

   This timely text is designed to expand the horizons of the average American school social worker by describing school social work services in nearly a dozen other nations around the world: the United Kingdom, Canada, Finland, Ghana, Argentina, Germany, Hong Kong, Malta, Hungary, Korea, and Japan. There is also a chapter on school social work in the United States. The idea for this book arose during the First International School Social Work Conference in Chicago in 1999.

Pahwa, B. A. (Ed.). (2003). *Technology-assisted delivery of school based mental health services.* New York: Hayworth Press.

   A deceptively slim paperback, this text provides a wealth of information on potential uses of technology by school social workers. The editor notes that school social workers still face a challenge in fully establishing themselves in the school setting and maintains that technology can provide them with new opportunities for delivering, documenting, and evaluating their services. Each chapter of the book presents a different means for doing so.

Sunderman, G., Kim, J., & Orfield, G. (2005). *NCLB meets school realities, lessons from the field.* Thousand Oaks, CA: Corwin Press.

   This book presents the original research conducted by members of the Civil Rights Project at Harvard University on the implementation of the No Child Left Behind law. It provides an overview of the levels of government involved—federal, state, local district, and school—and examines the issues raised, particularly the implications for minority and low-income students. The study involves six states: Arizona, California, Georgia, Illinois, New York, and Virginia. Two school districts are examined closely in each state.

CHAPTER 8

SUBSTANCE ABUSE SERVICES

OUTLINE

Dan Graves

DAN GRAVES

D an was so cold that he knew he might freeze. He looked down at his feet and remembered that he had given his boots to an old man by the train station. Now his broken shoes did little to protect his feet from the snow on the streets. If he could just keep walking, he would not freeze. If he could get a drink, he would feel warm. Dan saw a familiar figure, stooped and hacking with a cough, turn into the alley behind the library, his hand in his pocket. Dan followed, and soon both men were sitting in George's cardboard-box shelter, sharing a bottle of brandy. It warmed them as they talked about better times. George had been a preacher in Mississippi until he came north in search of a secure job. That was around 1990, and the secure job had never materialized. Alcohol had eased his disappointment, but it never erased the memories of the family he had left behind.

Dan, at 23, was much younger and was not ready to give up hope. True, he had left his wife . . . well, not really. Angela had told him to leave because of his drinking. He wouldn't believe that he had a drinking problem. He thought it was her imagination. But thinking about Angela hurt too much; he'd better have another drink of that brandy. George had fallen asleep, Dan noticed. Dan looked around for some newspapers to cover George, to keep the cold out, but he saw none. He was feeling sleepy himself, his body exhausted from walking all day on the cold city streets.

When the police found George and Dan, both men were unconscious. For the paramedics who were called, this was the third conveyance of street people to hospitals that evening. The first call had led them to a white woman with a baby, both with frostbite; the baby was listed in serious condition. The second call involved an African American man, but he had not been drinking, and—although suffering from malnutrition and exposure—he had been admitted in stable condition. George and Dan, also African Americans, were in more serious condition. George had no heartbeat; Dan's was very weak.

St. Francis Hospital was very busy with emergencies that night, but when Dan and George were brought in, the staff rallied. Dan had hypothermia (extreme loss of body temperature) and frostbite; one foot looked very damaged. He was admitted to the hospital for further care. After 10 minutes of effort by the emergency room medical staff, George was pronounced dead. It was a bitter cold night in Chicago.

Two weeks later, Dan was talking with the social worker at the Salvation Army Emergency Lodge. Dan had arrived at the shelter the previous afternoon, having been referred there by the alcoholism counselor at the hospital. Madeleine Johnson, the shelter's social worker, knew about the treatment program he had begun at the hospital, but she questioned him again to gather more information about his drinking history. Dan instinctively liked this African American social worker, but he found himself somewhat irritated by the persistence of her questions. He found he could talk fairly easily about his days drinking with high school friends when he was 17. It was much more difficult to talk about what happened later. Admitting that he had lost two good jobs as a computer programmer because of his drinking was definitely not pleasant. But it was true. Having to talk about all this was so hard!

But most difficult and painful to admit was what his drinking had done to his marriage. Angie was so beautiful, and their love had been so deep, so incredible. His pain was unbearable when he thought about Angie. The social worker probed this painful area too, and she made him talk about Angie and the last time he had spoken with her. For 3 months after Angie had asked Dan to leave and he had begun living on the streets, he would phone her from time to time. He tried to make her believe that he was managing just fine. But he had not telephoned her from the hospital, and he had not given anyone her name, even when he was in critical condition and needed surgery to remove the frostbitten toes of his left foot. Following surgery, he entered the AA program at the hospital. Here he realized and admitted out loud for the first time that he had let alcohol ruin him, that he was an alcoholic. Now, at the Salvation Army Emergency Lodge, he was determined to continue attending AA meetings. The program made sense to him even if it was humbling to have to admit, in front of a group, what alcohol had done to his life.

Madeleine Johnson, the Salvation Army social worker, described the AA meetings held every evening at the Emergency Lodge. Dan said that he was serious about ending his drinking. He planned to attend the meetings daily. They also discussed how they would work together to locate employment opportunities for Dan as soon as the doctors said he was well enough to work. When Dan missed an AA meeting on the third day of his stay at the Emergency Lodge, the social worker asked to see him. Dan knew that Madeleine was disappointed that he had missed the meeting; that was a goal he had set for himself. But he was angry too. He claimed that the meetings were not intended for Black men and that he was not—and probably never would be—comfortable with the group. He told her about the comments made by several of the men. It was clear they did not want minority members, especially Blacks, in their group. Stan, an older man, had been especially outspoken; most of the others, even the two Puerto Ricans, had sided with Stan.

Then Madeleine revealed that she herself was a recovering alcoholic. She too attended meetings and needed the support of others to prevent a return to active drinking. Some AA groups did not meet her needs as an African American woman and a professional person, so she had searched out and found a group that was right for her. Dan was stunned by her admission, her honesty. After further discussion Dan resolved to return to AA meetings, but he planned to explore other groups as soon as he was able to walk better on his healing foot.

In the weeks that followed, Dan did attend meetings faithfully. Through meetings and through his interviews with the social worker, Dan grew to better understand himself and his reaction to alcohol. Madeleine Johnson was a BSW with 4 years' experience at the Emergency Lodge. She was able to help Dan acknowledge his anger about the misunderstandings and prejudices against African American people that he encountered in the AA group and among other residents of the shelter. Dan's trust in Madeleine grew as he discovered that she shared his deep concern about the people like George, even families with children, who were living on the streets.

Dan learned from another Emergency Lodge resident that Madeleine and the other social workers had written a grant proposal that just last week had been approved for funding to begin a health care program for homeless people. They would need volunteers, Dan thought. Perhaps there was something he could do to help. He would silently dedicate his volunteer work to his friend George.

After Dan had lived at the shelter for 3 weeks, his doctor at St. Francis Hospital said that he could return to work soon. Madeleine and Dan had been talking about Dan's future plans. Now they developed a strategy that involved temporary employment in a service-industry job and evening classes to enable Dan to get back into the computer field. Dan was encouraged to find that the social worker did not want him to settle for a service-industry job for good. But he did need to start somewhere, and he would need income immediately to pay rent for a single room. Dan began searching the classified ads in the newspaper for a job that was near public transportation. Within a week he was hired at a fast-food restaurant. Dan knew that it was only temporary; he had other plans.

Dan registered for classes at the community college immediately. On the day that he began his computer class, he telephoned Angie. He had found a single room that he could afford with his minimum-wage job; he was leaving the shelter the next day. Angie was clearly reluctant to believe that Dan was really no longer drinking. She had heard that story before. Still, she was relieved to hear from him and to know that he was OK. She seemed excited about his computer class. Later, as he was leaving the shelter, Dan thanked Madeleine Johnson. She encouraged him to stay in touch with her when he returned for AA meetings and the volunteer work that he would soon begin. Dan sensed her sincerity when she wished him well in the new life he was beginning. In his heart Dan wished her well too, for now he understood the special lifelong demands imposed by addiction to alcohol. ■

THE PROFESSION'S HISTORY IN THE SUBSTANCE ABUSE FIELD

Social workers need to value their clients as unique human beings and to believe in the potential growth and contribution of each client. Dan Graves's social worker did this well. Madeleine Johnson was not burned out by the broken promises of numerous alcoholic clients. Unfortunately, however, social workers and other human service professionals in the past often held very negative attitudes toward this client population. As a result, potential clients and their families sometimes were refused treatment or were shunted to the least experienced staff. One reason for professionals' avoidance of substance abuse clients was the frustration of working with abusers who regularly denied drinking to excess or who denied abusing other substances. Today this attitude is giving way—somewhat—to a better understanding of why and how people (and not just substance abusers) use resistance and denial. To gain a perspective on the change that is taking place, let us review the history of social work in the field of substance abuse.

Mary Richmond: An Early Leader

The history of the social work profession in the substance abuse field began with the early social work pioneer, Mary Richmond. She proposed use of the word *inebriety* to replace *drunkenness* and the word *patient* to replace *culprit* in social work practice. She incorporated the new terminology in an interview guide that she devised for assessment of clients. This instrument has much to recommend it even today. Sections of

Richmond's interview guide focused on heredity of the inebriate, duration of the drinking behavior, causal factors, drinking habits (when, where, and so forth), the physical condition of and any current medical treatments needed by the person, and a description of the social conditions in which the person lived. Richmond's insights into the human condition enabled her to elicit information about the client's employment, home and family life, use of drugs in combination with alcohol, and even the potential use of alcohol by women to help them nurse their babies (Richmond, 1917).

As the director of the Russell Sage Foundation's Charity Organization Department in New York City, Mary Richmond was a highly respected and influential social worker. She was also noted for her work as a writer and teacher and is said to have contributed substantially to the acceptance of social work as a profession. Her sensitive discussion of social work practice with "the inebriate" may have helped to move social workers away from the extremely rigid, moralistic view of substance abusers that was held by contemporary society in the early 1900s.

An Uneven Evolution for the Profession

Social work literature from 1920 to 1950 contains little reference to intervention aimed at helping alcoholic or drug-dependent persons. Instead of working with the chemically dependent client, social workers tended to work with the spouses or families of such persons. In 1952, when New York University was requested by the U.S. Public Health Service to investigate juvenile drug use, the faculty felt as though they were "exploring a virtually unknown territory" (Chein, 1956, p. 50).

Similarly, in 1956 Catherine M. Peltenburg wrote in *Social Casework* that the few psychiatrists, psychologists, and social workers who did work with alcoholic patients in clinic settings had to deal with their own attitudes—with their feelings that alcoholism was a moral weakness and that alcoholic patients were morally depraved and lacked character. Jean Sapir's 1957 article urging social workers to help change public attitudes toward alcoholism is a classic in the field of social work and substance abuse; it was also one of the first articles that described an effective working relationship between social work and Alcoholics Anonymous and an attempt to differentiate those clients who could benefit from referral to AA from those who would not be appropriate candidates for this form of intervention.

In 1970, important legislation was passed that was to affect the delivery of services, including social work services, to alcoholic clients. The Comprehensive Alcohol Abuse and Alcoholism Prevention, Treatment, and Rehabilitation Law was the first piece of legislation that recognized alcohol dependence as an illness in need of treatment. The law established the National Institute on Alcohol Abuse and Alcoholism at the federal level, and it authorized grants to help the states develop alcoholism prevention and treatment programs. With such strong leadership from the federal government, many programs were initiated across the country.

Responding to the new federal initiative, the Council on Social Work Education commissioned a text to assist social work educators; the book, *Alcoholism: Challenge for Social Work Education*, was published in 1971 (Krimmel). This innovative work was useful to the schools that began offering courses on alcoholism because it provided excellent content about working with alcoholic clients and their families, community resources, and alcoholism and poverty.

With the election of Ronald Reagan as president and the new era of diminished federal funding of substance abuse prevention and treatment, crime, drugs, and immigration began to be lumped together. Funding was increasingly shifted to military and police crackdowns on the import and sale of illegal substances and also to housing immense numbers of prison inmates whose sentences were drug related. Insurance companies' decisions to pay only for substance abuse care delivered in general hospitals led to closure of many residential treatment centers. In the 1990s, however, some new, short-term, community-based programs began to be developed. Social workers designed, implemented, and staffed many of these organizations.

In recent years, social workers have used the person-in-environment perspective in many ways in their work with addictions and substance abuse–related problems. This chapter will describe some of the prevention and treatment currently being done with culturally diverse populations, with youths as well as older adults, with persons whose substance abuse results in sentencing for criminal acts, and with some interventions that are still not generally well accepted in society. Today's social workers encounter substance abuse across all fields of practice because addiction is often present in relation to other health problems, such as various cardiac diagnoses, or because addictions are contributing to family problems that bring people into counseling, into the child welfare system, or into contact with an employee assistance program related to their employment.

The prevalence of addictions across social work practice is seen in recent research conducted by NASW, where it was found that 70 percent of social workers in their study group had worked in some way with substance abuse in the previous 12 months (Smith, Whitaker, & Weismiller, 2006). The Dan Graves case study at the beginning of this chapter provides one example of a social worker intervening with a substance abuse problem that was clearly a factor in this client's homelessness.

ROLES FOR SOCIAL WORKERS

Case studies, like that of Dan Graves, are interesting, but they also pose some problems. One potential problem is that readers might make inappropriate generalizations. In this case study, for example, one might conclude that all street people are alcoholics, which, of course, is not true. By this point you have read many case studies throughout the text, and you probably have developed the ability to think about them carefully and critically. It is important not to draw inappropriate inferences from case studies.

Another incorrect conclusion based on this case study would be that a history of substance abuse is a necessary background for a social worker. Madeleine Johnson, after all, was able to use her own alcoholism effectively in working with client Dan Graves. In reality, however, a social worker's effectiveness is based on the application of skill and knowledge, and a person's knowledge base is much broader and much deeper than his or her personal history. The other social workers at the shelter, those with no history of addiction, were also effective with their clients.

There was a time in the past when professionals did not understand chemical dependency and preferred not to work in this field. As a result, alcoholism counselors were mostly people who had no professional credentials but instead used their own life experience with addiction. Today, most counselors in the field are expected to obtain certification through substance abuse training programs. Most states have some form of counselor certification, but requirements vary from state to state, as does the designation of the certification. Certification generally requires up to 2 years of coursework and field work. Increasingly professionals in nursing, social work, psychology, occupational therapy, and other areas are adding state certification for alcoholism or other drug counseling to their credentials for working with this population.

Social workers in substance abuse treatment settings function as members of a team. The social worker may or may not assume primary leadership of the treatment team. Before any decisions about treatment are made, however, assessment occurs.

Assessment

In substance abuse work, assessment is complicated by the variety of substances used and abused. It is further complicated by the need to determine whether a pattern of addiction is involved or whether the use/abuse might be related to other causes such as a person's response to experiencing disaster or trauma. An understanding of the causes of addiction is only now evolving. Alcoholism, for example, has been known and studied for many years. Although initially it was thought to be "sinful" and a sign of "weak" character development, it is increasingly understood to be a constellation of many types of problems that have genetic, neurochemical, psychological, and environmental contributing mechanisms. A growing body of research points to the importance of genetic factors in substance abuse disorders, especially alcoholism. Genetic factors are a powerful force but "it is not likely that genetics alone will account for the full range of alcohol and drug problems" (Butcher, Mineka, & Hooley, 2008, p. 309). Psychosocial and environmental factors are also known to be powerful contributors, especially in relation to availability and motivation for drug use. Additionally, biological and biochemical changes in the brain of addicted persons can now be detected through sophisticated diagnostic tools. In fact, depletion of endorphins (body chemicals that produce "good" feelings and diminish pain) as a result of drug use is now verifiable, so it is not difficult to understand why the craving of addictions can be truly overwhelming (Leshner, 2006, as cited in van Wormer & Davis, 2008).

Multiple approaches to assessment exist. The *Social Work Dictionary* offers a helpful framework for assessment that has fairly clear indicators for intervention. Three types of alcoholism are proposed: primary, secondary, and reactive. **Primary alcoholism** is characterized by heavy drinking, often "in response to physiological withdrawal symptoms" (Barker, 2003, p. 338). The person with primary alcoholism "lives to drink." Primary alcoholism generally becomes apparent between age 25 to 35. A strong family history of alcoholism is common. This form of alcoholism may be genetically linked. Secondary alcoholism differs markedly from primary alcoholism in that a major psychiatric disorder precedes heavy alcohol use. Reactive alcoholism occurs shortly after severe trauma such as the murder or accidental death of a loved one. According to Barker, "After the traumatic event, the individual may or may not become and remain addicted to alcohol" (p. 360).

Generally the person with primary alcoholism will benefit from a period of hospitalization followed by counseling and/or group therapy as an outpatient. If secondary alcoholism exists and the patient has been drinking heavily, a brief period of hospitalization for detoxification may be needed, but the primary mental illness must then become the major focus of treatment. The person experiencing reactive alcoholism needs intervention that will help her or him to deal with the emotions and life situation resulting from the crisis that occurred; this client may need no hospitalization but may need intensive counseling and support. The drinking behavior will need to be closely monitored.

Although Madeleine Johnson, the social worker in the case study, was not employed in a substance abuse setting, she frequently encountered clients who were alcoholic. Alcoholism is more commonly found in social work practice than other forms of substance abuse are, and so this chapter gives more attention to alcoholism than, for example, cocaine abuse.

Medical facilities that treat substance abuse tend to rely on the American Psychiatric Association's *Diagnostic and Statistical Manual of Mental Disorders* (*DSM-IV-TR*) approach to assessment. The *DSM-IV-TR* identifies 11 substances—drugs that can be abused, such as alcohol—and describes criteria that differentiate abuse of these substances from dependence (a more serious condition). These criteria are explained in Exhibits 8-1 and 8-2. Alcohol dependence, using the criteria, is characterized by compulsive drinking that produces such symptoms as tolerance for alcohol, withdrawal from it, ineffective efforts to cut back on its use, and failure to change the drinking behavior despite evidence that it is causing serious difficulty. Alcohol abuse is the recurrent use of alcohol to the extent that repeated use results in an inability to fulfill normal role functions, or presents legal or social/interpersonal problems, or creates a hazard to self or others (American Psychiatric Association, 2000). Note that alcohol abuse does not produce the physiological ramifications that occur with alcohol dependence.

The American Medical Association has considered alcoholism a disease since 1956, and yet there has been no universally accepted definition of alcoholism. This text, then, defines alcoholism as the compulsive use of alcohol characterized by evidence of abuse or dependence, as defined by the *DSM-IV-TR*, and resulting in some level of personal and social malfunctioning.

It is, essentially, this understanding of alcoholism that underpins Madeleine Johnson's and other social workers' practice as they gather information for an assessment. The actual process of data collection, especially in substance abuse treatment facilities, is increasingly a multidimensional one. The biological dimension is assessed by reviewing the person's medical history and current health and nutrition. (Nutritional needs may be neglected during heavy and prolonged bouts of drinking.) A drinking history is obtained that incorporates responses to the following questions: "What does the client drink, how much, how often, when, where, and in conjunction

EXHIBIT 8-1

Criteria for Substance Dependence

A maladaptive pattern of substance abuse, leading to clinically significant impairment or distress, as manifested by three (or more) of the following, occurring at any time in the same 12-month period:

1. Tolerance as defined by either of the following:

   a. A need for markedly increased amounts of the substance to achieve intoxication or desired effect.

   b. Markedly diminished effect with continued use of the same amount of the substance.

2. Withdrawal, as manifested by either of the following:

   a. The characteristic withdrawal syndrome for the substance. [Each substance has two criteria for withdrawal: (1) cessation or reduction of use that has been heavy and prolonged and (2) specified mood and physiological changes.]

   b. The same (or closely related) substance is taken to relieve or avoid withdrawal symptoms.

3. The substance is often taken in larger amounts or over a longer period than was intended.

4. There is a persistent desire or unsuccessful efforts to cut down or control substance use.

5. A great deal of time is spent in activities necessary to obtain the substance (e.g., visiting multiple doctors or driving long distances), use the substance (e.g., chain-smoking), or recover from its effects.

6. Important social, occupational, or recreational activities are given up or reduced because of substance abuse.

7. The substance use is continued despite knowledge of having a persistent or recurrent physical or psychological problem that is likely to have been caused or exacerbated by the substance (e.g., current cocaine use despite recognition of cocaine-induced depression, or continued drinking despite recognition that an ulcer was made worse by alcohol consumption).

SOURCE: American Psychiatric Association. (2000). *Diagnostic and statistical manual of mental disorders* (4th ed., text rev.). Washington, DC: American Psychiatric Association, p. 197.

EXHIBIT 8-2

Criteria for Substance Abuse

1. A maladaptive pattern of substance use leading to clinically significant impairment or distress, as manifested by one (or more) of the following, occurring at any time in the same 12-month period:

   a. Recurrent substance use resulting in a failure to fulfill major role obligations at work, school, or home (e.g., repeated absences or poor work performance related to substance use; substance-related absences, suspensions, or expulsions from school; neglect of children or household).

   b. Recurrent substance use in situations in which it is physically hazardous (e.g., driving an automobile or operating a machine when impaired by substance use).

   c. Recurrent substance-related legal problems (e.g., arrests for substance-related disorderly conduct).

   d. Continued substance use despite having persistent or recurrent social or interpersonal problems caused or exacerbated by the effects of the substance (e.g., arguments with spouse about consequences of intoxication, physical fights).

2. The symptoms have never met the criteria for substance dependence for this class of substance.

SOURCE: American Psychiatric Association. (2000). *Diagnostic and statistical manual of mental disorders* (4th ed., text rev.). Washington, DC: American Psychiatric Association, p. 199.

with which other substances? What are the eating, sleeping, and drug-taking patterns? When did the drinking begin? Is the pattern daily or binge drinking? How about blackouts, tolerance, DTs, and hallucinations?" (van Wormer, 1995, p. 312). The biological assessment provides clues to medical treatment needs.

The psychological dimension reviews the client's mental health history to determine the possible presence of underlying mental disorder. Questions are asked about current level of anxiety, depression, and suicidal thinking as well as unresolved trauma or grief. The connection between alcohol and psychological functioning emerges when questions about psychological functioning shift to "reasons for starting, stopping, and resuming drinking" (van Wormer, 1995, p. 312).

The social dimension of assessment engages the client in a review of family, friends, co-workers, and other social network relationships. Who has or currently provides friendship and support? Where do stresses and tensions exist? Which relationships have been impacted by the person's drinking? Are there religious or other organizations or community memberships or involvement that serve to protect against drinking? What about spiritual beliefs and practices? Who and what matters to the client? A careful, thorough multidimensional assessment provides insight for the client as well as the professional staff (van Wormer, 1995).

The assessment process usually involves informal discussion as well as structured, predesigned questionnaires. Multiple assessment instruments have been developed, but most were created for use with white, male clients. The World Health Organization's Alcohol Use Disorders Identification Test, AUDIT (see Exhibit 8-3), is currently the only assessment instrument that has been validated across six countries: the United States, Kenya, Norway, Bulgaria, Mexico, and Australia. It is used internationally with women as well as men, for college students as well as older adults, and it has been translated into many languages. The first three questions of AUDIT provide data that may point to the existence of "hazardous" alcohol use, questions 4–6 evaluate risk of "dependence," and questions 7–10 evaluate "harmful" alcohol use. Hazardous, dependent, and harmful alcohol use are the categories used internationally instead of the "dependence" and "abuse" categories used in the United States. Hazardous is the least serious and dependence the most serious of the three levels. How is the AUDIT scored? A quick assessment might look only at the total score. A total score of 8 or above suggests the presence of alcohol use at least at the hazardous and possibly at the harmful level. A more careful look at scores for individual instrument items provides a more sensitive analysis. For example: a score of 1 or more on question 2 or 3 is a pretty good indication of alcohol consumption at a hazardous level. Any points scored on questions 7 to 10 are strong indicators that a harmful level has been reached. The AUDIT instrument is under continuous study. Refined approaches to its use can be explored at the World Health Organization (WHO) website: http://who.int (Babor, Higgins-Biddle, Saunders, & Monteiro, 2001).

Assessment instruments such as the AUDIT are intended to be only a part of a more comprehensive effort to understand the person who presents with a potential drinking problem. Social workers increasingly include questions in their interviews that probe the strengths in the person and his or her social environment, especially the factors that are most responsible for healthy functioning across all phases of the

EXHIBIT 8-3

The World Health Organization's Alcohol Use Disorders Identification Test (AUDIT)

Patient: Because alcohol use can affect your health and can interfere with certain medications and treatments, it is important that we ask some questions about your use of alcohol. Your answers will remain confidential so please be honest.

Place an X in one box that best describes your answer to each question.

Questions	0	1	2	3	4
1. How often do you have a drink containing alcohol?	Never	Monthly or less	2–4 times a month	2–3 times a week	4 or more times a week
2. How many drinks containing alcohol do you have on a typical day when you are drinking?	1 or 2	3 or 4	5 or 6	7 to 9	10 or more
3. How often do you have six or more drinks on one occasion?	Never	Less than monthly	Monthly	Weekly	Daily or almost daily
4. How often during the last year have you found that you were not able to stop drinking once you had started?	Never	Less than monthly	Monthly	Weekly	Daily or almost daily
5. How often during the last year have you failed to do what was normally expected of you because of drinking?	Never	Less than monthly	Monthly	Weekly	Daily or almost daily
6. How often during the last year have you needed a first drink in the morning to get yourself going after a heavy drinking session?	Never	Less than monthly	Monthly	Weekly	Daily or almost daily
7. How often during the last year have you had a feeling of guilt or remorse after drinking?	Never	Less than monthly	Monthly	Weekly	Daily or almost daily
8. How often during the last year have you been unable to remember what happened the night before because of your drinking?	Never	Less than monthly	Monthly	Weekly	Daily or almost daily
9. Have you or someone else been injured because of your drinking?	No		Yes, but not in the last year		Yes, during the last year
10. Has a relative, friend, doctor, or other health care worker been concerned about your drinking or suggested you cut down?	No		Yes, but not in the last year		Yes, during the last year
					Total

SOURCE: T. F. Babor, J. C. Higgins-Biddle, J. B. Saunders, & M. G. Monteiro. (2001). AUDIT, *The Alcohol Use Disorders Identification Test: Guidelines for use in primary care* (2nd ed.). WHO/MSD/MSB/01.6a. Geneva, Switzerland: World Health Organization.

person's life. Assessments that explore strengths in addition to the negative, problem-focused facts provide better balance and are often more respectful than the traditional substance abuse diagnostic process. For this reason, engaging people in their own assessment and possibly including close family members or friends can provide an understanding that leads to motivation for change and to an effective and realistic intervention plan.

Generalist Interventions

Once the social worker has made an assessment of the situation, the next step in the problem-solving process is to develop an intervention plan, sometimes referred to as a treatment plan. Because the problem, the person, and the situation are all unique, the intervention must be creative. An early decision that must be made is: where should the social work action be targeted? Is the person who is actively drinking or abusing another substance the appropriate "client"? Perhaps the entire family should be seen as a unit. Perhaps an organization, possibly a worksite, inherently promotes substance abuse (e.g., a brewery that encourages its employees to drink on the job); if so, quite a different intervention plan would be needed. Are new programs needed in the community? Perhaps vulnerable populations can best be reached through community outreach work.

Many different and sometimes overlapping interventions are available to the generalist social worker. The social worker selects one or more strategies based on compatibility with client needs, culture, and goals. Some possible intervention approaches include:

■ Behavioral approaches

■ Self-help groups

■ Family intervention

■ Group therapy

■ Chemical treatment (prescribed medications)

■ Therapeutic communities

■ Program development

■ Community outreach

Behavioral approaches to intervention seek to change behaviors that are harmful through the use of positive and negative reinforcement. Self-help approaches generally involve groups of persons with similar problems who use what they have learned to help each other. Social workers may initiate and lead such groups, or they may refer people to existing groups.

Interventions that include work with the family can confront patterns of interpersonal relationships and family communications that subtly encourage or excuse excessive alcohol consumption or drug use and abuse. Securing the family as an ally in treatment and support for the client can be highly beneficial. Group therapy conducted by social workers, psychologists, or other professionals focuses on the "whys" of drinking and chemical addiction. Feelings are also explored and worked with in a group environment that is at once supportive and confrontational.

Prescription medications are sometimes used alone or in conjunction with one of the other intervention approaches; they may produce unpleasant effects such as nausea if alcohol is used (Antabuse), or they may block the pleasurable sensation of opiates (Methadone). Therapeutic communities are live-in programs where the resident is intensely and repeatedly confronted by staff and other residents when his or her thinking or behavior is inappropriate. Always alert to the needs of the community, generalist social workers may focus their intervention on building bridges between vulnerable persons, such as people living in isolation or on the streets, and the services that can help them with substance abuse problems. Sometimes it is first necessary to create new services or to put established treatment programs into entirely new areas; suburban communities and rural areas are examples. Social work interventions typically do focus on work at several different systems levels, as Chapter 1 explained.

Individuals and Families Hospitalized patients who have undergone detoxification (medical treatment to remove or reduce the dangerous level of alcohol or drugs in the body) often initially need help with practical financial matters and with decisions such as where to live following discharge. The most effective intervention at this time occurs if clients are actively involved in decision making. People often are sick and uncomfortable during detoxification, and hospitalization is brief. Only very brief counseling takes place during hospitalization. Use of behavioral approaches, therapeutic communities, or other forms of intervention usually occurs in the recovery period following hospitalization. The focus of this intervention depends on the assessment, but it always incorporates the goal of helping the client to cope with everyday life without resorting to substance abuse.

Case management has been found to be a useful approach in practice with chemically dependent persons. Rapp (1997) describes his experience using a strengths-based model of case management with persons whose substance abuse has primarily been with crack cocaine. This approach was so different from and contrary to the medical models previously used with the clients that initially they were confused. It was very difficult for some of them to identify any personal strengths, any competence, even any good decisions that they had made. Rapp found that they responded well to this approach—case managers met with them in their own environments, developed relationships with them, and helped them obtain needed resources. Recent empirical research has demonstrated the effectiveness of strengths-based case management with crack cocaine–addicted veterans in improving levels of after-care treatment following hospitalization. Additionally, fewer incidents of relapse of drug usage or involvement in criminal behaviors were reported. The warm, genuine quality of the case management relationship was seen by the veterans as a key element in the success achieved (Rapp, 2006).

Much of the family therapy that has been done in conjunction with addictions has kept the person with the addiction at the center of the action, with family members learning behaviors that will confront, control, and support the addicted person. A new approach, based on the strengths perspective, gives credit to families that have endured and survived the stress and misery that accompanies addiction. Instead of viewing the family system as dysfunctional and family members as co-dependents, this approach helps family members identify the strategies they used to survive and manage the chaos that exists when there is substance abuse within a family. Reframing is used to relabel behaviors. The simple mechanism of replacing the term *relapse* with *lapse* recharges family energy to assist rather than punish and blame a family member. A "lapse," after all, is a setback, quite possibly one that might be predicted when battling addictions, yet one that is only temporary and can be managed. Family members are encouraged in their caring and support for each other. As healing occurs for the entire family, it is increasingly possible for the family to reclaim what was once lost through addiction: "the fun in life, one's sense of peace and safety, one's spirituality, one's wholeness" (van Wormer & Davis, 2008, p. 411).

Groups   Although empirical research has not yet demonstrated the superiority of group treatment over other forms of intervention, practical experience has shown that groups offer many advantages. Among the potential advantages of group intervention are the facts that they "alleviate the social stigma associated with addiction by providing social acceptance from peers and they facilitate identification with peers who are further along in recovery" (Smyth, 1995, pp. 2329–2330). Groups can also be confrontational, making denial of drug dependence less possible, and can help members achieve a level of self-awareness that is essential to the development of self-control.

Social workers use a variety of intervention approaches in their work with groups. Psychoeducational groups, often co-facilitated by a social worker and physician, frequently use a lecture format to teach members about addiction, including the body's reaction to alcohol and other chemical substances, the signs and symptoms of addiction, and the stress-reduction and other coping techniques that can be used in recovery. Therapy groups, on the other hand, use member involvement to provide feedback, confrontation, and support. Role-playing is sometimes used to help members learn new behaviors (Smyth, 1995).

Despite the advantages of group intervention, groups are not the best choice for all chemically dependent persons. Clients must be able to function well enough to tolerate the emotional intensity of group encounters. Chronically mentally ill persons, for example, might find some groups devastating. Usually, however, social workers can structure their groups to meet the needs of specific populations or persons.

Self-help groups such as Alcoholics Anonymous and Narcotics Anonymous, which will be discussed in further detail later in this chapter, typically involve persons who share the same problem and meet together for mutual assistance. Until recently, most self-help groups avoided involvement with professional people. After many years of antipathy between professional groups and such organizations as Alcoholics Anonymous, social workers and other professionals now recognize the value of self-help groups for specific clients, and they frequently refer people to them or combine another form of therapy with self-help group participation. Sometimes, too, social workers will initiate a group for this purpose and then guide the group in developing its own leadership and group processes.

Social workers help group members confront each other and also offer each other support and encouragement.

Changing Organizations and Communities   Effective organizational change can potentially benefit a far larger population than one-on-one counseling or group work. Social workers practicing from a generalist perspective often target an organization for change rather than an individual or a group. Social workers on the faculty of colleges and universities, for example, sometimes help to initiate support groups for students, faculty, and staff with chemical dependencies. Organizational change can result in new or improved prevention or treatment programs. Serving as consultants, social workers help businesses, industrial corporations, and unions to implement employee assistance programs (EAPs) that offer help to people involved in chemical abuse. Within alcoholism and drug rehabilitation centers, social work staff attempt to effect policies and procedures to ensure that service will be provided in a humane manner. Educational programs are also offered by the social work staff to help other staff of the rehabilitation center better understand and serve the patients, their families, and the community.

   Another role for social workers is community education. Seminars and workshops are offered by social workers in community centers, churches, or schools. In this manner, substance abuse prevention programs can target specific populations such as a youth group or older adults, religious groups, and ethnic or cultural populations. Educational programs may be offered in the language spoken by the group members, or a person from the group may serve as a cultural interpreter, ensuring that the content and communication are truly relevant. This kind of outreach work enables social workers to reach youth gangs, immigrants, and other populations that would be less likely to attend seminars at, for example, a hospital or university. Other social workers staff local and state alcoholism councils or mental health associations that distribute informational materials or develop media messages designed to prevent problem drinking and drug use.

Community outreach can also be used to try to engage people in substance abuse treatment. Contact can be made with homeless persons who are abusing alcohol or chemical substances by "street workers," social workers who visit sites where homeless people live or gather. Coffee and hot food are a good entrée, especially in cold weather. If community outreach had been available, Dan Graves's friend, George (from the case study), might not have died. Community outreach social workers do save lives through early detection and strong emotional support that brings people who are at risk into treatment centers. Ability to form trust relationships and engage even hard-to-reach people is critical to successful outreach work with homeless people and also with teen gangs. Recognizing that a considerable portion of health crises are related to (even generated by) substance abuse, social workers have also begun initiating assessment procedures in hospital emergency rooms in suburbs as well as central city areas. A physician's forceful recommendation for treatment can be a strong motivator.

Program development is another powerful intervention in the substance abuse field. In Louisville, Kentucky, for example, a substance abuse prevention program was brought to five sites, including two rural area sites 40 and 45 miles from Louisville, two suburban sites, and one inner-city site. Interestingly, all were church sites; program development involved securing the cooperation and sponsorship not just of individual churches but of interdenominational groups. Research subsequently demonstrated the effectiveness of the program in moderating drug and alcohol use of youths as well as increasing parental knowledge of alcohol and other drugs. The program also decreased the parents' own use of alcohol, improved family communication, and strengthened bonding relationships within the families (Johnson et al., 2000).

PREVENTION AND TREATMENT PROGRAMS

Prevention and Treatment in the United States

Prevention of chemical dependence focuses on education and research. All levels of society are targeted but colleges and universities, business corporations, health care settings, and schoolchildren are the primary populations served. Three large federal government organizations have assumed leadership in the prevention field.

The National Institute on Alcohol Abuse and Alcoholism (NIAA) is a part of the National Institutes of Health. It supports and conducts research into the causes and consequences of alcohol abuse. It publishes *Alcohol Health and Research World*, a good source of current research.

The National Institute on Drug Abuse (NIDA) is responsible for research on drug abuse. Its Medications Development Program specifically focuses on research pertaining to the use of medication in the treatment of drug addiction.

A third organization, the Center for Substance Abuse Prevention (CSAP), is the unit within the large Substance Abuse and Mental Health Services Administration (SAMHSA) that focuses on prevention efforts. It funds prevention programs, including the Community Partnership Program, which encourages coalitions of agencies to work together to implement substance abuse prevention programs. The National Clearinghouse for Alcohol and Drug Information (a good source of substance abuse materials for student term papers) is operated by CSAP. See the Internet Sites at the end of this chapter for the Internet addresses of these three organizations.

In local public schools, educational programming is aimed at preventing the use of drugs and alcohol by children of all ages. Substance abuse prevention is a role for school social workers (school social work was described more fully in Chapter 7). Social group work with schoolchildren, whether oriented toward socialization or therapy, routinely contains content related to drugs. This is also true of parent education or family life seminars presented by school social workers.

The treatment of substance abuse often begins with a brief hospitalization for detoxification to safely withdraw the person from drugs or alcohol. Detoxification may also be done on an outpatient basis, depending on the drugs used by the person and the risks involved in the medical treatment. Withdrawal from barbiturates, for example, requires hospitalization because it may result in life-threatening seizures. Until recently, a 30-day inpatient treatment program routinely followed detoxification. Cost containment policies of managed care have resulted in briefer inpatient treatment for most people today.

Outpatient or follow-up care is available in a wide range of settings: mental health centers, substance abuse clinics, "drunk-driving" programs, halfway houses, prisons, social service agencies, employee assistance programs, college and universities, and through private therapists in the community. Treatment tends to be highly multidisciplinary but often involves social workers. The approaches used in treatment also vary widely but may include education programs, biofeedback training, group therapy, family therapy, and intensive short-term programs. The goal of these programs is abstinence.

European Approach: The Harm Reduction Model

The two models of substance abuse prevention and treatment used most commonly in the United States are the abstinence model and the 12-step recovery program. Both seek a complete and total end to substance use. An alternative but controversial program that is used far more frequently in Europe, Canada, and Australia than in the United States is known as the harm reduction model.

European children grow up in a culture that incorporates alcoholic beverages in everyday life. "There is no negative stereotype attached to the act of drinking" (Loebig, 2000, p. 1). Some of these European countries have a more open attitude toward the rights of people to use other substances and many, but not all, have been prescribing Methadone for the treatment of addiction for a long time. Needle exchange programs, in which used needles are exchanged for sterile ones, are much more common in Europe than in the United States. This is the primary treatment for

San Francisco, California: Needle exchange program volunteer (facing camera) talks with drug user.

drug addiction in Switzerland, for example. Interestingly, it was the threat of an AIDS epidemic in Europe in the 1980s that generated a groundswell of support for harm reduction programs and policies. Instead of criminalizing drug use, many other countries began to view it as a medical or public health issue, not just to protect the health of the users but to protect the well-being of the public. Programs were set up in the community that provided a safe supply to drug users and also to health care professionals for monitoring the use of drugs. Some cities in the United States have begun to create similar programs (van Wormer & Davis, 2008).

From a social work practice perspective, the harm reduction approach is strongly grounded in the strengths perspective. Persons using or abusing drugs or alcohol are not labeled "alcoholic," "substance abuser," or other negative terms. Instead, respect and collaborative relationships are essential. Spiritual as well as social, psychological, and medical needs are met, but the client is in control and is afforded the opportunity of making decisions for him- or herself (van Wormer & Davis, 2008).

Does the harm reduction model work? San Francisco's AIDS Foundation HIV Prevention Project estimates that its needle exchange program has reduced new HIV infection by 30 percent (*SFAF HIV prevention project*, 2001). Data on the number of addicts per country show that countries with liberal harm reduction programs tend to have fewer drug addicts. The Netherlands, for example, had 1.66 drug addicts per 1,000 persons in its population, Belgium had 1.75, Germany had 1.38, compared with the United States's 6.36 (Loebig, 2000). Much more research is needed to evaluate the harm reduction model, but it does pose another alternative to the present prevention and treatment approach used in the United States.

EXHIBIT 8-4

The Legacy of "Bill W."

The history of the founding of Alcoholics Anonymous is an interesting one. Bill Wilson was a stockbroker with a string of failed business ventures and years of alcohol abuse when he met Dr. Robert Holbrock Smith, a proctologist and surgeon, who was a graduate of Dartmouth College and of Rush Medical College in Chicago. Dr. Bob's alcohol abuse was beginning to interfere with his medical practice. Talking together, they discovered, helped Bill Wilson deal with his compelling desire for a drink, and it helped Dr. Bob face and begin to deal with his own alcoholism. Bill W.—his "anonymous" name to others in the organization that came to be known as Alcoholics Anonymous—was gregarious, impulsive, and an inspirational speaker. Dr. Bob, a man of few words, avoided public speaking and left that function to Bill W. Dr. Bob's authority, however, molded the new Alcoholics Anonymous organization in many ways. Women were not admitted to AA for years because Dr. Bob opposed their inclusion, preferring to keep AA an exclusively male organization (Robertson, 1988).

Without media publicity, the notion of a person-to-person supportive network spread only gradually, and yet its appeal touched the lives of many people. By 1939 about 100 persons belonged to Alcoholics Anonymous. They pooled what they had learned from their own experiences and created the book *Alcoholics Anonymous,* a classic that is still known as "The Big Book." It describes the 12 steps, which is the basic process by which members had learned to keep themselves sober. After the publication of The Big Book, Alcoholics Anonymous grew rapidly. Five thousand people attended the 20th-anniversary convention in St. Louis in 1955; by 1957 Alcoholics Anonymous had grown to 200,000, with groups meeting in 70 countries. Today Alcoholics Anonymous has more than 2 million members throughout the world.

Alcoholics Anonymous

Although it began in the United States, Alcoholics Anonymous has spread throughout the world. Also known as the "12-Step Program," this organization has spawned mutual aid groups for friends and relatives of alcoholics (A1-Anon) and groups for the adolescent children of people with alcoholism (A1-Ateen). In addition, the Adult Children of Alcoholics organization assists people struggling with past childhood experiences that continue to damage their present adult relationships.

Narcotics Anonymous (NA) is structured like Alcoholics Anonymous and uses the same principles and philosophy as AA, including the 12 steps. Cocaine Anonymous functions similarly but is probably not as well known as NA. Alternative self-help groups have borrowed some of the AA philosophy but use other strategies. Rational Recovery, for example, is based on cognitive-behavioral theory that seeks to change self-defeating thinking patterns. Women for Sobriety emphasizes self-respect for women who abuse alcohol. Some groups have emerged that avoid the spirituality of AA and instead focus on personal responsibility. A brief history of Alcoholics Anonymous is provided in Exhibit 8-4.

EMPIRICAL RESEARCH

Much research has been undertaken to explore the effectiveness of different interventions. Walsh et al.'s 1991 research with clients who were given a choice in treatment programs demonstrated the effectiveness of inpatient treatment followed by mandatory AA attendance. The Gibbs and Hollister study of 1993 made an important contribution to the scientific literature by isolating four distinct types of alcoholic clients based on measures of social stability and intellectual functioning. Their attempt to determine which form of treatment best fit each typology was unsuccessful because of difficulties such as inability to randomly assign clients to inpatient versus outpatient treatment. Their findings, however, suggested that clients with strong social stability and intellectual functioning were 25 percent more likely to achieve sobriety at 6 months through outpatient as opposed to inpatient treatment.

The largest clinical research trial ever to be implemented regarding alcoholism, Project MATCH, attempted to match clients with the most effective treatment. This 8-year, rigorous, multidisciplinary research effort sought to determine which of its three treatment approaches was most effective with specific configurations of characteristics. The surprising result was that each of the three forms of treatment—cognitive-behavioral therapy, motivational enhancement therapy, and therapy aimed at facilitating clients' involvement in a 12-step program—"appeared to do quite well and, perhaps more importantly, patients' gains were well sustained throughout 39 months' follow-up" (Allen, 1998, p. 43).

Another contribution that research can make to the study of addictions is to provide clear, factual evidence of the impact produced. Social workers in child welfare, family services, the corrections system, schools, and domestic violence centers know so well the tragedy and pain caused by substance abuse and other addictions. A growing body of data now documents the harm that is done. Here is just a sampling of this evidence as reported by Butcher, Mineka, and Hooley (2008):

> Heavy drinking is associated with vulnerability to injury (Shepherd & Brickley, 1996) and becoming involved in intimate partner violence (O'Leary & Schumacher, 2003). . . . Depression ranks high among the mental disorders often comorbid with alcoholism. It is no surprise that many alcoholics commit suicide (Hufford, 2001; McCloud, Barnaby, et al., 2004). . . . Alcohol abuse is associated with over half the deaths and major injuries suffered in automobile accidents each year (Brewer, Morris, et al., 1994) and about 40 to 50 percent of all murders (Bennett & Lehman, 1996), 40 percent of all assaults, and over 50 percent of all rapes (Abbey, Zawacki, et al., 2001). (p. 302)

This kind of data draws attention to the compelling need to create treatment programs and social environments that effectively reduce the terrible damage and broken lives that lurk behind the numbers and percentages. That, in fact, is the essence of the harm reduction approach that exists in other countries and that is beginning to gain some attention in the United States. The harm reduction approach does not focus on what the very best outcome might be; it focuses on doing whatever works to reduce harm, harm to the person who is addicted and harm to everyone who will be affected by the addiction. The role of research, though, is to carefully evaluate the effectiveness of treatment, not only in terms of the individual receiving care, but also the effectiveness of prevention and treatment programs on families, communities, and society.

AT-RISK POPULATIONS

Generalist practice theory directs social workers to develop intervention plans based on a careful assessment of the individual client within the totality of her or his life situation. Logan, McRoy, and Freeman (1987) underscore the need for social workers to take into consideration the client's "age, ethnicity, gender, availability of other supports, and other factors such as the particular client's orientation to change and principal mode of learning" (pp.183–184) when developing intervention plans for chemically dependent clients.

When people abuse alcohol or other substances as a reaction to grief or the overwhelming trauma of disaster or war, this seems understandable to society. Less well understood are the socioeconomic stressors that also exist. Of the various professionals who work in the substance abuse arena, social workers probably have the best understanding of this. As Roffman (1987) states, "Regardless of their negative consequences, psychoactive drugs [and alcohol] are used excessively precisely because they are effective, if only temporarily, in reducing pain—including the pain of being poor" (p. 482).

Women and Children

Among the most vulnerable populations in the United States are addicted women and their children. The 2006 National Center for Health Statistics data demonstrate that a smaller percentage of women than men use alcohol or consume alcohol heavily (see Exhibit 8-5), yet women and their children are at risk. It is estimated that only a small portion of addicted women receive services. The reasons for this vary but include the outmoded societal attitude that it is acceptable for men to drink to excess but for women, especially mothers, to do so is immoral.

Downs and Miller, who have studied the effects of trauma, propose that a lifetime of traumatic abuse, which is the experience of many addicted women, "causes low self-esteem and self-disgust that presses these women into further abuse" (2002, as cited in van Wormer & Davis, 2008, p. 464). Earlier research demonstrated that women who are depressed often self-medicate with alcohol (Turnbull, 1988). Because alcohol itself is a central nervous system depressant, the result for these women is that they become further depressed. Research data from the 2005 National Survey on Drug Use and Health showed that persons who experienced major depressive episodes were statistically more likely to be dependent on alcohol or drugs than those persons who did not have this serious form of depression (SAMHSA, 2006, p. 8). Often suicide ideation and serious marital and family disruption occur before depressed women seek treatment. When depression occurs, too, relapse is likely. Clearly there is a need for careful assessment and early treatment of women who would be likely to turn or return to alcohol or other drugs.

Some women need counseling, probably with a female social worker, that focuses on childhood or current experiences with violence and victimization. Family and couple therapy are helpful to many women, as is parent training, given the guilt that addicted women experience because of their failures in this area. Rhodes and Johnson

EXHIBIT 8-5

National Center for Health Statistics 2006 Alcohol Consumption by Adults 18 Years and Over (in percentages)

Characteristic	Both Sexes			Male			Female		
	1997	2003	2004	1997	2003	2004	1997	2003	2004
Drinking Status									
All	100	100	100	100	100	100	100	100	100
Lifetime abstainer	21.4	24.9	24.6	14.1	17.8	17.8	27.8	31.3	30.6
Former drinker	15.8	14.3	14.5	16.4	15.2	14.9	15.4	13.6	14.4
Current drinker	62.8	60.8	60.8	69.5	67.1	67.3	56.8	55.2	54.9
Consumed 5 or more drinks on at least 1 day in past year									
Age:									
18–44 years	42.5	41.1	41.8	54.8	52.1	52.3	28.7	28.7	29.5
45–64 years	25.3	23.9	24.3	36.1	33.5	34.3	12.8	13.2	13.5
65 and over	11.2	8.4	8.9	17.8	12.5	13.9	4.3	4.2	3.7
Race/Culture:									
White only	33.3	31.9	32.5	44.4	41.3	41.9	20.9	21.4	21.9
Black or African American only	23.9	21.6	23.4	32.0	31.0	33.4	15.0	12.2	12.4
American Indian or Alaska Native only	54.4	34.1	33.2	70.5	43.8	43.7	37.6	23.1[*]	19.5[*]
Asian only	25.6	15.3	18.6	30.8	20.3	25.4	16.6	8.4[*]	6.1[*]
Hispanic origin and race:									
Hispanic or Latino	37.0	30.2	31.8	46.6	39.1	40.2	22.4	15.4	17.2
Mexican	39.1	34.2	36.6	50.2	43.0	45.3	20.3	18.2	20.1
Not Hispanic or Latino									
White only	33.2	32.3	32.8	44.5	41.9	42.5	21.0	22.1	22.5
Black or African American only	23.7	21.2	23.3	32.0	30.9	33.5	14.5	11.9	12.1

[*]Denotes an estimate that is not considered reliable.

SOURCE: National Center for Health Statistics. (2006). Table 68 Alcohol consumption by adults 18 years of age and over, by selected characteristics: United States, selected years 1997–2004, *Health, United States, 2006 with chartbook on trends in the health of Americans* (pp. 276–278). Retrieved July 3, 2007, from http://www.cdc.gov/nchs/data/hus/hus06.pdf#066

(1994) found that teaching women to accept that alcohol has taken power over their lives—which is a tenet of Alcoholics Anonymous and may be more useful with men— is potentially devastating to women. Instead, they encourage the use of empowerment approaches, helping women to acquire competence and self-esteem. Then, because addicted women are less likely than men to have health insurance, substance abuse intervention is needed in the places such women frequent: shelters, public health departments, and even jails.

Health care systems tend to be particularly punitive toward homeless women because they lack health insurance. If inpatient addiction care can be obtained, women's guilt may be compounded by the need to place their children temporarily in foster care. Much support is needed, and social workers can help the mothers understand that they are making painful but good decisions. Children who were neglected or abused are especially confused and vulnerable. The needs of these children must be addressed, and the children must be provided a safe environment, too. Group homes or community centers can sometimes be found that will offer nurturing posthospital care for recovering mothers and their children.

Fetal alcohol syndrome (FAS), the name given to the abnormalities in children that can result from heavy alcohol consumption during pregnancy, also places both women and children at risk. One Seattle study, for example, found that 75 percent of the mothers of the more severely damaged FAS children had died of alcohol-related causes within 6 years of their births (Streissguth, Clarren, & Jones, 1985).

Among the abnormalities that accompany FAS are growth deficiencies, mental retardation, characteristic facial features, cleft palate, small brain, and behavioral problems. These children require special care—sometimes institutional care—for many years. Physicians who have studied FAS persons into adolescence and adulthood have found that they sustained significant attention deficit and diminished intellectual ability and had problems with judgment. Sadly, as adults these persons are also very likely to abuse and become dependent on alcohol.

According to the National Women's Health Information Center, "Prenatal alcohol exposure is one of the leading known causes of mental retardation in the Western world" (2000, p. 2). At one time, fetal alcohol syndrome was thought to affect only children of very heavy alcohol abusers, but currently physicians are urging caution in the use of alcohol in any amounts during pregnancy. The U.S. Surgeon General has revised previous recommendations and now suggests nonuse of alcohol during pregnancy and even when trying to conceive. The governments of France and Canada also advise abstinence (Brown, 2006).

The increased media visibility given to the danger of alcohol consumption during pregnancy has had beneficial effects. While decline in consumption is clear, there remain at-risk groups such as pregnant women in the age range of 15 to 25 who, research shows, are more likely to binge drink and also use illicit drugs and smoke cigarettes than pregnant women in the 26- to 44-year age group (SAMHSA, 2004). Another very positive recent research report showed that brief counseling with low-income pregnant women at WIC (Women, Infants, and Children) community nutrition sites was highly successful in improving the outlook for the newborns. Following counseling, the pregnant women were five times more likely to abstain from alcohol than pregnant women who did not receive counseling. Babies born to the women who had participated in counseling had higher birth weights and the newborn mortality rates were actually three times lower than those for the women who received no counseling (O'Connor & Whaley, 2007).

Youths

Adolescents and young adults frequently use, even abuse, drugs and alcohol as a part of their developmental process. While this may not necessarily result in adult dependency, it may be associated with unsafe sexual activity leading to sexually transmitted diseases (such as HIV infection), and/or pregnancy as well as car accidents, drownings, and illegal activities. Government reports showed marked increase in the use of illicit drugs by 12- to 17-year-olds, from 5.3 percent in 1992 to 11 percent in 1997, followed by a gradual downward trend. This downward trend continues, slowly. The most recent National Survey of Drug Use and Health reports a continued decline from 2002 to 2005 (most recent data currently available) in use of alcohol, marijuana, hallucinogens such as Ecstasy, and the nonmedical use of prescription drugs. The one area that showed no change from 2002 was use of inhalants and cocaine. Among 18- to 25-year-olds, cocaine and nonmedical prescription drug use increased, too, but alcohol and marijuana use showed no change from 2002 (SAMHSA, 2006, p. 95). The 18- to 25-year-old group consistently comprises—by far—the heaviest users of illicit drugs, so prevention and treatment efforts focused on these youths remain a priority.

These "youth at risk" are the focus of Malekoff's study of preventive programs. He asks the question, "What differentiates youth who become alcohol and drug abusers from their contemporaries from similar backgrounds who do not?" (1997, p. 228). Among the protective factors his research suggests is the bonding that occurs between adolescents, especially those who are nondrug users, and bonding with adults. Malekoff suggests use of group work with at-risk youths—groups that are well planned, that engage the youths in activities that promote development of skill and competence as well as relationships, and groups that also involve family activities.

Native Americans

The case study at the beginning of this chapter suggests that racism and poverty can be factors in substance abuse. Native American women clearly belong to several at-risk groups and, perhaps not surprisingly, they have a high rate of children born with fetal alcohol syndrome. A recent research report published in the *Journal of General Psychology* indicated that Native Americans had the highest rate of alcohol use and the highest rate of FAS of all other ethnic groups studied. The report cautions, however, that it is important to understand Native Americans' misuse of alcohol within the context of their history of trauma, poverty, and numerous other factors (Szlemko, Wood, & Thurman, 2006).

A hospital-based program at the Tuba City Indian Medical Center in Arizona was successful in achieving abstinence from alcohol in 19 of 21 pregnant Navajo women who were at risk of delivering alcohol-affected infants. Statistically, more Navajo women abstain from alcohol than women in the general U.S. population, but heavy alcohol consumption exists among those women and families where poverty and social problems abound. The Tuba City program is noteworthy because of the incorporation of cultural sensitivity and respect, as was demonstrated in the hiring of Navajo staff and use of the Navajo language (Masis & May, 1991).

EXHIBIT 8-6

SOURCE: A. P. Streissguth, R. A. LaDue, & S. P. Randels. (1988). *A manual on adolescents and adults with fetal alcohol syndrome with special reference to American Indians* (2nd ed.). Washington, DC: U.S. Department of Health and Human Services, Indian Health Service.

This comprehensive ethnic- and gender-sensitive program had a remarkable level of acceptance among the women it served.

FAS, associated with excessive alcohol consumption, is not the only risk factor for American Indian or Alaska Native Peoples. They also have one of the highest rates of all illicit drug use. The result is exceptionally high rates of suicide, homicide, car accidents, and deaths associated with cirrhosis.

Hispanic Americans

The Hispanic population in the United States, according to the last census, is increasing more rapidly than most other population cohorts. The higher birthrate of this population results in a large youth cohort. Although Hispanic people have much lower rates of illicit drug use (7.6 percent past-month use in 2005) than Native Americans, African Americans, or Caucasians, the 12- to 17-year-old youth group reported 10.2 percent past-month use in 2004 and 9.4 percent in 2005 (SAMHSA, 2006, Tables G-11, p. 234, and G-12, p. 235). While lower than that of many other youth ethnic or white populations, the Hispanic rate of youth illicit drug use is of concern to Hispanic families.

Melvin Delgado, a social worker, reiterates the need for culture-specific services. Of special concern to him is the lack of understanding of the variances in Hispanic culture among treatment facilities and their failure to acknowledge the impact of acculturation. Delgado (1988) suggests five culturally specific content areas that should be explored in intake interviews with youthful Hispanic substance abusers:

1. Attempt to understand the patterns alcohol and drugs play in the context of the family: ceremonial use? religious prohibition?

2. Find out the extent to which the client identifies with ("owns") her or his Hispanic heritage. Does it represent pride or is it viewed as a deficit?

3. In what language can the client best express herself or himself? (This has important ramifications for counselor or group treatment assignment.)

4. How does the youth's social network relate to drinking or substance use? Does it support or fight against treatment?

5. What prior assistance, through both formal and informal mechanisms, has been attempted, and with what results?

African Americans

Significant efforts of African American churches and schools have resulted in a marked decline in the use and abuse of alcohol by African Americans. The most recent National Center for Health Statistics report (see Exhibit 8-5), however, does not show the very steep decline of the African American alcohol consumption rate from nearly 60 percent in 1979 to the most recently available report of 23.4 percent. This decline should be acknowledged because it is evidence of the success that can come from strong commitment and concerted community action. In the current report, African Americans still show a lower rate of use of alcohol than White, Hispanic, or Native American people (2006, Table 68). Despite this, African Americans continue to experience barriers to treatment facilities associated with lack of funds or health insurance. In addition, White and other ethnic professional staff often lack the cultural understanding needed to work successfully with African Americans with substance abuse disorders.

Exhibit 8-7 provides data from the National Survey on Drug Use and Health demonstrating variations in illicit drug use according to age and ethnicity. For African Americans as well as many of the other ethnic and age cohorts, there has been a slight increase in illicit drug use in the past few years; however, "the overall rate of current illicit drug use among persons aged 12 or older in 2005 (8.1 percent) was similar to the rate in 2004 (7.9 percent), 2003 (8.2 percent), and 2002 (8.3 percent)" (SAMHSA, 2006, p. 13). In the recent past, declines in illicit drug usage seemed most evident in the years of strong economic growth in America, where incomes increased across most segments of the population. Does the recent slight increase reflect higher rates of poverty for some portions of the U.S. population? It is too soon to know this, but

EXHIBIT 8-7

National Survey on Drug Use and Health, 2006; Illicit Drug Use* by Persons Aged 12 or Older by Demographic Characteristics: 2004 and 2005 (in percentages)

Demographic Characteristic	Lifetime 2004	Lifetime 2005	Past Year 2004	Past Year 2005	Past Month 2004	Past Month 2005
Total Age	45.8	46.1	14.5	14.4	7.9	8.1
12–17	30.0[b]	27.7	21.0[a]	19.9	10.6	9.9
18–25	59.2	59.2	33.9	34.2	19.4	20.1
26 or older	45.6	46.3	10.2	10.2	5.5	5.8
Gender						
Male	50.7	50.8	16.9	16.8	9.9	10.2
Female	41.1	41.6	12.2	12.1	6.1	6.1
Hispanic origin and race						
Not Hispanic or Latino	47.3	47.4	14.7	14.5	8.0	8.2
White	49.1	48.9	15.0	14.5	8.1	8.1
Black or African American	43.3	44.7	14.6	16.0	8.7	9.7
American Indian or Alaska Native	58.4	60.9	26.2	21.3	12.3	12.8
Native Hawaiian or Other Pacific Islander	**	54.3	**	15.5	**	8.7
Asian	24.3	28.1	6.9	7.1	3.1	3.1
Two or More Races	54.9[a]	45.8	21.0	19.1	13.3	12.2
Hispanic or Latino	35.4	37.3	12.9	13.9	7.2	7.6

*Illicit Drugs include marijuana/hashish, cocaine (including crack), heroin, hallucinogens, inhalants, or prescription-type psychotherapeutics used nonmedically.
[a]Difference between estimate and 2005 estimate is statistically significant at the 0.05 level.
[b]Difference between estimate and 2005 estimate is statistically significant at the 0.01 level.
**Low precision: no estimate reported.

SOURCE: Substance Abuse and Mental Health Services Administration. (2006). Table G.11 Illicit drug use in lifetime, past year, and past month among persons aged 12 or older, by demographic characteristics: Percentages, 2004 and 2005, p. 234. *Results from the 2005 National Survey on Drug Use and Health: National findings.* Office of Applied Studies, NSDUH Series H-30, DHHS Publication No. SMA 06-4194, Rockville, MD.

the National Survey on Drug Use and Health, a good source for this data, can be accessed at http://www.samhsa.gov.

Drug abuse, however, has had a devastating impact on African American families. Drug-related family violence and crime have resulted in the need for shelter care for women and children, imprisonment, and foster care for children. Cocaine abuse has led to addictions to other drugs, and also to HIV/AIDS and other infections and diseases. Families struggle to remain intact under the pressure of drug abuse. Grandparents and even elderly great-grandparents carry heavy burdens as they take on the care of children whose parent or parents are absent from the home (Ruiz, 2001).

Let us now turn to some other populations who are at risk for substance abuse but for whom data on use and abuse are less readily available. (See Exhibit 8-7.)

Lesbian Women and Gay Men

The government statistical reports cited for other groups record no data regarding alcohol or drug use or abuse by gay men and lesbian women. The absence of reliable data does not eliminate the possibility that "oppression of gay men and lesbian women and subculture support of drinking could produce higher rates of alcoholism among them. Internalized homophobia results in tremendous anxiety and self-hatred, sometimes assuaged by alcohol" (Anderson, 1995, p.209). Gay bars have served as places to socialize and, until the recent development of substance-free establishments, this has hampered the efforts of gays and lesbians who are in treatment.

The open hostility that lesbian women and gay men sometimes experienced at Alcoholics Anonymous meetings resulted in 1970 in the founding of Alcoholics Together, another 12-step program. But 12-step programs are no longer well accepted by many women, including lesbian women, because of the focus on admitting loss of control over one's life, identifying one's moral and character defects, and so forth. Some women find empowerment-based models more useful, and, for lesbian women at least, treatment models that incorporate political awareness and concepts of oppression may prove more effective (Saulnier, 1991).

Among the homosexual community, Black male alcoholics are at special risk of encountering misunderstanding and negative attitudes that can interfere with treatment. Not only do some substance abuse programs and professional staff display negativity, but the African American community is sometimes not accepting of homosexuality, and some members of the gay community are racially biased. Social work intervention must help these clients deal with their substance abuse and also help them locate and link with a positive support system and integrate their sexual identity with their racial identity (Icard & Traunstein, 1987).

Persons with Disabilities

Persons with disabilities—physical, cognitive, or psychiatric—may use or abuse drugs (sometimes their own prescriptions) and alcohol just to make their lives more bearable. If they become dependent on chemical substances, treatment is complicated because it must be adapted to the situation of the specific client. Co-existence of mental illnesses and chemical dependence, known as a **dual diagnoses,** requires well-coordinated treatment from both mental health and substance abuse programs. When these are not available within the same facility, careful attention must be given to ensure responsible coordination of treatment.

Among the homeless or people living on the streets it is estimated that roughly 10 to 20 percent are persons with dual diagnosis. Some are chemically dependent and have health problems and disabilities other than mental illness. Clearly it is extremely difficult for them to comply with treatment regimes or to keep scheduled appointments. Outreach work by social workers, other professionals, and volunteers is undertaken to try to bring some forms of health care to the streets. Concern about transmission of HIV infection through sharing of dirty needles has prompted needle exchange programs in some communities. The largest program, in San Francisco, is estimated to reduce HIV infection by approximately 30 percent (*SFAF HIV prevention project*, 2001).

BUILDING A KNOWLEDGE BASE

Social workers in virtually every setting and across all population groups encounter substance abuse. Students entering any of the social service or human service fields must prepare themselves to work with people who abuse chemical substances and with others who have been victimized by parents, spouses, friends, or employers who are dependent on drugs or alcohol.

Where do students find curriculum content on substance abuse? The response is that it permeates many of the courses in the liberal arts (courses such as sociology and psychology) and the courses taken in the social work major. Field placements may also expose students to practice with or on behalf of chemically dependent and alcoholic persons. Some field placements will be in substance abuse treatment programs in which the entire client population has abused alcohol and/or drugs. Elective courses on alcoholism or substance abuse may also be available.

Awareness of community resources for the prevention and treatment of substance abuse is also necessary. The case study used in this chapter portrays a social worker in an emergency shelter and her very effective work with an African American male alcoholic. A part of Madeleine Johnson's effectiveness was her ability to link Dan Graves to appropriate resources, not only to substance abuse treatment programs but also resources for employment and educational opportunities.

Their generalist professional education prepares BSWs to enter practice in a variety of settings with the expectation that they will continue to develop and refine their knowledge, especially in reference to the client population they serve. MSW candidates, on the other hand, add a specialization—possibly in substance abuse treatment—to their generalist practice base. An MSW with this area of specialization is more likely to take courses entirely devoted to substance abuse than is a BSW student or an MSW student who has chosen another specialization. Social workers meet their responsibility to continue their education through their own research, reading, seminars, and workshops.

SUBSTANCES OF ABUSE

Because substance abuse is encountered by social workers throughout social work practice, social workers need to have an understanding of the substances that are most frequently misused and abused. Exhibit 8-8 provides basic information about alcohol and drugs that are abused. The exhibit is a modified version of the classification created

EXHIBIT 8-8

National Institute on Drug Abuse Commonly Abused Substances

Drug	Method of Administration	Potential Consequences
Cannabinoids		
Hashish	Swallowed, smoked	Euphoria, slowed thinking, confusion, impaired balance, cough; impaired memory and learning; increased heart rate, anxiety; panic attacks; tolerance, addiction
Marijuana	Swallowed, smoked	As above
Depressants		
Barbiturates	Injected, swallowed	Reduced anxiety; feeling of well-being; lowered inhibitions; slowed pulse and breathing; lowered blood pressure; poor concentration; confusion; impaired coordination, memory, judgment; addiction; respiratory depression and arrest; life threatening withdrawal; death
Benzodiaze (tranquilizers: Librium, Valium, Xanax, Halcion)	Swallowed, injected	Sedation, drowsiness/dizziness
Flunitrazepam (Rohypnol: forget-me-pill, Mexican Valium, R-2, Roche) Associated with sexual assaults	Swallowed, snorted	Visual and gastrointestinal disturbances' urinary retention, memory loss for the time under the drug's effects
GBH (liquid ecstasy) Associated with sexual assaults	Swallowed	Drowsiness, nausea/vomiting, headache, loss of consciousness, seizures, coma, death
Methaqualone Injected, (Quaalude, Sopor)		Euphoria/depression, poor reflexes, slurred speech, coma
Dissociative Anesthetics		
Ketamine (Feline Valium, Special K)	Injected, snorted, smoked	Numbness, nausea, vomiting; at high doses: delirium, depression, respiratory depression and arrest
PCP and analogs	Injected, swallowed, smoked	Possible decrease in blood pressure and heart rate, panic, aggression, Violence, loss of appetite, depression
Hallucinogens		
LSD	Swallowed, absorbed through mouth	Altered states of perception and feeling; nausea; persisting perception disorder (flashbacks); numbness, weakness, tremors; persistent mental disorders
Mescaline (cactus, peyote)	Swallowed, smoked	Increased body temperature, heart Rate, blood pressure; loss of appetite, sleeplessness, numbness, weakness, tremors
Psilocybin (magic mushroom)	Swallowed	Nervousness, paranoic

(Continued)

EXHIBIT 8-8 *(Concluded)*

Drug	Method of Administration	Potential Consequences
Opioids and Morphine Derivatives		
Codeine	Injected, swallowed	Pain relief, euphoria, drowsiness, nausea, constipation, confusion, sedation, respiratory depression and arrest, addiction, coma, death
Heroin	Injected, smoked, snorted	Staggering gait, withdrawal symptons resemble flu but are not life-threatening, addiction
Morphine	Injected, swallowed, smoked	Depression, anxiety, withdrawal
Opium	Swallowed, smoked	Physically addicting, psychological dependence
Hydrocodone (Vicodin)	Swallowed	Pain relief, altered brain activity, physical dependence, addiction
Oxycodone HCL (Oxy, O.C.)	Swallowed, snorted, injected	Pain relief, physical dependence, addiction
Stimulants		
Amphetamine (Dexedrine, bennies, speed, uppers)	Injected, swallowed, smoked, snorted	Increased heart rate, blood pressure, metabolism; feelings of exhilaration, energy, alertness; weight loss, heart failure, nervousness, insomnia; aggression, tolerance, addiction, psychosis
Cocaine (blow, crack, rock, snow)	Injected, smoked, snorted	Anxiety, chest pain, respiratory failure, headache, strokes, nausea, seizures, panic attacks
MDMA (ecstasy, Eve, lover's speed, peace, STP)	Swallowed	Mild hallucinogenic effects, increased tactile sensitivity, cardiac toxicity, renal failure, liver toxicity, impaired memory and learning
Methamphetamine (Desoxyn, crystal, fire, ice, meth, speed)	Injected, swallowed, smoked, snorted	Aggression, violence, psychotic behavior, memory loss, cardiac and and neurological damage, tolerance, addiction
Other Compounds		
Anabolic steroids (Anadrol, Oxandrin, Durabolin, Depo-Testosterone)	Injected, swallowed, applied to skin	Hostility and aggression; adolescents: premature stoppage of growth; males: prostate cancer, reduced sperm production, shrunken testicles, breast enlargement; females: menstrual irregularities, development of beard and masculine characteristics
Inhalants (solvents: paint thinner, gasoline; gases: butane, propane, aerosol propellants)	Inhaled through nose or mouth	Stimulation, loss of inhibition; headache; nausea; loss of motor coordination, unconsciousness, weight loss, depression, memory impairment, damage to cardiovascular and nervous systems, sudden death

SOURCE: National Institute on Drug Abuse. (2007). *Commonly abused drugs*. Retrieved July 7, 2007, from http://www.drugabuse.gov/DrugPages/DrugsofAbuse.html

by the National Institute of Drug Abuse (NIDA). Exhibit 8-8 does not include all of the substances in the NIDA classification but, instead, it focuses on those most frequently misused. The major categories in Exhibit 8-8 are organized alphabetically by physiological function of the substance (the impact the substances will have on the human body).

Alcohol is the most abused substance, but it is not a drug and therefore is no longer included in the NIDA classification. Alcohol, often mistakenly believed to be an "up" drug, is, in reality, a depressant. It has potentially serious side-effects. Withdrawal from alcohol can actually result in death. Although there has been a decline in the use of alcohol, it continues to be used excessively, and it is the major substance that is abused in the United States and many other countries today.

The cannabinoids comprise the first major category in Exhibit 8-8. Marijuana, the most frequently used drug in this category and the most commonly used of all of the illicit drugs (used by 74 percent of all illicit drug users), comes from a hemp plant that is grown throughout the United States (SAMHSA, 2006). Marijuana may produce a sense of well-being and relaxation, but it also may result in social withdrawal, anxiety, and even paranoia. It has been found useful in the treatment of diseases such as glaucoma and for persons suffering from cancer. Its advocates seek legalization, especially for medical use of the substance. Its opponents seek stiffer penalties for its illegal use.

Depressants are drugs that depress the central nervous system. Physicians rely on these drugs to treat various conditions, such as epilepsy and anxiety, and for their anesthetic properties. Barbiturates, ("downers") are generally obtained through a physician's prescription (or several physicians' prescriptions). Most frequently, barbiturates are taken in pill form. If injected, they are most dangerous because of their immediate effect. Withdrawal has the potential for mental disorder, seizures, and even death. Barbiturates are often the drug used in suicides and mercy killings of animals as well as humans.

Tranquilizers and sleeping medications are milder depressants of the central nervous system. They are among the most frequently prescribed substances in the United States. These drugs can create psychological dependence, but they are most hazardous when combined with alcohol or other drugs, causing a condition referred to as **potentiation.** This term denotes the dramatically increased potential for serious consequences to the health and well-being of the user. Social workers have learned to inquire about prescription drug use when obtaining a drinking history. When central nervous system depressants are combined or taken with alcohol, they can be truly lethal. Women—perhaps because they see physicians more frequently than men do—are more likely than men to have prescriptions for the minor tranquilizers. They are more likely to become involved in **cross-addiction,** that is, addiction to two or more substances at the same time.

Dissociative anesthetics is a new category in the NIDA classification of commonly abused substances. These were formerly included in the hallucinogens category. Probably the most used of the dissociative anesthetics is PCP. These drugs were developed as anesthetics. They act on the brain to change the perception of pain and they also produce a sense of detachment from reality (National Institute on Drug Abuse, 2007).

Hallucinogens are drugs that produce sensory distortions (dreamlike experiences, visual and/or auditory effects). Heavy users of hallucinogens report flashback experiences months after the drug use. LSD (lysergic acid diethylamide), the well-publicized drug of the 1960s, is being used again today. More frequently, however, people are using a variety of other hallucinogenic chemicals that are synthesized in black-market and home laboratories and are sold on the streets.

The next major category of substances that social workers should be familiar with are the opioids and morphine derivatives. They are used medicinally to deaden pain. Heroin, morphine, and codeine are among the more commonly used drugs in this category, but the more recent additions include vicodin and oxycodone HCL. These painkillers have been in the news because of their admitted abuse by respected sports athletes. Because many of these drugs are injected, they present a significant danger for the spread of AIDS and other diseases. This class of drugs can also result in physical dependence and addiction. Serious consequences such as coma and death may result from overdose.

New production methods have resulted in increased purity and potency of heroin, raising the possibility of overdose. Sometimes heroin, like cocaine, is diluted with other substances to lower its cost to users and to increase profits for drug dealers; the user cannot immediately tell if the drug has been diluted. Morphine is illegal (when not prescribed by a physician), addictive, and hazardous because of the frequent use of unsterile needles for injection. Malnutrition often occurs because of the depressant nature of the drug and because addicts become so dependent on it that they are unable to take care of their own basic needs.

The next category is the central nervous system **stimulants.** These are drugs that produce energy, increase alertness, and provide a sense of strength and well-being. They are sometimes taken for weight loss. Illegally obtained methamphetamines are used by students and truck drivers, among others, to avoid sleep to complete work. The resulting errors in judgment range from a poor exam grade to highway fatalities. Ice is a form of methamphetamine that can be administered by injection, orally, inhaled, or smoked. An overdose can cause coma and death. Addiction occurs very rapidly, sometimes after only a single use.

Cocaine, once considered a narcotic, is now classified as a stimulant. Cocaine is well known to social workers as a cause of child abuse and neglect, family violence, suicide, and unprovoked shootings. Repeated or prolonged use of cocaine can produce physical and psychological intoxication and withdrawal symptoms, including suicide. Use of contaminated needles is of great concern. Cocaine combined with alcohol results in a dangerous level of toxicity. Crack is a less expensive pellet form of the more expensive and relatively pure powder forms of cocaine hydrochloride. Use of crack as well as powdered cocaine and prescription pain relievers increased minimally from 2004 to 2005, while use of ecstasy and methamphetamine remained unchanged (SAMHSA, 2006).

"Designer drugs" are a form of stimulants. They are chemically produced drugs that differ slightly from the illegal drugs that they were formulated to replicate. Often they are many times stronger than the drugs they imitate. Their potential danger is often underestimated. In some cases a single use can cause irreversible brain damage. Ecstasy is the designer drug used—sometimes in combination with marijuana, heroin, and cocaine—in rave parties that have spread across Europe and America.

"Club drugs" comprise a wide combination of drugs used at college parties, bars, and dance clubs. Some are used to enhance the highs produced by cocaine or to reduce the negative effects of crack. One of these is rohypnol, the "date rape" drug, a tablet that can be easily crushed and put into a drink. Its immediate effect is a sense of intoxication, relaxation, and drowsiness that can last for many hours. It can be fatal when used in combination with alcohol or another depressant (National Clearinghouse for Alcohol and Drug Information, 2000).

The final major category in the NIDA classification of commonly abused drugs is called "other compounds." This includes steroids, which are sometimes used by college and professional athletes to rapidly build muscle and physical strength. Of special concern with steroids are the aggressive behaviors and the physical changes that may occur. Inhalants form the other substance in this category. People inhale ("huff") such products as gasoline, ether, paint thinner, propane, and glue with mixed results. They may hope for a "high" or improved sexual performance, but they may experience blindness, conjunctivitis (eye infection), or simple disappointment. Youths aged 10 to 17 are especially vulnerable.

Despite the focus of this chapter, chemical substances are not the only forms of addiction. Worldwide, compulsive gambling has lead to bankruptcy for millions of persons. Sexual addictions have wreaked havoc in many families. Computer addiction is on the rise.

ENVIRONMENTAL PERSPECTIVES

The previous section of this chapter identified some of the major substances that are abused and explained the concerns and hazards of those substances. Earlier in the chapter, we identified populations that are at risk for substance abuse. Building on this groundwork, we now offer a brief look at the role environment plays in substance abuse. In social work, it is important to think about the interactions between persons and their environment. Sometimes environments—neighborhoods and communities—have profoundly negative and harmful impacts on people, and sometimes the environment can be nurturing and supportive of human well-being.

Neighborhoods were the focus of an ecological study published in 2006 that linked environmental conditions to deaths resulting from substance abuse. The study found that a low level of homeownership in certain New York City census tracts was correlated with exceptionally high rates of drug abuse and with what the study referred to as "drug dependence mortality." In the census tracts with the very lowest levels of homeownership, deaths from substance abuse were exceptionally high. The researchers' explanation for this finding was that in the absence of homeownership, levels of social control and social stability fell dramatically, leaving whole neighborhoods without needed human support and connectivity. The researchers also looked at land use and housing structures that created environmental conditions inviting drug usage. The study demonstrated that the presence of boarded-up, vacant homes (which intensified drug activity) was also significantly related to the high level of substance abuse deaths within these census tracts (Hannon & Cuddy, 2006).

Studies such as this one of specific New York City neighborhoods do teach us something important about the toxic effect of neighborhood and community land usage, but they also hold clues to how these environments can become stronger and healthier for people. The report of the drug dependence mortality study concludes by recommending policy initiatives that would increase homeownership. "Policies geared toward increasing homeownership in economically disadvantaged areas may contribute to decreases in drug dependence by encouraging community pride and decreasing levels of neighborhood social disorganization" (Hannon & Cuddy, 2006, p. 461). Creating policies or programs that reduce the number of boarded-up, abandoned buildings that facilitate drug activity was also recommended. The report authors concluded wisely: "While most policies addressing drug dependence focus exclusively on the rehabilitation of the individual, the revitalization and rebuilding of neighborhoods may also be a worthwhile approach" (p. 461).

In most parts of the United States, neighborhoods and communities are quite different today than they were a century ago. Today, we are much less connected with our neighbors and fellow citizens. This is reflected in the continuing declines in church attendance, political organization involvement, labor union membership, even bowling leagues. Families are spread out across the country and around the world. This leaves many communities, rural as well as metropolitan, with environments in which people are much more socially isolated than in the past. In many neighborhoods today, people are not invested in homeownership nor, for that matter, are they invested in their neighbors. These neighborhoods may not produce substance abuse mortality statistics like those in some New York City census tracts, but they may nonetheless provide community environments that fail to protect youths and adults, from addiction and all of its consequences.

This brief introduction of the ecology of substance abuse is now broadened through a cross-national review of several countries' efforts to deal with substance abuse issues.

SUBSTANCE ABUSE: A CROSS-NATIONAL PERSPECTIVE

We begin with Singapore, where drug addiction has been under relatively good control over the past several years. This has been achieved through drug laws that are considered among the strictest in the world. Still, challenges persist. The small ethnic Malay community in Singapore accounts for half of the drug addiction in the country. The "iron-fist" policies of Singapore are unique in the Asian region. Anyone found guilty of trafficking in large amounts of dangerous drugs is subject to the death penalty. Drug abusers identified through urine tests or medical exams are subjected to mandatory treatment. They are committed to a drug rehabilitation center for up to 36 months. Following a week-long "cold turkey" (medically supervised but using no medication) detoxification, they have another week to recover from their detoxification experience. The next phase of treatment emphasizes training in the legal ramifications and dangers of drug use. Psychological counseling and physical fitness training, including calisthenics, occurs in the third phase. In the final phase, 4 months into the program, education and work programs are utilized. Eventually, following a month-long prerelease camp, assignment is made to a community-based rehabilitation program that will be either a live-in halfway house or a residential-day program. Interestingly, the community-based rehabilitation program uses minimal counseling or social work intervention; instead, worship and religious education are emphasized, with Islam, Buddhism, and Christianity as the major religions utilized. There is also a final 2-year-long mandatory follow-up supervised program (Osman, 2002).

Germany stands in contrast to Singapore. Germany has a long-time history of alcohol and drug tolerance and has used social workers in drug prevention and treatment programs since the early 1900s. Within Europe, Germany and Sweden have an estimated drug dependence of 205 persons per 100,000 residents compared with only 164 in the Netherlands, 181 in France, 258 in Spain, and a surprising 461 in Switzerland. In schools, social workers are a part of the prevention effort. Teams of social work experts assist teachers in preparing educational programs for children. Social workers also build networks with local authorities that distribute informational materials at youth events, including raves. Outpatient treatment programs are said to be dominated by social workers, but they also provide case management and individual and group treatment in inpatient facilities, although social workers are only about 30 percent of inpatient staff. Social workers developed harm reduction techniques and helped establish "low-threshold" facilities that are easily accessible and that offer both day and night programs. Germany has an extensive network of treatment facilities. Those in metropolitan centers tend to be more complex. Alcohol treatment is handled in a rather traditional, counseling-focused manner with detoxification, if necessary, completed in a general hospital. Drug treatment in cities generally includes "the distribution of condoms and sterile needles; day and night shelters; injecting rooms; individual counseling and case management; medical services, including emergency treatment; methadone dispensaries; and treatment of HIV-infections and other chronic illnesses" (Vogt, 2002, p. 76). Persons may be sentenced for drug law violations including the use or sale of marijuana (Vogt, 2002).

Germany, and the Netherlands as well, utilize an environmental approach to a greater degree than a clinical approach to the treatment of substance abuse. Social workers are vitally involved in urban regeneration and the development of anti-poverty programs. A great deal of emphasis is placed on community work (Harrison & Straussner, 2002). The Netherlands has historically had one of the most open and liberal substance use/abuse environments, with a generous harm reduction program that documented positive effects on the health and the mortality rates of persons addicted to hard drugs. Now, however, some shifts are taking place to improve the safety and lower the crime rates in larger cities. This environmental approach is aimed at rehabilitating deteriorating city neighborhoods and reducing the poverty of inhabitants. Until 2001, persons addicted to drugs could not be forced to enter a treatment program even if they were in prison. In 2001 the law was changed to

Today, in many parts of the world, detoxification centers provide either a "cold turkey" approach using no medication or medication-assisted withdrawal prior to admitting a seriously drug-addicted person to rehabilitation.

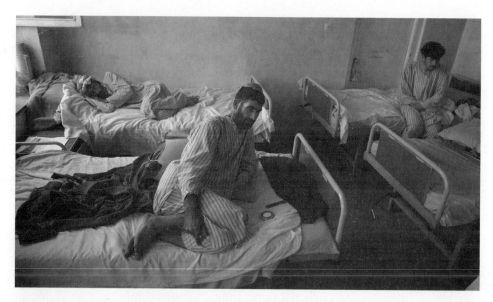

permit judges to require compulsory prison-based treatment. Nonetheless, tolerance is apparent in the continued growth of "user-friendly" places. These are locations where users can take drugs in a safe environment; in Rotterdam, some provide outreach and case management services. Rotterdam also has a facility designed for elderly drug addicts to receive their drugs in a secure location that meets their special needs as older adults. Social workers are involved across the broad range of Dutch substance abuse programs (de Koning & de Kwant (2002).

The social welfare policies of each country govern the availability and nature of substance abuse programs. These policies reflect the values of people within the country. In the Netherlands, we see increasing concern about public safety, resulting in a small shift toward legally mandating treatment. Ireland appears to be shifting away from a clinical approach to treatment (a U.S. model) toward increased focus on changing the environment. There also appears to be less support for use of law enforcement and prison sentences to treat addiction in a number of countries, including Australia and the United Kingdom (Harrison & Straussner, 2002).

U.S. SOCIAL WELFARE POLICY RELATED TO SUBSTANCE ABUSE

A brief review of history may help us understand how the United States arrived at its current social welfare policy concerning substance abuse and addiction. Shifts in public attitudes about criminalization of abuse are also interesting to consider. We can begin with the early colonists of our country.

The ship's log appears to provide evidence that the Pilgrims' diminished supply of food and beer resulted in their decision to land at Plymouth in 1620 rather than spending additional time exploring the coast of the New World (Kinney & Leaton, 1995).

During the late 19th century, the Industrial Revolution brought social turbulence and imposed strains on normal family life in the United States. Morphine, cocaine, and alcohol became available through new means of production, distribution, and marketing. Hollow needles were first used at this time to inject chemical substances. The chaos of the times was mirrored in disrupted family life. In the view of many who joined the social reform movement that had begun in the mid-1800s, domestic violence was incited by alcohol abuse. Women in those years were almost totally dependent on their husbands as providers for themselves and their children. Letters and diaries from the 1870s provide ample evidence of the wife and child abuse that brought thousands of women into the temperance movement (Lacerte & Harris, 1986).

Reform and Regulation

The Woman's Christian Temperance Union (WCTU) was founded in Cleveland in 1874 to pursue social reform, education, and legislation regarding alcohol abuse, which came increasingly to be seen as the root of all evil. Together with another powerful prohibitionist organization, the Anti-Saloon League, the WCTU rallied the vote and was largely responsible in 1919 for passage of the Eighteenth Amendment (commonly referred to as the Volstead Act), which prohibited the manufacture and sale of alcoholic beverages in the United States. However, Prohibition of the 1920s proved to be neither enforceable by the authorities nor fully acceptable to American society. It was repealed in 1933 by the Twenty-First Amendment. With the repeal of Prohibition, alcohol use increased steadily until the 1970s, when it began to level off. After some ups and downs into the 1980s, alcohol consumption began to decline.

Quindara, California: Members of the Temperance movement smashing the contents of a saloon.

Drug regulation in the United States was also influenced by the social reform movement that brought the WCTU into existence and that resulted in Prohibition. Opium was widely used in many parts of the world by the 1850s, and U.S. merchants joined in the lucrative opium trade. Drug use in general was common. Before 1900 narcotics were available from grocery stores and over the counter in pharmacies. Women used them to relieve discomfort related to menstruation and gave their children cough syrup containing opium. In fact, Coca-Cola's original formula contained cocaine.

Although the first U.S. tax on crude opium imports occurred in 1842, it was not until the Harrison Narcotics Act of 1914 that the use of narcotics for nonmedical purposes was prohibited. The public, which never completely supported the banning of alcohol, did support the suppression of narcotics. Federal laws resulted in increasing control of narcotics, with the 1956 Narcotic Drug Control Act providing the stiffest of penalties, including the death sentence for anyone convicted of selling heroin to a minor (Ray & Ksir, 1993).

Politics and Policy

The 1960s saw a massive increase in the use of drugs. Social reform efforts by the end of the decade resulted in the Comprehensive Drug Abuse Prevention and Control Act of 1970. This law shifted authority for control from the Department of the Treasury to the Department of Justice's Drug Enforcement Administration. The result was recodification of the substances, which separated alcohol and tobacco from drugs with a high potential for abuse; this left heroin, LSD, and marijuana in a category that brought penalties, including imprisonment, for their sale (1988 legislation added penalties for possession). Prevention and treatment funding was appropriated by the 1970 act, although alcoholism treatment centers had actually been developed shortly after the founding of Alcoholics Anonymous in 1935.

When the introduction of psychoactive drugs made methadone and antabuse available to treat heroin and alcohol abuse, new treatment programs emerged. The public became increasingly convinced that substance abuse was treatable. With the advent of the Reagan administration in the 1980s, however, the role of the federal government shifted away from a leadership role in treatment funding and toward use of law enforcement and prison sentences to curtail the use and sale of drugs.

Given the major focus on the prosecution and incarceration of drug users and suppliers, more prison facilities were constructed. Already overcrowded correctional facilities could not accommodate a rush of new offenders, and new facilities soon filled to capacity. In election after election, the public supported prison sentences as an answer to the perceived drug problem.

Despite the perception of the public, use of illicit drugs in the United States has actually declined markedly. The National Survey on Drug Use and Health changed its research design in 2001, making comparisons with previous years' data less accurate; however, some trends remain evident. Back in 1979, approximately 26 million people in the United States had used illicit drugs in the previous month (SAMHSA, 1998). By 2005 the reported figure was 19.7 million users, or 8.1 percent of the population over 12 years of age (SAMHSA, 2006). From 1979 to 2005, marijuana was overwhelmingly the most frequently used of all of the illicit drugs; in 1979 it was used by 76 percent and in 2005 by 74.2 percent of all illicit drug users (54.5 percent of whom used marijuana exclusively). Another way to look at this is that if 8.1 percent of the U.S. population used illicit drugs in 2005, 6.0 percent of the population used marijuana, 1.0 percent used cocaine, 0.3 percent used crack, 0.1 percent used heroin, 0.2 percent used methamphetamine, and 1.9 percent made illegal use of pain relievers (SAMHSA, 2006). Of course, this list is only a sampling of the illicit drugs being used, but it gives a sense of the proportionate use of various illicit substances.

　　The most constructive handling of alcohol and drug concerns remains a potent issue in politics, especially in the current politically conservative environment. Substance abuse is often linked in the media with crime and has been used to promote lengthy prison sentences. But political support for the War on Drugs continues, with billions of taxpayer dollars funding that war with Coast Guard vessels, assault helicopters, and NASA satellites in addition to all of the local law enforcement resources (McNeece & DiNitto, 2005). Meantime, of course, billions of dollars are paid in federal excise taxes by people who use and abuse legal substances of addiction, primarily alcohol. The government has become dependent itself—on income from alcohol—and Native American tribes as well as state governments rely on income from legal, although potentially addictive, gambling. Legalizing the use of marijuana remains an unresolved issue. Struggle over the legalization of marijuana for medical purposes (see the Up for Debate box) is a reflection of the interconnectedness of health and drug policies.

UP FOR DEBATE

Proposition: Use of marijuana should be legalized for medical purposes.

YES	NO
Legalization would allow doctors to practice medicine more humanely, relieving pain and reducing nausea and vomiting caused by anticancer drugs.	There is no empirical evidence that affirms the medicinal value of marijuana to humans.
Hundreds of patients and their doctors have filed applications seeking compassionate use of marijuana.	If use of marijuana for medical purposes were legalized, there would immediately be a demand to legalize it for recreational purposes.
A synthetic form of marijuana, Marinol, is available, but patients have found it to be less effective than marijuana in relieving pain.	Tax dollars should be spent on research to find new alternatives to marijuana.
Marijuana isn't nearly as potentially harmful as numerous other prescription medications in current use.	The Drug Enforcement Administration (DEA) is firmly opposed to making this illicit, potentially addictive drug available.

SOCIAL JUSTICE AND THE WAR ON DRUGS

Sometimes it is difficult to know why Americans are attracted to the notion of war or believe that war is the best approach to problem resolution. We've had a war on poverty, a war on terrorism, a war on drugs, and assorted other "wars." The War on Drugs was initiated by President Richard Nixon in 1971 to fight use and trafficking of illegal drugs. With the support of Congress, Nixon increased the criminal penalty for drug dealing. Subsequent presidents and Congresses have supported that war by stiffening penalties for use as well as selling drugs and by massively funding legal enforcement for interdiction of drugs coming into the country and imprisonment for drug abusers and drug traffickers within the United States (McNeece & DiNitto, 2005).

The War on Drugs has been popular with Congress to the extent that even the U.S. Sentencing Commission has begun to question some of the legislation that has been passed. According to van Wormer and Davis (2008), the War on Drugs includes several dimensions. The first relates to the mandatory minimum prison sentences for possession as well as sale of drugs. Incorporated in this dimension is the criminalization of drugs. This focuses the efforts of that war on use of the courts and prisons instead of the approach taken by some other countries that focus efforts on prevention and treatment ("criminalization" versus "medicalization"). The next dimension is one that gives clear preference to an abstinence approach rather than considering harm reduction. Next is the support for wide use of drug testing of individuals. The final dimension is the legislative as well as financial support for international interdiction, border surveillance to intercept drugs potentially entering the United States, and practices including wiretapping.

While billions of dollars have been spent on international interdiction in South American countries and in border surveillance, a more focused social justice issue relates to the lives of people who have been affected by the criminalization of drug use in the United States. Even though the War on Drugs has been popular, people in the United States are less and less supportive of incarceration for minor drug offenses. As long ago as 2001, it was reported that "the number of people entering prison for drug offenses has increased by more than *1,000 percent*" in the preceding two decades (Justice Policy Institute, as cited by McNeece & DiNitto, 2005, p. 241, emphasis added).

What has fueled the huge increase in sentencing and the phenomenal growth of the U.S. prison industry is the Anti-Drug Abuse Act of 1986, which established a framework of mandatory minimum prison sentences for offenses related to specific drugs. This law reserved the harshest sentences for crack cocaine offenses. In a 2007 report to Congress, the U.S. Sentencing Commission noted that the current federal sentencing policy was coming "under almost universal criticism from representatives of the Judiciary, criminal justice practitioners, academics, and community interest groups, and inaction in this area is of increasing concern to many, including the Commission" (U.S. Sentencing Commission, 2007, p. 2).

In the 2007 report to Congress, the U.S. Sentencing Commission requested that Congress enact a remedy for the "100-to-1" law now in existence. This law differentiates between crack cocaine and powder cocaine, providing a minimum 5-year mandatory sentence for a first-time offense (possession or trafficking) involving

5 grams or more of crack cocaine compared with the same minimum sentence for 500 grams or more of the powder form of cocaine. The result has been dramatically different sentences for people convicted of crack versus powder cocaine. The Sentencing Commission called for an end to this disparity and pointed out further that the quantity of crack cocaine that triggers the mandatory minimum provisions of current law are far smaller than the quantity required for powder cocaine. One hundred grams of heroin, for example, would be needed to result in the 5-year mandatory minimum sentence that is triggered by just 5 grams of crack cocaine (U.S. Sentencing Commission, 2007).

The social justice of sentencing disparity is certainly an issue. It looms larger and more serious when we look at the people who are most at risk of being incarcerated. Crack cocaine is most used by poorer, often inner-city, African American people, while the powder form of cocaine is more frequently associated with white, higher income, and often rural populations. The African American prison population, as a result, has grown significantly as a result of the War on Drugs. Women have become one of the fastest growing segments of the prison population. "Drug offenses account for around one third of women confined in state prisons and a majority in federal prisons" (van Wormer & Davis, 2008, p. 528). Families and children are always affected when a parent is imprisoned. The incarceration of the mother is likely to result in placement of the children out of the home and often a myriad of behavioral problems, too, for the children.

Will Congress repeal the mandatory 5-year sentence for possession of cocaine as the Sentencing Commission requested? Even the Sentencing Commission's 2007 report sounds dubious when it points out that "Congress has not acted on any of the various statutory recommendations set forth in the Commission's prior reports and expressly disapproved the Commission's guideline amendment addressing crack cocaine penalties submitted on May 1, 1995" (p. 1). Pressure is building for Congressional action. At the end of 2007, the United States Supreme Court, in *Kimbrough v. U.S.*, ruled that judges may use their discretion instead of following the minimum mandatory 5-year sentence for possession of 5 grams of crack cocaine. The Sentencing Commission immediately voted to retroactively implement this guideline amendment. The impact could be dramatic. Approximately 19,500 persons in federal prison could become eligible for sentence reduction, although the judicial review might take years to complete. The Sentencing Project, a Washington-based research and reform organization, estimated that reduced prison sentences could potentially save up to $1 billion in federal prison costs, and the early release of significant numbers of African American prisoners could reduce racial disparity in federal prisons (The Sentencing Project, 2007).

If Congress has failed to act on the federal government agency's recommendations for all of these years, it certainly is time for the people of this country to demand action. Social workers and social work students need to be much more aware of the social justice issues within the field of substance abuse. For the good of our clients and the good of our country, we need to take every opportunity to address social justice policy issues such as the crack cocaine minimum sentencing policies. (More discussion of the impact of drug offenses on prison populations can be found in Chapter 10 of this book.)

INTERNET SITES

http://www.samhsa.gov	Substance Abuse and Mental Health Services Administration Center for Substance Abuse Prevention
http://www.nida.nih.gov	NIDA (National Institute on Drug Abuse)
http://www.niaaa.nih.gov/	National Institute on Alcohol Abuse and Alcoholism
http://www.treatment.org	The Treatment Improvement Exchange
http://www.alcoholics-anonymous.org/	Alcoholics Anonymous World Services Inc.
http://www.nationalhomeless.org/publications/facts/addiction.pdf	Addiction Disorders and Homelessness
http://www.ca.org	Cocaine Anonymous
http://www.peele.net	The Stanton Peele Addiction Website
http://csdp.org/	Common Sense for Drug Policy
http://ncadi.samhsa.gov	National Clearinghouse for Alcohol and Drug Information
http://www.istss.org/resources/Traumatic_Stress_and_Substance_Abuse.cfm	The International Society for Traumatic Stress Studies
http://www.cnsaap.ca/cnsaap/Splash/	Canadian Network of Substance Abuse and Allied Professionals

SUMMARY

The setting for the chapter's case study is an emergency shelter, and the social worker is a BSW who is herself a recovering alcoholic. Madeleine Johnson's disclosure that she, too, is a recovering alcoholic helps Dan Graves to trust her. Dan decided to continue AA attendance while at the shelter. The client's housing, social, medical, financial, and educational needs are addressed, and the social worker then extends her concern to Dan's relationship with his wife, Angie.

The context for social work in this field of practice is explained through a brief discussion of history that acknowledges the contributions of Mary Richmond and other pioneers in substance abuse practice. In today's practice, substance abuse and addiction problems are found across all fields of practice. The roles and responsibilities of social workers are identified. The populations that are most at risk because of substance abuse, such as women and children, are introduced.

Social workers also need an understanding of the prevention and treatment programs that are available and the goals and philosophy of those programs. As programs evolve and change in the United States, it is often helpful to look at services being offered in other countries, services such as those in some European countries that emphasize the harm reduction model. This chapter introduces Alcoholics Anonymous, a program that has become international in scope.

The substances most frequently abused in the United States are identified. In addition to alcohol, the most commonly abused substance, some of the current "designer drugs" and "club drugs" are described. Environmental perspectives are explored.

Social welfare policy and the provision of funding for prevention and treatment programs are described in relation to the political context of U.S. society. A brief history of the profession of social work in this field of practice is presented.

Today there is a resurgence of interest in sub-stance abuse among social work students. This is hope-ful because the profession will look to them in the future to create humane programs that will be sensitive to the needs of women and children, minority groups, gay and lesbian clients, persons with disabilities, and other at-risk persons. Through research they will be able to add to our understanding of chemical depend-ency. They will have opportunities to educate the pub-lic and to advocate for laws and policies that advance social justice.

KEY TERMS

alcohol abuse, *p. 319*

alcohol dependence, *p. 319*

alcoholism, *p. 319*

cross-addiction, *p. 343*

depressants, *p. 343*

dual diagnosis, *p. 339*

fetal alcohol syndrome
  (FAS), *p. 334*

hallucinogens, *p. 344*

harm reduction model, *p. 328*

hypothermia, *p. 313*

potentiation, *p. 343*

primary alcoholism, *p. 318*

reactive alcoholism, *p. 319*

secondary alcoholism, *p. 319*

stimulants, *p. 344*

DISCUSSION QUESTIONS

1. In the case study, what are Dan Graves's chances for successfully dealing with alcoholism? Identify the factors that might help him attain success. What may prevent him from attaining a successful recovery?

2. What is a recovering alcoholic? How long does recovery take?

3. How have the patterns of drug and alcohol abuse changed over the history of the United States?

4. Identify substances discussed in this chapter that, if abused, can result in death.

5. Which populations or groups of people are at high risk in relation to substance abuse? Why?

6. Explain the differences between primary, secondary, and reactive alcoholism. Which kind of alcoholism did Dan Graves have?

7. What are some of the generalist practice interven-tions social workers may use in their work with chemically dependent clients?

8. What is the harm reduction model in the area of substance abuse services? How does it differ from the abstinence approach? Would there be any value in integrating the harm reduction model in U.S. programs?

9. Can you think of ways in which a generalist social worker could promote social justice in the field of substance abuse?

CLASSROOM EXERCISES

It is suggested that students break into small groups of three or four to discuss these exercises. It may be help-ful to choose a scribe to record and report interesting points to the class after the group discussion.

1. Why do you think people become addicted to alcohol and other drugs in the United States today?

2. Do you view substance abuse as a moral issue, a medical issue (physical illness), a law enforcement issue, or something else? What policies do you believe could best reduce drug use and abuse in this country?

3. How does the harm reduction model of substance abuse treatment in Europe differ from the abstinence model and the 12-step program of Alcoholics Anonymous in the United States? Which approach makes most sense to you? Why?

4. What do you think are the major reasons for the shortage of substance abuse treatment programs in the United States today? What do you think can or should be done about this issue?

RESEARCH ACTIVITIES

1. Gather information about your community's substance abuse programs. What are the names and locations of these organizations? What is the nature of the treatment provided? What is the cost? Will people who are uninsured be accepted?

2. Survey people of different ages and political persuasions on the issue of legalization of marijuana for medical purposes. Do your survey results suggest stronger support for or stronger opposition to legalization? Are the survey responses related to age or political preferences?

3. Review available local and national newspapers. Cut out all articles that pertain to substance abuse. Identify themes that relate to current or emerging political issues. (Example: automobile accidents caused by drunk drivers might relate to lack of substance abuse treatment resources, and that might connect with a political issue such as federal mental health parity legislation.) Then note how these themes might relate to the at-risk populations discussed in this chapter. Do any of these issues create concern for you as a potential social worker? Is there anything you can do in the political arena to advocate for the at-risk population?

4. Do library research to further your understanding of binge drinking, weekend rave parties, and drug abuse on college campuses. Then survey students on your campus and interview administrators such as the director of security about the prevalence of this activity on your campus.

INTERNET RESEARCH EXERCISES

1. As might be expected, the World Health Organization has a considerable amount of material on their website (http://www.who.int/substance_abuse/en/).

   a. The point is made that WHO is the only agency dealing with all psychoactive substances. What does this really mean? (Hint: Click "Terminology & classification"; then click "Psychoactive substances.")

   b. Click "Facts and figures." According to this site, how many people worldwide have alcohol use disorders?

   c. This agency includes "Volatile solvents" in their list of problem substances. Why?

2. The subject of "Club Drugs" is discussed at some length on a website sponsored by the Office of National Drug Control Policy in the Whitehouse in Washington, DC (http://www.whitehousedrugpolicy.gov/drugfact/club/index.html).

   a. What are the four substances listed in this article?

   b. According to their estimates, how many people age 12 and older have at some time tried ecstasy?

   c. What are the health effects of using ketamine?

3. The National Institute on Drug Abuse, a part of the National Institutes of Health, has a web page on methamphetamine (http://www.nida.nih.gov/drugpages/methamphetamine.html).

a. What are cited as the most effective therapies for methamphetamine addiction?

b. How does methamphetamine act on the brain and what are its long-term consequences?

c. What age group seems to have the highest use occurrence?

FOR FURTHER READING

McNeece, C. A., & DiNitto, D. M. (2005). *Chemical dependency: A systems approach* (3rd ed.). Boston: Pearson, Allyn & Bacon.

This is a very useful book for further reading or as a resource for term papers on topics related to substance abuse and addiction. The 16 chapters provide quite comprehensive treatment of the theories related to the causes and consequences of addiction, intervention, the legal and social policy context, and issues of chemical dependency in such special, at-risk populations as: youths, older adults, persons with disabilities, sexual minorities, and women.

Rapp, R. C. (2006). Strengths-based case management: Enhancing treatment for persons with substance abuse problems. In D. Saleebey (Ed.), *The strengths perspective in social work practice* (4th ed., pp. 128–147). Boston: Pearson, Allyn & Bacon.

Richard Rapp's writings on strengths perspective are always instructive and inspiring. His current work on strengths perspective in case management work with people who abuse various substances is very insightful. Recognizing that this population is one that is often believed to be "difficult and resistant," Rapp nonetheless turns to the client/social worker relationship as one of the key mechanisms that underpins effective treatment. As a result of his research, on which this article is based, Rapp concludes that "the warm, genuine and mentoring relationship noted by individuals in this study" (p. 146) should remain an integral part of either long-term or short-term case management with this population. The segments of client responses gleaned from the research and quoted in this article will be heartwarming and affirming to social workers and students alike.

Smith, D. C., & Hall, J. A. (2007). Strengths-oriented referrals for teens (SORT): Giving balanced feedback to teens and families. *Health & Social Work, 32* (1), 69–72.

This brief article offers for consideration a very hopeful strategy for delivering results from substance abuse evaluations to adolescents and their families and making effective treatment referrals. The strategy calls on elements of motivational interviewing to "elicit self-change statements through careful questioning and active listening" (p. 69). In this 1-hour interview, scaling questions from solution-focused therapy approaches may also be used to engage and motivate teens in ways that will increase the likelihood that they will follow through with recommendations for treatment.

Straussner, S. L. A., & Harrison, L. (Eds.). (2002). *International aspects of social work practice in the addictions.* New York: Haworth Press.

This book takes the reader beyond the academic literature on substance abuse produced in the United States. It offers perspective on how nations in many parts of the world evolved their policies and programs for dealing with substance abuse. The countries selected for inclusion enable the reader to see remarkable differences in the thinking and experience of other people of the world in reference to substance abuse. Articles for this text were contributed by persons, mostly social workers, from Germany, Israel, Ireland, the Netherlands, Singapore, as well as the United States.

van Wormer, K., & Davis, D. R. (2008). *Addiction treatment: A strengths perspective* (2nd ed.). Belmont, CA: Thomson Brooks/Cole.

Persons interested in the harm reduction approach will find this book especially useful because it develops harm reduction principles and interventions more clearly than most of the social work texts currently available. The final chapter also considers social policy from a harm reduction perspective. The book, however, is not focused on harm reduction. It, instead, explores the biological, psychological, and social dimensions of addiction and its treatment. Throughout, there exists an inherent respect for the person who is addicted, whether that addiction involves alcohol, drugs, gambling, food, or sex. This reflects the strengths perspective that imbues the book with life and hope.

CHAPTER 9

SOCIAL WORK WITH OLDER ADULTS

OUTLINE

Abbie Heinrich

ABBIE HEINRICH

A loud voice wailed persistently. Pat Smythe, BSW, who was toiling over some complicated paperwork at Oak Haven Nursing Home, tried to ignore it at first. He suspected the voice belonged to Abbie Heinrich. Abbie frequently turned on her call light and then yelled if help didn't come quickly. The care staff, occupied with other patients, took time to respond. To make matters worse, Abbie sometimes hit her call light button by accident. Rheumatoid arthritis had left her arms and legs severely contracted so that her movements were clumsy. Aides who responded to Abbie's light sometimes found they weren't needed. So they might ignore the light, muttering, "There she goes again."

Abbie's voice began to take on a hoarse, desperate tone. Pat decided to check on her himself. He put his paperwork aside and headed down the long hallway. He found a frail old woman lying flat on her back with her eyes closed but mouth wide open, emitting insistent cries.

"Abbie!" Pat called loudly, as she was hard of hearing. "What's going on?"

Abbie's eyes flew open, a startlingly clear blue beneath her crown of silver hair, direct and challenging. "Nobody comes when I turn on my call light," she accused, as articulate as any member of the staff. "I turned my light on over half an hour ago."

"I'm really sorry, Abbie," Pat said sincerely. "The aides must be very busy today. What do you need?"

"A pain pill," Abbie responded. "My back is hurting something terrible today." "I'll stop at the nursing station and let them know, Abbie," Pat said soothingly. After a few gentle assurances, he left to find assistance.

Pat found the charge nurse for Abbie's floor, Cindy Murphy, RN, down the hall, and told her about the request for a pain pill. Cindy said thoughtfully, "You know, Pat, Abbie has been asking for a lot more pain medication lately. Maybe we should reevaluate her level of need."

"She is due for a staffing soon," Pat replied. "Let's talk about her pain medication at the next meeting."

Pat was responsible for organizing quarterly meetings for all 80 of his clients, so he sent notices to Abbie's county social worker, Helen Haines, and to Abbie's only "family," a community volunteer named Harriet Locke who served as her power of attorney for health care. He checked back with Cindy, the nurse, and was able to schedule a meeting time that would work for everyone.

Organizing meetings took a lot of Pat's time, but his work responsibilities comprised a great deal more. He held conferences with families to help them understand issues such as living wills and powers of attorney. He mediated roommate disputes; counseled patients with personal problems; made referrals to other departments of the nursing home and to external resources, such as clinical social workers or psychiatrists; filled out numerous forms required by private insurance plans, Medicaid, and Medicare; and even, on occasion, used his handyman skills. For example, Pat had become proficient at cleaning filters in hearing aids and changing batteries, tasks too small to refer to the maintenance department. Needless to say, there was no such thing as a typical day for Pat Smythe at the nursing home.

Helen Haines, BSW, worked for the Department of Human Services in the rural county where Abbie Heinrich was born and raised. Helen was assigned to the unit serving people with developmental disabilities. Many of her 60 clients lived in family care homes out in the community. Helen was responsible for monitoring the care they received. Besides consulting with her individual clients, Helen needed to cultivate professional relationships with biological families, family care home staff, group home managers and staff, sheltered workshop managers and staff, state Developmental Disability Services Office personnel, social workers in nursing homes such as Oak Haven, and the like. Her work was complex and required facilitating cooperation among many different community agencies and staff to secure the best possible care for her clients. Helen's job title was case manager, but in addition to "managing cases," she frequently was involved in community organization work. For example, she often testified at county and state budgetary hearings, describing the need for additional services. She sometimes took clients with her to tell their stories. It distressed her that so many local residents attending the hearings opposed additional services for their vulnerable fellow citizens because of the fear of higher taxes.

A growing proportion of Helen's disabled clients were older adults. She found it necessary to consult regularly with social workers in nursing homes where many of her older clients resided. Once every year, for example, all nursing home clients had to be reassessed according to Medicaid regulations to make sure their placements and levels of care were appropriate.

Helen met with Pat Smythe at Oak Haven Nursing Home more frequently than she met with most nursing home workers. That was because Helen served as Abbie's power of attorney for financial matters, and also because Abbie Heinrich was an unusual case. She had absolutely no family left, and while totally bedridden, she was mentally sharp and needed to socialize. Only social workers were available to check that Abbie had sufficient clothing, to purchase personal toiletries, or to buy the occasional box of chocolates Abbie loved. Helen took more time helping Abbie than she actually had, meaning that she sometimes visited the old woman on her own time. The county discouraged case managers from visiting "unfunded clients" by assigning large case loads. Abbie was classified as an "unfunded client" because the county could not receive partial reimbursement from the state for the cost of supervisory visits by one of its case managers. Only clients participating in special programs providing "community care" were eligible for state funding (this will be explained in more detail later).

Helen knew that she was going beyond the requirements of her job description by visiting Abbie regularly. She also knew that in some ways she had a dual relationship with the elderly woman, a genuine closeness as well as a worker–client relationship, and that the social work code of ethics counseled caution with respect to dual relationships. But Helen had learned from experience that Abbie was much less depressed about her dependent condition when she received regular visits, and practically speaking, Abbie needed someone to buy clothing and other personal items for her. The NASW Code of Ethics states that the social worker's primary ethical responsibility is to promote the well-being of clients. Helen was doing just that.

Helen knew her attention and **advocacy** was crucial for Abbie. In the recent past she had advocated on Abbie's behalf with a psychiatrist, as the psychiatrist had prescribed medication for anxiety that gave Abbie terrible nightmares. Abbie had asked the psychiatrist to stop prescribing this medication, but instead he had prescribed an additional medication that was supposed to quell the nightmares. It didn't, and Helen feared from her extensive experience with older clients that two strong medications would be too much for Abbie's frail body. She discussed this problem with the psychiatrist, but he was unwilling to heed either her or Abbie's concerns. Finally, Helen persuaded Abbie's regular physician to take over all medication; this physician listened to Helen's suggestions and at last, Abbie could sleep again.

Helen knew Abbie needed her services, but still, given her ever-increasing work load, she had recently told the frail old woman that she might have to cut back on visits in the future. Abbie had been a client of Helen's county Department of Human Services for nearly 25 years. An only child, she had been crippled with polio when she was 3 years old. Her parents had cared for her at home for nearly 50 years, but then her mother had died and her father became too frail to carry on alone. County social workers placed Abbie in a group home where she had thrived. Abbie even participated in a sheltered workshop for a time and became a favorite because of her active mind and strong sense of humor. But, cruelly, disease struck again, this time in the form of rheumatoid arthritis. The group home could no longer meet Abbie's physical needs. At that time, Helen had hoped to place Abbie in a skilled family care home, but Abbie required 24-hour care. She needed to be turned regularly throughout the night to prevent bed sores, as she could no longer turn herself. If Abbie were to be placed in a skilled family care home and participate in a community day care program, the state would pay 60 percent of the cost, but the county would have to fund 40 percent. The county's portion would run more than $60,000 annually. The county, unfortunately, was having budgetary problems because more and more **frail elderly** and disabled people were requiring assistance. So Helen was told to place Abbie in a nursing home where Medicaid, funded by the federal government and the state, would pay the whole bill.

Helen had recently asked Pat Smythe if he could help her find a volunteer for Abbie, as Abbie's former power of attorney for health care, a retired social worker, was moving away. A new power of attorney was needed. Although Helen served as Abbie's power of attorney for financial matters, county policy would not allow her to take on both roles due to potential conflict of interest. Pat turned to the Volunteer Department, but there was no one available. He then tried the Department of Pastoral Care, and found Harriet Locke.

When the date for Abbie's staffing meeting arrived, Pat Smythe, Cindy Murphy, Helen Haines, and Harriet Locke all met at the old woman's bedside. Because Abbie was alert and capable, she was an integral part of her own staffing meeting. Pat initiated the discussion.

"Hello, Abbie," he began conversationally. "How are you today?"

"Not so good," Abbie replied. "The pain is bad again today."

"Where does it hurt, Abbie?" Pat asked.

"My back, mostly," she replied.

"On a level of 1 to 10, where '1' means no pain and '10' means such strong pain you can't bear it, where would you say your pain is today?" Pat inquired.

"It's about a 7," Abbie replied.

At this point Cindy, the nurse, joined the conversation. "Is your pain worse today than it was yesterday, Abbie?" she asked.

"It was about the same yesterday," Abbie replied. "My back hurts all the time."

The high pain level concerned everyone present, and it was decided that Cindy would consult with Abbie's doctor. Perhaps the pain medication needed to be changed or provided on a regular, scheduled basis.

Pat then asked Abbie if she had any other issues she wanted to discuss. Abbie complained that the nursing home staff were slow in responding to her call light. Cindy apologized, explaining that staff were busy but promising to ask the aides to respond to the light more quickly. Next, Abbie requested a different roommate, one that she could talk with, as her current roommate was deaf. She then remarked that her own hearing aid wasn't working properly and that she was almost out of her favorite hand lotion. Two of her best blouses hadn't returned from the laundry, and she was afraid they were lost.

Pat promised to investigate the whereabouts of the blouses and to check the hearing aid himself. He promised to have the hearing aid representative who came to Oak Haven every week take a look at the device if he himself couldn't fix it. Pat explained to Abbie that he couldn't provide a different roommate, however—there was no one else available. Softly, as an aside that Abbie couldn't hear, Pat explained to the others that Abbie needed a deaf roommate as she yelled so often that her two former roommates had requested different rooms.

Helen promised to purchase hand lotion and new hearing aid batteries using Abbie's tiny Medicaid allotment, which she managed as financial power of attorney.

Cindy offered another idea—she said she would ask the nurses' aides to greet Abbie and make a little fuss over her even when they were coming in to assist the roommate. That might help Abbie feel less lonely.

Helen had a sudden thought. "It's such a shame," she remarked, "that Abbie can't occupy her mind with reading. She used to love to read, but now she can't even hold a book."

"What about getting her recorded books?" Harriet, the new volunteer, suggested.

"That's not a bad idea," Pat replied. "The local library brings recorded books to the nursing home every 2 weeks. But we have a very limited supply of tape recorders and CD players to loan out here." He turned to Helen. "Does Abbie have enough money in her account to purchase a CD player of her own? CDs wouldn't need to be changed as often as tapes, and Abbie can't change anything by herself."

"I wish it were so," Helen replied. "I think Abbie would enjoy listening to books very much— but unfortunately, there is nowhere near enough money in her account."

Everyone looked sad as they remembered that Abbie was completely dependent on Medicaid and that Medicaid's personal allowance barely covered the cost of a haircut every couple of months.

"Tell you what," said Harriet. "if Abbie says she is interested in listening to recorded books, I'll ask her if she would accept a CD player as an early birthday present. I'd be glad to buy one for her."

"That's good news," Helen said quickly. "Listening to stories might help distract Abbie from her pain as well as provide her with something she could enjoy."

"I agree, I think listening to recorded books would be very good for Abbie," said Cindy, the nurse.

"If Abbie is interested," Pat said, "I can have the Activities Department put her name on their list for the library's outreach program right away. We could probably get some books for her next week."

"Abbie," Pat continued more loudly, turning to the older woman who was straining to hear, "I know it looks like we are plotting in whispers. I apologize. We're talking about books—do you think you might enjoy listening to recorded books, books you could listen to where you wouldn't need to use your hands to turn any pages?"

Abbie's blue eyes gleamed. Her mouth opened in a wide smile, showing every one of her false teeth. "Oh yes!" she said. "I used to love to read, especially mystery stories. Can you bring me mystery books? Lots of them?"

Then she paused and her face fell. "But how could I listen to them?"

Pat explained about the CD player.

And so it was decided. In Pat's next quarterly report, he recorded that Cindy would have Abbie's pain medication reevaluated, that Helen would bring needed personal supplies and that Harriet would provide a CD player. Pat would search for the missing clothes, check Abbie's hearing aid, and make a referral to the Activities Department so that she could receive recorded books from the library. Now, he reflected, all he had to do was meet the needs of his other 79 clients. ■

SOCIAL WORK WITH OLDER ADULTS: A BRIEF HISTORY

Probably most people require ongoing assistance of one kind or another as the years go by. Still, in the early 1800s, older adults in the United States were viewed in a positive light as survivors who had mastered the secrets of long life. By the turn of the 20th century, however, this view had changed. The focus was on the problems of elderly people, rather than their wisdom and strengths.

Social workers in the early years of the profession worked with older adults in institutions and in their own homes where possible, but such work was not emphasized as a special field until the numbers of elderly people began to increase significantly. Nathanson and Tirrito (1998) note that social work with older adults shifted focus over time. In the early years, the profession focused on alleviation of social ills through pursuit of social programs. Then, during the 1920s, the focus shifted to developing practice methods for work with individuals. One school, using Sigmund Freud's psychoanalytic theories, concentrated on treating individual psychopathology among older adults. A second school, the functional, emphasized utilizing health, growth, and self-determination along with social programs to help alleviate problems of older adults. Then, after the onset of the great depression in the 1930s, the emphasis shifted to alleviation of poverty.

Social workers have been instrumental in improving conditions for older adults. For example, Harry Hopkins, a famous social worker, led the nation's relief efforts during the great depression. Hopkins worked hard to achieve passage of the Social Security Act, crucial for the survival of many older Americans (*Hopkins led nation's relief effort*, 1998). Another social worker, Bernard E. Nash, organized the first White House Conference on Aging in 1961. This significant conference (which reconvenes every

10 years) led to such important legislation as Medicare and the Older Americans Act. Nash later became Executive Director of the American Association of Retired Persons (AARP) (*About Bernard Nash*, 2007). Rose Dobroff founded Hunter College of the City of New York's Brookdale Center on Aging in 1975 and served as its director until 1994. In 1995 Dobroff was appointed by President Clinton to the policy committee of the White House Conference on Aging and to membership on the Federal Council on Aging. She co-chaired the U.S. Committee for the Celebration of the United Nations Year of Older Persons in 1999 (*Rose Dobroff, DSW,* 2001).

Soon after the Great Depression, social work practice tended to focus once more on addressing the problems of individual older adults. In the 1960s, however, the War on Poverty inspired a shift back toward developing programs to alleviate the widespread social disadvantages they experienced. Legislation such as Medicare and the Older Americans Act (to be discussed later in this chapter) improved the lot of the elderly as a whole.

While today the profession maintains an interest in alleviating social ills, developing improved practice methods with older individuals has become the main focus again. This parallels the current national portrayal of poverty and other problems as private troubles rather than public issues.

The National Association of Social Workers has developed several continuing education courses to help social workers understand the most important issues surrounding working with older adults (Nadelhaft, 2005) and a new aging credential for social workers (Nadelhaft, 2006). The credentials include:

- Certified Social Worker in Gerontology (CSWG) at the BSW level.
- Certified Advanced Social Worker in Gerontology (CASWG) at the MSW level.
- Certified Advanced Clinical Social Worker in Gerontology (CACSWG) at the advanced clinical level.

THE IMPORTANCE OF GENERALIST SOCIAL WORK

Work with older adults requires practitioners who can operate from a generalist framework; every level of intervention is required, from individual to community. The generalist approach is illustrated well by the work of both of the social workers in this chapter's case study, Pat Smythe and Helen Haines.

Pat Smythe, for example, worked with all 80 of his clients on an individual basis. He frequently met with Abbie individually because she was so alert and yet so frustrated due to her pain and physical limitations. Pat met regularly with family members of most of his clients, answering questions and including them in care conferences. Abbie didn't have any family members left, so Pat took care to consult with Abbie's county social worker, Helen, and the new volunteer, Harriet. Pat used his group work skills effectively in leading quarterly staffing meetings and his organizational skills in arranging and coordinating those meetings. He also helped organize and coordinate a residents' council within the nursing home. In the wider community he, like Helen, lobbied at county and state levels for better funding for services for his indigent clients.

Helen Haines also took care to utilize every level of social work intervention. She met regularly on an individual basis with her clients with disabilities, their biological families, their foster families, their group home care staff, and the like. She organized or participated in care conferences for her clients on a regular basis, wherever they happened to live. She frequently intervened in various organizational settings where her clients were placed to improve the quality of their care—for example, when Abbie complained about the quality of the food she was provided at Oakwood Manor, Helen consulted with Pat Smythe, who called in the home's dietitian. At the community level, Helen frequently lobbied to increase funding to improve services for her clients. Where funding was not available, Helen was creative, sometimes calling on volunteers (see Exhibit 9-1).

EXHIBIT 9-1

Abbie and the Volunteer

"Abbie," murmurs the volunteer, Harriet, peering down into the old woman's face, noting the closed eyes and moving lips, "Today I've brought your DVD player." The CD player Harriet had brought previously had been a big success.

The blue eyes fly open, clear and bright as the Utah desert sky. Recognition dawns, and the eyes smile as wide as the mouth full of false teeth. "Oh, they're beautiful," Abbie says. She means the flowers the volunteer holds in her hands.

"For you, Abbie," Harriet says, lowering the flowers so the old woman can see them, her head still upon the pillow. "A bit of spring. Shall I put them in a vase for you?"

"Yes, yes," Abbie says, and when the flowers are in their vase and the conversation resumes, the volunteer says, again, "and today I've brought you your new DVD player, Abbie."

The blue eyes narrow. "I'm not so sure about that machine," she says. "I have my Bible channel on the TV, and I get the news, and the gospel, and that's what I want to hear."

"But Abbie," says Harriet, who has spent a weekend finding just the right DVD and a table stand for it small enough to fit in her half of the little nursing home room, "wouldn't you like to see movies? They'd show right on your TV screen. Like the movie *The Sound of Music*. Wouldn't you like to see that?"

"Saw it when I was younger," says Abbie. "Didn't like it. I like my Channel 30, where they teach every chapter of the Gospel. I think you should watch Channel 30. You know, only those who are saved are going to go to heaven. I've been praying for you, but it would help if you would watch Channel 30."

"But Abbie," says the volunteer, "we could get Gospel movies—maybe like *The Ten Commandments*. You'd have more choice of things you'd be able to watch."

"Saw it," she said. The blue eyes closed.

"But Abbie, remember your care conference last week, when the nurse and the social worker asked you about a DVD player and you said you might like one?"

"Well, I wasn't sure that day, and there was a lot else we were talking about, like fixing my hearing aid."

"Wouldn't you give the DVD a try, just once? Try something new?"

"Well, I suppose I might—but you know, I couldn't see it anyway."

"But Abbie, you watch TV all day!"

—And then the volunteer stops. Stares down at the ancient figure, tiny in the bed below her. Legs contacted into a frog-like heap beneath the blankets. Arthritic hands contracted into flannel-covered braces. Head propped carefully on a pillow on a hospital bed that has cranked lower year by year, year by year, easing pressure on a painful back.

Harriet suddenly sees Abbie's eyes in her own mind's eye—closed—always—when she comes to visit—the TV always on. She lowers herself by the bed, tips her head back where Abbie's is tipped and sees— only the ceiling, only the ceiling.

"Oh Abbie," Harriet sighs. "You don't watch TV at all, do you."

"Not any more," Abbie replies. "But I hear it. I hear my Gospel every day. And last week I saw an angel. Right in my room. She had the most beautiful smile."

"Tell you what, Abbie," says the volunteer. "I'll return the DVD."

SOCIAL WORK ROLES AND SERVICES FOR OLDER ADULTS

Social workers like Pat Smythe and Helen Haines must take on many roles when solving the complex problems that come their way. Creativity, flexibility, and dedication of purpose are required. In return, their work is constructive, rewarding, and often exciting. Results may be tangible and immediate or take considerable time, but older adults are often stimulating and appreciative clients.

Bellos and Ruffolo (1995) identify a variety of roles that social workers with older adults may assume and services in which they may become involved: **case management** (or coordination of care), advocacy, individual and family counseling, grief counseling, adult day care services, crisis intervention services, adult foster care services, adult protective services, respite care services, support and therapeutic groups, transportation and housing assistance, counseling, therapy, and advocacy services. These authors find that social workers constitute a significant portion of the network of service providers for older adults (see Exhibit 9-2).

Case management is probably the primary role utilized today by social workers in working with frail or ill older adults. Rosengarten (2000, p. 100) describes the goals of this kind of case management as:

1. Helping older adults remain safely, independently, and happily within their own homes and communities for as long as possible.

2. Helping older adults and their families to cope with transitions to more dependent status when needed (such as living with a family member or aide on a part-time or full-time basis; accepting nutritional and health care interventions; assisting with finances, transportation, and so on).

3. Helping those older adults and their families who need to consider a move to a more protected living environment, such as senior housing, enriched housing, a continuing care facility, or a nursing home.

Case managers also need to monitor client services to make sure they actually meet the needs of each particular client, and assist clients and their families to navigate

---

EXHIBIT 9-2

Social Work Roles with Older Adults

Case management	Adult foster care services
Advocacy services	Adult protective services
Individual and family counseling	Respite care services
Grief counseling	Support and therapeutic groups
Adult day care services	Transportation and housing assistance
Crisis intervention services	Psychotherapy

the increasingly complex systems of services, programs, and agencies that serve older adults (Austin and McClelland, 2003).

WHO ARE OUR OLDER ADULTS?

In terms of both total number and percentage of the population, more and more Americans are reaching the age of 65. In 1900, there were approximately 3.1 million Americans over 65, or about 4.1 percent of the population. By 2004, however, the percentage of Americans over 65 had more than tripled, comprising 12.4 percent of the population, about one person in eight, or 36.3 million. The population is expected to reach 55 million by 2020 (*A profile of older Americans*, 2005).

Should a person over 65 be considered "old"? Traditionally, 65 has been considered old indeed—time to retire, certainly. That is because life expectancy at the turn of the century was only 47 years. Today, however, life expectancy in the United States is 79.6 years for women and 74.2 years for men (*A profile of older Americans*, 2005). Perhaps surprising to some, the average life span of Americans is not the highest in the world. We do not even fall among the top 10 nations for longevity. Those are, respectively, Japan, Sweden, Hong Kong, Iceland, Canada, Spain, Australia, Israel, Switzerland, and France (Lamb, 2004).

American women who reach the age of 65 can expect to live another 19.8 years, and men who reach this age can expect to live another 16.8 years. Thus, 65 doesn't seem as old as it once did. The population of Americans over 65 is expected to exceed 70 million by 2030. The number of people over 100—64,658 in 2004—is expected to increase to more than 380,000 by 2030 (*A profile of older Americans*, 2005; Naleppa and Reid, 2003).

Geographical Distribution

Contrary to popular belief, most older adults do not move to warmer climates immediately upon retirement. In fact, older people are less likely to move than adults of other age groups; only about a quarter of those who do move go out of state. Still, about half of adults over 65 live in only nine states: California, Florida, New York, Texas, Pennsylvania, Ohio, Illinois, Michigan, and New Jersey. Looking at population patterns in a different way, in only eight states do older adults comprise 14 percent or higher of the total population: Florida, West Virginia, Pennsylvania, North Dakota, Iowa, Maine, South Dakota, and Rhode Island.

Most persons over 65 live in metropolitan areas today—about half live in the suburbs, 27.2 percent in central city areas, and 22.6 percent in nonmetropolitan or rural areas (*A profile of older Americans*, 2005).

Marital Status

Marital status is an important factor for older adults because at this stage of life a spouse is a significant resource for independent living. Women live longer on the average than men; nearly half of women over the age of 65 are widowed. Their chance of remarriage is low because there are nearly four times as many widows as widowers among older adults. The high proportion of women increases with age. Less than 30 percent of women over 75 live with a spouse, and half live alone (*A profile of older Americans*, 2005). Women generally take care of their husbands until they die, and then the women often have to cope on their own.

Employment

In general, labor force participation by older people has been falling. At the turn of the century, for example, two-thirds of men over 65 were employed; today, about 19 percent of men over 65 are employed. However, employment of women over 65 has shown a different pattern: it increased from about 8 percent in 1900 to over 10 percent in 1956; it fell to a low of 7.3 percent in 1985 and has fluctuated between 8 and 10 percent since 1988 (*A profile of older Americans*, 2005).

Because the huge baby boom generation will begin to reach the age of 65 in 2010, it is likely that more and more older adults will need to remain in the workforce, at least part-time. Traditional pension plans providing adequate income for retirement are becoming increasingly rare.

Economic Status

Economic concerns regarding the baby boom generation aside, statistics reveal increased economic security among people aged 65 and over in recent years. In 1960, fully a third of older Americans were poor. Their economic situation today has improved in large part due to federal government initiatives such as indexing Social Security benefits to inflation, Medicare, and Supplementary Security Income (see Chapters 3 and 6). The greater financial stability of older adults today has been widely publicized and unfortunately tends to pit the elderly against other groups competing for resources. However, many retired people experience great difficulty making ends meet.

In 2005, 10.1 percent of older Americans had incomes below the official U.S. poverty line, up slightly from the historic low of 9.7 percent in 1999 (*Poverty among individuals*, 2005). The poverty line, determined by multiplying the cost of the U.S. Department of Agriculture's emergency food basket times 3, assumes that people over 65 eat less than younger people. This may or may not be true for any given older adult and tends to result in poverty statistics that understate the actual prevalence and experience of poverty.

Members of ethnic minority groups and women are especially likely to be poor among older adults. For example, in 1999 the median net worth of households headed by older African Americans was $13,000, compared with $181,000 for households headed by older whites (*Facts and figures*, 2006). These figures are so shocking that the Administration on Aging adds a footnote asserting that they are not typographical errors. The percentage of elderly African Americans and Hispanics with incomes below the poverty level in 2004 (23.9 and 18.7 percent, respectively) was over twice as high as that for older whites (7.5 percent). Poverty increases with age and is highest among women who are members of ethnic minorities. Fully 39.9 percent of older Black and Hispanic women had incomes below the poverty line in 2004 (*Facts and figures*, 2006).

Social Security is a major source of income for more than 90 percent of older adults today, lifting many out of poverty. More than two-thirds receive more than half their income from the program. The average benefit in 2005 was $955 per month for a retired worker and $1,574 for a couple. More than three-quarters of Black and Hispanic elderly, and more than three quarters of all unmarried women, receive more than half their income from Social Security (*General information on Social Security*, 2006).

When the Social Security Act of 1935 was passed, it was not intended to be a sole source of income but rather to supplement people's pensions and savings. However, for many older adults, pensions and savings are nonexistent. The poorest elderly can receive Supplemental Security Income (SSI, see Chapter 3) in addition to any Social Security income for which they may be entitled, but SSI even in combination with Social Security does not raise its recipients' total income above the poverty line.

Housing

Despite the popular belief that most elderly people live in nursing homes, in fact, only 4.4 percent resided in one of these institutions at any given time in 2004; at least half of these institutionalized elderly suffered from Alzheimer's disease or other dementia (*A profile of older Americans*, 2005). The majority of older adults today live alone or in an independent household.

Older heads of household usually own their own homes (80 percent) rather than renting (20 percent); nearly three-quarters of these homeowners own their homes free and clear. Not surprisingly, their houses are older on average than those of younger people (median year of construction is 1965); 5.2 percent of the houses have physical problems such as rotting window frames or leaky roofs. More than one-third of older homeowners spend more than a quarter of their income on housing; three-quarters of renters spend more than a quarter of their income on housing (*A profile of older Americans*, 2005).

Although many of the poorest older Americans need safe, low-cost housing, the federal government has not invested in constructing additional units for decades.

Physical and Mental Health

The health of older adults is better than younger people may believe: in 2004, for example, 36.7 percent of all noninstitutionalized older adults rated their health as excellent or very good (compared with 66 percent of younger adults). But only a little over a quarter of older Blacks, Hispanics, and Native Americans reported their health as very good or excellent, as compared with nearly 40 percent of whites (*A profile of older Americans*, 2005).

Most older people experience at least one chronic health condition. Of these, the most frequently reported are hypertension, arthritis, heart disease, cancer, diabetes, and sinusitis. Approximately 27.3 percent of older adults between 65 and 74 who reside in the community have difficulty performing their **activities of daily living (ADLs),** such as cooking, eating, dressing, bathing, and toileting; the percentage increases dramatically as these adults grow older. Of older adults living in nursing homes, 93.3 percent have difficulty with one or more ADLs. Most of the institutionalized elderly today are over 85 years old (*A profile of older Americans*, 2005).

Despite the great improvement in availability of medical care for older adults through the Medicare and Medicaid insurance programs, which cover virtually all older people, the elderly today face substantial health costs that are not covered. Medicare premiums and co-insurance make appropriate medical care out of reach for many. Some older adults (approximately 61 percent) purchase additional private health insurance; the most impoverished of the older people still living out in the community (9 percent) receive assistance from Medicaid (*A profile of older Americans*, 2005). Still, millions of elderly have inadequate health insurance coverage. This is an important problem because chronic health conditions such as those listed earlier are persistent and afflict a large percentage. Such conditions can become long term, if not permanent, requiring adjustments in lifestyle and continuing care and attention.

Another problem for older people dependent on Medicare is the issue of prescription drugs. Until 2006, persons enrolled in Medicare received no assistance in purchasing prescribed medications. Finally, 40 years after Medicare was first enacted, a bill authorizing a drug benefit (known as Medicare Part D) was passed in 2005, taking effect in 2006. Indigent persons receiving Medicaid were enrolled automatically by the government; some older persons participating in Medicare HMOs (health maintenance organizations, discussed in Chapter 6) were also automatically enrolled. But of the older adults allowed freedom of choice, only about 1 million, or 4 percent, of the 25 million eligible signed on by the starting date. That is because the program is very confusing. Medicare Part D seems primarily designed to increase drug company profits: drug companies hired more than 800 lobbyists and spent more than $100 million in Washington to pressure Congress to insert language in Part D legislation that forbade the government to use its collective buying powers to negotiate prices or price controls (*The new Medicare "Part D" drug "benefit,"* 2006).

An early task of the Democratic Congress that took charge in 2007 was to confront the drug industry, so far without success as this chapter is being written.

Alzheimer's Disease   Alzheimer's disease is one of the most serious chronic conditions afflicting older adults today. It affects both physical and mental functioning. First described by Alois Alzheimer in 1907, the disease produces tiny lesions in the brain. It causes irreversible dementia, or loss of one's mental faculties. Symptoms of Alzheimer's disease are progressive; eventually, the afflicted person loses use of both body and mind. People with this condition generally live 4 to 6 years after diagnosis but some live as long as 20. Today more than 5 million people are affected, approximately 500,000 of them under 65 and 4.9 million over 65 (*What is Alzheimers*, 2007).

Alzheimer's disease is the most common cause of dementia in older persons, but it can be difficult to diagnose. There is no specific lab test that can confirm a diagnosis, and symptoms can be confused with depression, stroke, and many other debilitating conditions. Symptoms progress at different rates for different people and vary with the individual; one person may have difficulty with speech, for example, while another has difficulty with spatial relations and gets lost easily. Some people become severely depressed or agitated. Unfortunately, over time, every patient gets worse and eventually dies.

Despite the dismal long-term prognosis for Alzheimer's patients, new treatments are being developed that can help slow the progression of symptoms. These include medications for depression, psychosis, and agitation. While Medicare, Medicaid, and private insurance pay for much of the medical care, families assume most of the cost (which exceeds $100 billion nationally) and provide 75 percent of the personal care. Families of these patients need attention: at least half of primary caregivers develop significant psychological distress (Small et al., 1997; *Alzheimer's disease statistics*, 2006). Prolonged stress is likely to develop into physical illness.

Providing supportive care to families of Alzheimer's patients can be an important role for social workers; social workers can also help maximize the functioning of afflicted elderly people by helping them exercise whatever faculties they have left. Structured small-group activities are excellent for this purpose and are comparatively easy to organize in nursing home settings. Approximately half of nursing home residents suffer from Alzheimer's disease (Naleppa and Reid, 2003).

Mental Health Challenges The aging process is inevitably accompanied by personal losses. Body strength declines, for example, and one tends to suffer more chronic illness. Spouses, family members, and friends may die. Retirement brings loss of income and loss of the worker role; age discrimination limits one's ability to secure paying employment. The older adult gradually loses the necessary resources to remain independent. Independence, of course, is a major cultural measure of personal worth, and its loss undermines self-esteem. Chronic depression can result (Nathanson and Tirrito, 1998).

Of the elderly who become institutionalized in nursing homes, well over half suffer from cognitive deficit, or loss of mental acuity; only about 5 percent of community-based elderly people suffer from this condition. As discussed earlier, Alzheimer's disease is an increasing cause of mental confusion in older adults. In earlier stages of the disease, patients can be aware of their diagnosis; depression and anxiety are likely to follow. Support from social workers, along with medication (which social workers may monitor), can help ease the resultant emotional pain.

Ethnicity

The population of older Americans is becoming increasingly diverse. In 2004, for example, slightly more than 18 percent of persons over 65 were of ethnic minority heritage. By 2020 it is projected that 23.6 percent of the elderly will be of ethnic minority heritage, and the percentage is expected to increase substantially beyond that time. Of the total elderly population itself, African Americans constituted 8.2 percent. Hispanics (of any race) constituted 6 percent; Asian or Pacific Islanders, 2.9 percent; and Native Americans, less than 1 percent. Persons who identified themselves as belonging to more than one race constituted about 0.6 percent (*A profile of older Americans*, 2005).

Life-span expectations differ among various ethnic groups. For example, the average life span for African Americans is currently many years less than that for whites, 71.1 years on average as compared to 77.1 (*Facts and figures*, 2006).

OLDER ADULTS AND THEIR FAMILIES

Research on Family Strengths

There has been a myth in our times that Americans abandon their elderly parents, callously storing them away in nursing homes, never to see them again except perhaps at funerals. Although such tragedies undoubtedly do occur, research consistently refutes this myth with respect to most families. For one thing, older adults in need of long-term care have been relatively rare until recent times. Stories about families caring for parents until death in the early days of this country may have been true, but that death would probably have occurred rather quickly. The average life expectancy in 1900 was more than 25 years less than it is today. More families are caring for elderly members today than ever before, and for many more years. The monetary value of family care is estimated at $257 billion annually (*Providing care for another adult*, 2004). Many older adults are living so long today that a four-generation family is common; some families have five. Conner (2000) even offers a term for this type of structure: the "beanpole family."

Greene (2000) points out that family developmental tasks have traditionally centered on the nuclear family and child rearing. Families, however, also encounter developmental tasks in later life. Establishing a mutually satisfying parent–child relationship in later years involves the issue of dependency, a normal and important family process. Dealing with issues of dependency constructively involves both a realistic acceptance by the older adult of strengths and limitations and the ability of the adult child to accept a caregiving role. The adult child must also recognize his or her own strengths and limitations.

A proud family of four generations.

Unpaid informal support from family and friends is by far the most prevalent form of long-term care for older adults today. Older adults turn first to their spouses for assistance when needed, then their children, followed by friends and neighbors. Only when these potential resources are lacking or unable to assist do the elderly turn to formal service delivery systems (Naleppa and Reid, 2003).

Older Adults as Caregivers

Family members do not just assist their older adult relatives. Older adults are often caregivers themselves. First of all, many care for each other. Married elderly, for example, particularly women, frequently take care of a spouse through long-term illness, including dementia, right up until death brings release. Many others also care for relatives and friends.

Older people also frequently care for children. Sometimes they provide child care for grandchildren while the children's parents work. But more than that, today many families are headed by older adults who are assuming increasing responsibility for raising grandchildren. By 2003, 4 million children resided in households headed by grandparents, a 30 percent increase from the previous decade (Llana, 2006).

The primary reasons compelling many children to be cared for by their grandparents are substance abuse, incarceration of the parents, and child maltreatment. Custodial grandparents often suffer increased health problems because of their additional responsibilities. Others experience increased psychological distress and social isolation. Innovative programs have been developed in a few places to help support their caretaking efforts, such as case management, support groups, parenting skills groups, respite care, assistance with legal concerns such as adoption, and welfare benefits; informational audiotapes regarding health, caregiving, and well-being have been developed to assist (Kropf and Wilks, 2003).

Today older adults are adopting children more often. Many, for example, who were serving as foster parents in 1997, the year of the Adoption and Safe Families Act, decided to adopt their wards. This act encouraged states to speed up adoptions of children unlikely to have the opportunity to return to their biological families. Rather than risk losing the children in their care, many foster parents over the age of 60 decided to adopt. Because children older than 5 are considered hard to place, many of the older adults who applied were allowed to do so. Even an 80-year-old received permission to adopt (Stevens, 2001).

An unusual caretaking service by older adults is taking place in prisons today. Given the very long prison terms that are all too common today, more and more inmates are growing old and dying behind bars. Some prisons have developed hospice programs, and the response has been heartwarming. Not all inmate hospice volunteers are older adults themselves, but many are (see Exhibit 9-3).

Caregiver Stress and the "Sandwich Generation"

While millions of families provide care to their older members with goodwill and grace, providing help to older adults can be stressful. Activities of daily living such as

---

EXHIBIT 9-3

Older Inmates Help Others

Corrections departments began to recognize the need for hospice services in the mid 1980s; as the size of the U.S. prison population grew, longer sentences were mandated, and the number of older inmates mushroomed. Tougher attitudes toward crime meant parole boards were less likely to give "compassionate releases" to sick inmates. More began dying inside the walls (2,500 in 1998).

The first prison hospice programs opened in 1987. Now there are about 20, with at least a dozen more being planned. Oregon State Penitentiary trained its first inmate volunteers in 1999, using the same 36-hour course community hospice workers get. "It's amazing to watch men caring for other men," says Chaplain Judith Steele, who is on two interdisciplinary teams running the hospice. "In community hospices, most volunteers are women. . . . In here, men with tattoos, used to being macho and not showing emotion . . . you watch them tenderly shave their friends, or feed or bathe them. This program gives permission to an inmate to have empathy and demonstrate it. Nowhere else is that permission given—prison rules prevent you doing favors for other inmates."

SOURCE: Quoted from Jane Lampman. (2000, July 23). Caring for sick, prisoners learn compassion. *The Christian Science Monitor,* pp. 1, 4.

---

shopping, cooking, cleaning, helping with laundry, and bathing all take time and money. Even more time is required when caring for an elderly person who is ill.

A survey conducted jointly by the American Association of Retired Persons (which usually goes by the more familiar name, AARP) and the National Alliance for Caregiving estimates that there are more than 44 million Americans providing unpaid care to another adult. The study finds that almost 6 in 10 caregivers have responsibilities to an employer at the same time that they are providing unpaid care to a loved one. Most caregivers thus employed have had to make adjustments to their paid work life. Women provide the majority of unpaid caregiving, but men participate also; almost 40 percent of unpaid caregivers are male. The average length of care is 4.3 years, but caregiving lasts for more than 5 years in nearly a third of the cases (*Providing care for another adult,* 2004).

Many caregivers have children as well as older family members for whom to care: caregivers with responsibilities to both the generation above and below are known as the sandwich generation. Their conflicting duties create additional stress (see Exhibit 9-4). A survey conducted by the NASW with the New York Academy of Medicine in 2006 found that women of the sandwich generation have a higher level of stress than the rest of the population and are not as happy. Four in 10 have sought professional help to assist in coping with their heavy responsibilities; 2 in 10 have consulted a social worker. The survey indicated that only a little more than a third of respondents were aware that social workers provide assistance to aging adults and their caregivers, prompting the NASW to consider new ways to reach a wider percentage of this population (Stoesen, 2007).

Elder Abuse

Most families do their best to provide for their older members. But given the pressures of caregiving, it may not be surprising that reports of elder abuse are rising nationwide. A recent report estimates that somewhere between 1 and 3 million older

---

EXHIBIT 9-4

The "Sandwich" Generation

At issue is the cost of providing care to greater numbers of elderly. . . . The phenomenon is also putting a squeeze on more families, who find they are unprepared to handle the financial and emotional challenges of aging parents, growing children, and their own retirement. . . .

Colleen Galligan has first-hand knowledge of the challenges that can confront the sandwich generation. Last year her mother became physically unable to care for herself. Ms. Galligan and her three siblings shared the responsibility of caring for her, preparing meals, scheduling doctor's appointments, and finding someone to help during the day. Money was also tight.

"The most stressful thing to me was having small children and caring for mom at the same time because it put so much extra work on my husband," says Galligan, who also had a full-time job.

SOURCE: Quoted from E. L. Spaid. (1996, November 4). Florida leads states in effort to provide more elder care. *The Christian Science Monitor*, p. 3.

---

adults over 65 have been injured or mistreated by someone on whom they depended for care and protection (Schlesinger, 2006).

Abuse may occur in several ways (Kosberg & Nahmiash, 1996; Naleppa and Reid, 2003):

- Physical maltreatment, in which pain or injury is inflicted.
- Sexual abuse.
- Verbal or emotional abuse, in which a person is insulted, humiliated, or threatened.
- Material or financial abuse, in which money or property is misused.
- Passive or active neglect, or not providing adequate food, shelter, and other necessities for daily living.
- Violation of civil rights, or forcing someone to do something against his or her wishes.
- Self-neglect, in which a person retains responsibility for his or her own care but manages poorly in areas such as nutrition and hygiene.

Self-neglect, which is especially common among the elderly, can raise ethical dilemmas for social workers who serve this population. Many elderly people choose, for example, to live in their own homes, but they may grow too frail to cope well alone. Some suffer injuries that temporarily prevent them from being able to provide adequate self-care. Some elderly people in need refuse assistance even when it is offered; social workers can face difficult dilemmas involving client self-determination versus physical safety.

Increased social services to older adults, including day care for frail elderly and **respite care,** or temporary relief for their caregivers, could help prevent a large proportion of the elder abuse occurring today.

WORKING WITH OLDER ADULTS OF DIVERSE BACKGROUNDS

Ethnic and Cultural Minorities

The number of older adults who are members of ethnic minority groups is growing faster than average. Because of discrimination and other factors, minority elderly people are especially vulnerable to poverty and are likely to have an increased need for social services. The NASW (1994, pp. 17–18) has made the following recommendations for effective practice with minority elderly persons:

1. Presenting problems should be defined in terms of family and community systems and the culture, ethnicity, and heritage of the client.

2. Social work interventions should be based on the client's and the family's definition of problems, goals, needs, and solutions. Service plans should be based on the older person's strengths rather than deficits.

3. Programs should be preventive in nature whenever possible.

4. Services should be family and community based.

5. Service planning should be designed to enhance choices offered. For example, program options should include home health services, respite care, family support groups, and in-home care, along a continuum to nursing home care. Resource and program development activities should be undertaken to ensure the availability of services.

6. Services must be tailored to fit older people rather than forcing older people to fit into categorical services.

7. Services must be accessible.

8. Development of services should reflect appropriate roles for the life cycle of individuals.

Olson (2003) points out the sad fact that ethnic minorities have a greater need for services in their older years than whites due to the accumulated affects of discrimination and oppression, yet they have far fewer resources to obtain them. Older Black, Hispanic, Asian, and Native American women in particular suffer a high degree of poverty, which severely limits their options. Extended family networks provide as best they can, but loyal family caregivers, often also impoverished, thus undergo a heaven burden.

Gay and Lesbian Older Adults

Another minority that has had to learn to live in at least two different cultural systems simultaneously comprises gay and lesbian older adults. If they are female, persons of color, or poor, they have had to survive multiple barriers. Many have chosen not to reveal their sexual orientation in fear of rejection by family and friends. Yet many serve as caregivers for parents, spouses, or partners.

EXHIBIT 9-5

The R-E-S-P-E-C-T Model for Serving Older Gays and Lesbians

R—Review existing policies and practices at one's agency. How are lesbian/gay consumers treated at the present time?

E—Educate administration, staff, and residents about a range of taboo topics such as human sexualities and gender differences.

S—Share ideas and experiences for the unlearning of homophobia and heterosexism.

P—Promote diversity and prevention of homophobic practices. Illustrate the comparison between heterosexism and other "isms" such as racism, sexism, and classism.

E—Explore and evaluate areas for continued learning and teaching.

C—Change belief systems and taboos that devaluate diversity, including sexual diversity.

T—Transition to a diversity-friendly facility that offers support and attention to older gays and lesbians.

SOURCE: P. Metz. (1997). Staff development for working with lesbian and gay elders. In J. K. Quam (Ed.), *Social services for senior gay men and lesbians* (pp. 35–45). New York: Hawthorn Press.

Gay and lesbian older adults have the same concerns as all older adults: health care, housing, employment, transportation, and so forth. They need support, both formal and informal, to help cope with the ongoing concerns of old age. This represents a challenge for social workers because many gays and lesbians choose to remain invisible due to fear of social stigma and prejudice. Many remain isolated and alone (Kochman, 1997).

Schope (2005) has found that gay men and lesbian women differ in their perceptions of the aging process. Gay men tend to have more negative views of aging and to consider themselves "old" as early as age 39. Lesbians, on the other hand, reject what they view as male bias regarding age. Some even form social organizations with names such as CRONES or OWLS, terms honoring old age. Schope concluded that gay males in particular face a difficult future, especially as AIDS has devastated their support networks.

Metz (1997), given his perception of the needs of this vulnerable population, recommends a model called R-E-S-P-E-C-T in meeting their special needs (see Exhibit 9-5).

EMPOWERMENT PRACTICE

Social workers are encouraged to use an empowerment model when working with older adults, to help them enhance coping skills through consciousness raising, education, and support. Healey (2003) suggests that empowerment with older adults should include three basic strategies: assisting older adults, individually and collectively, to define their own needs; promoting conscious awareness of social and economic injustice; and encouraging political action.

Senior centers can be effective settings to assist older adults, providing supportive environments to engage in consciousness-raising and promoting political action about issues of importance to older adults. Encouraging older persons to join advocacy groups such as the AARP or the Gray Panthers can also aid in the process of empowerment.

Empowerment practice can assist older adults to advocate for government policies to improve the conditions of their lives.

SOCIAL POLICY AND OLDER ADULTS: PAST TO PRESENT

Family Care

Historically, before governmental social policies dealing with older adults were developed, services to the elderly were provided almost entirely by their families. This was workable because of the short life span that was the norm at that time and because there were many tasks an elderly parent or relative could perform as a way of reciprocating.

By the late 1800s, however, industrialization had changed family patterns. Grown children tended to move to the cities. Individual achievement as a value took precedence over loyalty to one's extended family. The nuclear family supplanted the extended family as the primary locus of responsibility. Changes such as these undermined family support systems for older adults. The need for new forms of support began to appear. In early times, the only alternatives were the church or almshouse. Later, pension plans were established in some countries.

Early Pension Plans

Germany initiated a compulsory pension program in 1889 that provided a regular source of income for older, retired workers. Employers, workers, and the state each contributed equal amounts to the financing. Britain introduced a pension program in 1908, which permitted general tax revenue to be transferred to elderly poor persons (Huttman, 1985). By comparison, the United States has been slow in developing universal pension plans for the elderly. Some states had pension plans by the 1920s, but they all required a means test (only people with very low incomes could qualify).

Not until the Great Depression did this country enact a nearly universal pension plan for the elderly, via the Social Security Act of 1935. The intent of Title II of this act was to stabilize income for older Americans without the appearance of the "dole," or a government handout. People were required to contribute to Social Security through a special tax during their working life. Thus, they could perceive the program as a contributory "insurance" plan, not charity. Workers who were required to pay Social Security taxes were eligible to receive benefits after retirement, whether rich or poor. In 1939, coverage expanded to include widows and children. Eventually, many other categories such as self-employed people, farm and domestic workers, government workers, the military, and religious personnel were included (Huttman, 1985).

Trends in American Private Pensions

In recent generations, American workers grew accustomed to receiving not only government Social Security benefits but substantial retirement benefits from the companies for which they worked most of their lives. This situation is changing rapidly, however.

Not only do workers tend to change jobs frequently today, due to both personal choice and involuntary layoffs, but companies have seriously underfunded the private **pensions** they have promised. About 44 million Americans are covered by company pension plans today, but these plans are underfunded by about $450 billion. The federal government guarantees benefits through the Pension Benefit Guarantee Corporation (PBGC) but this entity currently faces a $23 billion gap between obligations and income (Smoothing the way to retirement pay, 2006).

In late 2006 the federal government passed the Pension Protection Act, requiring employers to fund pension plans fully (up from 90 percent). While this legislation should help protect American taxpayers from having to subsidize underfunded company pension plans, an expected side effect will be that fewer companies will offer such plans (Trumbull, 2006). Many Americans will need to finance their own retirement in the coming years.

Social Security Today

Social Security is a federal **entitlement program,** a program in which a legal right to receive benefits has been bestowed by law on people who meet certain eligibility criteria. (These criteria vary with the law and the program.) Because of the increasing financial insecurity many older people are experiencing due to loss of traditional pension plans, Social Security benefits are more important today than ever before. They are indexed to inflation, which can help keep poverty at bay. Indexing, however, has become a political football in recent years as conservative politicians attempt to chip away at the program.

Almost all retired persons receive Social Security benefits today. The program, however, was designed only as a supplement to private pensions and personal savings. Americans are poor savers, however, and while more than 80 percent of employees in 1980 worked for companies that provided pensions, only slightly more than 20 percent do so today. Most employees must now save for their own retirement, usually through **tax-sheltered annuities** such as 401(k) plans. Employers often offer to match employee contributions to such plans, but the investment risk lies entirely with the employee (Magnusson, 2006). Thus more and more people are likely to reach retirement age with insufficient funds.

The Social Security program itself is not in any immediate danger financially, despite political wrangling. Social Security taxes generate a substantial surplus at this time. The surplus is invested in government Treasury bonds. By approximately 2017, income from Social Security tax revenue will be less than benefits paid out, so some of the Treasury bonds will have to be redeemed (*General information on Social Security*, 2006). By approximately 2040, the Treasury bonds will be used up; at that time income from Social Security taxes are projected to cover about 70 percent of the benefits owed (*Our fight, keeping Social Security strong*, 2007).

Conservatives, including the commission appointed by the George W. Bush administration, argue that the program should be privatized to allow maximum returns to investors (those who happen to be lucky). However, Jeanne C. Marsh, in an editorial in *Social Work* (2005) points out the dangers of such a plan. Because retiree benefits would continue to be paid in full for a time, while a percentage of worker payments would be diverted to private accounts, the cost to taxpayers would be enormous, up to

$17 trillion. At the same time, retirement security for the average worker would be greatly reduced due to the risks of the stock market.

Decisions regarding Social Security are extremely important, because the program helps support more than retired workers. More than a third of beneficiaries are disabled workers, spouses of retired or disabled workers, and survivors of deceased workers (including their minor children and the widowed parent).

Most people of liberal or progressive political persuasion argue that Social Security is sound as is and can be saved with very slight adjustments in the tax base. Currently, for example, that portion of a wealthy person's income exceeding $90,000 is not subject to the Social Security tax. Including higher incomes in the tax levy would go a long way toward financing the program well into the future.

Supplemental Security Income

Supplemental Security Income (SSI), another federal entitlement program, was initiated in 1972 as an amendment to the Social Security Act of 1935. As explained in Chapter 3, this program was developed to reduce the stigma of public assistance for poor people falling into three categories: the elderly, the blind, and the disabled. It established uniform national eligibility requirements and benefits. Stigma was reduced by allowing people to apply for SSI benefits through federal Social Security offices rather than local "welfare" offices. Benefits, however, although federally established and administered, remain very low.

Housing Assistance

Older adults pay a higher percentage of their income for housing than younger people. To assist with this problem, the Federal Housing Assistance Program, through the U.S. Department of Housing and Urban Development (HUD), subsidized nearly 2 million apartments for poor people, about half of them for the elderly, for many years (Salamon, 1986). However, the Reagan administration slashed HUD funding after the 1980 election; the funding losses have never been restored. In addition, many units of public housing have been demolished as unsafe. Thus, affordable housing has been increasingly out of reach for all of the nation's poor, including older adults. A Republican Congress tried to cut HUD funding entirely in recent years; to save the department, the Democratic Clinton administration converted its programs into a system of block grants to the states. But in 1996, Clinton signed a bill permitting no new applications for rental assistance (Popple & Leighninger, 1999). The Republican G. W. Bush administration continued to reduce funding for low-income housing.

Medicare and Medicaid

Before 1965, most health care costs for older adults were paid by the elderly themselves, with the result that many lacked any care at all. This situation greatly improved after the 1965 passage of Medicare, Title XVIII of the Social Security Act. As noted elsewhere in this book, all persons over 65 qualify for Medicare benefits whether they have paid into the Social Security system or not and whether they are poor or not.

Part A of Medicare pays for hospital care and some follow-up care. Part B pays for some outpatient hospital care and some physicians' services (the elderly must pay a special premium to receive Part B coverage). Neither Part A nor Part B of Medicare pays for prescription drugs, however—a major problem for many older adults with chronic health issues. Nor is nursing home care covered unless licensed nursing services (such as drawing blood) are required. Even then, the number of days covered for nursing home care is limited to 100, and a very small percentage of the actual cost is paid.

Because of rising costs of the Medicare program, benefits frequently change. Medicare Part C offers additional options designed to cut costs, such as health maintenance organizations (HMOs) for older adults. According to Olson (2003), the HMO option did not cut Medicare costs, however. Instead, these programs tended to accept only healthier adults—and so, made large profits. In general, elderly persons today must pay increasingly large **deductibles** (the portion of a given medical expense that must be paid up front before the Medicare program will contribute) and increasing **co-insurance** (percentage of the overall bill). See Chapter 6 for a more complete discussion.

Medicare Part D was enacted in 2005, effective in January 2006. As noted previously, few older adults enrolled voluntarily due to the complexity of the program (indigent adults, those already on Medicaid, were enrolled automatically). Most states offered more than 50 options under private insurance plans. How could an older adult, especially those in their 80s and 90s, make an informed choice?

Those who did make a choice found the "doughnut hole" in drug coverage a shock. The "doughnut hole" is a new concept in health insurance. After $2,500 has been spent on prescription medications for any given person, insurance coverage stops until the enrollee has paid $3,600 out-of-pocket (the doughnut hole). Even more confusing, the initial $2,500 includes not only the out-of-pocket co-pay required of the enrollee (approximately 25 percent of $2,500) but also the benefits paid out by the insurance company. So the average enrollee, after paying a relatively small out-of-pocket total co-pay, enters the doughnut hole. The enrollee then has to pay the full cost of prescription drugs until paying out $3,600. Coverage then resumes with a 5 percent co-pay (Barry, 2006).

With the exception of some HMO plans, Medicare leaves substantial health care costs unmet so that people who can afford to do so purchase private supplementary health insurance policies to cover some of the gaps.

Medicaid came into being in 1965 through an amendment to the Social Security Act, Title XIX. Title XIX was passed at the same time as Medicare, Title XVIII. Medicaid was designed and added specifically to aid older adults with low incomes. This is the program that paid for nursing home care for Abbie Heinrich of our chapter's case study. Medicaid is administered under each state's public welfare system, and benefits differ from state to state. Costs are shared between state and federal governments.

Since 1993, a federal law has required that states recover the money spent on long-term care of a Medicaid beneficiary after the beneficiary dies. In many cases, the only asset to seize is the deceased recipient's former home. This requirement is exempted if a surviving spouse or child under 21 lives in the home, but in many cases the person living there is an adult child who cared for the deceased for many years. He or she may have given up a former home and a paying job to serve as caregiver. If the adult child cannot buy the deceased parent's property, he or she will have to leave. Often the families involved are pitifully poor—the average monetary recovery per state is only about $5,000. Thus, to fatten state coffers, an indigent family loses its only asset (Green, 2006).

Medicaid pays for certain hospital expenses, physicians' expenses, prescription drugs, nursing home fees, and other health-related services. Benefits have been changing in recent years, and in general poor people are being required to pay more of their own fees as part of cost containment legislation.

Food Stamps

Food stamps, also discussed in Chapter 3, are another federal entitlement program available to poor older adults. Eligibility requirements involve both income and the number of persons in a given household who presumably share income. While only a small proportion of eligible older people apply for food stamps, nearly 1.5 million households containing elderly people report inadequate nutrition to maintain good health. Reasons for not applying for food stamps include lack of information, application anxiety, the stigma of charity, and expected low benefits. Older persons who apply tend to be extremely poor, with household incomes averaging about $605 per month. Households receive an average of $166 a month in food stamps; persons living alone, nearly 80% of applicants, receive $44 in stamps (*FRAC special analysis fact sheet*, 2006).

Because so many Americans of all ages are hungry, applications for food stamps have been increasing in recent years. But the Republican administration of George W. Bush has regularly proposed reducing funding for the program.

Current Innovative Programs and Alternative Lifestyles

A major challenge faced by older people is the prospect of living alone when family members have scattered or died. Co-housing is a concept developed in the United States by architect Charles Durant of Berkeley, California, who imported the idea from Denmark in the 1980s. Co-housing helps meet many needs for approximately 5,000 older Americans today, and an additional 100 co-housing communities are currently in development. People work together for 2 years, designing their housing together with the assistance of architects skilled in creating shared living spaces (Brown, 2004). There is now a National Shared Housing Resource Center that helps people (not only older adults) locate shared-living opportunities (Cox, 2005; National Shared Housing Resource Center, 2006).

Many communities are developing volunteer "friendly visiting" programs such as Little Brothers–Friends of the Elderly in Jamaica Plain, Massachusetts. Volunteers are matched with older adults living alone who otherwise would rarely have opportunity for social interaction (Gardner, 2006).

Loneliness among older people is not just an American problem, but worldwide. For example, a 79-year-old man put himself up for adoption in Italy. Although this man owned several pets and a treasured book collection, he felt so desperate for human contact after his wife's death that he advertised in a newspaper, offering to pay a healthy monthly fee to live with a family and teach their children. Fortunately, the man received a new home where his talents were wanted and appreciated, and the issue of the plight of the elderly gained new attention in Italy (Aire, 2004).

MORE FEDERAL LEGISLATION RELATING TO OLDER ADULTS

The Older Americans Act

The mid-1960s were important years for the elderly. The Older Americans Act of 1965 focused on coordinating comprehensive services for all people over 60, not just the poor. It established the Administration on Aging at the federal level and authorized state units and local area agencies on aging. These units assess the needs of the older adults and try to develop programs to meet them. State and local autonomy is permitted within federal guidelines. In 1993, President Clinton raised the position of commissioner of the Administration on Aging to an assistant secretary level (Torres-Gil & Puccinelli, 1995).

Amendments to the act in 1981 established priorities: information and referral services (including those for non-English-speaking elderly), transportation, in-home assistance (homemakers, health aides, visiting and telephone reassurance efforts), and legal services. Nursing home ombudsman programs (programs to investigate complaints) were required, as were nutrition programs.

Funding under the Older Americans Act has always been low. Still, it supports nutrition programs, senior centers (which often house the nutrition programs, consisting of low-cost congregate meals for all persons over 60), and information and referral services. In 1999 the National Family Caregiver Support Program was authorized under the act, calling for coordination between state and other community service programs to provide support services for caregivers. However, funding levels continue to decrease under Republican control of the federal government (Older Americans Act, 2006).

In these times of social service cutbacks, many argue that services should be provided only for older adults who are also poor or disabled. However, others point out that two-tiered services separate people according to economic status, place a stigma on services, and result in competition for scarce resources instead of cooperative self-help efforts. National organizations such as the AARP and the Gray Panthers support offering services to all elderly people. (See the Up for Debate box.)

The Social Services Block Grant

Before the 1970s, people who applied for financial assistance received services from social workers in public welfare departments, who routinely assessed social service needs while determining eligibility for financial aid. However, beginning in the early 1970s, eligibility for financial aid was determined by clerical staff who made no further assessment of need (Cox & Parsons, 1994).

Social services for older adults began to be funded by the Social Services Block Grant in the mid-1970s. It is a limited source of financing for homemaker services and adult day care. Originally known as Title XX of the Social Security Act, implemented in 1975, this program was renamed and modified under the Omnibus Budget Reconciliation Act of

UP FOR DEBATE

Proposition: Services under the Older Americans Act should be means-tested.

YES	NO
Funding under this act is low, so that services should be limited to the most needy.	All older Americans benefit from balanced meals and an opportunity for social interaction.
Taxpayers are unwilling to subsidize services for all elderly.	All taxpayers will one day be elderly. Services for all can help make old age a rewarding experience for everyone.
Poor elderly need help the most.	Services limited only to the poor separate people according to economic status and place a stigma on services.
Because money is scarce, it should be targeted to poor people.	Limiting services to the poorest people pits the non-poor against the poor, rather than encouraging all older adults to develop cooperative self-help efforts.
Taxpayers may resist using tax dollars to provide universal services for all older adults.	If most taxpayers know they will be denied services when they get old because they are not poor enough, no wonder they protest using tax money to provide these services for others.

1981 (Eustis, Greenberg, & Patton, 1984). Funding is very limited, and states are allowed freedom in determining how to use it (Karger & Stoesz, 1998).

VALUES AND PUBLIC POLICY

Funding for programs for older adults involves national policy choices; such policy choices translate into dollar terms the values of those who determine the policy. Should all American older adults be offered tax-supported services such as congregate meals, for example, or only the poorest, frailest elderly? Is it important for all older adults to have access to balanced meals along with a social group experience, or should these services be limited to the poor? Research can provide helpful data, but even the selection of questions for research is guided by values.

The debate around privatizing Social Security relates much more to values than to real financial concerns. Conservatives who want to privatize the program are primarily interested in promoting the free enterprise system so that the stock market gets the money contributed for retirement rather than the government. Under their plan, people who invest the most successfully will benefit the most. Liberals are more concerned about providing a reasonable standard of living for all older adults, their survivors, and people disadvantaged due to disabilities.

The "Continuum of Care": Prolonging Independence

Most older adults want to maintain independence as long as possible. Recognition of this preference has led to the concept of the continuum of care. Highly relevant is the principle of "least restriction: the least that will get you the most is the appropriate intervention" (Huttman, 1985). Generally, whatever can be done to enable the elderly person to remain in his or her own home setting (the least restrictive environment) is appropriate.

Exhibit 9-6 illustrates the major components of a long-term continuum of care for older adults. The diagram illustrates how many services for the elderly can fit into

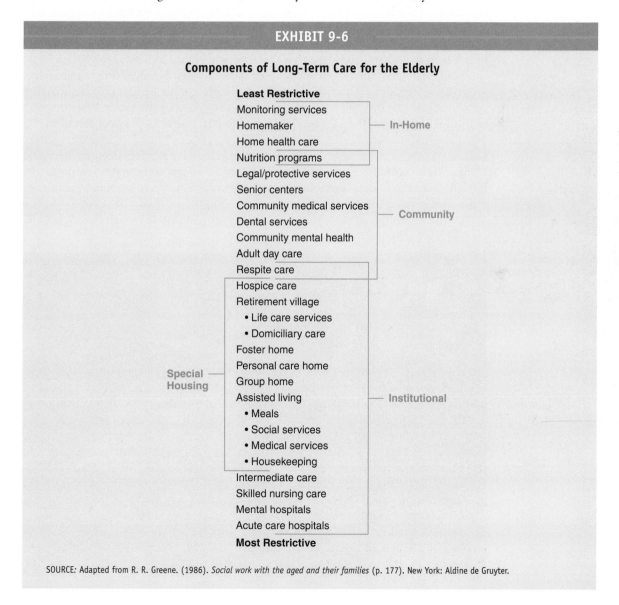

EXHIBIT 9-6

Components of Long-Term Care for the Elderly

Least Restrictive

Monitoring services
Homemaker ⎫ ─ In-Home
Home health care
Nutrition programs
Legal/protective services
Senior centers
Community medical services ⎫ ─ Community
Dental services
Community mental health
Adult day care
Respite care

Hospice care
Retirement village
  • Life care services
  • Domiciliary care
Foster home
Personal care home
Special ─ Group home
Housing   Assisted living
  • Meals ─ Institutional
  • Social services
  • Medical services
  • Housekeeping
Intermediate care
Skilled nursing care
Mental hospitals
Acute care hospitals

Most Restrictive

SOURCE: Adapted from R. R. Greene. (1986). *Social work with the aged and their families* (p. 177). New York: Aldine de Gruyter.

more than one category; for example, nutrition programs can be offered either in the home or in the community, perhaps at a senior center. The following sections briefly describe each major category of care.

In-Home Services   Monitoring services usually involve telephone calls to make sure that an elderly person is alive and well and to provide support and reassurance. Today, electronic devices are available where the push of a button alerts special services to investigate potential emergencies.

Homemaker services involve housecleaning, laundry, shopping, minor home repairs, yard work, and other routine chores. A more intensive kind of homemaker service may involve personal care, such as help with bathing and dressing. Home health aides provide medically oriented care, under the supervision of a skilled nurse. Home health aides may change bandages, give injections, and take a client's blood pressure.

Medicare and Medicaid pay for some of these services, but eligibility requirements are complicated and restrictive. Sometimes elderly people can receive homemaker services at low cost by applying to an agency partly funded by the Older Americans Act or the Social Services Block Grant. Most need to purchase these services privately.

Community Services   Nutrition programs can help older adults remain in their own homes. Meals on Wheels is a well-known example. In some communities, programs funded under the Older Americans Act provide congregate meals at senior centers or other sites 5 days a week.

Senior center activities promote social interaction among older adults.

Occasionally, family or other caretakers abuse or neglect older people. Protective services for the elderly are a fairly new phenomenon; in 1968 fewer than 20 communities had such programs (Dunkel, 1987). Today, however, almost every state requires helping professionals to report suspected abuse or neglect of older adults.

Senior centers are important means for older adults to maintain social interaction. Many are privately funded and administered by organizations such as churches or by local cities or counties. Some centers receive funding through the Older Americans Act or Social Service Block Grants.

Community medical and dental services include private-pay arrangements that older adults finance themselves as well as public services financed partly by Medicaid and Medicare. An important public policy issue involves how much of their own medical costs the elderly should have to finance themselves.

Community mental health services can help older adults cope with various stresses of living, including the stress of caring for a spouse who is ill. Mental health services also can assist other family caregivers. For example, a daughter or a daughter-in-law may have to give up a paying job and most personal freedom to provide round-the-clock care for an elderly relative. Mental health services may assist the caretaker (see Exhibit 9-7).

Adult day care services provide regular programming outside the home to supervise and maintain elderly persons who cannot get through the day alone. Many older adults who spend their days in adult day care programs live with relatives who regularly assist them but must work during the day.

Institutional Services　Some institutions, including nursing homes, offer a service called respite care, whereby an elderly person resides in the institution for a few days, a week, or even a month. This temporary arrangement allows family caretakers to take a break, go on vacation, or otherwise "recharge their batteries" physically and emotionally. After the respite, the elderly person returns home to their care. Many institutions also offer day care services as described above.

The next several categories in Greene's continuum of care (Exhibit 9-6) are institutional, in that they involve long-term care outside the older person's home, but Greene also places them in the subcategory of special housing. The first of these is hospice care, an institutional service that, when available, is provided to elderly people

---

EXHIBIT 9-7

Common Community Settings for Working with Frail Older Adults

- Home bound services such as Meals on Wheels
- Outreach/case-finding programs
- Elder abuse programs
- Financial management programs
- Legal services programs such as legal aid and eviction prevention programs

- Mental health programs
- Adult protective services
- Guardianship programs

SOURCE: Karen Bassuk & Janet Lessem. (2001). Collaboration of social workers and attorneys in geriatric community based organizations. *Journal of Gerontological Social Work, 34*(3), 103, 104.

(and others) who are dying. Medicare will pay for hospice care for elderly persons whose prognosis indicates that they have 6 months or less to live. (Medicare covers the medical charges, but not room and board.) Many hospices are contained entirely within hospitals or nursing homes. However, hospice care is sometimes provided in small homelike facilities or even in patients' own homes; that is why Greene also includes it as special housing. The purpose of hospice care is to help the patient die with dignity, with as little pain as possible.

The next item with both institutional and special housing aspects is the retirement village. Many retirement villages offer lifetime care with a continuum of services; many are private, nonprofit arrangements established by religious denominations. Older adults who are economically advantaged may purchase lifetime rights to an apartment or other housing unit. Some such programs offer the option of purchasing congregate meals. Many include a domiciliary option, or a large housing unit where a number of elderly people live and are offered personal assistance and meal services. The most advanced retirement villages include skilled nursing home care as needed.

Some older adults reside in foster homes or in small group homes, where they can receive individual attention and protection if needed, as long as ongoing medical attention is not required. Others live in larger **personal care homes,** which usually provide meals and are sometimes called nursing homes because the services of nurse's aides are available to help with bathing, eating, dressing, and the like. Technically speaking, however, a personal care home is not a nursing home because very limited nursing care is available.

An increasing demand for community living options for older people who need some level of assistance, but do not need an environment dominated by nursing requirements, has led to the recent development of an option known as **assisted living.** Assisted living is a step between independent living and living in a nursing home. The term became recognized nationally after the Assisted Living Federation of America was incorporated in 1992 (About ALFA, 2007). Older adults who reside in assisted living settings have their own small apartments including kitchens, bedrooms, and bathrooms. The environment is much more attractive than a room (usually shared) in a personal care home. Yet the same services are available: assistance with cooking, shared meals when desired, assistance with **activities of daily living** (dressing, bathing, laundry, housekeeping, etc.), and occasional nursing care as needed. Unfortunately, assisted living is usually available today only to people with significant financial means.

The institutional settings that provide the most restrictive environments for care of older adults are nursing homes and hospitals. Most elderly people do whatever they can to avoid them. However, as living into one's 80s and 90s is becoming common, an increasing number of older adults do face an eventual move to a nursing home. These facilities provide the only reasonable alternative to 24-hour family or hospital care when an elderly person is very ill or very frail. This is the setting that provided life-giving care to Abbie Heinrich of our chapter's case study.

Fortunately, nursing homes now are professionally organized and staffed. Many, especially the nonprofits, provide responsible services along with opportunities for older adults to enjoy the companionship of peers. "Intermediate care" and "skilled nursing care" are categories that reflect the level of nursing care provided. The former is less intensive than the latter; monthly fees are lower. Abbie Heinrich, with her extensive physical challenges, required the highest level of skilled nursing care (see Exhibit 9-8).

Unfortunately, because many nursing homes are administered by for-profit private organizations today, staffing levels are low to increase profits. Nonprofit homes provide nearly an hour more care per resident per day and nearly twice as much care from registered nurses. Federal rules require only 8 hours of registered nursing and 24 hours of licensed nursing care per day in any given facility, so large homes can have the same size staff as small ones. Many states have their own regulations, but state inspectors underreport deficiencies due to staff shortages of their own (Nursing homes, 2006).

Cuts in Medicaid reimbursements have contributed to nursing home understaffing. Olson (2003) reports that 90 percent of nursing homes are understaffed, resulting in widespread problems. Nearly a third were cited for physical, sexual, and verbal abuse between 1999 and 2001 according to a study commissioned by U.S. Representative Henry Waxman. This incidence was double that found in a 1997 study. Concerned by the data, Waxman introduced the Nursing Home Quality Protection Act of 2001, but it died in committee (Olson, 2003). More recent conditions are no better (Nursing homes, 2006). Nursing homes should be utilized only when less restrictive alternatives have been exhausted.

Rural versus Urban Issues   Services to assist older adults to live independently in the community are scarce almost everywhere, but gaps in the continuum of care are far more likely to occur in rural areas (see Exhibit 9-6). Even where important programs such as congregate meals and adult day care exist within a given rural county, transportation over long distances may be required to obtain them; thus, many seniors and their families are effectively blocked from participating in their benefits. Many rural areas are lacking in crucial services such as senior centers with congregate meals, Meals on Wheels, affordable housekeeping help, medical screening services,

---

EXHIBIT 9-8

Making a Home Out of a Nursing Home

[Dr. William] Thomas believes that the three plagues of loneliness, helplessness, and boredom afflict most nursing homes. "Often medications are used to make deficiencies in the environment less noticeable," he says. "We try to cover up the loneliness with pills."

With this research behind him, Thomas and his colleagues brought 12 dogs, 20 cats, and more than 600 birds to live in three nursing homes in upstate New York in 1993. (Other programs offer weekly or monthly pet visits, but Thomas wanted to provide permanent companions.) Employees filled the halls with hundreds of plants and invited elementary school students to join junior–senior gardening clubs. By 1995, the death rate at all three locations had dropped 25 percent and the residents used half as much medication. "People had a reason to get up each day," says Thomas. "They simply got hooked on living again."

SOURCE: Quoted from Kari Watson Culhane. (2000, April). A real home. *Natural Health,* 80.

adult day care programs, and the like. Yet there is a greater concentration of elders in rural than urban areas (Butler and Kaye, 2004; Hong, 2006). The result is that too many seniors in rural areas who become frail and ill find that their only option is to enter a nursing home.

Coming to Terms with Long-Term Care

We usually do whatever we can, both personally and collectively as a society, to live longer lives—and we are succeeding. That is the good news. Ironically, however, it is also bad news in some ways. Longer lives present new problems. Long-term care is a major one. It requires considerable financial outlay for which most of us are unprepared and raises important issues regarding quality of life.

Nearly 1.6 million older adults reside in nursing homes today; more than half are over 85 years old (*A profile of older Americans*, 2005). Yet despite questionable care, the average cost of nursing home living is very high, ranging somewhere between $50,000 and $70,000 annually. Most elderly adults cannot afford to pay, so a majority receive help from Medicaid (they must spend virtually all of their savings first). A few have private long-term care insurance to assist. Medicare is not a serious resource because it covers only short periods of skilled nursing home care after a hospital stay (see Exhibit 9-8).

Medicaid payments to nursing homes are lower than the fees charged to private clients, and they do not usually cover the full cost of care. Most nursing homes, therefore, accept private-paying clients first. When their money runs out, they turn to Medicaid. Most nursing homes will allow these people to stay, but had they originally applied as Medicaid clients, their chances of admission would have been minimal. Frail older adults who have experienced lifelong poverty find nursing home care very difficult to obtain. Abbie Heinrich was lucky—she was admitted to Oak Haven many years ago when Medicaid payments still met the true cost of care.

The social worker is very important in assisting the older adult to adjust to the nursing home setting.

Long-term care at home is very costly as well. Clearly, there is a mismatch between the reality of the cost of care and the ability of many elderly to finance it. In response to this dilemma, private long-term care insurance policies are increasingly available, but many people cannot afford them. Badly needed today are means of providing adequate financial assistance to the elderly for long-term care. Making private insurance plans affordable, perhaps with a government subsidy, would be a first step. More adequate government assistance is clearly needed.

END-OF-LIFE ISSUES, RELIGION, AND SPIRITUALITY

Death and Dying

Older adulthood involves many life changes, as noted previously. The possibility of death begins to feel very real. By this time the older person has lost members of his or her family, and probably friends. Coping with such loss often awakens spiritual concerns—not only for the older adult but for the social worker. Questions may arise such as "Does life have meaning?" "Does *my* life have meaning?" "Will death be the end?" "What, if anything, comes next?" Even if clients do not ask these questions aloud, both they and their social workers may wonder.

Spirituality and Religion

Naleppa and Reid (2003) suggest that spirituality and religion are important to older adults since they address questions such as those just listed. However, social workers have tended to avoid discussions of these issues, referring them instead to the clergy. It is, of course, important to involve clergy where available. Still, many clients do not belong to a church and feel embarrassed about asking to see a clergyperson who is unknown. The social worker, on the other hand, may be a person with whom they already feel comfortable, so workers are encouraged to discuss spiritual issues if requested.

Of concern, of course, is that social workers and clients may have very different religious orientations. Religion involves a formal belief system as taught by a particular church or theological tradition, whereas spirituality refers to a process involving a universal search for meaning. It is important for social workers not to impose religious beliefs on clients. However, in many instances workers and clients share similar beliefs. For example, a comparative study by Hodge (2003/2004) found that social workers in the United States share similar concepts of human nature with nonsocial workers (more good than corrupt) and God (more like father than mother, more like judge than lover). Social workers, on the other hand, are less likely to view the Bible as the literal word of God.

Regardless of a social worker's religious orientation, it is entirely possible to assist clients—even of very different traditions—to cope with spiritual issues. Encouraging clients to reminisce about their lives can help them work through meaning-related questions, for example. Allowing clients to talk about their beliefs, whatever they may be, can help them clarify these beliefs in a manner that may comfort them.

Social workers may find it helpful to clarify their own religious and/or spiritual beliefs. A spiritual grounding can help a worker cope with the fact that clients die, for example. Many other professionals grapple with religious and spiritual issues, of course. For example, Herbert Benson, a prominent physician who became famous for his scientific studies of the relaxation response, spent many years studying comparative religion. That is because he found that the relaxation response enhanced healing, and he recognized that there were many parallels between the relaxation response and the affects of prayer. He wrote in *Timeless Healing* (1996) that:

> Every culture had religious or secular practices that consisted of two basic steps—a repetitive focus and a passive attitude toward intrusive thoughts. There was a transforming power in prayer, no matter what the words, from a Hindu prayer to the Catholic "Hail Mary, full of grace," from Judaism to Buddhism, Christianity, and Islam. There were multitudes of descriptions of the peaceful state these religious practices elicited. (p. 199)

Benson hypothesized that human beings are physically "wired for God," and that the transcendent experience shared by various religious traditions and spiritual practices may be part of our genetic inheritance. Evidence of such a possibility is presented by Newberg, D'Aquili, and Rause (2001), in their book *Why God Won't Go Away*. These scientists found that the hypothalamus in the brain can produce transcendent experiences. Under a shutdown of neural input, as can occur during contemplative practice, silent prayer, or meditation, the "left orientation area" of the hypothalamus is unable to find the boundaries of the body so that the person feels a sense of unity with the universe. The result can be a profound spiritual experience, and a lessened fear of death.

Western science and religious traditions may argue the meaning or even the existence of a "biology of belief," but at the very least, learning to use the relaxation response in any form can be an effective self-care tool for the social worker.

End-of-life decisions can be particularly challenging. Some clients, usually when suffering extreme pain, ask for assistance in ending their lives. How is a social worker to respond? The NASW, in its *Standards for Social Work Practice in Palliative and End of Life Care*, "does not take a position concerning the morality of end of life decisions, but affirms the right of the individual to determine the level of his or her care" (Mackelprang & Mackelprang, 2005). One state, Oregon, permits people who are suffering and who have a life expectancy of less than 6 months to ask their doctors for medication to end their lives. Oregon's Death with Dignity Act was recently upheld by the U.S. Supreme Court in the *Gonzales v. Oregon* case (Stoesen, 2006). While it is important for social workers to assist their clients to identify all options available to them, advocacy regarding pain management is especially important. People in terminal situations who are not in pain are much more likely to choose to live as long as possible.

There is an interesting literature on *near*-death experiences (NDEs), which seem to help reduce the fear of dying for both social worker and client. The near-death experience, in which all vital signs have ceased but the person is later revived, was first studied by sociologist Raymond Moody (1976). The phenomenon has been investigated since by many others. It is described by scientist and author Dean Radin (2006) as follows:

> NDEs involve a sequence of distinctive experiences: finding oneself floating above the body, moving down a tunnel, being immersed in an intense beautiful light, interacting with deceased relatives or loved ones, and sometimes having to decide whether to return to the body or to continue on the disembodied journey. Those who come back to report the NDE often express deep regret at finding themselves embodied again because the out-of-body state is usually experienced as exceedingly blissful. (pp. 40–41)

Radin reports that in three studies of 496 patients with cardiac arrest (Dutch, British, and American), between 11 and 18 percent of patients had an NDE. Profound, positive personality changes were present in these people at follow-up studies 2 and 8 years later.

Does this mean that some part of the personality survives death? Not necessarily, as oxygen deprivation can trigger similar results. Yet patients who have registered as clinically brain dead on electronic monitors have later reported these experiences. How can a dead brain experience anything at all? Arguments are ongoing and the studies that they instigate are intriguing.

Hospice Services and Complementary Therapies

Hospice services are designed to assist people to cope with the dying process in a more humane and personal way than can be provided in traditional hospitals. The catalyst for the hospice movement in the United States was Dr. Elizabeth Kubler-Ross, who published her famous book, *On Death and Dying*, in 1969. In it she lamented the mechanized treatments provided by traditional hospitals and advocated for care of the whole person, including psychological and spiritual needs. The first hospice in the United States was opened in 1974 (Seeber, 1995); today, 43 states offer these services (Hospice Services of America, 2006).

Hospice services include medical care and psychological and spiritual counseling for patient and family and bereavement services for the family after the patient has died. Pain management is a primary concern. Patients can be accepted by hospice programs when life expectancy is 6 months or less and comfort rather than cure is the goal. Hospice care may be offered in one's own home or in homelike residential facilities; many services are covered under Medicare (Hospice Services of America, 2006).

An important complementary therapy offered in many hospices today has been developed by Therese Shroeder-Sheker. Shroeder-Sheker worked in a nursing home during her college career and was saddened to see people die alone and afraid. She began to sing to her patients as they lay dying. Eventually she founded the Chalice of Repose project, teaching others how to use music to ease the transition of the dying. Many scientific studies have demonstrated that music can help ease pain—physical, psychological, and spiritual. The instrument primarily suggested for this purpose is the harp, given its particular vibrational effect on the human body, but other instruments including the human voice are used also (Shroeder-Sheker, 2001). Chalice of Repose served as a catalyst for the development of several related projects such as the Music for Healing and Transition Program (MHTP) developed by Melinda Gardner in New York.

AN INTERNATIONAL PERSPECTIVE: THE NETHERLANDS

Provisions for older adults in the United States today could clearly be improved, and research regarding services provided by other nations may provide ideas. The AARP surveyed 16 industrialized nations (including the United States), weighing 17 criteria, and concluded that the country that provides the best care for its older citizens in the early years of the 21st century is The Netherlands (Edwards, 2004).

Social policy in The Netherlands is designed specifically to prevent social exclusion of older persons. The central government provides a policy framework that specifies the various responsibilities of finance agencies and service providers. Older people are encouraged to make their own decisions regarding the services they need and where and how they want to live. "Custom-made care," or care designed to meet the needs of each unique individual, is a central concept in The Netherlands' social policy. Another concept is that care should be "demand driven": the supply of care should meet the demand or need (Ex, Gorter, & Janssen, 2004) rather than being limited by a set budget allocation.

All older adults in The Netherlands receive a full old-age pension at age 65 whether or not they have worked outside the home (approximately $1,000 for a single person, $1,400 for a couple, married or not), but they must have lived in the country for at least 50 years between the ages of 15 and 64. Every older adult also receives a $700 "holiday allowance" in May, in time for a spring celebration. Seven days' free travel are provided on the nation's efficient railway system, and museums, movies, concerts, and holiday motels offer discounts. Government health insurance covers not only medical care, including prescription drugs, with tiny co-payments but also hospital care and coverage for nursing care if needed, both short and long term.

Such comprehensive services can be provided to older people in The Netherlands because the government controls almost all health care costs (drugs, physicians' services, hospital care, etc.). Taxes are higher than in the United States, but public attitudes support this trade-off. In general, younger people support generous treatment of older adults because older people are viewed as having earned assistance; they also recognize that the time will come when they themselves will need help (Edwards, 2004).

Interestingly enough, The Netherlands, like the U.S. state of Oregon, allows older people who are in extreme pain to request medication from their physicians to enable a peaceful death by choice. The Netherlands' law is broader than Oregon's, in that the excruciating pain justifying such a request may be psychological, not just physical. Two independent physicians, one of whom is a psychiatrist, must review and accept the request in order for it to be carried out (Mackelprang & Mackelprang, 2005).

SOCIAL WORK WITH OLDER ADULTS: A GROWING FUTURE

Older adults in this country and around the world are growing in number and proportion every day. Even with the predictable waxing and waning of public financing for social services for the elderly, reflecting shifts in the values of the politicians in power and the people who elect them, older adults are developing growing political sophistication. As a group, they are making themselves heard at all levels of government. Their needs are many. Thus, employment for social workers in the field of aging will probably continue to grow well into the foreseeable future.

Social workers who work with older adults encounter a varied and challenging client population. These are people who have led full lives and have developed the wisdom and perspective that come with many years on this planet. Elderly people are fascinating, enriching clients who can enlighten social workers as well as command their skills.

On the other hand, probably no other field of social work requires so much soul-searching on the part of the practitioner. Older adults are manifestly nearing the end of their journey on earth, and this certainty makes many thoughtful workers ponder the "meaning of it all."

INTERNET SITES

http://www.aahsa.org/	American Association of Homes and Services for the Aging
http://www.alz.org/	The Alzheimer's Association
http://www.agesocialwork.org/	The Association for Gerontology Education in social work.
http://www.elderweb.com/	ElderWeb (a research site for both professionals and family members looking for information on elder care and long-term care)
http://www.caregiver.org/	Family Caregiver Alliance
http://www.geron.org/	The Gerontological Society of America
http://www.ncoa.org/	The National Council on the Aging
http://www.ifa-fiv.org/en/accueil.aspx	International Federation on Aging
http://www.nih.gov/nia/	National Institute on Aging
http://www.aoa.dhhs.gov/	Administration on Aging
http://www.gswi.org	Geriatric Social Work Initiative
http://www.socialworkers.org/practice/aging	NASW areas of practice—Aging

SUMMARY

The case study of Abbie Heinrich, a severely disabled older adult, illustrates some of the challenges faced by older people today—health problems, poverty, and lack of living family members to name a few—as well as the challenges faced by the social workers who serve them.

Currently, more than 12 percent of the population of the United States is over 65, or about one person in eight. The number of people over 65 is expected to double by 2030, to about 70,000 at that time, constituting more than one person in five. This growing group of older persons, while resilient and self-sufficient in many cases, challenges the nation's social service system. The risk of poverty increases with age and is especially serious for members of ethnic minority groups and women. Those with lower incomes suffer the greatest problems in terms of health and adequate housing.

Many families are active in helping their older members cope with their special needs. Because people are living longer, more families are contributing to the care of elderly relatives than ever before, and for many more years. Middle-aged children, especially middle-aged women, often find themselves part of the "sandwich generation," those who have children to care for in addition to elderly relatives. Social workers can help many families cope with the stresses involved in intergenerational care.

Social workers are encouraged to use an empowerment model when working with older adults, assisting them to advocate for themselves and to utilize whatever resources are available. Pension plans and federal entitlement programs such as Social Security, Supplemental Security Income, housing assistance, health insurance, and food stamps help elderly people meet financial and material needs to some extent. Limited services such as information and referral, congregate meal programs, low-cost homemaker aids, and protective services are provided under the Older Americans Act and the Social Services Block Grant. However, need for services far outstrips supply, and a large burden of care today falls upon families, creating intergenerational stress.

The concept of the continuum of care, designed to help older adults maintain independence for as long as possible, includes in-home services, community services, special housing, assisted living, and institutional services. Whenever possible, older adults should be helped to remain in the least restrictive environment.

Given increasing longevity, the need for careful attention to long-term care is growing in importance, not only for individuals but for families and society as a whole. While an impressive continuum of care has been developed, we have not yet managed to come to terms with financing and quality-of-life issues. Another challenge is recognition of the spiritual needs of older adults, a responsibility no longer assigned to clergy alone. Social workers themselves may find themselves spiritually challenged as they work closely with clients who are facing a final transition.

The chapter concludes with a description of services to older adults provided in The Netherlands, considered the best place to grow old today according to a recent study by the American Association of Retired Persons. While services to the elderly are not nearly so comprehensive in the United States, social work practice with older adults is still likely to grow rapidly in this nation because of the increasing number of people who are elderly, frail, and in need of ongoing assistance.

KEY TERMS

activities of daily living
  (ADLs), *p. 369, 388*

advocacy, *p. 361*

assisted living, *p. 381, 388*

case management, *p. 366*

case manager, *p. 360*

charity, *p. 382*

co-insurance, *p. 370, 381*

continuum of care, *p. 385*

deductible, *p. 381*

empowerment, *p. 377*

entitlement program, *p. 379*

frail elderly, *p. 361*

health maintenance
  organization, *p. 370*

insurance, *p. 360, 370*

least restrictive environment,
  p. 385

DISCUSSION QUESTIONS

1. Approximately what percentage of the U.S. population is over the age of 65 today? About what percentage will be over 65 in the year 2030?

2. Why is it more likely that older women will live alone than older men? Who are more likely to be poor: older men or older women? Why?

3. What is meant by the statement "More families are caring for elderly members than ever before, and for many more years"? Why is this happening?

4. Is Social Security intended to be the sole source of support for older adults? What does this mean about the level of benefits provided? How likely do you think it is that older adults will have other sources of income in the future?

5. What types of programs are funded by the Older Americans Act of 1965? In general, has funding for these services been adequate? Why or why not? Are funds increasing or decreasing today? What major questions does the chapter raise about the funding of these services?

6. How do national values affect federal policies relating to the elderly? What major questions are being debated today? How will the answers to these questions affect specific services for the elderly? How might policy relating to the elderly in general affect social work practice options (or resources) available to assist particular elderly people in need?

7. Describe the continuum of care services that can help older adults maintain independence as long as possible.

8. How does the concept of the least restrictive environment reflect the social work ethical principle of self-determination?

9. In what ways does work with older adults tend to raise issues of religion and spirituality? Are social workers encouraged to talk about these issues with their clients? Why or why not? How does hospice care relate to these issues?

10. If community care is cheaper per person than care in a nursing home, do you think that more community care could still end up costing the nation more overall? If so, how? Do you think the social work profession would support more funding for community care even if it did end up costing more? Why or why not? Support your answer with a discussion of professional values.

CLASSROOM EXERCISES

It is suggested that students break into small groups of three or four to discuss these exercises. It may be helpful to choose a scribe to record and report interesting points to the class after the group discussion.

1. Review the arguments, pro and con, for means-testing services provided under the Older Americans Act. One or more groups should then develop as many additional arguments as possible to support means testing, and one or more groups should develop as many additional arguments as possible against it. Then, each group should choose a spokesperson to represent its ideas in a classroom debate or panel discussion.

2. Discuss various policy options for making Social Security more financially sound. Include those identified by the AARP (check their website for their newest ideas) and any other options you can think of. Which policies make the most sense to you? Why? Which make the least? Why?

3. Imagine that you have the power to establish national policies that will solve the long-term care problem for older adults in the United States. What policies will you implement? Why?

RESEARCH ACTIVITIES

1. Find out if your community, or one nearby, has a local area agency on aging established under the Older Americans Act. Visit the agency, and find out about the services it offers. Interview a staff member to learn about staff roles. What was the educational background of the staff person you interviewed?

2. Visit a local nursing home. Interview a social worker on staff. What are the roles of this worker? Next, interview a nursing home resident. What does the resident think about the services he or she receives? What would the resident like to be different at the home?

3. Find out if there is a retirement village near your community that provides a range of residential options for older adults. What is the range of services offered? Are there any gaps in service that you can identify? Interview a resident. How does resident satisfaction compare with that of the nursing home resident you interviewed earlier?

INTERNET RESEARCH EXERCISES

1. The National Institute on Aging addresses many problems of older people (http://www.nia.nih .gov/AboutNIA).

   a. How long has the NIA been in existence?

   b. Subsequent legislation made it the primary federal agency for what disease research?

   c. In addition to its research, what other mission does the NIA serve?

2. In July 2005, a White House Conference on Aging was held. The final report and recommendations can be found at http://depts.washington.edu/ geroctr/Resources4/SWAging/ WHCoAMiniConWorkforceRecommend.doc.

   a. The first recommendation relates to education. How will the third point of implementation affect you as a social worker?

   b. The second recommendation speaks to recruitment and retention. What would make you, as a social work student, get excited about the field of geriatric social work?

   c. The third recommendation refers to "Interdisciplinary Teams." How would you define this term, and why is it important?

3. The Healthy Aging Project, a combined effort of 10 European countries, the World Health Organization and the European Union among others, has some very interesting material on aging. Its recommendations can be found at http://www.healthyageing.nu/upload/pdf/ Chapters%20from%20the%20report/ 18.%20Recommendations.pdf.

   a. "Older people are of intrinsic value to society." This is one of the five core principles of healthy aging as stated in this document. Comment on this statement in terms of your own experience.

   b. Another core principle is heterogeneity. "Old people" are often treated as a homogeneous group. What are the dangers in this?

   c. This paper lists 10 priority topics for action. What three topics do you think should be given the highest priority and why?

FOR FURTHER READING

Butler, S., & Kaye, L. (Eds.) (2003). *Gerontological social work in small towns and rural communities*. New York: Haworth Press

This book combines studies of subgroups of small town and rural older adults with chapters directing attention to specific service networks. Chapters address various intervention models and the special nature of social work practice in rural areas. It concludes with a section addressing future social work training needs and recommentations for changes in social policy

Cox, C. (2005). *Community care for an aging society*. New York, Springer.

This text examines various factors that contribute to the needs of older persons and the ways in which society responds to various impairments related to aging. Social policies and services that address needs of the aged are examined in-depth, along with contemporary innovations that hold promise to improve independence and well-being among older adults.

Holosko, M., & Feit, M. (Eds.). (2004). *Social work practice with the elderly*, 3rd ed. Toronto: Canadian Scholars Press.

The editors of this text have carefully focused on what is right with services to the elderly rather than what is wrong. The first section provides an in-depth overview of current social work practice with older adults. The second section provides a description of 10 different practice settings utilizing social work skills. The last section discusses directions social work practice may need to take in future years.

Leichsenring, K., & Alaszewski, A. M. (Eds). (2004). *Providing integrated health and social care for older persons, a European overview of issues at stake*. Burlington, VT: Ashgate.

Social services and health care provisions are compared and contrasted in this text for nine different European countries: Austria, Denmark, Finland, France, Germany, Greece, Italy, The Netherlands, and the United Kingdom. The text notes that while there have been many innovations and improvements in the integration of health and social services for older adults during the past 20 years, provisions for care are currently decreasing all over Europe.

Naleppa, M., & Reid, W. (2003). *Gerontological social work, a task-centered approach*. New York: Columbia University Press.

Part 1 of this book provides a foundation for gerontological social work practice, including a demographic profile of older adults and a description of the network of potential service providers. Part 2 discusses a task-centered model for practice with the elderly. Part 3 examines various tasks that must be addressed to accomplish a successful aging process, including financial management, ensuring safety, arranging appropriate living accommodations, and securing resources to meet health and mental health needs.

Olson, L. (2003). *The not-so-golden years: Caregiving, the frail elderly, and the long-term care establishment*. Lanham, MD: Rowman & Littlefield.

This powerful book weaves together the complex issues related to care of older persons in the United States and the structures, values, and norms on which policies and programs are based. Long-term care is placed in the context of the American health care system and the larger political economy. Strategies for change are offered in the final chapter, including an overhaul of nursing homes, deprivitization of services, and a total reevaluation of the importance of care. The book calls for a universal system of care for vulnerable persons with impairments, regardless of age.

CHAPTER 10

CRIMINAL JUSTICE

OUTLINE

Alan Martin

History of Social Work in Criminal Justice

Components of the Criminal Justice System

Law Enforcement

The Courts

The Correctional System

The Juvenile Justice System

Value Dilemmas for Social Workers

Social Work with Groups and
Organizations

Environmental Perspectives

Crime and Communities at Risk

*Community Strengths, Restoration,
Spirituality, and Resilience*

Promoting Social Justice

Social Welfare Policy in Criminal Justice

The Prison Population

The Death Penalty

Social Policy and Juvenile Justice

Populations at Risk

ALAN MARTIN

Alan Martin slumped in his chair and sighed. Then he picked up the file again. Another new case had just been added to his already overloaded caseload. You're letting yourself burn out, he thought. Then, reminding himself that he was just tired but he could go home soon, he picked up the telephone and dialed the number he had found in Brian Cook's folder. He talked briefly with Brian's mother, Laura Cook, scheduling an office appointment with Brian for Friday. The file showed that Brian had been released on parole from the state juvenile corrections center just 5 days ago. He had served 2 years of a 5-year sentence for selling illicit drugs. He had apparently been a model prisoner.

The telephone rang and Alan reached for his notepad . . . an emergency; the police had just arrested another of his clients, a 13-year-old, for selling cocaine at the bus stop across the street from a school. There had been a scuffle, weapons were involved; one officer and the 13-year-old were badly injured and being transported to the hospital by ambulance. A picture of 13-year-old Ramon flashed through his mind: a bright, defiant, angry kid whose father died 6 months ago. Without hesitation Alan replied to the voice on the phone: "I'll be at the hospital in 10 minutes." It was very late when Alan finally got home that night.

Alan Martin was an experienced BSW social worker who had worked in the criminal justice field for 6 years now, initially in adult probation and parole and, for the past 6 months, in Youth Correctional Services. Alan was respected by his colleagues, police, and the judges. Among his clients he was viewed as tough, demanding, and fair. Once actively involved with NASW and careful to sustain continued professional learning activities, Alan had gradually drifted away from identification with his profession and, in fact, had forgotten to renew his NASW professional membership. Alan felt vaguely unsettled with his life and his work.

On Friday, minutes before Brian Cook's scheduled appointment, Alan pulled out his file. Brian's 14-year-old face stared back from the photo taken at the time of his arrest 2 years ago. This image was quite a contrast to the older-looking, broad-shouldered, passive but mistrustful person he had met at the correctional facility 2 weeks ago. Kids who weren't criminals before they arrived at that place were quite likely to be so by the time they were released, Alan thought as he snapped the file closed and went out to get Brian from the drab, vaguely filthy waiting room.

Their first session in Alan's office included a review of the parole contract. Brian's cool, almost sullen expression was annoying. Alan found himself talking loudly, lecturing Brian about the consequences of failure to abide by the terms of the contract. He told Brian about the procedure for providing a urinalysis to check for drugs each time he came in. He was angered by Brian's comment: "So, you don't trust me. I told you I don't do drugs." "No, I don't trust you," he responded, using the very words he didn't like but often heard other parole officers use. Further annoyed with himself for having said this, Alan changed the subject to school. Brian said that he had enrolled and started attending classes this week but hated the school. Alan ignored this, instead warning Brian about associating with anyone related to his conviction, especially Shari, the girl for whom he had purchased drugs.

After Brian left the office Alan returned the telephone call that had come in from Ramon's mother. She was at the hospital; Ramon was not doing well but she couldn't understand the doctor's explanation about what was happening to him. Alan decided to stop by the hospital during his lunch break. The expression of the policeman guarding the room told Alan that all was not well. One look at Ramon's face, contorted with pain and discolored by jaundice, confirmed that Ramon was in serious condition. Alan beckoned Ramon's mother to follow him. Tearfully she told him that in her heart she did not think that Ramon was going to live. She didn't know what was wrong; she was terrified. Alan searched frantically for a nurse, finally finding one who would talk with them. The nurse was dignified but cold. Ramon had developed an infection related to the gunshot wound in his abdomen. He was not responding to antibiotics. His lab reports this morning were very bad. She certainly didn't know why these teenage criminals thought they could get away with fooling around with guns. As she turned to leave, Alan heard her say, "Sometimes they have to pay the price." Struck to the core by her remark and instantly, painfully aware of the negative attitudes he had been developing, he turned to Ramon's mother, hugging her to defend her from the added pain of the nurse's remark. He took her to a quiet corner, explained what the nurse had said about the seriousness of the infection, and sat with her for a time while she cried. Alan left when Mrs. Perez's sister arrived. That night Ramon died.

Thoughts about Ramon's tragic death and the judgmental attitude of the nurse remained with Alan for weeks. Attending Ramon's funeral service both refreshed him spiritually and strengthened his determination to fight for real justice, a justice built on dignity and respect for people, not on retribution and various prejudices. Alan made time at night to do a bit of reading—some light short stories that were delightful and refreshing and some professional articles from social work journals. Rereading the NASW Code of Ethics renewed Alan's awareness that as a professional person he was responsible for the quality of his own practice. In his work with his clients Alan consciously struggled to become more self-aware and more attuned to the reality of their lives.

On the day that Brian Cook was scheduled to see him again, Alan received a report from the school indicating that Brian was not attending classes. This was a violation of his parole contract, and it also raised questions about what he was doing with his time. Was he back into the drug scene again? Alan confronted Brian with all of this. To his annoyance, Brian insisted that he was attending school. Brian added: "I know you won't believe me about this. You don't believe anything that I say." Alan showed him the report, but Brian still insisted that he was attending school even though he hated it. Then, despite the report, Alan decided to suspend his disbelief until he and Brian could check out the report together. Brian was quite surprised when Alan proposed this but readily agreed to wait while Alan met with his next client. Then they drove to the school in Alan's car.

On the drive Alan encouraged Brian to talk about his classes. By the time they reached the school it seemed more and more likely that Brian really had attended at least some of his classes. They were fortunate in being able to meet briefly with two of Brian's teachers, who affirmed that Brian had indeed been in class. Both gave Brian suggestions about how to improve his work. When Alan presented their case to the school attendance clerk, she reviewed her records and found that a mistake had been made.

Back in the car, Brian smiled for the first time. He said, "This time truth was on my side." Alan agreed. Suddenly Brian's expression changed. He said, "I can understand better now about truth. . . . I was lied to and I actually did lie to you, too." He explained that Shari had promised him when he was convicted that she would be true to him while he was away. He counted on that. Since getting out he had been trying to contact her but she wasn't returning his phone calls. Today he found out that she was pregnant and due to have a baby shortly. So he had been lied to. And he had lied to Alan, too, when he agreed not to contact Shari. When Brian looked up at Alan, there was pain in his eyes. It was quiet in the car for several minutes; Alan let the silence hang in the air unbroken, feeling Brian's pain. Then he said, "OK, Brian let's start over now . . . and we'll begin by trusting each other." ■

HISTORY OF SOCIAL WORK IN CRIMINAL JUSTICE

The history of the profession in the very interesting field of criminal justice is one that has slowly evolved out of a distant past when punishment for misdeeds was instantaneous and severe. Archaeological findings have provided evidence of the use of beatings and slavery for those who violated societal norms in ancient times. In the enlightened period of Greek civilization, around 400 BC, new ways of looking at criminal behavior emerged. Hippocrates insisted that natural causes, rooted in the environment and in the family, shaped behavior more significantly than did evil spirits.

Evidently such enlightenment failed to continue, for by the Middle Ages in Europe severe punishments were being used: branding, cutting out an offender's tongue, public hanging, beheading, or burning at the stake. In the 1600s many of these punishments were brought to America by the colonists. Following the Revolutionary War in America, the Pennsylvania Quakers became alarmed about the harshness of punishments being used. "They argued that offenders might be reformed through segregation from the evil influences of other persons and the opportunity to become penitent (thus the term *penitentiary*)" (Galaway, 1981, p. 259). This, then, was the precursor of the present prison system.

In France the Napoleonic Code of 1807 created a new and more humane approach to Western society's thinking about criminal justice for children. The Napoleonic Code established a minimum age at which children could be charged and punished for offenses. Thus was born the principle of differentiating juvenile from adult crime. Separate correctional facilities for children—facilities then known as refuges—began to be provided for children in the United States in the early 1820s. These privately funded, supposedly charitable organizations unfortunately grew into large institutions characterized by severe discipline.

John Augustus, a Boston shoemaker, is credited with the establishment of probation. In 1841 Augustus requested permission of the courts to serve as surety—to accept personal responsibility and provide supervision—for a man charged with drunkenness. That first successful experience led Augustus to continue his work with other offenders. In 1869 the first formal position for probation work was created by the Commonwealth of Massachusetts; the agent was required to appear at criminal trials of juveniles, to locate suitable homes for them, and to supervise them. In 1878 Boston began to provide probationary supervision for adult offenders.

During the mid-1800s, people in England began to realize that the concept of transporting convicts to other lands was not an effective approach to the problem. Captain Alexander Maconochie, who was responsible for the British penal colony on Norfolk Island in the South Pacific, devised and promoted a concept of conditional release for prisoners. The first correctional system in the United States to experiment with the concept was the Elmira Reformatory in New York State in 1877. The use of parole soon became an accepted principle in corrections in the United States.

By the early 1900s, juvenile courts began to be established across the United States. A special concern of juvenile courts was provision of competent, professional service for children. These courts looked to the new profession of social work for staff to assist juvenile court judges. In contrast, the adult probation and parole agents of the time represented a variety of disciplines but tended to use sheriffs and people with police experience. Gradually this area too was professionalized, but even today probation and parole agents come from a variety of disciplines with quite different philosophical approaches to criminal justice.

Women such as Jane Addams of Hull House and Edith Abbott, dean of the School of Social Service Administration at the University of Chicago, provided much of the leadership, teaching, and research in correctional social work in its early days. Abbott, for example, studied crime and incarceration of women during the Civil War and World War I. Florence Kelley, another of the Hull House residents, was an attorney who advanced the social work profession through the creation of the U.S. Children's Bureau and by developing training programs for the Children's Bureau staff. She also worked to develop child labor laws (Edwards, 1991, as cited in Barker & Branson, 2000). The social work profession, in its infancy, was also assisted by another attorney, Sophonisba Breckinridge, who helped bring training of social workers into universities and, in fact, became the dean of one of the earliest schools of social work, the University of Chicago's School of Social Service Administration (Quam, 1995, as cited in Barker & Branson, 2000). The early schools of social work taught courses on law and social work and, indeed, much of early social work practice was within courts, child welfare agencies that involved court investigations, and probation and parole systems.

Social casework was introduced within the U.S. Bureau of Prisons in the 1930s. By that time society had begun to accept Freudian concepts of causation of behavior. Increasingly, counseling for prisoners incorporated some of this theory. The federal prisons were fraught with riots resulting from overcrowding, understaffing, and overall poor prison conditions. Reform efforts introduced social casework as part of a rehabilitation effort. Kenneth Pray, a community organizer and educator, helped to clarify the role of social casework in the prisons with his writings in the 1940s (1945).

Police social work programs grew out of demonstration projects initially funded by the federal government, generally by the Law Enforcement Assistance Administration in the 1970s. Harvey Treger, of the Jane Addams School of Social

Social workers in prison or probation and parole settings advocate for prisoners, help them remain linked to their families, provide substance abuse counseling and education programs, and work toward constructive behavioral changes.

Work at the University of Illinois, is probably the most significant figure in the development of this field. Victim/witness programs were also initially created through governmental funding.

Innovations that occurred in probation and parole in more recent years include the use of home confinement, electronic monitoring, intensive supervision as a substitute for incarceration, and restitution. Victim/witness programs, police social work, alternatives to incarceration, and forensic social work have also continued to evolve. All of these programs brought opportunities for new approaches to practice for social workers in the corrections field. The expansion of prison privatization resulted in custodial care with minimal attention to prisoner rehabilitation. Many of the private prison facilities were located in southern states but were frequently used to house prisoners from northern states. The frail linkages between prisoners and their families became even more tenuous.

Today the criminal justice system is reacting to public sentiment through harsh sentencing and long prison terms, but there are calls for reform. Today, too, social workers are renewing their interest in criminal justice fields of practice such as police social work, probation and parole, victim/witness assistance programs, domestic violence services within district attorney's offices, and alternative-to-incarceration programs. Out of this renewed interest and increased opportunities is emerging a new specialty area of **forensic social work,** which is not yet well defined. It does, however, incorporate expertise in legal matters related to child welfare, juvenile offenses, divorce issues such as custody determination, and various areas of dispute negotiation (Barker, 2003; O'Neil, 2003). The social work perspective that looks at poverty, prejudice, housing, education, and family support needs to become a part of public policy debate. Hopefully the social work profession will join with other professions such as law, psychiatry, and criminal justice to challenge the punitive and ultimately destructive direction criminal justice policy has taken. The field of criminal justice could be a very exciting arena for new social justice activism and reform!

COMPONENTS OF THE CRIMINAL JUSTICE SYSTEM

Alan Martin, the social worker in the chapter case study, was experienced in the adult as well as juvenile corrections systems. In his practice Alan Martin worked with all of the subsystems of the criminal justice system. Sometimes referred to as the three Cs (cops, courts, and corrections), the criminal justice system in the United States grew out of the system brought to this country by colonists from England. Over time it developed into a complex and somewhat fragmented system, with separate subunits that did not always interact effectively. It acquired a strange and somewhat inconsistent combination of goals: to punish, to deter crime, to rehabilitate, and to remove criminals from society. Today, social workers are engaged in all three areas of the U.S. criminal justice system.

Specific laws and regulations pertain to each of the criminal justice system areas. Social workers can expect to learn the laws and regulations that guide the area of the criminal justice system in which they work. A police social worker will develop an understanding of arrest procedures, statutory rape laws, and laws pertaining to child and spouse abuse. A social worker serving as a parole agent, such as Alan Martin in the case study, will become familiar with the administrative law that defines the responsibilities of probation and parole agents, with parole contracts, and with revocation procedures.

Two terms that will be used in the remainder of this chapter, and that should be understood by informed citizens, need further definition: *misdemeanor* and *felony*. A misdemeanor is a relatively minor offense but certainly more serious than a misdeed; it is punishable by fines, probation, or a relatively brief jail or prison sentence unless taken to extreme or done repeatedly. A felony is a serious crime. Murder, rape, and armed burglary are felonies, while defacing public property is a misdemeanor. Assault could be a misdemeanor, while aggravated assault (involving deadly force or intent to rob, kill, or rape) would be considered a felony. Under federal law and also in many states, the consequence of a felony is a prison sentence of one or more years; the most extreme penalty for a felony is the death penalty. Professional people, such as social workers, may be prohibited from being licensed or certified to practice in their state if they have a criminal record.

Two additional terms, *probation* and *parole*, were encountered in the Alan Martin case study, and these terms will be used frequently in this chapter. It is important to understand the differences between the two. Probation is a sentence, following conviction for a crime, in which the offender is ordered to undergo supervision for a prescribed period of time instead of serving that time in prison. The supervision is provided by a court-designated probation officer who may be a social worker. Parole is defined as "the release of a prisoner before completion of full sentence because of good conduct in prison, promised good conduct, and continued supervision by an officer of the legal system (often a social worker) once out of prison" (Barker, 2003; pp. 315–316). Note that the person who has been paroled has served time in prison; probation normally does not require prior imprisonment.

Let us now examine the three major components of the criminal justice system in the United States and the interesting ways in which social work as a profession has found a niche in each of these areas.

Law Enforcement

When we speak of law enforcement, we are essentially referring to the police. The police, as law enforcement officers, comprise the first of the three areas of the criminal justice system. What exactly is the role of the police? It is much broader than most citizens realize.

Police are responsible for responding to citizens' complaints and for questioning and apprehending persons. Before charging a person with a crime, however, police have considerable decision-making responsibility. Exhibit 10-1, for example, illustrates the decisions made by police in 2005 for the juvenile offenders they took into custody. Note that more than two-thirds of these youths were turned over to the juvenile courts, 20.2 percent were handled within the police department and released, and 7 percent were referred to criminal or adult courts; this compares with 50.8 percent of juveniles referred to juvenile courts, 45 percent handled within the police department and released, and 1.3 percent referred to criminal or adult courts in 1972 (Pastore & Maguire, 2006, Table 4.26.2005). Police decide whether a charge is warranted or another alternative might be considered. Current law determines the officer's decision. Prevailing public sentiment or the political climate might also

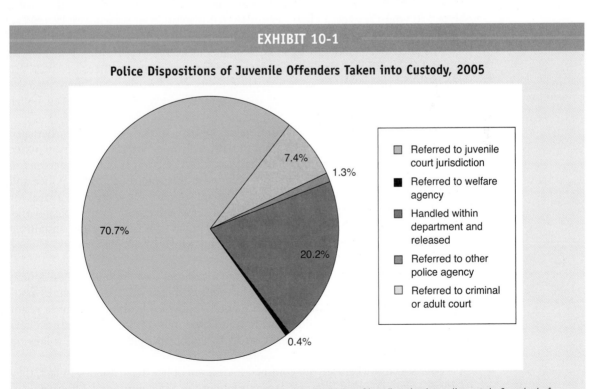

EXHIBIT 10-1

Police Dispositions of Juvenile Offenders Taken into Custody, 2005

- 7.4%
- 1.3%
- 70.7%
- 20.2%
- 0.4%

Legend:
- ☐ Referred to juvenile court jurisdiction
- ■ Referred to welfare agency
- ▨ Handled within department and released
- ▨ Referred to other police agency
- ☐ Referred to criminal or adult court

SOURCE: A. L. Pastore & K. Maguire. (Eds.). (2005). Table 4.26.2005 Percent distribution of juveniles taken into police custody. *Sourcebook of criminal justice statistics online*. Washington, DC: U.S. Department of Justice, Bureau of Justice Statistics. Retrieved June 19, 2007, from http://www.albany.edu/sourcebook/pdf/t4262005.pdf

be influential. Often it is a matter of chance, of visibility (as in a "high-crime" neighborhood that is under greater scrutiny than other areas), or of past behavior that determines whether a violation of the law even results in contact with the police. Shopkeepers, school authorities, and neighbors may be more prone to call the police in some parts of the city or community than in others.

In addition to responding to criminal complaints, police are also responsible for keeping the peace. In this role they encounter families in crisis, domestic violence, suicidal behavior, and substance abuse. One of the frustrations of police officers is that they receive little recognition by the community or even by the police system itself for the human services they routinely provide.

Police social work is the practice of social work within police departments, courthouses, or in jails. Police social work is still a relatively underdeveloped area of social work practice, but it appears to be an expanding area of the profession. Police and social workers share a common concern about personal and family crisis situations. A considerable portion of police calls is of a social service nature, because people are most likely to call the police when they don't know where else to turn for help. In communities where police social workers are available, dispositions of cases frequently results in redirection from the criminal justice to the social service system.

When social workers were first employed by police departments, they were assigned to youth services. Their tasks included resolution of parent–child conflicts; referral of children to child guidance or child psychiatric clinics; assessment of child abuse, neglect, and abandonment situations; and a variety of crisis roles. Police social workers have proven their value in domestic dispute situations. Because these are some of the most dangerous cases for police, police social workers' ability to ease the tension in such situations, as well as to assess and intervene, has impressed police departments.

Nonetheless, conflicts of roles and values remain sources of difficulty between police and social workers. Police did not initially welcome "interference" from police social workers. Over the years, police had found satisfaction in helping persons in crisis, and they were not always eager to relinquish this role. Even today, police and social workers may occasionally differ on the appropriate disposition of a case, or they may disagree about who has authority to make the decision. Police social workers continue to have concern about maintaining their own integrity and sustaining their values, especially the values of dignity and worth of all persons and clients' rights to self-determination.

In recent years police social workers' responsibilities have expanded. Assessment and counseling are increasingly provided for police officers when the pressures associated with police work threaten to create mental or physical health problems or result in inability to make rational judgments in tense situations. Police officers are vulnerable to the same kind of posttraumatic stress that other people experience following encounters with violence, disasters, or other life-threatening events.

Police social workers are not confined to desks in police departments. In fact, they are increasingly involved in crime prevention work in the community. Often, a team consisting of a social worker and a police officer seeks to prevent crime through educational programs provided to youth groups, in the schools, or to civic associations.

Today, suburban police systems are in the forefront of community organization work, with police personnel participating in and often leading community action efforts related to crime prevention, the development of youth services, and even the reform of mental commitment laws. Their professional education makes police social workers especially well suited for such responsibilities.

The Courts

Courts exist at the federal, state, and local levels, and they range from municipal courts to the highest court in the land, the U.S. Supreme Court. Courts have two primary functions: civil and criminal. Civil functions deal with the rights of private citizens and may result in fines or monetary damages. Criminal functions involve determination of guilt or innocence; punishment such as a prison sentence may result. In the criminal court system, a case begins with an arrest.

Some persons may have charges against them dropped, and therefore they discontinue their involvement in the criminal justice system. In fact, at each step along the way—from the point of police questioning through arrest, charging, and sentencing—a certain percentage of persons exit the system. Only a fraction of those initially detained for questioning are actually found guilty and incarcerated. In this "criminal justice funnel," the top of the funnel represents all the crimes that have been committed. The people who exit the system along the way are found in the slanting sides of the funnel. At the bottom of the funnel are those persons actually prosecuted and sent to prison—approximately 3 percent. As research studies described later in this chapter suggest, racial biases may be among the factors that influence decisions at each step from questioning through incarceration.

Social workers are increasingly found in the courts of America, where they serve in several interesting ways. One role for social workers is work with and on behalf of victims of crime. Social workers were among the pioneers of victim/witness programs. These programs, often housed in the local district attorney's office, assist people who are intimidated by the legal process. Programs to help battered women through the court system were among the first to emerge. Today social workers assist victims of domestic abuse to obtain restraining or harassment no-contact orders, and they serve as client advocates in the courts. Persons who are injured in crimes are also provided services that emphasize compassion, affirmation, and emotional support.

Testifying in court is a responsibility for social workers in child and family services and corrections, and in forensic social work, this is a primary area of expertise. NASW has a variety of resources that help to prepare social workers, beginning with how to deal with receipt of a **subpoena** (an order to appear in court on a specified date). Another role for social workers in the court system is that of work on behalf of the court in conducting a **presentence investigation.** If a case goes to court and the offender is convicted, a presentence investigation may be requested by the judge. Presentence investigations are conducted by probation officers, many of whom are social workers; the investigations typically involve both office and home visits with family members, the client, and other collaborative sources. The report is likely to be very detailed and comprehensive, including a social history and descriptions of the offender's home and work environment, education and employment, and physical or mental health problems, as well as an identification of existing social supports. The concluding recommendation often evaluates "the merits and risks of keeping an offender in the community. Recently this has been especially important in cases involving the physical and sexual abuse of children, where the needs of the victim constitute a major factor in the presentence investigation" (Isenstadt, 1995, p. 71).

Forensic social workers in private practice (often part-time) may also be requested by the court to conduct a presentence investigation or they may be asked to obtain information from the family of, for example, a child who has been physically or sexually abused. Sometimes the forensic social worker may be asked by the court to recommend "ways to resolve, punish, or rehabilitate those found guilty of crimes or negligence in civil actions" (Barker & Branson, 2000, p. 16). If the forensic social worker recommends community service, for example, the court may further ask that social worker to facilitate and monitor the sentence.

When the court decides to sentence a convicted person, the result may be a jail term, probation, or imprisonment. Note that there are significant differences between jail and prison. A **jail** is a correctional facility used for short sentences or for detaining persons while they await a court hearing. A **prison** is used for lengthier sentences, generally for a number of years. In passing sentence, judges are required to abide by the legal code, which provides parameters for length of imprisonment; therefore, judges' options are somewhat limited.

In recent years, courts have used various alternatives to prison. They are less costly than prison and they are a good deal more humane than a prison sentence. Any alternative program mandated by the court is usually attached to a sentence of probation. **Community-service sentencing** is an alternative that has come into use in many areas. It usually requires the offender to work without pay in a private or governmental human service organization for a specified period of time. **Restitution** programs require that offenders, adult as well as juvenile offenders, compensate their victims (usually monetarily) for the losses suffered as a result of the criminal offense. Restitution is most frequently used in conjunction with property crimes, which are the most prevalent of all crimes committed (Butts, 1995). It has often been the experience of social workers that the monetary payment made by the offender has less long-range meaning than the experience of facing the victim, explaining the offense, and seeking to restore the loss.

The Correctional System

The **correctional system** is that part of the criminal justice system that uses imprisonment, probation, parole, and various alternatives to change the behaviors of persons convicted of crime. The two major components of the correctional system in the United States are prisons and community-based programs. Each of the 50 states has its own correctional system with varying structures, sanctions, and administrative laws. The federal government has the Bureau of Prisons, which operates the federal prison system and is a component of the U.S. Department of Justice, and a federal probation system operated by the courts. In addition, the Department of Defense maintains military prisons. States have their own correctional systems; at the local level, some counties and cities also operate correctional facilities and probation departments. There is considerable variety of organizational structures as well as weak linkages among these many systems.

Prisons　Across jurisdictional systems, prisons are classified as minimum-, medium-, and maximum-security facilities. Until recently, all prisons were owned and administered by governmental bodies, but private enterprise has created a very profitable prison industry in some parts of the country. There has been considerable construction of new prisons, yet they tend to be extremely overcrowded, housing populations in excess of their capacity day in and day out. Juvenile facilities are separate from prisons for adults. They too are seriously overcrowded, presenting the same health, safety, and security problems found in adult facilities. Smaller, community-based correctional programs serve as prerelease centers, halfway houses, and group homes.

The various jurisdictions have different procedures for assigning persons to correctional facilities. Often newly sentenced persons are observed in specially designated reception facilities for several weeks while vocational and psychological testing is done to help select the most appropriate prison facility. Social workers participate in the evaluation procedure, gathering social-history data or supplementing information already available if a presentence investigation was done.

With the burgeoning rate of imprisonment of women (see Exhibit 10-2), the classification of women prisoners is receiving increased attention. Farr, for example, notes that the same classification system tends to be used for both male and female prisoners, yet research demonstrates that women prisoners are significantly less of a threat to other inmates or to the outside community, should they escape. Instead of basing the system on risk, Farr calls for a prison classification system for women based on need. She recommends substance abuse treatment, obstetric and gynecological health care, improving the connections between women and their children, instituting parenting skills training, and treatment for the mental disorders that appear to be more prevalent among women prisoners (2000).

Prison social workers are prisoners' links to their home community. In women's prisons, for example, it is often the prison social worker who communicates with the foster care agency when children have been placed in care pending the mother's release from prison. Family members often have great difficulty accepting the imprisonment. Feelings of anger, abandonment, fear, and denial have to be worked with. Just as families need to make very difficult adjustments when a member is imprisoned, other social, emotional, and economic adjustments are required when release from prison is anticipated. It would be wonderful if all prisons had social workers with sufficient time to provide these services. The reality is that some prisons have no social work staff at all, and other prisons have so few social workers that staff must carefully prioritize their tasks.

Although social workers are members of the prison staff, they do serve as communication facilitators between inmates and other prison staff. As advocates for prisoners, social workers attempt to secure resources, such as access to scarce educational or vocational programs. Social workers advocate with prison administrators

EXHIBIT 10-2

Sentenced Female Prisoners under Jurisdiction of State and Federal Correctional Authorities, 1925–2005

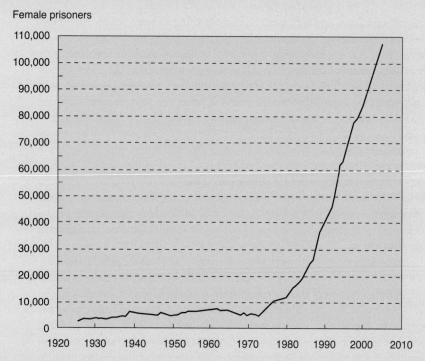

Female prisoners

SOURCE: Adapted from K. Maguire & A. L. Pastore. (Eds.). (2001). Figure 6.2. Sentenced female prisoners under jurisdiction of state and federal correctional authorities on December 31. *Sourcebook of criminal justice statistics 2000* (p. 505). Washington, DC: U.S. Department of Justice, Bureau of Justice Statistics. Retrieved January 12, 2002, from http://www.albany.edu/sourcebook/1995/pdft/6002.pdf; and A. L. Pastore & K. Maguire. (Eds.). (2005). Table 6.41.2005, Female prisoners under jurisdiction of State and Federal correctional facilities. *Sourcebook of criminal justice statistics online*. Washington, DC: U.S. Department of Justice, Bureau of Justice Statistics. Retrieved June 19, 2007, from http://www.albany.edu/sourcebook/pdf/t6412005.pdf

for changes in policies or procedures affecting the inmate population. They also promote an exchange of information between families of inmates (especially children in foster care) and the prisoners. During medical emergencies, prison social workers provide updated medical information between family members and prisoners and, if appropriate, with other segments of the prison community.

Prison riots have demonstrated the role of social workers in negotiation. Social workers have been selected by prisoners to present their issues to administrators and to the outside world. At the same time, social workers become the spokespersons for hostages taken in riots. Given the serious overcrowding of prisons today, most prison facilities experience tension and violence almost daily. Fighting between prisoners is a common occurrence.

Hans Toch's 1977 description of the prison environment remains true today: "Jails and prisons . . . have a climate of violence which has no free-world counterpart. Inmates are terrorized by other inmates, and spend years in fear of harm. . . . Such fears cause problems beyond the immediately obvious ones. In prison, fear is a stigma of weakness, and it marks men [and women] as fair game for exploitation" (p. 53).

Violence in prisons is not limited to inmate-inflicted abuse, nor is it only a function of modern times. Inmates of some of the early prison facilities were forced to work as servants in the homes of wardens, where many abuses were suffered, including beatings and death for disobedience. Female prisoners have always been subject to sexual abuse. Lawsuits filed on their behalf and public investigations into such abuses have resulted in the implementation of procedures that require a formal hearing and response to the complaints of inmates in correctional facilities, but this has not eliminated exploitation or violence.

The absence of heterosexual outlets encourages same-sex relationships in prisons and jails. These relationships may provide some level of comfort and closeness, but they may also produce jealousies, heated altercations, and acts of reprisal for unfaithfulness. Especially in prisons that are overcrowded, rape also occurs, sometimes with extensive physical injuries.

In prison and jail facilities social workers seek to reduce violence by building bridges between inmates and staff, by helping prisoners develop or enhance their sense of self-worth, and by reducing the inmates' sense of powerlessness. In their practice with prisoners, social workers often focus on creating behavioral change, seeking to improve problem-solving skills and to apply these skills in day-to-day institutional decision making. Behavior rehearsal and role-playing are used to teach new behaviors or to modify existing actions. Educational and skill-building programs are implemented. Alcohol and substance abuse group treatment is provided for persons with problems in these areas. Techniques including reality therapy, behavior modification, transactional analysis, and educational programs are used, depending on the social worker's level of skill and on inmates' needs.

Community-Based Corrections   **Community-based corrections** are programs that provide an alternative to incarceration. Probation and parole, the major community-based programs, require ongoing supervision until the original sentence is concluded. The person providing that supervision is generally referred to as a parole (or probation) agent or officer. Preferences regarding the use of "agent" or "officer" vary among the many federal, state, county, and city jurisdictions; we will use "agent." Very often, although not always, the probation or parole agent is a BSW or MSW social worker. Most state probation and parole positions require a bachelor's degree in social work or criminal justice. Sometimes a related degree is acceptable. Median annual earnings are around $40,000 (Bureau of Labor Statistics [BLS], 2007). Federal positions require 1 year of graduate courses in addition to the bachelor's degree; again, a degree in social work or criminal justice is preferred.

While parole provides for the early release of a prisoner from a penal institution, probation permits the offender to avoid imprisonment, remaining in the community to serve her or his sentence. Both parole and probation are conditional; that is, if the terms of the probation or parole agreement are violated, the offender may be subject to **revocation** (may be returned to prison for the remainder of the sentence). The terms of the agreement are identified in a contract signed by the client and the agent. A typical contract is shown in Exhibit 10-3. Note that space is provided for specific terms for the individual client. Exhibit 10-4 illustrates a set of specific terms that might be used with someone convicted of a sex offense.

Helping the person to meet the terms of the probation or parole agreement is a key function of the social worker. In truth, the client's life is subject to almost continuous scrutiny by the social worker. Developing a relationship of trust with a corrections client is not always easy. It requires skill and commitment from the social worker.

Alan Martin, the social worker in the case study, carried many of the responsibilities of both parole agent and probation agent. As a professional social worker in the role of parole agent, Alan Martin sought to apply the knowledge, values, and skills that he had learned while in college. He used the same problem-solving steps cited in Chapter 1, a process that underpins all generalist social work practice. If Brian Cook had been sentenced by the judge to probation instead of prison, Alan Martin might have been assigned as his probation agent. The role of the probation agent is very similar to that of the parole agent, so Alan would have engaged Brian in the same problem-solving work that was done during Brian's parole.

The correctional system requires the agent, in this case Alan Martin, to assist the client in meeting the terms of the probation agreement. The same contract form, citing the very same terms, may be used for both probation and parole, as is the case with the contract shown in Exhibit 10-3. Some correctional systems, however, use separate forms. The probation client generally has not left his or her home community as a result of the conviction and sentence; therefore, the agent has the advantage of working with a person who is still connected to family, neighborhood, and job or school. The pressing need to find housing or employment—so often the case with parole clients—is not usually present, nor is reintegration into the community an issue to be worked through.

Probation and parole agents often have extremely large caseloads. They range widely, from 20 to 100 clients. This makes it difficult for some agents to know their clients well. Often they use much of their time managing crises and barely spend more than 15 minutes with the client who reports for scheduled monthly meetings. Technology—computers, cell phones, fax machines—help probation and parole agents handle heavy workloads. Some agents may use technology to work, in part, from their homes (BLS, 2007).

Probation and parole departments have analyzed the work load and have found that there are identifiable corrections populations that need more time and greater expertise than others. Accordingly, some jurisdictions have created separate units to work with mentally ill offenders, for example, or those whose crime involves substance abuse or sex offenses. Social workers in specialized units usually have a smaller caseload; frequently they have MSW degrees plus experience.

One approach to minimizing **recidivism** (the repetition of criminal behavior resulting in return to prison or reinstatement of a prison sentence) is **risk rating** in which clients with higher risks of recidivism are placed under closer and more

EXHIBIT 10-3

Probation/Parole Rules

DEPARTMENT OF CORRECTIONS Division of Community Corrections DOC-10 (Rev. 12/2008)	**WISCONSIN** Administrative Code Chapter DOC 328 & 332 Federal Law 42 U.S.C. ss 290DD-3, 290ee-3 Federal Regulation 42 C.F.R. Part 2

RULES OF COMMUNITY SUPERVISION

OFFENDER NAME	DOC NUMBER

Notice: If you are on parole and sentenced for crimes committed on or after June 1, 1984, or have chosen to have the new Good Time Law apply to your case and you violate these rules, the highest possible parole violator sentence will be the total sentence less time already served in prison or jail in connection with the offense.

As established by Administrative Rule DOC 328.11, you have an opportunity for administrative review of certain types of decision through the offender complaint process.

The following rules are in addition to any court-ordered conditions. Your probation, parole, or extended supervision may be revoked if you do not comply with any of your court-ordered conditions or if you violate any of the following rules.

1. You shall avoid all conduct which is in violation of federal or state statute, municipal or county ordinances, tribal law or which is not in the best interest of the public welfare or your rehabilitation. Some rules listed below are covered under this rule as conduct contrary to law and are listed for particular attention.

2. You shall report all arrests or police contact to your agent within 72 hours.

3. You shall make every effort to accept the opportunities and counseling offered by supervision.

   The confidentiality of drug, mental health, and alcohol treatment records is protected by Federal and/or state laws and regulations. Generally programs you are involved in may not say to a person outside the Department of Corrections that an offender is attending the program, or disclose any information identifying him/her as a drug/alcohol abuser unless: 1) You consent in writing; or 2) The disclosure is allowed by a court order; or 3) The disclosure is made to medical personnel in a medical emergency or to a qualified personnel for research, audit, or program evaluation; or 4) You commit or threaten to commit a crime either at the program or against any person who works for the program. Programs that contract with the Wisconsin Department of Corrections can release information to Wisconsin Department of Corrections staff.

   Violation of the Federal law and regulations by a program is a crime. These regulations do not protect any information about suspected child abuse or neglect from being reported under state law to appropriate authorities.

   Refusal to sign the consent for releasing information, including placement for treatment, shall be considered a refusal of the program.

4. You shall inform your agent of your whereabouts and activities as he/she directs.

5. You shall submit a written report monthly and any other such relevant information as directed by your agent.

6. You shall make yourself available for searches or tests ordered by your agent including but not limited to urinalysis, breathalyzer, DNA collection and blood samples or search of residence or any property under your control.

7. You shall not change residence or employment unless you get approval in advance from your agent, or in the case of emergency, notify your agent of the change within 72 hours.

8. You shall not leave the State of Wisconsin unless you get approval and a travel permit in advance from your agent.

9. You shall not purchase, trade, sell or operate a motor vehicle unless you get approval in advance from your agent.

10. You shall not borrow money or purchase on credit unless you get approval in advance from your agent.

11. You shall pay monthly supervision fees as directed by your agent in accordance with Wis. Stats. s.304.073 or s.304.074, DOC Administrative Rule Chapter 328.043 to 328.046 and shall comply with any department and/or vendor procedures regarding payment of fees.

12. You shall not purchase, possess, own or carry any firearm or any weapon unless you get approval in advance from your agent. Your agent may not grant permission to carry a firearm if you are prohibited from possessing a firearm under Wis. Stat. s. 941.29, Wisconsin Act 71, the Federal Gun Control Act (GCA), or any other state or federal law.

13. You shall not, as a convicted felon, and until you have successfully completed the terms and conditions of your sentence, vote in any federal, state or local election as outlined in Wisconsin Statutes s.6.03(1)(b).

14. You shall abide by all rules of any detention or correctional facility in which you may be confined.

15. You shall provide true and correct information verbally and in writing, in response to inquiries by the agent.

16. You shall report to your agent as directed for scheduled and unscheduled appointments.

17. You shall submit to the polygraph (lie detector) examination process as directed by your agent in accordance with Wisconsin Administrative Code 332.15.

18. You shall pay fees for the polygraph (lie detector) examination process as directed by your agent in accordance with Wisconsin Administrative Code 332.17(5) and 332.18 and shall comply with any required Wisconsin Department of Corrections procedures regarding payment of fees.

19. You shall follow any specific rules that may be issued by an agent to achieve the goals and objectives of your supervision. The rules may be modified at any time, as appropriate. The specific rules imposed at this time are stated below. You shall place your initials at the end of each specific rule to show you have read the rule.

I have reviewed and explained these rules to the offender.		I have received a copy of these rules.	
AGENT SIGNATURE	AREA NUMBER	OFFENDER SIGNATURE	DATE SIGNED

SOURCE: Provided by Peggy Kendrigan, State of Wisconsin Department of Corrections, Division of Community Corrections. (2007). Wisconsin Administrative Code. Madison, WI.

EXHIBIT 10-4

Standard Sex Offender Rules

DEPARTMENT OF CORRECTIONS
Division of Community Corrections
DOC-10SO (Rev. 12/2006)

WISCONSIN
Administrative Code
Chapter DOC 301, 328, 332
Federal Law
42 U.S.C. ss 290DD-3, 290ee-3
Federal Regulation
42 C.F.R. Part 2

STANDARD SEX OFFENDER RULES

OFFENDER NAME

DOC NUMBER

Notice: If you are on parole and sentenced for crimes committed on or after June 1, 1984, or have chosen to have the new Good Time Law apply to your case and you violate these rules, the highest possible parole violator sentence will be the total sentence less time already served in prison or jail in connection with the offense.

As established by Administrative Rule DOC 328.11, you have an opportunity for administrative review of certain types of decision through the offender complaint process.

The following rules are in addition to any court-ordered conditions. Your probation, parole or extended supervision may be revoked if you do not comply with any of your court-ordered conditions or if you violate any of the following rules.

1. You shall have no contact with _____ nor any prior victims of your offenses nor their family members without prior agent approval. This includes face-to-face, telephone, mail, electronic, third party, or "drive by" contact.

2. You shall have no contact with anyone under the age of 18 without prior agent approval and unless accompanied by an adult sober chaperone approved by your agent. This includes face-to-face, telephone, mail, electronic, third party, or "drive by" contact.

3. You shall not establish, pursue, nor maintain any dating and/or romantic and/or sexual relationship without prior agent approval.

4. You shall fully cooperate with, participate in, and successfully complete all evaluations, counseling, and treatment as required by your agent, including but not limited to sex offender programming. "Successful completion" shall be determined by your agent and treatment provider(s). If sex offender treatment is required, you must attend and account for the details of the behavior committed in your conviction offense(s). Failure to admit the offense(s) or provide a detailed description will be considered a violation of your supervision and may result in disciplinary action including the recommendation for revocation of your supervision. Information revealed in treatment concerning your conviction offense(s) cannot be used against you in criminal proceedings.

5. You shall not reside nor "stay" overnight in any place other than a pre-approved residence without prior agent approval. "Overnight" is defined as the daily period of time between the hours of _____ p.m. and _____ a.m. unless redefined by your agent in advance.

6. You shall permit no person to reside nor stay in your designated residence between the hours of _____ p.m. and _____ a.m. without prior agent approval.

7. You shall not possess, consume, nor use any controlled substance nor possess any drug paraphernalia without a current prescription from a physician from whom you are receiving medical treatment. Verification must be provided to your agent as directed.

8. You shall not possess nor view any sexually explicit material-visual, auditory, nor computer-generated-without prior agent approval.

9. You shall seek, obtain, and maintain employment as directed by your agent. You shall obtain agent approval before accepting any offer of employment and prior to beginning any volunteer work.

10. You shall not purchase, own, nor manage any residential rental properties without prior agent approval.

11. You shall fully comply with all sex offender registry requirements as applicable and directed by your agent and/or required by statute. You shall immediately respond to all correspondence from the Sex Offender Registry Program.

12. You shall fully comply with Wisconsin Statute 165.76 requiring a biological specimen to be submitted to the State Crime Lab for DNA testing as applicable and as directed by your agent.

13. You shall pay all court ordered financial obligations and treatment co-payments as directed by your agent in accordance with your established payment plan.

14. You shall not purchase, possess, nor use a computer, software, hardware, nor modem without prior agent approval.

I have reviewed and explained these rules to the offender.		I have received a copy of these rules.	
AGENT SIGNATURE	AREA NUMBER	OFFENDER SIGNATURE	DATE SIGNED

SOURCE: Provided by Peggy Kendrigan, State of Wisconsin Department of Corrections, Division of Community Corrections. (2007). Milwaukee, WI.

frequent supervision. A risk-rating assessment form similar to the one shown in Exhibit 10-5 is now used in most state and county probation and parole departments as well as in Canada and Australia. Considerable work by the National Center for Crime and Delinquency and other corrections agencies has been done to validate the risk assessment instruments that are used. A score of 15 or higher on the form in Exhibit 10-5 would suggest the need for a maximum level of supervision; scores of 7 to 14 support a median level; and a score of 6 or below would normally result in a minimal level of probation or parole supervision. Generally, a minimum level of supervision or monitoring would involve contacts only once every 3 months, although more frequent telephone or mail-in reports might be required. By contrast, a maximum level of supervision could involve office visits every 2 weeks and possibly a home visit every month (Kendrigan, personal communication, Jan. 2, 2008).

An offender may also be placed in a specialized category of probation known as **intensive probation.** Offenders who have committed violent crimes or who have displayed violence or hostility and are considered to be of high risk are candidates for intensive probation. As the name implies, this form of probation utilizes frequent client contacts—daily or at least several contacts per week. Intensive probation is more cost efficient than imprisonment and provides a relatively high level of community protection. It is also useful with special client populations such as chronic abusers of alcohol or drugs (Butts, 1995).

Before concluding this discussion of probation and parole, it is important to note the considerable policing power of the corrections social worker. No other area of social work practice gives the social worker so much police authority. "In most jurisdictions the probation and parole officer not only performs supervision, surveillance, and counseling roles, but also has the authority to handcuff, search, arrest, and seize property and otherwise restrict clients' freedom" (Netherland, 1987, pp. 356–357). The agent also has the right to recommend a client's return to prison if terms of parole are not met. Agents may require clients to participate in treatment such as substance abuse counseling or batterers' group therapy. This power cannot be taken lightly.

Several other forms of community-based corrections programs exist. Some, such as victim–offender mediation and restitution, have already been described. Several others are informal diversion, community service, and house arrest. Informal diversion is used with first offenders or for minor offenses and is most common in juvenile justice systems. With informal diversion, an authorized intake worker (sometimes a social worker) or officer obtains agreement from the offender to abide by the law and, possibly, to make restitution, in lieu of being prosecuted for the offense. This is humane and cost effective. Community service may be a component of diversion, or it may be the sentence following conviction. It requires unpaid labor that is useful to the community and that, when possible, utilizes the offender's knowledge or skills. With house arrest, offenders are confined to their homes with electronic surveillance ensuring that they do not leave. Wrist or ankle bracelets are widely used and effective in confining offenders. Advances in telephone and computer in-home surveillance are expected to expand the use of house arrest as a form of community-based corrections.

Despite the media's fascination with some situations in which crime occurs during probation or parole, there is a growing body of empirical research demonstrating that

EXHIBIT 10-5

Admission to Adult Field Caseload

DEPARTMENT OF CORRECTIONS	ADMISSION TO ADULT FIELD CASELOAD		WISCONSIN

Division of Community Corrections
DOC-502 (Rev. 7/96)
ASSESSMENT OF OFFENDER RISK

OFFENDER NAME — Last — First — MI — DOC NUMBER — **A**

DATE PLACED ON PROBATION OR RELEASED ON PAROLE IN WISCONSIN (MM/DD/YY) — AGENT LAST NAME — AREA NUMBER

FACILITY OF RELEASE — CODE — DATE COMPLETED (MM/DD/YY)

SCORE

(Select the appropriate answer and enter the associated weight in the score column.)

Number of Address Changes in last 12 Months: (Prior to incarceration for parolees)
- 0 None
- 2 One
- 3 Two or more

Percentage of Time Employed in Last 12 Months: (Prior to incarceration for parolees)
- 0 60% or more
- 1 40% - 59%
- 2 Under 40%
- 0 Not applicable

Alcohol Usage Problems: (Prior to incarceration for parolees)
- 0 No interference with functioning
- 2 Occasional abuse; some disruption of functioning
- 4 Frequent abuse; serious disruption; needs treatment

Other Drug Problems: (Prior to incarceration for parolees)
- 0 No interference with functioning
- 1 Occasional abuse; some disruption of functioning
- 2 Frequent abuse; serious disruption; needs treatment

Attitude:
- 0 Motivated to change; receptive to assistance
- 3 Dependent or unwilling to accept responsibility
- 5 Rationalizes behavior; negative; not motivated to change

Age at First Conviction: (or Juvenile Adjudications)
- 0 24 or older
- 2 20 - 23
- 4 19 or younger

Number of Prior Periods of Probation / Parole Supervision: (Adult or Juvenile)
- 0 None
- 4 One or more

Number of Prior Probation/Parole Revocations: (Adult or Juvenile)
- 0 None
- 4 One or more

Number of Prior Felony Convictions: (or Juvenile Adjudications)
- 0 None
- 2 One
- 4 Two or more

Convictions or Juvenile Adjudications for: (Include current offense, Score must be either 0,2,3, or 5.)
- 0 None of the Offense(s) stated below
- 2 Burglary, theft, auto theft, or robbery
- 3 Worthless checks or forgery
- 5 One or more from the above categories

Convictions or Juvenile Adjudication for Assaultive Offense within Last Five Years: (An offense which involves the use of a weapon, physical force or the threat of force)
- 15 Yes
- 0 No

TOTAL _____ Total all scores to arrive at the risk assessment score

CASE FILE

SOURCE: Provided by Peggy Kendrigan, State of Wisconsin Department of Corrections, Division of Community Corrections. (2007). Milwaukee, WI.

probation and parole do work. This research is finding that some programs provided in prison, such as sex offender treatment, are much less effective in reducing further offenses than cognitive-behavioral programs provided while offenders are living in the community. Shock probation and Scared Straight (programs that incite fear to prevent crime) and correctional boot camps were also found to be ineffective with youths or adults (MacKenzie, 2000).

The Juvenile Justice System

The juvenile court system evolved from quite a different philosophy than the adult court system and came out of the pioneering and social reform work of Jane Addams and Hull House workers, among others. Established in 1899 in Chicago, it was born of the belief that children were not fully developed human beings capable of making judgments about their behavior or controlling their lives in the same way adults were expected to do. Juvenile courts were designed to intervene when children misbehaved or were in need of protection. There was a strong belief that children could be rehabilitated. Treatment was stressed, as well as separation of the child from adult court systems. Juvenile court proceedings were conducted informally, often without legal representation.

While Jane Addams and her Hull House colleagues in Chicago spearheaded social reform including the founding of the first juvenile court in 1899, Margaret Murray Washington (wife of Booker T. Washington) was actively pursuing similar goals in the South. The pioneers of this movement were later referred to as the "child savers," because their efforts led to the establishment of child labor laws, kindergartens, compulsory school attendance, and, perhaps their most ambitious project, the development of a juvenile justice system (Moon, Sundt, Cullen, & Wright, 2000). Removing children from the adult court and prison system was a major breakthrough. It required the skill of noted civic leaders like Margaret Murray Washington, whose personal involvement led to the development of Mt. Meigs Reformatory for Juvenile Law-Breakers in Alabama, which became a state institution in 1911, and the Mt. Meigs Rescue Home for Girls (Dickerson, 2001).

Children's courts and juvenile justice systems were gradually implemented in all parts of the country, and social workers were a major presence in the day-to-day operation of many of these programs. The juvenile justice system continued to grow. In the 1960s, a major philosophical shift occurred. After two landmark Supreme Court decisions, primarily the 1967 case, *In re: Gault*, formal legal processes were instituted within juvenile courts, affording children increased legal protections. No longer could the courts imprison or detain children without due process. An **adversarial court** evolved in which attorneys representing the prosecution and attorneys representing the defense were permitted to engage in cross-examination. Children's courts quickly lost their former informal environment in which parents, children, judges, and social workers talked across a table. Constitutional rights and legal processes increasingly became paramount. Legal issues emerged relating to detention, search and seizure, and, most recently, questions about transfer of children to adult courts.

Today, youth encounters with the juvenile justice system proceed through several phases: arrest, intake, detention, adjudication, and disposition. Behaviors in violation of the law bring youths into contact with the police. The officer determines whether to file charges. While there is considerable variability across states in the United States, most youths who come in contact with police are not arrested but are instead given a warning, or the problem is resolved in some other way. The Juvenile Justice and Delinquency Prevention Act of 1974 discontinued the earlier practice of jailing youths for offenses such as curfew violations and truancy and required that arrested youths be separated from adults in jails or prisons. As a result, juvenile detention centers were constructed. They are now the locations that receive arrested youths. In rural areas, where juvenile facilities do not exist, youths may be held in jails, but they are kept in cells separate from adults.

Following arrest an intake process is begun. It may take only a few minutes or may take up to several days to complete. The intake process will conclude with a decision to detain, dismiss, or make some other disposition of the case. The risk-and-needs assessments that are increasingly part of the intake process may affect the disposition decision. Juvenile court or probation officers (often social workers) generally conduct the intake-and-assessment process. The data collected include any history of past offenses, violent or aggressive behavior, mental health or substance abuse needs, family or peer problems, educational deficits, medical problems, and sexual abuse history. In addition, information is gathered from parents, police, schools, and other health and social service organizations (Mears & Kelly, 1999).

Sometimes **detention** (placement in a juvenile jail facility) is used on a temporary basis while the intake process is being completed. It is also used when there is reason to believe that the youth will not return for the assigned court date. Home detention, possibly supplemented with use of an electronic wrist or ankle monitor, may be used as an alternative. Social workers in juvenile detention centers provide individual and group counseling, often with a behavior change focus. Juvenile court work ideally includes service to families as well, but significant staff shortages often preclude the provision of significant family service.

Adjudication, the next phase, refers to the decisions made by the juvenile court judge when the charge against the youth is reviewed. The court may decide to drop all charges, but if instead the youth is found guilty, sentencing follows. The **disposition** of a case entails the carrying out of the court order. Probation is the most common sentence in juvenile courts. It is similar to adult probation and may require regular monthly contacts or more intensive and frequent meetings with a probation agent, who is often a BSW social worker. Restitution and/or community service may be a component of probation or may be court ordered as an alternative to probation. If the assessment done at intake identified need for mental health or substance abuse treatment, placement in a community-based residential treatment program or group home may be court ordered. Serious crimes or frequent offenses may result in sentencing to a secure juvenile prison, commonly referred to as a training school. Sentencing is for a specified number of years. Training schools are typically designed as a series of cottages, a school, and administrative facilities, all enclosed by walls topped with razor wire. Parole, which resembles probation, typically follows incarceration. Another possible disposition of a juvenile justice case is waiver to adult court for sentencing. This action, which is used with increasing frequency, is generally reserved for serious or violent criminal behavior. Serious and violent crimes, however, have actually declined.

VALUE DILEMMAS FOR SOCIAL WORKERS

Opportunities abound for social workers in the field of criminal justice. Not only does this field offer stimulating practice, but there are also employment opportunities at all levels of federal, state, and local government as well as with private organizations. Salaries tend to be good, and there are additional opportunities for advancement to administrative positions. But refer back to Exhibits 1-5 and 1-7 in Chapter 1 and you will find that only a small percentage of social workers enter this field, although a larger percentage of BSWs than MSWs do so. One of the reasons for this may be the value dilemmas that confront practitioners.

The use and abuse of authority represent one of the most consistent value dilemmas for social workers in correctional settings. For one thing, the legal system within which the corrections social worker functions gives the probation or parole agent substantial policing authority and responsibilities, and this may well conflict with—or at least appear to conflict with—the professional obligations to a client that are defined in the NASW Code of Ethics.

The Code of Ethics's strong emphasis on confidentiality presents a dilemma since social workers in criminal justice settings are required to testify, as requested by the courts, regarding their contacts with offenders and to report any new or suspected offenses. This requirement may place special strain on the relationship between social worker and client. Hard decisions sometimes have to be made by the social worker. If a teenaged girl, on probation for running away, admitted to a probation officer that she had been running away because of her father's sexual abuse, the social worker would feel sad about having to violate the confidence so painfully shared by the teenaged girl, but there would be no doubt that this situation would have to be reported and assessed further.

The profession of social work has long struggled with the issue of coercion in help-seeking. Mandatory, or involuntary, clients, for example, are people who are required by the law to see a social worker or other professional person. Social workers believe that motivation for change is not encouraged when the client is coerced to seek help. Forcing a client to see a social worker on a regular basis, as occurs in probation and parole situations, can result in "conning," where clients learn to "play the game," telling social workers just what they want to hear and nothing more. Sometimes it seems that the criminal justice system has succeeded remarkably well at educating offenders in such avoidance behaviors.

On the other hand, many of the clients seen by social workers and other human service professionals have been forced by some circumstance to seek help. Although a couple may seek marriage counseling from a family service agency voluntarily, the chances are good that one of the marital partners has insisted on counseling as a condition for the continuance of the relationship.

Mandated services can result in a very difficult issue for social workers: the issue of social control. In correctional settings social workers become agents of social control, enforcing specified behaviors from unwilling clients. Social workers ask: Is this a professional, even an ethical role? Hutchison responds that "social workers in mandated settings must acknowledge that they represent society's need, as well as desire, for a functional level of social stability" (1987, p. 587). She further suggests that there are always limits to individual self-determination, since human beings live in societal systems that are defined by their attempt to meet the greater good of the entire community. Sometimes societal systems are repressive, abusive, and unjust. Social workers do not wish to become agents of repression or even of a system that enforces a questionable status quo. Provided this is not the case, Hutchison believes that the social control role is legitimate if it is practiced with care and critically analyzed and if the social worker also seeks changes within the organization needed to humanize it and make it responsive to the needs of its clients as well as the larger society.

SOCIAL WORK WITH GROUPS AND ORGANIZATIONS

Although the case study and most of the discussion to this point have focused on correctional social work practice with individuals and families, there is a growing trend toward work with groups and with entire organizations.

Social work practice with sexual abuse and domestic violence victims as well as perpetrators is often most effective when groups are used. Mothers of sexually abused children, for example, have been helped through the use of groups. Because the mothers' inability to let go of their anger and guilt negatively affected the children's ability to continue their progress toward recovery, mutual aid groups were offered to the mothers. These groups proved to be extremely valuable in helping the mothers talk with each other very openly and in considerable detail about the abuse that another person (often the father or mother's boyfriend) had inflicted on their child. The strong empathy that the mothers offered each other enabled many to heal (Oliphant, 1994).

Similarly, groups for women sexual abuse survivors helped them share intimate, painful experiences of devastation they had never revealed before. They, too, learned to deal with their anger and grief as they learned self-forgiveness and ability to empathize deeply with others (Schiller & Zimmer, 2005). As they regained self-respect, they were significantly better able to nurture their children. Group work with men who have abused others in intimate relationships, interestingly, works with some similar themes. Although they were typically court-mandated, these men's fear of intimacy, angry feelings, and lack of self-respect emerged in group sessions. The detailed and painful sharing of ugly past experiences of their own abuse of others was made possible by the emotional environment of the group. These men were able to regain self-respect as they learned to control their behaviors. The social worker's use of strengths perspective helped them learn about and use the gentle, nurturing part of themselves whether or not they were ever able to return to the relationships that they had abused (Trimble, 2005).

Group work has been shown to be especially useful in prisons. Unfortunately, social workers in prisons are few in number compared with the burgeoning population of new prison admissions. Historically, women's prisons have provided even fewer social services than have prisons that house men. As a result, opportunities for individual counseling in prison facilities are limited. Group work has been found to be a useful alternative, and some believe that it is the treatment of choice in institutional settings.

Problems with anger management may have led to the offense that precipitated incarceration, but it may also be a complication of daily life in prison. In prison, for example, it is not uncommon for guards to demand that a work task, such as scrubbing a floor, be repeated several times even though it was satisfactorily completed initially. An inmate's personal possessions may be taken by other inmates or even by guards when similar prison materials (e.g., a radio) are missing. An inmate may have to share a small cell with a mentally ill or disabled person who is verbally or physically abusive, or an inmate who urinates in bed. Anger, frustration, depression, and mental deterioration are common in prisoners.

Groups can help prisoners verbalize their upset and dissatisfaction. Groups can sometimes be used for advocacy purposes too. Wardens and other prison authorities may be more open to hearing complaints from a group, especially one with a professional staff leader, than from individual prisoners. In this case, the social worker can use generalist practice skills to help make the organization—the prison—more humane, more just, and more responsive to the needs of its client population.

Group work can also be the primary problem-solving approach used in community-based homes for adolescents just released from correctional institutions. Because peer influence is so significant during adolescence, group work can sometimes be more beneficial than individual work with this age cohort. Establishing communication and relationships with withdrawn, socially immature teenagers is often an important goal for social workers in group homes.

Group home placement can be a desirable intervention plan, but a limitation is the high rate of staff turnover. To keep the group home or community-based correctional facility functioning, the social worker must tackle organizational tasks such as training the youth care staff, helping them understand and work more effectively with the residents. Youthful residents of group homes are often violent, impulsive, and very difficult for staff to work with; therefore, group sessions, in which problems of the home or the unit are discussed by staff and residents, are beneficial. The ability of the staff and the group home as an organization to meet the needs of this complex resident population depends heavily on the effectiveness of the social worker.

Social workers work with organizations in other ways as well. When social workers are the administrators of community-based correctional facilities and group homes, they are responsible for the budget, for recruitment and supervision of staff, and for the quality of care provided. A BSW holding the middle-management position of house manager is responsible for the day-to-day operation of the home, for direct supervision of staff, and for program planning for the residents. Whether serving as a house manager, an administrator, or a parole agent, the social worker has a professional responsibility to help make her or his organization as humane, just, and responsive to clients as possible.

ENVIRONMENTAL PERSPECTIVES

Criminal justice is a field of social work practice that brings police, police social workers, and probation and parole agents into communities that are known to people of those communities as high crime areas. Prison staff, including social workers, psychologists, nurses, and others also work in institutional environments where there is risk of violence and where prison inmates are often housed in degrading, even unclean conditions. The social work person-in-environment perspective implies that we need to consider the impact on our clients of the physical space in which they live and work.

Crime and Communities at Risk

Too often in social work we tend to ignore the immediate environments where, in Dennis Saleebey's words, "people live out the rhythms and tempos of their daily lives—rooms, apartments, office cubicles, cars, atria, restaurants, bars, gardens, city blocks, hallways, neighborhood stores, waiting rooms, malls, cells, and the like" (2006, p. 242). We could argue about whether crime causes deterioration in neighborhoods or whether neglected neighborhoods cause crime, but it is pretty clear that dilapidated, poorly cared for properties and crime generally co-exist.

In probation work, social workers' responsibility to their employing organization (usually the county, state, or federal government) is to try to prevent additional criminal activity in the persons they are supervising. When the social worker probation agent visits the client, however, many problems emerge in addition to the crime that resulted in a sentence of probation. Often the client's environment is filled with guns, drugs, and violence. Family, school, and even employment (if the client is lucky enough to still have employment) may actually promote rather than deter criminal activity. Sometimes neighborhoods are so unsafe that even police do not visit them alone.

Why are these communities and the families that live within them at risk? There are probably many factors involved, but now special concern is being voiced about the new threat. The steep increases in imprisonment of youth and young adults as a result of drug-related arrests, especially crack cocaine arrests in inner cities over the past 10 or more years, have had serious consequences for the fabric of community health and well-being: " . . . if one examines data on the residences of the individuals sent to jail or prison, one can begin to understand the impact of imprisonment at the block level. Predictablty, some blocks in urban America 'send' disproportionately high numbers of individuals (mostly men) to be housed in America's far-flung network of prisons and jails. Yet, the sheer magnitude of these local effects is staggering" (Travis, 2004, p. 188). In Brooklyn, New York, for example, it was found that in many city blocks, one out of every eight parenting-age man is sent to jail or prison every year.

The consequences of these policies for the communities hardest hit are almost beyond comprehension. What does it mean to grow up in a neighborhood where, if you are a young boy, there is such a high likelihood that you and many of your peers will go to jail or prison? What does it mean, if you are a girl, to realize that the young men of your neighborhood are often in and out of prison? What does it mean for so many children to be raised by grandparents? What does it mean for the economies of these already impoverished communities to have so many men (and an increasing number of women) sent to prison during the years when they should be learning a trade, establishing a work identity, providing for self and family? (Travis, 2004, pp. 188–189)

The profound impact of a decade of exceptionally high levels of incarceration and lengthy prison sentences, although strongly felt in neighborhoods and communities, has not yet been well portrayed in the professional literature or the national media. It does exist. It does have consequences.

A potential relationship between the United States's switch to unleaded gasoline and the unexpected decline in crime in the early 1990s is now being considered a possible indicator of the linkage between environment and crime and also the benefit that environmental protection can produce. A *New York Times* article reported on Amherst economist Jessica Wolpaw Reyes's findings that carefully and systematically tracked the surprisingly low criminal activity in the teen population born after leaded gasoline was phased out in the United States (Hoffman, 2007). The *Times* article noted that countries like the United Kingdom and Australia, which switched to unleaded gas more recently than the United States, should soon be seeing a reduction in crime, while Indonesia and Venezuela, which only recently discontinued use of leaded gasoline, should experience a decline in crime among teens in another 20 years. The teen crime rate was studied because this tends to be the age group with the highest level of violent crime. Studying crime statistics cross-nationally should provide intriguing data for environmentalists and criminal justice experts alike in the years ahead.

Community Strengths, Restoration, Spirituality, and Resilience

Dennis Saleebey, whose strengths perspective enriches social work practice today, is a firm believer that small changes in environment can bring big changes in the behavior of people. Citing what he refers to as the "Broken Windows" theory, he suggests that creating small changes, such as repairing or replacing broken windows, in areas where crimes occur reap dividends in crime reduction. "If a neighborhood or space looks like no one cares for or about it, then criminals are less likely to be restrained in their activities there" (2006, p. 242).

The strengths perspective tells social workers that all social systems (individuals, families, groups, organizations, and communities) have strengths. We sometimes have to look hard to find them. Supposedly "bad" or "high crime" neighborhoods have strengths, too. They have churches, schools, hard-working people, children full of energy and spirit. Often they contain large, old, ornamented, beautifully designed housing stock. Sometimes small changes, such as fixing a sagging porch or painting a picket fence, can mobilize other improvements in a community and contribute to an overall change in the neighborhood environment. Green space can be created out of

Green spaces and urban beautification or gardening projects provide an alternative to bars as places for people to congregate.

abandoned parking lots. Flower or vegetable gardens add color and beauty. They present an alternative to bars as places for people, old and young alike, to congregate, coming out of the fearful isolation of their homes to chat, share stories, and nurture helping neighborly networks.

Some of these exciting changes are already under way because churches, youth, and neighborhoods have begun to rally "their internal resources to save their neighborhoods from the onslaught of violence" (Travis, 2004, p. 177). In addition to green spaces, block watches, tenant organizations, and local business improvement organizations have sprung into being through the efforts of local community residents.

Churches have been a wellspring of energy and creativity in promoting community health and healing in many areas. While many American religious denominations have promulgated policy statements in support of restorative justice, the American Baptist Church provides resources to enable churches to mediate community conflicts, especially those involving cultural differences. To sustain or rebuild family relationships, some churches have developed programs that enable children to visit parents in prison. Others have provided church space for free health clinics, child care centers, food pantries, and as meeting places for women's alcohol and drug support groups, youth groups, even for probation and parole agents to meet with their clients. The Catholic bishops' statement, *Responsibility, Rehabilitation and Restoration: A Catholic Perspective on Crime and Criminal Justice* (2000, cited in Misleh & Hanneman, 2004), resulted in funds being allocated to local community efforts toward prisoner rehabilitation and restoration of safe, viable neighborhoods. Volunteers from many Christian and other denominational groups are increasingly working with local residents to build the capacities of neighborhoods and to change American social welfare policies that exacerbate poverty (Misleh & Hanneman, 2004).

The emerging resiliency of neighborhoods affected by crime and the resurgence of faith community resources could not have come at a better time. The extraordinarily high rates of incarceration are just now beginning to pose new challenges: prisoners are reaching the end of their sentences and are being released to the community, some on parole but many with no mandated ongoing supervision because their sentences have been served in full. In the next section of this chapter we will glimpse the nature of prison life that these people have experienced.

PROMOTING SOCIAL JUSTICE

As communities, aided by social workers, other professional people, denominational groups, and other volunteers, undertake the challenge of reintegrating large numbers of persons coming out of prison, it will be important to understand the injustices that people experience within prison systems. The environment of prisons in the United States and in many other countries as well makes them breeding grounds for abuses of many kinds.

Amnesty International is a private, nonprofit organization that operates worldwide to secure human rights. It has a large international membership base of individuals as well as student chapters on university campuses around the globe. This organization has exposed inhumane treatment in prisoner of war camps, the detention of political prisoners of conscience, and executions without trial by the Taliban in Afghanistan. In 2000 Amnesty International filed a briefing with the United Nations, alleging that treatment of prisoners in the United States was in violation of the United Nations Convention against Torture and Other Cruel, Inhuman or Degrading Treatment or Punishment. When the United States had ratified this UN convention in 1994, it had agreed to abide by the principles of the convention.

Amnesty International's listing of concerns included the following:

■ Beatings, excessive force and unjustified shootings by police officers.

■ Physical and mental abuse of prisoners and detainees by prison guards, including use of electroshock equipment to inflict torture or ill-treatment, and cruel use of restraints.

■ Sexual abuse of female prisoners by male guards.

■ Prisoners held in cruel conditions in isolation units.

■ Ill-treatment of children in custody.

■ Failure to protect prisoners from abuses by staff or other inmates.

■ Inadequate medical or mental health care and overcrowded and dangerous conditions in some facilities.

- Racist ill-treatment of ethnic or racial minorities by police or prison guards.

- Ill-treatment of asylum seekers held in detention, including in adult jails.

- Cruel conditions on death row and violations of human rights standards in the application of the death penalty. (Amnesty International, 2000, p. 1)

Amnesty International (AI) made numerous recommendations for improvement in U.S. correctional facilities. The development of standards for care of prisoners based on internationally accepted human rights standards, improvements in training of correctional officers, prohibition of torture and ill-treatment, and banning of dangerous restraint procedures were among the recommendations. AI also recommended that only female officers be used to guard female prisoners and that routine shackling of pregnant prisoners during labor and immediately after birth be discontinued. Further, AI recommended that children be incarcerated only as a last resort and that solitary confinement of children be used only as a last resort and the death penalty be discontinued for children and the mentally retarded (2000).

Social workers can promote social justice for prisoners by supporting Amnesty International's efforts. Indeed, social work students on many college and university campuses are working with AI campus chapters to secure humane treatment of prisoners. Action is also being targeted at specific areas of injustice. The New Mexico Chapter of NASW, for example, has developed a coalition of social workers, clergy, and other human rights activists to target the New Mexico state death penalty. According to the chapter executive director, "If we do not take a position against state-sanctioned capital punishment, then we become part of the problem" (Beaucar, 1999, p. 13).

In Michigan the increasing imprisonment of women, especially drug-dependent pregnant women, resulting from nationwide tougher sentencing for drug-related crime concerned social workers. They were aware of the lack of prenatal care in prisons, the high rate of infant mortality, the serious complications of pregnancy for women prisoners, and the inhumane treatment of women prisoners during labor and following delivery. A group of Michigan social workers engaged a Detroit city council member, a coalition of community leaders, and the state Department of Corrections in the development of WIAR, the Women and Infants at Risk program. Social work students did much of the research and organizing work for this project. Especially alarming to them was their finding that in Michigan "women in labor were secured in 'belly chains' while being transferred to the hospital, and a corrections officer—male or female, depending on who was on duty—remained with the client through the birth and the entire hospital stay" (Siefert & Pimlott, 2001, p. 130). The mothers were separated from their babies after a brief hospitalization and returned to the prison. The WIAR project was housed in a residential facility in a Detroit neighborhood. The women who qualified for the program were moved to the WIAR home, provided with maternity clothes (not normally available to prisoners), engaged in prenatal classes, linked with prenatal health care in the community, and given nutritional supplements. When the women went into labor, they were admitted to the local hospital where they delivered their babies. They were not chained or shackled during transport, labor, or following delivery. They returned to the WIAR facility and were

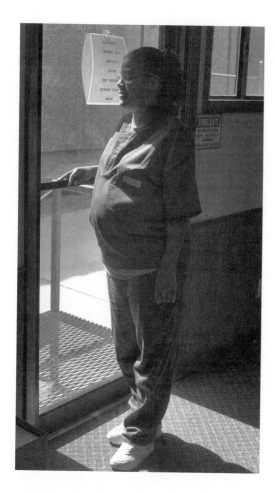

Stephanie Pierre is nine months pregnant and is serving time at the Colorado Women's Correctional Facility. She will give her baby to the New Horizons Ministries, a Mennonite ministry that cares for children who have parents in prison.

able to care for their babies for a full month before returning to a reduced level of work responsibilities. The WIAR program, which continues now after 10 years of operation, also provides GED classes, substance abuse treatment, and counseling. Referring to poor, drug-dependent, pregnant women prisoners, two of the social workers involved with this project concluded: "We hope that social workers in all states will take leadership in addressing the needs of this growing population by reforming punitive and ineffectual policies and instituting constructive and humane programs" (Siefert & Pimlott, p. 133).

SOCIAL WELFARE POLICY IN CRIMINAL JUSTICE

Punitive programs or rehabilitative programs—what do we want for our country? What type and location of prisons do we want: community-based or massive prisons far from population centers? Decisions about these social policies are made by the people we elect to office. The way we vote and how we interact with our elected representatives determine the nature of our criminal justice system.

The liberal and conservative political ideologies concerning incarceration are summarized by McNeece (1995):

> *Liberals* assume that most of the defects of human behavior have their origins in the social environment. . . . Liberals assume that incarceration should provide treatment to rehabilitate, reeducate, and reintegrate offenders into the community. *Conservatives* support the notion of retribution or just deserts, not necessarily as vengeance, but because it serves utilitarian purposes as well. Punishment is not only proper, but necessary, because it reinforces the social order. Deterrence is an expected outcome of incarceration, because punishing offenders for their misdeeds will reduce both the probability of their repeating the act (specific deterrence) and the likelihood of others committing criminal acts (general deterrence). (p. 61)

The strength of political conservatives in recent years has resulted in more use of imprisonment, longer sentences, and less concern about rehabilitation. This approach, however, ignores the simple fact that after a severe prison sentence and with minimal rehabilitation or preparation, most prisoners will someday be released back into the community. What kind of security or protection does this provide our communities? Is this true social or criminal justice?

The Prison Population

The increasing rate of incarceration is demonstrated in Exhibit 10-6. Comparing the 1970 data with those of 2006 (most recently available) shows an astounding rise in the prison population: from 200,000 persons in state and federal prisons to 1,556,518, or a rate of 96 per 100,000 persons in the population to 497 per 100,000 by 2006. The rate of imprisonment always varies from state to state within the country. In 2006 Maine and Rhode Island had imprisonment rates of only 141 and 175, respectively, while Louisiana had a rate of 835 and Texas had a rate of 687 persons imprisoned per 100,000 people in their resident population (Sabol, Minton, & Harrison, 2007).

One result of increasing taxpayer support going to prison construction, staffing, and maintenance is that decreasing portions of governmental budgets become available for allocation to universities, social service programs, health care, and other needs. Another result is that an entire new industry has evolved: private, for-profit prisons. In 1999 more than 138,000 prisoners were held in private prisons, 71,250 in prisons owned by Corrections Corporation of America alone. These numbers declined briefly as states opened numerous new prison facilities. By 2006, nearly 112,000 state and federal prisoners were housed in private prisons, 85 percent of which were state prisoners. Recently, there has been a gradual increase in the number of federal and state inmates housed in private facilities (Sabol et al., 2007). Corrections Corporation of America (CCA), the founder of the private prison system, can accommodate 72,500 prisoners in 65 facilities. According to CCA's website, CCA is now the "fifth largest corrections system in the country, behind only the federal government and three states" (2007, p. 1).

EXHIBIT 10-6

Number of State and Federal Prisoners per 100,000 Residents, 1920–2006

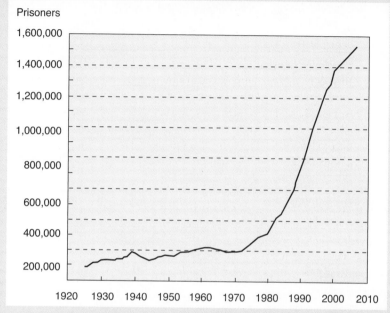

SOURCE: W. J. Sabol, T. Minton, & P. M. Harrison. (2007, June). *Prison and jail inmates at midyear 2006*. Retrieved July 26, 2007, from http://www.ojp.usdoj.gov/bjs/pub/pdf/pjim06.pdf. K. Maguire & A. L. Pastore. (Eds.). (2001, February 2). Figure 6.1, Sentenced prisoners under jurisdiction of state and federal correctional authorities on December 31. Retrieved January 12, 2002, from http://www.albany.edu/sourcebook/1995/pdf/16001.pdf

Public pressure for mandatory sentences, "truth in sentencing" (sentences with no parole), and waivers of juvenile offenders to adult courts continues although some voices for criminal justice reform are beginning to be heard in political debate. Violent crime rates have fallen considerably since 1993, making the 2003 rate one of the lowest in history, but the rate for robbery increased in 2004 and 2005, resulting in a slight increase in the violent crime rate for those 2 years (most recent data available). Most other violent crime categories, such as forcible rape, property crime, and burglary, either remained at previous levels or declined in the 2004–2005 period (U.S. Department of Justice [DOJ], FBI, 2007).

An increasing rate of imprisonment is not unique to the United States, but the United States has had the highest rate of incarceration of all countries in recent years and continued to do so in 2006, which was the most current data available at the time of this writing (Walmsley, 2007). Comparative figures for selected other countries are provided in Exhibit 10-7. It is interesting to note that in the 1990s, Russia's rate of imprisonment was higher than that of the United States and, before apartheid ended in South Africa, that country had the highest incarceration rate in the world (Mauer, 1994).

EXHIBIT 10-7

Incarceration Rates for Selected Nations, 2006
(per 100,000 Persons in the Population)

United States	738
Russian Federation	611
Singapore	350
South Africa	335
Poland	230
Libya	207
Mexico	196
Brazil	191
New Zealand	186
England/Wales	148
Argentina	140
Zimbabwe	120
China	113
Canada	107
Germany	95
Egypt	87
Sweden	82
Norway	66
Japan	62
Cambodia	58
India	30
Nigeria	30
Faeroe Islands (Northern Europe)	23

SOURCE: R. Walmsley. (2007, January 29). *World prison population list* (7th ed.). London: King's College, International Centre for Prison Studies.

Since the early 2000s, the world prison rate (the average of all countries) has remained at approximately 140 incarcerations per 100,000 persons in the population. In 2006 the rate for England and Wales of 148 was slightly above the mid-point; however, more than 60 percent of the 214 countries studied had rates below 150. This is quite a contrast to the United States's imprisonment rate of 738 in 2006. (The figure of 736 used in the world prison population research reflects persons in jails as well as state and federal prisons, which is why it is larger than the previous figure used earlier for U.S. state and federal imprisonment rates.) The United States, China, and Russia combined hold just about half of the total number of persons held in prison in the world (Walmsley, 2007).

The Death Penalty

Another social policy issue relates to **capital punishment**, the death penalty. Since its founding, the ultimate penalty for criminal conduct in the United States has been death. Public sentiment regarding use of the death penalty, however, has vacillated over time. It remains a hotly debated issue. Comments in favor of the death penalty and in opposition to it include:

"There are plenty of innocent people being killed by those on parole. . . . The only cure for this kind of sickness is death. I know I may sound hard and cruel—but I for one, have had enough!" (From a feedback forum, *Detroit News*, March 2, 1999)

"I like it the way it is." (Comment by Governor George W. Bush of Texas at the time that a law prohibiting execution of the mentally disadvantaged was defeated)

"We oppose the death penalty not just for what it does to those guilty of heinous crimes, but for what it does to all of us: It offers the tragic illusion that we can defend life by taking life." (Most Rev. Joseph A. Fiorenza, President, National Conference of Catholic Bishops/U.S. Catholic Conference, 1999)

" . . . in Canada, the death penalty has been rejected as an acceptable element of criminal justice. Capital punishment engages the underlying values of the prohibition against cruel and unusual punishment. It is final and irreversible. Its imposition has been described as arbitrary and its deterrent value has been doubted." (Supreme Court of Canada; all quoted in Robinson, 2001, p. 2)

As the final quote suggests, Canada does not have capital punishment. Nor do many of the other industrialized nations of the world. Some nations refuse to extradite prisoners to the United States because of the U.S. death penalty. Many U.S. organizations—including the National Association of Social Workers, the American Bar Association, the American Civil Liberties Union (ACLU), and various religious organizations—are now calling for the suspension or discontinuation of the death penalty. Inadequate legal representation for poor persons, racial bias, execution of child criminals, execution of mentally impaired persons, and execution of innocent persons are among the concerns of opponents to the death penalty. In recent years, DNA testing has confirmed the innocence of a number of persons sentenced to death. The ACLU has called for a moratorium on capital punishment in the United States.

From a human rights perspective, progress has been made. In 2005, the United States Supreme Court struck down the juvenile death penalty by a narrow 5–4 decision, citing as unconstitutional the state laws authorizing capital punishment for 16- and 17-year-old offenders. At that time, "the United States was one of only six countries in the world in which the juvenile death penalty was lawful. The United States has been responsible for two-thirds of the juvenile executions worldwide since 2002" (Human Rights Watch, n.d., p. 4). There appears to be declining sentiment in favor of the death sentence, yet 38 states and the federal government have capital punishment statutes. As Exhibit 10-8

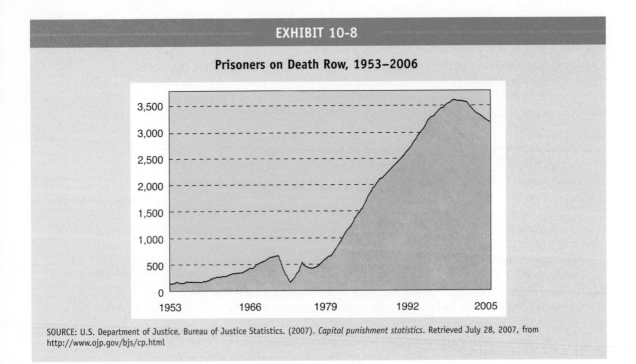

EXHIBIT 10-8

Prisoners on Death Row, 1953–2006

SOURCE: U.S. Department of Justice, Bureau of Justice Statistics. (2007). *Capital punishment statistics*. Retrieved July 28, 2007, from http://www.ojp.gov/bjs/cp.html

demonstrates, the number of prisoners on death row in the United States has begun to decline, with 3,254 persons on death row at the beginning of 2006, 66 fewer than the previous year. In 2006, 53 persons were executed, the majority by lethal injection (one by electrocution). Texas executed the largest number of persons (24) (U.S. DOJ, BLS, 2007). Arguments for and against capital punishment are shown in the Up for Debate box.

Capital punishment for mentally ill persons has become a current social policy issue. In July 2007, the American Civil Liberties Union joined the Tennessee Post-Conviction Defender Office to urge the state's Criminal Appeals court to reverse the death sentence of a schizophrenic, delusional man, Richard Taylor, who was on that state's death row. Citing the case of Kelsey Patterson, a 50-year-old man diagnosed with paranoid schizophrenia, who was executed by the state of Texas in 2004, Amnesty International is also working toward a ban on use of capital punishment for persons with mental illness. This is clearly a thorny issue; mental illness ranges widely, from forms of illness that can be well managed to circumstances of truly severe impairment. Decisions would have to be made, too, about those persons who became mentally ill while in prison versus those who, like Kelsey Patterson, clearly demonstrated profound mental illness at the time of the offense. Kelsey Patterson was apprehended as he walked naked down a street near his home on a warm fall afternoon, mumbling incoherently. He had committed a double murder for which no clear motive was established. Complicating the issue is the fact that "mental health experts believe that many mentally ill prisoners would never have ended up on death row in the first place if they had been able to find treatment when they were free" (Malone, 2005, p. 21).

UP FOR DEBATE

Proposal: The death penalty should be abolished in the United States.

YES	NO
The death penalty is cruel and inhumane, a fact that is acknowledged by almost all other industrialized countries in the world.	The death penalty is "just rewards" for the crime of murder.
Governments have no more right to take a life than does a person.	Each government has a right and an obligation to determine appropriate sentences. In the United States, the Supreme Court has ultimate authority to determine the constitutionality of laws enacted by state courts.
Capital punishment does nothing to protect citizens against crime.	As a result of capital punishment, thousands of people have been executed over the years, all of whom represented a threat to society.
As DNA evidence has demonstrated, there is always the potential for execution of an innocent person.	With technology such as DNA laboratory findings, there is very little likelihood of state execution of innocent persons.
There is clear racial, socioeconomic, and even geographic discrimination in the way in which offenders reach death row and are subject to execution.	The majority of persons subject to the death penalty and executed by the United States are White males.
Capital punishment is a failed, morally wrong social policy.	The death penalty should be expanded to include accomplices and others indirectly involved in committing a murder.

Social Policy and Juvenile Justice

Since 1994, juvenile crime has declined steadily and has fallen to a level last seen in the 1970s. In 2006, the U.S. Department of Justice reported that the number of murders committed by juveniles could be accounted for, in part, by the decline in murders of minority males by other minority males. Only one-fourth of the youths who offended when they were 16 to 17 years of age offended again as young adults (ages 18 to 19). Youth gangs remained active in urban communities; however gangs declined in nonurban areas (U.S. DOJ, 2006).

Despite the decline in juvenile offenses, public attitudes continue to support punitive policy for youths. Many professional persons involved with juvenile justice, however, hold a different perspective.

Jensen and Howard (both social workers) propose that juvenile justice decisions should be based on our knowledge "about the social conditions that place youths at risk of delinquency" (1998, p. 331). This includes such factors as poverty, family instability, and substance abuse. They suggest developing prevention programs targeted at youths known to be at high risk for antisocial behavior and investing in community economic development aimed at providing opportunities for young people. Jensen and Howard warn that "juvenile justice policy reform should not be solely determined by the characteristics of a relatively small number of violent and chronic offenders" (p. 332).

Scott and Grisso write from their perspectives as an attorney and a psychiatrist when they express concern that "the current landscape of juvenile justice reform suggests a view of delinquent youth as appropriately subject to adult punishment and procedures and thus as indistinguishable in any important way from their adult counterparts" (1998, p. 1). They urge the incorporation of understandings from developmental psychology in social policymaking. Scott and Grisso point to statistics that show that delinquent behavior is both fairly common in adolescence and likely to conclude as youths become young adults. Adolescents' knowledge base and decision-making abilities are sufficiently immature, they state, that it impairs their ability to make sound judgments when they are read their rights, at arrest, and in their ability to stand trial. Sometimes immature judgment is also involved in the behavior that leads to arrest. They conclude that severe sanctions (transfer to adult courts, imprisonment in adult jails, severe sentences) on youths for first offenses, even for serious crimes, will be in the best interests neither of the youths nor of society. Not surprisingly, they are opposed to the termination of separate juvenile and adult justice systems in the United States.

Differences between juvenile and adult prisons account for some of the risks that await juvenile offenders who are sentenced to adult correctional facilities. Inmates in adult prisons tend to be much older, while juvenile offenders are usually between 15 and 17 years old. According to Myers, "Older offender ages are correlated with greater size and physical strength, longer and more violent criminal histories, and more experience with incarceration, meaning transferred and incarcerated youths are exposed to a different type of criminal than typically exists in juvenile institutions" (2005, p. 100). The sheer size of adult facilities, often holding upward of 1,000 prisoners, further complicated by overcrowding, creates an environment that, at best, fails to nurture rehabilitation. In fact, studies have shown that juveniles placed in adult prisons are more likely than those in juvenile facilities "to be sexually assaulted, attacked by inmates, beaten by staff, perceive unfair treatment, and commit suicide" (Gottfredson & Barton, 1993, as cited in Myers, 2005, p. 101).

Populations at Risk

The demographics of crime and crime victimization are not very well understood. Which populations are most at risk of being victims of crime? Data from the 2006 Bureau of Justice Statistics' crime victimization report demonstrated racial disparity among victims of violent crime; 27 out of 1,000 Black persons experienced violent crime compared with a rate of 20 for Whites, but 83.6 for persons of two or more races, and 13.9 for all other races. Across all categories of violent crime (includes rape/sexual assault, robbery, aggravated and simple assault, and personal theft) except robbery, persons of two or more races were considerably more likely to be victimized than persons of any single race (Catalano, 2006).

Poor people, too, were more likely to be victims of violent crime than those who were not poor. Those households with incomes of less than $7,500 in 2005 had a violent crime rate of 37.7 (37.7 crimes per 1,000 persons) compared with a rate of 16.4 for households with an annual income of $75,000 or more. This disparity is significant because it demonstrates how much more likely extremely low income families are to experience crime victimization than households of greater means. Another interesting finding from this portion of the report was the amazing decline in violent crime victimization over time. Back in 1994, households with less than a $7,500 annual income had a victimization rate of 86.0, while households with an income of $75,000 or more had a rate of 39.5. The decline in violent crime victimization was statistically greatest for upper-income households, those with incomes of $75,000 or more per year. Property crime victimization rates, too, declined markedly since the 1990s, with upper-income households also benefiting most and poor people benefiting least in this decrease of crime (Catalano, 2006).

Imprisonment rates provide another perspective on the demographics of crime and of victimization. In the United States, the rate of incarceration of African American males is shocking: 836,800 African American men were in a state prison or jail compared with 718,100 white men and 426,900 Hispanic men in 2006; 11.7 percent of all Black men in the 25 to 29 age group were incarcerated; Black men were incarcerated in 2006 at 6.5 times the rate of White men! Black women, too, were imprisoned at exceptionally high rates: approximately four times the rate of White women and twice the rate of Hispanic women (Sabol et al., 2007).

Does this mean that African American men and women actually commit more crime? What does all of this mean to social workers? Social workers are committed to working with poor people. Given the huge overrepresentation of minority groups among the poor and the fact that crime is one way of surviving poverty, then perhaps the data may represent reality. If this is the case, then social workers must be aware of this reality. On the other hand, racially discriminatory behavior from the time an arrest decision is made through sentencing may also profoundly affect the data.

Many other at-risk populations exist within the criminal justice system. Women, for example, are a growing segment of the prison population and, as was demonstrated in an earlier section of this chapter, women prisoners have many unmet health needs.

Paralleling the increase of older persons in the general population is an increase of the elderly in prisons. One study of older male prisoners in Iowa found that they had few visitors. Health care problems included incontinence (the inability to control bowel movements or urination), hearing and vision loss, stiffness and inflexibility, cardiac disease, and high blood pressure (Colsher, Wallace, Loeffelholz, & Sales, 1992). Most prisons are not adequately staffed to deal with problems of advancing age and disability.

Racial profiling is another practice that continues to put selected people at risk despite many law enforcement organizations' efforts to change these behaviors. **Racial profiling** "occurs when race is used by law enforcement or private security officials, to any degree, as a basis for criminal suspicion in non-suspect specific investigations" (Amnesty International USA, 2007a, p. 1). Initially, racial profiling emerged in relation to police decisions concerning arrests for traffic violations. This came to be known as "driving while Black." Clearly, racial profiling can put minority people at risk of search, arrest, and ultimately of imprisonment. Racial profiling expanded in scope immediately after the terrorist attacks of September 11, 2001, and it remains a reality with the U.S. military action under way in various parts of the world plus terrorist activities threatened or occurring globally. According to Amnesty International USA, "the number of American ethnic, racial, and religious groups whose members are at high risk of being subjected to this scourge has increased substantially" (2007b, p. 1).

GLOBAL PERSPECTIVES

The world we live in has become increasingly small. Events that take place in one country are now communicated almost instantly around the globe. The injustice that has been practiced in the United States's criminal justice system has been critically observed by people in other countries. In 1995, for example, the United Nations conducted a review of the human rights situation and found the United States to be in violation of international law, the International Covenant on Civil and Political Rights, which bans the execution of juveniles. The United States Supreme Court did finally take action to ban the execution of juveniles, but not until 2005. "Today the treatment of prisoners regarding extreme overcrowding and limited physical activity, the death penalty, and Native American rights are among the human rights that are under international scrutiny for the first time" (van Wormer, 2004, p. 166). The international community has also expressed alarm with the U.S. detention of noncitizens suspected of terrorist acts and the use of military commissions to try cases of noncitizens.

The United Nations Universal Declaration of Human Rights of 1948, and its more recently developed sections related to the rights of women, children, and trafficked persons, provides a basis for agreed-upon international guidelines to human rights. While the United Nations does not have strict enforcement powers, it does set goals for nations and requests progress reports on identified needs. Member states of the United Nations also seek to hold other nations to the principles affirmed in this document. The United States signed the Universal Declaration of Human Rights; however, the U.S. Senate has never ratified it, leaving the U.S. position something less than totally affirming. Nonetheless, the Universal Declaration of Human Rights remains a respected legal instrument that is used to effect change globally.

In many respects, the NASW Code of Ethics parallels the Universal Declaration of Human Rights as it asserts the rights and dignity of all persons and calls social workers to culturally competent practice. The entire final section of the Code of Ethics, which deals with social workers' ethical responsibilities to the broader society, appears to have been written from a global social justice perspective. The social justice issues that this chapter has identified within the criminal justice area are clearly addressed, whether from a national or an international perspective. The Code requires that social workers "improve social conditions in order to meet basic human needs and promote social justice," that social workers "promote policies that safeguard the rights of and confirm equity and social justice for all people" and also that "social workers should act to prevent and eliminate domination of, exploitation of, and discrimination against any person, group, or class on the basis of race, ethnicity, national origin, color, sex, sexual orientation, age, marital status, political belief, religion, or mental or physical disability" (NASW, 1999).

The human rights perspective of the NASW Code of Ethics invites social workers to think globally and to appreciate the interdependence of all people and all nations. Increasingly, social workers in all parts of the world are expressing concern about criminal child labor that operates on an international level. This includes drug trafficking, smuggling goods of various kinds across borders, as well as petty theft. "International commercial sexual exploitation of children exists in all regions and countries" of the world, according to the organization known as ECPAT, End Child Prostitution, Pornography, and Trafficking (as cited in Lyons, Manion, & Carlsen, 2006, p. 151). According to Lyons, Manion, and Carlsen, authors of *International Perspectives on Social Work: Global Conditions and Local Practice*, the commercial exploitation of children has become a multi-billion-dollar international industry that involves traveling businessmen, military personnel, and the tourism industry. Children's rights are further violated if they are charged with treason and sentenced to death, as has occurred in Uganda, or incarcerated on genocide-related charges, which has been the case in Rwanda.

In 2004, the organization Terre des Hommes estimated that more than 100,000 children are trafficked (moved—sometimes by force—from one location to another for commercial purposes) each month (Dottridge, as cited in Lyons et al.). UNICEF suggests that Europe may currently be the biggest market, with women and children coming in from poorer countries to the east, some former states of the Soviet Union (UNICEF UK, 2003, as cited in Lyons et al.). Distinctions among international child adoptions, fostering, smuggling, and even trafficking are sometimes less than clear in today's world. For women, distinctions among voluntary migration, forced migration, smuggling, and trafficking for sexual, entertainment, or housework purposes are also sometimes unclear. The United Nations Office on Drugs and Crime currently has an initiative under way to stop global human trafficking, and this organization works with nongovernmental agencies and religious denominations to educate communities about this issue. Few local social service organizations, however, focus selectively on these internationally linked human rights issues. Today, international social work is literally coming to the doorstep of social workers everywhere; increasingly, we need to anticipate and be prepared to assist persons whose human rights have been denied in our global society.

INTERNET SITES

http://www.aclu.org	American Civil Liberties Union
http://www.ncjrs.gov	National Criminal Justice Reference Service
http://www.unodc.org/unodc/index.html	United Nations Office on Drugs and Crime

http://www.sentencingproject.org/	The Sentencing Project
http://nofsw.org	National Organization of Forensic Social Work
http://www.angelfire.com/wy/nainmatessupportgrp/index.html	Thundering Drums, American Indian Prisoner Support Group
http://www.religioustolerance.org/execute.htm	Religious Tolerance: Facts about Capital Punishment
http://www.kcl.ac.uk/depsta/rel/icps/home.html	International Centre for Prison Studies
http://www.buildingblocksforyouth.org/justiceforsome	Building Blocks for Youth and Justice for Some
http://www.deathpenaltyinfo.org/	Death Penalty Information Center
http://www.pbs.org/wgbh/pages/frontline/angel	Frontline: Angel on Death Row

SUMMARY

Alan Martin, the social worker in the case study, was experienced in the field of criminal justice. He had worked in the adult justice system before taking his current position with juvenile justice. In fields of social work practice such as criminal justice, where social work is not necessarily the primary profession, it takes special effort to sustain professional self-awareness; Alan Martin had begun to lose his professional identification and was becoming tired and unmotivated. Fortunately for Brian Cook and for Alan's future clients, he was able to confront and not to become lost in the pain of one client's tragic death. Instead, Alan Martin forced himself to reconnect with his professional knowledge base, including a strengths perspective that did not devalue his clients.

The complexities of the criminal justice system are introduced with an examination of its three major components: law enforcement, the courts, and the correctional system. The juvenile system, including its own courts and correctional programs, is also presented. While both BSWs and MSWs are employed in police departments and the courts, it is correctional systems that offer most of the social work employment opportunities today. In fact, many more social workers are employed in probation and parole than in prison facilities.

This chapter offers readers not only an introduction to the population served but also the value dilemmas and role conflicts that social workers in the correctional field experience. Generalist social work practice with individual clients as well as practice with groups, organizations, and within the community are described. Special attention is given to the juvenile justice system and work with youthful offenders because this is an area that often appeals to social workers and that has historically held more career opportunities for social workers.

The environments in which criminal justice programs operate is described, because this is a field of social work practice that challenges social workers with risks as well as rewards. These environments include jails, prisons, and local communities; they sometimes present danger. Communities known as "high-risk" neighborhoods are also shown to possess strengths in their people, their churches, and in sometimes untapped resources. Many of these communities have shown amazing resilience in the face of significant loss of young, parenting-age adults to incarceration. But challenges lie ahead as potentially large numbers of people will soon be released from prison and will need assistance in successfully reintegrating into the community. The experiences these people have had in the prison system are described, and it is apparent that many will be reentering society with little by way of rehabilitation. Punitive juvenile justice policies are also discussed.

A brief historical overview of criminal justice efforts was provided as a context for the evolution of social work within this field of practice. The perspective of social work, rooted in its knowledge of community and social as well as psychological systems, is somewhat unique within criminal justice. It is, nonetheless, a perspective that is needed—one that could challenge the system to seek new approaches and the kind of reform that would ensure true social as well as criminal justice. This field of practice offers career opportunities and exciting challenges for social workers.

The social policy context of corrections is frustrating and challenging for social workers with the current emphasis on punishment (even execution) of offenders rather than prevention and rehabilitation. Issues of poverty and racism that affect both the victims and the perpetrators of crime call out for social justice. Populations that were shown to be at special risk were people who are poor or elderly, African American males, and the youths, especially young women who are now increasingly housed in adult prisons.

The chapter concludes with a consideration of the interdependence of the global community in which we live and practice our profession of social work. It is pointed out that the injustices of the U.S. criminal justice system are not unknown to the rest of the world. The United Nations Universal Declaration of Human Rights was introduced and linkages to the NASW Code of Ethics were noted. The Code of Ethics calls social workers and students alike to act to prevent social injustice globally as well as locally. Several areas of international social injustice related to crime are described, including the trafficking of women and children. Social workers are urged to internationalize their thinking as they practice their profession.

KEY TERMS

adjudication, *p. 420*

adversarial court, *p. 419*

capital punishment, *p. 433*

community-based
  corrections, *p. 413*

community-service
  sentencing, *p. 410*

correctional system, *p. 410*

detention, *p. 420*

disposition, *p. 420*

felony, *p. 406*

forensic social work, *p. 405*

intensive probation, *p. 417*

jail, *p. 410*

misdemeanor, *p. 406*

parole, *p. 406*

police social work, *p. 408*

presentence investigation, *p. 409*

prison, *p. 410*

probation, *p. 406*

racial profiling, *p. 437*

recidivism, *p. 414*

restitution, *p. 410*

revocation, *p. 414*

risk rating, *p. 414*

subpoena, *p. 409*

DISCUSSION QUESTIONS

1. Speculate about the future of Brian Cook. What are his chances of leading a law-abiding life and avoiding return to prison?

2. What will the social worker, Alan Martin, need to do to prevent burnout?

3. How does probation differ from parole?

4. What is the benefit to a community of having police social workers? Are there police social workers in your community? What are their roles?

5. Why does a court request a presentence investigation? How detailed is this kind of report? What would be the outcome for the client if the social worker's presentence investigation report were poorly written or inaccurate or failed to include significant data?

6. Explain the function of a prison social worker.

7. What trends have emerged in the rate of imprisonment in the United States? How does the U.S. rate of imprisonment compare with that of other countries?

8. What racial or ethnic group has been most victimized by crimes of violence? What group has the highest rate of imprisonment? How can this be explained?

9. What social justice issues exist in the field of criminal justice?

10. What strengths might exist in neighborhoods that are described by the media as "high crime" areas?

11. How could social workers and social work student organizations join in the international effort to stop human trafficking or work on behalf of global human rights?

CLASSROOM EXERCISES

It is suggested that students break into small groups of three or four to discuss these exercises. It may be helpful to choose a scribe to record and report interesting points to the class after the group discussion.

1. This chapter states that only a small percentage of social workers enter the field of criminal justice, possibly due to value dilemmas. Identify major social work values that might interfere with practice in the criminal justice area, and discuss ways in which they could be put into action to the fullest possible extent.

2. Minorities are disproportionately incarcerated not only in this country but abroad. Discuss evidence cited in this chapter pertaining to the United States.

3. Discuss concerns with U.S. prisons that have been identified by Amnesty International and this organization's recommendations for improvement. How can social workers promote social justice for prisoners?

4. What are some unforeseen results of increased taxpayer support going to the building and maintenance of prisons? For example, how does prison spending affect public support of universities? Hospitals? Other important social institutions? Do you think this is a good trade-off? Why or why not?

RESEARCH ACTIVITIES

1. Use community resource directories and focused telephone contacts to identify the various organizations that are directly or indirectly involved with criminal justice in your community. Which of these employ social workers? Consider interviewing a social worker to learn about his or her professional responsibilities.

2. Based on the findings from your research of the community, determine whether private (for-profit) enterprise has entered the correctional field in your community or whether your local/state corrections programs send prisoners to private enterprise facilities in other areas. What effects, if any, do you expect this trend to have on offenders and their families?

3. Review and analyze current media reports related to criminal justice. How are victims of crime presented? How are the persons who committed the crimes presented? In media coverage of criminal justice programs or proposed policies or programs, is funding for rehabilitation programs described? Based on your media research, what kind of actions should social workers (and students) be taking to fight for social justice?

INTERNET RESEARCH EXERCISES

1. As a social worker it is important to be familiar with the sources of information that may be required by your clients. One such source is the National Criminal Justice Reference Service (http://www.ncjrs.gov/index.html).

   a. What is the NCJRS? (Hint: click on "About NCJRS.")

   b. What is the most frequently asked question of NCJRS? (Hint: click on "Search Q. & A.")

   c. How do you think you might use this service in your work as a professional social worker? How as a student?

2. The U.S. Department of Justice, through the Office for Victims of Crime, funded a 3-year

demonstration project with the Texas Chapter of the National Association of Social Workers (http://www.ovc.gov/publications/bulletins/NASWvictimassistance/ncj210592.pdf)

   a. What were the four objectives of this project?

   b. Why were social workers chosen to participate in this project?

   c. What do you feel would be the primary satisfaction in working in victim assistance? What is the primary drawback?

3. *Social Work Today* has an article in their archives regarding new opportunities for social workers in the area of criminal justice (http://www.socialworktoday.com/archive/swnov2006p34.shtml).

   a. What activities would you imagine a social worker in the offender reentry field would pursue?

   b. According to this article, what is the connection between a Girl Scout Troop in Austin, Texas, and the criminal justice system?

   c. What sort of challenges do you think police social workers would face in their work?

4. Cognitive interviewing is the subject of an article, "Social Research Update," published at the University of Surrey in Guildford, England (http://sru.soc.surrey.ac.uk/SRU50.html).

   a. What is cognitive interviewing?

   b. Once the interviewee has been encouraged to recall an experience and has gotten into the subject, should the interviewer seek clarification on certain points? Why?

   c. While the thrust of this article is using CI as a research tool, how do you feel your routine client interviews might be improved using some of the aspects of this technique?

FOR FURTHER READING

Judah, E. H., & Bryant, M. (Eds.). (2004). *Criminal justice: Retribution vs. restoration*. New York: Haworth Press.

   The editors of this text, a social worker and a Catholic priest, have gathered a collection of articles that offer a remarkably fresh, hopeful, yet scholarly perspective on criminal justice practice. They speak the language of values, reconciliation, restoration, faith, forgiveness, and struggle. With the insight of very seasoned professionals in the criminal justice field, Judah and Bryant have come to the conclusion that restorative justice could hold the seeds of a better way of providing justice than the policies and practices that currently characterize the field of criminal justice in the United States.

Lyons, K., Manion, K., & Carlsen, M. (2006). *International perspectives on social work: Global conditions and local practice*. New York: Palgrave Macmillan.

   The three authors of this book are as international as the topic they address: all are social workers but they come from the United Kingdom, Canada, and the United States—and one currently resides in New Zealand. This book is exceptionally well researched. It addresses an amazing span of content that reflects social policy and practice internationally. The authors' knowledge of international organizations, governmental as well as nongovernmental, and their work is impressive. The first portion of the book examines three related concepts: globalization, inequality, and loss. The remainder of the text focuses on the workings of globalization and the ramifications for social workers who work with communities during war and other conflicts, migration both forced and voluntary, the exploitation of children and women, and the global spread of disease. The final chapter encourages social workers to incorporate more environmental content in practice and teaching and urges all social workers to develop an international perspective to their practice.

Myers, D. L. (2005). *Boys among men: Trying and sentencing juveniles as adults*. Westport, CT: Praeger Publishers.

   This book is written from the perspective of a criminologist, not a social worker. The author directs the doctoral program in criminology at Indiana University of Pennsylvania. The book, laced with case studies, is well researched and scholarly yet highly readable. Myers walks the reader through the history of the juvenile court system in the United States, with its efforts to rehabilitate and to punish, to crack down on juvenile crime, and to elicit positive behavioral change. The reader follows Myers to the conclusion that adult courts and prisons are clearly not an appropriate answer to the needs of juvenile offenders.

Saleebey, D. (Ed.). (2006). *The strengths perspective in social work practice* (4th ed.). Boston: Pearson, Allyn & Bacon.

Saleebey, the originator of the strengths perspective that has had such a positive impact on social work education and practice in the past decade, continues to build and advance the theory base of this perspective in the 4th edition. In Part One of the text, Saleebey introduces the strengths perspective and the language of strengths, contrasting this to the medical, or pathology, model that has dominated social work practice for years. Another chapter by Blundo describes the fundamental shift in thinking needed to truly embrace and implement the strengths perspective and move toward a solution-focused, collaborative model of practice. Part Two focuses the reader on the strengths of indigenous people. Part Three, Chapters 5 to 15, examines implementation of a strengths-based approach to practice including practice with individuals, families, and communities. Every chapter in this text breathes fresh ideas and energy into a form of social work practice that truly respects, values, and empowers the people we serve as social workers.

Scott, E. S., & Grisso, T. (1997). The evolution of adolescence: A developmental perspective on juvenile justice reform. *Journal of Criminal Law and Criminology, 88*(1), 137–189.

The authors, a professor of law and a professor of psychiatry, make a remarkably compelling argument for the continuation of separate juvenile and adult court systems in the United States. They apply a coherent, in-depth analysis of the understandings derived from developmental psychology to the criminal proceedings that occur at all phases from arrest to incarceration in juvenile justice systems.

van Wormer, K. S., & Bartollas, C. (2007). *Women and the criminal justice system* (2nd ed.). Boston: Pearson, Allyn & Bacon.

This book is emphatically feminist, in the best possible sense of the term. It seeks to explain and describe the involvement of women in the criminal justice system—women who commit crime and women (lawyers, social workers, jail officers, correctional officers, and wardens) who work within the criminal justice system. New to the second edition of this excellent text are chapters on feminist theories, delinquency behaviors across the lifespan, restorative justice programs, substance abuse, and victimization of women. The entire text is enriched with a global perspective that provides examples of some of the best practices today in the criminal justice field.

CHAPTER 11

DEVELOPMENTAL DISABILITIES AND SOCIAL WORK

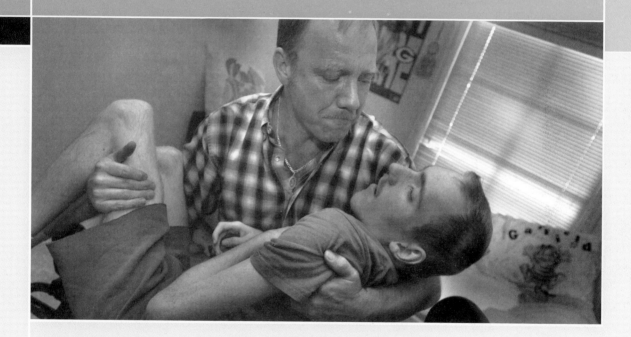

OUTLINE

Mary and Lea Perkins

MARY AND LEA PERKINS

Mary Perkins called the Department of Social Services (DSS) early one morning. Her teenage daughter, Lea, had been sexually assaulted by an unknown person during the night. The attack had taken place on the front steps of the family apartment. Mary had already called the police, but then she decided to call the DSS as well, because she believed that Lea was out of control and needed help. The girl had disobeyed Mary's curfew rules again, contributing to her traumatic experience. Moreover, she had skipped school almost daily for months. Mary asked the DSS for help in supervision. She knew the department offered these services because her older daughter, Lorraine, already received them. Lorraine had been arrested for drug possession the year before, and DSS supervision had been ordered by the court under a CHIPS petition (child in need of protection).

Shortly after Mary's call for help, a neighbor called to report Mary herself for neglect, complaining that the mother was rarely home and allowed her children to "run wild all day." The case was scheduled for investigation. The social worker making the initial contact regarding Lea found a mother who was overwhelmed by the demands of parenting three children, Lorraine, 16, Lea, 14, and Jeff, 11. Mary was openly seeking assistance. The children's father was not a resource for her. Alcoholic and unemployed, he had abused the mother physically and emotionally for years. Mary had recently secured a divorce; social workers at a local women's shelter had assisted her. With three children to support on her own, Mary worked long hours every day to try to make ends meet.

Because of Mary's admitted lack of control, Lea was at risk for foster placement. The case was contracted out to a private agency according to a service agreement reflecting the current trend toward privatization. The agency assigned the case to its Home Base program, which provided intensive in-home intervention designed to prevent foster placement. According to the agency's contract with DSS, services could be provided in the home setting for up to 3 months, for 4 hours per week.

If in-home intervention failed, foster care would follow. The Home Base program assigned the case to one of its social work student interns, Jenny Chambers.

New to her internship, Jenny felt understandably anxious when she read the referral information. She tried to make an appointment right away, but the Perkins's telephone had been disconnected. Jenny sent a note to schedule a late-afternoon appointment, when she hoped Mary would be home from work. Thankfully, she was. Mary met Jenny at the door and invited her in graciously. With an embarrassed smile, she raised her arms upward in a helpless gesture, motioning at the room around her. It was in total disarray. Clothes lay scattered all over the floor and dishes overflowed the sink. "I'm so sorry," Mary said softly. "I tried to clean up last night for your visit, but the children wouldn't help, and they messed everything up again today. I might as well not have bothered."

Jenny took a deep breath and smiled at the mother warmly, complimenting her on the one item she could see giving her an opportunity to do so, an appealing family picture hanging on the wall.

Mary began to talk about her troubles. Jenny soon learned that the family not only lacked a telephone but heat as well. In addition, the rent was 3 months overdue, and the landlord was threatening eviction. Mary cried as she told Jenny that as her bills piled up, she simply did not know what to do so she threw them in a grocery bag and tossed the bag in her bedroom closet. That way she could pretend they were gone. But the children made her so nervous she withdrew into the bedroom early in the evening and shut the door. Part of this problem was that two teenaged boys, Lorraine's boyfriend and one of his buddies, stayed in the apartment most of the time. They had been rejected by their families, and Mary felt sorry for them. To add to the confusion, Lea had recently thrown a frying pan at a friend's mother during an argument and had been arrested for assault. The neighbor had taken out a restraining order, and there would be a court appearance for Lea soon.

Jenny's social work courses at school had prepared her to look for strengths and resilience. She was grateful, as otherwise she suspected she would feel overwhelmed listening to Mary's situation. She began consciously searching for strengths. She already knew of one: Mary had read Jenny's note and kept her appointment. There were several others. Mary had tried to clean her apartment for Jenny's visit. Two of her three children were attending school. She wanted to hold her family together. Prior to the neglect charge, Mary had had the strength to request assistance for Lea. Now that the DSS was considering foster placement, Mary was willing to do whatever she could to prevent that from happening. She worked long hours due to economic necessity, not because she wanted to neglect her children. She was managing a full-time job responsibly. Like many poor people, she was generous, sharing her meager resources with two needy teens who were not even related to her.

Jenny next talked with Mary about Lea. Mary felt sorry for her daughter about the sexual assault but was also angry with her, as Lea had disobeyed Mary's curfew rules. Jenny asked how Lea usually behaved. Mary described Lea as "out of control, disrespectful, and nasty." Mary frankly stated that she felt exhausted from trying to function as a parent. But she did not want to "lose" her daughter, as so many of her neighbors had lost their children. Lea could be killed or injured on the street, for example. She could end up in foster care due to the neglect charge or to repeated truancy. Mary said that Lea probably refused to go to school because she was a very poor student.

On a hunch, Jenny asked Mary about her own experience as a student. To her surprise, she learned that this mother had an intellectual disability. School had been a desperate struggle for her, but a special education program had been opened when she was in her early teens. A teacher had referred her for evaluation, and she was placed in a class for children with mental retardation. While ashamed at first, Mary began to blossom with the new attention she was receiving. During her senior year, she participated in a school-to-work program, where she learned to assist in a physician's office. That education had served her well: Mary worked in a physician's office still.

Was it possible that Lea had an intellectual disability too, Jenny wondered? Could a special education placement make a positive difference for her? Certainly a referral for assessment was in order. And what about Mary's unusual coping style? Could her disability help explain the bag of unopened bills? Jenny also learned that Mary was taking prescribed medication for anxiety. Anxiety, too, could affect Mary's coping skills.

Before Jenny left her appointment with Mary, she made another to talk with Lea. When she returned 2 days later, Lea was waiting for her. A slim, appealing young girl with auburn hair and expressive blue eyes, she was dressed in baggy jeans, an old sweatshirt, and torn sneakers. Lea told Jenny straight away that she was tired of being poor and wanted to move out of the "ghetto," as she described her neighborhood. People who lived there were looked down upon as "criminals or bums." Lea admitted that she used alcohol to feel better and had been drunk the night of the sexual assault. She was having difficulty sleeping now because of flashbacks and nightmares. She admitted that she was fighting a lot at home and had recently been arrested for attacking a friend's mother.

Jenny recognized the emotional turmoil Lea was experiencing and the associated behavioral problems. However, she also recognized many strengths. Lea had kept her appointment with Jenny and talked to her with surprising candor for a first interview. She could express her feelings verbally. She was aware that some of her behavior was inappropriate. She was aware of her external environment and its dangers, even though she was careless about protecting herself. Lea also expressed a strong interest in sports. Jenny thought this might help lure the young girl back to school.

Jenny met next with Mary and Lea jointly. Together an intervention plan was developed, including a contract that was signed by all parties. The contract called for (1) school attendance and educational testing for Lea; (2) house rules for Lea; (3) consequences for Lea if she did not follow the rules, which Mary must enforce; (4) therapy for both mother and daughter; and (5) convincing DSS not to place Lea in foster care (this was the component that motivated Lea to agree to the other conditions).

To make the contract feasible, Jenny assisted the family in dealing with some very practical matters: the rent, the telephone, and the heat. She reviewed with Mary every bill in the grocery bag. She role-played talking with the landlord and encouraged Mary to approach the man in person. A payment plan for the back rent was successfully negotiated. Next, Jenny encouraged Mary to talk with the telephone company. A payment plan was worked out and service restored. Jenny found a state energy assistance program and encouraged Mary to call for more information. Mary did so, and her heating bill was substantially reduced with funds from the energy assistance program. Another payment plan was worked out. Heat was restored.

But if Mary were to meet the conditions of the payment plans for rent, telephone, and heat, something would have to be done to balance her income and expenses. So Jenny helped Mary develop a budget. That involved a great deal of effort. While many single mothers are unable to make ends meet due to inadequate wages, Jenny suspected that Mary might have an especially difficult time due to her intellectual disability. So she showed Mary how to write her income and expenses on paper and how to record her payments. To help cut expenses, she shopped for groceries with Mary and showed her how to compare prices and use coupons. She even helped Mary plan simple meals, demonstrating how she could save money by avoiding fast-food takeouts.

Through these efforts, Jenny and Mary together realized that feeding two extra teenagers was impossible on Mary's income. Moreover, Mary recognized that their presence had a lot to do with her withdrawing to her bedroom every evening. With Jenny's coaching, she found the courage to tell the boys that they would have to find another place to stay. Jenny offered to help them approach their parents or to refer them for foster care. The boys opted for help in talking to their parents and soon went home.

Now Jenny decided it was time to clean up the Perkins apartment, if Mary was interested. She was. Jenny moderated a family meeting, where Mary assigned regular chores to herself and the children. Together, they drew up a chart to record their accomplishments, displayed conspicuously on the refrigerator. While Jenny did much of the initial cleanup work with the family, gradually they took over.

Getting Lea to go to school or to attend therapy was not easy. The girl finally agreed to attend school only after her probation officer threatened to put her in juvenile detention if she didn't. (Lea had been put on probation for the frying pan incident shortly after Jenny began working with the family.) She then agreed to attend if Jenny would accompany her. Jenny agreed, and then referred Lea for a special education evaluation. Only after several meetings with Jenny, the special education staff, and Lea would Lea attend school on her own. Jenny also found she had to accompany Lea to her first few therapy sessions.

Assessment by the special education program determined that Lea did not have an intellectual disability. Her intelligence tested above average, in fact. However, she did have another disability, emotional disturbance (ED). Lea demonstrated disturbance in three environments: school (truancy), home (disobedience), and community (fighting behavior). Moreover, Lea's therapist submitted a diagnosis of PTSD, or posttraumatic stress disorder. The PTSD related not only to the recent sexual assault but to prior physical and sexual abuse by her father, which the therapist reported to DSS for further investigation. Lea soon began receiving special services at the school and became a much happier person. She joined the girls' basketball team, making new friends. Her grades improved dramatically. Lea's lively blue eyes flashed with pride as she told Jenny about her new accomplishments.

To Jenny's dismay, however, Mary Perkins initially did not follow through with parts of her contract, either. She did not attend therapy, nor did she often enforce consequences when Lea broke house rules. Lea continued to roam the streets at night, and because the rapist remained at large, danger was real. Jenny sometimes wondered if foster placement might not be appropriate after all. Mary seemed to say one thing and do another with respect to her daughter. Jenny later wrote, in an assignment for her university program, "At these times I was forced to trust in the love between daughter and mother and hope that they, with assistance, could find balance and safety. I had to believe in the process of treatment, in healing, and in resiliency" (Stites, 2001, p. 23).

Believing in the power of a strengths-based approach, Jenny continued to meet and talk with Mary regularly. She learned that Mary had suffered physical and sexual abuse from her own father. Jenny was then able to help the mother understand Lea's trauma (and need for firm parental protection) in terms of her own. Jenny helped Mary understand that she needed to serve as a role model for her daughter and to maintain consistent discipline to help Lea gain a sense of security and importance. Finally, Mary began to attend therapy, which helped her deal with long-term anxiety and develop the strength to enforce her own house rules.

As the initial 3-month contract with DSS came to a close, Jenny did not believe that either Mary or Lea was ready to carry on without assistance. She applied for, and received, a 6-week extension. By the end of that time, the situation had stabilized. Lea was attending school every day on time, participating in the ED program, and actually earning A's. Mother and daughter were attending therapy regularly, reporting that it was useful. Mary was writing down on paper her behavioral expectations and consequences for Lea and enforcing them. She was discussing possible alternative living situations for Lea if her expectations were not met. Lea was following the house rules.

Termination wasn't easy for anyone. Lea, in fact, said she felt "sad and out of control" when Jenny reminded her that their time was coming to a close. Jenny helped Lea recognize that she had many other caring people in her life now, such as her therapist and the special education staff. She reminded Mary and Lea that they could call the agency for services again if needed, but that she herself would no longer be an intern there. Jenny was sad at the end of her allotted time with the family, as she had grown fond of every member.

A few weeks later, Jenny's supervisor visited the family to evaluate Jenny's work. In response to her questions, Mary replied, with tears in her eyes, that Jenny had been "an awful nag, but we miss her terribly." ■

SERVICES FOR PEOPLE WITH DISABILITIES: A BRIEF HISTORY

Throughout most of history, very little has been done for persons with disabilities. At one extreme (ancient Sparta), individuals unfortunate enough to have an obvious disability were left outside to die of exposure. Native Americans, on the other hand, allowed people with disabilities to live unharmed as children of the Great Spirit.

There are a few early recorded efforts to make special provisions for persons with disabilities. In the 1300s, a colony of persons with mental retardation was established in Belgium, and in 1325 King Edward II of England issued a statute distinguishing between people with mental retardation and those afflicted with temporary mental illness. He established guidelines to protect the rights of "idiots" and to provide for their daily care (Dickerson, 1981). Later on, the Elizabethan Poor Law of 1601 provided limited food and shelter for people with disabilities (along with the poor, the mentally ill, and the sick). Apparently, no thought was given to providing services or education to improve the lives and opportunities of such individuals.

France provided the pioneers who first educated persons with disabilities. Jacob Rodriguez Pereira demonstrated that people with speech and hearing problems could be taught to read words and to add simple numbers. By the late 1700s, Pereira had become so famous for his work that he was honored at the court of King Louis XV. Later, in the early 1800s, Jean-Marc-Gaspard Itard took on the education of a young boy, about 12 years old, whom he named Victor. The boy had been discovered living in a forest in France in 1799, and Itard hoped to help him learn how to function as a normal human person. Itard worked intensively on this goal for about 5 years. The extent of Victor's mental retardation was too great, however, and Itard initially considered the project a failure. However, he was able to teach Victor basic self-care skills such as feeding and dressing. The boy remained mute but learned to read and write a few words. The French Academy of Science, impressed by Itard's accomplishments, recognized him and asked him to write a report. The result became a classic, *The Wild Boy of Aveyron* (Patton, Blackbourn, & Fad, 1996).

Another Frenchman, Itard's student Edouard Seguin (who was also influenced by Pereira), worked with small groups of children with mental retardation in a hospital in Paris in the mid-1800s. Seguin demonstrated that these children could be taught to speak, read, obey instructions, and accomplish simple tasks.

Training Schools

At the same time Seguin was working with retarded children in Paris, a Swiss physician named Johann Guggenbuhl started a residential facility for people afflicted with cretinism. Cretinism is common in mountainous regions of Europe. Caused by a thyroid deficiency, it results in severe mental retardation and physical crippling. Guggenbuhl was inspired by a religious vision; he was determined to prove that these people could be taught. Guggenbuhl succeeded in his long-term goal, stimulating further work with people with disabilities all over the world, including the development of training schools in the United States. In the short run he ran into trouble, however, partly because he misunderstood the causes of cretinism. Like others of his time, Guggenbuhl thought the condition was caused by poor diet, unclean air and water, and lack of sunlight. He corrected these problems in his training school but promised too much in too short a time. His facility was closed in 1858.

In 1848, Dr. Samuel Gridley Howe, an American reformer, traveled to Europe and visited Guggenbuhl's training school and Seguin's hospital program. Back in the United States, he lobbied for funds to begin similar work. He established training schools for children with disabilities in Massachusetts, New York, and Pennsylvania during the late 1840s and early 1850s. These schools were small and usually served fewer than 20 children each; their goal was to prepare children with disabilities (such as vision impairment or mild mental retardation) for productive adult lives in the community. Admission was limited to those children who were considered to have the most potential for rehabilitation and eventual discharge.

Seguin emigrated to the United States in 1848 after the rise of Napoleon III, a dictator with whom he had political and religious differences. As Seguin became active in the early movement establishing training schools for children with disabilities in America, he advocated for small facilities, each ideally serving no more than 200 children, so that each child could receive individual attention and planning. He suggested that these institutions be built near cities and towns so that younger children could receive instruction by parents, who, in turn, could be coached by the training staff of the school. Seguin's intent was that children should be returned to the community when they gained sufficient skills (Switzky, Dudzinzki, Van Acker, & Gambro, 1988).

Protective Asylums

Because of the lack of other resources for people with developmental disabilities in the community, the vision of the training school as a small institution to educate a few disabled children for community living soon was overwhelmed by demand for protective shelter for disabled people of all kinds. By the 1870s, parents and relatives were begging the schools to take on the daily care of their family members with disabilities.

The training schools quickly turned into huge impersonal institutions. They tended to be built in rural areas, which isolated the residents from the rest of society. To reduce costs, higher-functioning residents were set to work the land, so their education was abandoned in favor of using their abilities as a means of producing income for the asylums. Other talented residents were required to cook, clean, and provide personal care for the less able. Thus, tax input to support the institutions could be kept low, reducing taxpayers' complaints.

Custodial care, rather than education or rehabilitation, became the purpose of these large asylums. By the late 1860s, Samuel Gridley Howe was advocating that the institutions be closed. He urged that their residents be reintegrated into society rather than being segregated into the cheaply built, warehouse-style, oppressive facilities designed to provide mass management rather than individualized care.

The Eugenics Movement

The institutions were not closed, however. The next period of history was one that demeaned people with developmental disabilities and tended to keep them not only socially isolated but also despised. By the 1880s, social Darwinism was in full swing. Its advocates took Charles Darwin's fascinating discoveries regarding evolutionary trends in whole physical species and inappropriately applied them to single individuals within the species called *Homo sapiens* in a way Darwin never intended. Social Darwinists preached that because persons with disabilities were "inferior," they were second-class citizens, and taxpayers should not be required to assist them. In fact, it was better that they be allowed to die off according to "natural law."

Members of the eugenics movement whipped up a hysteria of fear regarding people with disabilities. A book in 1883 by the English scientist Francis Galton, a cousin of Darwin, asserted that people with mental retardation committed terrible crimes and that "morons" were multiplying like rabbits compared with the rest of the population. Galton insisted that retarded people were spreading venereal diseases and sexual immorality. Frightened by such assertions, eugenicists (people who believed that human perfection could be achieved if those they regarded as defective were eliminated) clamored successfully for massive sterilization of people with retardation (Patton et al., 1996). They called for confinement of people with disabilities in segregated, jail-like institutions from which there could be no escape without sterilization. Obviously, social Darwinists and eugenicists found natural allies in one another.

The eugenics movement took strong hold in both the United States and Europe in the late 19th and early 20th centuries, and many people today are still in the sway of its viewpoint. Perhaps its most horrific manifestation was Hitler's "final solution" in the 1930s and 1940s. It is estimated that Hitler slaughtered 250,000 people with disabilities in pursuit of his idea of perfection (Rothman, 2003).

A third social influence tending to demean people with disabilities was the development of the standardized intelligence test. The most famous IQ test of the time was devised by the French psychologists Alfred Binet and Théodore Simon. It was in widespread use by the early 1900s. The intelligence tests placed powerful labels such as "moron" on individuals with mental retardation and tended to set in stone other people's ideas of the potential of a person with disabilities. "Once feebleminded, always feebleminded" became a belief of the times. With such an outlook, why establish educational or rehabilitative programs for people with handicapping conditions?

Between 1880 and 1925, institutions for people with disabilities grew into huge facilities designed for subhuman "animals"; the model was that of the hospital, where everyone residing therein was viewed as "sick"; where living units were called "wards"; and where the residents were prevented from "hurting themselves" by being confined to locked wards with barred windows, little or no furniture, and nothing in the way of comfort or hope. Dehumanizing routines removed almost all opportunity for persons with disabilities to learn to live like people without disabilities; the "inmates" or "patients" truly seemed subhuman by the time the institution was through with them (Switzky et al., 1988).

New Research, New Attitudes

In 1919, W. E. Fernald published a study of what happened to 1,537 residents with disabilities who were released from institutions between 1890 and 1914. He delayed publication of his results because they astonished him; he had previously supported the "social menace" theory. Fernald found that most of the men and women released exhibited socially acceptable behavior. Few married or bore children; many became self-supporting. Fernald conducted another study in 1924 of 5,000 children with mental retardation in Massachusetts schools and found that fewer than 8 percent exhibited any kind of antisocial behavior (Switzky et al., 1988).

Other studies of the time demonstrated similar results. For example, Z. P. Hoakley investigated people discharged from public institutions in 1922 to determine how many had to be readmitted within 1 year; his results demonstrated that only 6 percent of males and 13 percent of females had to be readmitted. H. C. Storrs investigated 616 adults discharged from an institution in New York State in 1929 and found that only 4 percent had to be readmitted (Willer & Intagliata, 1984).

Attitudes toward people with disabilities began to improve in the 1920s, partly as a result of research but mostly because of the passage of time and the gradual dying down of the eugenics hysteria. Institutions made attempts to "parole" their highest functioning residents into the community, at first to relatives' homes and later, by the 1930s, to family care homes. Some institutions developed "colony" plans that relocated residents to smaller institutions intended to provide more nearly normal, but still supervised, living arrangements. Some of the "colonies" were farms, where residents could be nearly self-supporting; some were located in towns, where residents could work in factories.

Economic factors interfered with the process of **deinstitutionalization.** The Great Depression of the 1930s made it impossible to find community-based jobs for all who could perform them. World War II improved public attitudes toward the disabled because so many war veterans came home with disabilities, but the war effort itself drained money away from other pressing social needs. Although the rate of institutional growth slowed during the 1940s, admissions to institutions continued to exceed discharges during this entire period, despite attempts at community placement (Willer & Intagliata, 1984).

Normalization and the Deinstitutionalization Movement

Normalization is a concept that was first developed in the Scandinavian countries in the 1950s. The principle can be summarized as "making available to persons with mental retardation, as well as to persons with other handicapping conditions, patterns and conditions of everyday life that are as close as possible to the norms and patterns of mainstream society" (Switzky et al., 1988, p. 32). The idea took shape in the 1950s and continues to evolve today.

Normalization involves the recognition that people with disabilities are people first—people who simply happen to have physical or mental disabilities with which they must cope. They deserve caring, humane assistance. Parent groups such as the National Association for Retarded Citizens (organized in 1950, known today as the American Association on Intellectual and Developmental Disabilities, or AAIDD), as well as professional organizations such as the NASW, have provided leadership in this direction. The goal has not yet been achieved, but steps are being taken in the right direction, as illustrated in the case of Sandra McLean in Chapter 2 and Mary and Lea Perkins in this chapter's case example.

Normalization for a person with disabilities requires a plan of care providing for education, training in daily living skills, community-based rather than institutional care, and an opportunity for employment or some other occupation designed to maximize one's potential for independent living. Deinstitutionalization of persons with disabilities came to be perceived as part of the overall thrust of the 1960s toward upholding the rights of minority groups. Funding has been a continual problem in achieving this goal, however, as also is illustrated in the McLean case in Chapter 2. Zoning is another barrier keeping group homes for people with disabilities out of residential neighborhoods. Both problems illustrate that people without disabilities still discriminate against those who are less fortunate.

Deinstitutionalization as a Goal

An important piece of legislation, the Developmental Disabilities Act of 1969, called for establishing planning councils and advocacy agencies in every state. The act helped create a service structure that could help make deinstitutionalization a realistic goal (Parkinson & Howard, 1996). Also very important was the Rehabilitation Act of 1973, which established the first community-based Centers for Independent Living (CILs). Where available, CILs today provide information and referral services, peer support, and independent living and self-advocacy training for people with disabilities (Putnam, 2007).

The deinstitutionalization movement accelerated during the 1970s and 1980s. This acceleration was spurred in part by court decisions. For example, in 1971 a class action lawsuit was initiated on behalf of patients with mental illness at Bryce State Hospital and residents with mental retardation at the Partlow State School, both in Alabama. The decision of the U.S. Supreme Court in *Wyatt v. Stickney* (1972, cited in Willer & Intagliata, 1984) affirmed not only that institutionalized people have a constitutional right to habilitation services (services designed to help one achieve and maintain one's maximum level of functioning) but also that mildly or moderately

Parent discusses needs of disabled child living at home with social worker.

retarded persons should be admitted to institutions only if this is the least restrictive environment available (Willer & Intagliata, 1984).

The economic climate of the early 1970s also helped the deinstitutionalization movement. The economy was strong, helping provide funding for staff to organize community placement and permitting employment for the more independent of those discharged. That deinstitutionalization occurred at a dramatic rate has been well documented by research. Between 1967 and 1988, for example, the percentage of people with developmental disabilities residing in institutions dropped from 85 percent to 34 percent (Wolfe, 1992).

Figures such as these probably overstate the reality experienced by people with disabilities, however. As inflation became a severe problem in the late 1970s, the coalition fueling community placement (political conservatives who desired reduced government spending and liberals who wanted more humane care) fell apart (Segal, 1995). Many people simply were shifted from large state institutions to private custodial settings such as nursing homes because they were cheaper. Many of the new settings provided inadequate services for the population they absorbed. It has been suggested that "reinstitutionalization" better describes what actually happened to many people (Johnson & Surles, 1994).

SOCIAL JUSTICE AND SOCIAL WORK ROLES WITH PEOPLE WHO HAVE DISABILITIES

Who are our citizens with disabilities today? How is *disability* currently defined? Is a "disability" the same as a "developmental disability"? According to Putnam (2007):

> The phrase "persons with disabilities" includes individuals who have a mental or physical impairment that substantially limits one or more major life activities, have a record of such an impairment, or are regarded as having such an impairment.

This is the broadest definition of disability in U.S. law and is found in the Americans with Disabilities Act (1990). The definition of developmental disability is more narrowly defined. In general, a person with a developmental disability is considered to have a severe chronic disability attributable to mental or physical impairment (or a combination of both) that is manifested before she or he is 22 years of age and is likely to continue indefinitely. (p. 6)

Putnam (2007) points out that disability may be viewed as a "mismatch" between a person's abilities and his or her environment. In other words, where there is a problem related to disability, that problem is a result of the interaction between person and environment, and not the individual's issue alone. Along these same lines, May (2005) asserts that "disability" and "impairment" are not inherently linked. These observations are important. Mary Perkins, for example, with her developmental disability of mental retardation, could have functioned without assistance in a less complex environment and would not have been viewed as impaired. Lea Perkins would not have even developed her disability of emotional disturbance had she been fortunate enough to live in a safe environment. Once Lea received supportive services, she could function as well as any other teenager. As another illustration, while Sandra McLean (introduced in Chapter 2) was disabled severely enough that she could not have survived without assistance, an accommodating environment allowed her to function much more normally, feeding, toileting, and dressing herself independently.

Social Justice Concerns

As indicated in Exhibit 11-1, persons with disabilities frequently experience discrimination. It is important, therefore, for social workers to recognize that social justice issues are inherently involved in working with this significant minority, a population at risk. Advocacy is a very important role for the social work professional, and it is important for the worker to assess a disabled client's environment for strengths, resources, and limitations as well as the client's own strengths, resources, and limitations.

Smart (2001) reminds us that there are four important resources professionals can bring to their work with clients who have disabilities: hope, ideas, understanding of the prejudices and discrimination they face, and a willingness to stand by them. Jenny Chambers, in her work with Mary and Lea Perkins, exemplifies these resources well. The results of her intervention demonstrate what an enormous difference a social worker (even a social work intern) can make in people's lives. Without Jenny's assistance and advocacy, the Perkins family would almost certainly have been evicted from their apartment, landing homeless on the dangerous streets. Lea Perkins would probably never have received the structured support she needed to go back to school. She and her sister Lorraine might well have ended up "institutionalized" in juvenile detention for truancy and drug dealing.

Social workers have worked with people with disabilities in a variety of roles over many years. Early in the history of the profession, the Charity Organization Society (COS) workers investigated the needs of disabled people. Their work was described by Mary Richmond in her classic text, *Social Diagnosis* (1917). Richmond, a leader in the COS, devoted an entire chapter to "The Insane—The Feebleminded."

EXHIBIT 11-1

A Disability Paradigm

The disability paradigm states that the study of the experience of people with disabilities focuses on the following variables which impinge on the phenomenon of disability and interact with each other and other human characteristics: (1) the process in which the performance of social roles and tasks produced discrimination; (2) the discriminatory treatment of people with disabilities produced by the organization of society; (3) the recognition that an impairment does not imply tragedy and a low quality of life; (4) the stark reality that people with disabilities are an oppressed minority which experiences discrimination; (5) the need of all people, including people with disabilities, for various services in order to live independently; (6) the realization that all people have agendas so that the unstated assumptions of disability policy must be revealed; (7) the knowledge that people over time move on a continuum from non-disabled to disabled so that eventually everyone experiences disability; (8) the rejection that there is "normal" human behavior on which social policy can be based; and (9) the all pervasiveness of discrimination against persons with disabilities.

SOURCE: Quoted from G. May. (2005). Changing the future of disability. In G. May and M. Raske (Eds.), *Ending disability discrimination, strategies for social workers* (pp. 82–83). Boston: Allyn & Bacon.

Traditionally, however, social workers have tended to work with people with disabilities in institutional settings such as hospitals and nursing homes. That is because disabled persons have routinely been institutionalized in the past, given the attitudes of the wider society. Severely disabled persons tend to reside in institutions even today, and social workers are employed in these settings. Their roles with the disabled are multifaceted, including providing direct services to clients, program development, administration, and evaluation. As direct service providers, social workers usually function as members of rehabilitation teams, engaging in assessment and referral, education, and advocacy. Usually they are the only members of the team with knowledge and responsibility to focus on the social needs of their clients (Beaulaurier & Taylor, 2001).

Today, more and more social workers are working with people with disabilities who are living out in the community, as illustrated by this chapter's case study. As the service system continues to shift from an institution-based model toward a community-based one, social work roles have evolved to encompass increasing amounts of "boundary work," or intervention between and among social systems. Such work includes educating people with disabilities and their families about their civil rights and about appropriate programs and services in the community that may be of assistance. Important social work roles involve information and referral services, social brokerage between families and larger systems, and advocacy (Freedman, 1995). Assisting in the development of new or additional services and programs that are widely needed is another important role.

Beaulaurier and Taylor (2001) offer a useful framework for services intended to assist people with disabilities:

1. Expand their range of options and choices.

2. Prepare them to be more effective in dealing with professionals, bureaucrats, and agencies that often do not understand or appreciate their heightened need for self-determination.

3. Mobilize and help groups of people with disabilities to consider policy and program alternatives that can improve their situation. (p. 81)

Within the community, then, social workers need to assist clients with disabilities to advocate for programs and services that will allow them to maintain their sense of personal dignity and maximize their independence. Within the family, social workers can be helpful in assisting parents to develop positive expectations toward their children with disabilities and to cope with the ongoing stresses of daily living. Individual, group, and family counseling may be helpful, as can parent training groups and parent-to-parent programs. Respite care opportunities and other supportive services such as day care may be crucial in ensuring the success of family care. A systems-based, empowerment approach that recognizes and builds on family strengths is recommended (Freedman, 1995). Martha Raske (2005) offers an important perspective regarding how various theories of intervention can be blended to best serve clients with disabilities (see Exhibit 11-2).

A fairly new role for the social worker in the area of disabilities is that of **job coach**, or employment specialist, in a supported employment setting. **Supported employment** is a vocational option that provides individualized supports to people with disabilities so they can achieve their goals in the workplace, especially integrated settings where people with disabilities work alongside those without disabilities. The role of job coach helps ensure the success of supported employment. This specialist provides direct services to the consumer such as skill assessment, locating jobs, contacting employers, making job placement arrangements, providing onsite training, assisting with work-related issues, and providing other types of support as needed (Wehman, Inge, Revell, & Brooke, 2007).

Genetic counseling is another important role for social workers in this field. Scientific knowledge of genetics and its impact on birth defects is expanding exponentially. Genetic counseling translates scientific knowledge into practical information. Genetic counselors work with people who may be at high risk for inherited disease or abnormal pregnancy, assessing their chances of having children who are affected (*Genetic counseling*, 2007). (See the Up for Debate box.)

Spirituality Issues

People with disabilities confront special challenges, and spiritual sustenance can help them meet these challenges. Morrison-Orton (2005) conducted an important study to find out what, if any, strategies involving spirituality and/or religion were utilized by social work practitioners in assisting disabled clients. She conducted in-depth interviews with 15 rehabilitation specialists. Sadly, she found that not a single one was aware of the many empirical studies showing a positive relationship among spirituality, religion, belief, and healing (Benson, 1996; Dossey, 2003; Schlitz & Amorok, 2005).

EXHIBIT 11-2

Blended Theories in Disability Practice

Model	Key Concepts	Basic Principles	Practice Strategies
Strengths perspective	Hope Transformation	1. People/communities have capacities, talents, and resources. 2. Trauma/impairment viewed as potential opportunities/challenges.	1. Strengths first in assessment. 2. Client dreams documented.
Empowerment	Oppression Power	1. People are experts regarding their own conditions. 2. Problems are located in the structure of society/organizations. 3. Focus of attention on oppression and marginalized groups.	1. Collaborative problem solving. 2. Consciousness raising. 3. Targets of change = individuals and society. 4. Group work.
Resiliency	Survival	1. People with disabilities have found ways to master their own life experiences. 2. Focus on client survival techniques.	1. Make resiliency part of client's self-concept. 2. Reframe negative into pride of survival.
Disability discrimination model	Discrimination Impairment	1. Disability is socially constructed. 2. Disability is a diverse experience.	1. Develop receptive environments. 2. End discrimination. 3. Focus on pride/accomplishment.
Medical model	Diagnosis Scientific method	1. Medical care is part of holistic services. 2. Systematic review of signs and symptoms shape diagnosis and treatment.	1. Assess and treat for acute care needs. 2. Differential diagnosis and prescribed treatment protocols.

SOURCE: Quoted from M. Raske. (2005). The disability discrimination model in social work practice. In G. May and M. Raske (Eds.). *Ending disability discrimination, strategies for social workers* (pp. 106–107). Boston: Allyn & Bacon.

However, Morrison-Orton did find that 11 of the 15 participants believed that the helping relationship itself was spiritual and that the relationship was the catalyst for positive change. She writes:

> Overall it can be said that the participants went through three stages during the interview. In sequence all but one person went through the same process. The first step in the sequence was the initial denial of any and all use of spiritual or religious strategies. Second was awareness that they could not separate themselves from their spiritual or religious beliefs. Therefore, they did engage in spiritual or religious ways of behaving that enhanced their skills as rehabilitation professionals and were used in their own personal coping with this sometimes-

UP FOR DEBATE

Proposition: Genetic testing should be encouraged for people planning to have children.

YES	NO
Genetic testing can help reduce the overall incidence of developmental disabilities.	Any life is worthwhile, even one with a disability.
A life with a disability may bring much struggle and little satisfaction.	Many people with disabilities express strong satisfaction with their lives.
Family members, especially caregivers of people with disabilities, experience heavy burdens.	Many families find special rewards in providing care to members with disabilities.
Society as a whole is burdened by the special needs of people with disabilities.	People with disabilities are citizens who have the right to full participation in society like all other citizens.

difficult work. Third was the insight that they directly used the strategies in practice with clients. Related to this was the dawning belief that there should be more training (in these areas) while they were in school and on-going professional education once they left school. (2005, p. 32)

EDUCATION FOR WORK WITH PEOPLE WHO HAVE DISABILITIES: CSWE STANDARDS

Social work education can offer an excellent background for working with people with disabilities because of its person-in-environment perspective. But the profession has been slow in recognizing the opportunities and need for work in this area. Educational Policy and Accreditation Standards of the Council on Social Work Education (CSWE) included "disability" as a category for which programs are required to provide learning contexts to promote understanding and nondiscrimination only as recently as 2001 (May & Raske, 2005; CSWE, 2001).

According to May and Raske (2005, p. 148), content on disability has tended to be confined to diversity content courses, "already chock full of mandates and advocacy for including numerous discreet populations thought to be 'at risk' as a consequence of their membership in identified out groups. A sad consequence of this reality is that disability content is irregularly included and education is frequently superficial."

As Morrison-Orton (2005) notes in the study discussed earlier, education in the role of spirituality would be very beneficial for social workers who work with people with disabilities. But in this area and others, social work education has a long way to go to provide students with a satisfactory understanding of the strengths and needs of disabled clients. Students who aspire to work in the field of disabilities are encouraged to augment their formal education through outside reading, discussion with experienced professionals, attending workshops, and the like.

EXHIBIT 11-3

NASW Standards for Service

1. All social workers working with developmentally disabled clients shall possess or acquire and develop knowledge about developmental disabilities.

2. All social workers shall subscribe to a set of principles regarding developmental disabilities which should underlie their practice.

3. Social work practice and research shall seek to prevent or reduce the incidence of developmental disabilities.

4. All social workers shall participate in an interdisciplinary approach to serving the needs of developmentally disabled people.

5. The functions of the social work program shall include specific services to the client population and the community.

SOURCE: Quoted from R. Freedman. (1995). Developmental disabilities, direct practice. In R. L. Edwards (Ed.). *Encyclopedia of social work* (19th ed., Vol. 1, p. 724). Washington, DC: NASW Press.

NASW STANDARDS FOR SERVICE

The National Association of Social Work's standards for professional service reflect the need for social workers who are involved with disabled people to have generalist knowledge and skills. In 1982 the NASW collaborated with the American Association on Mental Deficiency to develop specific standards. These are summarized in Exhibit 11-3.

The NASW provides extensive interpretations of these standards. Services described include outreach, identification of individuals at risk, community liaison work, coordination of services, advocacy, and discharge planning. Services also include policy development, program planning and administration, research, and program evaluation.

TYPES OF DEVELOPMENTAL DISABILITIES

Some disabilities are so obvious that everyone agrees the person so affected is, indeed, "disabled." A clear example of such a disability might be a bone deformity such as a club foot that makes it difficult for the afflicted individual to walk. On the other hand, some disabilities, while just as real, are much less visible. For example, today certain children are diagnosed with "learning disabilities" through painstaking assessment of problems in reading, spelling, writing, and so on. These disabilities would not be evident in a preliterate society.

In addition, some disabilities are truly disabling but are not "developmental." A person seriously injured in midlife as a result of an automobile accident may be disabled, but the disability is not defined as developmental. According to the federal definition of **developmental disability,** the condition must occur before the affected individual has reached the age of 22.

How developmental disability is defined is not just an academic exercise. The definition affects real people in very real ways. For example, funds reserved for special education services for people with developmental disabilities may be spent only for those who qualify for that funding under the legal definition. A person who needs reeducation in midlife due to injury from severe physical or sexual abuse will not qualify for the same services in the public schools that assisted both Mary and Lea Perkins from this chapter's case study.

Some states define developmental disabilities according to category—for example, mental retardation or cerebral palsy. Persons who fall into these categories are eligible for whatever financial aid is provided by state law for such classifications. The federal definition of disability, on the other hand, is functional. The Developmental Disabilities Assistance Bill of Rights defines *developmental disabilities* as disabilities that are severe and chronic in nature. Furthermore, they are caused by either mental or physical impairment, or both; present themselves before the person becomes 22; have a strong probability of continuing for the rest of the person's life; and significantly limit a person's ability to carry on major life activities, including the ability to live independently and earn a living. Developmental disabilities also include disabilities that require some kind of intervention, care, or treatment for a long duration, if not for life. (Mackelprang & Salsgiver, 1999, p. 147).

For a given person to qualify for federal funds, his or her disability must be severe in function and the functional impairment must be chronic (of extended duration). Therefore, a person who might qualify categorically for state aid because of a mild disability might not qualify for federal aid.

With these considerations of definition in mind, let us examine 10 diagnostic categories of developmental disabilities (see Exhibit 11-4). We will also discuss fetal alcohol syndrome and cocaine and other drug-affected babies.

Intellectual Disability or Mental Retardation

Intellectual disability or mental retardation is caused by a wide variety of factors. Sometimes it results from injury at birth, as in the case of Sandra McLean in Chapter 2's case study. Sometimes the mother has had a serious illness during pregnancy (measles is a well-known example). Sometimes, as in Down's syndrome, the cause is genetic and involves chromosomal abnormalities. Sometimes the problem involves inadequate nutrition for the pregnant mother, a terrible potential side-effect of poverty. Early infant

---

EXHIBIT 11-4

Major Categories of Developmental Disabilities

Mental retardation (intellectual disability)	Epilepsy
Cerebral palsy	Traumatic brain injury
Autism	Learning disabilities
Orthopedic problems	Emotional disturbance
Hearing problems	Co-occurrence of disabilities

nutrition has an effect as well, as does early sensory stimulation. A mother's drinking, smoking, or drug use may result in retardation of her child. Some conditions are reversible with early intervention. Myriad factors—some identifiable, some not—may affect a young child's mental development.

A child who has an intellectual disability is unable to learn at the rate most children do or cannot apply what is learned in the normal way to requirements of daily living. Preschoolers with this diagnosis tend to learn more slowly than other children to crawl, sit, walk, and talk. Such school-aged children have difficulty developing academic skills and often social skills as well. Such adults have trouble living and working independently in the community, although they may do well with supervision and other assistance.

The American Association on Intellectual and Developmental Disabilities, or AAIDD (previously the American Association for the Mentally Retarded, or AAMR), revised its definition of mental retardation in 2002 to the following (*Definition of mental retardation*, 2002):

> Mental retardation is a disability characterized by significant limitations both in intellectual functioning and adaptive behavior as expressed in conceptual, social, and practical adaptive skills. This disability originates before the age of 18. A complete and accurate understanding of mental retardation involves realizing that mental retardation refers to a particular state of functioning that begins in childhood, has many dimensions, and is affected positively by individualized supports. As a model of functioning, it includes the contexts and environment within which the person functions and interacts and requires a multi-dimensional and ecological approach that reflects the interaction of the individual with the environment, and the outcomes of that interaction with regards to independence, relationships, societal contributions, participation in school and community, and personal well being.

The AAIDD suggests that, in determining if a person has an intellectual disability and in developing a support plan, one must (*Fact sheet: Frequently asked questions about mental retardation*, 2002):

1. Evaluate limitations in present functioning within the context of the individual's peers and culture.
2. Take into account the individual's cultural and linguistic differences as well as communication, sensory, motor, and behavioral factors.
3. Recognize that within an individual limitations often coexist with strengths.
4. Describe limitations so that an individualized plan of needed supports can be developed.
5. Provide appropriate personalized supports to improve the functioning of persons with mental retardation.

While the criteria for diagnosing mental retardation is generally a score of 70 or less on an IQ test, the AAIDD cautions that the IQ score is only one aspect of determining the presence or absence of an intellectual disability. Limitations in adaptive behavior skills and evidence that the disability occurred at a young age are also significant. Both Sandra McLean of Chapter 2's case study and Mary Perkins of this chapter's case study suffered from intellectual disabilities. Sandra's disability was profound, but Mary's was mild and with appropriate support she could live a normal life.

Cerebral Palsy

Cerebral palsy results from damage to the brain, usually before or during birth. It takes three major forms: spasticity, dyskinesia, and ataxia (described later). Some people manifest elements of all three forms. Cerebral palsy may affect the entire body or only parts, such as various limbs. Spasticity is the most common form of cerebral palsy. Movement is difficult, slow, stiff, and sometimes jerky. Dyskinesia, on the other hand, is a manifestation in which movement may be continuous but random and uncontrolled, especially under stress. Facial features may move in an uncontrolled manner as well. The walking gait is lurching. Ataxia is the least common form of cerebral palsy and is primarily a balance disorder; children with this disability may walk with feet spread wide apart for stability.

Approximately 2 to 3 children in 1,000 have cerebral palsy. Causes include infections to the mother during pregnancy, insufficient oxygen reaching the fetus, premature birth, lack of oxygen to the baby during birth, blood diseases, and other birth defects. About 10 percent of children with this disability acquire it after birth. Approximately 500,000 children and adults in the United States have cerebral palsy today. Risk is particularly great with premature and low-birthweight children. For those who develop cerebral palsy after birth, head trauma and brain infection are the most frequent causes.

Cerebral palsy is often accompanied by other disorders. For example, about half the victims suffer mental retardation. Fortunately, however, about half of children diagnosed with mild cerebral palsy seem to outgrow their symptoms (*Cerebral palsy*, 2004).

Autism

Autistic children are often described as being in a "world of their own." At birth these children may appear perfectly normal, and they may continue to appear perfectly normal for the first year or two. Then the parents will become disturbed by the child's repetitive motions and apparent inability to hear. Hearing tests will reveal, however, that the child does hear but pays attention to random sounds rather than to meaningful words. Language development is delayed, and the child may only repeat back exactly what is said, without apparent comprehension of meaning (such repetition is called *echolalic speech*). Mental retardation often accompanies autism, although intellectual functioning is difficult to test because of the child's language delays and behavior abnormalities. Autistic children do not respond positively to attention; instead, they withdraw and often behave violently or fearfully when approached. Such behavior, of course, can be heartbreaking to the parents (McDonald-Wikler, 1987).

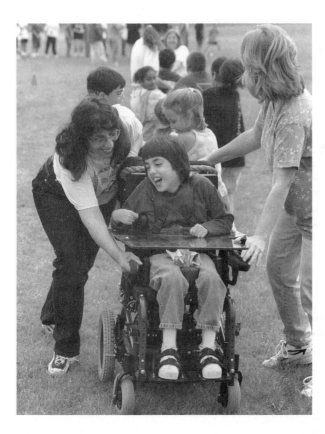

A mainstreamed fifth grader with cerebral palsy participates in a tug-of-war in her wheelchair, helped by teachers during a school field day competition.

Autism is a pervasive developmental disorder affecting 2 to 6 children per 1,000 in the United States. Perhaps autism can more accurately be described as a "spectrum," as symptoms fall along a continuum from mild to severe. Rates today are about four times higher than 30 years ago. Some suspect environmental factors, particularly mercury (*Children with autism get their day in court*, 2007). However, better reporting may explain much of the increase. Symptoms include (*Autism*, 2007):

1. Difficulties interacting with others and making friends.
2. Communication problems, both with spoken language and nonverbal gestures.
3. Insistence on sameness.
4. Repetitive movements, such as hand flapping or frequent tantrums.
5. Some degree of mental retardation or learning disabilities in most (but by no means all) affected children.

Children with Asperger syndrome share some of the features of autism but have normal intelligence and learn to speak at the expected age.

The causes of autism are not understood. At one time, parents were blamed for being aloof and unresponsive, but this theory has been proved false. Today, complex genetic factors are suspected, with possible complications from environmental sources. Early intensive interventions can make an important positive difference. With appropriate services and supports, most families are able to raise their autistic children at home.

Orthopedic Problems

Orthopedic problems include a wide variety of physical disabilities, such as problems with physical functioning of bones, joints, and muscles. Spina bifida is a well-known example. A child with this condition is born with an incomplete spinal column so that nerve impulses cannot reach the legs and the child cannot walk. Other examples of orthopedic problems include bone deformities, missing limbs, club feet, or extra fingers and toes. Some such problems can be corrected at birth by surgery or more gradually by corrective appliances such as braces.

Children with minor orthopedic problems may not be classified as developmentally disabled because functional impairment is not severe enough to meet the definition. Other children with severe orthopedic problems may receive services under a different classification (e.g., cerebral palsy). For this reason, the exact prevalence of orthopedic problems in the United States is difficult to determine.

It should be kept in mind that children with physical impairments may experience rejection, embarrassment, feelings of insecurity, stigma, and so forth (Patton et al., 1996). Social workers need to be sensitive to the emotional challenges that these children face in addition to the physical ones.

Hearing Problems

Hearing problems can cause massive developmental disabilities. This happens because speech and language are so important to cognitive development and social functioning and because hearing loss impedes language development. Children who are hearing impaired are often diagnosed incorrectly as having mental retardation because their language development is so grossly delayed that they cannot be tested accurately. Without language development, the thinking process may be hampered as well.

Hearing loss may range from mild to profound. Conductive hearing loss occurs when something interferes with sound passing through the outer or middle ear so that sound does not reach the inner ear. Such conditions may include wax, infections, or ruptures of the eardrum, and they are usually treatable. Sensorineural hearing loss usually occurs when the hair cells in the inner ear cannot detect incoming vibrations or when neural impulses are not transmitted to the brain. Some children suffer from both conditions, called mixed hearing loss.

Hearing loss may be present at birth (congenital hearing loss) or developed later in life. It is one of the most common birth defects, affecting approximately 3 to 4 in 1,000 newborns (*Hearing loss*, 2004).

Epilepsy

According to the Epilepsy Foundation (*Understanding epilepsy*, 2007), epilepsy is the most common neurological disorder in children. It is the third most common disorder in adults, after Alzheimer's disease and stroke. More than 3 million people suffer from epilepsy in the United States today, and nearly a third are children. Many other people have epilepsy that is undetected and untreated; at least 25 million Americans will have a seizure at some point in their lives. There is no known cause for about 70 percent of epilepsy cases; the rest seem to be caused by tumor or stroke, head trauma, poisoning, infection, or maternal injury.

The Epilepsy Foundation defines the disorder as follows:

> Epilepsy is a medical condition that produces seizures affecting a variety of men-
> tal and physical functions. It is also called a seizure disorder. A seizure is caused by
> a brief, strong surge of electrical activity involving part or all of the brain. When
> a person has two or more seizures without a clear cause (e.g. alcohol withdrawal)
> it is considered to be epilepsy.
>
> Seizures can last from a few seconds to a few minutes. They can have many
> symptoms, from convulsions and loss of consciousness to some that are not
> always recognized as seizures by the person experiencing them *or* by health care
> professionals: blank staring, lip smacking, or jerking movements of the arms and
> legs. (*Understanding epilepsy*, 2007)

Two types of seizures are particularly well known: grand mal and petit mal. A grand mal seizure is also called a convulsion. The afflicted person thrashes around on the ground for a few minutes and may be unconscious for a period of time afterward. This is the type of seizure experienced by Sandra McLean of Chapter 2. A petit mal seizure is less dramatic. There is a lapse of consciousness for a few seconds, during which the person appears to be staring or daydreaming. Petit mal seizures may occur several times a day. They disturb the afflicted person because they interrupt ongoing activities and thinking and tend to result in memory loss.

In another type of seizure, called a drop attack, the legs simply give way and the afflicted person drops to the ground. The attack lasts only a minute or two. Children with this disorder usually wear protective helmets.

Traumatic Brain Injury

Traumatic brain injury includes any trauma to the head that causes brain damage. Brain injuries generally occur in three ways: through blunt injuries, as when the head is hit by a fixed or moving object (such as a windshield or a baseball bat); penetrating injuries, as when the head is penetrated by an object such as a bullet; and compression injuries, as when the head is crushed.

Head injuries may result in fractures or broken or dented skull bones. Loose bone fragments may place pressure on the brain. Concussion, or temporary loss of consciousness, may occur. Severe blows may cause contusions, or bruising of the brain tissue. Lacerations of the head may tear brain tissue.

Traumatic brain injury may result in a variety of disabling conditions such as impaired judgment, memory loss, agitation, confusion, lack of inhibition, and short attention span (*Fact sheet on traumatic brain injury*, 1999). Persons with moderate to severe traumatic brain injury may experience a serioius headache that continues to worsen, repeated vomiting, convulsions or seizures, dilation of one or both pupils of the eyes, slurred speech, loss of coordination, and increased confusion. Approximately half of severely head-injured patients will require surgery to remove ruptured blood vessels or contusions (NINDS traumatic brain injury information page, 2007).

Learning Disabilities

Some children have disabilities that interfere with their ability to read, write, spell, or do mathematical calculations. They may also have trouble listening, speaking, or thinking. Often these children appear perfectly normal until they go to school, where they encounter a whole new set of demands. They score normally on IQ tests, but somehow they do not seem to perceive written language in the same way that other children do. While they may be able to read written words, many cannot translate their meaning. No matter how hard they try, these children seem unable to learn in the usual way. Although there is much about learning disabilities that we do not understand, a number of techniques have been devised to help children so afflicted.

The Learning Disability Association of America defines *learning disability* as "a neurological disorder that affects one or more of the basic psychological processes involved in understanding or in using spoken or written language. The disability may manifest itself in an imperfect ability to listen, think, speak, read, write, spell or to do mathematical calculations" (*Learning disabilities*, 2004). The legal definition of learning disability varies from state to state. In general, for regulatory purposes, the inability to learn cannot be the result of low intelligence, socioeconomic circumstances, or poor sensory skills. The most frequent method of identifying learning disabilities involves measuring and comparing ability and achievement in the school setting. Thus, the disabilities are rarely identified before a child goes to school.

Learning disability is an umbrella term encompassing a number of more specific disabilities such as dyslexia, a language and reading disability; dyscalculia, a disability involving math skills; and dysgraphia, a disorder resulting in illegible handwriting.

Emotional Disturbance

Many terms have been used to describe emotional or behavioral disorders, but the term currently used in the Individuals with Disabilities Education Act (IDEA) is *emotional disturbance*. IDEA defines this disability as follows (*Emotional disturbance, fact sheet 5*, 2004):

> a condition exhibiting one or more of the following characteristics over a long period of time and to a marked degree that adversely affects a child's educational performance—

- An inability to learn that cannot be explained by intellectual, sensory or other health factors.

- An inability to build or maintain satisfactory interpersonal relationships with peers and teachers.

- Inappropriate types of behavior or feelings under normal circumstances.

- A general pervasive mood of unhappiness or depression

- A tendency to develop physical symptoms or fears associated with personal or school problems.

Families who have children with emotional disturbance often need help in understanding their children's condition and in learning how to cope effectively. This chapter's case study, Mary and Lea Perkins, illustrates such a situation.

Fetal Alcohol Syndrome; Cocaine and Other Drug-Exposed Babies

Babies who are born affected by alcohol, cocaine, and other drugs are a growing concern in the United States. Each year, 40,000 newborns show some degree of alcohol-related damage. Many women are aware that heavy drinking can cause harm, but far fewer realize that light to moderate drinking can be harmful depending on the developmental stage of the fetus. Between 1,000 and 6,000 babies are born with fetal alcohol *syndrome* (FAS) annually, a combination of physical and mental birth defects, and the rest have fetal alcohol *effects* (FAE), or lesser degrees of alcohol-related damage (*Drinking alcohol during pregnancy*, 2007). In addition, many thousands of women use cocaine and/or other drugs such as heroin or Ecstasy during pregnancy, also placing their unborn children at serious risk of birth defects (*Illicit drug use during pregnancy*, 2006).

Fetal alcohol syndrome involves both physical and mental birth defects. Babies born with FAS are abnormally small at birth and remain below normal in size. They usually have flat cheeks, small eyes, and short, upturned noses. Most have small brains and a degree of mental retardation. Poor coordination, a short attention span, and behavioral problems are characteristic of FAS. Babies born with FAE have some, but not all, of these difficulties. The effects of FAS and FAE are lifelong.

Mothers who drink heavily (four to five drinks daily or more) have a very high risk of giving birth to an infant with FAS, but even a single drink at a critical time during pregnancy can cause problems. Alcohol passes through the mother's placenta into the developing fetus, whose immature organs cannot break the substance down as fast as the mother's can. Hence, the alcohol level in the baby's blood may exceed that of the mother's and may result in irreversible damage. Unfortunately, cocaine and other drugs also pass through the mother's placenta into the fetus. Drugs can trigger labor so that many cocaine or other drug-exposed babies are born prematurely. Those who survive are likely to have brain damage causing mental retardation, cerebral palsy, and visual and hearing impairments. Cocaine babies tend to have small heads, which possibly indicate small brains. Many appear to experience drug withdrawal; the babies are irritable and jittery, making it difficult to bond with parents or other caretakers.

While substance abuse during pregnancy clearly places a mother's infant at risk, there is increasing evidence today that substance abuse by fathers also increases the risk. More research is needed.

Overall Prevalence and Co-occurrence of Disabilities

In 2003, the U.S. Census Bureau conducted the American Community Survey in which families were asked about the incidence of disabilities in their members 5 years of age and over who were *not* institutionalized. In that year, nearly 37.5 million people over age 5 were reported to have a disability as defined by the study. Approximately 2.7 percent involved a self-care disability, 5.1 percent a mental disability, 9 percent a physical disability, and 4.1 percent a sensory disability. Almost 40 percent of persons over 65 reported that they had a disability, clearly demonstrating that this condition increases with age (Weathers, 2005).

As another measure of prevalence of disability, in 1998 12 percent of White students were enrolled in special education classes, 1.2 percent being identified as having an intellectual disability. Fourteen percent of African American students were enrolled in special education programs in that year, 2.6 percent being identified as having an intellectual disability (Mendez, 2004). Sadly, according to the National Education Association, enrollment in special education has risen 30 percent since then (*Special education*, 2007).

Many people suffer from more than one disability at the same time, a condition known as *co-occurrence* of disability. Sandra McLean, introduced in Chapter 2, suffered from both epilepsy and mental retardation. Persons with cerebral palsy and autism frequently experience mental retardation. Children with FAS and those who are exposed to cocaine characteristically suffer multiple disabilities. It is important to remember that all disabilities involve psychological and social dimensions. Professional intervention must involve attending to the whole person.

HUMAN DIVERSITY, POPULATIONS AT RISK, AND SOCIAL JUSTICE: UNFINISHED BUSINESS

Persons with disabilities can be viewed as members of diverse populations, in particular as members of diverse populations that are at risk because of discrimination by the wider society. Ongoing discrimination is clearly a social justice issue. As discussed previously, it has led to disabled people being warehoused for years in prisonlike facilities. People with severe disabilities are frequently still institutionalized today, often in private nursing homes that have few facilities for this population. Social workers are urged to advocate for all persons with disabilities and to prevent institutionalization wherever possible. Today people with disabilities are advocating for control of their own lives, understanding that they are "within the realm of legitimate human diversity" (see Exhibit 11-5).

EXHIBIT 11-5

An Open Letter: Autism from Autistics

The last several years have brought about an unprecedented rise in public awareness about the autism spectrum. Regrettably, that awareness has come with significant misinformation. Media representations of the autism spectrum consistently bring new messages of panic and tragedy. The television informs us the odds of a child achieving any one of a number of improbable events—starring in a Broadway show being one example—as compared to the much more likely odds of having a child with autism. The intended effect is clear. It is a call for parents to be afraid—if you dream for your child, if you aspire for them to achieve great things, then you should also fear for them, lest the tragedy of autism take them too. However, the truth of the matter is that we who are ourselves on the autism spectrum view ourselves in a very different fashion.

The truth is that while living with autism can be difficult, it is by no means the death sentence that many make it out to be. The autism spectrum is wide and diverse, and even those with what is viewed as the most "severe" symptoms may have a high quality of life. Furthermore, as people on the spectrum have grown increasingly self-aware and knowledgeable about their own neurological types, a true community has grown. The autistic community—made up of people on the spectrum ourselves rather than the relatives, professionals and others who claim to speak for us—has adopted a drastically different view of the spectrum that deserves to be heard.

We view our differences as within the realm of legitimate human diversity. Like the differences of race, religion and gender that have long been accepted in human society, we seek true acceptance for our differences—not just awareness. Furthermore, in demanding tolerance for neurological diversity, we seek acceptance on our own terms. The aim of all education and medicine directed towards autism must be to improve quality of life while respecting the differences of the individual—not to remove autistic traits simply because they diverge from the norm.

Too many use autism as an excuse to sell quack treatments and ineffective and often inhumane pseudoscience that exploits families and individuals. If 1/10th of the money spent on the quest for a "cure" to make autistic individuals behave as if they were neurologically typical was spent on the many promising avenues in assistive technology and other means to improve quality of life, far more people on the spectrum would be communicating and living successful lives today. It is imperative that we change the agenda on autism to make that possibility a reality.

As individuals on the autism spectrum, we believe that we have the right to choose instead of being chosen for. Those of us that are strong advocates realize that this is a civil rights movement, fighting for the basic rights to freedom that this country and all free human societies are based on. We are witnessing a historical perspective that parallels that of previous struggles by minority groups to create a society tolerant of their differences. With our perspective coming out publicly it will bring balance to a world of misinformation and hope for those that have been afforded none by this current atmosphere of panic and tragedy. The world we seek sometimes seems far away, but our dream—to live in a place tolerant of neurological diversity—is well worth a long struggle.

SOURCE: R. Snyder and A. Ne'eman. (2007, July 10). *Autism from autistics.* Retrieved July 11, 2007, from the Autistic Self Advocacy Network website, http://www.autisticadvocacy.org/

Preventing institutionalization requires a continuum of care available in the community. Fortunately, the service system moved from the primarily institution-based model in place prior to the late 1960s to a community-based model in the 1970s and 1980s (Freedman, 1995). The positive change was advanced by the Developmental Disabilities Act of 1969 and the Americans with Disabilities Act (ADA) of 1990, which will be discussed later in this chapter. It was further advanced in 1999 by the Supreme Court's Olmstead decision. This decision, *Olmstead v. L.C.*, interpreted Title II of the ADA to require states to provide services in the "most integrated setting" appropriate for a given person (Rothman, 2003).

The Continuum of Care

The continuum of care begins at home, the least restrictive, most normal environment in which children can be raised. Respite care to help prevent burnout of family caregivers can be crucial to the success of care in the home. Adults with disabilities may be able to live independently in homes or apartments of their own with appropriate assistance. Other reasonably independent adults may do well in boardinghouse-type arrangements, with room, board, and a minimum of supervision. Days may be spent in activity centers, regular employment, or sheltered workshops (places of employment that provide special training and services for people with disabilities) or supported employment in integrated work settings, as discussed earlier.

Foster homes, or family care homes, are the next step along the continuum of care. They provide familylike settings with foster parents. Lea Perkins would have been placed in one had her own mother not been able to improve her parenting skills. Next, somewhere near the middle of the continuum of care, are small group homes. These facilities are staffed by aides and skilled professionals who provide care, supervision, and training for up to eight people.

Nearing the institutional end of the continuum are nursing homes. Nursing homes range from those providing only room, board, and minor personal assistance to those offering skilled nursing care for persons with extensive physical needs. When large numbers of people with disabilities were moved to nursing homes in the 1970s, many of these facilities developed special programs for them. Unfortunately, however, many did not, and almost 20 years passed before federal Medicaid regulations required special certification and appropriate programming.

At the far end of the continuum of care are the large state institutions, where people with disabilities reside in highly restrictive, regulated environments. Today, most people who live in these facilities have severe and multiple disabilities.

Research Suggests Direction for Service Improvement

For family care to have the best chance for success, specialized services are often needed. However, a study by Christopher Petr and David Barney (1993) found that parents received limited help from professionals and may have even experienced adversarial treatment. For example, some professionals recommended institutional placement when the family desired additional home-based services. Sometimes, however, home-based services were recommended but simply did not exist or were financially out of reach because private insurance refused to pay.

The situation has not improved much, if at all, since the time of Petr and Barney's study. For example, Doris Mitnick, a social worker who has worked with children with chronic illness for more than 15 years, finds (Stoesen, 2005):

> The biggest lack is not in the strengths of the family. It's the strengths of community resources. Things just keep getting tighter and tighter. (The lack of) resources in the community and state is the biggest challenge families face. . . . That's where our development needs to be—in community resources and the creative application of those resources.

Community resources are clearly a serious issue, but unfortunately families find that working with professionals, including social workers, is difficult as well. Even a social worker suddenly thrust into the role of client finds the transition from professional to "parent of disabled child" a daunting experience (see Exhibit 11-6).

Providing Supportive Services to Diverse Families: A Chinese Illustration

Barnwell and Day (1996) point out that to intervene successfully, social workers and other professionals must understand that the values and experiences of the families they deal with may be very different from their own. Moreover, family needs change over time. Services required to cope successfully with infants with disabilities, for example, are very different from those required to meet the needs of adolescents, adults, or the elderly.

These authors note that different ethnic and cultural groups utilize professional services at different rates and provide professionals with different amounts and types of information. They point out that service systems tend to be designed according to White, middle-class values yet the values of other groups may differ. Cultural sensitivity is required to help develop service systems that are responsive to the needs of diverse families with members who have disabilities. Cultural perspectives differ as to the meaning of disability, the causes of disability, and the appropriate roles of families with respect to disability. What may be experienced as a terrible tragedy in one culture may in another be experienced as God's will and an opportunity to serve. Professional intervention must take account of these cultural differences.

EXHIBIT 11-6

How Parents View Professionals

Janice Fialka, a social worker, gave birth to a son with disabilities. She writes: "I had been a practicing social worker—what I was struck by was that I was in a waiting room where I had taken teen moms, and there I was, sitting as a client. I was quite humbled and very aware that I did not choose to be there. When I was the social worker, I made a conscious choice.

However, when you're the parent, especially in the early years during the transition—when it's not your choice—you're not so eager to join into this dance."

One night Fialka wrote a poem, "Advice to Professionals who Must 'Conference Cases,'" as a way to get her feelings onto paper. The poem reads, in part,

Please give me back my son
undamaged and untouched by your labels, test results
descriptions and categories
If you can't, if you truly cannot give us back our son
then just be with us quietly
gently and compassionately as we feel.

SOURCE: Quoted from L. Stoesen. (2005, March). Children with disabilities: a family affair. *NASW News*, p. 4.

Liu (2005) offers an interesting illustration of differing cultural perceptions of disability from a Chinese point of view. In many areas of China, Liu writes, disability is viewed as a punishment for sins committed in past lives—sins committed either by the disabled person or by that person's parents. Thus, a stigma is attached to disability, and families experience a sense of shame, guilt, and fear of social disgrace. A Taoist priest may be sought to perform rituals to try to seek a cause or a solution.

Because the family is the most fundamental unit of society among the Chinese—three generations living in one household is still common—it is important for the professional to do whatever possible to establish a strong working relationship with extended family members. Liu points out, however, that the family in China today is diverse given the 10-year cultural revolution that separated many families and undermined respect for the elderly. The one-child-per-family policy has also undermined the traditional family system. Hence, the social worker must carefully assess family structure as part of the intervention process. Competence in the Chinese language is also helpful to achieve best outcomes (see Exhibit 11-7). Social workers need, with great sensitivity, to help the family understand the cause of disability from a more neutral (less blaming) point of view and to discuss possible treatment options.

Asian Americans: A Brief History

People of Chinese descent comprise the largest subgroup of Asian Americans in the United States today. Asian Americans as a whole comprise approximately 5 percent of the population. Their number totals approximately 15.4 million persons, of whom

---

EXHIBIT 11-7

Cross-Cultural Competence from a Chinese Perspective: Sun

I worked as a case manager for a 25-year-old woman, Sun, a Chinese American who was legally blind, nonverbal, and diagnosed with moderate mental retardation. Sun was able to understand Cantonese, which was the only language that her parents spoke, and a few words in English. She responded to questions by nodding, shaking her head, or making certain sounds. When I started working with her, she had been attending, for a few years, a traditional day treatment program for people with mental retardation. She seemed to be comfortable there, but on the occasion of a home visit to see her and her parents in their Chinatown apartment, it became apparent that Sun's parents really preferred that she attend a special school for the blind. They said that even though they had this wish for a long time, they were not able to make their needs known because of language barriers.

Sun's past case managers spoke only English. They would periodically check as to whether Sun's parents were satisfied with the day treatment program, and the parents would always say "yes," unable to express their wish for a more appropriate setting for their daughter. I worked with Sun's parents and located an excellent program for adults and children with visual impairment. Sun was transferred to this program and appeared to be happier because she was more comfortable with the environment and was able to engage in activities designed for the blind. Sun has been attending the special program ever since.

SOURCE: G. Z. Liu. (2005). Best practices, developing cross-cultural competence from a Chinese perspective. In J. Stone (Ed.), *Culture and disability, providing culturally competent services* (pp. 78–79). Thousand Oaks, CA: Sage.

3.3 million are Chinese (U.S. Census Bureau, 2007). Other Asian Americans originate from Japan, India, and the Pacific Islands.

The Chinese were the first Asian people to come to America in large numbers. They arrived in relatively recent times, toward the middle of the 19th century, attracted by economic opportunity. In Hawaii the Chinese worked as sugar plantation laborers, and in California they took part in the Gold Rush of 1849. Many became construction workers for the Southern Pacific Railroad. Their success led to fear of competition, which culminated in the Chinese Exclusion Act of 1882, barring further immigration. People of Chinese descent were denied citizenship and the right to intermarry (Lum, 1992).

Large numbers of Japanese emigrated during the early 20th century, in response to the need for farm workers in California. The Immigration Act of 1924 closed the door to immigration of Asians after that time, however. This law set low immigration quotas for dark-skinned people of all nationalities and excluded Asians entirely. Then, after the bombing of Pearl Harbor in 1941, Japanese Americans were forcibly interned in camps for the duration of World War II. Their property was liquidated and never returned. Although the U.S. Supreme Court in 1944 declared this treatment unconstitutional, not until 1988 were petitions for redress of grievance accepted by Congress. The settlement even then was token, $20,000 for each living survivor.

The 1965 Immigration Act changed U.S. policy to make it more equitable to people of diverse racial and ethnic heritages. Political refugees from the Philippines and Korea included many educated Asian professionals at that time. Then the Vietnamese War brought waves of refugees from Vietnam, Laos, and Cambodia, particularly after the fall of Saigon in 1975. The early refugees were highly educated people who had been allies of the Americans, but later refugees included less privileged people who have experienced much more difficulty adjusting to life in the United States.

Traditional values strongly affect Asian family life today. These values include deference to parental authority and the expectation that children will sacrifice personal ambition to meet family needs. Families may experience stress when children encounter other values and begin to question differences. Overall, however, Asian Americans have achieved considerable success in their adopted country: nearly half of those 25 and older have achieved a baccalaureate degree, and median family income is highest of that of any racial group (U.S. Census Bureau, 2007).

Empowerment, Self-Determination, and Self-Advocacy

Empowerment is an attitude, a process, and a set of skills involving the ability to gain some control over valued events, outcomes, and resources. Empowerment requires genuine choices and the power to make one's own decisions (Gilson, 1998) and is strongly in accord with social work's professional value of self-determination.

People with disabilities, like other people, want to have as much control over their own lives as possible. Segal, Silverman, and Tomkin (1993, p. 706) point out that even people with severe disabilities have "potential for self-determination, provided that they have access to support services, barrier-free environments, and appropriate information and skills." The desired outcome is independent living wherever possible.

The empowerment model strongly encourages self-advocacy among people with disabilities, both as individuals and in groups. Self-advocacy in fact has become a national movement, modeled after the civil rights movement. The AAIDD describes some of the goals (*Fact sheet: Self advocacy*, 2005):

> When we speak of "the civil rights movement," "the parents movement," or "the independent living movement," we are referring to something like a crusade, powered by people who have been directly affected by unfair attitudes and practices, which has fostered change in our society. Similarly, the self-advocacy movement has redefined the "disability problem" as being less about rehabilitation and more about equality. People involved in the movement are very clear about not wanting to be called retarded, handicapped or disabled or to be treated like children. They are clear that self advocacy represents "rights" not "dependence"—the right to speak out, the right to be a person with dignity, the right to make decisions for themselves and others.

The concepts of empowerment, self-determination, and self-advocacy do not mean that society (or social workers) should abandon people with disabilities to struggle alone. It means, instead, that society must recognize that the impaired individual is not the problem; the problem is an environment that discriminates, does not provide viable choices, and does not meet the special needs of all its citizens.

Self-advocacy goes beyond individuals advocating for themselves alone. It also involves groups of people with disabilities working together to fight discrimination, gain more control over their lives, and work together toward greater justice in society. According to the AAIDD, a national organization called Self-Advocates Becoming Empowered was formed in the United States in 1991. By 1993, there were at least 37 statewide self-advocacy organizations. Numbers of local chapters continue to grow, with some states having as few as 3 and others as many as 75. In addition, many other self-advocacy groups operate independently or are attached to different organizations assisting people with disabilities. Such collective efforts can lead to important new legislation bringing changes in social policy. The disability rights movement described next is an example.

THE DISABILITY RIGHTS MOVEMENT, SOCIAL POLICY, AND APPROPRIATE TERMINOLOGY

Disabilities have been viewed historically as medical problems or personal tragedies. This prevailing view began to be challenged in the 1960s, when, along with other minority groups, people with disabilities sought to redefine their identities and to change popular perceptions of the sources of their problems (Christensen, 1996). By the late 1960s, first in Scandinavia and then in the United States, a disability rights movement developed, advocating that people with disabilities should be seen as "subjects in their own lives rather than simply as objects of medical and social regimes of control" (Meekosha & Jakubowicz, 1996, p. 80). Community prejudice and discrimination were overtly identified as major barriers preventing people with disabilities from taking control of their own lives, as were stereotypes portrayed in the popular media.

The crux of the new thinking, as noted by Beaulaurier and Taylor (2001), was that an individual's impairment in itself was not so much the problem as the lack of accommodation provided by the wider society. Lack of accommodation was not so much a result of hostility as from simple failure to consider everyone's needs. So those who became involved in the disability rights movement determined to get the requirements of people with disabilities onto the national agenda.

In the United States, the disability rights movement promoted deinstitutionalization and independent living and helped secure the passage of the Developmental Disabilities Act of 1969. The movement was strengthened in the 1960s by the civil rights movement. Then, in the late 1960s and early 1970s, thousands of veterans returned from the Vietnam War with extensive disabling conditions, both physical and emotional. Their added influence helped achieve passage of the federal Rehabilitation Act of 1973. Title V of this act prohibits recipients of federal funds from discriminating against people with disabilities in employment, education, or services.

The Rehabilitation Act of 1973 was followed in 1975 by the Developmentally Disabled Assistance and Bill of Rights Act, and the Education for All Handicapped Children Act, which later became the Individuals with Disabilities Act or IDEA (Meekosha & Jakubowicz, 1996; Asch & Mudrick, 1995; Pardeck, 1998; Rothman, 2003).

As publicly signaled by the changing terminology in the IDEA, sensitivity is needed with respect to terminology. Certain commonly used phrases and adjectives can be experienced as demeaning and inappropriate. For example, as in IDEA, the word *handicap* should be replaced by the more neutral term *disability*. Biased phraseology such as *suffer from*, *crippled by*, and *victim of* should be avoided; a person "has" a disability; he or she isn't necessarily "afflicted" with it or "suffering" from it; a "client" becomes a "consumer" (Pardeck, 1998).

A social worker with severe disability displays sophisticated interviewing skills.

Another major piece of legislation promoting disability rights, the Americans with Disabilities Act (ADA), was passed in 1990; it was greatly strengthened by the Civil Rights Act of 1991. These acts are described next.

THE AMERICANS WITH DISABILITIES ACT OF 1990 AND THE CIVIL RIGHTS ACT OF 1991

The Americans with Disabilities Act was designed to assist all people with disabilities, not just those with developmental disabilities. Its purposes are identified in its Section 2 as providing a mandate for ending discrimination, providing enforceable standards of treatment for disabled people, and creating a central role for the federal government in enforcing these standards (see Exhibit 11-8).

The Americans with Disabilities Act can help people in very concrete ways, as illustrated by the following true story:

> A young woman employed at a Milwaukee Target store sat quietly in her wheelchair by the employee entrance before work one day. Unable to open the door by herself, she waited for someone to walk by and hold the door open for her. The individual who helped her that day happened to work for the State of Wisconsin.
>
> After asking the woman how long she had been waiting to enter the building, the man instructed the store management to address the problem. Shortly after the incident, plans to install an electronic door opener began. (ADA rules out discrimination, 1993)

Without the Americans with Disabilities Act, neither the young woman in question nor the state employee would have had the legal clout to insist on an electronic

---

EXHIBIT 11-8

The Americans with Disabilities Act Recognizes Discrimination

Section 2 of the Americans with Disabilities Act states, among other things, that:

 . . . historically, society has tended to isolate and segregate individuals with disabilities, and, despite some improvements, such forms of discrimination against individuals with disabilities continue to be a serious and pervasive social problem; discrimination against individuals with disabilities persists in such critical areas as employment, housing, public accommodations, education, transportation, communication, recreation, institutionalization, health services, voting, and access to public services.

Unlike individuals who have experienced discrimination on the basis of race, color, sex, national origin, religion, or age, individuals who have experienced discrimination on the basis of disability have often had no legal recourse to redress such discrimination. . . .

SOURCE: Quoted from Section 2, "Findings and Purposes," Public Law 101–336, Americans with Disabilities Act of 1990.

opener for an employee of this Target store. However, Title I of the act makes new requirements of employers. One is that "employers with 15 or more employees may not discriminate against qualified individuals with disabilities." Another is that "employers must reasonably accommodate the disabilities of qualified applicants or employees, including modifying work stations and equipment, unless undue hardship would result" (*Americans with Disabilities Act fact sheet*, 1990). The law intends that required accommodations should be reasonable. Existing physical barriers, for example, need to be remedied only if this can be done without much difficulty or expense.

Other titles of the Americans with Disabilities Act call for reasonable access to public services (e.g., special accommodations as needed to allow usage of buildings, buses, and trains) and accessibility to public accommodations such as restaurants, hotels, theaters, schools, day care centers, and colleges and universities. Also, telephone companies must provide telecommunications services for hearing-impaired and speech-impaired persons.

Students may be interested to know that the ADA requires educational institutions to make reasonable modifications if these would not fundamentally alter a program or cause undue financial hardship. Such modifications could include reassigning classrooms to ensure accessibility, providing exams at different times or places, or offering early registration for classes (Pardeck, 1998).

The Civil Rights Act of 1991 greatly strengthened the ADA by allowing jury trials and compensatory and punitive damages in accord with those available to minorities under the Civil Rights Act of 1964. Complaints are handled by the Equal Employment Opportunity Commission (EEOC). By the fall of 1996, fully 70,000 complaints had been filed, and recently, nearly a quarter of the EEOC's caseload is comprised of discrimination complaints under Title I of the ADA (Pardeck, 2005). Interestingly enough, a large number of job discrimination suits were filed with the EEOC by people with disabilities that no one anticipated because they were previously, to all intents and purposes, hidden. The first plaintiff to win a monetary award, for example, experienced job discrimination related to a diagnosis of cancer (Pardeck, 1998).

Pardeck (2005) notes that over the years, the Supreme Court has had a profound effect on the ADA. Some rulings have strengthened certain aspects of the law, but other decisions have limited its impact by narrowing the definition of disability. As an example, one setback involved the case of Edna Williams, who was diagnosed with carpal tunnel syndrome. She sued her employer, Toyota Motor Corporation, seeking accommodation at work under the Americans with Disabilities Act. The U.S. Court of Appeals for the Sixth Circuit ruled in favor of Ms. Williams, but the Supreme Court overturned that decision in early 2002, stating that because Ms. Williams's disability did not restrict her from performing other manual tasks central to daily life, her disability was not serious enough to qualify her for the protections of the ADA (Richey, 2002).

An important decision strengthened aspects of the law in 2004, however. The Supreme Court upheld the right of disabled individuals to sue states for equal access to public services and facilities. Sadly, the decision was only 5–4, and the swing vote was made by Sandra Day O'Connor, who has since left the court. A 5–4 decision today would likely go the other way, given that President Bush has appointed an extremely conservative replacement for former Justice O'Connor. But due to the 2004 decision, people who are paraplegic (such as George Lane of Tennessee, who filed suit) should no longer have to crawl up to the second floor of a courtroom (Richey, 2004).

GLOBAL EFFORTS ON BEHALF OF PEOPLE WITH DISABILITIES

Discrimination against people with disabilities is not confined to the United States. Rather, it is a worldwide phenomenon. For this reason, the United Nations, an international organization often more visionary than its individual member states, determined to address the matter in 2006.

The outcome was the Convention on the Rights of Persons with Disabilities (2007). According to the AAIDD:

> The Convention on the Rights of Persons with Disabilities and its Optional Protocol was adopted on 13 December, 2006, at UN Headquarters in New York, and was opened for signature on 30 March, 2007. There were 82 signatories to the Convention, 22 signatories to the Optional Protocol, and 1 ratification to the Convention. This is the highest number of signatories in history to a UN opening day. It is the first comprehensive human rights treaty of the 21st century—it marks a "paradigm shift" in attitudes and approaches to persons with disabilities.
>
> The Convention is intended as a human rights instrument with an explicit, social development dimension. It adopts a broad categorization of persons with disabilities and reaffirms that all persons with all types of disabilities must enjoy all human rights and fundamental freedoms. It clarifies and qualifies how all categories of rights apply to persons with disabilities and identifies areas where adaptations have been made by persons with disabilities to effectively exercise their rights and areas where their rights have been violated, and which must be reinforced.

Clearly, the United Nations has developed an important international focus on the issues and rights of persons with disabilities. How well the Articles of the Convention will be translated into action in participant nations around the world remains to be seen.

VALUE DILEMMAS AND ETHICAL IMPLICATIONS

Both personal and professional values come into focus in social work with people with developmental disabilities. Today, because of new knowledge of genetics and new medical procedures, value issues in this field are more complex than ever. For example, genetic counseling makes it possible for a couple to know beforehand if they run a substantial risk of abnormality in a pregnancy. Should a concerned couple seek this type of information? What should they do if a substantial risk is identified?

Complex Issues

A procedure called amniocentesis can identify many types of fetal abnormalities during a pregnancy. Corrective measures may possibly be taken in utero. Sometimes, however, nothing can be done for a deformed or otherwise abnormal fetus. Should such a pregnancy be continued? Does this question involve absolute principles? Or can it involve consideration of probable quality of life for the fetus and the family?

Social workers advocate self-determination. But who is the client engaging in self-determination? The person with the disability (such as Sandra McLean, in Chapter 2) or the family providing necessary care (such as frail Mrs. McLean and college-bound Susan)? Lea Perkins in this chapter's case study or her family (specifically in this case, her mother, Mary)? Individual and family systems are both legitimate focuses for intervention, and the various systems might make different choices. Whose choices should be honored?

But perhaps these aren't the right questions. Perhaps if society provided sufficient supports to family caregivers, sufficient options such as universal access to respite care and day care services, choices could be made that would satisfy every member of a family, including the person with disabilities. Increasing options requires action in a larger arena. The NASW Code of Ethics provides a guide to expanding choice (see Exhibit 11-9).

The Americans with Disabilities Act of 1990 and the Civil Rights Act of 1991 are important examples of legislation aimed at improving social conditions and promoting social justice for people with developmental disabilities. This minority group was publicly recognized and provided with significant legal protections under these laws. People with disabilities themselves, their families, social workers, and many, many others participated in the effort that resulted in these new laws.

Social workers may assume policy-oriented roles directly by taking on administrative positions such as that of Stephanie Hermann described in Chapter 2. Even from direct-service positions, however, social workers may help create change by doing such things as writing informed letters to their agency administrators or to

---

EXHIBIT 11-9

Social and Political Action

The NASW Code of Ethics, provision 6.04, as quoted in part here, strongly advocates expansion of choice to make self-determination a more realistic opportunity for client systems.

(a) Social workers should engage in social and political action that seeks to ensure that all people have equal access to the resources, employment, services, and opportunities they require to meet their basic human needs and to develop fully. Social workers should be aware of the impact of the political arena on practice and should advocate for changes in policy and legislation to improve social conditions in order to meet basic human needs and promote social justice.

(b) Social workers should act to expand choice and opportunity for all people, with special regard for vulnerable, disadvantaged, oppressed, and exploited people and groups.

SOURCE: National Association of Social Workers. (1996). *NASW code of ethics*. Washington, DC: NASW Press.

influential legislators. They may serve as expert witnesses at legislative hearings. Social workers may be even more active in creating policy by running for and holding public office. There is a great deal of work that still needs to be done with, and on behalf of, people with disabilities.

Current Trends

Because community care today so often means ongoing care by the family, a major trend is respectful collaboration between families and professionals. The strengths, or empowerment, model has helped encourage a new paradigm in which families are viewed as competent, full partners in professional service, as illustrated in this chapter's case study with Mary and Lea Perkins. The role of social workers is primarily to assist families and consumers of services to meet their own goals. Mutual respect, trust, and open communication are imperative, as well as an atmosphere in which cultural traditions, values, and diversity are acknowledged and honored (Rothman, 2003).

Another major trend is the increasing lifespan of people with disabilities, made possible by advances in medicine. The 2003 American Community Survey identified fully 13.5 million *noninstitutionalized* people over 65, almost 40 percent of citizens of that age group, who indicated that they had a disability (Gold, 2005). Who will care for these citizens when they can no longer care for themselves?

As family caregivers age themselves and foresee a time when they will no longer be able to care for their disabled children or elderly family members with disabilities, future planning becomes a major concern for them. A survey taken a few years ago found more than 60,000 people with developmental disabilities on waiting lists for residential services in 37 states (*Aging*, 2001, 6). Housing for people with disabilities is thus in very short supply. The Older Americans Act provides important family supports in some areas of the country: senior centers, nutrition sites, homemaker services, home-delivered meals, and case coordination. But funding remains very low, and in many places waiting lists are long (see Chapter 9). Typically, even disabled persons who have worked their entire lives have little or no retirement income to help finance their own futures, having worked for minimal wages or no pay at all in sheltered workshops.

As a further potential problem for older workers with disabilities, a recent study by the General Accounting Office, an investigative arm of Congress, concluded that if the Social Security plan pushed by President George W. Bush were adopted by Congress, people with disabilities would lose out. Benefits would have to be cut because the system would lose too much money as it became diverted to private accounts (Torres-Gill, 2007). Fortunately, however, the Republican version of Social Security "reform," *privatization*, seems unlikely to be passed, at least during the Bush administration.

Families today are bearing increasing burdens of the cost of care for elderly people with disabilities, and as family caregivers themselves age, how long they will be able to carry on is an unanswered question. Only about 25 percent of noninstitutional care has been publicly subsidized in recent years (Hooyman & Gonyea, 1995), and government funding for this purpose has been decreasing since the turn of the century as a continually increasing proportion of the federal budget is allocated to "guns" rather than "butter."

In addition to families bearing increasing burdens of costs of care for elderly people with disabilities, they are also bearing a greater proportion of costs of children with disabilities. According to Mannes (1998), approximately 14 percent of the projected savings from welfare reform was expected to come from reductions in SSI (Supplemental Security Income; see Chapter 3), payments formerly provided for families with disabled children. The rationale was that eligibility criteria for disabilities were considered too lenient. Soon after passage of the welfare reform law, more than 135,800 children with disabilities lost their benefits. They had disorders that were primarily "mental," including retardation, learning disabilities, and attention deficit disorders. The average benefit lost was $410 per month, which was originally intended to help families meet the higher costs associated with raising children with disabilities (Feldmann, 1997).

As in so many areas of need today, the general trend is to rely on families to finance or provide care for their own, whether they can actually do so or not.

INTERNET SITES

http://www.aamr.org	American Association on Intellectual and Developmental Disorders
http://www.marchofdimes.com	March of Dimes
http://www.autisticadvocacy.org	The Autistic Self Advocacy Network
http://www.autism-society.org/site/PageServer	Autism Society of America
http://www.epilepsyfoundation.org	Epilepsy Foundation
http://www.ninds.nih.gov	National Institute of Neurological Disorders and Stroke
http://www.braintrauma.org	Brain Trauma Foundation
http://www.ucp.org	United Cerebral Palsy
http://www.ed.gov/about/offices/list/osers/nidr/Index.html	National Institute on Disability and Rehabilitation Research
http://www.ldanatl.org	Learning Disabilities Association of America
http://www.nichcy.org	National Information Center for Children and Youth with Disabilities
http://www.nea.org	National Education Association
http://www.wapd.org	The World Association for People with Disabilities

SUMMARY

This chapter begins with a case study that illustrates contemporary, community-based social work with people with disabilities. Mary Perkins has an intellectual disability. She has been served in the past by a special education program that prepared her for gainful employment, and she is doing well at her paying job.

Mary's daughter Lea, however, has suffered traumatic abuse resulting in emotional disturbance and ongoing truancy. The family is experiencing myriad other difficulties as well. Through intensive family-based intervention, a young social work intern, Jenny Chambers, assists Mary to develop the skills required to keep her family together and to remain in their own apartment. She engages Lea in a special education program at school where the girl begins to excel.

While social workers traditionally have worked with people with disabilities primarily in institutional settings, today their services are becoming increasingly community based. Social workers assist families to expand their options so that far more often today, children with disabilities are raised at home. Social workers assist individuals with disabilities and their families to advocate for their own ideas and choices, deal constructively with bureaucratic agencies, and join with others in promoting new policies and programs that can maximize their options.

By examining the differences between categorical and functional definitions of disability, we see why such differences are important in terms of funding resources and eligibility for service. Ten major categories of developmental disability are then discussed: intellectual disability or mental retardation, cerebral palsy, autism, orthopedic problems, hearing problems, epilepsy, traumatic brain injury, learning disabilities, emotional disturbance, and co-occurrence of disabilities. Fetal alcohol syndrome and cocaine and other drug-affected babies are also discussed.

Until comparatively recently, little has been done for persons with disabilities. For centuries, people with mental retardation and other disabilities were cruelly incarcerated. Reformers such as the Frenchmen Pereira, Itard, and Seguin worked to demonstrate that people with disabilities can be taught. Huge institutions replaced training schools, however, and not until the 1920s did research contribute to a change in public opinion. In recent years, the concept of normalization has spurred efforts toward removing people with disabilities from large institutions and placing them back in the community, ideally in homelike settings with special provisions to meet their needs.

Efforts toward home care have been hampered by lack of resources in the community. The Education for All Handicapped Children Act of 1975 (currently known as the Individuals with Disabilities Education Act), its 1986 amendment extending service to infants and toddlers, the Americans with Disabilities Act of 1990, and the Civil Rights Act of 1991 were discussed as examples of enabling legislation providing legal bases for equal opportunity and empowerment for people with disabilities. However, competition for scarce resources makes implementing the full intent of these laws difficult. The recent Convention on the Rights of Persons with Disabilities, adopted by the United Nations in 2007, lends hope that this population at risk will receive increasing social justice efforts around the world in the coming years.

The NASW has developed standards for service for working with people with disabilities and their families. The chapter presents these standards and also discusses how professional values and ethics guide contemporary practice efforts in this field.

Opportunities for social workers to work with people with disabilities are growing. More community-based services are needed, not only for younger people with disabilities but for ever-increasing numbers who survive into old age. A continuing problem is underfunding for community-based services, however, and recent legislation known as welfare reform has decreased rather than increased funding and the opportunities that funding can provide for this diverse population.

KEY TERMS

accommodation, *p. 477*

continuum of care, *p. 472*

deinstitutionalization, *p. 453*

developmental disability, *p. 461*

empowerment, *p. 475*

family care homes, *p. 472*

genetic counseling, *p. 458*

habilitation, *p. 454*

job coach, *p. 458*

normalization, *p. 454*

rehabilitation, *p. 451*

respite care, *p. 472*

sheltered workshop, *p. 472*

supported employment, *p. 458*

DISCUSSION QUESTIONS

1. Discuss the concept of in-home intervention for families experiencing such severe difficulties that placement of a child outside the home is a strong possibility. Then consider the Perkins family case specifically. Do you think the cost of providing in-home services was worthwhile to the wider community that financed them? Why or why not? Do you think foster placement for Lea would have been a better plan? Why or why not?

2. Not many years ago, most children with disabilities were placed in institutions. How do you think this plan would have worked for Mary Perkins? For Lea? Explain your reasons.

3. What are 10 major diagnostic categories of developmental disability? Briefly describe each one. What types of disabilities are found in babies with fetal alcohol syndrome and those who have been exposed to cocaine? By what age must a disabling condition be diagnosed to be considered "developmental" according to the federal definition?

4. Some states define developmental disabilities by category, but the federal government defines them by function. Using the federal government's definition, what kind of disabled person do you think may tend to be ineligible for federal assistance in the United States? Why?

5. How did social Darwinism, the eugenics movement, and the development of the IQ test all tend to influence society's treatment of people with developmental disabilities? How did these concepts play out in mid-20th-century Germany?

6. How did research findings during the 1920s, and the return of veterans injured in World War II, influence perceptions of the disabled?

7. Explain the concept of normalization. When and where did it develop? How does it affect care-planning efforts for disabled people in the United States today? Why?

8. Why is the generalist approach appropriate for social work practice with people with disabilities?

9. In what ways does the Americans with Disabilities Act of 1990 recognize people with disabilities as a minority group in need of protection? How is this act strengthened by the Civil Rights Act of 1991?

10. What are some of the major contemporary roles for social workers involved with the disabled?

11. How do social work values and the NASW Code of Ethics guide practice in the field of developmental disabilities, according to this chapter? What are the NASW standards for service?

CLASSROOM EXERCISES

While not required, it is suggested that students break into small groups of three or four to discuss these exercises. It may be helpful to choose a scribe to record and report interesting points to the class after the group discussion.

1. While most children with developmental disabilities are being raised at home today, the bulk of government funding still goes to care in institutions. Many people believe that families are supposed to provide for their own, so low levels of government assistance to those with disabled members living at home are not a problem. What do you think? Why?

2. People involved in the disability rights movement believe that their primary problem is not the disability itself but the failure of the environment to provide satisfactory accommodations. The movement teaches that for people with disabilities to be empowered, realistic options and choices must be available and that these should be a right, not a privilege. Many people without disabilities, however, disagree, due to the cost and inconvenience of providing accommodations. What do you think? Why?

3. Many older people with disabilities are facing destitution in old age as their family caregivers grow too old to care for them and alternative housing is in short supply. Their earnings have been too small to provide for retirement. Imagine that you have the power to create ideal social policies to deal with this situation. What policies will you develop? Why?

RESEARCH ACTIVITIES

1. With permission from your campus administrators, spend a day on your college campus using a wheelchair. Find out how easy or difficult it is for you to get around campus and attend your classes. Write a report about your experience, and submit it to the administrators (and perhaps your campus newspaper).

2. Visit a local nursing home that has a specialized unit for people with disabilities. Talk with some of the residents about how they like living there.

Interview the social worker to find out how well he or she thinks the services offered at the home meet the needs of the residents.

3. Interview various members of a family caring for a person with a disability, including the person with the disability. How do the perspectives of the different family members differ? What resources from the community are available to assist? What resources does the disabled person or the family feel are needed but are not available?

INTERNET RESEARCH EXERCISES

1. The Nemours Foundation has a site in which they discuss Down's Syndrome (http://www.kidshealth.org/parent/medical/genetic/down_syndrome.html).

   a. What is Down's Syndrome?

   b. What causes it?

   c. What are the physical characteristics common to children with Down's Syndrome?

2. An Australian website, Centre for Developmental Disability Studies, presents some useful information about developmental disability (http://www.cdds.med.usyd.edu.au).

   a. What is the mission of this organization?

   b. What is their definition of "developmental disability"? (Hint: click on "What is DD?")

   c. List five conditions cited as resulting in potential developmental disability.

3. Congress continues to amend the Individuals with Disabilities Eduation Act (IDEA). An overview of the act as of April 2007 can be found at http://edlabor.house.gov/publications/IDEAOverview.pdf.

   a. What is the basic purpose of this law?

   b. How many students were excluded from public education due to what some people considered disabilities according to this site?

   c. Who determines the eligibility for inclusion under the current law?

FOR FURTHER READING

May, G. E., & Raske, M. B. (Eds.). (2005). *Ending disability discrimination, strategies for social workers*. Boston: Allyn & Bacon.

   This work provides social workers with a new framework for conceptualizing disability in contemporary U.S. society. The Disability Discrimination Model integrates social work theories, such as empowerment and the strengths perspective, with new insights from disability studies to reshape social work practice and policy regarding disabilities. Its eight

chapters by various authors illustrate the evolution of thought toward the new paradigm described by the editors as the "Disability Discrimination Model."

Murphy, J. W., & Pardeck, J. T. (Eds.). (2005). *Disability issues for social workers and human services professionals in the twenty-first century*. New York: Hayworth Press.

   This edited volume explores several topics critical to the field of disability in the 21st century. Topics are explored at the practice, policy, program, and theoretical levels. Issues examined include the role of religion and spirituality in working with people with disabilities, the use of medication, the impact of cultural diversity, the importance of civil rights, and the recent effects of managed care. The information provided is critical for social workers and other human service workers today.

Putmam, M. (Ed.). (2007). *Aging and disability, crossing network lines.* New York: Springer.

This book brings together research findings and expert opinions into a comprehensive analysis of the issues involved in working across aging, developmental disability, and physical disability service networks. Section one provides an illustrative case study and current challenges in this area. Section two evaluates common agendas across aging and disability consumer populations and service networks. Section three discusses the work of moving partnerships forward through research, evaluation, and policy interventions.

Mackelprang, R., & Saisgiver, R. (1999). *Disability: A diversity model approach in human service practice.* Pacific Grove, CA: Brooks/Cole.

This text is written primarily for students preparing for careers in the human services with people with disabilities, including social work. The book is organized into three sections. The first creates a context that recognizes social devaluation of people with disabilities and suggests a need for an aggressive political action to overcome oppression. The second examines various groupings of disabilities and provides personal accounts from people who experience them. The third section discusses human service practice with persons with disabilities in social context.

Rothman, J. C. (2003). *Social work practice across disability.* Boston: Allyn & Bacon.

This book is designed to assist social workers and social work students to practice in a sensitive and effective manner with people with disabilities. The author takes great care to illustrate how the kind of disability, the limitations experienced, environmental factors, the family and social milieu, and personality characteristics and identity create a unique experience with disability for each person. While there are common themes—the experience of difference, stigma, frustration, oppression, empowerment through activism—each person "lives" disability differently.

Pardeck, J. T. (1998). *Social work after the Americans with Disabilities Act: New challenges and opportunities*

for social service professionals. Westport, CT: Auburn House.

Pardeck's goal in writing this book was to inform social workers about the mandates and requirements of the Americans with Disabilities Act of 1990. He has done this well, including chapters that explain the provisions of the act, discuss its impact on social service agencies in particular, and explore the importance of advocacy with respect to the act. The book also describes the impact on education.

Smart, J. (2001). *Disability, society, and the individual.* Gaithersburg, MD: Aspen.

This book examines the disability experience from the point of view of the individual with the disability. It also discusses how disabilities are viewed by the wider society and then considers the relationship between the two perspectives. Part I provides a detailed definition of disability. Part II examines the impact of social prejudice on people with disabilities, and Part III examines the impact of the disability itself on people with disabilities and their families.

Stone, J. H. (Ed.). (2005). *Culture and disability, providing culturally competent services.* Thousand Oaks, CA: Sage.

The theme of cultural competence is increasingly important in the delivery of social work services in the United States and elsewhere in the world. This book attempts to help practitioners develop such competence. The first three chapters describe the relationship between culture and disability as well as the role of service providers in communicating across cultures. The following seven chapters provide information about specific cultural groups that account for large proportions of recent immigration into the United States.

Wehman, P., Inge, K., Revell, W. G. Jr., & Brooke, V. (2007). *Real work for real pay, inclusive employment for people with disabilities.* Baltimore: P. H. Brookes.

The employment of people with disabilities directly into the labor force is not easy. Attitudes of businesspeople and professionals, knowledge of capacity and rights, funding, work preparation and retention strategies, and diversity issues are just a few of the challenges involved. The purpose of this book is to provide a comprehensive resource on inclusive employment. It discusses important values, behavioral tools for change, assistive technology for change, and policy directions. Case studies and program tables illuminate the concepts in each of the 17 chapters.

PART III

A LOOK AT THE FUTURE

The future: what will it hold? The world sometimes seems utterly chaotic but, in fact, existing forces are the catalysts for powerful change that will drive and define our evolving future. We will begin this final section of the book by exploring several powerful forces that are energizing, shaping, and propelling transformation in the world. We will think about how social workers are involved in this change and consider implications for the profession of social work and for the people we serve. We will also identify some of the emerging issues that will create ethical and value dilemmas for social workers.

Chapter 12 begins by looking at the remarkable human diversity that is rapidly changing the face of America, a diversity flavored by culture, race, ethnicity, age, spirituality, and numerous other facets of humanity. Next, the political scene is considered: how are strong political currents shaping the opportunity system for people, especially for the poor? Connected to political trends are economic forces: how will a volatile economy affect people in the United States and elsewhere in the world? Chapter 12 also explores technological advances and considers the ethics of evolving technology for practice. Biomedical advances represent another force that will challenge humanity and will affect the social work profession in countless ways. Chapter 12 focuses on biomedical advances in the areas of human reproduction, genetics, and organ replacement.

Our consideration of the future would not be complete without at least a glance at the future of the social work profession. The text authors suspect that students who are considering social work as a career will have interest in predictions about future employment opportunities. So, the text concludes with some final comments on social work employment projections from the U.S. Department of Labor. ∎

CHAPTER 12

FUTURE CHALLENGES AND CLOSING NOTES

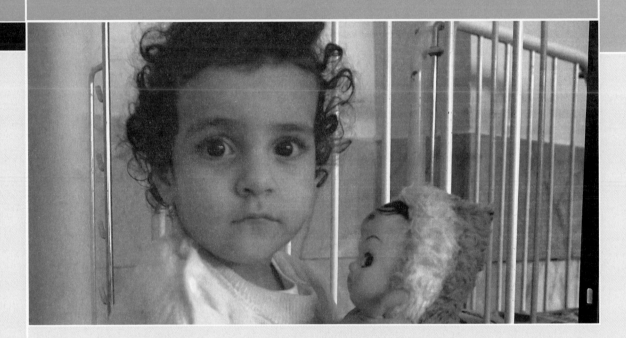

OUTLINE

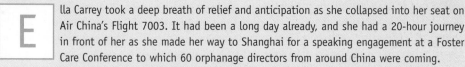

ELLA CARREY: SOCIAL WORKER IN AN INTERNATIONAL ARENA[1]

Ella Carrey took a deep breath of relief and anticipation as she collapsed into her seat on Air China's Flight 7003. It had been a long day already, and she had a 20-hour journey in front of her as she made her way to Shanghai for a speaking engagement at a Foster Care Conference to which 60 orphanage directors from around China were coming.

"This is downright crazy," Ella thought. "How did I ever get myself into this? What am I doing going to *China*?" She reflected that her growth as a social worker had brought her to this moment in her career.

Ever since she had been on a church-sponsored mission trip in eastern Europe and spent a week rocking babies in an overcrowded orphanage as a young college student, she had wanted to become a social worker and work in an orphanage. She proudly completed her BSW degree in her early 20s and worked in the public foster care system. Later, she placed older children in adoptive homes at a Michigan faith-based child welfare agency. While she enjoyed her jobs, the orphaned children consumed her mind and her plans.

In addition to a few donations, Ella eventually saved enough money to move to Romania, fulfilling her long-time dream. There she connected with a local nongovernmental organization (NGO) and spent almost every day at a 300-bed orphanage for children ages 0 to 3. It was heartbreaking to see so many abandoned infants and toddlers and realize that the few orphanage workers could not possibly provide for all their needs. Alongside the local staff, she fed, changed, and played with the children. From her education and experience, she knew that their development was severely delayed and learned that the typical "rocking" behavior was due to lack of stimulation. Infants even stopped crying as their needs went unmet. Ella started Romanian language classes so that she could communicate with the children and staff. With the extra attention, it was satisfying to see that some of the children showed vast improvement.

Ultimately, Ella realized that she and the small staff could not ever hope to give adequate attention to all of the children, and more and more were entering the institution. Additionally, with the attention, some of the children had actually become *more* demanding, fussing to be held. Instead of the frightening silence of the massive wards and the blank stares of neglect, some of the children started to cry when she left the room, and this irritated the already overworked staff. Sadly, she had to say good-bye to the older children as they "graduated" to different institutions, making room for more infants who quickly filled the empty beds. Feeling like a gerbil on a treadmill, Ella realized that the micro-level work with the children, while extremely important, would never be enough.

---

[1] The Ella Carrey case study was contributed by Pamela Awtrey Harrington, MSW, of Grand Rapids, Michigan. Ms. Harrington, has had extensive international social work practice experience in countries including Sri Lanka, Romania, and China.

"Great," she commiserated with a friend, exhausted and discouraged. "What do I do now? I've got 300 kids and this is only one orphanage in one country. There has got to be a better way."

From this conviction, Ella decided to mobilize resources on the mezzo level. Based on her own profound experiences, she organized teams of American students to come. Volunteers brought stimulating toys, disposable diapers, mobiles, and supplies and stayed to work with groups of children. She even found a network of artists to paint colorful murals on the dingy walls. Through the local NGO, a few of the young children were even adopted by American or western European families, and Ella helped facilitate those adoptions, trying to use the standards of practice she had learned in her previous jobs back in Michigan.

Frequently, parents or grandparents of children would come from long distances by train to visit. Ella was curious about their lives, and by this time she knew enough Romanian to converse with them. Often destitute, the relatives seemed to truly love their children but believed that the orphanage was a better option than home. She discovered that the law allowed a child to be maintained in the orphanage system if a parent visited at least once every 6 months; otherwise, a child was considered legally abandoned and paperwork could begin that allowed for the domestic or international adoption of the child.

As Ella learned more about the culture and history of Romania, she realized that the communist regime that controlled the country until 1990 strongly encouraged large families in an effort to increase the population and the independence of the country. Severe punishments were imposed for families who used any kind of birth control. Large families were honored, and if they could not be sustained through small, government-controlled salaries, the option of institutional care for children was provided. Staffed by medically oriented professionals, children could be fed, clothed, and educated. Doctors encouraged "special" institutions for children with disabilities, where the risk of medical problems could be managed more easily than in family homes in rural areas that offered few services. For some citizens, though, life became even more difficult as communism lost power and the country's economy convulsed with change and transition. Poverty became rampant, even for those fortunate enough to be employed in the new capitalistic open market. Old beliefs die hard, and years later, the post-communist-era orphanages were still considered to be viable and even loving alternatives for children.

Thus, for a period of time, Ella felt that she reached the pinnacle of her life's calling through her fulfilling orphanage work. She thought about starting her own orphanage, where children could grow up in a consistent, nurturing environment. She loved the Romanian culture, made friends, and enjoyed making a difference in the lives of so many.

But there was a dark side. Even with the additional help and resources, Ella knew in her heart that, as the United Nations Convention on the Rights of the Child affirms, every child is entitled to grow up in a family, not an institution. Even if hundreds of children were adopted every year, it would be a mere drop in the bucket compared with the total numbers languishing in institutions. And other disturbing scenes began to plague her mind: in the capital city, she saw numerous teenagers who were "emancipated" from the orphanages, many of them with their own babies and no means of support other than begging. She was repulsed knowing that some of these young people were seen as fair game for sexual predators and was aware that the vast water and sewer structure under the city was considered home to many. She saw the institution-induced mental retardation and heard about "Reactive Attachment Disorder" caused by lack of appropriate care by one person. She began wondering how many of the children were truly "orphans" rather than victims of poverty and the country's difficult past. Could it be that the entire *system* needed to change and become child-focused?

Through a consortium of local and international agencies, Ella discovered that she was not alone in these reflections. With great interest, she joined a team of professionals to write a proposal for a grant offered by the federally funded U.S. Agency for International Development (USAID). In partnership with the Romanian government and in anticipation of the 2007 accession to the European Union, she and her colleagues created alliances and were eventually awarded a grant to implement a macro-level demonstration model of community-based services that would eventually reduce the need for institutions.

Using her professional social work knowledge, skills, and values, together with her language and cultural competence, Ella was ideally suited to work alongside the Romanian staff in this task. Realizing that it would be difficult to do, Ella nonetheless moved her relentless effort away from the children in orphanages and instead concentrated on working with the newly decentralized governmental entities in the community. In a sense, her client shifted from the institutionalized child to the "client" of government. While there was much initial resistance to change, prevention services were established, deinstitutionalization services were created, and children were reunited with their birth families. Foster care laws and standards were written based on a western European model, and many of the children who could not return home, even those with disabilities, were placed and monitored in families. In accordance with government policy, permanency planning was introduced and domestic adoption encouraged. Independent living skills trainings were offered to young adults aging out of the system. Counties began to shift funding to a community-based model instead of institutional care.

At the end of the rewarding 3-year grant period, Ella decided to return to the United States to enroll in an advanced-standing MSW program. She continued to explore global options for children and avidly read everything she could find on the subject. She joined an electronic list serve, participated in video conferences in eastern Europe, and engaged with internationally adopted children and their families.

Now, 7 years after leaving Romania, Ella was equipped with her MSW and a supervisory foster care job at the state level. International work had profoundly changed her perspective and continued to enthuse her. She jumped at the chance to share her de-institutionalization and foster care experiences with orphanage directors in China. The most populous country in the world, China is being revolutionized by lightening-fast economic and demographic change, profoundly affecting its families everywhere. After carefully researching the cultural considerations that brought China to its current crossroads in children's services, it was clear that there were major and pervasive differences in the macro-level situations between countries. What were the common principles? Ella recognized that China ratified the Convention on the Rights of the Child. But in her work with Chinese orphanage directors, how would she be able to relate to their government's "one child" policy? How could she discuss human rights? What about the gender biases that filled institutions with so many females?

She certainly did not wish to replicate the American foster care situation with all its challenges—including foster care "drift," where children move from one home to another, always in search of permanency. At the same time, she pondered the potential for conflicts between her Western perspective and Asian culture and knew her experiences would not totally "fit" the Chinese context. But she was also aware of the immense interest in the budding social work profession in China, and she could respectfully offer her expertise along with the lessons that she had learned. She could engage in a universal conversation about the best interests of children in need of families. There would be plenty of time for the conference participants to explore options of "best practice models" that could be created out of their own ancient culture with its wisdom, and she anticipated that her role would be learner as well as teacher. Within the context of internationally accepted conventions and agreements, Ella knew that her focus would be to see as many children as possible grow up in families of their own. With this passion, she believed that she could make a difference to some of the hundreds of thousands of Chinese children.

Drifting off to sleep on her flight high above the international waters of the Pacific Ocean, Ella smiled in satisfaction and recognized that she had become part of a global social work movement. ■

SOCIAL WORK: PROFESSION AT THE EDGE OF CHANGE

Ella Carrey is a compassionate, ethical, competent social worker. She is also attuned to change, adventuresome, willing to take risks, and ready to use promising opportunities when they emerge. She cares deeply about the children of the world and their families. Ella is confident in her social work knowledge and skills. The profession's values are her values. She is also very committed to a lifetime of learning and humble in her awareness that she does not have all of the answers, but she can learn. Ella is creative. She is fully aware that her efforts to help people will not always work; when they don't, she is ready to look for new interventions. As a generalist social worker, Ella may begin her work with individuals and their families. At the same time, she may also be seeking change within organizations, sometimes the very organization that is her employer. Because she is a generalist, Ella may also begin her work not at the individual or family level but at the community or governmental level. Change that will truly help people often needs to be made at the larger social system level. Ella, as a social worker, is committed to helping people, and she is ready to work where change is needed, even if this is not within her own familiar local environment or her own country. Social work is, at its core, a change profession.

Author Ann Fadiman (1997) describes her position as the storyteller, a perspective very much like that of the social worker:

> I have always felt that the action most worth watching is not at the center of things but where edges meet. I like shorelines, weather fronts, international borders. There are interesting frictions and incongruities in those places, and often, if you stand at the point of tangency, you can see both sides better than if you were in the middle of either one. (p. viii)

Indeed, a stream of exciting, sometimes frightening, highly energized forces is rapidly reshaping our world. Perhaps Ella Carrey represents the social work profession at this confluence of change. Like Ella Carrey, social workers live with change every day. Social workers also create change. Key to much of the change taking place in the world today is cultural transformation and globalization.

In the next 10 years, the United States will become far more culturally diverse than it is today, and social work practice will be at that confluence of change. This is not an easy or comfortable place to be. The profession of social work will be challenged by a society that still does not understand it or its clients well. Education will be needed to dispel the stereotype of the welfare worker (social worker) dispensing "the dole" to lazy, fraudulent recipients (clients). This book attempts to destroy such stereotypes by providing extensive case studies that illustrate the true nature of social work practice and the people social workers work with. The people in the case studies—the clients as well as the social workers—were drawn from real-life situations. These are people of dignity. They do not fit into stereotypes. Instead, the varying circumstances of their lives lead naturally into an exploration of the values, social policy issues, research findings, practice, and history of the profession of social work.

Just as the clients did not fit into any preconceived stereotype, neither did the case study social workers. Certainly they did not fit old stereotypes such as the welfare worker or the lady bountiful. Neither, however, does social work fit the image of a glamorous, high-status profession. In reality, social work is not the right profession for everyone. This will be more true in the years to come than it has ever been in the past. At the heart of the social work profession lies a set of values that ultimately guide practice. Concern for the poor, the oppressed, those discriminated against, and those in pain and most at risk is central to the mission of social work. Belief in the dignity and worth of every human being is not merely a philosophical stance; it is—and must be—inherent in all social work practice. Social workers of the future will need to fight to make social institutions more humane and more responsive to human needs. Their commitment to social and economic justice will need to be carried out in action, not just in silent intent.

Many persons considering a career in social work will find that the value base of the profession is inconsistent with their own values, and they will need to look for another career. Those who enter social work will find that the profession is strongly influenced by various outside forces: demographic trends, political trends, economic conditions, technological advances in science and health care, and environmental concerns, just to name a few. These forces contain energy that drives change. When these forces overlap and intermingle, they sometimes build momentum that speeds change. Increasingly, they are not contained within national borders but, instead, operate globally. They are among the forces that futurists analyze when they seek to forecast change that will take place in the next 5 to 25 years on this planet.

This chapter, then, is about change. It cites the work of social workers, other researchers, and of futurists. Futurists are people who study global trends to predict the nature of life in the future. They do not predict specific future events but instead provide alternative scenarios. True futurists are exceptionally well educated, often holding several PhD degrees; they are fluent in multiple languages; and they often live and work in several different countries. The chapter uses the work of futurists as well as other writers and researchers to examine trends in the United States and other parts of the world and to generate thinking about the implications of these trends for the profession of social work.

Futurists' Perspectives on Globalization

The term **globalization** has come to have different meanings within different contexts. One futurist, James Canton, believes that this concept is still relatively new and will evolve broader meaning over time. He sees globalization currently as "a new synthesis of ideas, trade, communications, and collaboration that should promote future global prosperity, freedom, and opportunity" (2006, p. 183). Canton's definition of globalization stresses the interconnectedness of all regions and people of the world, resulting from technological advances in communication and transportation; his definition seeks a positive outcome. The usual way that the media deals with the topic of globalization today is one that emphasizes international commerce, a much narrower view than the one held by Canton.

John Naisbitt, another futurist, considers the question: does globalization imply Americanization? In many parts of the world there is growing public animosity to the expectation that globalization will result in the adoption of American culture everywhere. Naisbitt's perspective on globalism, however, is different. He astutely points to the paradox that "America itself is changing more dramatically than America is changing the world. It is the world that is changing the world" (2006, p. 179). It is his contention that the United States itself is undergoing rapid and profound change primarily as a result of immigration, which we will discuss in this chapter in more detail shortly. Naisbitt also points out that everywhere in the world, people are actually working hard to strengthen or regain their cultural connections and identities. They are seeking to retain their native language, even while learning another or several other languages. They are actively ensuring that their children learn the history and traditions of their culture and heritage. Cultural and ethnic communities are celebrating festivals with traditional music, food, drink, and spiritual practices. Communities are safeguarding historical central city areas and architectural treasures through protective legislation.

But futurists, other researchers, and the media have not yet agreed on a definition of globalization. The absence of a precise definition could, perhaps, be attributed to the multiplicity of forces driving global change as well as the fact that globalization is itself a process that is ever evolving. So, where did globalization actually begin? Two sociologists, Hewa and Stapleton, note that from early human history forward, people have changed locations, often crossing geographic as well as tribal or national borders. This process of human movement, communication, and development of social relations increased markedly during the 20th century. Hewa and Stapleton define globalization as "a growing 'sense of interconnectedness of humankind' around the globe" (2006, p. 4). Critical to their definition is the concept of an exchange of ideas and values that crosses national borders and creates global communities.

Instead of letting ourselves think of globalization as merely a form of modernization or just from the perspective of commerce and trade, a more informed understanding of globalization considers four central themes:

1. Globalization is, in fact, a sustained process that has been under way across human history.

2. Globalization includes economics but, perhaps more importantly, it includes the communication of culture, values, technological advances in communication and transportation, and urbanization.

3. Globalization as a process does not move in a single direction (e.g., top-down) but instead is multidirectional.

4. This process has an impact on local and global dimensions alike, not as a clash with one victor, "but in the reconstitution of both." (Grew, 2006, p. 17)

National and International Strategic Planning

The interdependence of the world can no longer be questioned. Nonetheless, each country seeks to guide the direction the future will take. In the United States, the U.S. Government Accountability Office (GAO) is responsible for helping Congress oversee federal programs and engage in planning based on unbiased data. The GAO's 2007–2012 Strategic Plan was developed within a context of global awareness. The GAO was surely aware that currently the United States is the only superpower in the world. In the recent past, Russia was considered equal in power to the United States. Other power blocks now exist, such as the European Union, but the United States remains the only single country currently in the position of dominance. This position places special responsibility on the United States (Walker, 2007).

Several of the key themes identified by the GAO as likely to shape the future of the nation and of the world include security threats, fiscal as well as environmental sustainability, issues pertaining to economic growth, societal change stemming from demographic change, managing advances in science and technology, and ensuring quality of life for U.S. citizens. The entire strategic plan of the GAO for the years 2007 to 2012 is based on these themes. The report concludes with a dramatic statement: "Nothing less than a transformation in the people, processes, and technology used to address public goals is necessary to address the demanding policy goals facing the nation in a time of rapid change" (Walker, 2007, p. 31).

Internationally, other countries also develop strategic plans for the future, often emphasizing similar concerns. On a global scale, the United Nations in 2000 articulated a set of goals with 2015 as the target date for accomplishment. This goal statement was adopted by all member nations. In the years that followed 2000, the world experienced terrorism, wars, earthquakes, and other natural and manmade disasters that could have totally defeated efforts to attain the goals. In 2007, the United Nations published a midpoint report. It demonstrated some surprising progress as well as areas of serious concern. A brief review of the goals will demonstrate similarity to the themes in the United States GAO strategic plans (Ki-Moon, 2007).

Goal 1 of the UN development plan was to eradicate extreme poverty and hunger. This was an area in which some progress was made. Between 1990 and 2004, according to the United Nations' midpoint report, extreme poverty declined from nearly one-third of the world's population to less than one-fifth. In sub-Saharan Africa, however, the poverty rate declined by only 6 percent; this region lags behind others in reaching the goal that had been set. Goal 2, to achieve universal primary school education, demonstrated improvement: by 2005, 88 percent of the world's children were enrolled in primary schools compared with 80 percent in 1991. The promotion of gender equality and empowerment of women, Goal 3, also

Extreme poverty and maternal mortality (women dying from complications of pregnancy and childbirth), as well as malnutrition and diseases resulting from tribal wars, remain critical issues in many parts of the world.

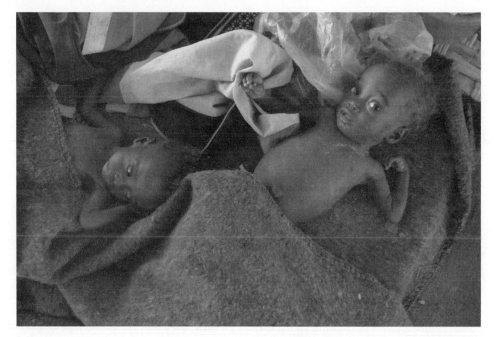

demonstrated improvement in the number of women who are participating in politiacal activity; in some countries, where in the past only men were permitted to run for political office, women have now achieved seats in the parliament. Goal 4, the reduction in child mortality, has also shown positive results: child mortality has declined globally with deaths due to child killers such as measles declining most dramatically (Ki-Moon, 2007).

The improvement of maternal health, Goal 5, has not demonstrated positive results. According to the United Nations report: "over half a million women still die each year from treatable and preventable complications of pregnancy and childbirth" (Ki-Moon, 2007, p. 5). Women in sub-Saharan Africa are most at risk. Reversing the spread of HIV/AIDS by 2015, Goal 6, has shown no progress. In fact, the number of deaths from this disease worldwide increased from 2.2 to 2.9 million by 2006, with increases in prevalence of the disease especially noted in Asia and Africa. In one year alone, 2005, "more than 1.5 million children had lost one or both parents to AIDS" (p. 5). Goal 7, the final goal, also had negative results. Ensuring environmental sustainability, as reflected in increasing deforestation and providing access to safe drinking water and basic sanitation, were not on target for achievement by 2015.

Globalization: Relevance to Social Work

The 2001 terrorist attacks on the World Trade Center in New York and the Pentagon in Washington, DC, awakened people in the United States, including social workers, to globalization in a new and dangerous form. Americans came to realize that even as a world superpower, they were vulnerable to international terrorism. The military campaign to end terrorism that has stretched out for years following the 2001 attacks in the United States has not satisfactorily answered important questions about why terrorism exists. What nourishes, supports, and sustains it? While social workers don't have answers to these questions, social workers do understand that frustrations related to poverty, economic exploitation, differences in religion and in worldview, among others, drive much of the unrest and strife in the global environment in which we all live.

Social workers, in concert with other health and human service professionals, play a key role in the healing and transformation of the world. This has been true since the days of Jane Addams and the pioneers of the social work profession. Social workers from the United States act internationally, as Ella Carrey in this chapter's case study illustrates, as well as at home. The cross-national practice experience of Lyons, Manion, and Carlsen, authors of *International Perspectives on Social Work*, lead them to believe that "social work across the globe is now operating under different conditions, which produce new social problems—or exacerbate old ones. Social [work] professionals therefore need to review services and practices in the light of international events and perspectives. For some, this entails working in international settings, but for others it means incorporating internationalized perspectives into local practice" (2006, p. 1). They view globalization as a form of interdependence in which "global events and processes now impact on individuals, communities, and societies everywhere" (pp. 1–2).

Social work is, indeed, a profession at the edge of change. As the world around us changes, so must our profession. As we prepare for the future, the values of the social work profession—service, social justice, dignity and worth of all persons, and the importance of human relationships—remain as beacons, guiding our actions and our practice. Standard 6 of the NASW Code of Ethics reminds us that social workers have ethical responsibilities, not just to our individual clients, but to the broader society on local as well as global levels (NASW, 1999).

Globalization will remain a theme throughout the remainder of this chapter. It will emerge frequently as the chapter addresses five major forces that are energizing, shaping, and transforming the world. We will begin with what is arguably the most significant transforming force: demographic change. Following this, the chapter will consider other forces of change: political trends, economic conditions, biomedical and scientific advances, and environmental sustainability.

DEMOGRAPHIC TRENDS

For peace and justice to prevail, there must be a new and respectful attention to human diversity. The case study at the beginning of this chapter was chosen because of its international focus.

Ella Carrey's cross-national practice reflected the shift in the social work profession from a "casework" approach that focused on individual people to emphasis on practice that is able to move comfortably across social systems. This more nimble generation of practitioners works with individuals, families, groups, organizations, communities, or even larger societal systems, often with several systems at once, depending on what is needed to prevent or resolve problems. Adapting to the needs of changing client populations is essential to effective practice in an increasingly diverse society.

Demographics, the study of population characteristics and trends, is an area of considerable interest to researchers and futurists who monitor patterns of change from which they develop forecasts of the future. Perhaps one of the most significant forces creating change today, change that will carry into the next 40 or 50 years, is that of the demographics of the United States. The U.S. Census Bureau, which charts population shifts, predicts that by the year 2050 Whites will remain a slim majority of only 50.1 percent, having declined from 69.4 percent in 2000 (2004a). In reality, the "new" multicultural world that is predicted may be new for some people, but not for all. Already, in some parts of the country, there is so much diversity that there is no single majority population. Other parts of the United States have few non-White residents. Rapidly changing demographics, however, will become increasingly apparent in the next few decades. The social work profession, with a value system that respects diversity and with historical roots in practice across cultures, should be well positioned to take on the challenges that lie ahead. Other demographic trends that will influence social work practice are the increase in our elderly population, evolutions in American family structures, and the changing immigrant and refugee population.

A Multicultural America

Although White Americans made up 85 percent of the U.S. population in 1950 (U.S. Bureau of the Census, 1950, pp. 90–91, 109–111), White, non-Hispanic persons constituted 69.4 percent in 2000 (U.S. Census Bureau, 2004a).

The ethnic makeup of the country is continuing to change, rapidly. Writing about the ramification of this shift, Farai Chideya (1999) observes:

> This is uncharted territory for this country, and this demographic change will affect everything. Alliances between the races are bound to shift. Political and social power will be reapportioned. Our neighborhoods, our schools and workplaces, even racial categories themselves will be altered. Any massive social change is bound to bring uncertainty, even fear. But the worst crisis we face today is not in our cities or neighborhoods, but in our minds. (p. 5)

Her vision is that the new generation, the millennium generation of 15- to 25-year-olds that is already far more culturally diverse than any previous generation, will create a future that is less negatively biased on issues of race. In 1997, Nancy Gordon, Associate Director for Demographic Programs, U.S. Bureau of the Census, reported to the House Committee on Government Reform and Oversight that the number of mixed-race persons in the U.S. quadrupled between 1970 and 1990 (as cited in Chideya, p. 38). Even the matter of classifying persons by the U.S. Census Bureau is more complex today because many people are not able to identify with any single racial category. After a hard-fought battle, the Census Bureau declared that for the first time in its history, the 2000 census would permit people to "check more than one box under race—for example, 'white' and 'Asian'" (Chideya, p. 40). The result was that 6,826,228 persons did check the "two or more races" box. Although this represented only 2.4 percent of the total population, it was double the number of American Indian, Alaskan Native people, Native Hawaiian, and all other Pacific Island people combined (U.S. Census Bureau, 2000).

Americans have typically thought about race in terms of Black and White. This tends to be how race is covered in the media. The reality, though, is that America is really very diverse. The 2010 census data is likely to show that 13.1 percent of the population is Black, 15.5 percent is Hispanic, 4.6 percent is Asian, and an additional 3 percent includes all other races except White. The White population is likely to have declined from 69.4 percent in 2000 to 65.1 percent in 2010. The Asian and Hispanic populations are currently the fastest growing in the United States, according to the Census Bureau (2004a).

The social work profession was birthed in a spirit of reform and celebration of multiculturalism, as revealed in the history sections of past chapters of this text. The Council on Social Work Education has written curriculum standards that ensure inclusion of human diversity content in all baccalaureate and master's degree programs. Ethnic sensitive approaches to social work practice are now taught in schools of social work that link knowledge of culture and ethnicity with understandings of social class differences (Devore & Schlesinger, 1999). In many ways, social work as a profession has meant being an advocate and supporter of human diversity.

But there is much more for social work to do to create a just society, and the predicted transformation of our country's ethnic and cultural makeup will challenge the profession to become much more proactive. An ethnoconscious approach might be the strategy of the future for the social work profession. This theoretical construct incorporates ethnic sensitivity with empowerment tactics that build upon appreciation for the strengths already existing in ethnically diverse communities (Gutierrez & Nagda, 1996). An ethnoconscious approach would insist, for example, that the organizations that deliver social work services reflect the ethnic makeup of the community served by the agency. From agency board members to executives, supervisors, and staff, human diversity would be clearly present. This organization of the future would be "dually focused on bringing about social change and providing empowering programs and services to its clientele" (Gutierrez & Nagda, 1996, p. 206). Linked not only to its service community, but also to the region, nation, and other countries, the organization and its social workers could take on human problems in the lives of people as they live in families and function in groups, organizations, and entire communities.

The Graying of America

As indicated in Chapter 9, "Social Work with Older Adults," a significant shift in the age of the population has also taken place in the United States. During the colonial period of American history, approximately half the population was under the age of 16, and relatively few persons lived to age 65. By 1900 about 4 percent of the population was 65 years of age or older. In 1970 the proportion of persons 65 or older had grown to 9 percent. By 2000 this had increased to 12.4 percent (34,991,733 persons), and estimates for the year 2050 indicate that the population aged 65 and older is expected to reach 86 million; this will represent 20.7 percent (U.S. Census Bureau, 2004b). A surprise in the 2000 census was the finding that the aged-65-and-older population was actually found to have increased "at a slower rate than the overall population for the first time in the history of the census" (U.S. Census Bureau, 2001a).

Despite a long history of age discrimination in the United States (unlike most Asian countries, where age is revered), the new and rapidly growing cohort of older adults may produce shifts in ageism attitudes. Today's older adults are quite different from previous generations. They have achieved higher levels of education than their predecessors, they generally have a higher level of income and buying power, and they are politically active. They have fewer disabilities, and if disabilities do occur, they have better designed equipment (e.g., motorized wheelchairs) to enable them to sustain an active lifestyle. The baby boomers, who will start reaching their 65th birthdays in 2011, "promise to further redefine what it means to grow older in America" (U.S. Census Bureau, 2007b).

Today social workers provide financial counseling, recreation and wellness programs, housing assistance, advocacy (especially in relation to health care), adult protective services, counseling, and case management. People who compose the oldest cohort of the elderly, those 85 years and older, require the greatest number of services. As Exhibit 12-1 indicates, this segment of the elderly population is growing most rapidly. Because of advanced age, these people are more likely to have cognitive disorders such as Alzheimer's disease as well as physical disabilities, so they require care that is physically and psychologically demanding for caregivers. Intervention, then, would seek to strengthen bonds of intergenerational caregiving as well as economic and social service policies to ensure good quality of life.

A demographic characteristic that influences the planning and delivery of social services to the elderly is the lifespan of women. Women tend to outlive men by several years and they also tend to marry men who are several years older, so it is common for women to outlive their husbands by 10 years or more. Women are more likely than men to have to deal with the complex health, economic, and housing problems of old age, first as caregivers of others and later as receivers of care.

The complex problems of aging require social workers to have both a sound understanding of the aging process and a broad generalist practice background that enables them to work simultaneously with individual clients, families, and community systems. Fortunately, the number of students interested in social work with older adults has increased in recent years. Encouraged by the financial support of organizations like the Hartford Foundation, schools of social work have increased the aging content in required courses, and some have also added elective courses on social work with older adults. More field placements in aging, too, are now available. As a result, it appears that the new generation of social workers will be

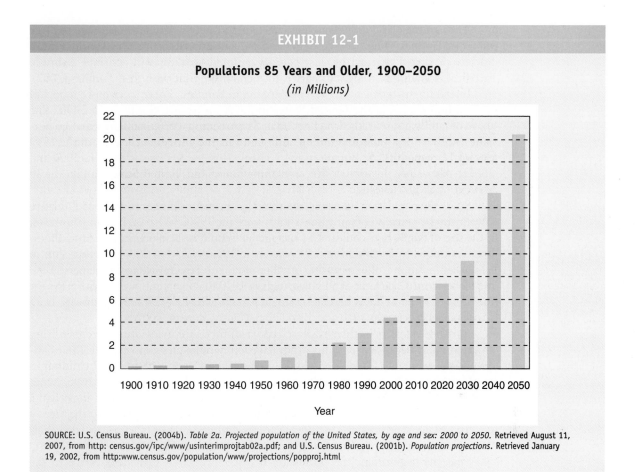

EXHIBIT 12-1

Populations 85 Years and Older, 1900–2050
(in Millions)

SOURCE: U.S. Census Bureau. (2004b). *Table 2a. Projected population of the United States, by age and sex: 2000 to 2050*. Retrieved August 11, 2007, from http: census.gov/ipc/www/usinterimprojtab02a.pdf; and U.S. Census Bureau. (2001b). *Population projections*. Retrieved January 19, 2002, from http:www.census.gov/population/www/projections/popproj.html

better prepared for work with older adults, especially when the older adult population is increasing and the number of social work positions in this field is growing substantially.

The Evolving American Family

The American family has undergone considerable change, and it continues to evolve. In the 1980s, some writers predicted the imminent collapse of the traditional American family. Such gloomy reports, however, were replaced in the 1990s by analysts' recognition of a renewed valuing of family life. In a 1994 article in *The Futurist*, for example, Cetron pointed out that family issues such as "long-term health care, day care, early childhood education, anti-drug campaigns, and drug-free environments" had come to dominate the 1990s (p. 8). Families were valued once again by society.

The vast majority of these are persons living alone. Society has continued to place value on families. This trend is expected to continue. Recently the World Future Society predicted that as the 21st century unfolds, workers will continue to make sacrifices, sometimes in higher salaries, to spend more time with their families (2007).

Interesting patterns have been developing in families. There were more than 114 million households in the United States in 2006, up from 105 million in 2000. The share of family households, which stood at 81 percent in 1970, had fallen to 67.6 percent in 2006. This was a continuing, although relatively small decline, from the 1990 rate of 71 percent (U.S. Bureau of the Census, 1998; U.S. Census Bureau, 2000 and 2007a). Also, since the early 1990s, nonfamily households have remained a bit over 30 percent of all households.

So, as the population increases, the trend has been for families to exist, with relative stability in the percent of family households since the 1990s. What is changing, however, is the size of family households. The average household is shrinking in size. Households have continued to decline from 3.14 persons in 1970 to 2.57 in 2006. Another shift in family composition is the increasing number of households consisting of one person living alone: from 17 percent of all households in 1970 to 26 percent in 2006. Surprisingly, the number of households headed by single parents actually grew only minimally, from 5 to 9 percent, between 1970 and 2006 (U. S. Census Bureau, 2007d).

As other chapters in this text have reported, there are many grandparents raising children today because drugs and AIDS have left parents unable to care for their children. Approximately 5.7 million children under age 18—8 percent of all children in the United States—lived in a household that included a grandparent in 2006. More than half of these children actually lived in the grandparent's home, and most had a parent living there, too (U.S. Census Bureau, 2007d). This is increasingly the face of poverty. Many sacrifices are made by parents and grandparents to try to keep their families intact or to try to help young parents to continue their education.

Since its beginnings, the profession of social work has provided service to the American family. As families and societal conditions changed over time, the profession found that it needed to rethink how it worked with families. In the past two or three decades, for example, the profession switched from strongly encouraging unmarried mothers to place their babies for adoption to helping families to remain together. Federal legislation, much of which was promoted by social workers, also resulted in renewed efforts to keep families together. The 1978 Indian Child Welfare Act, for example, discouraged adoption of Indian children into non-Indian families and gave tribes limited funds for family support services. The 1980 Adoption Assistance and Child Welfare Act was considered benchmark legislation for its attempt to ensure permanent families for children. The 1997 Adoption and Safe Families Act furthered commitment to adoption rather than long-term foster care by shortening the time limits of foster care and speeding up the adoption process.

This sounds quite wonderful, but there is another perspective on adoption that social workers must consider. Some cultures define family differently from the nuclear family concept that is valued by people of White, European descent. African Americans, for example, have traditionally valued the extended family. The Association for Black Social Workers has articulated clear preference for kinship care over adoption. Kinship is a broad concept, incorporating persons related by blood or legal ties, plus persons related by strong affectional ties (Holody, 1999, p. 7). Poverty is often a factor in preventing or discouraging biological parents from meeting agency behavioral demands that would allow them to reunite with children placed in foster care. Especially for minority families, poverty is also a factor in discouraging relatives from seeking legal adoption. But bonding with family members, permanency of care, and uninterrupted cultural identity are all potentially available through kinship care, which often occurs as long-term foster care (Holody, 1999).

Kinship care versus adoption is only one of many challenges that social workers of the future will confront. Families clearly are changing. The family of the future is likely to be diverse in culture and ethnicity, in age, and in structure (single-parent, two-parent, gay- or lesbian-parented, or a kinship unit). Nonrelative members of households may continue to increase in low-income families.

Social work research and practice over the past 10 years has provided considerable insight into the remarkable strengths of families. This has led to a new paradigm in which social workers are shifting away from focusing on problems and dysfunction to an acknowledgement of the assets and resilience of families. Out of this new way of thinking has evolved ways of working with families in which collaboration and partnership are emphasized. Caring professional relationships with children and families are paired with high expectations. Similarly, social workers have learned that it is critical to support not only family members but also the people outside the family (teachers, caregivers, mentors, etc.) who nurture, educate, socialize, and often transform the lives of children. Finally, helping families requires lobbying for and even creating programs that ensure the existence of basic social and economic resources to all families (Benard, 2006).

In thinking about social work with families in the years ahead, Karen Holmes (1996) suggests that in the future, social work practice

> will be characterized by a renewed professional commitment to social and economic justice. As the gap between the haves and have-nots widens, we will be challenged to move more assertively toward achieving a just and equitable society. . . . . In our work with families of all kinds, we will be challenged to accept and appreciate diversity in its many forms. (p. 178)

The Changing Immigrant and Refugee Population

The demographic trends that we have looked at so far include multicultural diversity, aging, and evolving patterns in families. Immigration, the final process affecting change, will contribute dramatically to the increasing multiculturalism of the United States in the very near future. Immigration, however, is not happening in America alone. This is a worldwide phenomenon, and it is yet another way in which regions of the world are increasingly interconnected. Actually, throughout history patterns of human migration have evolved, often reflecting events such as war, famine, natural disasters, and religious or political persecutions. The early history of the United States is replete with descriptions of waves of immigrations.

People arrived on U.S. shores to seek a fortune; for adventure; or as indentured servants, slaves, or promised brides. When the Cold War that followed World War II ended, the breakup of the former Soviet Union created massive poverty, prompting large numbers of persons to seek a better life in other parts of the world, including the United States. In the 1990s, war in Kosovo brought masses of new refugees to western European countries, many of which were already tense from episodes of anti-refugee ethnic violence. Precipitated by civil unrest, thousands of additional people around the globe have become displaced in recent years. The United States has admitted some of these refugees. Canada and several European countries have also done so, and they have provided the newcomers with quite generous welfare programs.

People, in general, enter another country through three legal means: immigration, asylum, or as a refugee. An **immigrant** is someone who moves to another country for the purpose of settling there permanently. **Asylum** is a protected status that is granted only on a case-by-case basis to persons who can substantiate serious, possibly life-threatening political persecution. **Refugees** are people who leave their country "because of persecution or a well-founded fear of persecution on account of race, religion, nationality, membership in a particular social group, or political opinion" (Bruno, 2006, p. 1).

Applications for refugee status in the United States are processed by the State Department before entry to the United States. Persons seeking asylum, on the other hand, may already have arrived in the United States, or they may be physically present at a border. Persons who persecuted others are not accepted for either asylum or as refugees. Once they have been admitted and lived in the country for 1 year, both refugees and persons accepted for asylum may apply for permanent resident status (Bruno, 2006). If granted, they then have a "green card"; after 5 years, they may apply for full (naturalized) citizenship.

The U.S. Congress sets the refugee admission ceiling each year, generally at approximately 70,000, and that policy has remained fairly constant; approximately 10,000 persons are admitted under asylum status each year. In the aftermath of the terrorist attacks on the United States in 2001, refugee admissions were temporarily suspended, new security procedures were implemented, and applications were much more cautiously screened. The number of persons accepted as refugees plunged from 73,000 in 2000 to 27,000 in 2002, and it reached only 53,800 in 2005 (most recent data available; Bruno, 2006).

In addition to these legal forms of entry there is, of course, illegal immigration. The United States has implemented border patrols, specialized policing, and considerable legislation to stop illegal immigration from Mexico, El Salvador, Guatemala, Cuba, and Haiti. While many people do enter the United States over guarded land or water routes, which is the way illegal immigration is often portrayed in the media, others arrive quite legally. They simply overstay the expiration of their employment, student, or other legal visa. The disparity between countries' standards of living and economic well-being will remain the catalyst for continued immigration, legal and illegal, into the United States and other industrialized countries for years to come.

Until the 1970s, persons who became U.S. citizens came primarily from European countries. The 1970s saw a considerable increase in the number of Asian immigrants, and Asian immigrants continue to make up a significant portion of new U.S. citizens. Beginning in 1996, there was a shift to Latin American immigration, which continues to this day. In 2006, the citizenship data, by continent, indicated that 36.6 percent of new citizens came from Asia; 31.8 percent from North America; 15.3 percent from Europe; with smaller portions coming from Africa, South America, and other regions. (Latin America is split between North and South America; if Latin American citizenship was reported as a whole, it would be larger than the Asian citizenship data.) According to the U.S. Department of Homeland Security, the leading countries from which new citizens came in 2006 were Mexico, India, the Philippines, China, and Vietnam (Simanski, 2007).

The sharp increase in citizenship and naturalization beginning in 1996 and its uneven pattern are depicted in Exhibit 12-2. Changes in law, crackdowns on illegal immigration, and worldwide migration pressures account for the volatile shifts in citizenship patterns in recent years. Immigration has become a huge political issue, not just in the United States, but worldwide. According to the International Organization for Migration (IOM), "migration is a catalyst for change and development, and in a world that is changing at a lightning pace, not harnessing the power of migration is shortsighted" (McKinley, n.d.).

EXHIBIT 12-2

Naturalized United States Citizens: Fiscal Years 1907–2006
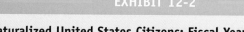
(in Thousands)

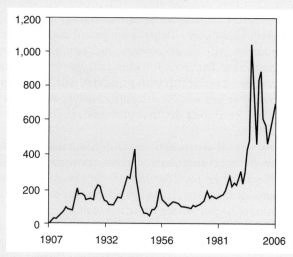

SOURCE: U.S. Department of Homeland Security. (2007, May). *Figure 1, Persons naturalized: Fiscal years 1907 to 2006*. Retrieved August 14, 2007, from http://www.dhs.gov/xlibrary/assets/ statistics/publications/Natz_01_Sec508Compliant.pdf

This nongovernmental organization works at the global level to resolve the deep social and political rifts occurring in many countries where migrants, often without legal documentation or work permits, compete for extremely low paying jobs with higher paid, more educated, native laborers. The failure of many countries to provide legal options for immigration has resulted in migrants' use of expensive and potentially life-threatening smuggling networks to seek employment. Often, however, they find themselves at the margins of society and open to exploitation of many kinds. The IOM visualizes a possible solution in the development of an international circulatory migration program that uses technology to determine where the mismatch exists between labor shortages on the one hand and eager laborers on the other. Under this plan, which the IOM has actually implemented in Italy, Canada, and Spain, migrants would be assisted to obtain temporary employment and later return to their own country. Data banks would enable potential employers, individuals, even countries to access information about regional and national migration laws. The IOM is seeking assistance from the World Bank and the United Nations to move this plan forward (McKinley, n.d.). IOM's proposal is, indeed, a creative, fresh approach to the volatile international migration issue.

In the United States, the foreign-born population tends to be young, be employed in service industries, have less education than the native population and, not surprisingly, be at increased risk of poverty (Larsen, 2004).

Kemp, writing in *Futures Research Quarterly*, predicts that increasing numbers of immigrant persons in U.S. cities "will create new demands for more specialized public services such as the need to hire more bilingual employees, implement cultural diversity programs, and evidence equity in the delivery of existing services to citizens" (2000, p. 23). There is a message in this prediction for social work students and for social workers. Bilingual social workers may be in even greater demand in the future than they are currently. The profession also needs to be able to recruit people who reflect the culture of the immigrant newcomers. Kemp anticipates that East and West Coast port cities will see an influx of immigrant groups. Existing ethnic communities will likely expand, and new ethnic communities may emerge. Kemp expects that day care for children, youth and teen programs, community policing, and low-cost health care programs will be implemented. Throughout the United States—in schools, health care centers, shelters, and advocacy programs—social workers are among the first professional persons to assist new residents with resettlement.

As advocates for at-risk and vulnerable populations, social workers may be called on increasingly in coming years to assist immigrants, refugees, and asylum-seekers. Social workers will be involved in resettlement work. Social workers may also help organizations such as church groups to sponsor new immigrants or asylum-seekers. In international social service agencies such as the Red Cross, social workers will communicate across borders to keep relatives linked, especially during disasters or in the event that a person becomes a prisoner of war. Program planning will be undertaken, too, to assist communities in providing for the child care, health, and other needs of new immigrants.

POLITICAL TRENDS

Politics is the basis for the second major force that will generate change in the future. Political trends and political balance of power shift over time, and these shifts have enormous impacts on the health, welfare, criminal justice, and educational services that are available to people. Of course, these same shifts also determine social work employment opportunities. Looking back over the past several decades, it is apparent that politically conservative forces were gaining power in elections in many countries, including the United States. In America, the political liberalism of the Kennedy and Johnson administrations during the 1960s gave way, even when Democrats were elected to office. As Chapter 2 of this text explained, neoliberals such as Bill Clinton took a more favorable stance toward big business and supported reduction of government aid to poor people. Voter support for conservative policies, which grew stronger in the 1990s, had enormous impact on the political decisions that brought welfare reform into being.

Welfare Reform and Poverty

Welfare reform was a popular political movement that swept the United States in the 1990s and brought about the TANF (Temporary Assistance for Needy Families) program. Prior to the passage of legislation that created TANF, an AFDC (Aid to Families with Dependent Children) program provided federal money to states, giving states considerable discretionary power to administer their own financial assistance programs. The TANF program has been referred to frequently in this text. A feature of TANF that did not exist in AFDC was a lifetime limit of 60 months on benefits. Under TANF, too, parents may be required to work after 24 months of assistance, and TANF assistance could be cut off for a variety of reasons—if a family failed to cooperate with the work requirement, for example, or if a teen mother stopped attending school. Discontinuation of benefits for failure to comply with TANF requirements became known as **sanctioning.** If another child was born while a family was receiving TANF, the state was not obliged to provide any additional assistance for the newborn. With a significant level of funding provided to states to design and administer their own TANF programs (which most states renamed to reflect their state's philosophy), some states provided child care funding and other services to encourage rapid transition to work from welfare.

The TANF program has achieved success by most counts. The U.S. Department of Health and Human Services 2006 report to Congress cited a continuing decline in welfare caseloads since the beginning of the TANF program. The average monthly number of cases in 2003 was 2,027,600 compared with 2,060,300 in 2002. The average monthly TANF income was $354; the maximum payment was $521 for a family of four or more children (U.S. Department of Health & Human Services [DHHS], 2006).

Several trends related to TANF welfare reform emerged from this report. "Child-only" cases had increased from 36.6 percent in 2002 to 38.6 percent in 2003; in these cases no adult receives TANF income, which may reflect parents who are ineligible because of noncitizenship, receipt of disability, or a variety of other reasons. Provision of welfare to children only is surfacing as a trend. The child poverty rate increased from 16.7 percent in 2002 to 17.6 percent in 2003. Only 17.9 percent of the cases that were closed in 2003 resulted from employment, also an emerging trend. An additional 23.9 percent were closed because of failure to comply with TANF program requirements (generally this relates to work requirements). TANF's 5-year lifetime benefit limit took effect for the first time in 2002. Of the cases closed in 2003, less than $\frac{1}{2}$ of 1 percent of cases were closed for this reason, but an increasing percentage is likely in future years (U.S. DHHS, 2006).

Welfare reform is sure to be targeted in political debates as the declines in TANF case closures begin to level off. While a clear trend is not yet entirely verifiable, there is growing concern that a portion of people receiving assistance have serious barriers to employment and self-sufficiency. A 2007 Urban Institute analysis (Acs & Loprest, 2007) of TANF data found an increase from 22 to 30 percent of TANF cases with health conditions that limited employability and an increase from 39 to 43 percent of recipients who failed to complete high school (a factor that reduces likelihood of employment) between 2000 and 2005. Numerous other circumstances affect ability to work: mental health or substance abuse problems, a history of imprisonment, recent exposure to domestic violence, and learning disabilities. TANF is a social program that is affected by changes in the economic cycle of the country. When the economy is "soft," or slowing down, jobs are lost or harder to find and TANF cases increase (Acs & Loprest, 2007). Even the educational attainment of recipients increases during difficult economic conditions.

The 2006 legislation that reauthorized the TANF program through 2010 added some rule changes. As of 2007, the requirement for work participation was substantially increased for TANF recipients. The reauthorization act reached beyond the TANF program and effectively discontinued the financial assistance programs that some states had created, which exempted families applying for federal disability assistance (SSI) from work requirements. While the Social Security Administration is trying to process applications more quickly, it has taken from several months to 3 years before SSI checks begin to be received (Wamhoff & Wiseman, 2005/2006). This additional crackdown in the 2007 TANF reauthorization legislation has earned the "work or starve" label from some observers.

So, despite apparent success, the TANF program also has critics who are increasingly concerned about issues such as work requirements that probably cannot be met, the program's ability to sanction recipients who fail to comply with regulations, and the 5-year lifetime limit. States, having enjoyed power and control in administering the program, are also increasingly concerned about their future ability to deal with potentially large numbers of "hard-core poor" families who will not be able to transition from TANF to employment. Issues of social welfare tend to polarize Americans, but it is very likely that the political process will soon need to take on some difficult issues regarding poverty, welfare reform, and TANF.

Social workers need to become more involved in the political arena, because political forces, of course, will continue to determine the availability of human services in our country and in the nations of the world. If social workers truly care about people and about social change, they will not sit idly by, merely providing psychotherapy for the emotional and physical pain suffered by the victims of politics and poor public policy; instead, they will assume responsibility for their own political behavior and will also empower their clients to engage in the democratic process.

Privatization of Social Services

Privatization of social services is one of the results of the shift toward an increasingly conservative political environment. This trend can be seen in the advent of corporate prison systems, for-profit child abuse services, and states contracting for social services instead of sustaining their own social service programs. Group homes are another example of privatization. Twenty years ago, foster group homes for teenagers, developmentally disabled adults, and the elderly were almost exclusively operated by state and county welfare departments or nonprofit agencies. In most communities today, only a small portion of the group homes are run by nonprofit organizations. Instead, most are owned and operated by private corporations, often headed by social workers. The same is true of residential treatment centers for emotionally disturbed children. Substance abuse programs—once provided almost exclusively by tax-supported hospitals or denominational facilities—have become big business and are being marketed aggressively. Chapter 10 described the marked growth of a for-profit prison industry in the United States.

The entrepreneurial practice of social work has also expanded significantly, especially for MSWs. Social workers in private practice offer their services for a fee in much the same way that physicians or attorneys in private practice do. Often health insurance policies cover the cost of counseling through social workers. *The Social Work Dictionary* defines private practice as "the provision of professional services by a licensed/qualified social worker who assumes responsibility for the nature and quality of the services provided to the client in exchange for direct payment or third-party reimbursement" (Barker, 2003, p. 339).

Privatization has undoubtedly benefited the private practice of social work and nonprofit agencies as well by providing clients and income. The most significant ramification of privatization, however, is a change in philosophy regarding the provision of service to clients. With privatization, public investment is shifted away from administering and sustaining public social service programs to purchasing the same service from a private source. Service is terminated when the contract is completed, often with no provision for follow-up care. On the surface, this may look like economic efficiency, but when vulnerable populations such as the frail elderly or emotionally disturbed children are involved, such apparent efficiency may actually be detrimental to clients. Neither economic nor human justice interests are served when clients' well-being suffers because of disrupted or prematurely discontinued service. What is needed instead is service that is efficient, effective, humane, and readily available—whether it is delivered through a public or private agency or through a professional person in private practice.

The trend toward privatization in human services, whether prisons or family therapy, breaks with a long tradition of tax-supported public services delivered without the cost and the potential conflicts of interest of the for-profit, entrepreneurial enterprise. This trend raises concerns about the inherent values of human service organizations. Is monetary profit the primary goal, or are the best interests of the client the real goal? While moving more and more into for-profit practice, the profession of social work nevertheless maintains a somewhat skeptical stance about it. Of concern is the potential that social workers might lose their traditional commitment to advocacy, to social change, to social and economic justice, and to service to vulnerable populations.

The political drive to shift public health and social services to the private sector remains very strong. Yes, it can save money for taxpayers by reducing personnel costs and fragmenting services, but at a substantial cost of the quality of services. Although professional people may be accused of being self-serving, they will need to become proactive to ensure that the quality of professional services provided in the private sector is not further jeopardized and that public social services continue to exist. An important responsibility of government is to ensure the quality of life and well-being of its citizens.

Women's Issues

The profession of social work, because it serves many poor and vulnerable women and is comprised of significant numbers of women, is awakening to the needs of women and their struggle for equality. Even in the past, social work pioneers such as Jane Addams and Florence Kelley of Chicago's Hull House were leaders in the struggle for the right to vote and for equality for women. Despite public ridicule and even imprisonment in the early days of the women's movement, these women and the men that supported them succeeded in 1920 in obtaining passage of the Nineteenth Amendment to the U.S. Constitution—the right to vote for women.

The next effort of women, to pass the **Equal Rights Amendment (ERA)** prohibiting discrimination on the basis of gender, was not as successful. The effort to achieve the ERA was immense, with huge political rallies, statewide and regional conventions, parades, and much demonstration of public support. In 1972 Congress did pass the ERA, but it was defeated when the necessary number of states failed to ratify this proposed amendment to the U.S. Constitution.

Another gain for women, although a painfully slow one, has been the narrowing of the wage gap between men and women. Using the most current data available at the time of writing, Exhibit 12-3 documents the progress that has taken place in narrowing the wage gap between American women and men. It is also important to note that real annual wages have actually fallen for men and women who have lost jobs since 1980 because dramatically increased international trade has expanded the supply of low-skill, low-wage workers producing goods for the American market.

The wage data shown in Exhibit 12-3 is expanded for the year 2005 (most currently available data) in Exhibit 12-4. Exhibit 12-4 is a clear demonstration of the considerable income differences associated with further education. The shocking differences in the wages of females and males at each level is heightened by a close examination of the growing differentials as women and men obtain some college education, then among college graduates, with the most significant difference by far demonstrated among women and men who have earned graduate or professional degrees (U.S. Census Bureau, 2006). The assumption that additional education and credentials narrows the gender wage gap is simply not true.

EXHIBIT 12-3

Wage Gap by Gender

Median Annual Earnings of Full-Time Workers by Sex: 1960–2005

Year	Women's Earnings as a % of Men's	Earnings in Real Dollars	
		Women	Men
1960	60.7%	$11,003	$18,175
1970	59.4	13,719	23,105
1980	60.2	13,589	22,587
1990	71.6	15,166	21,177
1995	71.4	14,762	20,667
2000	73.0	27,355	37,339
2001	76.3	29,215	38,275
2002	76.6	30,203	39,429
2003	75.5	30,724	40,668
2004	76.6	32,285	42,160
2005	77.0	31,858	41,386

SOURCE: National Committee on Pay Equity. (2006). *The wage gap over time: In real dollars, women see a continuing gap.* Retrieved August 17, 2007, from: http://www.pay-equity.org/info-time.html; U.S. Census Bureau. (2006). *S2001.Earnings in the past 12 months (in 2005 inflation-adjusted dollars); Data set: 2005 American Community Survey.* Retrieved August 17, 2007, from http:www.factfinder.census.gov/servlet/STTable?_bm=y&-geo_id=01000US&-qr_name=ACS_2005_EST_G00_S2001&_ds_name=ACS_2005_EST_G00_

EXHIBIT 12-4

Wage Gap by Gender and Educational Attainment

Population 25 Years and Over with Earnings: 2005

Educational Attainment	Total	Female	Male
Less than high school	$18,435	$13,067	$22,138
High school graduate (includes equivalency)	25,829	20,179	31,683
Some college or associate's degree	31,566	25,736	39,601
Bachelor's degree	43,954	36,250	53,693
Graduate or professional degree	57,585	47,319	71,918

SOURCE: U.S. Census Bureau. (2006). *S2001.Earnings in the past 12 months (in 2005 inflation-adjusted dollars); Data set: 2005 American Community Survey.* Retrieved August 17, 2007, from http:www.factfinder.census.gov/servlet/STTable?_bm=y&-geo_id=01000US&-qr_name=ACS_2005_EST_G00_S2001&_ds_name= ACS_ 2005_EST_G00_

As pronounced as the wage differences are for upper income women, poor women are most at risk of being economically exploited. With low-wage competition from lesser developed nations, the U.S. economy attempts to locate potential low-wage employees wherever possible. This may mean recruiting migrant workers, or it may mean employing persons who are TANF recipients. The 2006 TANF reauthorization act, with its tightening of work requirements, pushes many recipients into low-wage jobs.

Not surprisingly, inequality in wages became a political issue that women's organizations in particular targeted for change. As women's professional groups such as the 70,000-member Business and Professional Women/USA (BPW/USA) joined with labor unions and other politically active women's groups, the pragmatic concept of pay equity emerged. Pay equity is defined by the National Committee on Pay Equity as

> a means of eliminating sex and race discrimination in the wage-setting system. Most women and people of color are still segregated into a small number of jobs— such as clericals, service workers, nurses and teachers. These jobs have historically been undervalued and continue to be underpaid because of the gender and race of the people who hold them. Pay equity means that the criteria employers use to set wages must be sex and race neutral. (*Questions and answers on pay equity*, 1998, p. 1)

With more women than ever in the workplace, pay equity is one political issue that will be on the agenda of women in the future.

Historically and currently, men far outnumber women in legislative offices in the United States, but women are becoming a political force in state legislatures, and they are now challenging men in races for the highest political offices in this country. The next decade seems poised to produce many exciting political races with high-powered women running effective campaigns for key offices. In 1984 the United States had its first female vice presidential candidate, Geraldine Ferraro. Following her defeat, no woman ran again for this level of office until the presidential candidacy of Hillary Clinton in 2008. But women are on the move. The 110th Congress (2007) included a record number of women—16. Notable among them is Nancy Pelosi, the first female Speaker of the House. Also notable is a social worker, and the longest serving of current women senators, Barbara Mikulski of Maryland. Senator Debbie Stabenow, from Michigan, is another social worker. Of the eight social workers in the U.S. House of Representatives in the 110th Congress, five are women (Lewis, 2007; NASW, 2007).

Meanwhile, in developing countries as well as industrialized parts of the world, women have been elected as presidents and prime ministers. Countries such as Switzerland, Pakistan, Ireland, Norway, and Great Britain have had women presidents and prime ministers.

ECONOMIC TRENDS

The people served by social workers, especially generalist baccalaureate social workers, are often poor people. Of course, social workers work with all sectors of society and all people are affected by the economy, but poor people and near-poor persons are likely to be most dramatically impacted by economic conditions. Not surprisingly, political forces and economic conditions are strongly interrelated. And now more than ever, events and conditions in other parts of the world affect our lives. In the past decade there has been an expansion of industrialization around the globe, especially in third world countries, in eastern Europe, and in the former Soviet Union. Some of the industrialization exploited the masses of poor people in emerging countries, luring them into urban areas and leaving their villages and farms bereft of able-bodied workers. In the United States, economic development has increasingly moved from central-city areas to suburbs and from northern to southern states.

During the late 1980s in the United States, the combination of economic stress coupled with a large federal budget deficit and a conservative administration led to major reductions in federal funding of social service programs. Social service programs were, in fact, among the first government programs to be cut back as the Reagan administration attempted to deal with recession. A significant change was taking place in the economy of the country. **Underemployment**—which is employment at or near minimum wage, often part-time and without health insurance or other benefits—had begun to replace unemployment. The numbers of employed persons receiving financial and medical assistance and food stamps increased, while the unemployment rate decreased dramatically. Food pantries provided groceries, and community feeding programs served meals to the families of employed persons whose income was inadequate to meet their daily needs. Advocates of the poor spoke out against the administration's cuts in social services, especially programs for the poor. One such advocate wrote:

> What first appeared as the Reagan Administration's war against the poor and the welfare state has now emerged as a broader national policy of social underdevelopment that affects most Americans. The deliberate policy of disinvesting in social programs has created a skyrocketing social deficit (the gap between met and unmet social needs), a bipolar structure of income distribution and a shrinking middle class. . . . It affects not only the social welfare system but the broader quality of life in urban and rural America, the way income is distributed, and the structure of U.S. social classes. (Iatridis, 1988, p. 11)

Meanwhile, a very small portion of the U.S. population had doubled its income in a single decade, ending in the late 1980s; the poorest 20 percent of the population, however, saw their share of the national income fall from 5.1 percent in 1980 to 4.5 percent by 1991. By the mid-1990s these economic conditions resulted in increased homelessness, which had become shockingly visible even in the nation's capital. The *New York Times* reported:

> Attention to homeless issues had been heightened in Washington, D.C., by the Nov. 29 discovery of the body of a homeless woman, Yetta Adam, outside the headquarters of the Department of Housing and Urban Development, the federal agency in charge of housing policy. (Major new spending, 1994, p. A18)

For many Americans the 1990s brought increased prosperity and a surge in consumer products. The number of households with telephones, televisions, cars, computers, and air-conditioning increased. When the federal welfare reform law, Temporary Assistance for Needy Families, was passed in 1996, it was heralded as an end to poverty in the United States. TANF caseloads did continue to decrease, unevenly and at an increasingly slower pace, for years.

Changes in the country's economic condition affected the program, with slow economic cycles resulting in increases in applicants. With economic recessions always a specter on the horizon, the Children's Defense Fund (n.d.) concludes: "Our nation needs to rebuild a better safety net—one that can withstand the challenges of a recession." Most social workers who make home visits and work with people in poverty would certainly agree: a better safety net surely does need to be built for American families, especially those whose low wages support the American economic system. Social workers find people living in overcrowded homes, where multiple generations of family members attempt to share meager resources. Illness from infectious diseases, family discord, and even domestic violence may result.

The food needs of low-income people in America are routinely monitored and reported by the U.S. Department of Agriculture. Its recent report finds 11 percent of all U.S. households experiencing **food insecurity,** defined as insufficient access to "enough food for an active, healthy life" (2007). The U.S. Department of Agriculture also provides international food insecurity data from 70 low-income countries. It found that between 2005 and 2006, the number of hungry people in these countries rose from 804 million to 849 million. Its projections suggest that "by 2016, the number of hungry people is projected to decline in all regions, except sub-Saharan Africa" (Meade, Rosen, & Shapouri, 2007).

The global economic interdependence in food insecurity issues is abundantly clear in a recent report of the International Food Policy Research Institute. Its study found that the U.S. farm sector could increase its profits from agricultural exports if there were even small reductions in the level of poverty in low- and middle-income countries of the world—just dollars per day. "One of the first things very poor people do when they have additional income is increase their food consumption" (as cited in Bread for the World Institute, 2007, p. 55). China and India, for example, have become customers of American food exports in just the last few years, as income has increased in both countries.

Probably the most crucial economic trend that has affected people in the United States and that will shape the future is that of distribution of income and wealth. In recent years, Americans have become increasingly aware that income inequality exists in the United States. In this country, we are much less comfortable talking about income disparity or social class differences than people in other countries, where social class differences much more overtly shape politics. Rich or poor, most people in America like to consider themselves part of the middle class. An examination of the data, however, tells a different story.

According to an analysis of 2005 tax returns, the top 1 percent of U.S. households reported 21.8 percent of all pretax income (which included capital gains). This was more than twice the percentage of pretax income of the 1970s (Piketty & Saez, as cited in Hartman, 2007). Another perspective on the shift in income distribution is provided by the U.S. Census Bureau's report: "Between 1979 and 2005, the top 5 percent of American families saw their real incomes increase 81 percent. Over the same period, the lowest-income fifth [of the population] saw their real incomes decline 1 percent" (Census Bureau, Historical Income Data, as cited in Hartman, p. 134). Other indicators of wealth and income disparity (wages, stock ownership, personal savings) tell the same story. Despite fluctuations in the overall economy of the country, income disparity has been quietly but steadily increasing.

What does this mean for the future? Obviously, the persons with the lowest income will be most vulnerable. These are often the people social workers serve. They are the people social workers seek to empower. Perhaps middle-income people, with growing awareness of their own potential vulnerability, will increase their support for the pro-poor, poverty reduction programs and other social programs that are so necessary for the well-being, not just of the poor, but of all people.

TECHNOLOGICAL AND BIOMEDICAL ADVANCES

The fourth major trend or force influencing and shaping the future is that of technological and biomedical advancement. The evolution in these areas in the past decade has generated energy and knowledge that will continue to produce new products, software, and biomedical options in the near future. The ongoing change in these areas will influence social work practice and challenge the profession in many ways.

Information and Communication Technology

Today's social work students are more computer literate than any cohorts of students that preceded them. Their college class assignments involve them with word-processing and Internet searches. Increasingly, they will be asked to run statistical analyses for their research projects and work with spreadsheet and database programs. Before they graduate from college, they will become proficient with library electronic databases such as *Social Work Abstracts*, which is available in many college and university libraries.

As a profession, however, social work was slow to adopt computers, and some small agencies are still, only now, beginning to use databases, spreadsheets, and word processing to manage their administrative work and case records. A legitimate concern of some agency directors was that storage of clients' records in computer databases might be very efficient, but it could also present risks to confidentiality. On the other hand, computerized databases, e-mail, chat rooms, and other technology resources actually help keep social workers connected and may remedy one of the most serious problems in social work: fragmentation of services.

Access to information about social work agencies, services, and even social work employment opportunities is readily available on the Internet to students and social workers, and social workers increasingly refer clients to these same sources. While it is true that computer access is still not available to all of the people social workers see, this is less and less true as libraries and other public services make computers available. Even older adults in nursing homes are learning to use computers, so computer literacy is rapidly expanding. Social work practice has been enriched through the use of computerized client self-assessments that screen for anxiety, depression, and chemical dependency. A survey of the clients of an employee assistance agency found that some had initially turned to websites for help "because they had issues too embarrassing to share face to face" (O'Neil, 2002, p. 14). This poignant description of vulnerability, added to the fact that Internet counseling is rapidly increasing, underscores the importance of social workers adhering to strict ethical guidelines when using electronic technology.

Today's office technology—including computers, fax machines, cell phones, telephone answering machines or answering services, voice mail, and all other electronic equipment—is a potential source of ethical problems. The current NASW Code of Ethics, located in the Appendix of this book, holds social workers responsible for protecting confidentiality for clients, which includes accepting responsibility for the careful use of current technology in handling client records. Security systems are available within computer software or agency computer network systems. Social workers need to ensure that they have access to security systems that protect confidential documents.

Increasingly sophisticated software is being developed that can assist social workers in assessing client problems, developing intervention plans based on well-researched evidence of potential outcomes, and evaluating the results of their interventions. Online groups dealing with specific issues such as breast cancer or children who are school phobic are now being used and are likely to be further developed rapidly. They are inexpensive for clients with computer access, and they usually function within a time frame that fits today's hectic lifestyles.

Social action, advocacy, and policy research also benefit dramatically from the availability of shared databases, from programs that permit statistical analysis of massive amounts of statistical data, and from the ease of computer-assisted international communication. Online databases available through the Internet are rich sources of data for social workers. Technological advances in computers, fax transmission, and long-distance telephone access will continue to affect the way social workers "do business" each day. These tools are fostering globalization at a rapid rate, and for creative social workers, their potential uses in organizational, community, and even global systems change efforts are nearly unlimited.

Biomedical Technology

Technological advances in medicine continue to startle the world—and to bring both hope and havoc to the lives of patients and their families. Social workers in health care settings very quickly encounter the ethical and personal dilemmas precipitated by advances in medicine, but across social work settings all social workers can anticipate working with people whose lives are affected by advances in medical technology.

Organ Replacement   Organ transplantation, an area that continues to evolve, involves social workers as key members of the medical team. Social workers are called upon to bridge the communication gap between the highly specialized medical

Technological advances in medicine affect lives and offer dramatically changed futures for children as well as adults of all ages.

professionals and the persons so vitally affected—such as organ recipients and family members of the potential organ donor. Social workers help family members understand the medical situation, the decisions that need to be made, and the potential ramifications. Simultaneously, they help people deal with the overwhelming emotions of such health crisis situations.

Many lives could be saved today if organ donors could be found, but only a small fraction of donors are found in countries like Canada or the United States, where reluctance to consent to organ donation seems especially strong. In some countries—Austria, Spain, and France, for example—presumed consent is practiced. In these countries, the assumption is that you have granted consent unless you have indicated the contrary, in writing (Hawaleshka, 2005). In the absence of sufficient replacement organs, biomedical research is moving at a rapid pace to research potential solutions. Futurists like James Canton predict that stem cell technology will generate these organs and more. By 2030, Canton (2006) suggests stem cell treatment may be able to offer:

■ New organs, including hearts and lungs.

■ New bone growth for legs, arms, and backs.

■ New sensory functions and optic nerves to restore eyesight.

■ New cancer treatments.

■ New nerves to heal muscles and to restore movement.

■ New cells to offset the aging brain. (p. 136)

Tissue engineers have already made progress in research with stem cells that could be manipulated to develop the capacity to reproduce or heal organs. In Scotland, for example, scientists have learned to reproduce from stem cells the cells that are found in the brain and central nervous system. It is believed that this discovery could lead to the development of new cell-based drugs that could be used to treat Parkinson's and Alzheimer's diseases. In London, researchers converted stem cells into the type of cells that line a critical functioning portion of the human lungs. This could lead to cell therapy for lung tissue destroyed by cancer or even eventually generate entire replacement lung organs. Bone marrow transplants, one of the cell-based therapies, are already in use today (Tucker, 2006).

Complex ethical questions, however, already abound in the area of human organ replacement. In the United States, historically, society has approved the donation or selling of blood, sperm, and bone marrow, but selling vital body organs that cannot be easily replaced, organs like kidneys or livers, is not legal in the United States. In some other parts of the world, especially in very poor countries, people desperate for income sell their vital organs at considerable risk. Moldova, a country that was formerly a part of the Soviet Union, is such a place. Here, poor people sell their kidneys for $3,000, mostly to prosperous Asians. They may be paid in full, as promised, but often they are not. Lacking adequate medical care, the donor may encounter prolonged illness following surgery or may die. Other countries that are sources of human "spare parts" are Brazil, the Philippines, and Argentina. There seems to be evidence that China may be selling the vital organs of its prisoners (*Human organs for sale*, 2001). If the United States were to change its policy about sale of vital human organs in the future, this would undoubtedly be a concern for social workers. Shouldn't we also be concerned about these practices in other parts of the world?

Ethical issues regarding human embryo stem cell research also have been intensely debated in the media for the past several years. In considering the arguments for and against use of stem cells, it is important to understand the difference between embryonic and adult stem cells. A fertilized human egg is made up of cells, pluripotent cells, that are not yet differentiated into distinct, separate body organs—that occurs beginning in the 9th week following conception—but which have the potential to do so. If placed in a laboratory culture dish and provided the right environment, they will continue to divide and produce more pluripotent cells, but they are not able to form organs without further treatment. These are the so-called embryonic stem cells that have greatest potential for research. Multipotent cells, which are known as adult stem cells, are taken from various parts of the human body, but the most useful sources are from bone marrow or from the umbilical cord or placenta. In the United States, there is opposition to use of embryonic cells because this use destroys the fertilized egg that would otherwise have potential to develop into a human being. The U.S. government has not outlawed stem cell research, but it has placed restrictions on it. Meanwhile, other countries, notably the United Kingdom, are aggressively and competitively moving ahead with stem cell research aimed at advancing treatment for cancer, Alzheimer's disease, and numerous other human organ malfunctions (Wagner, 2007).

Biomedical ethics groups are engaged in serious and deeply emotional considerations of myriad difficult questions engendered by stem cell research, questions such as when human life begins, when it becomes sacrosanct, whether an embryo has different value as a living being than a fetus or a newborn child, and whether one human life can ethically be sacrificed to save the life of another. These are tough questions!

Genetic Research   Significant advances have also been made in genetics, thanks to the **Human Genome Project.** The Human Genome Project was an international effort, initiated in 1990, to seek significantly greater understanding of human genetics that could ultimately cure diseases and promote health and longevity. A **genome** is an organism's DNA that contains the genetic instructions responsible for developing and directing the activities of that organism. It is made up of 3 billion twisted strands of chemicals that exist in the 23 pairs of chromosomes within human cells (National Human Genome Research Institute, 2006). The Human Genome Project was completed in 2003.

It was an amazing feat involving the collaboration of researchers around the world, and it was possible only because of information technology that enabled large computers and robots to analyze massive amounts of data. Its findings are being explored but have already led to the development of more than 1,000 genetic tests that aid diagnostic studies or reveal specific genetically linked risk factors. More than 1,800 disease genes have already been discovered (National Institutes of Health, 2006). There are already genetic tests to determine the potential for such conditions as cystic fibrosis, Huntington's disease, sickle-cell anemia, and certain kinds of cancer (some forms of ovarian, colon, and breast cancer). As genetic information becomes increasingly available, it raises difficult spiritual, emotional, and ethical questions, "such as whether to go ahead with a pregnancy or whether to inform existing children and siblings of their risk" (Dahinden et al., p. 24). Because the meaning of genetic risk carries such significance and potentially involves multiple generations of family members, social workers and other allied health professionals often become involved.

The ethical and social quandaries of women seeking genetic testing for breast or ovarian cancer were studied by Tovia Freedman (1998), a social worker. Two segments from her research interviews reveal the emotion experienced by these women:

> I do not want to carry on another generation of cancer. Should my daughter be told not to have children? It feels like a death sentence. There is uncertainty and the never knowing.
>
> There is tyranny involved because the technology is available. I feel that it would be stupid of me not to avail myself of it. If there is anything that I can do to assure myself that I do not have to share my mother's fate, that I won't die a horrible death from ovarian cancer, I will do it. I don't want to be in the position down the road of beating my head against the wall and saying, "Why didn't I do this?" (pp. 216–217)

Social workers help people understand what genetic testing means, the kinds of information that can come from the tests, and how it can be used. They help family members resolve the issues that testing results bring, the multigenerational consequences of information suggesting susceptibility to disease. The social worker is not usually the actual genetics counselor—that person is a medical specialist. But the social worker provides the supportive relationship, assists with panic or psychological crises that result, and assists the family after the information is given to them. Genetic testing is commercially available and costly. Its current lack of availability to all socioeconomic groups raises ethical questions for social workers.

Completion of the Human Genome Project is only the beginning of extensive research by government as well as business and private research organizations around the world. Pharmaceutical corporations have clinical trials under way for drugs that will effectively target individuals' specific genetic makeup. New modes of delivery of drugs will enable them to take effect very quickly and be more effective than medications that are currently available. Exhibit 12-5 reflects the possibilities that may be realized in the next 50 years as a result of the Human Genome Project and related research. An additional consideration for the future, however, is that "the increasing ability to connect DNA variation with non-medical conditions, such as intelligence and personality traits, will challenge society, making the role of ethical, legal and social implications research more important than ever" (National Institutes of Health, 2006, n.p.)

Human Reproduction   The area of human reproduction has been affected dramatically, too, and future advances may result in quite complex moral and ethical issues. Currently multiple for-profit organizations exist (many are advertised on Internet websites) that offer infertile persons alternatives for parenthood. Among the alternatives are surrogate parenting, human egg donation (or sale), and embryo transfer. In **surrogate parenting,** a woman agrees to be impregnated and to release the baby that

---

EXHIBIT 12-5

The Next 50 Years of Medical Science: The Impact of the Human Genome Project

Individualized analysis based on each person's genome will lead to a very powerful form of preventive medicine. We'll be able to learn about risks of future illness based on DNA analysis. Physicians, nurses, genetic counselors, and other health care professionals will be able to work with individuals to focus efforts on the things that are most likely to maintain health for a particular individual. That might mean diet or lifestyle changes, or it might mean medical surveillance. But there will be a personalized aspect to what we do to keep ourselves healthy. Then, through our understanding at the molecular level of how things like diabetes or heart disease or schizophrenia come about, we should see a whole new generation of interventions, many of

which will be drugs that are much more effective and precise than those available today.

We are entering a new age of discovery that will transform human health. Our eventual knowledge about the workings of the genome has the potential to fundamentally change our most basic perceptions of our biological world. It is difficult to predict what will be learned and how future knowledge will be applied, but there can be little doubt that understanding the genome will revolutionize our concept of health and improve the human condition in remarkable ways.

SOURCE: National Human Genome Research Institute. (2006, December). *The Human Genome Project completion: Frequently asked questions.* Retrieved August 20, 2007, from: http://www.genome.gov/11006943

she delivers to the person(s) who contracted with her for this purpose. In human egg donor programs, the egg, also called ovum, of a donor is surgically implanted in anther woman who is unable to produce her own ovum; she may then be able to conceive a baby through sexual intercourse. Embryo transfer involves surgical implantation in a woman of another woman's egg that has been fertilized by her husband's, partner's, or a donor's sperm (*Glossary of terms*, 2001).

As of 2006, a landmark year in the world of assisted reproductive treatment, more than 3,000,000 babies had been born as a result of one or more forms of assisted reproductive technology (Rathode, 2006). Most infertility is successfully treated with medication or surgery; therefore, people seeking more involved procedures, such as in vitro fertilization using sperm banks or human egg donors, are likely to have to pay large fees (generally not covered by insurance). The Ethics Committee of the American Society for Reproductive Medicine reports that if fees in excess of $5,000 for an egg (oocyte) donor are requested, they should be questioned, and fees in excess of $10,000 are not appropriate (2007). Often not mentioned in this discussion is the fact that egg donation is painful and risky for a woman. It involves repeated injections of hormones over several weeks, followed by surgery and the possibility of severe pelvic pain, bleeding, cysts, and some forms of cancer. Low-income women, especially in the United States where this procedure is not legally regulated, are at greatest risk of exploitation (Krimbell, as cited in Levine, 2004).

Cloning is an asexual, as compared with a sexual, form of reproduction. Animals have been cloned, so why not humans? That, at least, is a question asked by futurists. In human cloning, an embryo grows from either a male or female stem cell and then is implanted in a woman so that it can be brought to term and delivered as a newborn infant. This "clonal embryo" does not carry the genetic makeup of two persons; it

---

UP FOR DEBATE

Proposal: In the future, humans should be cloned the way animals are now.

YES	NO
Children would not be born with inheritable diseases or defects.	Cloning may not totally prevent defects and may, in fact, result in tragic malformations.
Regulating human reproduction has so many benefits to humankind that it should be mandatory.	Moral and spiritual values that view God as the creator should prevail over procedures that science makes possible.
Cloning should be allowed in order to obtain the most perfect human specimen.	Who is to determine the "perfect" human? Is the perfect human a mighty warrior or a peace maker, an intellectual giant, or a nurturer?
The health, longevity, and economic benefits of cloning are obvious.	Human variety and diversity are such valuable traits that they should be cherished, not obliterated.

consists of the genes of only the person who donated the stem cell. Obviously these genes could also be scientifically engineered or altered so that the child will not carry a predisposition to known diseases. There could potentially also be alterations to determine sex of the child, hair color, intelligence, body type, and numerous other traits. Or the child might be a true clone, identical to the "parent." Another type of cloning that is also likely to be developed is therapeutic cloning, where the tissue that results from the stem cell growth is used to replace organs or held indefinitely to permit creation of future organs, should there be a need (*Human cloning and genetic modification* 2002). The Up for Debate box suggests some of the arguments that are inevitable as cloning possibilities draw near. What a strange and fascinating future awaits us!

ENVIRONMENTAL SUSTAINABILITY

Social work, with its person-in-environment perspective, is poised to reclaim its historical involvement with the physical environment. The profession is awakening to the enormous impact of current and past environmental degradation on humanity. Increasingly, there are calls for a fresh generation of leaders who will revitalize the social work literature and enrich social work practice with a holistic, planetary view of practice (Besthorn & Canda, 2002; Holland, 2005). A future for the profession is envisioned, where the ecological, social, and spiritual dimensions of practice will be merged and strengthened. Increased involvement with the environment, possibly including planned experiences with natural and wilderness areas, will be built into social work practice. People—social workers as well as clients—will be helped to achieve ecological awareness and a sense of responsibility for the environment. A fundamental shift is needed in the way much of the world views its relationship with living things and with nature; the profession of social work will need to incorporate this awareness into its ecological theoretical perspective (Besthorn, 2002; Besthorn & Canda, 2002).

Throughout this text, environmental issues have been shown to be relevant to social work practice and social welfare policy. The person-in-environment perspective that is central to social workers' thinking was introduced early in the text and carried into many of the different fields-of-practice chapters. Now, as the text concludes, we consider what the future holds in terms of the environment for our clients, ourselves, and the world we live in.

Environmental sustainability is a major concern for futurists. Canton, for example, lists among his "top ten threats that could kill America's future" the possibility of an environment so damaged that it could cause significant reduction to the quality of life and even the public health and well-being of Americans (2006). The earth, even today, is being increasingly overwhelmed by pollutants of various kinds. Around the world, carbon is currently being produced in twice the amount than oceans and forests can absorb, and that amount is likely to soon quadruple if current trends continue, according to Glenn and Gordon (2006). Global climate change is likely to threaten both coasts of the United States as well as coastlines in many other countries with

Urban renewal or beautification service projects are increasingly initiated by social work students as they demonstrate campus leadership for "green" (environmental) concerns.

flooding. Blyth is one of several futurists who contemplate a post-petroleum world, where there will not be sufficient gasoline to fuel even hybrid cars and where some communities that rely on petroleum products to fuel their cars, farm implements, and other industries will become ghost towns. Some small communities in Arizona, for example, are viewed as too dependent on automobiles to survive (2006).

The earth's inherent self-regulating mechanisms, however, do not have to be totally overwhelmed by pollutants and chemicals of modern living. Efforts are increasing worldwide to save the planet. The European Union has assumed a remarkable leadership role with its precautionary principle that holds all nation-members of the EU to regulations that will not permit "economic activity, regardless of how lucrative or beneficial it might be, [to] be allowed to compromise the integrity of the life-support systems that make up the indivisible biosphere in which we all dwell, and from which we draw our sustenance" (Rifkin, 2004, p. 338). Nations that wish to become EU members, too, must clean up their environments and initiate earth-friendly ecological practices.

As the social work profession assumes increasing responsibility for practice, social policy development, and research that supports environmental sustainability, it could be guided by the following set of core assumptions developed by Coates and Leahy (2006):

- *Interdependence*: a holistic systems approach.
- *Care*: the earth exists to be shared and cared for by all.
- *Emergence*: the universe, earth, and all people are always undergoing development.

These basic assumptions are easily taught to clients or used in educational programs. They blend social work values with respect for the environment and all beings. In acknowledging the interdependence of all living things, people are seen as connected to each other and to the life of the planet. When people or the environment is endangered, nurturing and care are needed. Social workers can help others develop capacity to care for other people and other living things. Coates and Leahy believe that "caring for 'others' can be an expression of our spirituality as it helps us to transcend an exclusive self-interest" (2006, p. 7). They conclude that just as earth and the universe are continually evolving so, too, every human being is also experiencing development. As social workers help their clients and communities achieve recognition of their role in nature and the environment so, too, can social workers experience a new emergence as we become actors in the work of creating an environment that truly respects and nurtures all people and all living beings.

Before turning to a look at the future of the social work profession, a listing of Internet sites related to content areas in this chapter is provided. These sites were selected to enable readers to pursue topics of interest. Some of the sites provide a different perspective from those presented in the text.

INTERNET SITES

http://www.ornl.gov/sei/techresources/ Human_Genome/home.shtml	Human Genome Project Information Site
http://www.genome.gov	The National Human Genome Research Institute
http://www.pay-equity.org/	National Committee on Pay Equity
http://www.ifg.org	The International Forum on Globalization
http://archives.cnn.com/2001/HEALTH/01/15/growing.bone/	CNN Report on Neo-Organs
http://www.nci.nih.gov/cancertopics/Genetic-Testing-for-Breast-and-Ovarian-Cancer-Risk	Genetic Testing for Breast and Ovarian Cancer Risk
http://www.nlm.nih.gov/medlineplus/genesandgenetherapy.html	Medline Plus—Genes and Gene Therapy
http://www.cancer.gov/cancertopics/factsheet/Therapy/gene	Gene Therapy for Cancer: Questions and Answers
http://www.wiley.co.uk/genetherapy/clinical/	Gene Therapy Clinical Trials Worldwide
http://stemcells.nih.gov/info/basics/basics3.asp	Stem Cell Basics—The National Institutes of Health
http://health.iafrica.com/doconline/general/neworgans.html	Can We Grow Organs
http://www.pbs.org/saf/1107/features/body.htm	The Bionic Body—The Body Shop

THE FUTURE OF THE SOCIAL WORK PROFESSION

Throughout this chapter, we explored several powerful forces—demographic, political, and economic trends, technological and biomedical advances, and issues of environmental sustainability—that will affect life on the planet in the next 5, 10, 20 years, or more. We now narrow our focus and briefly look at the future for the social work profession.

The organization that undoubtedly has the greatest amount of data on which to build future employment projections for social work or any other profession or occupation is the U.S. Department of Labor's Bureau of Labor Statistics (BLS). If BLS statistics are one criterion of predictability, then the profession of social work is likely to remain healthy and in existence for a long time. In its most recent report, the BLS noted: "Employment for social workers is expected to increase faster than the average for all occupations through 2014" (Bureau of Labor Statistics, 2006, p. 4). The BLS publication, the *Occupational Outlook Handbook*, is a good source of information on trends in employment. According to this publication, changing demographics in the United States and technological advances are creating new and expanding existing niches for social work employment. Even today, the BLS notes, agencies in many parts of the country are struggling to fill social work vacancies. Services to older adults will need to expand as the U.S. population ages. The BLS predicts that growth will take place in home health care, in assisted living, and within hospice programs. Other areas that are expected to expand include substance abuse services, schools, employee assistance programs, and alternatives to incarceration for persons convicted of certain drug offenses.

Detailed information from the BLS as well as NASW's manpower survey can be found in Chapter 1 of this text. NASW's Center for Workforce Studies plans to collect and disseminate data on a continuing basis, so NASW will be another good source of information on trends related to social work employment.

The rosy employment data, of course, are not the only predictors of the future for social work. While a need clearly will continue to exist for social workers, there is a clear need for the profession to define itself much more clearly for the public. Nurses, teachers, librarians, dentists, and accountants all have clear, if not always correct, images in the public. Social work is not well understood, nor is occupational therapy, psychology, or professional counseling.

One of the reasons people have difficulty understanding social work is the reality that the social work profession is, in Leon Ginsberg's terms, "a mammoth occupation" (2005, p. 8). The profession functions across a very diverse array of fields of practice. Chapters 4 through 11 in this text presented social work in family and children's services, in mental health, in health care, in schools, in substance abuse services, with older adults, in criminal justice settings, and in the field of developmental disabilities. These are stable fields of practice that are traditional within social work. Other

areas of practice, such as employee assistance programs or genetic counseling, are more recent. Some social workers specialize, while others are generalists. Specialty areas of practice sometimes result in social workers identifying solely with their specialty or with their position title, such as psychotherapist, professor, addictions counselor, or case manager. As the chapter case study demonstrates, social work is both local and global. The breadth of social work as a profession is truly both a strength and an exciting challenge.

The future of the profession depends greatly on its ability to attract students who identify with the values, ethics, and the profession of social work. This new generation of social workers will help the profession to evolve and become even more committed to social and economic justice, equality, and social change. To make change happen, social workers need to add the dimension of policy practice to their intervention roles. This means that while working with individual persons, families, or groups, social workers are simultaneously seeking to create or improve policies or programs. To do so, they may actively support legislation or organizational policies that will result in the resources and programs that are needed to ensure a good quality of life for clients and, indeed, for all Americans. Policy practice might also include voter registration, speaking before a city council meeting, giving testimony at a state legislative committee, and offering community education programs. Social workers of the future will actively and effectively participate in their communities.

To prepare for the exciting challenges of the future, social work education will need to retain a firm hold on its values and ethics but change some parts of the curriculum. Practice courses will need to incorporate more content on empowerment, advocacy, coalition building, and legislative lobbying. Field placements should engage students in direct services to clients but also ensure that all students learn about and take appropriate action to create or support (or oppose) legislation that will affect the lives of the people they serve. Social work courses will need to broaden the human diversity content they incorporate, paying increased attention to spirituality, economic differences, ability/disability, new immigrant and refugee populations, and evolving family systems. Fluency in Spanish may become a requirement in some social work programs as Spanish-speaking populations become a larger presence in many parts of the United States. Computer and technology skills will expand students' access to information. The social work curriculum will develop students' ability to organize, analyze, and effectively use information as well as the technology tools that will increasingly be used to deliver services. Social work courses of the future will also increasingly incorporate global content and will build upon multicultural, international, and historical content from courses taken in the liberal arts. As military might is built in many parts of the world and security technology is developed to defend against possible biological and chemical terrorists, the social work curriculum may add a new dimension of study. Peace studies—alternatives to the use of violence to resolve conflict in families, communities, and worldwide—could become a focus for social work education of the future.

The profession of social work is probably one of the most difficult to practice. It is demanding and frustrating. It is not always well understood. Sometimes it is poorly paid. But it is potentially the most rewarding and enriching profession that anyone could choose. It also provides a unique opportunity to participate in the creation of a future society, one that we would choose for ourselves as well as for the people we serve.

KEY TERMS

adult stem cells, *p. 520*
asylum, *p. 506*
cloning, *p. 523*
demographics, *p. 500*
egg donor programs, *p. 523*
embryonic stem cells, *p. 520*
embryo transfer, *p. 523*
Equal Rights Amendment
(ERA), *p. 512*

ethnic sensitive approaches,
p. 501
ethnoconscious approach,
p. 501
food insecurity, *p. 516*
futurists, *p. 495*
genome, *p. 521*
globalization, *p. 495*
Human Genome Project, *p. 521*

immigrant, *p. 506*
kinship care, *p. 504*
pay equity, *p. 514*
private practice, *p. 511*
privatization, *p. 511*
refugees, *p. 506*
sanctioning, *p. 509*
surrogate parenting, *p. 522*
underemployment, *p. 515*

DISCUSSION QUESTIONS

1. How do you respond to people who think that social workers are welfare workers who dispense "the dole" to lazy, fraudulent people?

2. Identify several personal values that would be inconsistent with the values of the social work profession. Speculate about what might happen if persons with these values prepared for a career in social work.

3. What demographic changes are occurring in the United States? Why is this relevant to social work practice? How are the planning and delivery of social work services influenced by demographic trends?

4. Outline the political shifts that have taken place in the past 25 years. How would you characterize the current political environment? Identify current key political issues that have consequences

for the people that social workers serve. Thinking about political forces, what implications do you see for the future of the social work profession?

5. What is the difference between unemployment and underemployment? Which of the two is most likely to be an issue in the United States in the next 5 years? In other parts of the world?

6. In what ways is the American family changing? What implications does this change have for social work practice?

7. Who are America's newest refugees? Where do they come from? Why are they fleeing their homeland? Are they seeking haven in other countries, too? Can you think of ways in which social workers will be able to assist them in the

United States? In what ways might they enrich our country?

8. The privatization of social services has been discussed in several chapters in this book. Explain what is meant by privatization. How does it affect social work practice? Can you cite examples of conflicts between social work professional values and the movement toward privatization? Can you think of any advantages of privatized or entrepreneurial social services?

9. How do women's wages in the United States compare with those of men? How do you explain this discrepancy? Do you think that this will change? How? When?

10. What are the various ways in which social workers and social work students use computer technology? Are there risks in the use of computers and other technology in social service agencies? How can the risks be minimized? How do you think

technology will affect social work practice in the next decade?

11. What environmental issues affect the lives of social work clients? Do you think it would be possible to involve clients in environmental change efforts? How might this be done?

12. Almost every day there seems to be an announcement of yet another breakthrough in medical science. What biomedical advances do you think will occur in the next decade? What implications might they have for social work practice? Would you anticipate any ethical or moral dilemmas relative to these new technologies?

13. As you complete this text, you may be thinking about your own future career plans. Considering what you now know about the social work profession, is this a career area that you wish to pursue? What concerns do you have? What satisfactions might a social work career hold for you?

CLASSROOM EXERCISES

It is suggested that students break into small groups of three or four to discuss these exercises. It may be helpful to choose a scribe to record and report interesting points to the class after the group discussion.

1. Why does the author of this chapter believe that social work is not the right profession for everyone? What qualities, characteristics, or commitments help make a good fit between person and profession?

2. Many people in the general public have little understanding of the social work profession. What have you learned from this text that would help you explain the profession to others? How do you

think that the profession of social work can more creatively and effectively educate the public?

3. If conditions of poverty, inequality, and conflict continue to worsen in this world, immigrants are likely to increase in number and in need. How might social workers become involved in addressing this worldwide issue?

4. Why do many political conservatives consider TANF a success, while many liberals, especially traditional liberals, do not? What is your own perspective? In particular, what do you believe is the more important goal, to eliminate welfare programs or to eliminate poverty? Why?

RESEARCH ACTIVITIES

1. Experiment with being a policy practitioner. Select an issue or a piece of legislation that will have impact on at-risk or vulnerable people. Review newspaper and news media coverage of your issue, noting the arguments in favor and those in opposition. Look at the historical

development of the issue. Use the NASW Code of Ethics as a screen to filter the various perspectives and arguments related to your chosen issue. Think through what you have learned, and determine what your position is. Then communicate your position to a legislator who should be involved with this issue. State your position convincingly and seek the appropriate action from your legislator. Request a response.

2. The text provided information about the changing demographics of the United States. Is your community also experiencing increasing diversity? What data can you obtain about the demographics of your community (or your university) over the past 10 years?

3. Interview one social worker each from the public sector (perhaps a county or state social services office), the nonprofit sector (e.g., a denominational agency or the American Red Cross), and a social worker in a private for-profit practice or agency setting. Obtain information about the populations they serve and the nature of the services they provide. Note any discernible differences in their attitudes about their clients. Ask them to identify any changes they have experienced in the past 5 years regarding the financing or funding of their services.

INTERNET RESEARCH EXERCISES

1. How are older Americans doing in the new century? The Federal Interagency Forum on Aging Related Statistics website has some answers. Go to http://www.agingstats.gov/agingstatsdotnet/ Main_Site/default.aspx. Click on "Older Americans Update 2006: Key Indicators of Well-Being." Then click on "download" for Entire Chartbook—Full Text PDF. Examine each of the "indicator" subsections as you look for answers to the following questions:

   a. What will be the changes in the makeup of the racial and ethnic cohorts of older Americans in the future? (Hint: indicator 2.)

   b. What is the projected life expectancy for persons age 65 in 2003? What was it in 1900? (Hint: indicator 13.)

   c. Indicators 17 and 18 relate to memory impairment and depressive symptoms. What general conclusion can you draw relative to gender from these two indicators?

2. The subject of genetic testing is briefly explained on a governmental laboratory website (http://www.lbl.gov/Education/ELSI/genetic-testing.html). Use that site to locate answers to the following questions:

   a. Is genetic testing highly reliable? Why?

   b. List and explain briefly three types of genetic testing.

   c. What are the three ethical, legal, and social issues in genetic testing as specified in this website?

3. Multiculturalism is discussed in a powerful way on the Canadian Heritage website (http://www.canadianheritage.gc.ca/progs/multi/what-multi_e.cfm).

   a. What are the stongest points you receive from a reading of this page?

   b. Click on "Canadian Diversity: Respecting our Differences." What importance does this website give bilingualism?

   c. Does the existence of constitutional measures and legislation achieve the results of true multiculturalism? If not, what else is required?

4. An interesting organization typifying both the concern with environmental issues and a just society can be found at http://www.worldwatch.org/.

   a. Click "About Worldwatch" and then "Mission." How would you characterize the mission of this organization? How would you compare their approach to an organization like Greenpeace?

   b. Click on "Green Activities." Discuss the practicality and ease with which the procedures they have put in place could be applied to your college or workplace.

   c. Click on: FAQ. How is Worldwatch funded?

FOR FURTHER READING

Abramovitz, M. (1998). Social work and social reform: An arena of struggle. *Social Work, 43*(6), 521–526.

Abramovitz's works are always an inspiration, and this article is no exception. Of special interest in this article is a remarkably comprehensive history of social work activism, rich historical material that should be treasured and nourished by the profession but that is largely undocumented in current social work texts. The author concludes by challenging social workers to forgo silence in the face of inhumane social conditions and instead to keep the voice of change alive by active political involvement.

Gaskell, G., & Bauer, M. W. (Eds.) (2006). *Genomics and society: Legal, ethical and social dimensions*. London: Earthscan.

The editors of this book provide a wide range of perspectives on the legal, ethical, and social science implications of the global advancement in the science of genomics. The contributors to the text are all social scientists from North America, Europe, and Japan. The major sections of the text deal with emerging issues and debates related to organ replacement, bioethics, and genetics; the efficacy of public opinion; and five excellent articles that capture a global perspective.

Ginsberg, L. (2005, Spring). The future of social work as a profession. *Advances in Social Work: Special Issue on the Futures of Social Work, 6*(4), 7–16.

Ginsberg succinctly addresses what he sees as major trends that will influence the future of the social work profession in the next several decades. In discussing the influence of politics, he explores the shift from federal government leadership to the primacy of state governments as current and future sources of power. State licensure of social workers is noted as a powerful force in the profession. Ginsberg also deals with ideological conflicts that are likely to have major influence in the future: same-sex unions, health care, multiculturalism, and religious and political fanaticism.

Rifkin, J. (2004). *The European dream: How Europe's vision of the future is quietly eclipsing the American dream*. New York: Jeremy P. Tarcher/Penguin.

Jeremy Rifkin is one of the most respected social thinkers of our time. He has contributed much to current thinking about the future. In this fascinating book, he contrasts the American dream, one of belief in the possibility of each individual to attain success (usually defined as financial success), with an emerging European vision. The European dream emphasizes global cooperation and interconnectedness. It gives preference to community relationships instead of individual autonomy and material wealth, and it respects human rights over property rights. Rifkin's focus in this book is far broader than just America and Europe. The book is global in perspective, and it is further enriched by themes of spirituality, multiculturalism, and appreciation for natural environments.

Van Hook, M., Hugen, B., & Aguilar, M. (Eds.). (2001). *Spirituality within religious traditions in social work practice*. Pacific Grove, CA: Brooks/Cole.

The rapidly increasing diversity of religions in the United States has caught the social work profession off guard. Consistent with Freudian perspectives adopted early in the profession's history, social work has tended to avoid the religious or faith dimensions of people's lives. Now the profession is awakening to its responsibility to understand, appreciate, and utilize the beliefs of clients as a resource in meeting their needs. The editors clarify the differences between spirituality and religion. Social work contributors representing 11 different religions present an introduction to faith and religious practices as diverse as Lakota, Hinduism, Confucianism, Catholicism, Judaism, Islam, African American Baptist, and Seventh-day Adventist. They write of their own personal religious experiences, and they offer implications for the ways in which the religion can be a source of help and healing for its believers. This book provides refreshing insight and begins to fill a gap that must be addressed by social work education.

CODE OF ETHICS OF THE NATIONAL ASSOCIATION OF SOCIAL WORKERS

Approved by the 1996 Delegate Assembly and revised by the 1999 NASW Delegate Assembly.

OVERVIEW

The *NASW Code of Ethics* is intended to serve as a guide to the everyday professional conduct of social workers. This *Code* includes four sections. The first section, "Preamble," summarizes the social work profession's mission and core values. The second section, "Purpose of the *NASW Code of Ethics*," provides an overview of the *Code*'s main functions and a brief guide for dealing with ethical issues or dilemmas in social work practice. The third section, "Ethical Principles," presents broad ethical principles, based on social work's core values, that inform social work practice. The final section, "Ethical Standards," includes specific ethical standards to guide social workers' conduct and to provide a basis for adjudication.

ABOUT NASW

The National Association of Social Workers (NASW) is the largest organization of professional social workers in the world. NASW serves nearly 160,000 social workers in 56 chapters throughout the United States, Puerto Rico, the Virgin Islands, and abroad. NASW was formed in 1955 through a merger of seven predecessor social work organizations to carry out three responsibilities:

- Strengthen and unify the profession.
- Promote the development of social work practice.
- Advance sound social policies.

Promoting high standards of practice and protecting the consumer of services are major association principles.

PREAMBLE

The primary mission of the social work profession is to enhance human well-being and help meet the basic human needs of all people, with particular attention to the needs and empowerment of people who are vulnerable, oppressed, and living in poverty. A historic and defining feature of social work is the profession's focus on individual well-being in a social context and the well-being of society. Fundamental to social work is attention to the environmental forces that create, contribute to, and address problems in living. Social workers promote social justice and social change with and on behalf of clients. "Clients" is used inclusively to refer to individuals, families, groups, organizations, and communities. Social workers are sensitive to cultural and ethnic diversity and strive to end discrimination, oppression, poverty, and other forms of social injustice. These activities may be in the form of direct practice, community organizing, supervision, consultation, administration, advocacy, social and political action, policy development and implementation, education, and research and evaluation. Social workers seek to enhance the capacity of people to address their own needs. Social workers also seek to promote the responsiveness of organizations, communities, and other social institutions to individuals' needs and social problems.

The mission of the social work profession is rooted in a set of core values. These core values, embraced by social workers throughout the profession's history, are the foundation of social work's unique purpose and perspective:

- Service.
- Social justice.
- Dignity and worth of the person.
- Importance of human relationships.
- Integrity.
- Competence.

This constellation of core values reflects what is unique to the social work profession. Core values, and the principles that flow from them, must be balanced within the context and complexity of the human experience.

PURPOSE OF THE *NASW CODE OF ETHICS*

Professional ethics are at the core of social work. The profession has an obligation to articulate its basic values, ethical principles, and ethical standards. The *NASW Code of Ethics* sets forth these values, principles, and standards to guide social workers' conduct. The *Code* is relevant to all social workers and social work students, regardless of their professional functions, the settings in which they work, or the populations they serve.

The *NASW Code of Ethics* serves six purposes:

1. The *Code* identifies core values on which social work's mission is based.

2. The *Code* summarizes broad ethical principles that reflect the profession's core values and establishes a set of specific ethical standards that should be used to guide social work practice.

3. The *Code* is designed to help social workers identify relevant considerations when professional obligations conflict or ethical uncertainties arise.

4. The *Code* provides ethical standards to which the general public can hold the social work profession accountable.

5. The *Code* socializes practitioners new to the field to social work's mission, values, ethical principles, and ethical standards.

6. The *Code* articulates standards that the social work profession itself can use to assess whether social workers have engaged in unethical conduct. NASW has formal procedures to adjudicate ethics complaints filed against its members. In subscribing to this *Code*, social workers are required to cooperate in its implementation, participate in NASW adjudication proceedings, and abide by any NASW disciplinary rulings or sanctions based on it.

The *Code* offers a set of values, principles, and standards to guide decision making and conduct when ethical issues arise. It does not provide a set of rules that prescribe how social workers should act in all situations. Specific applications of the *Code* must take into account the context in which it is being considered and the possibility of conflicts among the *Code*'s values, principles, and standards. Ethical responsibilities flow from all human relationships, from the personal and familial to the social and professional.

Further, the *NASW Code of Ethics* does not specify which values, principles, and standards are most important and ought to outweigh others in instances when they conflict. Reasonable differences of opinion can and do exist among social workers with respect to the ways in which values, ethical principles, and ethical standards should be rank ordered when they conflict. Ethical decision making in a given situation must apply the informed judgment of the individual social worker and should also consider how the issues would be judged in a peer review process where the ethical standards of the profession would be applied.

Ethical decision making is a process. There are many instances in social work where simple answers are not available to resolve complex ethical issues. Social workers should take into consideration all the values, principles, and standards in this *Code* that are relevant to any situation in which ethical judgment is warranted. Social workers' decisions and actions should be consistent with the spirit as well as the letter of this *Code*.

In addition to this *Code*, there are many other sources of information about ethical thinking that may be useful. Social workers should consider ethical theory and principles generally, social work theory and research, laws, regulations, agency policies, and other relevant codes of ethics, recognizing that among codes of ethics social workers should consider the *NASW Code of Ethics* as their primary source. Social workers also should be aware of the impact on ethical decision making of their clients' and their own personal values and cultural and religious beliefs and practices. They should be aware of any conflicts between personal and professional values and deal with them responsibly. For additional guidance social workers should consult the relevant literature on professional ethics and ethical decision making and seek appropriate consultation when faced with ethical dilemmas. This may involve consultation with an agency-based or social work organization's ethics committee, a regulatory body, knowledgeable colleagues, supervisors, or legal counsel.

Instances may arise when social workers' ethical obligations conflict with agency policies or relevant laws or regulations. When such conflicts occur, social workers must make a responsible effort to resolve the conflict in a manner that is consistent with the values, principles, and standards expressed in this *Code*. If a reasonable resolution of the conflict does not appear possible, social workers should seek proper consultation before making a decision.

The *NASW Code of Ethics* is to be used by NASW and by individuals, agencies, organizations, and bodies (such as licensing and regulatory boards, professional liability insurance providers, courts of law, agency boards of directors, government agencies, and other professional groups) that choose to adopt it or use it as a frame of reference. Violation of standards in this *Code* does not automatically imply legal liability or violation of the law. Such determination can only be made in the context of legal and judicial proceedings. Alleged violations of the *Code* would be subject to a peer review process. Such processes are generally separate from legal or administrative procedures and insulated from legal review or proceedings to allow the profession to counsel and discipline its own members.

A code of ethics cannot guarantee ethical behavior. Moreover, a code of ethics cannot resolve all ethical issues or disputes or capture the richness and complexity involved in striving to make responsible choices within a moral community. Rather, a code of ethics sets forth values, ethical principles, and ethical standards to which professionals aspire and by which their actions can be judged. Social workers' ethical behavior should result from their personal commitment to engage in ethical practice. The *NASW Code of Ethics* reflects the commitment of all social workers to uphold the profession's values and to act ethically. Principles and standards must be applied by individuals of good character who discern moral questions and, in good faith, seek to make reliable ethical judgments.

ETHICAL PRINCIPLES

The following broad ethical principles are based on social work's core values of service, social justice, dignity and worth of the person, importance of human relationships, integrity, and competence. These principles set forth ideals to which all social workers should aspire.

Value: *Service*

Ethical Principle: *Social workers' primary goal is to help people in need and to address social problems.*

Social workers elevate service to others above self-interest. Social workers draw on their knowledge, values, and skills to help people in need and to address social problems. Social workers are encouraged to volunteer some portion of their professional skills with no expectation of significant financial return (pro bono service).

Value: *Social Justice*

Ethical Principle: *Social workers challenge social injustice.*

Social workers pursue social change, particularly with and on behalf of vulnerable and oppressed individuals and groups of people. Social workers' social change efforts are focused primarily on issues of poverty, unemployment, discrimination, and other forms of social injustice. These activities seek to promote sensitivity to and knowledge about oppression and cultural and ethnic diversity. Social workers strive to ensure access to needed information, services, and resources; equality of opportunity; and meaningful participation in decision making for all people.

Value: *Dignity and Worth of the Person*

Ethical Principle: *Social workers respect the inherent dignity and worth of the person.*

Social workers treat each person in a caring and respectful fashion, mindful of individual differences and cultural and ethnic diversity. Social workers promote clients' socially responsible self-determination. Social workers seek to enhance clients' capacity and opportunity to change and to address their own needs. Social workers are cognizant of their dual responsibility to clients and to the broader society. They seek to resolve conflicts between clients' interests and the broader society's interests in a socially responsible manner consistent with the values, ethical principles, and ethical standards of the profession.

Value: *Importance of Human Relationships*

Ethical Principle: *Social workers recognize the central importance of human relationships.*

Social workers understand that relationships between and among people are an important vehicle for change. Social workers engage people as partners in the helping process. Social workers seek to strengthen relationships among people in a purposeful effort to promote, restore, maintain, and enhance the well-being of individuals, families, social groups, organizations, and communities.

Value: *Integrity*

Ethical Principle: *Social workers behave in a trustworthy manner.*

Social workers are continually aware of the profession's mission, values, ethical principles, and ethical standards and practice in a manner consistent with them. Social workers act honestly and responsibly and promote ethical practices on the part of the organizations with which they are affiliated.

Value: *Competence*

Ethical Principle: *Social workers practice within their areas of competence and develop and enhance their professional expertise.*

Social workers continually strive to increase their professional knowledge and skills and to apply them in practice. Social workers should aspire to contribute to the knowledge base of the profession.

ETHICAL STANDARDS

The following ethical standards are relevant to the professional activities of all social workers. These standards concern (1) social workers' ethical responsibilities to clients, (2) social workers' ethical responsibilities to colleagues, (3) social workers' ethical responsibilities in practice settings, (4) social workers' ethical responsibilities as professionals, (5) social workers' ethical responsibilities to the social work profession, and (6) social workers' ethical responsibilities to the broader society.

Some of the standards that follow are enforceable guidelines for professional conduct, and some are aspirational. The extent to which each standard is enforceable is a matter of professional judgment to be exercised by those responsible for reviewing alleged violations of ethical standards.

1. SOCIAL WORKERS' ETHICAL RESPONSIBILITIES TO CLIENTS

1.01   Commitment to Clients
Social workers' primary responsibility is to promote the well-being of clients. In general, clients' interests are primary. However, social workers' responsibility to the larger society or specific legal obligations may on limited occasions supersede the loyalty owed clients, and clients should be so advised. (Examples include when a social worker is required by law to report that a client has abused a child or has threatened to harm self or others.)

1.02   Self-Determination
Social workers respect and promote the right of clients to self-determination and assist clients in their efforts to identify and clarify their goals. Social workers may limit clients' right to self-determination when, in the social

workers' professional judgment, clients' actions or potential actions pose a serious, foreseeable, and imminent risk to themselves or others.

1.03   Informed Consent

(a) Social workers should provide services to clients only in the context of a professional relationship based, when appropriate, on valid informed consent. Social workers should use clear and understandable language to inform clients of the purpose of the services, risks related to the services, limits to services because of the requirements of a third-party payer, relevant costs, reasonable alternatives, clients' right to refuse or withdraw consent, and the time frame covered by the consent. Social workers should provide clients with an opportunity to ask questions.

(b) In instances when clients are not literate or have difficulty understanding the primary language used in the practice setting, social workers should take steps to ensure clients' comprehension. This may include providing clients with a detailed verbal explanation or arranging for a qualified interpreter or translator whenever possible.

(c) In instances when clients lack the capacity to provide informed consent, social workers should protect clients' interests by seeking permission from an appropriate third party, informing clients consistent with the clients' level of understanding. In such instances social workers should seek to ensure that the third party acts in a manner consistent with clients' wishes and interests. Social workers should take reasonable steps to enhance such clients' ability to give informed consent.

(d) In instances when clients are receiving services involuntarily, social workers should provide information about the nature and extent of services and about the extent of clients' right to refuse service.

(e) Social workers who provide services via electronic media (such as computer, telephone, radio, and television) should inform recipients of the limitations and risks associated with such services.

(f) Social workers should obtain clients' informed consent before audiotaping or videotaping clients or permitting observation of services to clients by a third party.

1.04   Competence

(a) Social workers should provide services and represent themselves as competent only within the boundaries of their education, training, license, certification, consultation received, supervised experience, or other relevant professional experience.

(b) Social workers should provide services in substantive areas or use intervention techniques or approaches that are new to them only after engaging in appropriate study, training, consultation, and supervision from people who are competent in those interventions or techniques.

(c) When generally recognized standards do not exist with respect to an emerging area of practice, social workers should exercise careful judgment and take responsible steps (including appropriate education, research, training, consultation, and supervision) to ensure the competence of their work and to protect clients from harm.

1.05 Cultural Competence and Social Diversity
(a) Social workers should understand culture and its function in human behavior and society, recognizing the strengths that exist in all cultures.
(b) Social workers should have a knowledge base of their clients' cultures and be able to demonstrate competence in the provision of services that are sensitive to clients' cultures and to differences among people and cultural groups.
(c) Social workers should obtain education about and seek to understand the nature of social diversity and oppression with respect to race, ethnicity, national origin, color, sex, sexual orientation, age, marital status, political belief, religion, and mental or physical disability.

1.06 Conflicts of Interest
(a) Social workers should be alert to and avoid conflicts of interest that interfere with the exercise of professional discretion and impartial judgment. Social workers should inform clients when a real or potential conflict of interest arises and take reasonable steps to resolve the issue in a manner that makes the clients' interests primary and protects clients' interests to the greatest extent possible. In some cases, protecting clients' interests may require termination of the professional relationship with proper referral of the client.
(b) Social workers should not take unfair advantage of any professional relationship or exploit others to further their personal, religious, political, or business interests.
(c) Social workers should not engage in dual or multiple relationships with clients or former clients in which there is a risk of exploitation or potential harm to the client. In instances when dual or multiple relation-ships are unavoidable, social workers should take steps to protect clients and are responsible for setting clear, appropriate, and culturally sensitive boundaries. (Dual or multiple relationships occur when social workers relate to clients in more than one relationship, whether professional, social, or business. Dual or multiple relationships can occur simultaneously or consecutively.)
(d) When social workers provide services to two or more people who have a relationship with each other (for example, couples, family members), social workers should clarify with all parties which individuals will be con-sidered clients and the nature of social workers' professional obligations to the various individuals who are receiving services. Social workers who anticipate a conflict of interest among the individuals receiving services or who anticipate having to perform in potentially conflicting roles (for example, when a social worker is asked to testify in a child custody dispute or divorce proceedings involving clients) should clarify their role with the

parties involved and take appropriate action to minimize any conflict of interest.

1.07   Privacy and Confidentiality

(a) Social workers should respect clients' right to privacy. Social workers should not solicit private information from clients unless it is essential to providing services or conducting social work evaluation or research. Once private information is shared, standards of confidentiality apply.

(b) Social workers may disclose confidential information when appropriate with valid consent from a client or a person legally authorized to consent on behalf of a client.

(c) Social workers should protect the confidentiality of all information obtained in the course of professional service, except for compelling professional reasons. The general expectation that social workers will keep information confidential does not apply when disclosure is necessary to prevent serious, foreseeable, and imminent harm to a client or other identifiable person. In all instances, social workers should disclose the least amount of confidential information necessary to achieve the desired purpose; only information that is directly relevant to the purpose for which the disclosure is made should be revealed.

(d) Social workers should inform clients, to the extent possible, about the disclosure of confidential information and the potential consequences, when feasible before the disclosure is made. This applies whether social workers disclose confidential information on the basis of a legal requirement or client consent.

(e) Social workers should discuss with clients and other interested parties the nature of confidentiality and limitations of clients' right to confidentiality. Social workers should review with clients circumstances where confidential information may be requested and where disclosure of confidential information may be legally required. This discussion should occur as soon as possible in the social worker–client relationship and as needed throughout the course of the relationship.

(f) When social workers provide counseling services to families, couples, or groups, social workers should seek agreement among the parties involved concerning each individual's right to confidentiality and obligation to preserve the confidentiality of information shared by others. Social workers should inform participants in family, couples, or group counseling that social workers cannot guarantee that all participants will honor such agreements.

(g) Social workers should inform clients involved in family, couples, marital, or group counseling of the social worker's, employer's, and agency's policy concerning the social worker's disclosure of confidential information among the parties involved in the counseling.

(h) Social workers should not disclose confidential information to third-party payers unless clients have authorized such disclosure.

(i) Social workers should not discuss confidential information in any setting unless privacy can be ensured. Social workers should not discuss confidential information in public or semipublic areas such as hallways, waiting rooms, elevators, and restaurants.

(j) Social workers should protect the confidentiality of clients during legal proceedings to the extent permitted by law. When a court of law or other legally authorized body orders social workers to disclose confidential or privileged information without a client's consent and such disclosure could cause harm to the client, social workers should request that the court withdraw the order or limit the order as narrowly as possible or maintain the records under seal, unavailable for public inspection.

(k) Social workers should protect the confidentiality of clients when responding to requests from members of the media.

(l) Social workers should protect the confidentiality of clients' written and electronic records and other sensitive information. Social workers should take reasonable steps to ensure that clients' records are stored in a secure location and that clients' records are not available to others who are not authorized to have access.

(m) Social workers should take precautions to ensure and maintain the confidentiality of information transmitted to other parties through the use of computers, electronic mail, facsimile machines, telephones and telephone answering machines, and other electronic or computer technology. Disclosure of identifying information should be avoided whenever possible.

(n) Social workers should transfer or dispose of clients' records in a manner that protects clients' confidentiality and is consistent with state statutes governing records and social work licensure.

(o) Social workers should take reasonable precautions to protect client confidentiality in the event of the social worker's termination of practice, incapacitation, or death.

(p) Social workers should not disclose identifying information when discussing clients for teaching or training purposes unless the client has consented to disclosure of confidential information.

(q) Social workers should not disclose identifying information when discussing clients with consultants unless the client has consented to disclosure of confidential information or there is a compelling need for such disclosure.

(r) Social workers should protect the confidentiality of deceased clients consistent with the preceding standards.

1.08 Access to Records

(a) Social workers should provide clients with reasonable access to records concerning the clients. Social workers who are concerned that clients' access to their records could cause serious misunderstanding or harm to the client should provide assistance in interpreting the records and consultation with the client regarding the records. Social workers should limit clients' access to their records, or portions of their records, only in exceptional circumstances when there is compelling evidence that such access would cause serious harm to the client. Both clients' requests and the rationale for withholding some or all of the record should be documented in clients' files.

(b) When providing clients with access to their records, social workers should take steps to protect the confidentiality of other individuals identified or discussed in such records.

1.09 Sexual Relationships

(a) Social workers should under no circumstances engage in sexual activities or sexual contact with current clients, whether such contact is consensual or forced.

(b) Social workers should not engage in sexual activities or sexual contact with clients' relatives or other individuals with whom clients maintain a close personal relationship when there is a risk of exploitation or potential harm to the client. Sexual activity or sexual contact with clients' relatives or other individuals with whom clients maintain a personal relationship has the potential to be harmful to the client and may make it difficult for the social worker and client to maintain appropriate professional boundaries. Social workers—not their clients, their clients' relatives, or other individuals with whom the client maintains a personal relationship—assume the full burden for setting clear, appropriate, and culturally sensitive boundaries.

(c) Social workers should not engage in sexual activities or sexual contact with former clients because of the potential for harm to the client. If social workers engage in conduct contrary to this prohibition or claim that an exception to this prohibition is warranted because of extraordinary circumstances, it is social workers—not their clients—who assume the full burden of demonstrating that the former client has not been exploited, coerced, or manipulated, intentionally or unintentionally.

(d) Social workers should not provide clinical services to individuals with whom they have had a prior sexual relationship. Providing clinical services to a former sexual partner has the potential to be harmful to the individual and is likely to make it difficult for the social worker and individual to maintain appropriate professional boundaries.

1.10 Physical Contact

Social workers should not engage in physical contact with clients when there is a possibility of psychological harm to the client as a result of the contact (such as cradling or caressing clients). Social workers who engage in appropriate physical contact with clients are responsible for setting clear, appropriate, and culturally sensitive boundaries that govern such physical contact.

1.11 Sexual Harassment
Social workers should not sexually harass clients. Sexual harassment includes sexual advances, sexual solicitations, requests for sexual favors, and other verbal or physical conduct of a sexual nature.

1.12 Derogatory Language
Social workers should not use derogatory language in their written or verbal communications to or about clients. Social workers should use accurate and respectful language in all communications to and about clients.

1.13 Payment for Services
(a) When setting fees, social workers should ensure that the fees are fair, reasonable, and commensurate with the services performed. Consideration should be given to clients' ability to pay.
(b) Social workers should avoid accepting goods or services from clients as payment for professional services. Bartering arrangements, particularly involving services, create the potential for conflicts of interests, exploitation, and inappropriate boundaries in social workers' relationships with clients. Social workers should explore and may participate in bartering only in very limited circumstances when it can be demonstrated that such arrangements are an accepted practice among professionals in the local community, considered to be essential for the provision of services, negotiated without coercion, and entered into at the client's initiative and with the client's informed consent. Social workers who accept goods or services from clients as payment for professional services assume the full burden of demonstrating that this arrangement will not be detrimental to the client or the professional relationship.
(c) Social workers should not solicit a private fee or other remuneration for providing services to clients who are entitled to such available services through the social workers' employer or agency.

1.14 Clients Who Lack Decision-Making Capacity
When social workers act on behalf of clients who lack the capacity to make informed decisions, social workers should take reasonable steps to safeguard the interests and rights of those clients.

1.15 Interruption of Services
Social workers should make reasonable efforts to ensure continuity of services in the event that services are interrupted by factors such as unavailability, relocation, illness, disability, or death.

1.16 Termination of Services
(a) Social workers should terminate services to clients and professional relationships with them when such services and relationships are no longer required or no longer serve the clients' needs or interests.

(b) Social workers should take reasonable steps to avoid abandoning clients who are still in need of services. Social workers should withdraw services precipitously only under unusual circumstances, giving careful consideration to all factors in the situation and taking care to minimize possible adverse effects. Social workers should assist in making appropriate arrangements for continuation of services when necessary.

(c) Social workers in fee-for-service settings may terminate services to clients who are not paying an overdue balance if the financial contractual arrangements have been made clear to the client, if the client does not pose an imminent danger to self or others, and if the clinical and other consequences of the current nonpayment have been addressed and discussed with the client.

(d) Social workers should not terminate services to pursue a social, financial, or sexual relationship with a client.

(e) Social workers who anticipate the termination or interruption of services to clients should notify clients promptly and seek the transfer, referral, or continuation of services in relation to the clients' needs and preferences.

(f) Social workers who are leaving an employment setting should inform clients of appropriate options for the continuation of services and of the benefits and risks of the options.

2. SOCIAL WORKERS' ETHICAL RESPONSIBILITIES TO COLLEAGUES

2.01 Respect

(a) Social workers should treat colleagues with respect and should represent accurately and fairly the qualifications, views, and obligations of colleagues.

(b) Social workers should avoid unwarranted negative criticism of colleagues in communications with clients or with other professionals. Unwarranted negative criticism may include demeaning comments that refer to colleagues' level of competence or to individuals' attributes such as race, ethnicity, national origin, color, sex, sexual orientation, age, marital status, political belief, religion, and mental or physical disability.

(c) Social workers should cooperate with social work colleagues and with colleagues of other professions when such cooperation serves the well-being of clients.

2.02 Confidentiality

Social workers should respect confidential information shared by colleagues in the course of their professional relationships and transactions. Social workers should ensure that such colleagues understand social workers' obligation to respect confidentiality and any exceptions related to it.

2.03 Interdisciplinary Collaboration

(a) Social workers who are members of an interdisciplinary team should participate in and contribute to decisions that affect the well-being of clients by drawing on the perspectives, values, and experiences of the social work profession. Professional and ethical obligations of the interdisciplinary team as a whole and of its individual members should be clearly established.

(b) Social workers for whom a team decision raises ethical concerns should attempt to resolve the disagreement through appropriate channels. If the disagreement cannot be resolved, social workers should pursue other avenues to address their concerns consistent with client well-being.

2.04 Disputes Involving Colleagues

(a) Social workers should not take advantage of a dispute between a colleague and an employer to obtain a position or otherwise advance the social workers' own interests.

(b) Social workers should not exploit clients in disputes with colleagues or engage clients in any inappropriate discussion of conflicts between social workers and their colleagues.

2.05 Consultation

(a) Social workers should seek the advice and counsel of colleagues whenever such consultation is in the best interests of clients.

(b) Social workers should keep themselves informed about colleagues' areas of expertise and competencies. Social workers should seek consultation only from colleagues who have demonstrated knowledge, expertise, and competence related to the subject of the consultation.

(c) When consulting with colleagues about clients, social workers should disclose the least amount of information necessary to achieve the purposes of the consultation.

2.06 Referral for Services

(a) Social workers should refer clients to other professionals when the other professionals' specialized knowledge or expertise is needed to serve clients fully or when social workers believe that they are not being effective or making reasonable progress with clients and that additional service is required.

(b) Social workers who refer clients to other professionals should take appropriate steps to facilitate an orderly transfer of responsibility. Social workers who refer clients to other professionals should disclose, with clients' consent, all pertinent information to the new service providers.

(c) Social workers are prohibited from giving or receiving payment for a referral when no professional service is provided by the referring social worker.

2.07 Sexual Relationships

(a) Social workers who function as supervisors or educators should not engage in sexual activities or contact with supervisees, students, trainees, or other colleagues over whom they exercise professional authority.

(b) Social workers should avoid engaging in sexual relationships with colleagues when there is potential for a conflict of interest. Social workers who become involved in, or anticipate becoming involved in, a sexual relationship with a colleague have a duty to transfer professional responsibilities, when necessary, to avoid a conflict of interest.

2.08 Sexual Harassment
Social workers should not sexually harass supervisees, students, trainees, or colleagues. Sexual harassment includes sexual advances, sexual solicitation, requests for sexual favors, and other verbal or physical conduct of a sexual nature.

2.09 Impairment of Colleagues
(a) Social workers who have direct knowledge of a social work colleague's impairment that is due to personal problems, psychosocial distress, substance abuse, or mental health difficulties and that interferes with practice effectiveness, should consult with that colleague when feasible and assist the colleague in taking remedial action.
(b) Social workers who believe that a social work colleague's impairment interferes with practice effectiveness and that the colleague has not taken adequate steps to address the impairment should take action through appropriate channels established by employers, agencies, NASW, licensing and regulatory bodies, and other professional organizations.

2.10 Incompetence of Colleagues
(a) Social workers who have direct knowledge of a social work colleague's incompetence should consult with that colleague when feasible and assist the colleague in taking remedial action.
(b) Social workers who believe that a social work colleague is incompetent and has not taken adequate steps to address the incompetence should take action through appropriate channels established by employers, agencies, NASW, licensing and regulatory bodies, and other professional organizations.

2.11 Unethical Conduct of Colleagues
(a) Social workers should take adequate measures to discourage, prevent, expose, and correct the unethical conduct of colleagues.
(b) Social workers should be knowledgeable about established policies and procedures for handling concerns about colleagues' unethical behavior. Social workers should be familiar with national, state, and local procedures for handling ethics complaints. These include policies and procedures created by NASW, licensing and regulatory bodies, employers, agencies, and other professional organizations.
(c) Social workers who believe that a colleague has acted unethically should seek resolution by discussing their concerns with

the colleague when feasible and when such discussion is likely to be productive.

(d) When necessary, social workers who believe that a colleague has acted unethically should take action through appropriate formal channels (such as contacting a state licensing board or regulatory body, an NASW committee on inquiry, or other professional ethics committees).

(e) Social workers should defend and assist colleagues who are unjustly charged with unethical conduct.

3. SOCIAL WORKERS' ETHICAL RESPONSIBILITIES IN PRACTICE SETTINGS

3.01 Supervision and Consultation

(a) Social workers who provide supervision or consultation should have the necessary knowledge and skill to supervise or consult appropriately and should do so only within their areas of knowledge and competence.

(b) Social workers who provide supervision or consultation are responsible for setting clear, appropriate, and culturally sensitive boundaries.

(c) Social workers should not engage in any dual or multiple relationships with supervisees in which there is a risk of exploitation of or potential harm to the supervisee.

(d) Social workers who provide supervision should evaluate supervisees' performance in a manner that is fair and respectful.

3.02 Education and Training

(a) Social workers who function as educators, field instructors for students, or trainers should provide instruction only within their areas of knowledge and competence and should provide instruction based on the most current information and knowledge available in the profession.

(b) Social workers who function as educators or field instructors for students should evaluate students' performance in a manner that is fair and respectful.

(c) Social workers who function as educators or field instructors for students should take reasonable steps to ensure that clients are routinely informed when services are being provided by students.

(d) Social workers who function as educators or field instructors for students should not engage in any dual or multiple relationships with students in which there is a risk of exploitation or potential harm to the student. Social work educators and field instructors are responsible for setting clear, appropriate, and culturally sensitive boundaries.

3.03 Performance Evaluation

Social workers who have responsibility for evaluating the performance of others should fulfill such responsibility in a fair and considerate manner and on the basis of clearly stated criteria.

3.04 Client Records

(a) Social workers should take reasonable steps to ensure that documentation in records is accurate and reflects the services provided.

(b) Social workers should include sufficient and timely documentation of records to facilitate the delivery of services and to ensure continuity of services provided to clients in the future.

(c) Social workers' documentation should protect clients' privacy to the extent that is possible and appropriate and should include only information that is directly relevant to the delivery of services.

(d) Social workers should store records following the termination of services to ensure reasonable future access. Records should be maintained for the number of years required by state statutes or relevant contracts.

3.05 Billing

Social workers should establish and maintain billing practices that accurately reflect the nature and extent of services provided and that identify who provided the service in the practice setting.

3.06 Client Transfer

(a) When an individual who is receiving services from another agency or colleague contacts a social worker for services, the social worker should carefully consider the client's needs before agreeing to provide services. To minimize possible confusion and conflict, social workers should discuss with potential clients the nature of the clients' current relationship with other service providers and the implications, including possible benefits or risks, of entering into a relationship with a new service provider.

(b) If a new client has been served by another agency or colleague, social workers should discuss with the client whether consultation with the previous service provider is in the client's best interest.

3.07 Administration

(a) Social work administrators should advocate within and outside their agencies for adequate resources to meet clients' needs.

(b) Social workers should advocate for resource allocation procedures that are open and fair. When not all clients' needs can be met, an allocation procedure should be developed that is nondiscriminatory and based on appropriate and consistently applied principles.

(c) Social workers who are administrators should take reasonable steps to ensure that adequate agency or organizational resources are available to provide appropriate staff supervision.

(d) Social work administrators should take reasonable steps to ensure that the working environment for which they are responsible is consistent with and encourages compliance with the *NASW Code of Ethics*. Social work administrators should take reasonable steps to eliminate any conditions in their organizations that violate, interfere with, or discourage compliance with the *Code*.

3.08 Continuing Education and Staff Development

Social work administrators and supervisors should take reasonable steps to provide or arrange for continuing education and staff development for all staff for whom whey are responsible. Continuing education and staff development should address current knowledge and emerging developments related to social work practice and ethics.

3.09   Commitments to Employers
(a) Social workers generally should adhere to commitments made to employers and employing organizations.
(b) Social workers should work to improve employing agencies' policies and procedures and the efficiency and effectiveness of their services.
(c) Social workers should take reasonable steps to ensure that employers are aware of social workers' ethical obligations as set forth in the *NASW Code of Ethics* and of the implications of those obligations for social work practice.
(d) Social workers should not allow an employing organization's policies, procedures, regulations, or administrative orders to interfere with their ethical practice of social work. Social workers should take reasonable steps to ensure that their employing organizations' practices are consistent with the *NASW Code of Ethics*.
(e) Social workers should act to prevent and eliminate discrimination in the employing organization's work assignments and in its employment policies and practices.
(f) Social workers should accept employment or arrange student field placements only in organizations that exercise fair personnel practices.
(g) Social workers should be diligent stewards of the resources of their employing organizations, wisely conserving funds where appropriate and never misappropriating funds or using them for unintended purposes.

3.10   Labor–Management Disputes
(a) Social workers may engage in organized action, including the formation of and participation in labor unions, to improve services to clients and working conditions.
(b) The actions of social workers who are involved in labor–management disputes, job actions, or labor strikes should be guided by the profession's values, ethical principles, and ethical standards. Reasonable differences of opinion exist among social workers concerning their primary obligation as professionals during an actual or threatened labor strike or job action. Social workers should carefully examine relevant issues and their possible impact on clients before deciding on a course of action.

4.   SOCIAL WORKERS' ETHICAL RESPONSIBILITIES AS PROFESSIONALS

4.01   Competence
(a) Social workers should accept responsibility or employment only on the basis of existing competence or the intention to acquire the necessary competence.
(b) Social workers should strive to become and remain proficient in professional practice and the performance of professional functions.

Social workers should critically examine and keep current with emerging knowledge relevant to social work. Social workers should routinely review the professional literature and participate in continuing education relevant to social work practice and social work ethics.

(c) Social workers should base practice on recognized knowledge, including empirically based knowledge, relevant to social work and social work ethics.

4.02 Discrimination

Social workers should not practice, condone, facilitate, or collaborate with any form of discrimination on the basis of race, ethnicity, national origin, color, sex, sexual orientation, age, marital status, political belief, religion, or mental or physical disability.

4.03 Private Conduct

Social workers should not permit their private conduct to interfere with their ability to fulfill their professional responsibilities.

4.04 Dishonesty, Fraud, and Deception

Social workers should not participate in, condone, or be associated with dishonesty, fraud, or deception.

4.05 Impairment

(a) Social workers should not allow their own personal problems, psychosocial distress, legal problems, substance abuse, or mental health difficulties to interfere with their professional judgment and performance or to jeopardize the best interests of people for whom they have a professional responsibility.

(b) Social workers whose personal problems, psychosocial distress, legal problems, substance abuse, or mental health difficulties interfere with their professional judgment and performance should immediately seek consultation and take appropriate remedial action by seeking professional help, making adjustments in workload, terminating practice, or taking any other steps necessary to protect clients and others.

4.06 Misrepresentation

(a) Social workers should make clear distinctions between statements made and actions engaged in as a private individual and as a representative of the social work profession, a professional social work organization, or the social worker's employing agency.

(b) Social workers who speak on behalf of professional social work organizations should accurately represent the official and authorized positions of the organizations.

(c) Social workers should ensure that their representations to clients, agencies, and the public of professional qualifications, credentials, education, competence, affiliations, services provided, or results to be achieved are accurate. Social workers should claim only those relevant professional credentials they actually possess and take steps to correct any inaccuracies or misrepresentations of their credentials by others.

4.07 Solicitations
(a) Social workers should not engage in uninvited solicitation of potential clients who, because of their circumstances, are vulnerable to undue influence, manipulation, or coercion.
(b) Social workers should not engage in solicitation of testimonial endorsements (including solicitation of consent to use a client's prior statement as a testimonial endorsement) from current clients or from other people who, because of their particular circumstances, are vulnerable to undue influence.

4.08 Acknowledging Credit
(a) Social workers should take responsibility and credit, including authorship credit, only for work they have actually performed and to which they have contributed.
(b) Social workers should honestly acknowledge the work of and the contributions made by others.

5. SOCIAL WORKERS' ETHICAL RESPONSIBILITIES TO THE SOCIAL WORK PROFESSION

5.01 Integrity of the Profession
(a) Social workers should work toward the maintenance and promotion of high standards of practice.
(b) Social workers should uphold and advance the values, ethics, knowledge, and mission of the profession. Social workers should protect, enhance, and improve the integrity of the profession through appropriate study and research, active discussion, and responsible criticism of the profession.
(c) Social workers should contribute time and professional expertise to activities that promote respect for the value, integrity, and competence of the social work profession. These activities may include teaching, research, consultation, service, legislative testimony, presentations in the community, and participation in their professional organizations.
(d) Social workers should contribute to the knowledge base of social work and share with colleagues their knowledge related to practice, research, and ethics. Social workers should seek to contribute to the profession's literature and to share their knowledge at professional meetings and conferences.
(e) Social workers should act to prevent the unauthorized and unqualified practice of social work.

5.02 Evaluation and Research
(a) Social workers should monitor and evaluate policies, the implementation of programs, and practice interventions.
(b) Social workers should promote and facilitate evaluation and research to contribute to the development of knowledge.

(c) Social workers should critically examine and keep current with emerging knowledge relevant to social work and fully use evaluation and research evidence in their professional practice.

(d) Social workers engaged in evaluation or research should carefully consider possible consequences and should follow guidelines developed for the protection of evaluation and research participants. Appropriate institutional review boards should be consulted.

(e) Social workers engaged in evaluation or research should obtain voluntary and written informed consent from participants, when appropriate, without any implied or actual deprivation or penalty for refusal to participate; without undue inducement to participate; and with due regard for participants' well-being, privacy, and dignity. Informed consent should include information about the nature, extent, and duration of the participation requested and disclosure of the risks and benefits of participation in the research.

(f) When evaluation or research participants are incapable of giving informed consent, social workers should provide an appropriate explanation to the participants, obtain the participants' assent to the extent they are able, and obtain written consent from an appropriate proxy.

(g) Social workers should never design or conduct evaluation or research that does not use consent procedures, such as certain forms of naturalistic observation and archival research, unless rigorous and responsible review of the research has found it to be justified because of its prospective scientific, educational, or applied value and unless equally effective alternative procedures that do not involve waiver of consent are not feasible.

(h) Social workers should inform participants of their right to withdraw from evaluation and research at any time without penalty.

(i) Social workers should take appropriate steps to ensure that participants in evaluation and research have access to appropriate supportive services.

(j) Social workers engaged in evaluation or research should protect participants from unwarranted physical or mental distress, harm, danger, or deprivation.

(k) Social workers engaged in the evaluation of services should discuss collected information only for professional purposes and only with people professionally concerned with this information.

(l) Social workers engaged in evaluation or research should ensure the anonymity or confidentiality of participants and of the data obtained from them. Social workers should inform participants of any limits of confidentiality, the measures that will be taken to ensure confidentiality, and when any records containing research data will be destroyed.

(m) Social workers who report evaluation and research results should protect participants' confidentiality by omitting identifying information unless proper consent has been obtained authorizing disclosure.

(n) Social workers should report evaluation and research findings accurately. They should not fabricate or falsify results and should take steps to correct any errors later found in published data using standard publication methods.

(o) Social workers engaged in evaluation or research should be alert to and avoid conflicts of interest and dual relationships with participants, should inform participants when a real or potential conflict of interest arises, and should take steps to resolve the issue in a manner that makes participants' interests primary.

(p) Social workers should educate themselves, their students, and their colleagues about responsible research practices.

6. SOCIAL WORKERS' ETHICAL RESPONSIBILITIES TO THE BROADER SOCIETY

6.01 Social Welfare
Social workers should promote the general welfare of society, from local to global levels, and the development of people, their communities, and their environments. Social workers should advocate for living conditions conducive to the fulfillment of basic human needs and should promote social, economic, political, and cultural values and institutions that are compatible with the realization of social justice.

6.02 Public Participation
Social workers should facilitate informed participation by the public in shaping social policies and institutions.

6.03 Public Emergencies
Social workers should provide appropriate professional services in public emergencies to the greatest extent possible.

6.04 Social and Political Action
(a) Social workers should engage in social and political action that seeks to ensure that all people have equal access to the resources, employment, services, and opportunities they require to meet their basic human needs and to develop fully. Social workers should be aware of the impact of the political arena on practice and should advocate for changes in policy and legislation to improve social conditions in order to meet basic human needs and promote social justice.

(b) Social workers should act to expand choice and opportunity for all people, with special regard for vulnerable, disadvantaged, oppressed, and exploited people and groups.

(c) Social workers should promote conditions that encourage respect for cultural and social diversity within the United States and globally. Social workers should promote policies and practices that demonstrate respect for difference, support the expansion of cultural knowledge and resources, advocate for programs and institutions that demonstrate cultural competence, and promote policies that safeguard the rights of and confirm equity and social justice for all people.

(d) Social workers should act to prevent and eliminate domination of, exploitation of, and discrimination against any person, group, or class on the basis of race, ethnicity, national origin, color, sex, sexual orientation, age, marital status, political belief, religion, or mental or physical disability.

GLOSSARY

ableism A practice in which people without disabilities exclude and/or oppress those who do.

abuse The infliction of physical or emotional injury through beatings, corporal punishment, persistent ridicule and degradation, or sexual maltreatment.

accommodation Making environmental modifications in architecture, equipment, commercial structures, employment facilities, and so forth, to make them accessible to persons with disabilities.

ACSW This acronym designates membership in the Academy of Certified Social Workers. This certification is available to members of NASW who have an MSW degree, have 2 years of additional supervised social work practice, and have passed the ACSW examination.

active treatment Training, therapy, and services provided to people with disabilities to address any social, intellectual, or behavioral deficits and achieve the highest possible level of functioning.

activities of daily living (ADLs) Those daily activities such as dressing, eating, and bathing that a person must be able to perform to maintain independence.

acute care Health care facilities such as hospitals, outpatient clinics, and emergency rooms that provide immediate, short-term care.

acute traumatic stress Overwhelming physical and psychological distress that occurs during and immediately following disasters.

adjudication Decisions made by the juvenile court judge when a charge against a youth is reviewed. The court may decide to drop all charges, but if instead the youth is found guilty, sentencing follows.

adult stem cells Cells that can be taken from various parts of the human body for utilization in research related to advancing treatment for certain kinds of cancer, Alzheimer's disease, and other human organ malfunctions; bone marrow, the umbilical cord, or the placenta are currently the most common sources of adult stem cells.

advanced professional level The highest level in the NASW classification system of social work personnel. Possession of a doctoral degree, the Diplomate in Clinical Social Work, or other certification of advanced practice competence is required. A social worker at this level may conduct social welfare and program evaluation research, practice in highly specialized clinical areas, or teach in college or university social work education programs.

adversarial court A court setting in which there is opportunity for cross-examination by a prosecutor and a defense attorney. Although this procedure has been adopted in juvenile courts since the 1967 *Gault* decision, a much less formal court was envisioned when children's courts were first established.

advocacy Representing and defending the rights of individuals, groups, or communities through direct intervention.

advocate Someone who fights for the rights of others or fights to obtain needed resources.

affirmative action Procedures used to ensure opportunities such as employment, advancement, or admission to professional programs to people who have been discriminated against, such as women and members of minority groups.

ageism The practice of stereotyping people according to their age; frequently refers to prejudice against older adults.

Aid to Families with Dependent Children (AFDC) A government program authorized under the Social Security Act to provide income for dependent children of poor families and sometimes their parents. A means test and other eligibility criteria were required. Programs were administered by each state, and benefits varied by state. AFDC was eliminated in 1996.

alcohol abuse The recurrent use of alcohol to the extent that repeated use results in an inability to fulfill normal role functions, presents legal or social-interpersonal problems, or creates a hazard to self or others.

alcohol dependence The compulsive consumption of alcohol which, over a 12-month period, produces such symptoms as tolerance for alcohol, withdrawal symptoms, ineffective efforts to cut back on its use, and failure to change the drinking behavior despite evidence that it is causing serious difficulty.

alcoholism The compulsive use of alcohol characterized by evidence of abuse or dependence, resulting in some level of personal and social malfunctioning.

almshouse An institution or shelter, common before the 20th century, to house and feed destitute families and individuals.

alternative schools Schools that operate outside the regular public school system.

anxiety disorder The term used by the *DSM–IV* to describe a large number of anxiety-related states; these tend to be chronic or recurring experiences arising from unknown or unrecognized perceptions of danger or conflict.

assisted living Programs that provide accommodation for people who need help with activities of daily living such as dressing and bathing but do not need the high level of nursing care provided in a nursing home. Assisted living environments tend to provide comfortable, apartment-like units with private bedrooms and small kitchens. Many also provide restaurant-like dining rooms for those who no longer wish to prepare their own meals. Unfortunately, usually only persons with ample means can afford these accommodations.

asylum The protected legal status that is granted by the government on a case-by-case basis to persons who can substantiate serious, possibly life-threatening, political persecution. This status permits people to remain in the country for a specified period of time, but it may not afford them rights to citizenship.

basic professional level The entry-level classification for social work professionals developed by the NASW. The required credential is a baccalaureate degree from a college or university social work program that is accredited by the Council on Social Work Education.

behavioral health care A broad area of health care services often involving a combination of medication, various forms of psychotherapy or counseling, and patient education. Services are provided for persons with developmental disabilities, cognitive disorders, and mental illness or behavioral problems.

bilingual education Education provided in two languages, usually including the language spoken by the majority culture and one spoken by a minority group.

block grants An increasingly common system used by the federal government and sometimes by state governments in their budgetary processes. Through consolidating health, education, and social welfare budget items, the governmental decision makers can avoid earmarking funds for specific programs, thus retaining considerable control over the expenditure of such funds without submitting them to the political process.

broker A professional role in which the social worker uses the processes of referral and follow-up to ensure that a family or person obtains needed resources.

BSW A baccalaureate-level social worker.

capital punishment A sentence of execution; the death penalty.

capitated plans Coordinated and managed, prepaid health care plans in which clients are not permitted to receive services outside the plan.

career ladder The imaginary upward-directed steps that must be taken, as on a ladder, to advance in a profession or occupation. In some fields, career advancement is based on performance, while in others additional academic credentials must be completed.

case advocacy Advocacy strategies used to attain social and economic justice on an individual basis.

case management Coordinating all helping activities on behalf of a particular client or group of clients.

case manager In social work, the combination of counselor/enabler, advocate, and broker roles plus responsibility for planning, locating, securing, and monitoring services for people who are unable to do this because of ill health or frailties. Should not be confused with the term *case management* that is used by insurance companies and health care organizations to designate a process that seeks to restrict access to care.

cause advocacy Advocacy strategies used to attain social and economic justice for whole groups of people.

charity The donation of goods and services to those in need.

children at risk Children born to or residing with families suffering significant problems—such as poverty, disability or absence of a parent, and substance abuse—that tend to increase the probability of abuse or neglect.

client An individual, family, group, organization, or community who brings an issue to a social worker for professional assistance.

clinical social worker A social worker qualified to engage in psychotherapy; formerly referred to as a *psychiatric social worker.* The MSW is the minimal credential required. Private practice in clinical social work requires at least the ACSW.

cloning The procedure whereby the nucleus of a single cell is used to reproduce an entirely new organism with identically the same genetic makeup as the organism that provided the original parent cell.

codependent A relationship between two or more people to meet reciprocal needs, which often are unhealthy psychological or social needs. In alcoholism, codependents may be friends or family members who, sometimes unconsciously, subtly encourage or aid an alcoholic to persist in consuming alcoholic beverages.

co-insurance The percentage of an overall medical bill that a person must pay in addition to what his or her health insurance pays.

communicator The social work practice role involving clearly conveying information: verbally, nonverbally, and in writing.

community placement Arranging supervised care for children and adults with special needs in small-group and family-care homes rather than in large custodial institutions.

community-based corrections   Programs, such as probation and parole, that provide an alternative to incarceration.

community-service sentence   An alternative to imprisonment that requires work without pay in a human service organization for a specified period of time.

comparable worth   Also known as *pay equity*, this concept states that a person's wages or salary should be based solely on the value of the work performed rather than on other considerations. Recent comparable worth strategies have sought to correct the practice of paying low wages in occupations dominated by women.

conservative   A political perspective that is influenced by a desire to maintain the status quo and avoid change. The conservative view of human nature is pessimistic: that people will not work without economic insecurity and inequality to motivate them. Thus, conservatives tend to oppose government intervention in the economic market to aid poor people and, instead, may support tax breaks for the rich as incentives for investment.

continuum of care   Caregiving services that are coordinated to provide for a variety of client needs with minimal duplication or gaps in service.

correctional system   That part of the criminal justice system that seeks to change and improve the behaviors of convicted law offenders through imprisonment, parole, probation, and diverse community-based programs.

cost containment   Policies and procedures that seek to control rising costs. Health care organizations have been under considerable pressure from government and citizen groups to cut or at least stabilize health care costs.

counselor/enabler   The terms *counselor* and *enabler* tend to be used fairly interchangeably. The counselor or enabler role focuses on improving social functioning; affirming strengths; helping people deal with feelings; and coping with stress, crises, or changing life circumstances.

court   Public tribunals existing at the federal, state, and local levels that are mandated to deal with offenses against the nation or the state or with controversies among individuals.

cross-addiction   Addiction to two or more drugs. The combination of two or more drugs often results in more serious consequences than either drug would if used alone (this is known as *potentiation*).

cultural competency   The skill of communicating and working competently and effectively with people of contrasting cultures.

cultural conservatism   A political perspective in which single parenthood, sex outside of marriage, homosexuality, gay marriage, etc., are disapproved. Cultural conservatives favor government intervention restricting life choices such as these.

cultural pluralism   A model for understanding ethnic and racial diversity in which difference is expected and respected.

culture   The customs, habits, values, beliefs, skills, technology, arts, science, and religious and political behavior of a group of people in a specific time period.

decision tree   A schematic diagram resembling a tree, used to demonstrate the steps of decision making that people engage in when making career choices.

deductible   The amount of money an insured person must pay up front before an insurer will pay any portion of the remaining amount of the bill.

deinstitutionalization   A policy promoting the use of alternatives to institutional care. The process of releasing people who are dependent for their physical and mental care from residential-custodial facilities, presumably with the understanding that they no longer need such care or can receive it through community-based services.

delusions   Inaccurate but strongly held beliefs about reality, often with elements of persecution; delusional thinking suggests the presence of mental illness.

demographics   The study of population trends and statistics.

depressants   Drugs that depress the central nervous system.

detention   Placement in a juvenile jail facility.

detoxification   Medical treatment to remove or reduce dangerous levels of alcohol or drugs in the body and restore adequate physical and psychological functioning.

developmental disability   A condition that occurs as a result of disease, genetic disorder, or impaired growth pattern that is evidenced before adulthood. Such conditions include intellectual or cognitive disabilities, cerebral palsy, autism, orthopedic problems, hearing problems, epilepsy, traumatic brain injury, learning disabilities, fetal alcohol syndrome, cocaine exposed babies, and co-occurrence of disabilities.

Diagnostic and Statistical Manual of Mental Disorders (DSM)   A book (published by the American Psychological Association) providing comprehensive descriptions and classifications of various mental disorders, often used as a reference tool for diagnostic purposes. The fourth edition, revised, is often termed DSM–IV–TR.

diagnostic-related group (DRG) plan   A plan, introduced by the federal government in 1983, that provides payment to hospitals based not on the number of days or services provided but on a predetermined dollar amount per diagnosis. Hospitals that are able to discharge patients expeditiously, without using the prescribed dollar amount, are permitted to retain these funds. Criticism of this form of cost containment occurs when patients suffer complications resulting from premature hospital discharge.

Diplomate in Clinical Social Work A credential awarded by the NASW to social workers who have special qualifications for advanced clinical practice, including the MSW degree, 5 or more years of clinical practice, and successful completion of an advanced practice examination.

discharge planning A social service provided by health care social workers (although sometimes performed by other members of the health care team) focusing on postdischarge planning for a patient. Family members are extensively involved, along with the patient, if possible. Discharge planning is routinely utilized with Medicare patients but may involve patients of any age.

disposition Within the justice system, the carrying out of the court order; sentencing.

dual diagnosis The co-existence of mental illness and chemical dependence; this situation requires careful assessment and well-coordinated treatment between the substance abuse and mental health programs.

ecological perspective A way of perceiving and thinking that takes account of the totality or pattern of relations between organisms and their environments.

ecosystems perspective A perspective that maintains simultaneous focus on person and environment and is attentive to their interactions and adaptations.

educator A professional role involving teaching, coaching, or the provision of information.

egg donor programs The process by which the ovum (a human egg) of a donor is surgically implanted in another woman who is unable to produce her own ovum; the recipient may then be able to conceive a baby through sexual intercourse.

embryo transfer The surgical implantation in a woman of another woman's egg that has already been fertilized by her husband's, her partner's, or a donor's sperm.

embryonic stem cells The undifferentiated cells from a fertilized human egg that are considered to have great potential for research related to advancing treatment for certain kinds of cancer, Alzheimer's disease, and other human organ malfunctions; because these cells have the potential to differentiate and become a human embryo, there is considerable controversy over their use for research purposes.

emotional or behavioral disturbance A condition characterized by inappropriate or harmful behavior. In children, this diagnosis may lead to eligibility for special education services in a school setting. Eligible children demonstrate disturbed behavior in at least two or three environments: the school, the home, and/or the community.

empowerment A process through which people gain the strength to significantly alter the institutions that affect their lives.

English as a Second Language A special method of instruction in public schools used to teach children who do not speak English. The goal is to bring children up to grade level in English and into regular classrooms as soon as possible.

entitlement program A program providing services, goods, or money due to an individual by virtue of a specific status.

epidemiologists People who study the occurrence and distribution of disease within a population.

equal employment opportunity The right of all persons to work and advance on the basis of merit, ability, and potential.

Equal Rights Amendment (ERA) An amendment to the U.S. Constitution prohibiting discrimination on the basis of gender and providing equal protection of all constitutional rights to women. Although it was passed by Congress in 1972, the amendment failed to achieve the ratification of a sufficient number of states and hence did not become law.

ethics Behaviors prescribed by values.

ethnic group A population group that shares certain cultural characteristics that distinguish it from others, characteristics such as customs, values, language, and a common history.

ethnic sensitive approaches Strategies in social work practice that link knowledge of culture and ethnicity with understandings of social class differences; these approaches to practice reflect respect for and valuing of differences in people and communities.

ethnoconscious approach A theoretical construct that links ethnic sensitive approaches with empowerment tactics that build upon appreciation for the strengths already existing in ethnically diverse communities.

extrapyramidal symptoms The side effects of medication, generally psychotropic medication, that may include loss of balance, severe emotional reaction, nausea, or fatigue. Severe symptoms may require hospitalization and change of medication. The newer antipsychotic medications cause fewer negative side-effects than pharmaceuticals used in the past.

facilitator A professional role most frequently associated with group work; incorporates skills in convening groups, introducing members, promoting communication, and engaging members in planning, decision making, and goal attainment.

family care home A foster care home where unrelated persons are cared for in a family-like setting.

felony A serious criminal offense, generally punishable by a prison sentence. Murder, rape, and armed burglary are examples of felonies.

feminization of poverty   The increasing incidence of poverty among women, due to lower average wages than men and limited access to high-paying positions.

fetal alcohol syndrome (FAS)   A condition in which the fetus is damaged by the mother's alcoholism.

First Nations People   Also known as Native Americans, these were the first people to inhabit America.

food insecurity   A condition in which people do not have sufficient access to the quantity and quality of food needed to achieve a reasonably healthy life; the term used by the U. S. Department of Agriculture to denote insufficient access to enough food to sustain an active, healthy life.

forensic social work   An area of specialization in social work that is characterized by expertise in legal matters related to child welfare, juvenile offenses, divorce and child custody issues, and various areas of dispute negotiation.

frail elderly   Aged men and women who suffer from, or are vulnerable to, physical or emotional impairments and require services to ensure their well-being.

futurists   Persons who engage in serious, in-depth study of global trends to predict the nature of life in the future; they generally do not predict specific future events but instead provide alternate scenarios.

gay   A person whose sexual orientation is homosexual. This term usually refers to homosexual men.

generalist approach   An approach to social work practice drawn from social systems theory that uses an ecological perspective that is attentive to person and environment and their interactions. Generalist practice is based on research-guided knowledge and uses a planned change or problem-solving process to determine the level or levels of intervention—individual, family, group, organization, and/or community—appropriate to addressing the issues presented. It recognizes the profession's dual purpose and responsibility to influence social as well as individual change.

generalist social worker   A professional social worker who engages in a planned change process—discovering, utilizing, and making connections to arrive at unique, responsive solutions involving individual persons, families, groups, organizational systems, and communities. Generalist social workers respect and value human diversity. They identify and utilize the strengths existing in people and communities. Generalists seek to prevent as well as to resolve problems. Guided by the NASW Code of Ethics, generalists are committed to working for social justice.

genome   An organism's DNA, which contains the genetic instructions needed to develop and direct the activities of that organism; the DNA of humans exists within the 23 pairs of chromosomes within human cells.

genetic counseling   A service to help people translate scientific genetic findings into practical information. A genetic counselor works with individuals and/or families who may be at risk for an inherited disease or abnormal pregnancy, discussing the chances of having children who will be affected.

globalization   The interconnectedness of all regions and people of the world as a result of technological advances in communication and transportation; often thought of in terms of international commerce, this term also encompasses issues such as poverty and exploitation, religious movements, and terrorism.

guardian ad litem   A court-appointed attorney who represents the interests of a person considered incapable of managing his or her own affairs during litigation—for example, a minor child or an adult with mental retardation.

guilds   Fraternal organizations established during the Middle Ages to protect the interests of their members. Guilds were initiated by such occupational groups as craftspeople, artisans, and merchants. Over time, guilds began to provide death benefits to widows and orphans of deceased workers, and food and subsistence financial assistance to unemployed persons, thereby becoming the first form of employee assistance program. By the late Middle Ages, guilds had become a powerful political force in Europe.

habilitation   Services designed to help a person achieve and maintain his or her maximum level of functioning.

hallucinations   False perceptions of reality that result from mental illness, abuse of chemical substances, or damage to the brain. People who hallucinate sometimes respond to voices that they believe they hear; their behavior may be very inappropriate.

hallucinogens   A category of drugs that produce dream-like experiences and hallucinations involving visual and/or auditory effects. The effects of such drugs are not always predictable; they sometimes include gross distortions of reality, frightening visualizations, and mental confusion. Heavy use can intensify underlying mental disorders. LSD, mescaline, and psilocybin are hallucinogens. Some hallucinogens come from mushrooms and cacti, but increasingly they are manufactured in home laboratories and are sold on the black market.

harm reduction model   A variety of alternative but controversial substance abuse treatment programs that seek to limit the hazards (such as overdose deaths, spread of disease, car accidents) that can occur while people are using chemical substances. It is based on the philosophy that people can be withdrawn more safely, effectively, and humanely from chemicals if this process is done slowly.

health maintenance organizations (HMOs)   A type of insurance business that negotiates lower rates from doctors and other health care providers in return for providing these practitioners (and participating hospitals) with consumer volume. The consumers' use of the health care benefits outlined by the organization's promotional literature are usually closely monitored and restricted, often clashing with recommendations from the health care providers and the wishes of the consumers. Consumers may use only those health care providers with contracts with the health maintenance organization.

Health Security Act A proposal by the Clinton administration in 1991—ultimately withdrawn—to create a national health care system ensuring access to health care for all U.S. citizens.

hemodialysis A medical procedure in which the blood of a person with renal (kidney) disease is cleansed of toxins and impurities.

heterosexism The belief that people who are heterosexual are better in some way than people who are homosexual.

holistic The organic or functional relation between parts and wholes.

home health aide A person who is employed to provide personal care and assistance to an older adult or person with disabilities within that person's home. Generally, the level of care does not include skilled nursing care.

home health care Health care services, including social work, that are delivered to persons within their own homes.

homophobia The fear, dread, or hatred of people who are homosexual.

homosexual A person whose sexual orientation is toward members of that person's own gender.

hospice A program that cares for terminally ill people in an environment that is less restrictive than a hospital.

human diversity Normal variations among people reflecting differences in gender, genetics, ethnicity, cultural heritage, religious background, sexual orientation, age, and the like.

Human Genome Project A research effort coordinated by the U.S. Department of Energy and the National Institutes of Health to determine the makeup of human DNA. Half of the data produced are not yet sufficiently refined to be applied but will have implications for health care and disease prevention through genetic engineering.

human services worker A person who does not have traditional professional academic credentials but who, through experience, training, or education, provides helping services.

hypothermia Extreme loss of body temperature; this condition can result in death if not treated immediately.

immigrant Someone who moves to another country for the purpose of settling there permanently.

income maintenance Social welfare programs designed to provide individuals with enough money or goods and services to maintain a predetermined standard of living.

independent professional level A level of classification of professional social work personnel that requires 2 years of appropriately supervised practice following completion of a master's degree from a program accredited by the Council on Social Work Education. Generally, social workers who obtain the ACSW are classified at this level.

indeterminate sentence A sentence imposing imprisonment for a time period that is not fixed by the court but that instead is left to the discretion of prison authorities, who, however, must comply with broad parameters set by the court.

indoor relief A historically important form of social welfare benefit in which the recipient was required to reside in an institution (almshouse or workhouse) to remain eligible.

in-home services Services provided to assist families that have special needs to remain living together in their own homes. Services include homemaker aides, home health care, day care services, and the like.

insurance A program designed to protect people from the full consequences of the risks to which they are vulnerable, such as disability, death of a breadwinner, medical needs, and financial problems in old age. Covered individuals are required to make regular contributions to a fund set aside to pay for the claims of those insured.

intensive probation A specialized category of probation in which monitoring contacts occur very frequently and consistently, sometimes daily or at least several times a week. This form of probation is more cost effective than imprisonment. It provides a relatively high level of community protection when used with discretion.

intervention process A plan of action used by social workers to help create desired change involving several steps: engaging the client system, identifying and defining important issues, gathering and assessing data, identifying plans of action, contracting, implementing plans of action, evaluating outcomes, and terminating.

isms Prejudices common to large segments of society.

jail A correctional facility generally used for short sentences or for detaining persons while they await a court hearing. Prisons, by contrast, are used for lengthier sentences.

job coach An employment specialist in a supported employment setting.

juvenilization of poverty The increasing incidence of poverty among children, related to the feminization of poverty.

kinship care Care provided beyond the nuclear family to an inclusive family system that includes extended family members and also incorporates persons unrelated by blood or legal ties, that is, persons related instead by strong affectional ties.

lady almoner A forerunner of today's health care social worker. The original lady almoners were social workers from London's Charity Organization Society, who in the late 1800s interviewed patients at the Royal Free Hospital to determine which were eligible to receive free medical care. Lady almoners soon broadened their services to include advocacy, referral to other community resources, and patient education and counseling.

least restrictive environment The setting that provides the least interference with normal life patterns and yet provides the most important and most needed services to a given client.

legal minor A person too young to have the legal rights of an adult—usually a person under 18 years of age.

legal regulation The control of certain activities, such as professional conduct, by government rule and enforcement; governmental controls that limit access to use of professional titles such as *social worker* or *psychologist*.

legislative advocacy The process of lobbying for more responsive legislation.

lesbian A female whose sexual orientation is toward other females.

less eligibility The concept, based on the belief that pauperism is voluntary, that the condition of a poor person receiving "relief" should be worse than the condition of the poorest self-supporting worker in the community.

levels of intervention The systems with which social workers intervene or work: individual, family, group, organization, and community.

liberal or progressive A political perspective that supports government intervention in the economic market to help "level the playing field" for disadvantaged groups such as women or minorities. Persons of this perspective tend to believe that people are inherently good, are naturally industrious, and will work hard if conditions are humane. Liberals or progressives believe that it is conditions in the social environment that keep many poor people from achieving a decent standard of living.

lifestyle An individual's manner of living, which includes his or her choice of living single or coupled, orientation toward homosexual or heterosexual relationships, and the like.

long-term care Any combination of nursing, personal care, volunteer, and social services provided intermittently or on a sustained basis over a span of time to help persons with chronic illness or disability to maintain maximum quality of life.

mainstreaming In the context of educational policy, the term refers to a philosophy and practice in which children with disabilities—or children who are different from the majority in some special characteristic such as native language—should be educated in regular classrooms as much as possible.

mandatory client Also known as an *involuntary client*, this is a person who does not seek out services voluntarily but instead is required by an authority (e.g., a court) to obtain specified services. Persons on probation or parole are examples of mandatory clients.

means test Evaluation of a client's financial resources, using the result as the criterion to determine eligibility to receive a benefit.

Medicaid Title XIX of the Social Security Act, Medicaid is a federal program designed to provide health care for poor people of all ages.

medically indigent Persons who lack insurance coverage or other financial resources to cover the cost of medical treatment or hospitalization.

Medicare Title XVIII of the Social Security Act, Medicare is a federal program designed to provide health care for the elderly and for long-term disabled persons. Recent legislation has decreased Medicare coverage substantially, and older people especially are often surprised to learn how few hospital and nursing home bills are actually covered by Medicare.

mental disorder Impaired or dysfunctional cognitive or behavioral patterns that occur in individuals and that cause suffering, pain, or some level of disability.

Mental Health Bill of Rights Legislation that seeks to ensure consumers' rights to information, to a reasonable choice of providers and to emergency services, to participate in treatment decisions, to receive respectful care, and to appeal decisions of the mental health care plan.

Mental Health Parity Act of 2007 A U.S. Senate bill introduced in 2007 that sought to prohibit group health insurance corporations from initiating health care plans that were more restrictive of mental health or substance abuse coverage than their plans for physical health coverage.

minority group A group that has less power than the majority group so that members are relatively vulnerable to poverty and discrimination.

misdemeanor An offense that is considered to be relatively minor by the judicial system. Misdemeanors are generally punishable by fines, probation, or a short jail sentence; misdemeanors are contrasted with felonies, which are more serious offenses.

mood disorder   A commonly cited diagnostic category of DSM–IV that encompasses a broad range of dysfunctions of mood. The category includes very serious as well as relatively minimal dysfunctions such as depressive (low mood) and manic (abnormally high mood) states and bipolar states in which both depression and mania occur.

MSW   A social worker at the master's degree level of the profession.

multidisciplinary team (M-team)   A small, organized group of persons—each trained in different professional disciplines (e.g., teaching, social work, psychology) and each possessing her or his own skills and orientations—working together to achieve a common goal.

mutual aid   Reciprocal aid among members of a family, ethnic group, organization, or some such community.

National Alliance on Mental Illness (NAMI)   A mental health services consumer organization founded in 1979 to support research, education, social policy, and political activity that will enhance access to community-based mental health services.

national health insurance   A system that provides participation in comprehensive health care insurance for all citizens. The United States remains one of the few industrialized countries that has no national health insurance program.

national health service   A nation's ownership and administration of health care facilities and services that provide the complete range of health care to all citizens.

neglect   The failure of responsible persons to provide for the appropriate care of a dependent, including inadequate nutrition, improper supervision, and deficient health care.

neoconservative   A political perspective that arose in the mid-1970s that opposed government welfare programs for the poor and advocated ending entitlements to assistance under the Social Security Act for poor children and their parents. People of this perspective believe that public social welfare programs should be privatized.

neoliberal   Former liberals who decided that their best hope for election was to express more favorable attitudes toward big business and more caution about the role of big government.

nondiscrimination   Practices that avoid discrimination against minorities; laws that ban bias and require equal access to resources such as education and jobs.

normalization   Making available to persons with disabilities those conditions of everyday life that are as close as possible to the norms and patterns of mainstream society.

norms   Rules of behavior, both formal and informal, and expectations held collectively by a culture, group, organization, or society.

organ replacement   The removal of an organ or tissue from one body or part of a body followed by insertion of organ tissue from another body or body part.

organizer   A professional role most frequently associated with community intervention; incorporates skills in bringing together representatives of different groups or organizations to seek improvement in resources or to advance social justice. This role may also be used to effect policy changes within a social agency.

osteoporosis   A bone-thinning disease most commonly found in women over 50 years of age. Osteoporosis is a frequent cause of fractures in elderly persons.

outdoor relief   A form of welfare relief providing assistance outside of residential institutions (e.g., in one's home).

out-of-home services   Services provided to assist needy children and their families when families are no longer able to care for their children in the home. Such services include foster care (both short-term and long-term), institutional care, and the like.

palliative care   An active form of treatment to relieve pain and provide the best quality of life possible to persons who are terminally ill.

parole   The release of a prisoner by corrections officials before completion of the full sentence; supervision by persons designated by the court (often social workers) is generally required until the full sentence has been completed. Any violation of the terms of the parole agreement can result in return to prison for the remainder of the sentence (revocation).

pay equity   The policies and procedures used to ensure that sex and race discrimination are eliminated from wage-setting systems used by employers.

pension   A payment made regularly to an individual because of retirement, age, loss, or incapacitating injury or to dependents in the event of the holder's death.

pension plan   A plan or program designed to provide financial support for older adults who have retired from their former occupations.

permanency placement   Placement of children who, for whatever reason, cannot live with their biological parents, in permanent adoptive homes.

personal care home   A residential facility providing custodial care and supportive services such as assistance with meals, bathing, and dressing for elderly people. Nursing care provisions are limited or absent.

personality disorders   Deeply ingrained, inflexible, maladaptive patterns of relating to others that result in significant social impairment.

physical trauma   A wound caused by physical injuries. Fights, accidents, and rape cause physical trauma and may be accompanied by psychological pain.

planned change process Another term for intervention process; see intervention process.

police social work The practice of social work within police departments. Direct services are provided to persons accused of crime and to family members; some services may also be provided to victims and witnesses of crime and to police personnel to help them deal with crises, trauma, and stress. Community education and crime prevention work are frequently an additional responsibility.

policy practice Social work practice that involves participating in the political system to influence the direction and substance of social welfare policy to bring about systems change on behalf of people who are marginalized and disadvantaged.

political asylum A protected legal status granted by the U.S. government on a case-by-case basis to persons who can demonstrate persecution.

populations at risk Population groups at greater than average statistical risk of being poor or discriminated against socially or in job markets through no fault of their own. Children, women, the elderly, and members of racial and ethnic minority groups are examples of populations at risk.

posttraumatic stress disorder (PTSD) Acute and overwhelming physical and psychological distress lasting for a prolonged time (beyond 1 month) following a traumatic life event. Unless it is treated, PTSD may impair children as well as adults, making it nearly impossible for them to study, work, sustain parenting responsibilities, or even maintain self-care.

potentiation A dramatically increased potential for serious, even life-threatening hazards to health resulting from the combination of two or more chemical substances. Cross-addiction to tranquilizers and alcohol, for example, can result in loss of consciousness and body shutdown, requiring emergency medical attention.

poverty The lack of resources to achieve a reasonably comfortable standard of living. When poverty is extreme, basic needs such as food and shelter are not met.

poverty line The amount of income determined to be the absolute minimum necessary to meet basic survival needs such as food and shelter. It is determined by the cost of food (as established by the U.S. Department of Agriculture) multiplied by three.

poverty turnover rate The rate produced by determining the number of families rising out of poverty in a given year and the number of families replacing them by falling below the poverty line.

power of attorney A written statement legally authorizing another person to act in one's behalf; the term may also refer to the person who has been legally authorized to act in one's behalf.

practice concentration A concentration or focus (usually with advanced training) on a specific practice method, field of practice, or social problem area; characteristic of social workers with the MSW degree.

preferred practices Protocols or directives that set in place the specific practice to be followed for designated client problems; usually seen in short-term, highly focused interventions in mental health.

preferred provider organization (PPO) A model of managed health care in which patients receive relatively low-cost care through a network of hospitals, doctors, and other health care providers linked by contractual agreements. Patients may elect to receive care outside the PPO, but they will pay a higher proportion of the cost.

prejudice Beliefs or opinions formed before the facts are known.

presentence investigation An investigation—ordered by the court before sentencing—into the life situation of a person convicted of a crime. Presentence investigations are conducted by probation officers; they are comprehensive and include information concerning the offender's social history, home and work environments, educational and employment experiences, and physical or mental health problems. This report typically concludes with a recommendation to the judge regarding sentencing.

primary alcoholism A condition in which the abuse of alcohol is not a function of another psychiatric disorder nor the result of a life crisis that preceded the heavy drinking.

primary social work setting A setting that has a fundamental social work purpose (such as enhancing social functioning) and in which the majority of the staff are social workers.

prison A correctional facility where persons convicted of a crime are confined. Generally, prisons house persons whose sentences exceed 1 year, whereas jails hold persons who are awaiting trial or who have been sentenced for short durations.

private practice In social work, the autonomous provision of professional services by a licensed/qualified social worker who assumes responsibility for the nature and quality of the services provided to the client in exchange for direct payment or third-party reimbursement.

private trouble A trouble exclusively affecting a specific individual or family.

privatization The act of replacing government systems designed to meet the social welfare needs of people with private sector services. In the United States growth of for-profit human service organizations has resulted from social policies that support privatization.

probation   Suspension of a jail or prison sentence with an accompanying agreement that the offender will abide by all requirements of a court-appointed agent (often a social worker); violation of any terms of the probation agreement can result in return to court or incarceration.

problem-solving process   Another, more traditional term for intervention process; see *planned change process* or *intervention process*.

professional roles   The behaviors that are expected from persons who are sanctioned by society through education and legal certification to provide service in a specific profession.

progressive   Favoring, working for, or characterized by progress or improvement, as through political or social reform.

prospective payment system (PPS)   A system for paying hospitals a fixed amount regardless of the length of stay or the actual expense of caring for the patient.

protective services   Services—often including social, medical, legal, residential, and custodial care—that are provided to children whose caregivers are not providing for their needs.

psychological trauma   Shock or emotional pain that can have lasting effects if not treated promptly. Survivors of war or war-like life situations, automobile accidents, and rape are examples of persons who may need assistance with psychological trauma.

psychosis   A group of major mental disorders, either organic or psychological in origin, that includes impaired thinking, perception, and emotional response as well as regressive behavior and possibly delusions and hallucinations.

psychotherapy   An advanced form of counseling provided by certified professionals, including social workers; used to resolve or ameliorate mental health or psychosocial functioning problems.

psychotropic medications   Drugs prescribed by doctors to influence a patient's mental functioning, mood, or behavior. The symptoms of some forms of mental illness can now be well controlled by the use of psychotropic medications.

public assistance   A system of financial aid programs funded out of general tax revenues; people may receive benefits even if they have never paid any taxes. To qualify, one must fit a specific category (e.g., "elderly," "blind," "disabled") and must also pass a means test.

public issue   An issue, such as poverty, that affects so many people in a society that people come to perceive the problem as beyond the "fault" of each affected individual. For example, during the Great Depression of the 1930s, the perception of poverty as a public issue rather than as just a private trouble led to the creation of many national public works programs to provide jobs for people out of work.

Qualified Clinical Social Worker (QCSW)   A credential acquired through the NASW that requires 2 years of full-time or 3,000 hours of part-time post-MSW or postdoctoral clinical social work practice. Additional requirements include evidence of ongoing continuing education.

qualitative research   Systematic research based on data gathered from interviews and field study with individuals, families, groups, organizations, or communities.

quantitative research   Systematic research based on statistical, numerical data gathering and analysis to arrive at valid, reliable conclusions.

racial group   A population with distinct physical or biological characteristics that distinguish it from other populations.

racial profiling   Police targeting of someone for investigation or arrest on the basis of that person's race, national origin, or ethnicity.

racism   The belief that one race is superior to others.

radical   A political perspective that, like the liberal, tends to believe that people are inherently good and naturally industrious. However, radicals do not believe that social justice can be achieved under a capitalist system but, rather, that society must be entirely restructured to redistribute wealth and power among all the people.

reactive alcoholism   A condition in which heavy use of alcohol occurs following a severe life crisis. Treatment should focus on the resolution of the crisis rather than on the abuse of alcohol.

recidivism   The tendency of criminal offenders to relapse to former behavior, thus bringing them again to the attention of the courts and probably to reincarceration. The term is sometimes also used to describe the rehospitalization of chronically mentally ill persons or to describe any return to institutional care.

refugees   People who leave their country out of a fear of persecution based on religion, political affiliation, race, nationality, or membership in a particular group; they may be granted safety and legal approval to remain, at least temporarily, by another country.

rehabilitation   Restoring someone to a healthy and useful capacity or to as satisfactory a condition as possible.

religion   A system of beliefs such as the existence of a divine or superhuman power that must be worshipped and obeyed using certain rituals or patterns of conduct.

resident council   Commonly found in nursing homes but also found in other institutional or residential settings, this is a group that represents all the residents; it engages in negotiation with administration to ensure that residents' needs are met.

resilience   A person's ability to recover his or her strength and good spirits after challenges and setbacks.

respite care   Temporary personal care or short-term board away from home for people with disabilities, the frail elderly, or the terminally ill; this provides temporary rest and relief for their family caregivers.

restitution   The act of restoring to a person something that was stolen, removed, damaged, or destroyed. An enlightened approach, most often seen in juvenile courts, is a restitution program in which the offender is required to repay or replace items stolen or damaged (such as a bicycle, an automobile, or a VCR). Face-to-face contact with the victim of the offense often helps the offender understand the depth of hurt caused by her or his actions. Restitution programs are often administered or staffed by social workers.

revocation   A term used in corrections to describe the act of returning a paroled person to prison, thereby canceling parole. The right to revoke is granted to the parole agent by the legal system; revocation is used when there has been a serious violation or repeated less serious violations of the parole contract.

risk rating   A system used in corrections that assesses and rates the risk of recidivism to determine the amount and frequency of supervision needed by a client.

sanction   This term has two quite different meanings: (1) the acknowledgment or permission by an established authority for an organization or entity to carry forward a plan or an action; thus, it can be said that social work is sanctioned by society; (2) a response that penalizes an individual for failure to conform to established policies or procedures; NASW, for example, can sanction a member who is found to have violated the Code of Ethics.

sandwich generation   Adults who provide unpaid caregiving to older adults, usually parents or other relatives, who must also provide care for their own children. Many members of the sandwich generation also must hold paying jobs to make ends meet.

schizophrenia   A serious form of mental disease in which the person has lost the capacity to function normally; disturbances in communication, perception, and affect are commonly associated with schizophrenia, although the disease has several different forms.

School Social Work Specialist (SSWS)   A credential acquired through the NASW requiring completion of a minimum of 2 years of supervised school social work practice, post-MSW or postdoctoral degree, satisfactory completion of a specialized test, and submission of professional evaluations and references, as well as evidence of continuing education.

secondary alcoholism   A condition in which abuse of alcohol is related to a preceding and underlying psychiatric disorder, often depression. The primary mental illness must become the major focus of treatment.

secondary social work setting   A setting in which social work services support the primary purpose of the setting. For example, the primary purpose of a school system is educational; the primary professionals who carry out that purpose are teachers.

self-determination   An ethical principle of the social work profession which recognizes the right and need of clients to make their own choices and decisions.

sexism   The belief that one gender is superior to the other, usually that males are superior to females.

sexual orientation   An individual's erotic orientation toward heterosexual, homosexual, or bisexual behavior.

Sheltered English Immersion (SEI)   An educational model in which children who do not speak English are placed in classrooms where English only is spoken. Their teachers have training in working with non-English-speaking students.

sheltered workshop   A work environment that hires people with disabilities and provides special services enabling persons with handicaps to perform their work successfully.

shock probation   The practice of brief incarceration at the beginning of probation to frighten the offender into complying with the terms of the probation contract.

single-payer system   A health insurance system where one government-authorized insurance plan pays all hospital and other health care expenses directly; the Canadian system is an example.

social and economic justice   Fairness among people so that members of diverse population groups have an equal chance to achieve a reasonably comfortable standard of living.

social-emotional learning (SEL)   In the school setting, SEL involves recognizing emotions and using a variety of methods to regulate responses to stress such as contemplative practice or meditation and breathing exercises.

social insurance   Government programs to protect citizens from the full consequences of the risks to which they are vulnerable, such as unemployment, disability, death of a breadwinner, and catastrophic medical care needs. Typically, the government requires covered individuals to make regular contributions to a fund that, theoretically, is set aside and used to reimburse those who are covered by the plan for any losses they suffer as a result of covered risks.

social justice   An ideal condition in which all members of society have the same basic rights, protections, opportunities, obligations, and social benefits.

social service aide   An employee of a social agency hired not on the basis of academic credentials but for her or his unique life experiences. Social service aides may provide translation services, interpreting not only language but also cultural beliefs and practices. Aides typically assist clients with the completion of insurance and other complicated forms, provide other clerical duties, transport clients, and engage in community outreach efforts.

social service technician A paraprofessional employee of a social service agency who has completed a 2-year associate degree in community or human services work or who has completed a baccalaureate degree in a major other than social work. The technician assists clients in the completion of complex forms, helps with intake procedures, conducts noncomplex interviews, shepherds frail or disabled clients through financial aid applications, and processes some of the paperwork required by the agency.

social welfare A nation's system of programs, benefits, and services that help people meet those social, economic, educational, and health needs fundamental to the maintenance of society.

social work The major profession that delivers social services in governmental and private organizations throughout the world; persons educated for practice in this profession help people prevent or resolve problems in psychosocial functioning, achieve life-enhancing goals, and create a just society.

special education Educational services and programs designed to meet the needs of children with special needs, such as physical disabilities, learning disabilities, emotional or behavioral disturbances, speech and language problems, or pregnancy.

spirituality A personal quality or characteristic pertaining to the search for meaning. Spirituality may or may not involve religious practices or beliefs.

staffings Staff meetings, typically conducted on a regular basis, to assess, develop treatment plans, or monitor the care of clients.

stimulants Drugs that produce energy, increase alertness, and provide a sense of strength and well-being; one example is amphetamines.

strengths perspective A viewpoint encouraging social workers to focus on finding and highlighting client strengths as opposed to problems and limitations.

subacute center Health care facilities that provide intensive medical services for people who do not need to remain in the hospital but also may not need, or hopefully can avoid, long-term care.

subculture A smaller variant of a particular culture.

subpoena An order to appear in court on a specified date; failure to appear may result in a penalty.

subsidy Monetary aid to assist in the purchase of needed goods or services, usually provided by governmental

bodies to private organizations, programs, or persons according to specific eligibility guidelines.

supported employment A vocational option providing individualized supports to people with disabilities so that they can achieve their goals in the workplace.

surrogate parents Women who agree to be impregnated and to release the baby that they deliver to the person(s) who contracted with them for this purpose.

system A whole consisting of interacting parts such that a change in one part affects all others.

tax-sheltered annuity A government program with the purpose of assisting workers to have a source of income in retirement. Workers may have money deducted from their paychecks during their working years and deposited, tax-free, in a special account. Some employers match employee contributions. Money may be withdrawn in retirement (and in other special circumstances such as medical emergency) and is taxed at the time of withdrawal. Tax-sheltered annuity programs are becoming more important as retirement benefits from private employers become increasingly scarce.

Temporary Assistance for Needy Families (TANF) A program authorized by the federal government under the Personal Responsibility and Work Opportunity Act of 1996. States are allowed but not required to assist poor parents for up to 5 years in a parent's lifetime. Parents are required to work after 2 years of assistance.

terrorism The systematic use of fear, intimidation, and disruption of social systems, usually by politically motivated or criminal groups, to gain publicity or concessions. This is a violent form of social activism.

trafficking The use of physical or psychological coercion in transporting persons, often for financial gain, for commercial or sexual labor, or for the illegal adoption of children.

truancy The failure to attend school as required by law.

underemployment Employment at or near minimum wage, often part-time and without health insurance or other benefits.

universal coverage The assurance of health care for all people in need.

universal health care A government's policies and provisions that ensure health care benefits for all citizens at the same rate and without regard to their economic status.

universal programs Social welfare programs that are available to everyone in a nation who falls into a defined category; these programs are not based on financial eligibility.

vagrants   People who wander from place to place with no permanent home or job.

values   Preferred ways of believing.

voucher   A coupon or stamp worth a certain amount of money only if spent on specified services or products.

work ethic   A societal attitude that work is good and laziness is irresponsible.

workfare   A term used to describe social policies that require poor people to work to receive financial assistance.

workhouse   An "indoor relief" form of assistance common during the 18th century, in which poor people who received help had to live and work in special facilities.

working poor   Persons whose income from employment is not sufficient to meet their survival needs.

worldview   A comprehensive conception of the world especially from a specific standpoint (e.g., as shaped by a particular culture).

zero tolerance   A government policy requiring schools to expel any student caught carrying a weapon. Some schools have adopted zero tolerance policies for other types of infractions as well.

REFERENCES

CHAPTER 1

American Association for Marriage and Family Therapy. (2002). *FAQs on MFTs*. Retrieved January 4, 2007, from http://www.aamft.org/faqs/index_nm.asp

Association of Social Work Boards. (2006). *Licensing requirements*. Retrieved January 2, 2007, from http://www.aswb.org/lic_reqs.html

Barker, R. L. (2003). *The social work dictionary* (5th ed.). Washington, DC: NASW Press.

Biggerstaff, M. A. (1995). Licensing, regulation, and certification. In *Encyclopedia of social work* (19th ed., vol. 2, pp. 1616–1624). Washington, DC: NASW Press.

Buchan, V., Hull, G. H., Pike, C., Rodenhiser, R., Rogers, J., & Smith, M. (2006). BEAP total reports. *BPD Baccalaureate Education Assessment Project*. Retrieved January 6, 2007, from http://beap.socwk.utah.edu

Bureau of Labor Statistics, U.S. Department of Labor. (2006a). *Occupational outlook handbook: 2006–2007 edition, Psychologists*. Retrieved December 28, 2006, from http://www.bls.gov/oco/ocos056.htm

Bureau of Labor Statistics, U.S. Department of Labor. (2006b). *Occupational outlook handbook: 2006–2007 edition, Social Workers*. Retrieved August 16, 2006, from http://www.bls.gov/oco/ocos060.htm

Bureau of Labor Statistics, U.S. Department of Labor. (2006c). *Occupational outlook handbook: 2006–2007 edition, Tomorrow's jobs*. Retrieved November 25, 2007, from http://www.bls.gov/oco/pdf/oco2003.pdf

Community Action. (2005, May 23). *UK has social worker shortage, recruitment campaigns failing*. Retrieved December 28, 2006, from http://www.findarticles.com/p/articles/mi_mOLVZ/is_9_20/ai_n13800696

Cook, M. J. (2001, December 7). *Community psychology. . .What is it?* Retrieved January 4, 2007, from http://www.communitypsychology.net/cmmtypsych.shtml

Council on Social Work Education. (2001). *Council on Social Work Education: Educational policy and accreditation standards* (rev. October 2004). Alexandria, VA: Council on Social Work Education.

Council on Social Work Education. (2006, April). *Directory of accredited social work degree programs*. Retrieved January 3, 2007, from: http://www.cswe.org/0nav.htm

Farr, J. M., & Ludden, L. L. (2000). *Enhanced occupational outlook handbook* (3rd ed.). Indianapolis, IN: JIST Publishing.

Harvey, D. (2001). Social worker shortage: Illusion or reality? *Social Worker Today, 1* (7), 10–12.

Hecker, D. E. (2005, November) Employment outlook: 2004–14; Occupational employment projections to 2014. *Monthly Labor Review, 128*(11), 70–101.

International Federation of Social Workers. (2001, November 11). *Aims; General Infos*. Retrieved January 3, 2007, from http://www.ifsw.org

Kirst-Ashman, K. K., & Hull, G. H. (2002). *Understanding generalist practice* (3rd ed.). Pacific Grove, CA: Brooks/Cole.

Lee, N. (2006, May 16). *Social worker shortage slams state*. Retrieved December 28, 2006, from KGMB 9Local News website: http://kgmb/display.cfm?storyID=8183

Miley, K. K., O'Melia, M., & DuBois, B. (2007). *Generalist social work practice: An empowering approach* (5th ed.). Boston: Pearson/Allyn & Bacon.

Mizrahi, T., & Clark, E. J. (2003). *Social work speaks: National Association of Social Workers policy statements 2003–2006* (6th ed.). Washington, DC: NASW Press.

Morales, A. T., & Sheafor, B. W. (2002). *The many faces of social workers*. Boston: Allyn & Bacon.

Nadelhaft, A., & Rene, D. (2006, March 8). *Landmark study warns of impending labor force shortages for social work profession*. [Press release]. Washington, DC: National Association of Social Workers.

National Association of Black Social Workers (NABSW). (n.d.). *Code of Ethics. History*. Retrieved January 3, 2007, from http://www.nabsw.org

National Association of Puerto Rican & Hispanic Social Workers. (2007). *Membership; Mission*. Retrieved January 3, 2007, from http://www.naprhsw.org

National Association of Social Workers. (n.d.). *About NASW*. Retrieved January 2, 2007, from https://www.socialworkers.org/pressroom/features/ general/nasw.asp

National Association of Social Workers. (1996). *NASW Code of Ethics* (rev. 1999). Washington, DC: NASW Press.

National Association of Social Workers. (2006, March 8). *Landmark study warns of impending labor force shortages for social work profession*. Washington, D.C.: National Association of Social Workers.

National Association of Social Workers. (2007). *NASW Credentialing Center*. Retrieved January 11, 2007, from www.socialworkers.org/credentials/default.asp

News 24. (2006, March 28). *Social worker shortage critical.* Retrieved December 28, 2006, from the News 24.com website: http://www.news24.com/News24/ South_Africa/ News/0,2–7–1442_1906277,00.html

O'Neill, J. V. (2001). Chapters play helping role. *NASW News, 46*(10), 14.

Popple, P. R. (1995). Social work profession: History. In *Encyclopedia of social work* (19th ed., vol. 3, pp. 2282– 2291). Washington, D.C.: NASW Press.

SNP: It's Time. (2005, November 3). *Hyslop: Shortage of social workers is putting children at risk.* Retrieved December 28, 2006, from http://www.snp.org/press-releases/2005/ HYSLOP/

Thyer, B. A., & Biggerstaff, M. A. (1989). *Professional social work credentialling and legal regulation: A review of critical issues and an annotated bibliography.* Springfield, IL: Charles C. Thomas.

Whitaker, T., Weismiller, T., & Clark, E. (2006). *Assuring the sufficiency of a frontline workforce: A national study of licensed social workers, Executive Summary.* Washington, DC: National Association of Social Workers.

Woodside, M., & McClam, T. (2005). *Introduction to human services: Cases and applications.* Belmont, CA: Thomson/ Brooks/Cole.

CHAPTER 2

Abbott, A. (1999, October). Measuring social work values. *International Social Work, 42*(4), 455–470.

Abramovitz, M. (2000). *Under attack: Fighting back: Women and welfare in the United States.* New York: Monthly Review Press.

Bauerlein, M. (2006, July/August). Every breath you take: Air pollution kills tens of thousands of Americans each year. It doesn't have to be that way. *Sierra,* 56–62.

Berg-Weger, M. (2005). *Social work and social welfare, an invitation.* Boston: McGraw-Hill.

Compton, B., & Galaway, B. (1999). *Social work processes* (6th ed.). Pacific Grove, CA: Brooks/Cole.

Council on Social Work Education. (2001). *Educational policy and accreditation standards.* Alexandria, VA: CSWE.

Franklin, C., & Jordan, D. (1999). Advances in systems theory. *Family practice, brief systems methods for social work,* 397–425. Pacific Grove, CA: Brooks/Cole.

Germain, C. B., & Gitterman, A. (1995). Ecological perspective. In *Encyclopedia of social work* (19th ed., pp. 816–822). Washington, DC: NASW Press.

Ginsberg, L. (1998). *Conservative social welfare policy, a description and analysis.* Chicago: Nelson-Hall.

Glicken, M.D. (2004). *Using the strengths perspective in social work practice.* Boston: Allyn & Bacon.

Guralnik, D. (Ed.). (1984). *Webster's new world dictionary of the American language* (2nd ed.). New York: Simon and Schuster.

Johnson, M. J., & Rhodes, R. (2005). *Human behavior and the larger social environment.* Boston: Pearson.

Karger, J. K., & Stoesz, D. (2005). *American social welfare policy, a pluralist approach* (4th ed). Boston: Allyn & Bacon.

Kirst-Ashman, K., & Hull, G. (2006). *Understanding generalist practice* (4th ed). Pacific Grove, CA: Wadsworth.

Lampman, J. (2006, November 9). New sermon from evangel- ical pulpit: global warming. *The Christian Science Monitor,* pp. 13, 14.

Lerner, M. (2006). Surviving the great dying. In M. Schlitz & T. Amorok, with M. S. Micozzi (Eds.), *Consciousness and healing.* St. Louis, MO: Elsevier.

Lum, D. (2007). *Culturally competent practice, a framework for understanding diverse groups and justice issues* (3rd ed). Pacific Grove, CA: Wadsworth.

Miley, K. K., O'Melia, M., & DuBois, B. L. (2004). *Generalist social work practice* (4th ed.). Boston: Allyn & Bacon.

Norlin, J., Chess, W., Dale, O., & Smith, R. (2006). *Human behavior and the social environment, social systems theory* (5th ed.). Boston: Allyn & Bacon.

O'Driscoll, P. (2006, June 5). Spate of lawsuits target e-voting. *USA Today,* p. 1.

O'Murchu, D. (2000). *Religion in exile, A spiritual homecoming.* New York: Crossroad Publishing.

Popple, P. R., & Leighninger, L. (2005). *Social work, social welfare and American society* (6th ed). Boston: Allyn & Bacon.

Poulin, J. (2005). *Strengths-based generalist practice* (2nd ed). Pacific Grove, CA: Wadsworth.

Robbins, P., Chaterjee, P., & Canda, E. (2006). Systems theory. *Contemporary human behavior theory, a critical perspective for social work* (2nd ed). Boston: Allyn & Bacon.

Rothman, J. C. (2005). *From the front lines, student cases in social work ethics.* (2nd ed.). Boston: Allyn & Bacon.

Saleebey, D. (2006). *The strengths perspective in social work practice* (4th ed). Boston: Allyn & Bacon.

Schriver, J. M. (2004a). Paradigm thinking and social work knowledge for practice. *Human behavior in the social environment, shifting paradigms* (4th ed., pp. 105–166). Boston: Allyn & Bacon.

Schriver, J. M. (2004b). Global perspectives and theories. *Human behavior in the social environment, shifting para- digms* (4th ed., pp. 542–567). Boston: Allyn & Bacon.

Segal, E., & Brzuzy, S. (1998). *Social welfare policies, programs, and practice.* Itasca, IL: Peacock.

Shaefor, B. W., Horejsi, C. R., & Horejsi, G. A. (2000). *Tactics and guidelines for social work practice* (5th ed.). Boston: Allyn & Bacon.

Sommer, V. L. (1995). The ecological perspective. In M. J. Macy, N. Flax, V. L. Sommer, & R. Swaine (Eds.), *Directing the baccalaureate social work program, an ecological perspective* (pp. 1–15). Jefferson City, MO: Association for Baccalaureate Social Work Program Directors.

Stoessen, L. (2004, July). Collaborating with faith-based services. *NASW News,* p. 4.

Trumbull, M. (2007, May 16). Corporate concern on climate rises. *The Christian Science Monitor,* pp. 1, 10.

Tyuse, S. W. (2003). Social justice and welfare reform: a shift in policy. In J. Stretch, E. Burkemper, W. Hutchinson, & J. Wilson (Eds.), *Practicing social justice*. New York: Hayworth Press.

Wells, C. (1998). *Stepping to the dance: The training of a family therapist*. Pacific Grove, CA: Brooks/Cole.

Zastrow, C. H. (2007). *The practice of social work, applications of generalist and advanced content* (8th ed). Pacific Grove, CA: Brooks/Cole.

CHAPTER 3

Anti-torture efforts on Capitol Hill (2006, June). *FCNL Washington Newsletter, (708)*, 6, 8.

Association joins global coalition (2005, February 1). *NASW News*, 50(2), 1.

Bane, M. J. (2003). A Catholic policy analyst looks at poverty. In M. J. Bane & L. M. Mead, *Lifting up the poor* (pp. 12–52). Washington, DC: Brookings Institution Press.

Barker, R. L. (2003). *Social work dictionary* (5th ed.). Washington, DC: NASW Press.

Bartkowski, J. P., & Regis, H. A. (2003). *Charitable choices: religion, race and poverty in the post-welfare era*. New York: New York University Press.

Bernstein, R. (2007, May 17). *Minority population tops 100 million*. Retrieved June 12, 2007, from U.S. Census Bureau News, http://www.census.gov/Press-Release/www/releases/archives/population/010048.html

Bills tackle welfare, patient's rights. (1998, September). *NASW News*, p. 7.

Brieland, D. (1995). Social work practice: History and evolution. In R. L. Edwards (Ed.), *Encyclopedia of social work* (19th ed., vol. 3, pp. 2250–2255). Silver Spring, MD: NASW Press.

Bryner, G. (1998). *The great American welfare reform debate, politics and public morality*. New York: W. W. Norton.

Butler, R. (1994). Dispelling ageism: The cross-cutting intervention. In R. D. Enright Jr. (Ed.), *Perspectives in social gerontology* (p. 5). Boston: Allyn & Bacon.

Champagne, A., & Harpham, E. (1984). *The attack on the welfare state*. Prospect Heights, IL: Waveland, pp. 97–105.

Children's Defense Fund. (2004, August). *Where America stands*. Retrieved June 21, 2006, from http://www.childrensdefense.org/data/america.aspx

Civil liberties and human rights. (2004, September). *FNCL Washington Newsletter*, p. 8.

Democracy and the death tax (2006, June 12). *The Christian Science Monitor*, p. 17.

Despeignes, P. (2004, August 27–29). Census: poverty rose by million. *USA Today*, pp. 1, 48.

Eisler, R. (1987). *The chalice and the blade*. San Francisco: Harper.

FAQ: Who was poor in 2004? Retrieved June 20, 2006, from Institute for Research on Poverty website, http://www.irp.wisc.faqs.faq3.htm

Federico, R. (1984). *The social welfare institution* (4th ed). Lexington, MA: Heath, p. 94.

Feldmann, L. (2006, June 6). GOP targets gay marriage. *The Christian Science Monitor*, pp. 1, 10.

Fisher, G. M. (1998, Spring). Setting American standards of poverty: A look back. *Focus, 19*(2), 47–51.

Food stamp program annual summary (2007, April 26). Retrieved June 3, 2007, from the U.S. Department of Agriculture website, http://www.fns.usda.gov/pd/fssummar.htm

Francis, D. R. (2001, June 6). Women demolish more career barriers. *The Christian Science Monitor*, p. 4.

Francis, D. R. (2004, September 13). Shhh! The budget ax is poised. *The Christian Science Monitor*, p. 17.

Friends Committee on National Legislation. (2007). *FY 2008 federal budget president's proposal—percent of federal funds budget*. Retrieved June 2, 2007, from Friends Committee on National Legislation website, http://www.fcnl.org/pdfs/budget_graphs.pdf

General information on Social Security (2005: April) Retrieved June 16, 2006, from American Association of Retired Persons website, http://www.aarp/research/social security/general/aresearch-import-352-FS39R.html

Goldberg, G. (2002a). More than reluctant: the United States of America. In G. Goldberg & M. Rosenthal (Eds.), *Diminishing welfare, a cross-national study of social provision* (pp. 33–71). Westport, CT: Auburn House.

Goldberg, G. (2002b). Diminishing welfare: convergence toward a liberal model? In G. Goldberg & M. Rosenthal (Eds.), *Diminishing welfare, a cross-national study of social provision* (pp. 320–372). Westport, CT: Auburn House.

Goldberg, G., & Rosenthal, M. (Eds.) (2002). *Diminishing welfare, a cross-national study of social provision*. Westport, CT: Auburn House.

Grier, P. (2001, December 13). Fragile freedoms, which civil liberties, and whose, can be abridged to create a safer America? *The Christian Science Monitor*, pp. 1, 8, 9.

Harrington, M. (1962). *The other America, poverty in the United States*. New York: MacMillan.

Hodge, D. R. (2007, April). Social justice and people of faith: a transnational experience. *Social Work, 52*(2), 139–147.

Huang, C. (2007, April 19). The House of Representatives in Oregon passed a bill Tuesday to recognize same sex couples. *The Christian Science Monitor*, p. 3.

Karger, H. J., & Stoesz, D. (2006). *American social welfare policy, a pluralist approach* (5th ed.). Boston: Allyn & Bacon.

Kart, C. S. (1994). *The realities of aging: An introduction to gerontology* (4th ed). Boston: Allyn & Bacon.

Katz, M. B. (2001). *The price of citizenship*. New York: Metropolitan Books.

Kim, R. Y. (2001). The effects of the earned income tax credit on children's income and poverty: Who fares better? *Journal of Poverty, 5*(1), 1–22.

Kramer, S. (2004, August 5). Same sex marriage takes a hit. *The Christian Science Monitor*, pp. 1, 10.

Kozol, J. (1996). *Amazing grace*. New York: HarperCollins.

Johnson, N. (2000, November 2). *A hand up, how state earned income tax credits help working families escape poverty in 2000: An overview*. Center on Budget and Policy Priorities (online). Available http://www.cbpp.org/11–2–00sfp.htm

Labor Law Center (2007). *Federal minimum wage increase for 2007*. Retrieved June 2, 2007, from www.laborlawcenter.com/federal-minimum-wage.asp

Lieby, J. (1987). History of social welfare. In R. L. Edwards (Ed.), *Encyclopedia of social work* (18th ed., vol. 1, pp. 761–765). Silver Spring, MD: NASW Press.

Lum, D. (2007). *Culturally competent practice, a framework for understanding diverse groups and justice issues* (3rd ed.). Pacific Grove, CA: Wadsworth.

Marks, A. (2000, April 27). Vermont launches revolution by allowing same-sex unions. *The Christian Science Monitor*, p. 2.

May-Chahal, C., Katz, I., & Cooper, L. (2003). Social exclusion, family support and evaluation. In I. Katz & J. Pinkerton (Eds.), *Evaluating family support, thinking internationally, thinking critically* (pp. 45–65). West Sussex, UK: John Wiley.

McSteen, M. (1989). Fifty years of social security. In I. Colby (Ed.) *Social welfare policy: Perspectives, patterns, insights* (pp. 172–174). Chicago: Dorsey.

National Association of Social Workers, Office of Governmental Relations (1994, March). *Welfare reform principles*. Washington, DC: NASW.

National Coalition on Health Care. (2007). *Facts on health insurance coverage*. Retrieved June 2, 2007, from http://www.nchc.org/facts/coverage.shtml

Navetta, J. M. (2005, Spring). Gains in learning, gaps in earning. *Outlook, 99*(1), 11–13.

Nine million uninsured children need a solution now. (2007). Retrieved June 3, 2007, from Children's Defense Fund website, http://childrensdefense.org/site/PageServer.

Nomura, M., & Kimoto, K. (2002). Is Japanese-style welfare society sustainable? In G. Goldberg & M. Rosenthal (Eds.), *Diminishing welfare, a cross-national study of social provision* (pp. 296–319). Westport, CT: Auburn Press.

Oliver, R. (2007, April 25). Women short-changed—still. Retrieved April 27, 2007, from The Institute for America's Future website, http://www.tompaine.com/articles/2007/04/25/women_shortchanged_still.php

Over 13 million children face food insecurity. (June 2, 2005). Retrieved June 16, 2006, from Children's Defense Fund website, http://www.childrensdefense.org/family income/food security 2005.pdf

Pagels, E. (1979). *The gnostic gospels*. New York: Random House.

Pagels, E. (2003). *Beyond belief*. New York: Random House.

Paulson, A. (2006, June 12). A tighter rein on faith-based initiatives. *The Christian Science Monitor*, p. 3.

Paulson, A., & Stern, S. (2003, November 19). Landmark ruling on gay marriage. *The Christian Science Monitor*, pp. 1, 10.

Popple, P. R. (1995). Social work profession: History. In R. L. Edwards (Ed.), *Encyclopedia of social work* (19th ed., vol. 3, pp. 2250–2255). Silver Spring, MD: NASW Press.

Poverty among individuals by the official poverty measure, 2005. Retrieved June 3, 2007, from Institute for Research on Poverty website http://www.irp.wisc.edu/faqs/faq3/table1.html

Poverty threshold 2006. Retrieved June 3, 2007, from U.S. Census Bureau website, http:///www.census.gov/hhes/www/poverty/threshld/thresh06.html

Quadagno, J. (1982). *Aging in early industrial society: Work, family and social policy in 19th century England*. New York: Academic Press, p. 95.

Richey, W. (2007, June 29). Court rejects diversity plans. *The Christian Science Monitor*, pp. 1, 10.

Richey, W., and Feldman, L. (2006, June 12). Many perils at Guantanamo—for Bush, too. *The Christian Science Monitor*, pp. 1, 10.

Rocha, C. J., & McCarter, A. K. (2003/2004, Fall/Winter). Strengthening economic justice content in social work education. *Arete, 27*(2), 4–14.

Scherer, R. (2006, July 7). Two states say "no" to gay marriage. *The Christian Science Monitor*, p. 3.

Segal, E., & Brzuzy, S. (1998). *Social welfare policies, programs, and practice*. Itasca, IL: Peacock Publishers.

Senators urge native leaders to cry out louder (2004, March). *FCNL Washington Newsletter*, p. 6.

Skenazy, L. (2004, May 21) American equality? That's rich. *New York Daily News*, quoted in *The Daily News*, West Bend, WI, p. A6.

Stoessen, L. (2004, July). Collaborating with faith-based services. *NASW News*, p. 4.

Terzieff, J. (2007, June 1). Maloney and Ginsberg parry high court ruling. Retrieved June 5, 2005, from the Women's ENews website: http://www.womensnews.org/article/cfm?aid=3190

The state of America's children, 2005. Retrieved June 16, 2006, from Children's Defense Fund website, http://www.childrensdefense.org/publications/greenbook/default.aspx

Thompson, R. A., & Raikes, H. A. (2003). Children and welfare reform. In R. Gordon & H. Walberg (Eds.), *Changing welfare*. New York: Kluwer Academic/Plenum.

Trattner, W. I. (1999). *From poor law to welfare state* (6th ed.). New York: The Free Press.

Tropman, J. (1989). *American values and social welfare*. Englewood Cliffs, NJ: Prentice Hall, pp. 134–135.

Trumbull, M. (2007, July 24). Rising food prices curb aid to global poor. *The Christian Science Monitor*, pp. 1, 2.

Tyuse, S. W. (2003). Social justice and welfare reform: a shift in policy. In J. Stretch, E. Burkemper, W. Hutchison, & J. Wilson (Eds.), *Practicing social justice*. New York: Hayworth Press.

United Nations (1948). *Declaration of Human Rights*. Retrieved June 16, 2006, from http://www.un.org/overview/rights/html

USA news in brief (2006, November 17). *The Christian Science Monitor*, p. 3.

Whitaker, W., & Federico, R. (1997). *Social welfare in today's world* (2nd ed). New York: McGraw-Hill.

Wilensky, H., & Lebeaux, C. (1965). *Industrial society and social welfare*. New York: Free Press, pp. 138–139.

Wyers, N. (1987). Income maintenance system. In R. Edwards (Ed.), *Encyclopedia of social work* (18th ed p. 888). Silver Spring, MD: NASW Press.

CHAPTER 4

Abramovitz, M. (2000). *Under attack, fighting back: Women and welfare in the United States*. New York: Monthly Review Press.

Abramovitz, M. (2005, April). The largely untold story of welfare reform and the human services. *Social Work, 50*(2), 175–190.

Adoption and Safe Families Act clarifies child welfare commitments (1998, February). *Partnerships for Child Welfare, 5*(5), 3.

Allen, M., Kakavas, A., & Zalenski, J. (1994, Spring). Family preservation and support services. *The Prevention Report*. Iowa City: National Resource Center on Family Based Services, University of Iowa School of Social Work, p. 2.

Appleby, G., Colon, E., & Hamilton, J. (2001). *Diversity, oppression and social functioning*. Boston: Allyn & Bacon.

Axinn, M., & Levin, H. (1992). *Social welfare: A history of the American response to need* (3rd ed.). New York: Longman.

Belsie, L. (2001, March 14). Ethnic diversity grows, but not integration. *The Christian Science Monitor*, pp. 1, 4.

Benkov, L. (1994). Reinventing the family. In A. S. Skolnick and J. H. Skolnick (Eds.), *Families in transition* (10th ed.). New York: Longman.

Bernstein, R. (2007, May 17). *Minority population tops 100 million*. Retrieved June 12, 2007, from U.S. Census Bureau News, http://www.census.gov/Press-Releases/www/releases/archives/population/010048.html

Campbell, K. (2004, June 23). Welfare reform hasn't led to more marriage—yet. *The Christian Science Monitor*, p. 11.

Carter, B., and McGoldrick, M. (2005). *The expanded life cycle, individual, family, and social perspectives*. Boston, Allyn & Bacon.

Collins, C. (2005, January). N.H. adoptees gain access to records. *The Christian Science Monitor*, p. 14.

Delgado, M., Jones, K., & Rohani, M. (2005). *Social work practice with refugee and immigrant youth in the United States*. Boston: Allyn & Bacon.

de Silva, E. C. (2006, June). Human rights and human needs. *NASW News*, p. 3.

Diller, J. V. (1999). *Cultural diversity: A primer for the human services*. Pacific Grove, CA: Brooks/Cole.

Dossey, L. (1989) *Recovering the soul, a scientific and spiritual search*. New York: Bantam Books.

Dossey, L. (2003). *Healing beyond the body, medicine and the infinite reach of the mind*. Boston: Shambhala.

DukeMedNews (July 14, 2005). *Results of first multicenter trial of intercessory prayer, healing touch in heart patients*. Retrieved February 3, 2007, from Duke University Medical Center website, http://dukemednews.duke.edu/news/article.php?id=9136

Eighty-one years of paving the way, a history of family planning in America. (1997, Fall/Winter). *Planned Parenthood Today, 4*, 5.

Engbur, A., & Klungness, L. (2000) *The complete single mother*. Holbrook, MA: Adams Media Corporation.

Erickson, J. (2006a, Fall). FDA finally acts on emergency contraception with plan B approval. *National NOW Times*, p. 16.

Erickson, J. (2006b, Fall). NOW scores with U.N. human rights report. *National NOW Times*, p. 17.

First nationwide estimate of homeless population in a decade announced (2007, January). Retrieved January 14, 2006, from National Alliance to End Homelessness website, http://www.endhomelessness.org/content/article/detail/1443

Ford, P. (2005, June 2). Europe's balancing act. *The Christian Science Monitor*, pp. 1, 10.

Ford, P. (2006, April 17). In Europe, unmarried parents on rise. *The Christian Science Monitor*, pp. 1–12.

Francis, D. R. (2006, July 3). How to slow the population clock. *The Christian Science Monitor*, p. 15.

Gardner, M. (2001, April 18). What the Bush budget does for children. *The Christian Science Monitor*, p. 3.

Gardner, M. (2006, July 31). The problem of a pregnant pause. *The Christian Science Monitor*, pp. 13–14.

Gustavsson, N. S., & Segal, E. A. (1994). *Critical issues in child welfare*. Thousand Oaks, CA: Sage Publications.

Hays, S. (2007). Flat broke with children. In S. Shaw and J. Lee (Eds.), *Women's voices feminist visions* (3rd ed). (pp. 641–648). New York: McGraw-Hill.

Hands-on help for mothers (1997, August 18). *The Christian Science Monitor*, p. 1.

Home at last (2007). Retrieved February 4, 2007, from PBS website, http://www.pbs.org/now/shows/305/index.html

Hunger in America 2006. (2006). Hunger Study—2006. Retrieved January 14, 2006, from Hunger in America website, http://www.hungerinamerica.org/key_findings/

Jonsson, P. (2007, February 21). The homeless get counted. *The Christian Science Monitor*, pp. 2, 4.

Kadushin, A., & Martin, J. (1988). *Child welfare services* (4th ed.). New York: Macmillan.

Karger, J., & Stoesz, D. (1998). *American social welfare policy, a pluralist approach* (3rd ed.). New York: Addison Wesley Longman.

Kaufman, M. (2007, January 11). Climate change causes warmest year in 2006. *The Christian Science Monitor*, p. 2.

Kirchheimer, S. (2005, April). *The credit card sinkhole.* Retrieved December 4, 2007, from AARP Bulletin Online, http://www.aarp.org/bulletin/consumer/ec_sinkhole.html

Lindsay, R. (2002). *Recognizing spirituality, the interface between faith and social work.* Crawley, Western Australia: Western Australia Press.

Loeb, P. R. (1999). *Soul of a citizen, living with conviction in a cynical time.* New York: St. Martin's Griffin.

Logan, S. M. L., Freeman, E. M., & McRoy, R. G. (1990). *Social work perspective with black families: A culturally specific perspective.* New York: Longman.

Lum, D. (1992). *Social work with people of color: a process-stage approach* (2nd ed.). Pacific Grove, CA: Brooks/Cole.

Macdonald, G. (2004, Feb. 4). Is having a home a right? *The Christian Science Monitor*, pp. 15–16.

McKenzie, J. K., & Lewis, R. (1998). Keeping the promise of adoption and safe families act. *The Roundtable, 12*(1), 1–9.

Meyers, M., Han, W., Waldfogel, J., & Garfinkel, I. (2001, March). Child care in the wake of welfare reform: The impact of government subsidies on the economic well-being of single-mother families. *Social Service Review, 75*(1), 30–59.

Miks, J. (2006, December 20). Growing income inequality troubles Japanese. *The Christian Science Monitor*, p. 4.

Miller, S. (2005, August 22). Rise in homes with multiple generations. *The Christian Science Monitor*, p. 2.

Mink, G. (1998). *Welfare's end.* Ithaca, NY: Cornell University Press.

Nadakavukaren, A. (2006). *Our global environment* (6th ed.). Long Grove, IL: Waveland Press.

National Coalition on Health Care (2007). Facts on health insurance coverage. Retrieved June 2, 2007, from National Coalition on Health Care's website, http://www.nchc.org/facts/coverage.shtml

Ornes, S. (2007, February). The hole story. *Discover, Science, Technology and the Future*, 60–65.

Pardess, E. (2005). Pride and prejudice with gay and lesbian individuals. In C. L. Rabin (Ed.), *Understanding gender and culture in the helping process* (pp. 109–128). Belmont CA: Thompson Wadsworth.

Quarles, B. (1987). *The Negro in the making of America* (3rd ed.). New York: Macmillan.

Radin, D. (2006). *Entangled minds, extrasensory experiences in a quantum reality.* New York: Simon & Schuster.

Ramanathan, C. S., & Link, R. J. (1999). *All our futures: Principles and resources for social work practice in a global era.* Belmont, CA: Science and Behavior Books.

Reich, J. (2005). *Fixing families, parents, power, and the child welfare system.* New York: Routledge.

Richey, W. (2007, April 19). Court allows late-term abortion ban. *The Christian Science Monitor*, pp. 1, 2.

Ross, J. (2006, September 12). In Chile, free morning-after pills to teens. *The Christian Science Monitor*, pp. 1, 10.

Roth, C. (2006, Summer). War against reproductive rights surges through states. *National NOW Times*, pp. 1, 3.

Samantrai, K. (2004). *Culturally competent public child welfare practice.* Pacific Grove, CA: Brooks/Cole-Thompson Learning.

Savin-Williams, R., & Esterberg, K. G. (2000). Lesbian, gay, and bisexual families. In D. Demo, K. Allen, & M. A. Fine, *Handbook of family diversity* (pp. 197–215). New York: Oxford University Press.

Schlitz, M. (2005). Consciousness beyond death. In M. Schliz, T. Amorok, & M. Micozzi (Eds.). *Consciousness and healing, integral approaches to mind body medicine* (pp. 221–223). St. Louis, MO: Elsevier.

Schwartz, G., Simon, W., & Chopra, D. (2002). *The afterlife experiments.* New York: Atria Books.

Segal, E., & Brzuzy, S. (1998). *Social welfare policy, programs, and practice.* Itasca, IL: F. E. Peacock Publishers.

Smith, M. K. (1998, January). Utilization-focused evaluation of a family preservation program. *Families in society: The Journal of Contemporary Human Services*, 1–19.

Soss, J., Schram, S., Vartanian, T., & Obrien, E. (2004, Winter). Welfare policy choices in the states: does the hard line follow the color line? *Focus, UW Madison Institute for Research on Poverty 23*(1), 9–15.

Steinberg, D. (2006, November 17). When war and children collide. *The Christian Science Monitor*, p. 9.

Stoessen, L. (2005, March). Court reverses foster care decision. *NASW News*, p. 6.

Stoessen, L. (2007, March). Children said at higher risk in red states. *NASW News*, p. 11.

Trattner, W. I. (1999). *From poor law to welfare state: A history of social welfare in America* (6th ed.). New York: The Free Press.

Trumbull, M. (2007, January 2). Why consumers may show more discipline in 2007. *The Christian Science Monitor*, pp. 1, 2.

Trumbull, M. (2007, January 4). CEO pay may face squeeze. *The Christian Science Monitor*, pp. 1, 10.

Trumbull, M. (2007, February 2). Washington takes aim at C.E.O. pay. *The Christian Science Monitor*, pp. 1, 10.

United States fails to meet key health goals for infants and mothers. Retrieved January 13, 2006, from The Children's Defense Fund website, http://www.childrensdefense.org/site/News2?page=NewsArticle&id=6669

USA news in brief (2006, Nov. 17). *The Christian Science Monitor*, p. 3.

Van Wormer, K. (1997). *Social welfare: A world view.* Chicago: Nelson Hall Publishers.

Vives, O. (2007, Winter). NOW opposes anti-marriage ballot measures. *National NOW Times*, p. 3.

Yule, R. (2006, May/June). Super-wealthy families try to repeal estate tax. *Public Citizen News*, pp. 1, 11.

Watkins, S. A. (1990, November). The Mary Ellen myth: Correcting child welfare history. *Social Work, 35*(6), 501–503.

Where America stands (2004, August). Retrieved January 13, 2006, from The Children's Defense Fund website, http://www.childrensdefense.org/site/PageServer?pagename=data_america

Wright, J., Rubin, B., & Devine, J. (1998). *Beside the golden door: Policy, politics, and the homeless.* New York: Aldine de Gruyter.

CHAPTER 5

American Psychiatric Association. (2000). *Diagnostic and statistical manual of mental disorders* (4th ed., text revision). Washington, DC: Author.

Anello, E., Kirk, S. A., & Kutchins, H. (1992). Should social workers use the DSM-III? In E. Gambrill & R. Pruger, *Controversial issues in social work* (pp. 139–156). Boston: Allyn & Bacon.

Beers, C. (1908). *A mind that found itself.* New York: Longmans, Green, & Co.

Bentley, K. J., & Walsh, J. (2001). *The social worker and psychotropic medication: Toward effective collaboration with mental health clients, families, and providers* (2nd ed.). Belmont, CA: Brooks/Cole.

Brave Heart, M. Y. H. (2004). Incorporating native historical trauma content. In L. Gutierrez, M Zuniga, & D. Lum (Eds.), *Education for multicultural social work practice: Critical viewpoints and future directions* (pp. 201–211). Alexandria, VA: Council on Social Work Education.

Butcher, J. N., Mineka, S., & Hooley, J. M. (2008). *Abnormal psychology: Core concepts.* Boston: Allyn & Bacon.

Callicutt, J. W. (1987). Mental health services. *Encyclopedia of social work* (18th ed., Vol. 2, pp. 125–135). Silver Spring, MD: National Association of Social Workers.

Cunningham, P. J., & Freiman, M. P. (1997). Determinants of ambulatory mental health service use among school age children. *Medical Care, 31,* 409–427.

de Silva, E. C., & Clark, E. J. (2006). Mental health policy statement. *Social work speaks: National Association of Social Workers policy statements 2006–2009* (pp. 266–274). Washington, DC: NASW Press.

Eng, A., & Balancio, E. F. (1997). Clinical case management with Asian Americans. In E. Lee (Ed.), *Working with Asian Americans: A guide for clinicians* (pp. 400–407). New York: The Guilford Press.

Gelman, C. R., & Mirabito, D. M. (2005). Practicing what we teach: Using case studies from 9/11 to teach crisis intervention from a generalist perspective. *Journal of Social Work Education, 41*(3), 479–494.

Hollis, F. (1964). *Casework: A psychosocial therapy.* New York: Random House.

Johnstone, M. (2007). Disaster response and group self-care. *Perspectives in Psychiatric Care, 43*(1), 38–40.

Joint Commission on Accreditation of Healthcare Organizations. (1998). *Lexikon* (2nd ed.). Oakbrook Terrace, IL: Author.

KEN Publications/Catalog. (n.d.). *Final report, consumer bill of rights & responsibilities.* Retrieved August 25, 2001, from http://www.mentalhealth.org/consumersurvivor/billofrights.htm

Kirk, S. A., & Kutchins, H. (1992). *The selling of DSM: The rhetoric of science in psychiatry.* New York: Aldine de Gruyter.

Kutchins, H., & Kirk, S. A. (1989). Human errors, attractive nuisances, and toxic wastes: A reply to Anello. *Social Work, 34*(2), 187–188.

Kutchins, H., & Kirk, S. A. (1997). *Making us crazy: DSM—The psychiatric bible and the creation of mental disorders.* New York: The Free Press.

Leiby, J. (1987). History of social welfare. *Encyclopedia of social work* (18th ed., Vol. 1, pp. 755–777). Silver Spring, MD: National Association of Social Workers.

Lerner, M. D., & Shelton, R. D. (2001). How can emergency responders help grieving individuals? and How do people respond during traumatic exposure? *Trauma response info-sheet.* Retrieved September 29, 2001, from the American Academy of Experts in Traumatic Stress website: http://www.aaets.org

Lightman, D., & Waldman, H. (2007, May 12). Mental health bill: Is parity possible? *Hartford Courant.* Retrieved May 28, 2007, from http://www.courant.com

Lum, D. (1992). *Social work with people of color: A process-stage approach* (2nd ed.). Pacific Grove, CA: Brooks/Cole.

Lum, D. (1999). *Culturally competent practice: A framework for growth and action.* Pacific Grove, CA: Brooks/Cole.

Lum, D. (2007). *Culturally competent practice: A framework for understanding diverse groups and justice issues.* Belmont, CA: Thomson, Brooks/Cole.

Mankiller, W., & Wallis, M. (1993). *Mankiller: A chief and her people.* New York: St. Martin's Press.

Meyer, C. (1987). Direct practice in social work: Overview. In *Encyclopedia of social work* (19th ed., Vol. 1, pp. 409–422). Silver Spring, MD: National Association of Social Workers.

Mitchell, C. G. (1998). Perceptions of empathy and client satisfaction with managed behavioral health care. *Social Work, 43*(5), 404–411.

Moniz, C., & Gorin, S. (2007). *Health and mental health care policy: A biopsychosocial perspective.* Boston: Pearson, Allyn & Bacon.

National Alliance on Mental Illness. (2007). *About NAMI.* Retrieved April 28, 2007, from http:www.nami.org

National Association of Social Workers. (2007). *NASW Credentialing Center.* Retrieved January 22, 2007, from www.socialworkers.org/credentials/default.asp

National Institute of Mental Health. (2001, January 1). *Reliving Trauma.* Retrieved September 29, 2001, from http://www.nimh.gov/publicat/reliving.cfm

Oltmanns, F. F., & Emery, R. E. (2007). *Abnormal psychology* (5th ed.). Upper Saddle River, NJ: Pearson, Prentice Hall.

Pace, P. R. (2007). New York parity law signed. *NASW News, 52*(3), 7.

Perlman, H. H. (1957). *Social casework: A problem-solving process.* Chicago: University of Chicago Press.

Red Horse, J. (1988). Cultural evolution of American Indian families. In C. Jacobs & D. D. Bowles (Eds.) *Ethnicity and race: Critical concepts in social work* (pp. 86–102). Silver Spring, MD: National Association of Social Workers.

Reynolds, B. C. (1934). *Between client and community.* Silver Spring, MD: National Association of Social Workers.

Reynolds, B. C. (1942). *Learning and teaching in the practice of social work.* Silver Spring, MD: National Association of Social Workers.

Reynolds, B. C. (1935). *Social work and social living: Explorations in philosophy and practice.* New York: Citadel Press

Richmond, M. E. (1917). *Social diagnosis.* New York: Russell Sage Foundation.

Richmond, M. E. (1922). *What is social casework? An introductory description.* New York: Russell Sage Foundation.

Schopler, J. H., Abell, M. D., & Galinsky, M. J. (1998). Technology-based groups: A review and conceptual framework for practice. *Social Work, 43*(3), 254–267.

Social work in the public eye. (2002). *NASW News, 47*(1), 15.

Social work in the public eye. (2006). *NASW News, 51*(9), 11.

Susser, E., Schwartz, S., Morabia, A., & Bromet, E. J. (2006). *Psychiatric epidemiology: Searching for the causes of mental disorders.* New York: Oxford University Press.

Taft, J. (1933). *The dynamics of therapy in a controlled relationship.* New York: The Macmillan Co.

U.S. Department of Health and Human Services. (2001). *Mental health: Culture, race, and ethnicity—A supplement to mental health: A report of the Surgeon General.* Retrieved January 16, 2007, from http://mentalhealth.samhsa.gov/cre/ch4_historical.asp

Vastola, J., Nierenberg, A., & Graham, E. H. (1994). The lost and found group: Group work with bereaved children. In A. Gitterman & L. Shulman (Eds.). *Mutual aid groups, vulnerable populations, and the life cycle* (2nd ed., pp. 81–96). New York: Columbia University Press.

Wells, K., Klap, J., Koike, A., & Sherbourne, C. (2001). Ethnic disparities in unmet need for alcoholism, drug abuse, and mental health care. *American Journal of Psychiatry, 158,* 2027–2032.

Wilson, D. C. (1975). *Stranger and traveler: The story of Dorothea Dix, American reformer.* Boston: Little, Brown & Co.

World Health Organization. (2007). *Quantifying environmental health impacts.* Retrieved January 16, 2007, from http://www.who.int/quantifying_ehimpacts/global/en/

Wortsman, P. (2006). Alumni profile Ezra Susser: A life in epidemiology. *Alumni News and Notes: The College of Physicians & Surgeons of Columbia University, 26*(2). Retrieved April 4, 2007, from http:cumc.columbia.edu/news/journal/journal/-o/spring-2006/alumni.html

Wyffels, M. (2001, December 19). House-Senate Conference Committee votes down Domenici-Wellstone parity amendment. *NAMI: The nation's voice on mental illness, 02*(39). Retrieved January 1, 2002, from http://www.nami.org/update//20011219.htm

CHAPTER 6

Armstrong, P., Armstrong, H., & Feagan, C. (1998). The best solution: Questions and answers on the Canadian health care system. *Washington Monthly, 30*(4), 8–12.

Barker, R. L. (2003). *The social work dictionary* (5th ed.). Washington, DC: NASW Press.

Barnes, F. (1994, August 15). A White House watch: Left out. *New Republic, 211*(7), 15–17.

Berger, R. M. (1995). Habitat destruction syndrome [Op. Ed]. *Social Work, 40*(4), 441–443.

Besthorn, F. H. (2002). Radical environmentalism and the ecological self: Rethinking the concept of self-identity for social work practice. *Journal of Progressive Human Services, 13*(1), 53–72.

Bureau of Labor Statistics. (2006). Social workers. *Occupational outlook handbook, 2006–2007 edition.* Retrieved August 16, 2006, from http://www.bls.gov/oco/print/ocos060.htm

Cannon, I. M. (1952). *On the social frontier of medicine: Pioneering in medical social service.* Cambridge, MA: Harvard University Press.

CBC News. (2006, August 22). *Indepth: Health care.* Retrieved June 19, 2007, from http://www.cbc.ca/news/background/healthcare/

Center for Medicare Advocacy (2007). *Center for Medicare Advocacy testifies regarding Medicare Part D and Medicare Managed Care.* Retrieved June 16, 2007, from http://www.medicareadvocacy.org/PtDTestimony/PartD_07_05.03.Testimony.htm

Csikai, E. L., & Chaitin, E. (2006). *Ethics in end-of-life decisions in social work practice.* Chicago: Lyceum Books.

Davidson, T., Davidson, J. H., & Keigher, S. M. (1999). Managed care: Satisfaction guaranteed . . . Not! *Health & Social Work, 24*(3), 163–168.

de Silva, E. C., & Clark, E. J. (2006). Environmental policy (pp. 136–143); Hospice care (pp. 211–216). *Social work speaks: National Association of Social Workers Policy Statements 2006–2009* (7th ed). Washington, DC: NASW Press.

Devore, W., & Schlesinger, E. G. (1987). *Ethnic sensitive social work practice* (2nd ed.). Columbus, OH: Merrill.

Dziegielewski, S. F. (2004). *The changing face of health care social work: Professional practice in managed behavioral health care* (2nd ed.). New York: Springer.

Galambos, C. M. (Ed.). (2003). Building healthy environments: Community- and consumer-based initiatives. *Health & Social Work, 28*(3), 171–173.

Germain, C. B., & Gitterman, A. (1980). *The life model of social work practice.* New York: Columbia University Press.

Gorin, S. H. (2000). Progressives and the 2000 election. *Health & Social Work, 25*(2), 139–143.

Healy, T. C. (1998). The complexity of everyday ethics in home health care: An analysis of social workers' decisions regarding frail elders' autonomy. *Social Work in Health Care, 27*(4), 19–37.

Hoff, M. D., & McNutt, J. G. (Eds.). (1994). *The global environmental crisis: Implications for social welfare and social work.* Brookfield, VT: Avebury.

Hoff, M. D., & Rogge, M. E. (1996). Everything that rises must converge: Developing a social work response to environmental injustice. *Journal of Progressive Human Services, 7,* 41–57.

Jong-wook, L. (2003). *The world health report 2003: Shaping the future.* Geneva, Switzerland: World Health Organization.

Kawachi, I., Wilkinson, R. G., & Kennedy, B. P. (1999). Introduction. In I. Kawachi, B. P. Kennedy, & R. G. Wilkinson (Eds.), *The society and population health reader.* Vol. 1 (pp. xi–xxxiv). New York: New Press.

Keigher, S. M. (2000, February). Knowledge development. *Health & Social Work, 25*(1), 3–8.

Lyons, K., Manion, K., & Carlsen, M. (2006). *International perspectives on social work: Global conditions and local practice.* New York: Palgrave Macmillan.

McGinn, F. (1996). The plight of rural parents caring for adult children with HIV. *Families in Society, 77*(5), 269–278.

Medicare: The official U.S. Government site for people with Medicare questions. (2007). Medicare options compare: Supporting information. Retrieved December 9, 2007, from http://www.medicare.gov/MPPF/Static/tabHelp.asp

Mizrahi, T., Fasano, R., & Dooha, S. N. (1993). National health line: Canadian and American health care: Myths and realities. *Health & Social Work, 18*(1), 7–8.

Moniz, C., & Gorin, S. (2007). *Health and mental health care policy: A biopsychosocial perspective* (2nd ed.). Boston: Pearson, Allyn & Bacon.

Muennig, P., Franks, P., Jia, H., Luebetkin, E., & Gold, M. R. (2005). The income-associated burden of disease in the United States. *Social Science and Medicine, 61*(9), 2018–2026.

Munch, S., & Shapiro, S. (2007). Osteoporosis as the silent thief in women of all ages. *Health Section Connection, 1,* 1, 3–6.

National Assocation of Social Workers. (n.d.). *Social work services in nursing homes: Toward quality psychosocial care.* Retrieved June 7, 2007, from http://www.socialworkers.org/research/nasw Research/0605Psychosocial/default.asp

National Association of Social Workers. (1993). *NASW clinical indicators for social work and psychological services in nursing homes* (brochure). Washington, DC: Author.

National Osteoporosis Foundation (2007). *Fast Facts.* Retrieved June 5, 2007, from http://www.nof.org/osteoporosis/index.htm

Pistella, C. L. Y., Bonati, F. A., & Mihalic, S. (1999). Social work practice in a rural community collaborative to improve perinatal care. *Social Work in Health Care, 20*(1), 1–14.

Poole, D. L. (1995). Health care: Direct practice. In *Encyclopedia of social work* (19th ed., pp. 1156–1167). Washington, DC: NASW Press.

Reamer, F. G. (1993, July). AIDS and social work: The ethics and civil liberties agency. *Social Work, 38*(4), 414–415.

Rehr, H. (Ed.). (1994). *Medicine and social work: An exploration in interprofessionalism.* New York: Prodist Press.

Rehr, H., & Rosenberg, G. (1982). *Advancing social work practice in the health care field.* New York: Haworth Press.

Rehr, H., & Rosenberg, G. (2006). *The social work-medicine relationship: 100 years at Mount Sinai.* New York: Haworth Press.

Richman, J. M. (1995). Hospice. In *Encyclopedia of Social Work* (19th ed., pp. 1358–1365). Washington, DC: NASW Press.

Robert, S., & Norgard, T. (1996). Long-term care policy based on ADL eligibility criteria: Impact on community dwelling elders not meeting the criteria. *Journal of Gerontological Social Work, 25*(3/4), 71–91.

Saleebey, D. (2004). The power of place: Another look at the environment. *Families in Society, 85*(1), 7–16.

Skocpol, T. (1997). *Boomerang: Health care reform and the turn against government.* New York: W. W. Norton.

Slivinski, L. R., Fitch, V. L., & Wingerson, N. W. (1998). The effect of functional disability on service utilization: Implications for long-term care. *Social Work, 23*(3), 175–185.

Somer, E., Buchbinder, E., Peled-Avram, M., & Ben-Yizhack, Y. (2004). The stress and coping of Israeli emergency room social workers following terrorist attacks. *Qualitative Health Research, 14*(8), 1077–1093.

Susser, E., & Morabia, A. (2006). The arc of epidemiology. In E. Susser, S. Schwartz, A. Morabia, & E.V. Bromet (Eds.), *Psychiatric epidemiology: Searching for the causes of mental disorders.* (ch. 2). New York: Oxford University Press.

The Henry J. Kaiser Family Foundation. (2007) *Kaiser state health facts, 50 state comparisons: Medicaid payments per enrollee, FY 2004.* Retrieved June 17, 2007, from http://www.statehealthfacts.org/cgi-bin/healthfacts.cgi?previewid=252&action=compare&category=Medicaid+%26+SCHIP&subcategory=Medicaid+Spending&topic=Medicaid+Payments+per+Enrollee%2c+FY2004

United Nations Statistics Division. (2006). *Social indicators: Indicators on health.* Retrieved June 14, 2007, from http://unstats.un.org/unsd/Demographic/Products/socind/health.htm

USAID (2007). Trafficking in persons. *Women in development.* Retrieved June 14, 2007, from http://www.usaid.gov/our_work/cross-cuttingprograms/wid/trafficking/index.html

U.S. Census Bureau (2006, Auust 29). *Income climbs, poverty stabilizes, uninsured rate increases.* Retrieved June 18, 2007, from http://www.census.gov/Press-Release/www/releases/archives/income_wealth/007419.html

Wennemo, I. (1993). Infant mortality, public policy and inequality: A comparison of 18 industrialized countries 1950–1985. *Sociology of Health and Illness, 15,* 429–446.

Weiss, L. (1997). *Private medicine and public health: Profit, politics, and prejudice in the American health care enterprise.* Boulder, CO: Westview Press.

Wilkinson, R. G. (2005). *The impact of inequality: How to make sick societies healthier.* New York: New Press.

Wolfe, S. M. (2006). Outrage of the month: Massachusetts' mistake. *Public Citizen Health Research Group Health Letter, 22*(5), 10, 12.

World Health Organization (n.d.). *Linkages between health and human rights.* Retrieved June 14, 2007, from http://www.who.int/hhr/HHR%20linkages.pdf

CHAPTER 7

American Institute for Research. (1998). *Gender gaps: Where schools still fail our children.* Washington, DC: American Association of University Women Educational Foundation.

Baldauf, S. (1998, September 8). Public schools at a crossroads. *The Christian Science Monitor,* pp. 1, 18.

Bernstein, R. (2007, May 17). *Minority population tops 100 million.* Retrieved June 12, 2007, from U.S. Census Bureau News, http://www.census.gov/Press-Release/www/releases/archives/population/010048.html

Berkman, C. S., & Zinberg, G. (1997, July). Homophobia and heterosexism in social workers. *Social Work, 42*(4), 329–332.

Bishop, K. (2006). Family-centered services to infants and toddlers with or at risk for disabilities: IDEA 2004, Part C. In R. Constable, C. Massat, S. McDonald, & J. Flynn (Eds.). *School social work* (6th ed., pp. 189–204). Chicago: Lyceum Books.

Boyle-Del Rio, S., Carlson, R., & Haibeck, L. (2000, Fall). School personnel's perception of the school social worker's role. *School Social Work Journal, 25*(1), 59–75.

Burt, M., Resnick, G., & Novick, E. R. (1998). *Building supportive communities for at-risk adolescents.* Washington, DC: American Psychological Association.

Button, J., & Rienzo, B. (2002). *The politics of youth, sex, and health care in American schools.* New York: The Hayworth Press.

Caple, Frances S., & Salcido, Ramon M. (2006). A framework for cross-cultural practice in school settings. In R. Constable, C. Massat, S. McDonald, & J. Flynn (Eds.), *School social work* (6th ed., pp. 299–320). Chicago: Lyceum Books.

Constable, R. (2006). The role of the school social worker. In R. Constable, C. Massat, S. McDonald, & J. Flynn (Eds.). *School social work, practice, policy, and research* (6th ed., pp. 3–27). Chicago: Lyceum Books.

Constable, R. & Kordesh, R. (2006). Policies, programs, and mandates for developing social services in the schools. In R. Constable, C. Massat, S. McDonald, and J. Flynn (Eds.), *School social work, practice, policy, and research* (6th ed., pp. 123–144). Chicago: Lyceum Books.

Constable, R., & Thomas, G. (2006). Assessment, multidisciplinary teamwork, and consultation: foundations for role development. In R. Constable, C. Massat, S. McDonald, & J. Flynn (Eds.). *School social work, practice, policy, and research* (6th ed., pp. 283–320). Chicago: Lyceum Books.

Costin, L. (1987). School social work. In A. Minahan (Ed.), *Encyclopedia of social work* (18th ed., pp. 536–539). Silver Spring, MD: National Association of Social Workers.

Dr. Jocelyn Elders urges comprehensive sexuality education (2001, Spring). *Moving Forward,* 1.

Dupper, D. R. (2000). The design of social work services. In P. Allen-Meares, R. O. Washington, & B. L. Welsh, *Social work services in schools* (3rd ed., pp. 243–272). Boston: Allyn & Bacon.

Dupper, D. R. (2003). *School social work, skills and interventions for effective practice.* Hoboken, NJ: John Wiley & Sons.

Franklin, C. (2000). The delivery of school social work services. In P. Allen-Meares, R. O. Washington, & B. L. Welsh, *Social work services in schools* (3rd ed., pp. 273–298). Boston: Allyn & Bacon.

Freeman, E. M. (1995). School social work overview. In R. L. Edwards (Ed.). *Encyclopedia of social work* (19th ed., pp. 2087–2097). Washington, DC: NASW Press.

Freeman, E. M., Halim, M., & Peterson, K. J. (1998). HIV/AIDS policy development and reform: Lessons from practice, research, and education. In E. M. Freeman, C. G. Franklin, R. Fong, S. G. Shaffer, & E. M. Timberlake (Eds.). *Multisystem skills and interventions in school social work practice* (pp. 371–377). Washington, DC: NASW Press.

Ginorio, A., and Huston, M. (2001). *Si, se puede! Yes, we can, Latinas in school.* Washington, DC: AAUW Educational Foundation.

Hancock, B. (1982). *School social work.* Englewood Cliffs, NJ: Prentice Hall.

Hare, I., Rome, S., & Massat, C. (2006). The developing social, political, and economic context for school social work. In R. Constable, C. Massat, S. McDonald, & J. Flynn (Eds.). *School social work, practice, policy, and research* (6th ed., pp. 145–170). Chicago: Lyceum Books.

Harris Interactive (2001). *Hostile hallways, bullying, teasing, and sexual harrassment in school.* Washington, DC: AAUW Educational Foundation.

Hinkelman, J. M. (2005). Triple oppression. In Claire Low Rabin (Ed.). *Understanding gender and culture in the helping process* (pp. 167–185). Belmont, CA: Thompson Wadsworth.

Hobbins, W. (2007; April 16). Personal communication. Madison, WI.

Jolly, E. J. (2004, Spring). *Mosaic, an EDC report series.* Retrieved February 24, 2007, from the Mosaic Home/Educational Development Center, Inc. Home website, http://main.edc.org/Mosaic/Mosaic9/beneath.asp

Koch, K. (2000). School violence, are American schools safe? In D. Bonilla, (Ed.), *School violence* (pp. 5–33). New York: H. W. Wilson.

Kopels, S. (2000). Securing equal educational opportunity: language, race, and sex. In P. Allen-Meares, R. O. Washington, & B. L. Welsh, *Social work services in schools* (3rd ed., p. 216). Boston: Allyn & Bacon.

Llana, S. M., & Paulson, A. (2006, June 13). Bilingualism issue rises again. *The Christian Science Monitor*, pp. 1, 11.

Lewin, T. (2001, July 31). Surprising result in welfare-to-work studies. *New York Times*. Available, http://nytimes.com/2001/07/31/WELF.html?ex=9975930&ei=1&en=_14a580ab

Lum. D. (1992). *Social work with people of color: a process-stage approach.* Pacific Grove, CA: Brooks/Cole.

Mann, E., & Reynolds, A. (2006, September). Early intervention and juvenile delinquency prevention: evidence from the Chicago longitudinal study. *Social Work Research, 30*(3), 153–167.

Matuszek, T., & Rycraft, J. (2003). Using biofeedback to enhance interventions in schools. In Bhavana Pahwa (Ed.), *Technology-assisted delivery of school based mental health services* (pp. 31–56). New York: Hayworth Press.

Mercola, J. (2001, January 21). Chemical contamination linked to early puberty. Retrieved April 14, 2007, from Dr. Mercola's website, http://cmsadmin.mercola.com/2001/jan/21/chemicalspuberty.htm

Morrow, D. F. (1993, November). Social work with gay and lesbian adolescents. *Social Work, 38*(6), 655–660.

National Campaign to Prevent Teen Pregnancy (2007). *New survey of Latino teens shows that there is still work to do* and *foster care youth.* Retrieved February 4, 2007, from The National Campaign to Prevent Teen Pregnancy website, http://www.teenpregnancy.org.

O'Driscoll, P. (2007, April 20–22). Teen rant reminiscent of Columbine, shooters in both spewed contempt in recordings. *USA Today*, p. 1.

Paulson, A. (2005, March 25). Schools using many lessons from Columbine. *The Christian Science Monitor*, pp. 1, 10.

Paulson, A. (2006, September 5). Push to win back dropouts. *The Christian Science Monitor*, pp. 1, 11.

Paulson, A. (2007, January 8). Next round begins for No-Child-Left-Behind Law. *The Christian Science Monitor*, pp. 1, 10.

Pawlak, E., Wozniak, D., & McGowen, M. (2006). Perspectives on groups for school social workers. In R. Constable, C. Massat, S. McDonald, & J. Flynn (Eds.). *School social work, practice, policy, and reseach* (6th ed. pp. 559–578). Chicago: Lyceum Books.

Politics & Opinion. (2002). *National survey of Latinos.* Retrieved March 5, 2007, from the Hispanic Publishing Group/HispanicOnline.com website, http://www.hispaniconline.com/pol&opi/02_nat_survey_latinos.html

Rose, S. (1998). *Group work with children and adolescents, prevention and intervention in school and community systems.* Thousand Oaks, CA: Sage Publications.

Sappenfield, M. (2001, June 22). For more students, summer means—more school. *The Christian Science Monitor*, pp. 1, 9.

Sossou, M., & Daniels, T. (2002). School social work practice in Ghana: a hope for the future. In M. Huxtable and E. Blyth (Eds.). *School social work worldwide* (pp. 93–108). Washington, DC: National Association of Social Workers.

Special education and the Individuals with Disabilities Education Act (2007). Retrieved April 7, 2007, from the National Education Association website, http://www.nea.org/specialed/index.html?mode=print

Stoessen, L. (2006, July). Health focus of LGBQ workshop. *NASW News*, p. 5.

Study: Safe-sex programs don't increase sexual activity (2001, May 30). *The Daily News, West Bend, WI*, p. A 10.

Sunderman, G. L., Kim, J. S., & Orfield, G. (2005). *NCLB meets school realities, lessons from the field.* Thousand Oaks, CA: Corwin Press.

Tyre, P. (2006, January). *The trouble with boys.* Retrieved January 23, 2006, from Newsweek website, http://www.msnbc.msn.com/id/10965522/site/newsweek/

Wells, C. (1999). *Social work day to day, the experience of generalist social work practice* (3rd ed.). New York: Addison Wesley Longman.

CHAPTER 8

Allen, J. P. (1998). Project MATCH: A clarification. *Behavioral Health Management, 18*(2), 42–44.

American Psychiatric Association. (2000). *Diagnostic and statistical manual of mental disorders* (4th ed., text rev.). Washington, DC: American Psychiatric Association.

Anderson, S. C. (1995). Alcohol abuse. In *Encyclopedia of social work* (19th ed., pp. 203–215). Washington, DC: NASW Press.

Babor, T. F., Higgins-Biddle, J. C., Saunders, J. B., & Monteiro, M. G. (2001). *AUDIT, The Alcohol Use Disorders Identification Test: Guidelines for use in primary care* (2nd ed.). World Health Organization (WHO/ MSD/MSB/01.6a). Retrieved June 28, 2007, from http://whqlibdoc.who.int/hq/2001/WHO_MSB_ 01.6a.pdf

Barker, R. L. (2003). *The social work dictionary* (5th ed.). Washington, DC: NASW Press.

Brown, P. (2006). Drinking for two? *New Scientist, 191* (2558), 46–49.

Butcher, J. N., Mineka, S., & Hooley, J. M. (2008). *Abnormal psychology: Core concepts.* Boston: Pearson, Allyn & Bacon.

Chein, I. (1956). Narcotics use among juveniles. *Social Work, 1*(2), 50–60.

Delgado, M. (1988). Alcoholism treatment and Hispanic youth. *Journal of Drug Issues, 18*(1), 59–68.

de Koning, P., & de Kwant, A. (2002). Dutch drug policy and the role of social workers. In L. A. Straussner & L. Harrison (Eds.), *International aspects of social work practice in the addictions* (pp. 49–68). New York: Haworth Press.

Gibbs, L. E., & Hollister, C. D. (1993). Matching alcoholics with treatment: Reliability, replication and validity of a treatment typology. *Journal of Social Science Research*, *17*(1/2), 41–72.

Hannon, L., & Cuddy, M. M. (2006). Neighborhood ecoloy and drug dependence mortality: An analysis of New York City census tracts. *American Journal of Drug and Alcohol Abuse*, *32*, 453–463.

Harrison, L., & Straussner, L. (2002). Introduction. In L. A. Straussner & L Harrison, (Eds.), *International aspects of social work practice in the addictions* (pp. 1–5). New York: Haworth Press.

Icard, L., & Traunstein, D. M. (1987). Black, gay, alcoholic men: Their character and treatment. *Social Casework*, *68*(5), 267–272.

Johnson, K., Noe, T., Collins, D., Strader, T., & Bucholtz, G. (2000). Mobilizing church communities to prevent alcohol and other drug abuse: A model strategy and its evaluation. *Journal of Community Practice*, *7*(2), 1–27.

Kinney, J., & Leaton, G. (1995). *Loosening the grip: A handbook of alcohol information* (5th ed.). St. Louis: Mosby.

Krimmel, H. (1971). *Alcoholism: Challenge for social work education*. New York: Council on Social Work Education.

Lacerte, J., & Harris, D. L. (1986). Alcoholism: A catalyst for women to organize: 1850–1980. *Affilia*, *1*(2), 41–52.

Loebig, B. J. (2000). *European alcoholism and drug abuse perceptions*. Retrieved October 4, 2001, from http://www.geocities.com/bourbonstreet/2640/topic.htm.

Logan, S., McRoy, R. G., & Freeman, E. M. (1987). Current practice approaches for treating the alcoholic client. *Health and Social Work*, *12*(3), 176–186.

Malekoff, A. (1997). Group work in the prevention of adolescent alcohol and other drug abuse. In G. L. Greif & P. H. Ephross (Eds.), *Group work with populations at risk* (pp. 227–243). New York: Oxford University Press.

Masis, K. B., & May, P. A. (1991). A comprehensive local program for the prevention of fetal alcohol syndrome. *Public Health Reports*, *106*(5), 484–489.

McNeece, C. A., & DiNitto, D. M. (2005). *Chemical dependency: A systems approach* (3rd ed.). Boston: Pearson, Allyn & Bacon.

National Center for Health Statistics. (2006). Table 68 Alcohol consumption by adults 18 years of age and over, by selected characteristics: United States, selected years 1997–2004. *Health, United States, 2006 with chartbook on trends in the health of Americans* (pp. 276–278). Retrieved July 3, 2007, from http://www.cdc.gov/nchs/data/hus/hus06.pdf#066

National Clearinghouse for Alcohol and Drug Information. (2000, August 4). Prevention works! *Prevention Alert*, *3*(26). Retrieved from http://www.health.org/_govpubs/prevalert/v3i26.htm.

National Institute on Drug Abuse. (2007). *Commonly abused drugs*. Retrieved July 7, 2007, from http://www.drugabuse.gov/DrugPages/DrugsofAbuse.html

National Women's Health Information Center. (2000, October 23). *Alcohol abuse and treatment*. Retrieved October 6, 2001, from http://www.4woman.gov/faq/sa_alcoh.htm.

O'Connor, M. J., & Whaley, S. E. (2007). Brief intervention for alcohol use by pregnant women. *American Journal of Public Health*, *97*(2), 252–258.

Osman, M. M. (2002). Drug and alcohol addiction in Singapore: Issues and challenges in control and treatment strategies. In L. A. Straussner & L. Harrison (Eds.), *International aspects of social work practice in the addictions* (pp. 97–117). New York: Haworth Press.

Peltenberg, C. (1956). Casework with the alcoholic patient. *Social Casework*, *37*(2), 81–85.

Rapp, R. (1997). The strengths perspective and persons with substance abuse problems. In D. Saleebey (Ed.), *The strengths perspective in social work practice* (2nd ed., pp. 77–96). New York: Longman.

Rapp, R. C. (2006). Ch. 8: Strengths-based case management: Enhancing treatment for persons with substance-abuse problems. In D. Saleebey, *The strengths perspective in social work practice* (4th ed., pp. 128–147). Boston: Pearson, Allyn & Bacon.

Ray, O., & Ksir, C. (1993). *Drugs, society, & human behavior* (6th ed.). St. Louis: Mosby.

Rhodes, R., & Johnson, A. D. (1994). Women and alcoholism: A psychosocial approach. *Affilia*, *9*(2), 145–154.

Richmond, M. E. (1917). *Social diagnosis*. New York: Russell Sage Foundation.

Robertson, N. (1988). *Getting better: Inside Alcoholics Anonymous*. New York: Ballantine.

Roffman, R. A. (1987). Drug use and abuse. In *Encyclopedia of social work* (18th ed., Vol. 1, pp. 477–487). Silver Spring, MD: NASW Press.

Ruiz, D. S. (2001). Ch. 16: Traditional helping roles of older African American women: The concept of self-help. In I. Carlton-LaNey (Ed.), *African American leadership: An empowerment tradition in social welfare history* (pp. 215–228). Washington, DC: NASW Press.

Sapir, J. V. (1957). The alcoholic as an agency client. *Social Casework*, *38*(7), 355–361.

Saulnier, C. L. (1991). Lesbian alcoholism: Development of a construct. *Affilia 6*(3), 67–84.

The Sentencing Project. (2007, December 11). *United States Sentencing Commission approves crack reform for federal prisoners*. Retrieved December 21, 2007, from http://www.sentencingproject.org/NewsDetails.aspx?NewsID=530

SFAF HIV prevention project (needle exchange). (2001, May 20). Retrieved October 7, 2001, from http://www.sfaf.org/prevention/needlesexchange/

Smith, M. J. W., Whitaker, T., & Weismiller, T. (2006). Social workers in the substance abuse treatment field: A snapshot of service activities. *Health & Social Work*, *31*(2), 109–115.

Smyth, N. (1995). Substance abuse: Direct practice. In *Encyclopedia of social work* (19th ed., Vol. 3, pp. 2328–2337). Washington, DC: NASW Press.

Streissguth, A. P., Clarren, S. K., & Jones, K. L. (1985, July 13). Natural history of the fetal alcohol syndrome: A 10 year follow-up of eleven patients. *Lancet, 2*, 85–91.

Streissguth, A. P., LaDue, R. A., & Randels, S. P. (1988). *A manual on adolescents and adults with fetal alcohol syndrome with special reference to American Indians* (2nd ed.). Washington, DC: U. S. Department of Health and Human Services, Indian Health Service.

Substance Abuse and Mental Health Services Administration (1998). Table 11: Percentages reporting past month use of any illicit drug, by age group, race/ethnicity, and sex: 1979–1997. *Preliminary results from the 1997 National Household Survey on Drug Abuse* [Online]. Available: http://www.samhsa.gov/oas/nhsda/hnsda97/97tab.htm

Substance Abuse and Mental Health Services Administration. (2004). *National Survey on Drug Use and Health, the NSDUH Report: Pregnancy and substance use.* Office of Applied Studies. Rockville, MD.

Substance Abuse and Mental Health Services Administration. (2006). *Results from the 2005 National Survey on Drug Use and Health: National findings.* Office of Applied Studies, NSDUH Series H-30, DHHS Publication No. SMA 06–4194). Rockville, MD.

Szlemko, W. J., Wood, J. W., & Thurman, P. J. (2006). Native Americans and alcohol: Past, present, and future. *Journal of General Psychology, 133*(4), 435–451.

Turnbull, J. E. (1988). Primary and secondary alcoholic women. *Social Casework, 69* (5), 290–297.

U.S. Sentencing Commission. (2007, May). *Cocaine and federal sentencing policy.* Retrieved July 12, 2007, from http://www.ussc.gov/ r_congress/cocaine2007.pdf

van Wormer, K. (1995). *Alcoholism treatment: A social work perspective.* Chicago: Nelson-Hall Publishers.

van Wormer, K., & Davis, D. R. (2008). *Addiction treatment: A strengths perspective* (2nd ed.). Belmont, CA: Thomson, Brooks/Cole.

Vogt, I. (2002). Substance use and abuse and the role of social workers in Germany. In L. A. Straussner & L. Harrison (Eds.), *International aspects of social work practice in the addictions* (pp. 69–83). New York: Haworth Press.

Walsh, D. C., et al. (1991). A randomized trial of treatment options for alcohol-abusing workers. *New England Journal of Medicine, 325* (11), 775–782.

CHAPTER 9

A profile of older Americans: 2005. Retrieved June 18, 2007, from the Administration on Aging website: http://www.aoa.gov/PROF/Statistics/profile/2005/profiles2005.asp

About ALFA. (2007). Retrieved November 23, 2007, from Assisted Living Federation of America website, http://www.alfa.org/i4a/pages/index.cfm?pageid=3293

About Bernard Nash. (2006). Retrieved June 15, 2007, from the American Association for Retired Persons (AARP) website: http://www.aarp.org/money/careers/employerresourcecenter/bestemployers/bernardnash

Aire, S. (2004, September 23). A lonely Italian retiree puts himself up for adoption. *The Christian Science Monitor,* pp. 1, 4.

Alzheimer's disease statistics Fact Sheet. Retrieved July 31, 2006, from Alzheimer's Association website: http://www.alz.org/resources/FactSheets/FSAAlzhermerStats.pdf

Austin, C. D., & McClelland, R. W. (2003). Case management practice with the elderly. In M. J. Holosko and M. D. Feid (Eds.), *Social work practice with the elderly* (3rd ed., pp. 175–202). Toronto: Canadian Scholars Press.

Barry, P. (2006, June). *Medicare Part D, in and out of the doughnut hole.* AARP Bulletin, pp. 16–18.

Bellos, N. S., & Ruffalo, M. S. (1995). Aging: Services. In R. L. Edwards (Ed.), *Encyclopedia of social work* (19th ed., Vol. 1, pp. 165–171). Washington, DC: NASW Press.

Benson, H. (1996). *Timeless healing, the power and biology of belief.* New York: Scribner.

Brown, B. (2004, November). Communes for grownups. *AARP Bulletin,* p. 22.

Butler, S., & Kaye, L. W. (2004). Rurality, aging, and social work: setting the context. In S. Butler and L. W. Kaye (Eds.), *Geronological social work in small towns and rural communities* (pp. 1–18). New York: The Haworth Press.

Conner, K. A. (2000). *Continuing to care.* New York: Palmer Press.

Cox, C. (2005). *Community care for an aging society.* New York: Springer.

Cox, E., & Parsons, R. (1994). *Empowerment-oriented social work practice with the elderly.* Pacific Grove, CA: Brooks/Cole.

Dunkel, R. E. (1987). Protective services for the aged. In A. Minahan (Ed.), *Encyclopedia of social work* (18th ed., vol. 2, pp. 393–395). Silver Spring, MD: NASW Press.

Edwards, M. (2004, November–December). As good as it gets; what country takes the best care of its older citizens? *AARP Magazine,* pp. 47–53.

Elderly people were abused in almost one-third of the U.S.'s nursing homes. (2001, July 31). *The Christian Science Monitor,* p. 20.

Eustis, N., Greenberg, J., & Patton, S. (1984). *Long term care for older persons, a policy perspective.* Monterey, CA: Brooks/Cole.

Ex, C., Gorter, K., & Janssen, U. (2004). Providing integrated health and social care for older persons in the Netherlands. In K. Leichsenring and A. Alaszewski (Eds.), *Providing integrated health and social care for older persons,* (pp. 415–445). Burlington, VT: Ashgate.

Facts and figures: Statistics on minority aging in the U.S. (2006). Retrieved June 18, 2007, from Administration on Aging website: http://www.aoa.gov/prof/Statistics/minority_aging/facts_minority_aging.asp

FRAC special analysis fact sheet: food stamps and the elderly. (2006). Retrieved June 18, 2007, from Food Research and Action Center website: http://www.frac.org/html/news/fsp/fsfactselderly.htm

Freeman, M. S. (1998, December 2). Sharing a roof and a way of life. *The Christian Science Monitor*, pp. 11, 14–15.

Gardner, G. (2006, June 21). Independent but alone. *The Christian Science Monitor*, pp. 13–14.

General information on Social Security. (2006). Retrieved June 16, 2006, from AARP website: http://aarp.org/research/social security/general/aresearch-import-352-FS39R.html

Green, A. (2006, December 26). A flap over recouping costs of Medicaid. *The Christian Science Monitor*, p. 3.

Greene, R. R. (2000). *Social work with the aged and their families* (2nd ed.). New York: Aldine de Gruyter.

Healy, T. C. (2003) Ethical practice issues in rural perspective. In S. Butler and L. Kay (Eds.). *Gerontological social work in small towns and rural communities* (pp. 265–285). New York: The Hayworth Social Work Practice Press.

Hodge, D. R. (2003/2004). Points of spiritual congruence and dissimilarity: a comparative study. *Arete*, 27(2), 17–33.

Hong, L. (2006, June). Rural older adults' access barriers to in-home and community-based services. *Social Work Research*, 30(2), 109–118.

Hopkins led nation's relief effort. (1998). Retrieved June 15, 2007, from NASW website: http://www.socialworkers.org/ profession/centennial/hopkins.htm

Hospice Services of America (2006). *Hospice services and expenses.* Retrieved September 18, 2006, from http://www. hospicefoundation.org/hospiceInfo/services.asp

Huttman, E. (1985). *Social services for the elderly.* New York: Free Press.

Karger, H. J., & Stoesz, D. (1998). *American social welfare policy: A pluralist approach* (3rd. ed.). New York: Addison Wesley Longman.

Kochman, A. (1997). Gay and lesbian elderly: Historical overview and implications for social work practice. In J. K. Quam (Ed.), *Social services for senior gay men and lesbians* (pp. 1–10). New York: Haworth Press.

Kosberg, J. I., & Nahmiash, D. (1996). Characteristics of victims and perpetrators and milieus of abuse and neglect. In L. A. Baumhover and S. C. Beall (Eds.), Abuse, neglect, and exploitation of older persons (pp. 31–45). Baltimore: Health Professions Press.

Kropf, N. P., & Wilks, S. (2003). Grandparents raising grandchildren. In B. Berkman (Ed.). Social work and healthcare in an aging society (pp. 177–200). New York: Springer.

Kubler-Ross, E. (1969). *On death and dying.* New York: Macmillan.

Lamb, G. M. (2004, November 9). In some nations, the rise of "shortgevity." *The Christian Science Monitor*, pp. 13, 14.

Lampman, J. (2000, July 23). Caring for sick, prisoners learn compassion. *The Christian Science Monitor*, pp. 1, 4.

Llana, S. M. (2006, September 8). Seniors raising their grandkids get a new boost. *The Christian Science Monitor*, pp. 1, 2.

Mackelprang, R. W., & Mackelprang, R. D. (2005, October).

Historical and contemporary issues in end-of-life decisions: implications for social work. *Social Work*, 50(4), 315–323.

Magnusson, P. (2006, June). Today's do-it-yourself pension. *AARP Bulletin*, pp. 22–23.

Marsh, J. C. (2005, April). Bush plan takes security out of social security. *Social Work*, 50(2), 99.

Metz, P. (1997). Staff development for working with lesbian and gay elders. In J. K. Quam (Ed.), *Social services for senior gay men and lesbians* (pp. 35–45). New York: Hawthorn Press.

Moody, R. A. (1976). *Life after life: the investigation of a phenomenon—survival of bodily death.* Harrisburg, PA: Stackpole Books.

Mui, A. C., Choi, N. C., & Monk, A. (1998). *Long term care and ethnicity.* Westport, CT: Auburn House.

Nadelhaft, A. (2005). NASW launches "Understanding aging, the social worker's role." Retrieved December 15, 2005, from the National Association of Social Worker's website, www.socialworkers.org

Nadelhaft, A. (2006). NASW launches new aging credential for social workers. Retrieved May 3, 2006, from the National Association of Social Worker's website, www.socialworkers.org

Naleppa, M. J., & Reid, W. J. (2003). *Gerontological social work, a task centered approach.* New York: Columbia University Press.

Nathanson, I. L., & Tirrito, T. T. (1998). *Gerontological social work: Theory into practice.* New York: Springer.

National Association of Social Workers (1994). *Social work with older people: understanding diversity.* Washington, DC: NASW Press.

National Shared Housing Resource Center (2006). *Shared housing, more then just a place to live.* Retrieved August 10, 2006, from http://www.nationalsharedhousing.org/ index.html

Newberg, A., D'Aquili, E., & Rause, V. (2001). *Why God won't go away, brain science and the biology of belief.* New York: Ballentine Books.

Nursing homes, business as usual (2006, September). *Consumer Reports*, pp. 38–41.

Older Americans Act. Retrieved August 10, 2006, from Administration on Aging website http://www.aoa.gov/ about/legbudg/oaa/legbudg_oss.asp

Olson, L. K. (2003). *The not so golden years: Caregiving, the frail elderly, and the long term care establishment.* Lanham, MD: Rowman & Littlefield.

Our fight: keeping Social Security strong. (2007). Retrieved June 18, 2008, from AARP website, http://www.aarp.org/ money/social_security/a2004-10-22-ss_strong.html

Popple, P. R., & Leighninger, L. L. (1999). *Social work, social welfare, and American society.* Boston: Allyn & Bacon.

Poverty among individuals by the official poverty measure, 2005. Retrieved June 3, 2007, from the Institute for Research on Poverty website: http://www.irp.wisc.edu/faqs/faq3/ table1.htm

Providing care for another adult a second job for many, National Alliance for Caregiving/AARP study shows. (2004, April 6).

Retrieved June 17, 2007, from AARP website, http://www. aarp.org/research/press-center/presscurrentnews/ 2004–03–30-caregiving.html

Radin, D. (2006, September–November). Becoming mindful of consciousness. *Shift, at the frontiers of consciousness, 12,* 40–41.

Rose Dobrof, DSW. (2001). Retrieved June 15, 2007, from Next Age website, http://nextagespeakers.com/ rdobrof.htm.

Rosengarten, L. (2000). *Social work in geriatric home health care.* New York: Hayworth Press.

Salamon, M. (1986). Mind/body health in practice, taking care of the caregivers. *Mindbody Health Newsletter, 7*(3), 3.

Schlesinger, R. (2006, June). An expert's view of ageism: things aren't any better. *AARP Bulletin,* p. 6

Schope, R. (2005). Who's afraid of growing old? Gay and lesbian perceptions of aging. *Journal of Gerontological Social Work, 45*(4), 23–39.

Schroeder-Sheker, T. (2001). *Transitus, a blessed death in the modern world.* Missoula, MT: St. Dunstan's Press.

Seeber, J. (1995). Congregational models. In M. Kimble, S. McFadden, J. Eilor, & J. Seeber (Eds.), *Aging, spirituality and religion* (pp. 253–269). Minneapolis, MN: Fortress Press.

Segal, E., & Brzuzy, S. (1998). *Social welfare policy, programs, and practice.* Itasca, IL: Peacock Publishers.

Small, G.W., et al. (1997, October 22). Diagnosis and treatment of Alzheimer disease and related disorders: Consensus statement of the American Association for Geriatric psychiatry, the Alzheimer's Association, and the American Geriatrics Society. *Journal of the American Medical Association, 278*(6) (electronic version). Retrieved July 31, 2006, from http://www.alz.org/Resources/FactSheets/ Diagnosistreatment.pdf

Smoothing the way to retirement pay (2006, July 28). *The Christian Science Monitor,* p. 8.

Stevens, D. G. (2001, May 23). Elderly help fill adoption gap. *The Daily News,* West Bend, WI, p. A5.

Stoessen, L. (2006, June). Legal articles cover CIGNA case, end-of-life choices. *NASW News,* p. 10.

Stoessen, L. (2007, January). Stress on women studied. *NASW News,* pp. 1, 8.

The new Medicare (Part D) drug "benefit." (2006, January). *Health Letter, Public Citizen Research Group,* pp. 14–16.

Torres-Gil, F. M., & Puccinelli, M. A. (1995). Aging: Public policy issues and trends. In R. L. Edwards (Ed.), *Encyclopedia of social work* (19th ed., Vol. 1, pp. 159–164). Washington, DC: NASW Press.

Trumbull, M. (2006, August 18). Reform erodes future of pensions. *The Christian Science Monitor,* p. 2.

What is Alzheimers (2007). Retrieved June 18, 2007, from the Alzheimer's Association website, http://www.alz.org/ alzheimers_disease_what_is_alzheimers.asp.

CHAPTER 10

Amnesty International. (2000, May). *A briefing for the UN Committee against Torture.* Retrieved October 30, 2001, from http://www.web.amnesty.org/ai.nsf/indes/ AMR510562000

Amnesty International USA. (2007a). *Racial profiling.* Retrieved July 29, 2007, from http://www.amnestyusa. org/Domestic_Human_Rights/Racial_Profiling/page.do? id=11066

Amnesty International USA. (2007b). *Threat and humiliation: Racial profiling, national security, and human rights in the United States.* Retrieved July 29, 2007, from: http://www. amnestyusa.org/Racial_Profiling/Report_Threat_and_ Humiliation/page.do?id=1106664&n1=3&n2=850&n3= 1298

Barker, R. L. (2003). *The social work dictionary* (5th ed.). Washington, DC: NASW Press.

Barker, R. L., & Branson, D. M. (2000). *Forensic social work: Legal aspects of professional practice* (2nd ed.). New York: Haworth Press.

Beaucar, K. O. (1999). Effort against death penalty alters views. *NASW News, 44*(6), 13.

Bureau of Labor Statistics, U.S. Department of Labor. (2007). Probation officers and correctional treatment specialists. *Occupational outlook handbook, 2006–2007 edition.* Retrieved July 20, 2007, from http://www.bls.gov/oco/ ocos265.htm

Butts, J. A. (1995). Community-based corrections. In *Encyclopedia of social work* (19th ed., pp. 549–555). Washington, DC: NASW Press.

Catalano, S. M. (2006, September). *National crime victimization survey: Criminal victimization, 2005.* U.S. Department of Justice, Bureau of Justice Statistics. Retrieved July 28, 2007, from: http://www.ojp.usdoj.gov/bjs/pub/pdfcv05.pdf

Colsher, P. L., Wallace, R. B., Loeffelholz, P. L., & Sales, M. (1992). Health status of older male prisoners: A comprehensive survey. *Public Health Briefs, 82*(6), 881–884.

Corrections Corporation of America. (2007). *About CCA: CCA at a glance.* Retrieved July 27, 2007, from http://www. correctionscorp.com/aboutcca.html

Dickerson, J. G. (2001). Margaret Murray Washington: Organizer of rural African American women. In I. B. Carlton-LaNey (Ed.), *African American leadership: An empowerment tradition in social welfare history.* Washington, DC: NASW Press.

Farr, K. A. (2000). Classification for female inmates: Moving forward. *Crime & Delinquency, 46*(1), 3–15.

Galaway, B. (1981). Social service and criminal justice. In N. Gilbert & H. Specht (Eds.), *Handbook of the social services.* Englewood Cliffs, NJ: Prentice Hall.

Hoffman, J. (2007, October 21). Criminal element. *New York Times.* Retrieved December 26, 2007, from http://www. nytimes.com/2007/10/21/magazine/21wwln-idealab-t. html?ref=magazine

Human Rights Watch. (n.d.). *Did You Know?* Retrieved July 28, 2007, from: http://www.hrw.org

Hutchison, E. D. (1987). Use of authority. *Social Service Review, 61*(4), 581–598.

Isenstadt, P. M. (1995). Adult courts. In *Encyclopedia of social work* (19th ed., pp. 68–74). Washington, DC: NASW Press.

Jensen, J. M., & Howard, M. O. (1998). Youth crime, public policy, and practice in the juvenile justice system: Recent trends and needed reforms. *Social Work, 43*(4), 324–334.

Killias, M., Aebi, M. F., & Ribeaud, D. (2000). Learning through controlled experiments: Community service and heroin prescription in Switzerland. *Crime & Delinquency, 46*(2), 233–251.

Lyons, K., Manion, K., & Carlsen, M. (2006). *International perspectives on social work: Global conditions and local practice.* New York: Palgrave Macmillan.

MacKenzie, D. L. (2000). Evidence-based corrections: Identifying what works. *Crime & Delinquency, 46*(4), 457–471.

Maguire, K., & Pastore, A. L. (Eds.) (2001, February 2). Figure 6.1, Sentenced prisoners under jurisdiction of state and federal correctional authorities on December 31; Table 6.27, Rate (per 100,000 resident population) of sentenced prisoners under jurisdiction of state and federal correctional authorities on December 31. *Sourcebook of criminal justice statistics 2000.* Retrieved January 12, 2002, from http://www.albany.edu/sourcebook

Malone, D. (2005). Cruel and inhumane: Executing the mentally ill. *Amnesty International, 31*(3), 20–23.

Mauer, M. (1994). *Americans behind bars: U.S. and international use of incarceration, 1992–1993.* Washington, DC: The Sentencing Project.

McNeece, C. A. (1995). Adult corrections. In *Encyclopedia of social work* (19th ed., pp. 61–68). Washington, DC: NASW Press.

Mears, D. P., & Kelly, W. R. (1999). Assessments and intake processing: Emerging policy considerations. *Crime & Delinquency, 45*(4), 508–529.

Mesch, G. S., & Fishman, G. (1999). Entering the system: Ethnic differences in closing juvenile criminal files in Israel. *Journal of Crime and Delinquency, 36*(2), 175–193.

Misleh, D. J., & Hanneman, E. U. (2004). Emerging issues: The faith communities and the criminal justice system. In E. H. Jucah & M. Bryant (Eds.), *Criminal justice: Retribution vs. restoration* (pp. 111–131). New York: Haworth Press.

Moon, M. M., Sundt, J. L., Cullen, F. T., & Wright, J. P. (2000). Is child saving dead? Public support for juvenile rehabilitation. *Crime & Delinquency, 46*(1), 38–60.

Myers, D. L. (2005). *Boys among men: Trying and sentencing juveniles as adults.* Westport, CT: Praeger Publishers.

National Association of Social Workers. (1999). *Code of Ethics of the National Association of Social Workers.* Washington, DC: Author.

National Council on Crime and Delinquency. (n.d.). *Research capabilities: Offender risk and needs assessment.* Retrieved July 20, 2007, from http://www.nccd-crc.org/nccd/n_more_researchrisk.html

Netherland, W. (1987). Corrections system: Adult. In *Encyclopedia of social work* (18th ed., pp. 351–360). Silver Spring, MD: NASW Press.

O'Neil, J. V. (2003). Forensic field broader than most think. *NASW News, 48*(10).

Oliphant, J. (1994). Group work with victims of crime: Mutual aid in practice. In C. Sumner, M. Israel, M. O'Connell, & R. Sarre (Eds.), *International victimology: Selected papers from the 8th International Symposium: Proceedings of a symposium held 21–26 August, 1994.* Retrieved July 22, 2007, from http://www.aic.gov.au/publications/proceedings/27/oliphant.html

Pastore, A. L., & Maguire, K. (Eds.). (2006). Table 4.26.2005; Table 6.41.2005. *Sourcebook of criminal justice statistics* [online]. Retrieved July 19, 2007, from http:www//Albany.edu/sourcebook/

Pray, K. (1945). Place of social casework in the treatment of delinquency. *Social Service Review, 19*(2), 235–248.

Robinson, B. A. (2001, February 16). *Capital punishment: The death penalty.* Retrieved November 23, 2001, from http://www.religioustolerance.org/ecute.htm.

Sabol, W. J., Minton, T. D., & Harrison, P. M. (2007, June). *Bureau of Justice statistics bulletin: Prison and jail inmates at midyear 2006.* Retrieved July 26, 2007, from http://www.ojp.usdoj.gov/bjs/pub/pdf/pjim06.pdf

Saleebey, D. (Ed.). (2006). *The strengths perspective in social work practice* (4th ed.). Boston: Pearson, Allyn & Bacon.

Schiller, L. Y., & Zimmer, B. (2005). Sharing the secrets: The power of women's groups for sexual abuse survivors. In A. Gitterman & L. Shulman (Eds.), *Mutual aid groups, vulnerable & resilient populations, and the life cycle* (pp. 290–319). New York: Columbia University Press,

Scott, E. S., & Grisso, T. (1998). The evolution of adolescence: A developmental perspective on juvenile justice reform. *Journal of Criminal Law and Criminology, 88*(1), 137–189.

Siefert, K., & Pimlott, S. (2001). Improving pregnancy outcome during imprisonment: A model residential care program. *Social Work, 46*(2), 125–134.

State of Wisconsin Department of Corrections. (2007). Form DOC-10 (Rev. 12/2006): Rules of community supervision. Form DOC-10SO (Rev. 12/2006): Standard sex offender rules. Form DOC-502 (Rev. 1/03): Admission to adult field caseload: Assessment of offender risk. Wisconsin Administrative Code. Madison, WI: Author. Provided by Peggy Kendrigan, Division of Community Corrections.

Stein, J. (2000, July 10). The lessons of Cain. *Time*, pp. 84–85.

Toch, H. (1977). *Police, prisons, and the problem of violence.* Rockville, MD: National Institute of Mental Health, Center for Studies of Crime and Delinquency.

Travis, J. (2004). Building from the ground up: Strategies for creating safe and just communities. In E. H. Judah & M. Bryant (Eds.), *Criminal justice: Retribution vs. restoration* (pp. 173–195). New York: Haworth Press.

Trimble, D. (2005). Uncovering kindness and respect: Men who have practiced violence in intimate relationships. In A. Gitterman & L. Shulman (Eds.), *Mutual aid groups, vulnerable & resilient populations, and the life cycle* (pp. 352–372). New York: Columbia University Press.

U.S. Department of Justice, Bureau of Justice Statistics (2007). *Capital punishment statistics.* Retrieved July 28, 2007, from http://www.ojp.gov/bjs/cp.htm

U.S. Department of Justice, Federal Bureau of Investigation. (2007, June). *2006 crime in the United States: Preliminary annual uniform crime report.* Retrieved July 27, 2007, from http://www.fbi.gov/ucr/06prelim/ucrtable3.htm

U.S. Department of Justice, OJJDP Stastical Briefing Book. (2006). *Juvenile offenders and victims: 2006 national report.* Retrieved July 28, 2007, from http://ojjdp.ncjrs.org./ojstatbb/nr2006/index.html

van Wormer, K. (2004). *Confronting oppression, restoring justice: From policy analysis to social action.* Alexandria, VA: Council on Social Work Education

Walmsley, R. (2007, January 29). *World prison population list* (7th ed.). London: King's College, International Centre for Prison Studies.

CHAPTER 11

ADA rules out discrimination. (1993, October). *Update.* West Allis, WI: Advocates for Retarded Citizens, p. 1.

Aging, older adults and their aging caregivers, AAMR fact sheet (2001, March 6). Retrieved 2002, from the American Association on Mental Retardation website, http://161.58.153.187/Policies/faqaging.shtml

Americans with Disabilities Act of 1990. Section 2, Findings and Purposes. Public Law 101–336.

Americans with Disabilities Act fact sheet. (1990, September). Washington, DC: U.S. Architectural Board, p. 1.

Autism (2007). Retrieved July 9, 2007, from the March of Dimes website, http://www.marchofdimes.com/printableArticles/4439_10110.asp

Asch, A., & Mudrick, N. R. (1995). Disability. In R. L. Edwards (Ed.), *Encyclopedia of social work* (19th ed., Vol. 1, pp. 752–760). Washington, DC: NASW Press.

Barnwell, D. A., & Day, M. (1996). Providing support to diverse families. In P. Beckman (Ed.), *Strategies for working with families with disabilities* (pp. 47–65). Baltimore: Paul H. Brookes.

Baroff, G. S. (1991). *Developmental disabilities: Psychosocial aspects.* Austin, TX: ProEd.

Beaulaurier, R. L., & Taylor, S. H. (2001). Social work practice with people with disabilities in the era of disability rights. *Social Work in Health Care 32*(4), 67–91.

Bender, W. N. (1992). Learning disabilities. In P. J. McLaughlin & P. Wehman (Eds.), *Developmental disabilities: A handbook of best practices* (pp. 82–87). Boston: Andover Medical.

Benson, H. B. (1996). *Timeless healing, the power and biology of belief.* New York: Scribner.

Bishop, K. (2006). Family-centered services to infants and toddlers with or at risk for disabilities: IDEA 2004, Part C. In R. Constable, C. Massat, S. McDonald, & J. Flynn (Eds.). *School Social Work* (6th ed., pp. 189–204). Chicago: Lyceum Books.

Cerebral palsy. (2004). Retrieved July 9, 2007, from the March of Dimes website, http://www.marchofdimes.com/printableArticles/4439_1208.asp

Christensen, C. (1996). Disabled, handicapped, or disordered: What's in a name? In C. Christensen & F. Rizvi (Eds.), *Disability and the dilemmas of education and justice* (pp. 63–78). Buckingham, UK: Open University Press.

Children with autism get their day in court (2007, June 11). Retrieved July 4, 2007, from Dr. Mercola's website (quoting *Forbes* magazine of June 11, 2007), http:// v.mercola.com/blogs/PrintArticle.aspx?PostID=10994&SectionID=37

Convention on the rights of persons with disabilities (2007, June 7). Retrieved July 9, 2007, from the American Association for Intellectual and Developmental Disability (AAIDD) website, http://www.aamr.org/unresolution.shtml

Council on Social Work Education (2001). *Educational policy and accreditation standards.* Alexandria, VA: Author.

Definition of mental retardation (2002). Retrieved July 9, 2007, from the American Association on Intellectual and Developmental Disabilities (AAIDD) website, http://www.aamr.org/Policies/faq_mental_retardation.shtml

DeWeaver, K., & Kropf, N. (1992, Winter). Persons with mental retardation: A forgotten minority in education. *Journal of Social Work Education, 28* (1), 38–40.

Dickerson, M. U. (1981). *Social work practice with the mentally retarded.* New York: Free Press.

Dossey, L. (2003). *Healing beyond the body, medicine and the infinite reach of the mind.* Boston: Shambala.

Drinking alcohol during pregnancy (2007). Retrieved July 9, 2007, from the March of Dimes website, http://www.marchofdimes.com/printableArticles/14332_1170 asp

Emotional disturbance, fact sheet 5 (2004, January). Retrieved July 9, 2007, from the National Dissemination Center for Children with Disabilities website, http://www.nichcy.org/pubs/factshe/fs5txt.htm

Fact sheet on traumatic brain injury. (1999). Milwaukee, WI: ARC Milwaukee.

Fact sheet: Frequently asked questions about mental retardation. Retrieved July 9, 2007, from the American Association on Intellectual and Developmental Disabilities (AAIDD) website: http://www.aamr.org/Policies/faq_mental_retardation.shtml

Fact sheet: Self advocacy. (2005). Retrieved July 12, 2007, from the American Association on Intellectual and Developmental

Disabilities (AAIDD) website, http://www.aamr.org/Policies/faq_movement.shtml

Feldmann, L. (1997, October 24). Fraud-busters cut benefits for disabled children. *Christian Science Monitor*, p. 4.

Freedman, R. (1995). Developmental disabilities: Direct practice. In R. L. Edwards (Ed.). *Encyclopedia of social work* (19th ed., Vol. 1, pp. 721–728). Washington, DC: NASW Press.

Genetic counseling. (2007). Retrieved July 9, 2007, from the March of Dimes website, http://www.marchofdimes.com/printableArticles/4439_15008.asp

Gilson, S. F. (1998). Choice and self-advocacy, a consumer's perspective. In P. Wehman & J. Kregel (Eds.)., *More than a job: Satisfying careers for people with disabilities* (pp. 3–23). Baltimore: P. H. Brookes.

Gold, S. (2005, February 20). *2003 Census data for persons with disabilities*. Retrieved July 9, 2007, from the National Association for the Mentally Ill (NAMI) website, http://namiscc.org/Research/2004/2003-CensusData.htm

Habilitation plan administrator. (2001). Retrieved from the Washington State Department of Personnel website, http://hr.dop.wa.gov/lib/hrdr/speca/50000/56980.htm

Hearing loss. (2004). Retrieved July 9, 2007, from the March of Dimes website, http://www. marchofdimes. com/printableArticles/4439_1232.asp

Hooyman, N. R., & Gonyea, J. G. (1995). Family caregiving. In R. L. Edwards (Ed.), *Encyclopedia of social work* (19th ed., Vol. 1, pp. 951–957). Washington, DC: NASW Press.

Illicit drug use during pregnancy. (2006, November). Retrieved July 9, 2007, from the March of Dimes website, http://search.marchofdimes.com/cgi-bin/MsmGo.exe? grab_id=0&page_id=480&query=coc

Johnson, A. B., & Surles, R. C. (1994). Has deinstitutionalization failed? In S. A. Kirk and S. D. Einbinder (Eds.), *Controversial issues in mental health* (pp. 213–216). Boston: Allyn & Bacon.

Learning disabilities: Signs, symptoms and strategies (2004). Retrieved July 9, 2007, from the Learning Disabilities Association of America website, http://www.Idanatl.org/aboutld/parents/id_basics/print_Id.asp

Liu, G.Z. (2005). Best practices, developing cross-cultural competence from a Chinese perspective. In John Stone (Ed.) *Culture and disability, providing culturally competent services* (pp. 65–85). Thousand Oaks, CA: Sage.

Lift every voice: Modernizing disability policies and programs to serve a diverse nation. (1999, December 1). Washington, DC: National Council on Disability, p. 50.

Lum, D. (1992). *Social work with people of color: A process-stage approach* (2nd ed.). Pacific Grore, CA: Brooks/Cole.

Mackelprang, M., & Saisgiver, R. (1999). *Disability: A diversity model approach in human service practice*. Pacific Grove, CA: Brooks/Cole.

Mannes, M. (1998). The new psychology and economics of permanency. *The prevention report #2*. Iowa City: The University of Iowa National Resource Center for Family Centered Practice.

May, G.E. (2005). Changing the future of disability: the disability discrimination model. In G. May & M. B. Raske (Eds.). *Ending disability discrimination, strategies for social workers* (pp. 82–98). Boston: Allyn & Bacon.

May, G. E., and Raske, M. (Eds.). (2005). *Ending disability discrimination, strategies for social workers*. Boston: Allyn & Bacon.

McDonald-Wikler, L. (1987). Disabilities, developmental. In A. Minahan (Ed.), *Encyclopedia of social work* (18th ed., Vol. 1, pp. 423–431). Silver Spring, MD: NASW Press.

Meekosha, H., & Jakubowicz, A. (1996). Disability, participation, representation and social justice. In C. Christensen and F. Rizvi (Eds.), *Disability and the dilemmas of education and justice* (pp. 9–95). Buckingham, UK: Open University Press.

Mendez, T. (2004). A special compromise on education. *Christian Science Monitor*, pp. 11, 12.

Morrison-Orton, D. J. (2005). The use of religion and spiritual strategies in rehabilitation. In J. Murphy and J. Pardeck (Eds.). *Disability issues for social workers and human services professionals in the twenty-first century* (pp. 5–41). New York: Hayworth Press.

Murphy. J. W., & Pardeck, J. T. (Eds.). (2005). *Disability issues for social workers and human service professionals in the twenty-first century*. New York: Hayworth Press.

National Association of Social Workers. (1996). *NASW code of ethics*. Washington, DC: NASW Press.

NINDS traumatic brain injury information page. (2007). Retrieved July 9, 2007, from the National Institute of Neurological Disorders and Stroke website, http://www.ninds.nih.gov/disorders/tbi.htm

Oliver, M., & Sapey, B. (2006). *Social work with disabled people* (3rd ed.). New York: Palgrave Macmillan.

Pardeck, J. T. (1998). *Social work after the Americans with Disabilities Act*. Westport, CT: Auburn House.

Pardeck, J. T. (2005). An analysis of the Americans with Disabilities Act (ADA) in the twenty-first century. In J. Murphy and J. Pardeck (Eds.). *Disability issues for social workers and human service professionals in the twenty first century* (pp. 121–151). New York: Haworth Press.

Parent, W. S., Cone, A. A., Turner, E., & Wehman, P. (1998). Supported employment, consumers leading the way. In P. Wehman & J. Kregel (Eds.), *More than a job: Securing satisfying careers for people with disabilities* (pp. 149–166). Baltimore: P. H. Brooks.

Parkinson, C. B., & Howard, M. (1996). Older persons with mental retardation/developmental disabilities. In M. J. Mellor (Ed.), *Special populations and systems linkages* (pp. 91–101). New York: Haworth Press.

Patton, J. R., Blackbourn, J. M., & Fad, K. (1996). *Exceptional individuals in focus* (6th ed.). Englewood Cliff, NJ: Prentice Hall.

Petr, C., & Barney, D, (1993, May). Reasonable efforts for children with disabilities: The parents' perspective. *Social Work, 38*(3), 252–255.

Putnam, M. (2007). Moving from separate to crossing aging and disability service networks. In M. Putnam (Ed). *Aging and disability, crossing network lines* (pp. 5–17). New York: Springer.

Raske, M. (2005). The disability discrimination model in social work practice. In G. May and M. Raske (Eds.)., *Ending disability discrimination strategies for Social Workers* (pp. 106–107). Boston: Allyn & Bacon.

Richey, W. (2002, January 9). In workplace, tougher standards on job-related injuries. *Christian Science Monitor*, p. 2.

Richey, W. (2004, May 18). Court boosts civil rights law for disabled. *The Christian Science Monitor*, pp. 1, 10.

Richmond, M. (1917). *Social diagnosis*. Philadelphia: Russel Sage Foundation, p. 26.

Rothman, J. C. (2003). *Social work practice across disability*. Boston: Allyn & Bacon.

Schlitz, M., & Amorok, T. (2005). *Consciousness and healing, integral approaches to mind-body medicine*. St. Louis, MO: Elsevier.

Segal, S. P. (1995). Deinstitutionalization. In R. L. Edwards (Ed.), *Encyclopedia of social work* (19th ed., Vol. 1, pp. 704–711). Washington, DC: NASW Press.

Segal, S., Silverman, C., & Tomkin, T. (1993, November). Empowerment and self-help agency practice for people with mental disabilities. *Social Work, 38*(6), 705–708.

Smart, J. (2001). *Disability, society, and the individual*. Gaithersburg, MD: Aspen.

Snyder, R., & Ne'eman, A. (2007, July 10). *Autism from autistics*. Retrieved July 11, 2007, from the Autism Self Advocacy Network website, http://www.autisticadvocacy.org

Special education and the Individuals with Disabilities Education Act (2007). Retrieved April 7, 2007, from the National Education Association website, http://www.nea.org/specialed/index.html?mode=print

Stites, S. (2001). *Allyse* (unpublished paper). Northampton, MA: Smith College.

Stoessen, L. (2005, March). Children with disabilities: a family affair. *NASW News*, p. 4.

Stone, J. H. (Ed.) (2005). *Culture and disability, providing culturally competent services*. Thousand Oaks: CA: Sage.

Switzky, H., Dudzinski, M., Van Acker, R., & Gambro, J. (1988). Historical foundations of out-of-home residential alternatives for mentally retarded persons. In L. Heal, J. Haney, & Amado, A. (Eds.), *Integration of developmentally disabled individuals into the community* (2nd ed., pp. 19–35). Baltimore: P. H. Brooks.

Talbott, R. E. (1992). Communication disorders. In P. J. McLaughlin & P. Wehman (Eds.). *Developmental disabilities: A handbook for best practices* (pp. 98–100). Boston: Andover Medical.

Torres-Gill, F. (2007). Translating research into program and policy changes. In M. Putnam (Ed.). *Aging and disability* (pp. 245–262). New York: Springer.

Understanding epilepsy. (2007). Retrieved July 9, 2007, from the Epilepsy Foundation website, http://www.epilepsyfoundation.org/about/

U. S. Census Bureau (2007, May). *Asian/Pacific American Heritage Month*. Retrieved December 23, 2007, from the IM Diversity website, http://www.imdiversity.com/Villages/Asian/reference/census_asian_pacific_american_heritage_2007.asp

Weathers, R.R. II (2005). *A guide to disability statistics from the American Community Survey*. Retrieved July 10, 2007, from the Employment and Disability Institute Collection website, http://digitalcommons.ilt.cornell.edu/edicollect/129

Wehman, P., Inge, K., Revell, W. G. Jr., & Brooke, V. (2007). *Real work for real pay, inclusive employment for people with disabilities*. Baltimore: P. H. Brookes.

Willer, B., & Itagliata, J. (1984). *Promises and realities for mentally retarded citizens*. Baltimore: University Park Press.

Wolfe, P. S. (1992). Challenges for service providers. In P. J. McLaughlin & P. Wehman (Eds.), *Developmental disabilities: A handbook for best practices* (pp. 125–130). Boston: Andover Medical.

CHAPTER 12

Acs, G., & Loprest, P. (2007). *TANF caseload composition and leavers synthesis report*. Retrieved December 30, 2007, from: http://www.acf.hhs.gov/programs/opre/welfare_employ/tanf_caseload/reports/tanf_caseload_comp/tanf_caseload_final.pdf

Barker, R. L. (2003). *The social work dictionary* (5th ed.). Washington, DC: NASW Press.

Benard, B. (2006). Using strengths-based practice to tap the resilience of families. In D. Saleebey (Ed.)., *The strengths perspective in social work practice* (4th ed., pp. 197–220). Boston: Pearson, Allyn & Bacon.

Besthorn, F. (2002). Radical environmentalism and the ecological self: Rethinking the concept of self-identity for social work practice. *Journal of Progressive Human Services, 13*(1), 53–72.

Besthorn, F., & Canda, E. R. (2002). Revisioning environment: Deep ecology for education and teaching in social work. *Journal of Teaching in Social Work, 22*(1/2), 79–101.

Blythe, M. (2006). Will wind and biofuels be enough? *The Futurist, 40*, 28.

Bread for the World. (2007). *Healthy food, farms, & families: Hunger 2007*. Retrieved August 17, 2007, from http://www.bread.org/learn/hunger-reports/hunger-report-2007-download.html

Bruno, A. (2006). Refugee admissions and resettlement policy. *CRS report for Congress*. (Congressional Research Service; the Library of Congress). Retrieved August 13, 2007, from http://www.ilw.com/immigdaily/news/2006.0215-crs.pdf

Bureau of Labor Statistics, U.S. Department of Labor. (2006). *Occupational outlook handbook: 2006–2007 edition, social workers.* Retrieved August 16, 2006, from http://www.bls.gov/oco/ocos060.htm

Canton, J. (2006). *The extreme future: The top trends that will reshape the world for the next 5, 10, and 20 years.* New York: Dutton.

Cetron, M. (1994). An American renaissance in the year 2000: 74 trends that will affect America's future—and yours. *The Futurist, 28*(2), 27, 1A–11A.

Chideya, F. (1999). *The color of our future.* New York: William Morrow.

Children's Defense Fund. (n.d.). *Income support and welfare.* Retrieved August 17, 2007, from http://www.childrensdefense.org/site/PageServer?pagename=family-income_welfare_default

Coates, J., & Leahy, T. (2006). Ideology and politics: Essential factors in the path toward sustainability. *Electronic Green Journal, 23,* 1–20.

Dahinden, U., Lindsey, N., Chatjouli, A., Diego, C., Fjaestad, B., Matias, M., et al. (2006). Dilemmas of genetic information. In G. Gaskell & M. W. Bauer (Eds.), *Genomics and society: Legal, ethical and social dimensions.* London: Earthscan.

Devore, W., & Schlesinger, E. G. (1999). *Ethnic-sensitive social work practice* (5th ed.). Boston: Allyn & Bacon.

Ethics Committee of the American Society for Reproductive Medicine. (2007). *Financial compensation of oocyte donors.* Retrieved August 21, 2007, from http://www.asrm.org/Media/Ethics/financial_incentives.pdf

Fadiman, A. (1997). The *spirit catches you and you fall down: A Hmong child, her American doctors, and the collision of two cultures.* New York: Farrar, Straus and Giroux.

Freedman, T. G. (1998). Genetic susceptibility testing: Ethical and social quandaries. *Health & Social Work, 23*(3), 214–222.

Ginsberg, L. (2005, Spring). The future of social work as a profession. *Advances in Social Work,* 5–16.

Glenn, J. C., & Gordon, T. J. (2006). Update the state of the future. *The Futurist, 40*(1), 21.

Glossary of terms. (2001). Retrieved January 28, 2002, from the Fertility Institutes website, http://www.fertility-docs.com/glossary.html

Grew, R. (2006). Global history and globalization. In S. Hewa & D. Stapleton (Eds.), *Globalization, philanthropy, and civil society: Toward a new political culture in the 21st century* (pp. 15–32). New York: Springer.

Gutierrez, L., & Nagda, B. A. (1996). The multicultural imperative in human services organizations: Issues for the twenty-first century. In P. R. Raffoul & C. A. McNeece (Eds.), *Future issues for social work practice* (pp. 203–213). Boston: Allyn & Bacon.

Hartman, C. (2007). *By the numbers.* Retrieved August 17, 2007, from http://www.demos.org/inequality/ByNumbersMay31.pdf

Hawaleshka, D. (2005). I take that as a "yes." *Maclean's, 118*(38), 52.

Hewa, S., & Stapleton, D. H. (2006). Structure and process of global integration. In S. Hewa & D. Stapleton (Eds.), *Globalization, philanthropy, and civil society: Toward a new political culture in the 21st century* (pp. 3–13). New York: Springer.

Holland, J. (2005), The regeneration of ecological, societal, and spiritual life: The holistic post modern mission of humanity in the newly emerging planetary civilization. *Journal of Religion and Spirituality in Social Work, 24*(1/2), 7–25.

Holmes, K. A. (1996). Headed for the future: Families in the twenty-first century. In P. R. Raffoul & C. A. McNeece (Eds.), *Future issues for social work practice* (pp. 172–179). Boston: Allyn & Bacon.

Holody, R. (1999). Toward a new permanency planning: How kinship care can revitalize the foster care system. *Areté, 23*(1), 1–10.

Human cloning and genetic modification: The basic science you need to know. (2002, January 24). Retrieved January 28, 2002, from http://www.arhp.org/cloning/

Human organs for sale. (2001, July 21). Retrieved January 24, 2002, from the *Newsweek* website, http://www.msnbc.com/news/603127.asp

Iatridis, D. S. (1988). New social deficit: Neoconservatism's policy of social underdevelopment. *Social Work, 33*(1), 11–15.

Kemp, R. L. (2000). Cities in the 21st century: The forces of change. *Futures Research Quarterly,* 21–30.

Ki-Moon, B. (2007). *The millennium development goals report 2007.* New York: United Nations.

Larsen, L. J. (2004). *The foreign-born population in the United States: 2003.* Retrieved August 14, 2007, from http://www.census.gov/prod/2004pubs/p20–551.pdf

Levine, J. (2004). Genetic engineering threatens women's reproductive choices. In L. Gerdes (Ed.), *Genetic engineering: Opposing viewpoints.* Framington Hills, MI: Greenhaven Press.

Lewis, J. J. (2007). *Women in the United States Senate.* Retrieved August 17, 2007, from http://womenshistory.about.com/b/a/257491.htm

Lyons, K., Manion, K., & Carlsen, M. (2006). *International perspectives on social work: Global conditions and local practice.* New York: Palgrave Macmillan.

Major new spending urged for homeless. (1994, May 18). *New York Times,* p. A18.

McKinley, B. (n.d.). *Editorial: Looking at the bigger picture in migration.* Retrieved August 14, 2007, from the International Organizaton for Migration website, http://www.iom.int/jahia/jsp/index.jsp

Meade, B., Rosen, S., & Shapouri, S. (2007). *Food security assessment, 2006.* Retrieved August 17, 2007, from the U.S. Department of Agriculture website, http://www.ers.usda.gov/Publications/GFA18/

Naisbitt, J. (2006). *Mind set! Reset your thinking and see the future*. New York: HarperCollins.

National Association of Social Workers. (1999). *Code of ethics of the National Association of Social Workers*. Washington, DC: NASW Press.

National Association of Social Workers. (2007). *Social workers in federal office*. Retrieved August 17, 2007, from http://www.socialworkers.org/pace/fed_swers.asp

National Committee on Pay Equity. (2006). *The wage gap over time: In real dollars, women see a continuing gap*. Retrieved August 17, 2007, from: http://www.pay-equity.org/info-time.html

National Human Genome Research Institute. (2006, December). *The Human Genome Project completion: Frequently asked questions*. Retrieved August 20, 2007, from http://www.genome.gov/11006943

National Institutes of Health. (2006). *Human Genome Project fact sheet*. Retrieved August 21, 2007, from http://www.nih.gov/about/researchresultsforthepublic/Human GenomeProject.pdf

O'Neil, J. V. (2002). EAPs offer multitude of internet services. *NASW News*, *47*(1), 14.

Questions and answers on pay equity. (1998). Retrieved January 25, 1999, from http://www.Feminist.com/fairpay.htm

Rifkin, J. (2004). *The European dream: How Europe's vision of the future is quietly eclipsing the American dream*. New York: Jeremy P. Tarcher/Penguin.

Rathode, B. (2006, June 22). *Over 3 million babies born through IVF in 3 decades*. Retrieved August 21, 2007, from http://www.earthtimes.org/articles/show/7288.html

Simanski, J. (2007). Naturalizations in the United States: 2006. *Annual flow report*. (Office of Immigration Statistics, U.S. Department of Homeland Security.) Retrieved August 14, 2007, from http://www.dhs.gov/xlibrary/assets/ statistics/publications/Natz_01_Sec508 Compliant.pdf

Tucker, P. (2006). Technology: Embryonic stem cells promise new cures. *The Futurist*, *40*(2), 16–17.

U.S. Bureau of the Census. (1950). *Census of population: 1950* (Vol. II, Pt. 1, U.S. Summary, Table 38, pp. 90–91 & Table 61, pp. 109–111) and *U.S. census of population: 1950* (Special Reports: Nonwhite Population by Race, Table 2, p.16, Table 3, p.17, Table 4, p.18, and Table 5, p.19).

U.S. Bureau of the Census. (1998). Annual population estimates by sex, race and Hispanic origin, selected years from 1990 to 1998. *The official statistics*. Washington, DC: U.S. Government Printing Office.

U.S. Census Bureau. (2000). *Census 2000 national data. Projections of the resident population by age, sex, race, and Hispanic origin: 1999 to 2100*. Retrieved January 18, 2002, from http://www.census.gov

U.S. Census Bureau. (2001a). *Nation's median age highest ever, but 65-and-over population's growth lags, Census 2000 shows*. Retrieved January 19, 2002, from http://www.census.gov/PressRelease/www/2001/cb01cn67.html

U.S. Census Bureau. (2001b). *Population projections*. Retrieved January 19, 2002, from http:www.census.gov/population/www/projections/ propproj.html

U.S. Census Bureau. (2004a). *Table 1a. Projected population of the United States, by race and Hispanic origin: 2000 to 2040*. Retrieved August 10, 2007, from http: census.gov/ipc/www/usinterimpro/natprojtab01a.pdf

U.S. Census Bureau. (2004b). *Table 2a. Projected population of the United States, by age and sex: 2000 to 2050*. Retrieved August 11, 2007, from http: census.gov/ipc/www/usinterimprojtab02a.pdf

U.S. Census Bureau. (2006). *S2001.Earnings in the past 12 months (in 2005 inflation-adjusted dollars); Data set: 2005 American Community Survey*. Retrieved August 17, 2007, from http:www.factfinder.census.gov/ servlet/STTable?_bm=y&-geo_id=01000US&-qr_name=ACS_2005_EST_GOO_S2001&_ds_name= ACS_2005_EST_GOO_

U.S. Census Bureau (2007a). *America's families and living arrangements: 2006*. Retrieved August 11, 2007, from http://www.census.gov/population/socdemo/hh-fam/cps2006/tab/AVG1.xls and http://www.census.gov/population/socdemo/hh-fam/cps2006/tab/AVG2.xlls

U.S. Census Bureau (2007b). *Dramatic changes in U.S.A. aging highlighted in new census, NIH report*. Retrieved August 10, 2007, from http://www.census.gov/Press-Release/www/releases/archives/aging_population/006544.html

U.S. Census Bureau (2007c). *More than 300 counties now "majority-minority."* Retrieved August 10, 2007, from http://www.census.gov/Press-Release/www/releases/archives/population/010482.html

U.S. Census Bureau (2007a). *Single-parent households showed little variation since 1994, Census Bureau reports*. Retrieved August 11, 2007, from: http://www.census.gov/Press-Release/www/releases/archives/families_house-holds/009842.html

U.S. Department of Agriculture. (2007). *Food security in the United States*. Retrieved August 17, 2007, from http://www.ers.usda.gov/Briefing/FoodSecurity/

U.S. Department of Health and Human Services. (2000, August). *Temporary Assistance for Needy Families (TANF): Third annual report to Congress*. Retrieved January 21, 2002, from http:www.acf.dhhs.gov/programs/opre/director.htm

U.S. Department of Health and Human Services. (2006). *Temporary assistance for needy families (TANF): Seventh annual report to Congress*. Retrieved August 16, 2007, from http://www.acf.hhs.gov/programs/ofa/annualreport7/ar7index.htm

U.S. Department of Homeland Security. (2007, May). *Figure 1, Persons naturalized: Fiscal years 1907 to 2006*. Retrieved August 14, 2007, from http://www.dhs.gov/xlibrary/assets/statistics/publications/Natz_01_Sec508Complaint.pdf

Wagner, C. (2007, January–February). Values conflicts in stem-cell research. *The Futurist, 40*(1), 8–9.

Walker, D. M. (2007). *GAO: Forces that will shape America's future: Themes from GAO's strategic plan 2007–2012.*

Washington, DC: U.S. Government Accountability Office.

Wamhoff, S., & Wiseman, M. (2005/2006). The TANF/SSI connection. *Social Security Bulletin, 66*(4), 21–36.

World Future Society. (2007). *Forecasts: Top 10 forecasts from Outlook 2007; World trends & forecasts.* Retrieved August 11, 2007, from http://www.wfs.org/forecasts.htm

INDEX

CREDITS

Exhibit 3–11, p. 125: "FY 2008 Federal Budget—President's Proposal: Percent of Federal Funds Budget." Friends Committee on National Legislation. Reprinted with permission.

Exhibit 3–12, p. 129: National Association of Social Workers, "Welfare Reform Principles," *NASW Office of Government Relations*, March 1994. Used with permission.

Exhibit 4–2, p. 146: Excerpt from *The Convention on the Rights of the Child*, 1990. Secretary of the Publications Board, United Nations. The United Nations is the author of the original material. Reprinted by permission of The United Nations.

Exhibit 4–6, p. 159: © Mike Keefe, The Denver Post and PoliticalCartoons.com. Reprinted with permission.

Exhibit 4–8, p. 161: Brian Barling/© 2006 The Christian Science Monitor (www.csmonitor.com). All rights reserved.

Exhibit 5–2, p. 190: Reprinted with permission from the *Diagnostic and Statistical Manual of Mental Disorders*, Fourth Edition, Text Revision (Copyright 2000). American Psychiatric Association.

Exhibit 5–4, pp. 198–199: National Association of Social Workers, *Social Work Speaks*, 7th ed., Copyright 2006, pp. 271–272. Used with permission.

Exhibit 5–5, p. 200: A. Eng and E. F. Balancio, "Clinical Case Management with Asian Americans," in E. Lee, *Working with Asian Americans: A Guide for Clinicians*, The Guilford Press, 1997, pp. 403–404. Used with permission.

Exhibit 5–6, p. 203: M. D. Lerner and R. D. Shelton, "How Do People Respond During Traumatic Exposure?" *Acute Traumatic Stress Management*, The American Academy of Experts in Traumatic Stress, Inc., 2001. Used by permission of The American Academy of Experts in Traumatic Stress, Inc.

Exhibit 5–7, pp. 218–220: National Association of Social Workers, "Mental Health Bill of Rights Project," Copyright © 1999, pp. 1–3. Used with permission.

Exhibit 6–2, p. 239: National Association of Social Workers, *Social Work Speaks*, 7th ed., Copyright 2006, p. 190. Used with permission.

Exhibit 6–3, p. 248: National Association of Social Workers, *Social Work Speaks*, 7th ed., Copyright 2006, pp. 140–141. Used with permission.

Exhibit 6–4, p. 250: "Linkages Between Health and Human Rights" from World Health Organization (n.d.). Retrieved June 14, 2007, from http://www.who.int/hhr/HHR%20linkages.pdf. © World Health Organization.

Exhibit 6–6, p. 261: United Nations Statistics Division (2006). *Social Indicators: Indicators on Health*. Retrieved June 14, 2007, from http://unstats.un.org/unsd/demographic/products/socind/health.htm. The United Nations is the author of the original material. Reprinted by permission of The United Nations.

Exhibit 6–7, p. 262: United Nations Statistics Division (2006). *Social Indicators: Indicators on Health*. Retrieved June 14, 2007, from http://unstats.un.org/unsd/demographic/products/socind/health.htm. The United Nations is the author of the original material. Reprinted by permission of The United Nations.

Exhibit 6–8, p. 263: T. Mizrahi, R. Fasano, and S. M. Dooha, "Summary of Canadian Health System," *Health and Social Work*, NASW Press, Copyright ©1993, vol. 18 no. 1, pp. 7–8. Used with permission.

Exhibit 7–1, p. 280: D. Dupper. (2003). *School Social Work, Skills and Interventions for Effective Practice*. Hoboken, NJ: John Wiley & Sons, Inc., p. 12. Reprinted by permission.

Exhibit 7–5, p. 296: Deana F. Morrow, "Social Work with Gay and Lesbian Adolescents," *Social Work*, Social Work, November 1993, vol. 38, pp. 655–660.

Exhibit 8–1, p. 320: Reprinted with permission from the *Diagnostic and Statistical Manual of Mental Disorders*, Fourth Edition, Text Revision (Copyright 2000). American Psychiatric Association.

Exhibit 8–2, p. 320: Reprinted with permission from the *Diagnostic and Statistical Manual of Mental Disorders*, Fourth Edition, Text Revision (Copyright 2000). American Psychiatric Association.

Exhibit 8–3, p. 322: T. F. Babor, J. C. Higgins-Biddle, J. B. Saunders, & M. G. Monteiro (2001). AUDIT, The Alcohol Use Disorders Identification Test: Guidelines for Use in Primary Care (2nd ed.). WHO/MSD/MSB/01.6a Geneva, Switzerland: World Health Organization. © World Health Organization.

Exhibit 9–5, p. 377: P. Metz (1997), Staff Development for Working with Lesbian and Gay Elders, in J. K. Quam (Ed.), *Social Services for Senior Gay Men and Lesbians*, pp. 35–45. New York: Haworth Press. Used by permission of Haworth Press.

Exhibit 9–6, p. 385: R. R. Green, *Social Work with the Aged and their Families*, 1986, p. 177. Reprinted by permission of Transaction Publishers.

Exhibit 9–7, p. 387: Karen Bassuk and Janet Lessem, "Collaboration of Social Workers and Attorneys in Geriatric Community Based Organizations," *Journal of Gerontological Social Work*, 34, NAELA, 2001, pp. 103, 104. Used with permission.

Exhibit 9–8, p. 389: Kari Watson Culhane, "A Real Home," *Natural Health*, April 2000, p. 80. Used with permission.

Exhibit 10–7: p. 432: ICPS, "Incarceration Rates for Selected Nations," International Centre for Prison Studies, R. Walmsley (2007, Jan. 29). *World Prison Population List* (7th Ed.). Used by permission of the International Centre for Prison Studies.

Exhibit 11–1, p. 457: From Gary May & Martha Raske, *Ending Disability Discrimination: Strategies for Social Workers*, 1/e. Published by Allyn and Bacon, Boston, MA. Copyright © 2005 by Pearson Education. Reprinted by permission of the publisher.

Exhibit 11–2, p. 459: From Gary May & Martha Raske, *Ending Disability Discrimination: Strategies for Social Workers*, 1/e. Published by Allyn and Bacon, Boston, MA. Copyright © 2005 by Pearson Education. Reprinted by permission of the publisher.

Exhibit 11–5, p. 471: Ruth Snyder and Ari Ne'eman. "An Open Letter: Autism from Autistics." (2007, July 10). Autism from Autistics. Retrieved July 11, 2007, from the Autistic Self Advocacy Network website: http://www.autisticadvocacy.org/. Used with permission.

Exhibit 11–6, p. 473: L. Stoesen, "Children with Disabilities: A Family Affair, Working with Families Is a 'Dance Partnership.'" *NASW News*, vol. 50, no. 3, 2005. Copyright 2005, p. 4. Used with permission of National Association of Social Workers.

Exhibit 11–7, p. 474: Used with permission of Sage Publications, Inc. from Liu, G. Z. (2005). "Best Practices, Developing Cross-Cultural Competence from a Chinese Perspective." In John Stone (Ed.), *Culture and Disability, Providing Culturally Competent Services*, pp. 78–79; permissions conveyed through Copyright Clearance Center.